Thinking Government

Thinking

Government

Public Sector Management in Canada

Second edition

David Johnson

broadview press

Library and Archives Canada Cataloguing in Publication

Johnson, David, 1957-
   Thinking government : public sector management in Canada / David Johnson. — 2nd ed.

Includes bibliographical references and index.
ISBN 1-55111-779-7

   1. Public administration—Canada.   2. Canada—Politics and government.   I. Title.

JL108.J64 2006   351.71   C2006-900653-9

Broadview Press, Ltd.

is an independent, international publishing house, incorporated in 1985.

North America	UK, Ireland, and Continental Europe	Australia and New Zealand
P.O. Box 1243,	NBN International	UNIREPS
Peterborough, Ontario,	Estover Road	University of New South Wales
Canada K9J 7H5	Plymouth	Sydney, NSW, 2052 Australia
Tel: (705) 743-8990	PL6 7PY UK	Tel: + 61 2 96640999
Fax: (705) 743-8353	Tel: 44 (0) 1752 202300	Fax: + 61 2 96645420
	Fax: 44 (0) 1752 202330	info.press@unsw.edu.au
P.O. Box 1015	enquiries@nbninternational.com	
3576 California Road,		
Orchard Park, New York		
USA 14127		

customerservice@broadviewpress.com
www.broadviewpress.com

Broadview Press gratefully acknowledges the financial support of the Government of Canada through the Book Publishing Industry Development Program for our publishing activities.

Edited by Betsy Struthers.

Cover and interior pages designed and readied for the press by Zack Taylor. www.zacktaylor.com

Printed in Canada

Contents

Acknowledgements

This book is the result of years of thinking, writing, and teaching about public sector management in Canada. It has a genesis dating back over two decades, and I am indebted to so many people whose support has been integral to the realization of the first edition and to the completion of this second revised edition.

As I mentioned in my Acknowledgements to the first edition, I must mention those who taught me about Canadian government and politics and who instilled in me a love of knowing more about this country and how and why it works. I salute Ted Hodgetts, Carl Baar, Ken Kernaghan, Ron Manzer, Hudson Janisch, and Peter Russell. These men taught me how to think.

I must also express my gratitude to my colleagues and friends at Cape Breton University. As I was working on this second edition I always knew I had the support and encouragement of some very special people. In our Department of Political Science—Jim Guy, Brian Howe, Lee-Anne Broadhead, Andrew Molloy, Terry Gibbs, Tom Urbaniak, Garry Leech and Darrell Kyte. In our library—Laura Syms and Cathy Chisholm. And in the School of Business—Joanne Pyke.

No book can exist without a publisher, and the leadership and staff at Broadview Press have been wonderful as they have supported the coming into being of this second edition. A big thank you is extended to Michael Harrison for his vision and encouragement of what this book could be. And a number of people at Broadview have been pivotal in seeing this second edition come together, notably Greg Yantz, Betsy Struthers, and Zack Taylor. Without their support this book would not exist.

I also thank the anonymous reviewers who read the initial manuscript and whose constructive criticisms have made this a better book.

Countless students here at Cape Breton University also need to be acknowledged. My students over the years have been a very receptive audience and have helped me to sharpen my thinking and teaching with respect to Canadian government and its myriad power relations. This book has been written with students in mind. I have tried to produce a book that provides them with a solid foundation in Canadian public administration and public sector management while also being readable, accessible, and interesting. I believe it is important for all Canadians to be knowledgeable in the nature and working of government and the exercise of power in this society. Such knowledge is vital to our democratic purpose. I hope that this book is a modest means to that end. Of course, it is the students who are now reading this book who will be the best judges of whether I have succeeded in this endeavour.

And finally, once again, this book is dedicated to my dearest wife, Rosalie. Through all the ups and downs of writing and rewriting, Rosalie was a constant source of inspiration, encouragement, sound judgement, and good humour. She is my muse.

Introduction

This text deals with government, politics, public administration, and public sector management in Canada. While these subject matters are not ones that tend to be viewed in popular culture as inherently interesting, this attitude betrays a stunning lack of insight regarding the nature of our society and the importance of the role played by the state in the life of every Canadian. Whether we are aware of it or not, the institutions of the state, in one manner or another, and whether for good or ill, touch the lives of every man, woman, and child in this country, whether desired or not, on a continuous, daily basis. The state exists around every one of us all the time, and no study of government, public administration, and public sector management can be fruitfully entered into without a clear awareness of just how present and how important the state is and can be in the ordinary lives of Canadians. Most of us never consciously envisage the scope of the government presence in our routine lives, but to do so is enlightening and thought-provoking. Consider the following scenario as a typical Canadian begins the day and, perhaps without even noticing it, relates to a variety of state actors representing federal, provincial, and municipal governments, departments, regulatory agencies, and Crown corporations.

If you awaken to an electric alarm/clock radio you are interacting with a provincially-regulated power utility that provides your home with power. The price you are charged for this power is publicly regulated; the environmental, health, and safety standards to be met by the supplier are likewise set and overseen by a variety of public agencies; and—depending in which province you live—the actual supplier of the power may be a provincially owned Crown corporation: Ontario Power Generation, Hydro-Quebec, or SaskPower, to name a few.

If your radio comes on following the alarm, you may be listening to the CBC. If so, you are listening to programming coming from a federal Crown corporation—the Canadian Broadcasting Corporation—established and substantially funded by the government to provide high-quality radio and television services to all Canadians and, by so doing, promoting Canadian culture while enhancing public sensibility respecting this country by "interpreting Canada to Canadians." But, if you don't listen to CBC Radio but rather tune in to a private broadcaster, you are nonetheless in the presence of the Canadian state through the jurisdiction of the Canadian Radio-television and Telecommunications Commission (CRTC). This is a federal regulatory agency that oversees all radio and television broadcasting in this country produced by both public and private sector enterprises, that licenses and regulates all such undertakings, and that imposes Canadian content requirements on all broadcasters. Federal content rules legally stipulate the proportion of Canadian-generated content, including artistic performance and production, which must be broadcast over prescribed periods of time—daily, weekly, monthly, annually. Such rules are designed not only to promote Canadian artists in the fields of music and visual performance but also to promote Canadian-based radio and television programming of all types—current affairs, news, educational, general interest—that will assist us in becoming more aware of the country in which we live. Such Canadian content rules were largely designed to act as a counterbalance in some degree to the flood of American radio and television programming that inundates this country.

Once you are up and have turned on a light or two (public power utility generation and/or regulation, again), you will likely go to the bathroom, where you will again meet the state via the process of "waterworks." We in this country take for granted municipally delivered, clean, fresh water and sewage services until there is a problem with them when we find their absence quite unbearable. Most people in the world do not have regular access to the quality of waterworks we have come to expect, partly because most countries in the "developing world" do not possess the state infrastructure necessary for providing such public services. Of course, the Walkerton, Ontario water scandal of 2000 fundamentally challenged the faith of many Ontarians respecting the quality of drinking water in their province and the competence of those in the public and private sectors charged with maintaining necessary environmental and health standards for the supply of safe drinking water. The Walkerton scandal, moreover, served not only to highlight concerns respecting water quality but also to raise questions respecting the merits and demerits of the privatization and deregulation of such basic public services as the provision of clean drinking water. Subsequent problems relating to water quality in British Columbia, Saskatchewan, and Newfoundland have reinforced the magnitude of this issue.

Following your trip to the bathroom, you will get dressed. If your clothes are Canadian-made, the producer has likely benefitted from some form of federal or provincial industrial incentive package or taxation benefit; if they are American- or Mexican-made, their import into this country has been subject to the North American Free Trade Agreement (NAFTA), while if they are from elsewhere in the world, their import has been regulated by federal tariff policy. And, of course, there was the federal and provincial taxation you paid on them as purchased goods.

Next, you go into the kitchen for breakfast, and your connections to the state increase in myriad ways. All the food you have bought has been subject to federal or provincial agricultural health inspection to ensure that it is fit for consumption, and much of it also has been produced with the generous support of government-sponsored agricultural subsidies. All the appliances in your kitchen—the stove, refrigerator, toaster, microwave, electric kettle—also have been subject to product safety inspections by federal and provincial agencies to ensure, for example, that they will not electrocute you when you turn them on.

As you leave the door to head for work or school, you may travel in an automobile. If so, the production of that vehicle was subject to Canadian-American trade rules (if it is North American-made) or to Canadian tariff rules (if it was imported into this country from outside North America). If you travel via public transit, you are once again relating with an institution of the municipal or provincial government (GO Transit in Ontario, for example) that provides a public service supplemented both through user fees (tickets) and direct state subsidies. Regardless of whether you travel by private automobile or public transit, you will be travelling on public roads or perhaps rail lines created and maintained by provincial or municipal governments, with significant financial support for such transportation infrastructure deriving from the federal government.

If you work, the chances are you work in the private sector, but it is noteworthy that nearly 3,000,000 Canadians work within the Canadian state—the broad collection of federal, provincial, and municipal public service institutions in Canada (See Box 8.1 in Chapter 8). And remember, the Government of Canada is the single largest employer in the country with some 366,000 employees. If you do work in the private sector, that does not mean an end to this litany of state connections. All private sector employers, for example, are subject to federal or provincial labour relations laws, workers' compensation regulations, and human rights provisions. All employers must comply with pertinent workplace and product regulations, such as health and safety and environmental rules, as well as all federal, provincial, and municipal taxation requirements. The presence of the state here is not one solely of a burden on the private sector. All firms in the private sector can benefit from corporate taxation policies (and most do), and, depending on the nature of the industry, many firms can benefit from a wide variety of government policies and programs designed to support and promote the economic development of the private sector.

Finally, if you are a student travelling to a university or college, you are heading towards a unique institution of the broader public sector. While universities and colleges are not direct components of provincial public services, in that, for example, faculty are not members of any province's public service, these institutions are closely related to provincial governments in many ways. They are substantially funded by their provincial government (with a good portion of this money coming directly from federal government transfer payments). They also are legally established by their host provincial government since they are created and given degree-granting powers by an act of the provincial legislature. As such, universities and colleges are subject to broad regulatory oversight by their provincial governments with respect to matters as diverse as program curricula, presidential and board of governors/senate appointments, tuition frameworks, and student loan plans. Thus, if you are a student paying tuition, you have a very close relationship with the state.

The foregoing is illustrative of the many, diverse, often unseen, and little noticed ways in which people interact daily with the state and its broad administrative apparatus. The state is all around us helping to maintain our living standard, keeping us healthy, educating us, promoting our jobs. But it also at times irritates us by its imposition of laws and regulations and bothers us by its demands for revenues in the forms of taxation and user fees. Despite these "irritations," it is noteworthy that the policy fields in which Canadian governments act usually are desired and supported by most Canadians—hence, the state presence in the first place.

Our brief review illustrates state policy in the fields of public utility production and regulation, cultural policy promotion, public health and safety regulation, industrial support and economic promotion, environmental protection, transportation infrastructure promotion, public education, and, of course, public revenue generation. Policy fields not covered by this exercise but which are equally important to the lives of Canadians and their governments include such matters as policies on health care; public order, security, policing, and justice; defence; human rights; Aboriginal rights; language; multiculturalism; regional economic development; and public welfare, to name a few.

Not only is the scope of the major responsibilities borne by the state remarkable, but the problems and controversies in which governments find themselves embroiled while trying to fulfill all these responsibilities and duties are astonishingly complex. The central questions here become: Can and should governments be involved in all these policy fields? If so, how should they exercise their power? Upon what principles? With what means? To what ends? These are, of course, simple questions for which there are no easy answers.

Yet, these questions frame deeper and broader debates in public discourse respecting the role of government, the function of the public sector and public administration, and the desired nature and operation of public sector management. These debates tend not to garner great media exposure because they are neither as topical nor as dramatic as other stories. But these public discussions, involving political parties, governments, public interest groups, business groups, political commentators, certain media analysts, and concerned citizens, are in many respects more significant than "front-page stories" because they mark the political and governmental undercurrents upon which current public policy transpires.

Public debate often begins with pointed questions such as: Why can't governments do a better job of managing the economy, reducing taxes, and running their own administrative affairs efficiently and economically while providing good quality public services to Canadians? And why are there so many ethics scandals in government, such as the sponsorship scandal that plagued the Martin government in 2005? These questions lead to others: Why has the quality of public services declined in recent years? Why are taxes so high? Why do governments have such a problem relating to and understanding business and the needs of the private sector? Why are governments incapable of managing the public sector in as rigorous a manner as the private sector is administered? Why are governments so wasteful? These lead to more profound issues: Should the work of governments be drastically reconfigured and downsized? Should the public service be subject to major deregulation and privatization? Are there many economic and social policy functions currently in the hands of governments that could be more economically and efficiently run by the private sector? Should taxation levels be greatly reduced so as to benefit ordinary Canadians and Canadian businesses, thereby limiting the ability of governments to significantly intervene in the social and economic life of the country? In short, should the role of the state in society be fundamentally rethought and reordered to one more in keeping with a private sector view of social and economic relations and public policy? Would such changes in the policy and program orientation of the state make for more effective, responsive, and accountable government?

All these questions, however, elicit rejoinders and counter-questions from those critical of their rightward thrust. Has the quality of public services declined over the past decade? To what extent? And, if so, why? Are Canadian taxation rates exorbitantly high, and do we need tax cuts in order to restore national economic health while disciplining governments? Is it true that Canadian governments tend to be ignorant of, and unsympathetic to, the interests of the private sector? Or is the reverse actually the case: that our governments tend to be unduly solicitous of the welfare of Canadian business interests at the expense of the broader public interest? In this vein, is it also true that Canadian governments are generally uneconomic, inefficient, and ineffective in the administration and management of public services, or are such claims ideologically motivated by those seeking to limit the role of the state? Is it also true that governments are prone to ethics scandals or, in reality, is it the case that most politicians and public servants fulfill their public duties with honesty and integrity and that only a few "bad apples" taint the public perception of government for everyone? Finally, should the role of the state be re-evaluated? Do governments have a legitimate role to play in providing core health, educational, and welfare services to Canadians? Should governments also be promoting the economic well-being of Canada through a host of government-directed sectoral, industrial, and regional development programs? Would a more socially active and economically interventionist state lead to more effective, responsive, and accountable government?

Canadians hold widely diverging opinions regarding the quality of existing political and government leadership. They disagree about the capability or even about the desirability of existing public services and public sector management. They evaluate from different perspectives the impact and worth of the profound changes in government and public services over the past two decades. They debate what should be the desired relationship between the public and private sectors as well as between the state and its citizens. And, increasingly, we wonder whether Canadian governments are up to the task of providing innovative, intelligent, and effective public sector management capable of building and maintaining a bond of service, accountability, and respect with their citizens.

Textual Propositions

These questions are the starting point of this review and investigation of Canadian government, its public administration, and public sector management, and they will be returned to many times throughout the work. As we probe the nature and working of the Canadian state—primarily the federal government and its institutions—the following positions will be advanced.

1. The state is understood by Canadians to be important, yet of such complexity that its operational dynamics are difficult for most citizens to understand. Chapter 1 offers a basic introduction to the Canadian government; the paradox of public perception that it faces; the scope and presence of government in the life of this country's citizens; and the range of issues, policies, programs, and problems that governments, public services, and public sector management must daily confront.

2. Regardless of its complexity, the role of the state has always been central to political debate in this country, and this debate continues to divide public opinion. In Chapter 2, I will probe the various ideological positions regarding this matter and study how such ideas have had, and are having, a profound impact on the practical life of governments and their relationship to Canadians. While conservative, social democratic, and liberal ideological approaches to politics and the role of the state all have been significant to the development of Canadian public sector management, the most influential stream of thought has been liberalism, the approach of the broad political centre. Most governments in this country, and especially those in Ottawa, have sought to promote a balanced and moderate approach to socio-economic policy, seeking to balance fiscal prudence and concern for economic growth and stability with a recognition of the importance of progressive policies on social welfare, human rights, regional and cultural development, and environmental policy. Throughout this text, we will explore the ways in which Canadian federal governments have sought a liberal and pluralistic approach to managing public policy by promoting sound public administration through practical reasoning, adaptation, and response based on this awareness; that is, how the federal governments developed the ability to learn, understand, adapt, and synthesize practical knowledge and awareness with ideological and theoretical understandings of how the world works and how governments should respond to the needs of citizens.

While we have had many different governments in this country over the past half-century, they have tended to adopt a similar style of governance. We will explore this style, its evolution, and the tensions on it in a period of competing demands for a smaller, less costly government, yet one that provides greater services. These tensions between economical and effective government are accentuated when governments must balance concerns for fiscal prudence with competing demands for both enhanced national security against international terrorism and ongoing requests for enhanced social and environmental programming.

3. As viewpoints respecting the role of the state have waxed and waned, one core truth remains: the state always will have a major role to play in the life of Canadians. This means that public administration and public sector management will remain important and will continue to be important subjects of study for those wishing to know how this country is governed, why government power is exercised in certain ways and for whose benefit, and how the exercise of such power may be improved.

Chapters 3 and 4 offer a close view of the keystone institutions of the Canadian federal government and an assessment of the power relations within it. This will involve a study of prime ministerial power, cabinet decision-making, and ministerial responsibility, as well as an examination of the complex relationships between elected politicians and unelected public servants. Chapter 4 attends particularly to the current nature and working of the federal cabinet and the increasing concentration of political and administrative power in the hands of the prime minister and his closest associates. While the analysis of the federal order of government takes centre stage, much of the understanding gained in these chapters will relate also to provincial governments and their inner workings.

Chapter 5 provides an introduction to public sector management theory and a summary of major approaches to thinking about management, understanding public sector organizational behaviour, and improving the quality of public service policy-making and program delivery. This chapter devotes special attention to the unique nature of the public sector and its distinctiveness from the private sector. It contrasts the long-standing ideal of rational management and decision-making with the equally long-lasting notions of incrementalism, bounded rationalism, crisis management, and bureaucratic politics within the general theory and practice of public sector management.

4. A study of such power relationships and managerial thought necessitates a close study of certain core fields of public sector management. The managerial side of government is crucial to its effective functioning, yet it is precisely this feature of public administration that has generally been understood little by most Canadians while also being ignored by most previous studies of Canadian government. I seek to rectify this situation by

presenting a clear, relatively concise analysis and critique of the principal components of public sector management, namely, financial management, human resources management, administrative law, service delivery, public sector ethics, accountability, and leadership. And, once again, while the main focus of this attention is on the federal government and its administration, many of the organizational features, administrative dynamics, managerial issues, and basic power relations are applicable to provincial governments and their public services.

5. I aim to be both informative and critical. Major issues and debates arise in all the components of management listed above, with all of these fields becoming the subjects of much political and governmental thought and action. Thus, Chapters 6 and 7 address the key issues of financial management, including public sector budgeting; the nature of budget systems; deficit and debt control; fiscal restraint policy; and the choices that now present themselves to governments as they struggle to enter a new world of balanced budgets, surplus revenues, and new policy and program options.

Central matters of human resources policy are reviewed in Chapters 8 and 9, including human resources management systems, the nature of patronage, the role of the merit principle in hiring and promotion, the pros and cons of public service collective bargaining and public sector unions' right to strike, and contemporary issues surrounding the merits and demerits of affirmative action and employment equity policies.

It is also important to note, here, that this book has a designated "Thinking Government" web site (http://www.broadviewpress.com/thinkinggovernment/) that contains a variety of additional information relevant to the issues and materials addressed in this text. In particular, the web site contains an extra chapter that offers an introduction, for the non-lawyer, to the basic concepts of administrative law, the rationale for these legal obligations borne by the state and its officials, and an assessment of how and why these legal rules are important in establishing rights and duties for both government decision-makers and those affected by such decisions—everyone living in society.

The final three chapters of the book proper address a variety of other matters. Chapter 10 reviews contemporary developments in public sector management reform that are altering both the federal and provincial orders of government. I look at the concept of the reinvention of government, the theory of New Public Management, and the demonstrable impact that such reform initiatives have had on the actual practice of public administration and the thinking surrounding it. While these new approaches to government can be thought-provoking and have been influential to certain governments seeking to reconfigure their operations to enable themselves to "do more with less" in a period of fiscal restraint, they have also elicited major criticisms with respect to their theoretical underpinnings as well as their practical usefulness. I argue that, far from observing a re-invention of government, we have been witnessing a less dramatic yet significant reform of government over the past decade. While a fundamental transformation in the nature and role of government in this society is both unlikely and undesirable, we have nevertheless been witnessing significant changes to government with much debate ensuing as to their merits and demerits. Through all such changes governments are seeking ways to deliver policies and programs to Canadians by processes that are more economical, efficient, effective, respectful, and accountable. We will probe the nature of these actions and the future policy and management directions that the federal government is carving out for itself. We will devote specific attention to the issue of service delivery, a concern of growing importance to many government offices. We will focus attention on the actions taken by the federal government in seeking to improve the quality of services received by the public and how this goal is sought even within an environment of fiscal restraint.

Chapter 11 is a study of accountability and public sector ethics. These are related concepts; accountability has always been a central concern to governments, public sector management, and, indeed, the public. Accountability will be presented as an amalgam of ministerial responsibility, legal responsibility, and social responsibility, with governments and their public services being called upon to respond effectively to the demands of all three of these duties. Crucial in this are the concept and practice of public sector ethics. We will look at these concepts, their elusive yet defining features, and their continuing vital role in government and effective public sector management. I will stress the importance of ethics in government while also highlighting the difficulties that governments have in putting codes of ethics into practice.

Finally, in Chapter 12 I assess the future of public sector management in this country, devoting special attention to the characteristics of leadership within government. I will look closely at both good, effective leadership and at failed leadership. The study of bureaucratic pathologies found here is offered as a means towards understanding how good leadership can be understood and promoted. One of the key arguments flowing through this work is that we can and should have the highest calibre of leadership within our governments. As students we have a need to study the nature and practice of government leadership, and as citizens we have a duty to insist upon it.

And it is here where one of the key arguments of this work will be made. The paradox of perception versus reality regarding the state is not to be resolved only through the public's better understanding of the state, its role, and the strengths and limitations of public sector action. In addition to, and consonant with the need for, greater knowledge and education in the public is a need for governments in general and senior public service management in particular to become better leaders within the state and within this society. There is a need for these actors to strive not only to provide good, effective, and responsible administration of public services but to go beyond the normal routine of policy development and program implementation to become creative agents of governmental change and reform. Such actors need to be more visionary and proactive than in the past as they confront the challenges facing the country, address the generalized public apathy and cynicism directed to their work, and strive to provide good and necessary government services to a citizenship that still has very high expectations of what governments should be doing. Governments and public sector managers also need to be more forthright and persuasive in defending the role of the state in this society, even as that role is modified, reformed, and changed by the exigencies of an ever-changing socio-economic environment. The state will always be called upon to play a significant role in the life of this country; we need to ensure that the leadership of the state, and especially its permanent senior managerial ranks, are fully trained, capable, knowledgeable, and attuned to the many demands, obligations, and requirements of effective leadership. These officials undertake, on our behalf, a complex and important mission. We should appreciate this mission, we should understand the various approaches and debates to comprehending the work of government, and we should develop good, critical faculties in assessing the merits and demerits of government leadership.

We need to think about government just as we need a government that can think and act strategically and effectively, responsibly and responsively. All of this is a civic duty.

A Final Note: As you read through the text, note that key terms are highlighted in bold, with definitions provided at the end of each chapter. Relevant web sites are also listed at the end of each chapter. And don't forget to check out the Thinking Government web site for additional information and materials.

CHAPTER 1
Thinking about Canadian Society and Government

A puzzle exists with respect to how most Canadians view government, the public service, and **public sector management** in this country—a paradox in that two contradictory positions, beliefs, or viewpoints prevail, both of which, however, are commonly held to be true.

The first part of the paradox is that most Canadians, and likely many of the students who are beginning to read this book, have a skeptical, jaundiced, even cynical attitude towards government. Governments tend to suffer from a terrible public image of being big, complex, unhelpful entities whose work is slow, uneconomic, inefficient, incompetent, and wasteful. Government institutions likewise—departments, agencies, offices—are often viewed as being confusing, awkward, and bloated bureaucracies staffed by people—bureaucrats—who essentially are overpaid, underworked incompetents, more concerned with self-interest than serving the public interest. This critical and bitter assessment leads many people to think that governments basically are negative influences in society and that at best they must be endured, like high taxes, and at worst constitute part of the problem facing us as Canadians and are not a part of any solution. The mention of such concepts as public administration, public service, and public sector management tend to be met with dull or suspicious stares from most people. Public administration often is treated as a joke and the term "public service" laughed at as an oxymoron. Public sector management, in turn, is granted that most damning of modern epithets—"boring." Why would anyone be interested in anything as dull, uninteresting, lifeless, and even negative and useless as public sector management?

And yet, the second part of the paradox is that most Canadians and likely most students who are beginning to read this book take great pride in this country and the quality of life to be found here. Indeed, such beliefs periodically are reinforced when Canada is ranked by the United Nations as having among the highest quality of life of any country throughout the world. Most of us also take pride in the very favourable comparisons we draw between the quality of life in this country and that found in our southern neighbour. While we may have more in common with Americans than we usually like to admit, it is generally true that few of us actually desire to live in the United States or believe that the overall living standard in that country is superior to ours. When called upon to explain this, we tend to make reference to certain government policies, public services, and government programs as factors in elevating the quality of life in this country above that found there.

Most Canadians are proud of our health care system—a publicly administered and funded system guaranteeing to all Canadians a high calibre of medical care regardless of one's ability to pay for such services. We are also proud of our education system, one that provides all our children with primary and secondary education administered through a complex of public schools financed jointly by both provincial and federal governments. Our post-secondary education system also is praised for offering all students who meet the requirements of admission a valuable, life-enhancing education, with the majority of its costs borne by the **state.** Many of us comment favourably on basic elements of the broad state-established and -administered Canadian welfare system. The Canada Pension Plan and its Quebec counterpart offer retirement pension payments to all senior citizens, thereby providing them with a modicum of financial security in their later years. Federal employment insurance programs provide most Canadians facing unemployment with income support and a variety of job-related initiatives to help them return to the workforce. Provincial workers' compensation systems guarantee to all workers hurt while on the job that they will receive compensation for income lost and injuries sustained. Provincial welfare systems assure that all persons who fall upon hard times will be guaranteed basic food, clothing, and shelter so that no one need starve on the street. To these policies and programs could be added others that Canadians often mention when reflecting on the building blocks of our quality of life: gun control, human rights legislation, **multiculturalism** policy, environmental regulation, health and safety regulation, regional equalization, and support for Canadian arts and culture.

The intriguing point to notice is that all these features that distinguish Canadian reality are matters of public policy and public administration, the creations of governments, and the subject of public sector management. And all these policies and programs of social and economic importance to so many of us have been developed in direct response to social, economic, and political pressures arising from the Canadian public. In this sense, the state presence is substantial in this country because, in the past, most Canadians have been supportive of a significant development and growth of the state to meet certain needs and wants through the political and governmental process.

The irony here is that, while many Canadians value a wide range of the specific policies and programs provided by Canadian governments and hold high expectations of what the state should be doing to protect and promote the quality of life for themselves and others, these same citizens also are critical of, at times hostile to, and even cynical about, the actual institutions of the state from which they receive these services. My aim is to probe this puzzle and assess the contours of this paradox by offering a close review and analysis of government, public administration, and public sector management in Canada. Why do we find this paradox? How else might we understand the reality of government, public administration, and public sector management in this country? Is government really so important to the life of ordinary Canadians? If so, why the disconnection between perception and reality? Is there any merit to the critical, skeptical, cynical assessments of governments, public administration, and public servants? Is it true that governments are inherently uneconomic, inefficient, and ineffective? Is it true that public servants are essentially incompetent and non-productive? Or, are these viewpoints rooted in myth, founded in woeful ignorance of the nature of government, or wedded to ideological presupposition and deliberate political attack against the state? What truly is the nature of the state in Canada?

This question poses an array of related questions: What do governments do? How have their roles changed and evolved over the past century? What is the contemporary nature of government in this society? How does public sector management in this country work? How are public services organized, managed, and delivered? How do governments address such matters as financial management, human resources policy, administrative law, public service ethics, **accountability**, and leadership? Do Canadians receive the high quality of government services they expect? If not, if there are disconnections between expectations and performance, what may be done to fix this? How have governments been coping with contemporary pressures for public sector reform, and what are we to make of recent changes in government operations? What choices do we have with respect to what the role of the state should be? Can the nature and function of government be improved? Can public sector management be better organized so as to provide a higher calibre of public service leadership to the Canadian people? In short, should we expect more of governments? Can we expect more of governments?

1.1 Thinking about the State and Governance: The Challenge of Choice

These issues define most of the parameters of the public debate that has swirled about this country in recent decades about the role and function of Canadian governments. We confront important choices respecting the quality of governance this country possesses. A thorough understanding of government and public sector management is essential both to appreciating the history of political life of this country and to comprehending the current social, economic, and political dynamics that are shaping the evolution of our society.

As illustrated in the Introduction, it is actually quite easy to delineate the presence of the state in this society: it is all around us in a host of forms, institutions, and policies. What is much more difficult to do—and much more likely to elicit heated debate—is to try to delineate what the Canadian state should do with the many powers in its possession. In moving from the question of what is to what ought to be, the important matters of social action, managerial direction, political vision, and the overarching complexities of governing begin to emerge. As Rick Van Loon and Michael Whittington (1987: 1-18) have long argued, governing is all about making choices with regard to scarce resources so as to advance desired goals and to promote certain interests.

But what happens when there are multiple and incompatible goals, when competing interests strive to promote self-interest, often at the expense of others? What happens when Canadians confront a variety of options respecting possible government actions? The result is acrimony and tension as citizens and their political parties and governments debate their future. These omnipresent debates, however, ultimately culminate in some form of government decision-making. Policy and programs will be chosen and designed to gain specific goals and to serve particular interests deemed by the government of the day to be more worthy of support and advancement than other competing goals and interests. Such governmental calculations will always be founded upon a variety of considerations—professional, managerial, administrative, financial, policy orientation, ideological, and political. But choices will be made. And through such choices there will always be policy and program winners and losers.

The complexity of governing Canada, especially from the perspective of the federal government, can be quickly appreciated through a review of just some of the major socio-economic, political, and cultural tensions existing in this country. In all instances governments confront issues that are important yet divisive, issues which generate not only great public interest and political controversy but also strong public expectations that some form of government action—policy development and/or program enactment or administration—should be taken to address, resolve, or at least manage these tensions. Debate arises regarding how to interpret these tensions, how to achieve these administrative ends, and just what role governments can and should play in the development of necessary public policy.

1.2 Socio-Economic Policy: Thinking about Government Choice Amid Competing Options

Consider first the debates surrounding **socio-economic policy** and the differing understandings and expectations regarding governments, their work, and their future roles. Many people are very critical of attitudes in the past towards social and economic planning that called upon governments to play large roles in the everyday lives of citizens. These conservative critics bemoan the growth of the state since the end of the Second World War, the rise of government intervention in the economy through the means of regulation, the creation of **Crown corporations**, increased taxation, and the development of a wide variety of social welfare offerings to individuals as a matter of entitlement. These initiatives, it is argued, were not only poorly thought through but also put a great strain on the financial health of the country and its federal and provincial governments while promoting the growth of large, costly, and inefficient public sector bureaucracies that came to threaten the private sector principle of free enterprise (Campbell and Christian, 1996: 48-61; Jackson and Jackson, 1998: 397-98).

As the state grew, so the argument goes, governments became more and more removed from ordinary people and the "common sense" of market economics. Governments, often influenced or manipulated by the self-serving pleadings of special interest groups, seemed to believe that every perceived social or economic problem had a solution based on public sector intervention and the spending of public money. Of course, public servants themselves benefitted from ideas promoting the growth of the state, so they, too, became one of the forces pushing forward this **bureaucratization of society**. The end result was a bloated public sector, runaway government **deficits** and debts, increasing taxation levels, and the creation of an interventionist state that actually threatened the economic well-being of the country.

This view necessarily leads conservative critics to target the institutions and policies of governments themselves as the root cause of most of this country's problems over the past half-century and to focus accordingly on policy reforms. For those who believe that the growth of the state has been a problem, the solution is simple: cut government. We are all familiar with the basic policy prescriptions of this position: Crown corporations should be **privatized**, the economy should be deregulated, individual and corporate taxation rates should be dramatically reduced, government bureaucracies should be substantially downsized, public sector deficit spending should be eliminated if not outlawed altogether, public debts should be paid down, public services should be "rationalized" (i.e., reduced), and free enterprise should be enthusiastically promoted. In short, governments should be given a much smaller role to play in the life of society, while the private sector should be encouraged to assume a leading position in providing the goods and services that people need and desire (Johnston, 1996: 103-04; Nelson, 1995: 30-34).

Such conservative ideas have been very influential in this country over the past two decades, just as they have tended to dominate political and economic discourse and policy-making throughout the western world over this time period. All governments in Canada—federal, provincial, and municipal—have promoted many of these policy ideas in varying degrees of intensity, regardless of political affiliation. Indeed, the development of free trade policy on this continent, first with the Canada-United States Free Trade Agreement of 1989, followed by the creation of the NAFTA in 1993, is proof of the power of these ideas and how they can become entrenched both in international law and domestic public policy to affect this country for decades to come.

These ideas of **government restraint**, however, have not gone unchallenged. A variety of liberal and socialist viewpoints critical of such reduced-state, free-enterprise approaches and supportive of progressive government leadership persist. Advocates of a continued or even enhanced state role in this society and its economy promote a wide range of criticisms and alternatives. One is that cutbacks to government will necessarily mean cutbacks to health, education, and social welfare services, causing people in need of these services to suffer. Such government cutbacks, it is argued, have had and will have the effect of limiting hospital beds, cutting the numbers of nurses, and increasing waiting times for medical attention and physicians' services. Likewise, cutbacks will mean fewer teachers in schools, fewer books in school libraries, fewer special and extra-curricular programs, and indeed fewer schools. At the post-secondary level, budget cuts will result in fewer professors and instructors; poorer, more rundown infrastructure; and, of course, ever higher tuition fees. And for those concerned about welfare programs, government restraint policies simply result in fewer entitlements (welfare, unemployment insurance, workers' compensation, pension benefits) payable to smaller numbers of claimants (Swimmer, 1996; Prince, 1999).

Critics of conservative restraint policies assert that, far from cutting such programs, their funding should be escalated to meet the growing needs of those seeking the benefits of these public policy commitments. Not restricting attention to the policy fields already mentioned, advocates of a sustained if not greater state presence in society argue that a variety of other social and economic concerns need more, not less, government attention. Human rights activists—those concerned with the rights of ethnic and racial minorities, the mentally and physically handicapped, women, and others who historically have been marginalized by governments— claim that state funding for human rights policies should be increased, with the expectation that this would lead to more rigorous enforcement and promotion of human rights law and policy by both federal and provincial human rights commissions. Similarly, environmental advocates assert that environmental protection legislation across the country should be strengthened, that existing laws should be more rigorously enforced, and that federal and provincial departments of environment and their environmental protection regulatory agencies be given greater powers and more funding to facilitate their work. Likewise, promoters of labour reform stress that labour policy needs to be improved, that the right to unionize and to engage in free collective bargaining should be facilitated, that more public monies should be spent on federal and provincial labour relations and workers' compensation boards, and that state enforcement of labour standards and occupational health and safety guarantees should be escalated (Shields and Evans, 1998; Phillips, 1999: 380-88).

Of course, the conservative critics of increased state involvement in society contest all of these propositions, stressing that such proposals would result, once again, in greater public spending, bigger bureaucracies, higher taxation, larger public deficits and debts, and a more bothersome and interventionist state. In contrast to statist policy prescriptions for these areas of public concern, the advocates of smaller government and free enterprise tend to stress the need for governments to develop more effective means in the public or private sector to meet policy needs in these and other socio-economic policy fields, and for governments to do so by modelling their administration and management on proven and successful private sector approaches to policy and program delivery.

Defenders of the state presence in society, however, argue against all these ideas, stressing that they are essentially predicated on a narrow, ideologically right-wing perspective on social and economic life and that while the private sector may have a legitimate role to play in a modern, liberal democratic society, that role should not be allowed to overwhelm, undermine, and delegitimize the valuable function that can be assumed by the public sector. In promoting what they perceive as a broader, more ideologically progressive role for the state, advocates of increased state involvement in society stress the major function governments can serve in the economic life of society.

Rather than viewing the private sector as the star actor in the economy, those supportive of the state stress that governments have always had and still do have important responsibilities for furthering economic growth and stability, job creation, wealth generation and distribution, and regional economic development. These goals are viewed as being attainable through a variety of manners, but the most common and substantial policy instruments are the following:

1. *Public spending.* This allows governments to promote a certain firm, industrial sector, or entire region by such strategies as

- direct subsidization;
- incentive grants and loans;
- labour skills upgrading programs;
- research and development support;
- the promotion of export markets; and
- industrial infrastructure creation and support both through traditional actions, such as the building of airports, harbours, and highways, and new initiatives, such as creating and developing high-speed telecommunications networks.

BOX 1.1
Policy Instruments

Governments possess a variety of options when confronting any issue. In simple terms this means that they can take any number of actions depending upon how serious they consider an issue to be and the degree to which they believe the issue requires state attention, as well as the degree of state involvement they wish to bring to the management of the issue.

The full array of "Policy Instruments" available to governments have conventionally been viewed as nine in number, ranging from the slightest, involving the most minimal degree of state involvement through to the greatest, involving the most substantial degree of state involvement.

These are the nine Policy Instruments, ranging from the slightest to the most substantial:

- Do nothing; leave the matter to the private sector.
- Engage in symbolic state action; promote showpiece behaviour.
- Engage in policy exhortation; use the power of persuasion.
- Spend taxes; use the tax system to promote policy goals through tax credits/tax breaks/tax incentives.
- Engage in public spending; promote Canadian aims though programs directly funded by government.
- Regulate; promote policy aims by mandating and enforcing compliance with established regulatory frameworks.
- Impose taxation; promote policy aims by imposing tax burdens/punishments upon those engaged in actions deemed luxurious/extravagant/unnecessary/undesired.
- Seize ownership; promote policy aims through direct state intervention, control, and ownership over particular fields of socio-economic activity.
- Declare a state of emergency; assume full state control over the society and its economy.

how gov react

2. *Creative taxation policy.* Governments can provide favourable tax treatments, such as depreciation allowances, tax write-offs, and preferential rates, to particular firms, sectors, or regions deemed to be in need of special support. Such policies are designed to encourage new economic activities or to protect and enhance pre-existing business initiatives.

3. *Regulatory policy.* Public regulations can be developed whereby the behaviour of economic actors—governments, individuals, and firms—is restricted or enhanced to promote and defend desirable types of economic activity. Examples of such economic regulation are

- reforestation quotas for forestry companies;
- Canadian content and production standards for television and radio broadcasters;
- entry standards for certain professions;
- and legal and ethical standards for all entrepreneurs, licensed professionals, and self-governing professional associations.

Examples of such regulated fields include the medical, legal, and engineering professions, as well as service industries as diverse as taxi driving, the managing of restaurants and bars, and the practice of veterinary medicine.

4. *Tax penalties*. Taxation policy can be used not only to promote certain desired policy objectives but also to penalize certain less desirable activities, such as smoking or failing to comply with environmental regulations, or to generate revenue through elevated taxation rates on "luxury" goods or activities.

5. *Public ownership*. If a government deems that a particular economic sector or activity is of such public importance as to warrant or necessitate state involvement, the state can become directly involved in that sector or activity through the creation and operation of a Crown corporation. Historically, federal and provincial governments have not shied away from the creation of Crown corporations, classic examples being the Canadian National Railway (CN), Air Canada, the Canadian Broadcasting Corporation (CBC), the Canadian Wheat Board, the National Film Board (NFB), Petro-Canada, Canada Post, Enterprise Cape Breton Corporation, Ontario Hydro, Hydro Quebec, SaskTel, and all provincial liquor distribution commissions across the country. Some of these Crown corporations have been privatized, but others remain firmly under state ownership (Inwood, 1999: 216-21; Howlett and Ramesh, 1995: 80-83).

As supporters of an active state role in the economy have long proclaimed, the policy and program means available to governments wishing to intervene in the economic life of society are many and varied. Even following the 1990s, a decade of significant public sector downsizing by federal and provincial governments of all political persuasions, public pressure is increasing for governments to continue to make use of some or all of these instruments. As governments, especially the federal government, have generally tamed annual deficits and are beginning to realize balanced budgets if not substantial **surpluses**, they are now beset with competing demands as to how new revenues and surplus monies should be used. Name a policy field and you can find policy advocates pushing government to spend more on it. Thus, we see calls for increased public spending in health care, public education, public works, roads and transportation infrastructure, and environmental protection. In the fall of 2004, for example, the federal government and the provincial and territorial governments agreed to a new health, equalization, and territorial financing system that would witness an additional $75 billion in federal monies being directed to these policy fields over the following ten years. And yet this is only the beginning of the list. It can easily be extended to include demands for enhanced government spending in agriculture, natural resources development, fishery and forestry promotion, industrial development, the facilitation and promotion of high-technology industries, industrial and technological research and development, and the promotion of regional economic development. The terrorist attacks against the United States in the fall of 2001, of course, simply confirmed this logic. Following these tragic events, the federal government announced over $7.7 billion in new spending geared to promoting national defence, security and intelligence services, air transportation security, and enhanced border and immigration controls. We also see varying levels of support for greater or better **state regulation** in fields ranging from environmental protection and water quality assurance to natural resources development (forestry and fishery management in particular), through to public law and order (with specific reference to gun control), the regulation of pornography on the Internet, and the refinement of rules addressing the possession of soft drugs. Continued public interest in Crown corporation activity is seen in public debates on the proposed expansion of the CBC through additional cable networks, the ongoing question in various provinces as to whether provincial power corporations and liquor commissions should be privatized, and whether or not the Canadian Wheat Board should be disestablished (Canadian Centre for Policy Alternatives, 1998; Shields and Evans, 1998; Albo, Langille, and Panitch, 1993).

The pressures on governments to develop innovative ways to spend, tax, regulate, and engage in commercial activities are real and pervasive, and, with most governments entering into a realm of fiscal stability, it is intriguing to observe them wrestling with the competing demands for greater socioeconomic intervention versus staying the course on public sector restraint and continuing the reduction of the role of the state in society and the economy. From conservatives we hear calls for less government spending on most everything except defence and security policy; less regulation; the further **privatization** of Crown corporations, especially the provincial power-generating giants; and, most notably, vigorous demands for generalized and deep cuts to all individual and corporate taxation rates. Advocates of a smaller state stress that the single greatest cause of Canadian economic lethargy—slow growth, high unemployment, and the "brain-drain" to the south—is high taxation rates relative to the United States. These critics of the state suggest that governments should direct these surpluses both into deficit and/or debt reduction and into major taxation reductions across the board. Such policies would enhance the financial management profile of governments, reduce deficit and debt borrowing costs, and stimulate the private sector by pumping billions of dollars into the hands of individuals and corporations—the necessary stimulus to a Canadian social and economic renaissance. And, these conservative voices argue, a failure to follow this course of action will have equally dramatic negative economic and social effects: an interventionist model of public policy and public administration will inevitably result in

- ever higher and growing deficits;
- greater debts;
- a state once again characterized by its lack of economy, efficiency, effectiveness, and accountability;
- greater regulation and bureaucratic "red tape";
- slower economic growth;
- higher unemployment;
- higher taxes;
- a declining private sector;
- greater out-migration as the "brain-drain" towards the south of the border escalates; and
- the slow decline of Canadian living standards as this country becomes steadily poorer (Johnston, 1996:103-04; Flanagan, 1995; McCormack, 1996).

This policy position, of course, is vehemently scorned by the advocates of a sustained or even greater state role in society and the economy. Liberal or socialist critics of this free enterprise/market economics approach to public policy claim that the social and economic costs of such conservative restraint and taxation policies will be deteriorating conditions in all fields of public policy. The end results of this dynamic would be developments as diverse as two-tiered health care and education systems, as the rich seek superior private medical care and educational services; a growing privatization of services as traditional public services are redefined as commodities to be bought and sold, such as public order and security policy in "gated communities"; and the growing division between richer and poorer. It is feared that this, in turn, will lead to general increases in unemployment, poverty, family breakdowns, family violence, alcohol and drug abuse, prostitution, gambling, crime, and social violence, all leading to an increased need for private security and public law enforcement and penal incarceration, the decline of public safety, and the ultimate decline of Canadian living standards and quality of life as society here comes increasingly to resemble that in the United States. While most liberal and socialist critics of public policy stress that claims for enhanced defence and security spending are legitimate in view of 9/11, they also argue that "security" needs to be seen in a broader socio-economic context requiring governments to protect and promote health, education, welfare, and environmental programs as vital elements of a secure quality of life.

We have painted a stark and disturbing contrast between the policy positions of those for or against greater state involvement in society and the economy. Of course, neither side accepts as fair or accurate the worst-case scenarios of the other. Each stresses that its approach is necessary for the long-term social and economic welfare of the country—or province—and that serious problems await any government that fails to make the correct policy choices.

All governments face major tensions and sharp differences of opinion as they confront the questions of just what courses of action, what policy and program options, are truly in the best interests of the people within their jurisdictions. Governments must engage in the difficult process of governing complex societies and economies—societies and economies replete with numerous and competing political parties, business interests, public interest groups, media voices, and concerned individuals, each of whom will possess their own often entrenched understandings and expectations of what is right in public policy and management and what is wrong. And within this political environment, governments must make choices, often hard choices, with respect to the future of **public policy**, **program administration**, and public sector management. We will see in the next chapter that most governments, especially at the federal level, have sought to deal with these policy tensions by appealing to a moderate, centrist approach to decision-making, seeking to balance concerns for economic growth, stability, and governmental efficiency and economy with creative and relatively progressive policies on economic development, social and cultural policy, and environmental protection. In seeking a balance between demands for a very restrained, rather than a very active state presence, most governments simply reflect mainstream Canadian attitudes towards political balance and moderation. Of course, "the devil is often in the details," so that much Canadian political and governmental debate continues to swirl around the particulars as to how well any government has struck this balance, whether its policies and programs appropriately address the needs and concerns of the various competing interests in society, and whether such policies and programs serve the long-term best interests of the country and its citizens.

Thus, the work of any Canadian government in relation to the broad matters of socio-economic policy development and program management is very complex, and this applies even before we consider the social and economic problems unique to the Canadian federal government. Beyond the general social and economic policy debates confronting all Canadian governments, the federal government faces four ongoing challenges respecting public policy, public administration, public sector management, and government choice:

1. French-English relations and the issue of Quebec;
2. Canadian regionalism, regional disparities, and regional policy;
3. the United States and Canadian-American relations; and
4. Aboriginal policy and relations with **First Nations**.

1.3   French-English Relations and the Issue of Quebec

From the advent of Confederation to the present day, all federal governments have had to address the complex and often divisive relationships between French and English Canadians, between francophones and anglophones, and between Quebec and the rest of Canada (Dyck, 2000; Bothwell, 1998; McRoberts, 1993). This calls for government acts of exquisite balancing as the federal government seeks to serve the long-term well-being of all these forces while advancing its own policy agenda with regard to national unity. Such a balancing act can lead to the ruin of a government if and when its policy and program initiatives come to be widely viewed as undesirable, prejudicial, or disrespectful. Testaments to these realities are the political problems the Trudeau government encountered in the West and those the Mulroney government eventually faced throughout the country as their administrations sought to develop policies beneficial to both French and English Canadians.

The perpetual tension facing any federal government lies in its being called upon to serve and promote the interests of a majority English-Canadian population while also serving and promoting the interests of all the provinces, including, of course, Quebec. But Quebec is distinct, by virtue of the French pervading its history, its demographics, its culture, and its politics. Roughly 80 per cent of the population of Quebec is French Canadian, with many of these people viewing themselves as Québécois, a linguistic and ethnic cultural nationality composing a truly distinct society. To those who identify themselves as Québécois, Quebec is not to be seen as a province *commes les autres*, but as a nation within a nation, defined not only by its French language, culture, and history, but also by its politics of social and cultural survival in the face of English dominance both in Canada and throughout North America. Quebec, then, is to be viewed as a society needing and deserving various forms of special status, state action, and cultural protection so as to preserve and promote its distinct identity. In seeking to promote this political vision, most Québécois turn to the Quebec government as the actor that can best represent their needs and aspirations and which can most effectively advance a Québécois policy agenda.

However, the federal government has always and will always claim a role with respect to Quebec and the "French Fact" in this country. Simply put, Quebec is a constituent part of the greater Canadian whole; the province sends 75 members to the federal Parliament; the federal government is mandated to provide public policy and public services for Quebec just as for any other province; and, from the federal government perspective, there is more to the French Fact in this country than Quebec, just as there is more to Quebec than the French Fact, since roughly 20 per cent of the Quebec population is either anglophone or **allophone**. From the time of Confederation, successive federal governments have been concerned with the social development and economic growth of Canada overall as well as having to deal with Quebec. From the 1960s on, especially, federal governments have devoted considerable time and effort to the "national unity" issue as the rise of separatist sentiment in Quebec has marked a growing anxiety within the province respecting the future of the French language and culture within Canada and even the future constitutional status of Quebec within this country. The federal government's response to these pressures has been multi-faceted and significant in terms of public policy initiatives, though many on both sides of the issue will be critical of the substance of federal actions as well as of the time, money, and procedural effort devoted to these matters at the expense of other policy priorities. Federal initiatives have extended from various efforts at mega-constitutional reform involving both the federal and all provincial governments, to major new federal policy and program initiatives, to specific and more mundane matters of routine federal administration. The past 45 years have witnessed a litany of constitutional reform undertakings spearheaded by the federal government, but with only one set of negotiations, those of 1981, leading to a major amendment of the constitution resulting in the **Constitution Act, 1982**. It is this Act that, among other matters, provides the federal and provincial governments with a domestic amending formula governing future constitutional change and establishes the Canadian **Charter of Rights and Freedoms** as the primary source of legal entitlements for all those living in Canada. While this constitutional reform stands, to many observers, as the greatest accomplishment of the Liberal government of Pierre Trudeau, both his and other federal governments presided over a succession of constitutional failures with respect to the national unity issue over these years: the Fulton-Favreau initiative of 1964 (Pearson); the Victoria Charter of 1971 (Trudeau); and other failures in 1978 (Trudeau) and 1979 (Clark), with perhaps the most significant and most controversial, yet celebrated, failures being the 1987 **Meech Lake Accord** (Mulroney) and then again the 1992 **Charlottetown Accord** (Mulroney) (Russell, 1993).

During the Chrétien years of the 1990s the federal government stood back from proposing major constitutional amendments, preferring to address the Quebec issue through a so-called Plan A/Plan B approach to national unity (Gagnon, 1999; Archer *et al.*, 1999: ch. 3). According to Plan A, the federal government would provide (hopefully sound) social and economic policy throughout the country, including Quebec, with the aim of an improved quality of life for all people in this country and, by logical extension, declining support for sovereignty in Quebec as most Québécois come to realize they have more to gain by remaining a part of Canada than by separating from it. Plan B, deriving from the shock experienced by the Chrétien government and the rest of the country from the excruciatingly close result of the 1995 Quebec referendum, calls upon the federal government to "play hardball" with a Parti Québécois (PQ) government respecting any future sovereignty referendum. This Plan B approach, as endorsed by a Supreme Court of Canada judgement in 1998, stipulates

- that any future referendum must provide for a clear question on separation;
- that any Yes victory, to be legitimate, must be grounded on a clear majority and not a razor-thin margin of victory; and
- that the federal Parliament itself will play a role in deciding whether or not a referendum question is "clear" and a winning majority sufficient.

Finally, should both of these conditions be met through a future referendum, Plan B also stipulates that the federal government can and will enter into negotiations with a victorious PQ government but that all matters concerning a renewed relationship between Quebec and Canada will be subject to bargaining, including

- new international boundaries;
- the status of First Nations in Quebec;
- the possible partition of Quebec and the retention, within Canada, of anglophone and allophone dominant regions of Quebec; and
- any and all economic, financial, currency, and trade relations between a new Canada and a new Quebec.

These policy matters are mentioned here to highlight the past and present importance of such constitutional matters to the federal government and to the entire country. The federal relationship with Quebec, however, extends far beyond constitutional politics, with such issues representing only a small proportion of the federal government engagement with that province. The federal government has sought to provide good and effective governance to Quebec by recognizing through a variety of policy and administrative undertakings its obvious cultural distinctiveness and unique socio-economic needs (Dyck, 2000: ch. 5). Foremost among these are the cultural and linguistic concerns of French Canadians, both in Quebec and throughout the rest of the country, which the federal government addressed through the Official Languages Act, 1969. This Act establishes both French and English as the official languages of Canada and mandates the federal government to defend and promote these languages through policies and programs of bilingualism and biculturalism throughout the country. The Government of Canada, as an institution, is officially bilingual, bearing a general duty to provide public services to any person, anywhere in the country, in the preferred official language. While such policy has been defended by both Liberal and Conservative federal governments as protecting and promoting the interests of the French language, it is also hailed as being fair and even-handed to English Canadians in that it also specifically defends the interests of the English-Canadian and allophone minorities within the province of Quebec.

The key to understanding language policy in this country is to recognize the jurisdictional parameters of federal and provincial governments. The Official Languages Act is federal law, applicable to the federal government; it provides general linguistic entitlements to public services as offered by the federal government. While it makes French and English the official languages of Canada, this is a federal initiative only, in no way binding on provincial governments, each of which remains a fully sovereign political actor within its own fields of jurisdiction. Thus, while the federal government has been officially bilingual since 1969, only one other province, New Brunswick, followed suit in 1982. All other provinces have refrained from passing legislation declaring themselves to be officially bilingual, though some, such as Ontario and Manitoba, do provide significant levels of French-language services where population numbers warrant. And Quebec, once again, is a distinct case. By virtue of Bill 101, passed by the PQ government of René Levesque in 1977, French is the only official language of Quebec's provincial government; moreover, both the PQ and provincial Liberals during their recent terms of power have promoted the French language not only as the official language of the province but also as the official language of work and as a language requiring special priority in all public advertising. None of this should be interpreted as meaning that the English language has no role within the linguistic policies and programs of the government of Quebec. In consideration of its significant English-speaking minority, the Quebec government does provide a substantial range of health, education, and welfare services in English that rival and often surpass the level of minority French language services provided by the neighbouring government of Ontario. The existence of official provincial unilingualism in Quebec, however, does present the irony that within Quebec two official orders of language policy co-exist, in an understandably uneasy and sometimes confusing manner, as both federal and provincial governments advance differing policy objectives with regard to language and French-English relations.

As Québécois nationalist and separatist sentiment and political power has grown within Quebec over the past 50 years, it is also not surprising to observe that the federal government has devoted substantial attention to general socio-economic and cultural policy and programming within Quebec as a means of maintaining and enhancing the federal presence within the province. Such federal initiatives have provided

- arts funding to both French and English theatre, dance, and literary groups, as well as promoting and supporting the Quebec-based aircraft production and shipbuilding industries by way of federal subsidization;
- favourable taxation treatment;
- federal contract preference; and

BOX 1.2
The Sponsorship Scandal

Did federal policy to promote the role of the federal government in Quebec backfire in the years following the 1995 sovereignty referendum? Following the "near death" experience of that vote where the federalist side won by only a 1 per cent margin over the sovereigntist side (50.5 per cent to 49.5 per cent) the Chrétien government initiated the Sponsorship Program designed to promote the federal government's role in supporting cultural events in Quebec. The program had a budget of $250 million, to be used at the discretion of senior officials responsible for the program.

In her 2002 and 2004 reports into the Sponsorship Program, Auditor General Sheila Fraser vociferously attacked the administration of the program on the grounds that $100 million had been improperly used and manipulated, with much of this money finding its way into the hands of Quebec-based public relations firms with known ties to the federal Liberal Party. The auditor general famously remarked that senior federal bureaucrats broke "just about every rule in the book" in their management of the program.

As the media, the opposition parties, and many in the general public cried scandal, the Martin government accepted that something had gone terribly wrong with this program and in 2004 established a public inquiry led by Justice John Gomery to investigate the causes of any wrongdoing.

Prime Minister Jean Chrétien, however, always denied that there was a serious problem here and that any misuse of federal monies was the fault of junior officials who should be dealt with, if need be, by the criminal law process. As for the broader goals of the program, Chrétien and his defenders always said the program had to be understood in the context of the mid to late 1990s when the federal government desperately needed to raise its public profile in Quebec so as to combat the threat of growing public sympathy for separatism. From this perspective, the program accomplished its objectives. Support for sovereignty waned, the PQ lost power to the provincial Liberals in 2003, and as of 2005 the constitutional issue in Quebec lay dormant. As Chrétien's defenders long argued, if the cost of achieving this end result was some wasted money, it's a small price to pay for national unity. Do you agree with this logic? No.

- active federal support for regional development, job creation, and export promotion.

Through all its program activities, the federal government is always keen to promote its own role in providing services to the people of Quebec and in being, and being seen to be, a major player in the common life of the province. Such a presence and such recognition for this role are, after all, fundamental elements of Plan A, and all actions of the federal government in Quebec must be understood, and will be understood by political actors in the province, in light of the broader political and constitutional battle being waged by the federal government against the Québécois sovereigntist movement (Gagnon, 1999). However well-intentioned Plan A might be to Canadian federalists, its implementation was proven to be problematic, as the federal sponsorship scandal highlighted in Box 1.2 illustrates.

1.4 Regionalism, Regional Disparities, and the Politics of Regional Accommodation

The federal policy concern for Quebec, however, has often embittered many English Canadians who insist that the federal government devotes too much time, attention, and economic support to the interests of Quebec at the expense of other pressing needs in English Canada. This criticism highlights the second great challenge faced by all Canadian federal governments: the need to balance and serve the needs of all the major regions of this vast and diverse country while being seen to accomplish this difficult task in a fair and respectful manner (Jackson and Jackson, 1998: 99-105; Dyck, 2000: ch. 3).

Just as there is a French Fact in Canada, so, too, there is the factor of regionalism, which every federal government must address. The main regions—Atlantic Canada, Quebec, Ontario, the Prairies, British Columbia, and the Far North—are noteworthy not only for their historic senses of place and identity, but also for their distinctive socio-economic and cultural compositions and their frequently conflicting economic interests. It is often said that Canada is a difficult country to govern, and a quick review of the regional nature of this land and its politics explains why. The economy of Atlantic Canada is vastly different from that of Ontario, just as the economic interests of British Columbia and the Prairies have clashed with those of Quebec. The simple problem here is that differing regional economies exist within the same country, and these regional economies compete directly with each other, causing people, industries, and provincial governments in each region to call on the federal government to develop economic policies beneficial to them. Thus, public opinion on the Prairies supports the federal government's subsidies for grain producers, for example, while farmers in Quebec want federal agricultural funding to support the Quebec pork industry. Similarly, emerging high-technology and knowledge-based industries in Atlantic Canada desire federal financial support for their activities, even though their actions and success mean additional competition for similar firms in Ontario and British Columbia. And, naturally, public opinion in Ontario will generally support federal policies to bolster the economic strength and job-creation capacity of their province, which Ontarians view as the chief regional economic actor in the country, therefore deserving special consideration as the "motor" of the national economy.

The economic dominance of Ontario in the federation, on the other hand, provides a constant source of disgruntlement for those living outside the province. Many in the West have argued that federal economic policy beneficial to Ontario's manufacturing interests has systematically discriminated against the economic development of the Western provinces and their industrial diversification. In this respect, such historic federal economic policies as the **Crow's Nest Pass railway freight-rates** and oil and natural gas pricing arrangements, which culminated in the **National Energy Policy** of the early 1980s, still rankle Westerners. Such feelings of alienation, moreover, are not simply a Western Canadian phenomenon. There is a deep tendency among many Atlantic Canadians to view themselves and their economy as the forgotten members of the Canadian family; while the rest of the country prospers, so the Maritime lament goes, their unique economic problems receive haphazard and sporadic attention by the federal government, usually only in the lead-up to a federal election. Thus, concern for a federal commitment to promote and practise regional economic development beneficial to the economically disadvantaged peripheral regions of the country is a position not only of Atlantic public opinion but of Atlantic provincial governments as well.

Other provincial governments, however, may be hostile to the Atlantic Canadian interpretation of their economic plight and critical of federal **equalization policy** and greater federally funded regional development programs. Ontario, Alberta, and British Columbia (the richest provinces in the country) can claim that the economic difficulties faced by Atlantic Canada are "inherent" in that they derive from the region's geographic isolation, its historic reliance on natural resource industries now facing decline, and the rigidity of the region's labour market due to overly generous unemployment insurance and welfare payments. In fact, the latter are said to have the effect of leading unemployed or underemployed Atlantic Canadians to remain in the region rather than migrate to other parts of the country where local economies are stronger and jobs more plentiful. From this perspective, federal regional development initiatives are a part of the problem and not the solution, and such initiatives historically are criticized as a response to the political-electoral aims of specific federal governments rather than as cogent thinking about sound national economic policy. This critique of federal regional development policy often is couched in terms of fiscal management, with critics from the wealthier parts of the country complaining that their tax dollars should not be going to subsidize and maintain an approach to economic policy that is both very expensive and incapable of showing effective results.

Federal governments seek a balance between these sharply divided perspectives on federal regional development policy and the interprovincial tensions they elicit. Note, though, that the Atlantic provinces are not alone in their continued support for a strong federal presence in equalization and regional development initiatives; often, they are joined by the governments of Manitoba, Saskatchewan, and at times Quebec, provinces also often considered **"have-not" jurisdictions**. The economic fault-lines here are very much between the richer parts of the country and the poorer, with the latter seeking federal support in promoting their economic and industrial advancement, while the former at times complain that they are not only called upon to financially support economic development programs of questionable effectiveness, but that in so doing they are subsidizing the promotion of their own economic competitors. The friction between the "haves" and "have-nots" is thus understandable, if not very pretty, and it demonstrates the difficult balancing act the federal government performs as it seeks to serve and promote the best economic interests of all the regions of the country. While mention of federal regional development policy can still elicit sharp debate among Canadians with respect to its effectiveness, it is necessary to recognize that all Canadian governments, federal and provincial, are committed to the principle of equalization, with its history of initiatives dating back to the 1950s and enshrined in the Constitution Act, 1982. Despite interregional tensions, the federal and provincial governments have shown that they can work together on certain joint policy undertakings, although usually with much bureaucratic haggling and in-fighting.

Such interprovincial divisions of interest are also found in policy sectors far beyond the economy. The diverse socio-cultural and linguistic make-up of the country produces sharp tensions respecting a variety of issues. Linguistic rights and interest in policies of official bilingualism and biculturalism are of clear, if not uniform, importance in Quebec, New Brunswick, and the parts of Ontario and Manitoba with large francophone populations, but less so elsewhere in Atlantic Canada, Ontario, and the West. Immigration, multiculturalism, and race-relations policy may be of great significance in Toronto, Montreal, Vancouver, and other large urban centres that attract substantial numbers of immigrants, but less so

BOX 1.3

Population Distribution and Parliamentary Representation, 2004

Provinces/Territories	Population	% Total	H. of C. Seats	% of Seats
Newfoundland and Labrador	517,000	1.6	7	2.3
PEI	137,900	0.4	4	1.3
Nova Scotia	937,000	2.9	11	3.6
New Brunswick	751,400	2.4	10	3.2
Quebec	7,542,800	23.6	75	24.3
Ontario	12,392,700	38.8	106	34.4
Manitoba	1,170,300	3.7	14	4.5
Saskatchewan	995,400	3.1	14	4.5
Alberta	3,201,900	10.0	28	9.1
British Columbia	4,196,400	13.1	36	11.7
Yukon	31,200	0.1	1	0.3
Northwest Territories	42,800	0.1	1	0.3
Nunavut	27,500	0.1	1	0.3
Total	31,946,300	100%	308	100%

Sources: Statistics Canada, The House of Commons, 2004.

in rural and small-town Canada. Indeed, attitudes towards immigration, multiculturalism, and equality rights may be distinctly hostile among those Canadians who have little direct contact with recent immigrants and the New-Canadian experience. Likewise, the policy concerns of rural and small-town Canada on issues as diverse as gun registration, regional development, and public sector job decentralization differ greatly from those found in the great cosmopolitan centres.

Regardless of these differing and shifting regional viewpoints, the federal government is expected to govern in the best interests of all regions, while people, businesses, the media, and provincial governments in all regions will closely, if not jealously, review federal action to determine how well the government is serving its mandate and how fairly it is distributing economic, financial, and social benefits across the country. An additional complicating factor is the population imbalance between the regions. Ontario, with a population of roughly 12.4 million as of 2004, is a demographic giant compared to Prince Edward Island with a population of roughly 138,000. The four Atlantic provinces combined have a population of roughly 2.3

million, comparable to the population of the City of Toronto. The Greater Toronto Area (encompassing the 416 and 905 area codes) has a population of roughly 4.5 million, coming close to the population of the Prairies at 5.2 million. Quebec has a population of roughly 7.5 million, many of whom believe they constitute a distinct nation. British Columbia has a population of just over 4 million, Alberta 3.2 million, Manitoba 1.1 million, and Saskatchewan 995,000; the northern territories of Yukon, the Northwest Territories, and Nunavut combined have a population of just over 100,000 (Dyck, 2000: 44).

These figures are basic for a number of reasons. They highlight the vast discrepancies in demographic size between many of the provinces and regions, and they also are indicative of the differing scope and magnitude of regional economies. It is no wonder that Ontario is the economic powerhouse in the country, but it is equally noteworthy that Alberta and British Columbia are growing in size, both demographically and economically. The numbers are also indicative of the difficulties faced by the smaller provinces of Saskatchewan, Manitoba, and Atlantic Canada in promoting economic diversification through the development of secondary manufacturing and service industries when they have to compete against the established economic power and influence of much larger provinces and regions. And the federal government is called upon to oversee and manage these differing interests through its own policy and program decisions. All such federal actions must be understood also in light of a certain political and electoral logic. Just as the Canadian population is not evenly distributed across the country, so, too, there is a variation in electoral representation in the federal Parliament. As this country is a liberal democracy committed to the general principle of representation by population—one person, one vote—the corresponding political reality is that Ontario, with over one-third of the country's total population, dominates representation in the federal House of Commons with 106 of 308 seats, followed by Quebec with 75, British Columbia with 36, and Alberta with 28. The poorer, less populated provinces make up the rest of the seats with Manitoba and Saskatchewan having 14 each, Nova Scotia 11, New Brunswick 10, Newfoundland seven, Prince Edward Island four, and the Far North with three members of Parliament.

The political logic here is unmistakable. For a party to win federal power, it must, as a general rule, do quite well in Ontario and Quebec while gaining reasonable support in at least one other region. It is not necessary to win every region or province, with the "expendable" regions or provinces being those of smaller population size and fewer parliamentary seats. Hence, the long-noted and oft-lamented (by Atlantic and Western Canadians) dominance of Ontario and Quebec over the political attention and government agenda of the federal government.

1.5   Managing the Canadian-American Relationship

While Quebec and regionalism constitute historical policy concerns of the federal government, a third and rapidly evolving area is the Canadian relationship to the United States (Dyck, 2000: ch. 9; Jackson and Jackson, 1998: 553-60; Magnussen, 1999).

Canada has always possessed a complex relationship with its American neighbour. While we have always had close economic ties with the United States, most Canadian leaders since Confederation have promoted policies designed to establish a distinct Canadian economy. Likewise, we have always been greatly influenced by socio-cultural developments in the United States while seeking to maintain a Canadian society and culture separate from and hopefully better than the American. As most Canadians have shown national pride—in characteristically reserved terms—they also have demonstrated sympathy towards some basic policies designed to promote Canadian nationalism. In keeping with these sentiments, the federal government has been called upon to create policies, programs, and institutions to serve the general socio-economic interests of Canadians while also defending the uniqueness of Canada and promoting a Canadian national identity. Economic initiatives ranging from **the National Policy** of the Macdonald government to the **Foreign Investment Review Agency** (FIRA) and the National Energy Policy (NEP) of the Trudeau ministry— as well as the creation of such Crown corporations as Canadian National, Trans-Canada Airlines (later Air Canada), de Havilland, Canadair, Petro-Canada, and the Canadian Development Corporation—can all be seen as federal undertakings to promote the growth and development of the Canadian economy. But more than this, these initiatives and many others like them were promoted as ways of advancing distinctive Canadian approaches to building our economy so that substantial control over the future growth and development would rest in Canadian, and not American, hands, for the benefit of Canadian citizens.

Similar dynamics can be observed in the history of Canadian social and cultural policy. In confronting the power and pervasive influence of American social and cultural ideas, institutions, and practices in this country—from American dominance in television, movies, music, and publishing to the omnipresence of the American ideal of "life, liberty and the pursuit of happiness"—the federal government has defended and promoted uniquely Canadian social and cultural interests. The creation of policies on such issues as gun control legislation, universal and publicly provided health care, state-subsidized post-secondary education, Canadian content rules and regulations in broadcasting, and the establishment of public cultural institutions (the CBC, the NFB, the CRTC, and Telefilm Canada, to name a few) have all served distinct Canadian demands and needs. And they have all helped to distinguish Canadian society from that of the United States. Most Canadians, moreover, recognize and applaud such initiatives, stressing that a key role of the federal government is to defend our cultural identity, broadly defined, from being overwhelmed by American values and influences.

This role has become quite controversial over the past two decades as Canada negotiated and entered into free trade agreements first with the United States in 1989 and then with the United States and Mexico in 1993 (the NAFTA.) These agreements are designed to reduce and eventually eliminate tariff and non-tariff (subsidy and restrictive regulation) barriers to trade between the signatory nations, to ease the free flow of goods and services between the countries, to enhance the ability of private firms in any one country to do business in the others, and to restrict the ability of governments from any signatory country to intervene in the free operation of the continental economy so as to provide specific benefits to specific national firms. One of the policy thrusts of the free trade undertaking was to entrench free enterprise/market economic approaches to economic development throughout the continent. As a consequence, Canada has been drawn closer to the American dominant economic policy approach of supporting the private sector, supporting a more individualistic and business-oriented economic development, and downplaying the role of the public sector in such economic planning (Doern and Tomlin, 1991: ch. 12; Riggs and Velk, 1993).

This reality poses major challenges to many Canadians and to all Canadian governments. The magnitude of this orientational shift in economic and government policy was sensed in 1988, during the so-called "Free Trade" election, when the campaign became a virtual referendum on the merits and demerits of free trade with the United States, producing a contest that was one of the most bitter, passionate, and divisive elections in Canadian history. The Progressive Conservatives under the leadership of Brian Mulroney won that election, and the Canada-United States Free Trade Agreement was passed into law 1 January 1989. While we have been living with free trade for more than a decade, many Canadians remain very

BOX 1.4
In Defence of Canada

Pierre Trudeau once equated Canada living beside the United States as a mouse having to live beside an elephant. While the elephant will hardly ever notice the mouse, the mouse will always be sensitive to every move and twitch and grunt of the great beast for fear that inattention could prove fatal. Beyond the trade and economic and social policy issues mentioned in this chapter, the years following 9/11 have placed added stress on the Canadian-American relationship with respect to foreign policy, national defence, and border security. Since the fall of 2001, the American government has asked for Canadian support in the invasion and occupation of Afghanistan and Iraq, the strengthening of Canadian border security, and substantial Canadian involvement in American intercontinental missile defence programs.

These requests posed challenges to both the Chrétien and Martin governments since such initiatives tend to divide Canadians on what is the appropriate course of action for the Government of Canada to follow. The Chrétien government supported the invasion and lib-eration of Afghanistan, and Canadian military personnel have served numerous tours of duty in that country. Canada also beefed up its military spending in the immediate aftermath of 9/11 by some $8 billion while promising to further strengthen the Canadian armed forces. In its budget for 2005, the Martin government committed an additional $12 billion for national defence over the next five years. Yet the Chrétien government did not support the American and British invasion and occupation of Iraq in 2003, with this policy decision being widely popular among most Canadians. And Canadian involvement in an American-developed missile defence shield has always been controversial. These events and developments pose fundamental questions of national defence to Canadians and their federal government: What should be the desired role of the Canadian armed forces? More peacekeeping and national security or greater interoperability and common deployment with major American missions? Should Canadian defence spending be increased to address the "War on Terror" and concern for greater international insecurity, or are there other pressing social, economic, and diplomatic calls for additional governmental spending?

critical, or at least skeptical, of this policy, arguing that the supposed benefits of economic growth and job creation never materialized and that we, as a country, are slipping further and further into the American economic orbit while being subjected to a concomitant "Americanization" of Canadian society and social policy. This concern has only been exacerbated in recent years with the softwood lumber dispute and repeated American refusals to obey international trade rulings that run counter to preferred American outcomes. Furthermore, despite fervent Liberal opposition to free trade in 1988, this party also has come to embrace greater continental free trade policy, with the Liberal government of Jean Chrétien endorsing the NAFTA in 1993. While the federal New Democratic Party (NDP) still officially calls for the abolition of the NAFTA, all other major Canadian political parties, including even the Bloc Québécois, have come to accept it as a *fait accompli*, if not a great leap forward. The policy goal is to allow governments to manage the free trade relationship with our partner countries in such a way that benefits flowing to Canada will be maximized, while unique and distinct Canadian economic and social interests will be protected, as much as possible.

Free trade, of course, does have serious implications for all Canadian governments in that certain traditional forms of state support for Canadian economic and industrial development are now prohibited under the terms of the NAFTA; however, this agreement neither emasculates the economic powers of the federal and provincial governments nor prohibits governments from intervening in the economic life of society. Rather, the terms and conditions of free trade policy challenge governments in any of the signatory countries to be more precise, balanced, and fair in their development of economic and industrial promotion policy. Far from curtailing the role of the public sector in such economic and industrial development, free trade policy forces governments to be both more open and creative in devising means to provide state support to designated industrial sectors by way of a variety of public service programs generally available to all economic actors, domestic or foreign, in a given sector. The rules and regulations of free trade impose an even greater obligation on all Canadian governments—federal and provincial—to coordinate their economic policies *vis-à-vis* the United States, with the federal government in particular carrying not a diminished but an enhanced duty to promote Canada's economic and social interests in our relations with our southern neighbour. The policy capacity and managerial strength of Canadian governments are at a premium in this world of free trade as they must work to manage the historic relationship with the United States so as to maximize Canadian interests. And, as always, the federal government plays a leading role in this work, because Canadians continue to insist that, although we want the economic benefits to be derived from a strong continental economy, we also want to maintain a strong Canadian-influenced economy and our traditional social and cultural distinctiveness (Doern and Tomlin, 1991: ch. 11).

1.6 Addressing the First Nations

A fourth ongoing, and often difficult and controversial, policy concern of the federal government is its primary responsibility for managing the relationship between the First Nations and the Canadian state, including developing just Aboriginal policy, the fair negotiation of treaty and **land**

BOX 1.5
First Nation's Governments

One of the most important and challenging developments in the history of Canadian government is the current renaissance of First Nations' governments. The government relationship between Aboriginal and non-Aboriginal Canadians dates back centuries, with the most significant constitutional document of this relationship being the Royal Proclamation of 1763.

One vital element of this proclamation was the recognition by the British Crown of the existence of First Nations within what was becoming British North America. It also affirmed that the only legal foundation for the establishment of intergovernmental relations between the British government and these First Nations, including any transfer of land and responsibilities, would be through the establishment of treaties.

The history of the relations between these First Nations and first the British and then the Canadian federal and provincial governments has been generally woefully inadequate and even shameful. When these nations were colonized, many of the obligations that British and Canadian governments owed to them were ignored. But First Nations' governments never died away, and their leaders were successful in 1982 in gaining explicit recognition of Aboriginal Rights in Section 25 of the Charter of Rights and Freedoms as well as in Section 35 of the Constitution Act.

In the past two decades much has begun to change. In a number of landmark cases such as *Sparrow* (1990), *Delgum'ukw* (1997), and *Marshall* (1999), the Supreme Court of Canada has recognized the continuing constitutional validity of the Royal Proclamation of 1763 as well as of specific Aboriginal and treaty rights to engage in traditional ceremonial and economic activities. Many First Nations have also engaged in complex treaty negotiations or renegotiations respecting treaty rights, land claims, and the development of self-government.

We are witnessing a rebirth of Aboriginal nationalism. These First Nations and their governments confront many challenges. They must deal with federal and provincial governments that have not always proven supportive of Aboriginal concerns. They must also deal with non-Aboriginal Canadians who may be either ignorant or unsympathetic, or both, to the rights and interests of Aboriginal Canadians. And, just as importantly, First Nations' governments are called upon, by their own people, to undertake the process of governance and public sector management within their nations in conformity with the highest degrees of administrative competence, political accountability, and respect for the rule of law.

All Canadians, Aboriginal and non-Aboriginal, have important roles to play in the development and evolution of Aboriginal self-government as a way of addressing the quality of social justice and fairness in this country.

claim demands, and the promotion of systems of Aboriginal self-government (Dyck, 2000: ch. 4; Long and Dickason, 1996; Asch, 1997).

The historic relations between the Canadian government and the Aboriginal peoples of this land have been characterized by the manipulative, abusive, and imbalanced power relationship between the dominant white society and the First Nations. The revival of First Nations' nationalism over the past 30 years has forced Canadian governments—especially the federal government—to recognize and acknowledge the injustices of this past relationship and to redress and reform it through new and better ways of managing Aboriginal policy.

Among these are the negotiation or renegotiation of **treaty rights** and **land-claim demands**. In many cases in the past, treaties were entered into by British and Canadian governments, which failed to comply with their obligations. In other cases, Aboriginal leaders either did not understand the language and, therefore, the terms of the treaties or were forced to sign to get some help for their peoples ravaged by hunger, deprivation, illness, and disease. The fairness and legitimacy of many treaties are also questionable, due to differing cultural understandings respecting such matters as individual and collective rights, land ownership, private property entitlements, and the concept of **Aboriginal Title**. In many other instances, in British Columbia or the Far North for example, treaties were never entered into at all, with the result that First Nations' lands were simply occupied by white settlers in the absence of any formal legal process. Given these problems with the treaty process as well as the many social and economic problems experienced by many First Nations, the federal government is committed either to the renegotiation of existing treaties or the negotiation of first treaties. Of course, such contemporary treaty negotiation is complex and fraught with controversy. Governments must address such matters as Aboriginal land claims, the establishing of First Nations on sufficient territory to be economically viable, the balancing of ownership rights to hitherto Crown lands and natural resources, the determination of financial compensation for past injustices and lost entitlements, and the provision of current fiscal support for the operational management of First Nations. With respect to any one of these issues, governments are hard pressed to determine what is both just and constitutionally required for First Nations and also politically acceptable to the non-Aboriginal majority. The debate with respect to the Nisga'a Comprehensive Treaty of 1999 within British Columbia highlights all of these problems.

The federal government and most provincial governments are committed to the negotiation and creation of systems of **Aboriginal self-government**. This commitment poses great challenges to Aboriginal and non-Aboriginal officials and citizens, as debates are entered into about the precise meaning of self-government, the merits and demerits of various models of self-government systems, and the nature of the political, economic, and legal relationships that will be created through such systems. These relationships can and will govern such matters as the equality rights of Aboriginal men and women, the legal and political rights of non-Aboriginal peoples residing on First Nations' territory, the applicability of the Charter of Rights and Freedoms to First Nations, and the constitutionality of race-based approaches to rights entitlements. Moreover, both the federal and First Nations' governments need systems of public sector management that will further Aboriginal self-government, stabilize the policy and administrative relationships between these governments, and enable First Nations and governments to provide effective, responsible, and accountable public administration for their people. The challenges are great. After devolving or returning administrative authority to the leadership of the First Nations, the federal government is then expected to recognize the legitimacy of First Nations' governments and to work cooperatively with them in the administration of government services, such services still largely funded by federal money. In turn, First Nations are called upon to develop the managerial expertise to administer their affairs in accordance with all standard expectations of just and effective public administration. With their federal and provincial counterparts, First Nations' governments are expected to adhere to all established concepts of administrative fairness and competence, with the same traits of economy, efficiency, and democratic accountability displayed in their governmental decision-making. And, just as federal and provincial governments have often struggled to live up to these standards, so also have First Nations' governments been subjected to criticism from their citizens who demand greater accountability from their elected leaders.

As both federal and provincial governments on one side and First Nations' governments on the other have been working to develop better means of relating to one another and of promoting better means of accountability between themselves and the people they serve, they have also been confronted with a unique and difficult problem in providing public services to Aboriginal Canadians. While many of the developments regarding Aboriginal self-government relate to the devolution of political authority to First Nation band governments on reserves, the troubling reality is that, in most provinces, almost half of the Aboriginal population is not living on reserves. Aboriginal and non-Aboriginal governments must develop ways of providing needed public services to these urban Aboriginal peoples in keeping with the principles and practices of self-government and sound program management. As we will observe in Chapter 11, many contemporary reforms in public sector management over the past decade, especially in relation to decentralization, participatory management, enhanced accountability, and communication and service responsiveness, are of significant interest to those who are concerned with building systems of public services and lines of communication between First Nations' governments and their often scattered populations. In some ways, these old-yet-also-new governments are on the cutting edge of public sector management reform and innovation.

1.7   Government Capacity, Accountability, and Public Sector Management

It is not surprising that interest in governmental capability and accountability has increased in the past quarter-century not only among the general public but in political parties, interest groups, the media, and the public service itself. This dynamic has led to substantial undertakings with respect to the nature and working of public sector management by Canadian governments to enhance and improve their capacity to provide effective policy and program administration. Over the past two decades, for example, all governments in this country have been influenced by a new approach to thinking and doing public administration. This approach, known as the **New Public Management** (NPM), adopts a rather conservative frame of reference, stressing that governments need to be more businesslike in their undertakings, learning from and emulating the private sector in much of their work, and even transferring to private hands responsibilities that were traditionally seen as essential duties of the public sector. As interest in the NPM increased over these years, we have observed an increasing interest in such public policies as privatization, deregulation, contracting-out, commercialization and user fees, decentralization, and the overall downsizing of the public sector. All these actions were seen by advocates of the NPM not only as a means of eliminating horrendous public sector deficits and controlling related debts, but of putting public sector management on a new, more creative footing.

According to these analysts, whose work will be assessed more fully in Chapter 10, governments should be just as creative, dynamic, and competent as their private sector counterparts. As such, management in the public sector should be just as devoted to the concerns of economy, efficiency, and effectiveness as can be found in the private sector, without abandoning the social and economic needs of the broad public—hence, the now familiar refrain that governments and their management and staff must be prepared to "do more with less." And by doing so, as the defenders of the NPM assert, governments can reclaim their damaged credibility in the eyes of the public, can become significant actors once again in the public life of this country, and can become far more accountable and responsive to the people they are called upon to serve.

All these claims, however, are highly contested by the critics of the NPM who see this approach as a not-so-veiled threat to the integrity and role of the public sector by treating it as a poor imitation of the private sector and not as a separate entity with distinct and valid forms of reasoning, problem-solving, and decision-making. The unique reality attending management within the world of public administration, democratic government, and parliamentary politics legitimizes and necessitates forms of management different from those in the competitive marketplace. This debate is rejoined in Chapter 10, for it has become one of the great debates that has dominated Canadian political discourse for well over a decade and is one likely to continue to preoccupy political thought and action.

This debate, in theory, poses important questions respecting the type of government and public services that Canadians want. And it is this debate that we see reflected in such diverse issues as the modernization of health care, educational, and social assistance policy through to public concern for the maintenance and regulation of drinking water quality; the deterioration of public infrastructure, especially roads, bridges, and waterworks systems; and the growing concern respecting environmental protection and the quality of life within the environment. All these matters relate to the quality of our governments and public services and, thus, to the quality of systems of accountability respecting the governments. Accountability, then, becomes the one great theme flowing through all issues pertaining to governments and through any analysis of governments and their management of public duties. All governments will seek to be accountable to the needs and wishes of the public they serve, and all governments will routinely claim that they are so accountable. Any study of government must address the concept of accountability, its meaning, and the degree to which governments live up to this expectation. These matters are complex, subject to much discussion, debate, and differences of opinion, as governments face competing demands with respect as to how they can and should be accountable.

These are the demands that all governments face:

- that they must provide excellent policies and services delivered in the most economical and efficient manner possible;
- that their policy and program developments be responsive to general public needs while also serving the needs of various special interests;

- that their role within the state be intelligently designed and operated to strike a balance between the needs and interests of the public and private sectors;
- that their actions and those of their public servants be consistent with the rules of administrative law, as well as with newly developing rules governing public sector ethics;
- that their decision-making be more open and transparent than ever before, subject to much more interest group and general public participation than has ever been the case in the past;
- that they must exercise sound and prudent financial management of the public's money and that their budgetary practices must be open, honest, and fiscally responsible;
- that their personnel management must reflect the legitimate promotion of a professional and competent public service, broadly representative of, and sensitive to, the community it serves and that practices of nepotism, favouritism, and patronage must be disavowed and prohibited; and
- that while they provide strong and capable executive and administrative leadership with respect to all of these matters, they will establish administrative systems conducive to efficient and effective decision-making that is wise, just, rational, far-sighted, and advances the long-term interests of Canadians.

In addition, the federal government must provide sound and fair management towards Quebec and national unity, towards all Canadian regions and federal-provincial relations, and towards relationships with the United States and with the First Nations.

This is a tall order. Indeed, as Jeffrey Simpson (2001) has argued, governments face demanding yet desirable expectations for a reason. They are guardians yet also servants of the public trust. The demands placed upon Canadian governments are many and varied, and public expectations for quality in policy and program services are very high. This is altogether fitting and proper in a society with high aspirations, a social conscience, and dedication to democratic principles. Public sector management will go a long way to either promoting, or detracting from, a government's ability to live up to these public expectations. Hence, the focus of this text is not only on the general nature of government in this society and the role of the state, but also upon the nature of public sector management in Canada, the quality of its working, and the debates respecting the ways and means of its improvement. How successful are our governments in living up to all these expectations? To begin this analysis of Canadian government and public sector management, the next chapter turns to the political and ideological foundation of government in this country, assessing the competing schools of thought respecting the role of the state in society and the corresponding duties and responsibilities to be borne by the public sector and its managers.

Key Terms

Aboriginal Self-Government: The initiative for the members of First Nations to gain full responsibility for managing their own social, economic, and political affairs free from the control of federal or provincial governments; for First Nations to govern themselves.

Aboriginal Title: The constitutional concept that First Nations retain an inherent Aboriginal and religious relationship of care, concern, and responsibility for protecting and preserving their lands for future Aboriginal generations. While Canadian law recognizes that title can be extinguished by clear and explicit treaty provisions, this point remains debatable in Aboriginal constitutional discourse.

accountability: The duty owed by public officials—elected politicians and public servants—to abide by the concepts of ministerial responsibility, the Rule of Law, and social responsiveness. Accountability is a complex concept in both theory and practice and is explained in greater detail in Chapter 11.

allophones: Those persons living in Quebec whose mother tongue is neither French nor English.

bureaucratization: The dynamic that occurs when social and economic affairs are increasingly subject to the growing influence and/or control of the state and its institutions.

Charlottetown Accord: A constitutional amendment proposal of 1992 supported by the Mulroney government and all provincial governments of the time; it was designed to, among other features, recognize Quebec as a distinct society, decentralize federal powers, create an elected Senate, and recognize Aboriginal self-government. This accord was defeated in a national referendum in the fall of 1992.

Charter of Rights and Freedoms: The constitutional declaration of fundamental rights and freedoms possessed by all Canadians that must be respected by all Canadian governments and their officials. The Charter was brought into force as part of the Constitution Act, 1982.

Constitution Act, 1982: The constitutional agreement signed by the federal government and all provincial governments with the exception of Quebec that resulted in the patriation of the constitution, the establishment of a constitutional amending formula, and the creation of the Charter of Rights and Freedoms.

Crown corporations: Commercial enterprises established and owned by either the federal or provincial state but which possess relative operational autonomy from the government of the day.

Crow's Nest Pass Policy: Federal railway freight policy designed in the late nine-teenth century to promote the industrial development of central Canada by arti-ficially lowering the costs of transporting manufactured good to the West from the East while artificially raising the costs of transporting manufactured goods from the West to the East.

deficits: The budgetary dynamic when expenditures and other financial liabilities exceed revenues resulting in the need to borrow money to meet financial obliga-tions, with such borrowing resulting in an accumulating debt.

equalization policy: Federal policy now enshrined in section 35 of the Constitu-tion Act, 1982, designed to provide federal funding to "Have-Not" provinces so as to bring their revenues up to the national provincial average required to pro-vide basic public services at a level of quality comparable to the national aver-age.

First Nations: The term given, in general, to specific Aboriginal groups who formed societies and possessed systems of government predating the arrival of Euro-pean settlers.

Foreign Investment Review Agency (FIRA): A federal regulatory agency estab-lished by the Trudeau government designed to screen, analyze, and even pro-hibit foreign, and especially American, direct investment in Canada so as to promote the Canadianization of the national economy. FIRA was abolished by the Mulroney government.

government restraint: The policy of governments restricting and/or downsizing social and economic spending initiatives and promoting privatization and dereg-ulation as a means of reducing government spending, cutting deficits, and limit-ing the scope of government involvement in the social and economic life of a country.

"have-not" jurisdictions: Those provinces whose ability to levy taxes so as to fund basic public services falls below the national provincial average of revenue gen-erating capacity.

land claim demands: The claims, advanced by the leaderships of various First Nations, to better arrangements with the federal government respecting the allo-cation of land rights between Aboriginal and non-Aboriginal populations, and the compensation owing to First Nations for lands relinquished by them or improperly seized from them in the past.

Meech Lake Accord: A constitutional amendment proposed by the Mulroney gov-ernment in 1987 and supported by most provincial governments over the late 1980s. This Accord would have recognized Quebec as a distinct society and would have witnessed a decentralization of federal powers to the provinces. This proposal died in 1990 when it failed to gain unanimous provincial approval.

multiculturalism: Federal and provincial policy designed to defend and promote acceptance of a pluralist and welcoming appreciation that Canadian culture is composed of multiple linguistic, ethnic, religious, national, and social groups.

National Energy Policy: A policy of the Trudeau government in the early 1980s designed to promote the Canadianization of the national energy sector by impos-ing greater federal taxes on oil and gas, largely generated in Western Canada, and enhancing the role of the then federal Crown corporation Petro Canada in the development and sale of oil and gas. This policy was greatly reviled in Western Canada.

National Policy: A national economic development policy designed by the government of John A. Macdonald to promote Canadian industrialization by imposing high tariffs on imported American manufactured goods resulting in Canadian firms having a protected Canadian market.

New Public Management: An approach to public sector management that emerged in the 1980s and that was designed to promote greater economy, efficiency and effectiveness in government by stressing that the public sector should adopt certain of the techniques and behaviours of the private sector while also granting public servants much greater operational freedom in undertaking their actions, subject to the overall control of elected politicians. This concept is dealt with at greater length in Chapter 10.

privatization: The act of governments divesting themselves of Crown corporations.

program administration: The managerial concept of taking public policy and implementing it in the real world. The technique of using the tools of financial management, human resources management, and operational management so as to develop the ways and means of being able to deliver, and administer, programs to the public that meet the goals of public policy.

public policy: The broad understandings, priorities, goals, and objectives that a government entity will possess with respect to a given field of human activity and governmental interest. Public policy refers to a set of understandings respecting what should be the ends of governmental actions in a given field; program administration deals with the implementation of the managerial means to attain those ends.

public sector management: The administrative functioning of the state and its officials. Public sector management will deal with the methods and techniques by which state officials will organize themselves so as to be able to implement public policies. Public sector management will traditionally focus on the mobilization of financial resources (budgeting policy), human resources (personnel policy) and operational and strategic leadership.

socio-economic policy: Those policies of the state designed to address social (health, education, welfare, environmental and cultural) concerns as well as their inter-relationship to economic (trade, business, income, commercial and tax) concerns.

state: That part of society comprising the broad public sector as opposed to the private sector; that part of society based upon the institutions of government. The Canadian state can be understood as comprising all those institutions accounted for and controlled and directed by the federal government, all provincial and municipal governments, and all First Nations' governments. One can also refer to the federal state as being all the public institutions in the federal realm and to a given provincial state as referring to all the public provincial and municipal institutions in that given province.

state regulation: Public mandates and requirements established by either federal or provincial law designed to control, direct, influence, and shape the actions of individuals, private firms, or related government institutions so as to achieve a public purpose set by the responsible government.

surpluses: The budgetary dynamic when revenues exceed expenditures and other liabilities resulting in the possession of excess, or surplus, monies at the end of a fiscal year, with such surplus monies then being available for new spending.

treaty rights: Those entitlements respecting land, social services, and economic rights extended to First Nations and their members by virtue of legal agreements entered into by the leaders of First Nations and representatives of the Crown.

References and Suggested Reading

Albo, Gregory, David Langille, and Leo Panitch, eds. 1993. *A Different Kind of State? Popular Power and Democratic Administration.* Toronto: Oxford University Press.

Archer, Keith, Roger Gibbins, Rainer Knopff, and Leslie A. Pal. 1999. *Parameters of Power: Canada's Political Institutions.* 2nd ed. Toronto: Nelson.

Asch, Michael, ed. 1997. *Aboriginal and Treaty Rights in Canada: Essays on Law, Equality and Respect for Difference.* Vancouver: University of British Columbia Press.

Bothwell, Robert. 1998. *Canada and Quebec: One Country; Two Histories.* Rev. ed. Vancouver: University of British Columbia Press.

Campbell, Colin, and William Christian. 1996. *Parties, Leaders, and Ideologies in Canada.* Toronto: McGraw-Hill Ryerson.

Canadian Centre for Policy Alternatives, and Choices: A Coalition for Social Justice. 1998. *Alternative Federal Budget Papers 1998.* Ottawa: Canadian Centre for Policy Alternatives.

Doern, G. Bruce, and Brian W. Tomlin. 1991. *Faith and Fear: The Free Trade Story.* Toronto: Stoddart.

Dyck, Rand. 2000. *Canadian Politics: Critical Approaches.* 3rd ed. Toronto: Nelson.

Flanagan, Tom. 1995. *Waiting for the Wave: The Reform Party and Preston Manning.* Toronto: Stoddart.

Gagnon, Alain-G. 1999. "Quebec's Constitutional Odyssey." In James Bickerton and Alain-G. Gagnon, eds., *Canadian Politics.* 3rd ed. Peterborough, ON: Broadview Press. 279-300.

Howlett, Michael, and M. Ramesh. 1995. *Studying Public Policy: Policy Cycles and Policy Subsystems.* Toronto: Oxford University Press.

Inwood, Gregory J. 1999. *Understanding Canadian Public Administration: An Introduction to Theory and Practice.* Scarborough, ON: Prentice Hall Allyn and Bacon.

Jackson, Robert J., and Doreen Jackson. 1998. *Politics in Canada: Culture, Institutions, Behaviour and Public Policy.* 4th ed. Scarborough, ON: Prentice Hall Allyn and Bacon.

Johnston, Larry. 1996. *Ideologies: An Analytical and Contextual Approach.* Peterborough, ON: Broadview Press.

Long, David, and Olive Dickason. 1996. *Visions of the Heart: Canadian Aboriginal Issues.* Toronto: Harcourt Brace.

Magnussen, Warren. 1999. "State Sovereignty, Localism, and Globalism." In James Bickerton and Alain-G. Gagnon, eds., *Canadian Politics.* 3rd ed. Peterborough, ON: Broadview Press. 57-78.

McCormack, Peter, 1996. "The Reform Party of Canada: New Beginning or Dead End?" In Hugh G. Thorburn, ed., *Party Politics in Canada.* 7th ed. Scarborough, ON: Prentice Hall Canada. 352-63.

McRoberts, Kenneth. 1993. *Quebec: Social Change and Political Crisis.* 3rd ed. Toronto: McClelland and Stewart.

Nelson, Ralph. 1995. "Ideologies." In Robert M. Krause and R.H. Wagenberg, eds., *Introductory Readings in Canadian Government and Politics.* 2nd ed. Toronto: Copp Clark. 25-40.

Phillips, Susan. 1999. "Social Movements in Canadian Politics: Past Their Apex?" In James Bickerton and Alain-G. Gagnon, eds., *Canadian Politics.* 3rd ed. Peterborough, ON: Broadview Press. 371-92.

Prince, Michael J. 1999. "From Health and Welfare to Stealth and Farewell: Federal Social Policy, 1980-2000." In Leslie A. Pal, ed., *How Ottawa Spends 1999-2000: Shape Shifting; Canadian Governance Toward the 21st Century.* Toronto: Oxford University Press. 151-98.

Riggs, A.R., and Tom Velk. 1993. *Beyond NAFTA: An Economic, Political and Sociological Perspective.* Vancouver: The Fraser Institute.

Russell, Peter H. 1993. *Constitutional Odyssey: Can Canadians Become a Sovereign People?* 2nd ed. Toronto: University of Toronto Press.

Shields, John, and B. Mitchell Evans. 1998. *Shrinking the State: Globalization and Public Administration "Reform."* Halifax: Fernwood Publishing.

Simpson, Jeffrey. 2001. *The Friendly Dictatorship.* Toronto: McClelland and Stewart.

Swimmer, Gene. 1996. "An Introduction to Life Under the Knife." In Gene Swimmer, ed., *How Ottawa Spends 1996-1997: Life Under the Knife.* Ottawa: Carleton University Press. 1-38.

Related Web Sites

CANADIAN GOVERNMENT
<http://www.canada.gc.ca>

CANADIAN GOVERNMENT AND POLITICS
<http://www.canoe.ca>
<http://www.culture.ca>
<http://www.politicswatch.com>
<http://www.canadiansocialresearch.net>

CHAPTER 2
Competing Ideologies of Government and Public Service

The state is a major player in our society. Governments and their administrative functions are omnipresent in the routine life of every Canadian, and debates about desired public policies are ongoing, as individuals, business corporations, interest groups, the media, political parties, and governments wrestle with fundamental political issues: What type of society do we want to live in? What should be the appropriate balance between individual and collective rights and duties? What should be the appropriate role of the public sector in this society?

These questions are crucial not only to the nature and working of governments in this country, but also to the ways in which people think about politics and power. In thinking about government and public sector management it is important always to bear in mind that these matters exist in an inherently political world. Politics and political ideas are at once the foundation stones of governments and the material from which approaches to desired public policy and public sector management are fashioned. It is impossible to think about governments and their work without knowing the ideas, interests, and values that condition all governments. This chapter examines the many linkages between politics, ideology, policy, and management. By probing the ideological foundations of Canadian politics and government one can discern the seeds of the paradox outlined in Chapter 1.

Canadian political culture contains different strains of thought respecting the role of the state and the working of government. Some of these ideas are very hostile to a large state presence in this society, while others are hostile to a minimalist state presence. In the interplay of these competing ideas, most Canadians seek a moderate, balanced, middle ground. It is this middle ground, the politics of centrism, that has defined the work of most governments in this country, especially at the federal level.

2.1 A Parliamentary Primer and the Centrality of Politics

Governments exist, in simplest terms, to provide leadership to a society and its economy. In Canada, the federal Parliament and the provincial assemblies are the legislative arms of the Canadian state. They are the focal point for the organization of competing parties, political debate, and regular democratic elections. Through the electoral process, citizens determine which party and, consequently, which party leader they wish to lead the federal government and their respective provincial government for a maximum five-year term of office. Once elected to office by winning a majority or at least a plurality of the seats in Parliament or the legislature, the leader of the winning party usually will be called upon by the governor general—or by the lieutenant-governor in a province—to form a government. This is accomplished by the party leader, the prime minister or premier, choosing a cabinet. The now governing party then takes control of the executive and administrative institutions of the federal or provincial state and undertakes its responsibilities in policy-making and program implementation. As the governing party works to fulfill its duties, its actions will be scrutinized closely by opposition parties, those parties that ran behind the winning party but that won some level of representation in Parliament or the legislature. Such representation provides the opposition parties with an institutionalized accountability function: the parliamentary opposition holds the governing party to account for its exercise of power. In parliamentary theory and practice, the government—the executive branch—must be accountable to Parliament or the provincial legislature—the legislative branch—for all of its actions. Ministers of the Crown must sit in the legislature, and they must be prepared to answer questions regarding their conduct of government business, to debate the merits and demerits of new policy and administrative initiatives, and to have all new government legislation reviewed and voted on by the members of Parliament or the legislative assembly.

This brief overview of parliamentary procedure is a reminder of the centrality of politics to the working of any government. The point is basic, yet it deserves reiteration, for it marks a fundamental point of distinction between public sector and private sector management. At the core of public sector management is the factor of politics. Depending on the changing currents and undercurrents of political favour governments rise and fall, prime ministers and premiers come and go, and various approaches to policy, policy-making, and program implementation wax and wane. Everything governments do, and don't do, can be reduced to political explanations, because governments are forged out of the processes of party politics and democratic elections. The behaviour of governments is always judged in a political forum, and the assessment of the decision-making of any government is an inherently political act.

This must be the case because of the essential nature of government. In contrast to the work of business enterprises and private sector management, where the prime focus of attention is the continued viability of the individual firm, its profitability, and rate of return of investment to owners and shareholders as measured by the precise logic of the "bottom-line," the work of governments and public sector management is centred on the much more ambiguous world of party politics, political debate, and the assessment of the "public interest." Parties vie for government power on the grounds that any one party can provide—can "promise"—an approach to public policy and public administration superior to those approaches offered by other parties. This is the essence of party competition: parties compete with one another for the favour of public opinion by struggling to capture the hearts and minds of ordinary Canadians, or at least a winning plurality of the will of the voting public, by packaging and promoting certain policy and program messages and goals, which each party believes will garner maximum sympathy and support from the general public. Such party competition is ongoing, year-in and year-out, though it reaches a periodic climax during election campaigns, when the electorate is called upon to exercise a choice by casting ballots to determine the composition of a new Parliament or legislative assembly and, thus, either to confirm the continuation in office of the old, pre-existing government or to elect a new government to office.

Political belief and political action is vital to the unfolding saga. Parties compete against one another with respect to policy ends and means, broad ideological beliefs, proven political and managerial records, and demonstrated experience in political and government leadership. Differing alternatives to public policies, the assessment of the role of the state, and the manner by which government will be used to promote certain policy objectives become the staples of political and electoral debate. Unlike strategic policy debates with respect to institutions operating in the private sector, such debates in the public sector address matters of broad public policy. Rather than dealing with matters of profit and loss, in which the measure of success and managerial competence is explicitly quantifiable and verifiable, governments, by their very nature, must address broad socio-economic and cultural matters that do not possess any such clear and generally agreed-upon measures of success.

Common indications of success for a government are not whether it turned a profit or not, but whether it promoted economic growth, maintained and enhanced the quality of social welfare, strengthened justice, and generally nurtured and improved the quality of life of its citizens. While governments in the 1990s and the first years of this new century came to be increasingly concerned with eliminating public sector deficits and running balanced or even surplus budgets, they faced public pressures

- to marry policies of fiscal restraint with other policies designed to help the disadvantaged;
- to promote and strengthen the quality of services in the fields of health, education, and welfare; and
- to elevate public services designed to enhance the quality of human rights and environmental, cultural, and Aboriginal policy, to name just a few major policy fields.

And, of course, following the terrorist attacks of 9/11, the federal government was called upon to enhance the quality of policies and programs for national defence, security and intelligence services, air transportation safety, and border security. With respect to all these policy goals, however, terms such as "promote," "maintain," "enhance," "quality," "help," "strengthen," and "elevate" are subjective. Any assessment as to whether any one government has successfully achieved any of these ends is a matter of political judgement and interpretation through which differing persons can and likely will—reasonably or unreasonably—disagree, because they bring differing political and philosophical understandings to the qualitative assessment of what is and is not good government, good public policy, and good public sector management.

As parties compete with one another for favourable public opinion ratings, political influence, and ultimately the attainment of government power, this competition will be significantly affected by each party's broad approach to public policy. Parties contest for power in a political arena in which they are called upon to address the grand questions of public life:

How should the economy be organized and managed? Should free enterprise and a market economy be promoted or controlled and regulated? Should individual liberty be given higher priority than social equality, or vice versa? Can some balance be struck between these two positions? If so, how? Should governments play an active role in the promotion of economic development, the generation of wealth, and its distribution, or should such matters be left to the working of the private market? Should governments play an active role in providing all citizens with equal entitlements to state-provided health, education, and welfare services, or can such services be provided better by the private sector? Ultimately, all these matters return to the question of the state, its role in society, and the policy directions that it ideally should follow.

All such questions, and many more like them, form the broad foundation of political life and public discourse in this society, and it is through such debate that parties seek to distinguish themselves, and their leadership, as being the ones that deserve to be entrusted by the electorate with the reins of government power. The quest for such power is a political dynamic, centering on many of the classic questions of political philosophy. In addressing these broad questions respecting the ideal nature of government, the role of the state, and the relationship to be desired between the private and public sectors, between the individual and the collectivity, between individual rights and social duties, we observed the emergence of a number of ideological schools of thought that define or sharpen differing viewpoints while bringing some level of philosophic coherence to an often raucous public debate. While the ideological spectrum is wide, three schools of thought have dominated Canadian political discourse and resultant government policy and program development for well over a century: these are conservatism, socialism, and liberalism (Horowitz, 1996; Johnston, 1996; Bazowski, 1999; Nelson, 1995; Campbell and Christian, 1996).

2.2 Conservative Thought and the State

On the right of the political spectrum in this country stands **conservatism**. This school of thought encompasses a set of ideas that promote the principles of individualism, tradition, liberty, competition, self-interest, private property, and a social order founded on respect for the past, individual freedom and responsibility, free enterprise, and a pro-business economic climate. Central to modern conservative thought is individualism. The individual is perceived as the fundamental building-block of society; indeed, to conservatives, society is nothing but a collection of varied and self-directing individuals, and it is these individuals who are the driving force of social progress (Johnston, 1996: 93-104; Dyck, 1996: 394-97).

Individuals, in conservative thought, are conceived as rational and self-interested persons who know best how to live their own lives with no need for others, and especially not the state, to tell them how to do so. Conservatism generally stresses that each person is responsible for his or her own life and its well-being and that every person must have the socio-economic and political freedom to make the most of his or her own opportunities. Every individual should be free to "ride to the top" in life; to acquire wealth, prestige, and personal power; and to make use of these acquisitions as he or she deems fit. The converse of this, however, is that nothing can be guaranteed in life and that all individuals are also free to fail, to stumble to the bottom, to find poverty and insignificance if they fail to make the best of the opportunities presented to them.

Social life, in conservative thought, is a grand competition, a form of social Darwinism, in which individuals struggle among themselves for the good material things in life. All individuals are responsible for their own welfare, and, in the quest to promote their own well-being, individuals are expected to rely on their own determination, capabilities, and effort. Those who show drive and fortitude, who set personal goals and consistently struggle to achieve these goals, will prosper in life because they create and maintain their own well-being through their own hard work. Conversely, those who have less drive and fortitude, who are less interested in personal advancement through education and work experience, for example, or who are less adept at struggling for success, will fall short in this race for individual well-being; according to conservative logic, such persons have no one to blame but themselves for their own misfortune. Conservatives do believe in the principle of equality but understand it primarily in terms of equality of opportunity. So long as everyone has an equal chance in the "race of life," society has essentially fulfilled its moral obligation to its citizens.

Within this conservative world of competition, the struggle is inherently one for material success and acquisition. People compete for wealth, possessions, and money with a very basic evaluating system: How much material wealth can one amass? Accordingly, modern conservative thought places great stress on the sanctity of private property and the right of individuals to gain, maintain, and manipulate private property as they themselves deem most appropriate to maximize their own individual self-interest. It is this concern for the private use of property that draws conservative thought towards the concept of capitalism.

As individuals seek to advance their own material self-interest through the attainment of private wealth, the logical extension of this reasoning is that they should be free to enter into business arrangements with one another, to form enterprises, to engage in the production and sale of all legally permissible goods and services, to manage their firms as they see fit, and to gain and enjoy the fruits of their labours. Such individual entrepreneurs should also be free to hire others to work for them or to engage in contractual relations with other firms, with all such business relationships ultimately governed by the dictates of market economics—supply and demand, rational individual decision-making, and freedom of choice.

Conservative interest in individualism, materialism, and private property leads inexorably to support for free enterprise and the interests of businesses operating within the private sector. Conservative thought stresses the need for individuals and corporations to be free to engage in business with the minimum of restraints imposed by governments. Thus, regulation on the activities of actors in the private sector should be minimal, taxation rates should be as low as possible, and governmental activity should be undertaken with a concern for promoting an economic climate conducive to private sector investment, growth, and financial reward.

2.2.1   Conservatism, the Role of the State, and Public Policy

Given the conservative perspective regarding the primacy of individualism, liberty, and private sector interests, the corresponding role of the state is predictable: the good state is the state that governs least. Governments should see their role, first and foremost, as protecting and advancing individual freedom and business interests. This implies the development of public policies that respect the principles of conservatism discussed above. Public policy should be designed to promote individual responsibility, to advance individual initiative, and to reward individual hard work. Governments should see their prime role as promoting the equality of individuals and guaranteeing to all individuals equality of opportunity. All individuals should know that they have an equal opportunity to compete in the "race of life," that they are free to promote their self-interest, and that the state will encourage such fair competition through its support of the working of business (Campbell and Christian, 1996: 48-54).

In advancing such a free enterprise and market-oriented approach to social and economic relations, conservative thought stresses that all state economic and regulatory policy should be designed to facilitate the interests of the private sector and those individuals competing within it. The role of the state, at best, is to establish and oversee a set of basic rules and laws establishing a free economic marketplace through the creation of property rights, corporate laws, the enforcement of private legal contracts, the fair regulation of the stock market, the free flow of property and money, the maintenance of a stable currency, and the promotion of trade and commerce. The duty of the state is to limit as far as possible all other economic regulation, to have as little impact as possible on the economic behaviour of market actors, and especially to impose the least possible degree of regulation on labour, occupational health and safety, consumer protection, and environmental standards.

The fundamental conservative aim is to ensure that the public sector plays only a minor role in the economy once a free market system has been established and given legal sanction and protection. Beyond this, the state is essentially a provider of those basic public services that cannot be effectively and/or comprehensively delivered by the private sector: law and order, national defence, international relations, trade policy, currency and monetary policy, public infrastructure development, and, historically, public education. Overarching these activities, however, the state is to respect the primacy of the private sector as the key economic and social player in society; this means also that the officials of the state are supposed to recognize their secondary and subordinate role in the life of society as a sponsor and promoter of the private sector. Thus, conservative economic policy directs governments to respect the interests of private capital, so that rules regarding domestic and foreign investment, trade, property rights, and capital accumulation and transfer across international borders should be as unrestricted as possible; hence, the policies of free trade, the free flow of international capital, and prohibitions on state policies designed to restrict such freedoms (Nelson, 1995: 30-34).

In keeping with these regulatory and economic policy priorities, conservative thought also stresses the importance of governmental financial prudence. Governments should exert as minimal an impact on society as possible, including a very limited financial impact. Taxation rates should be as low as possible not only to impose a limited financial burden on the private sector, but also to limit the flow of revenue to the state and, thus, by extension, to limit the size of the public sector and the range of activities the government undertakes. Governments should perform only a limited number of public duties, as enumerated above, which traditionally have fallen within the purview of the state; all other matters, both as matters of principle and sound practice, should be reserved to the working of the private sector. And in everything that governments do, conservative thought stresses the pre-eminence of fiscal prudence. The organizations of the state should spend as little as possible on running government programs, and all governments should live within their means. Ideally, governments should avoid deficit financing and the creation of public debts that must ultimately be paid for by higher taxation or reduced public services, or both. Governments should refrain, as a matter of principle, from creating expensive state-run social and economic programs, allowing, wherever possible, for the private sector to provide the goods and services needed by people in this society. Conservatives will claim that governments have consistently shown themselves to be inefficient and uneconomic providers of most public services, whereas the private sector can and will and should be allowed to bring the ethos of the private market to bear in providing them.

This approach to financial management, however, is more than just a method to minimize the scope of government spending in society and thus of taxation rates. While these financial motives are major aspects of conservative thought, so, too, is the desire to promote, wherever feasible, the concepts of individual responsibility and of reliance on private means to address social needs. Since individuals should take primary responsibility for their own lives, when various economic problems emerge in society solutions to these problems should be sought first and foremost through the working of the private sector. If individuals face economic and related social problems—poverty, bad jobs, poor working conditions, undesirable housing, limited education, few opportunities for social betterment—they should look first to themselves for solutions rather than turning to the state to provide relief. For conservatives, the essential and most effective response to all these and so many other problems is their traditional recipe for success: individual hard work, perseverance, personal improvement through education and skills-training, seeking and getting better jobs and better housing, and an overriding personal commitment to succeed. If and when social and economic problems are simply too big or too general for individuals to cope with on their own, the next level of support should come from the broader private realm of extended families, charities, and religious organizations—the traditional givers of social support. It is to these institutions, not to the state, that people should turn when they have problems that are beyond their capabilities to solve (Johnston, 1996: 95-100).

Likewise, for broader economic and social problems that not even these institutions can effectively address on their own, such as environmental pollution, crime, and perceived sub-standard health care and educational systems, creative private actions and public policies designed to introduce and promote private sector solutions should be advanced. With respect to environmental policy, such solutions can range from individually oriented recycling and waste reduction initiatives to industrially oriented policies of transferable pollution credits designed to financially benefit environmentally friendly firms while fiscally penalizing polluting firms. With respect to crime, many conservatives mention the role that private security firms can play in providing security services to individual homes and private businesses, including the merits of "gated communities" to which access is specifically restricted by the stakeholders of the estates. Many conservatives also favour the value of creating private sector alternatives to existing and failing public sector systems of such service delivery; hence, their support for private health care clinics, private hospital care, and private schools, colleges, and universities.

This emphasis on individual responsibility and private means for addressing problems also prevails in contemporary conservative social thought, but it is here that contemporary conservatism reveals a schism between those who view themselves in general terms as conservatives and those who are avowed **social conservatives** (Johnston, 1996: 101-03). Social conservatives place greater stress on the importance of social policy and moral issues than on matters of general economic policy, asserting that concerns respecting abortion, pornography, family breakdown, gun control, capital punishment, and the growing secularization of society must take precedence in government policy-making. Social conservatives express a need to return to what they consider traditional conservative values—values rooted in conservative religious belief in general and often evangelical Protestant fundamentalism in particular. Social conservative policy agendas associated with the "religious right" are devoted to such causes as outlawing abortion, banning pornography, promoting traditional "family values," and supporting "get tough" approaches to crime, including advocacy for capital punishment. While social conservatives often turn to the state and state power to develop and enforce laws to advance their social agenda, their attitudes to the individual and the state are rather contradictory in that, with regard to such policy matters as abortion and pornography, they reject the idea that the individual should be left free to decide how best to address these matters. This rather contradictory attitude deepens when those desiring state leadership with respect to certain moral issues also speak of the dangers of a socially intrusive state and seek to restrict the role of the state in social life by opposing state-enforced gun control, resisting secularization in public schools, and supporting faith-based (particularly Christian) approaches to education.

BOX 2.1
Evolving Conservatism

The organizational voice of Canadian conservatism has undergone major changes in recent years with these changes posing significant questions to conservatives in particular and Canadians in general.

Over 2003-04 the Progressive Conservative Party of Canada and the Canadian Alliance Party merged into the new Conservative Party of Canada. This new party, under the leadership of Stephen Harper, is designed to "unite the right" in this country and provide Canadian voters with an effective alternative to the long-governing Liberals. But the Conservatives face some serious ideological and practical questions of policy.

Should the Conservative Party be more moderate and centrist in its policy and program orientation, accepting the broad contours of Liberal social and economic policy, while stressing that Conservatives could manage the federal government better than the Liberals, thereby positioning the Conservatives as a balanced and reasonable challenger to the electoral hegemony of the Liberal Party of Canada? Or would such a move to the centre represent a denial of basic conservative values?

Should the organizational voice of Canadian conservatism be more doctrinaire and right-wing, presenting Canadians with a sharply different set of policy and program approaches from those advocated by the Liberals? Should the Conservatives stress policies of greater tax cuts, debt repayment, the downsizing of government, privatization, deregulation, the promotion of more "market-oriented" approaches to health care, and the promotion of family values, while increasing military spending and closer interaction with the United States on defence policy and the "War on Terror"?

Which of these two competing approaches would be more likely to appeal to most Canadian voters? And can the Conservative party maintain the unity of Conservatives, social Conservatives, and Red Tories?

Most conservatives, however, shy away from the fundamentalist and contradictory fervour of the social conservatives, their often puritanical social policies, and their prioritizing of social policy over general economic policy. Most conservatives seek more moderate approaches to deal with existing social problems and tend to downplay the moral and religious side of these issues (to the disgust of social conservatives). Despite these differences in policy approach, both social and moderate conservatives share certain core individualist beliefs with respect to how social problems should be addressed—they both emphasize the roles of private actors as means to resolving such problems. Nonetheless, if some form of collective action is considered to be necessary, most conservatives again stress the importance of traditional private institutions acting as the problem-solvers, the mediators, and the conciliators of social problems. Hence, the long-standing conservative interest in having such institutions as the family, the churches, local autonomous community groups, and charitable organizations play a lead role in addressing such matters as teen pregnancy, responsible gun ownership, social discrimination, and caring for the socially and economically disadvantaged.

Another sub-school of conservatism meriting attention is **Red Toryism** (Horowitz, 1996: 149-54; Campbell and Christian, 1996: 25-30). This term, in its more modern connotation, is used to describe those conservatives who, while generally believing in the virtues of individualism, free enterprise, private property, and the leading role of the private sector in the economy, also believe that there is an important collectivist side to social and economic life. This collectivist side is usually defined by Red Tories as nationalism or provincialism, those felt ties of shared culture, identity, and interests that connect people to one another in ways that transcend individualist relations. The nation, or the province, as a collective whole, is given a special place in Red Tory thought: the long-term interests of the nation or province should always be a priority for those living within that collectivity. While the private sector can and should be turned to as a means to serve these long-term interests, if it proves itself either unwilling or unable to meet important ends necessary to the well-being of the nation or province, then the state itself, as the collective representation of the nation or province, should become the means of fulfilling these needs. Thus, Red Toryism is that branch of conservatism willing, at times, to endorse a collectivist vision of the country, or of a province, while being fully prepared to embrace statist instruments to advance broad collective goals with regard not only to economic development but also to the promotion of social welfare and the defence of Canadian nationalism and culture in the face of external threats. To Red Tories, whose representatives range from prime ministers John A. Macdonald to John Diefenbaker, such threats historically have come from the United States and have required the active role of the federal government to develop policies and programs designed to defend Canadian national interests.

Through all of this conservative thinking, however, one feature stands in sharp relief: the institutions of the state should be turned to only as a last resort for dealing with social and economic problems. Ideally, people acting in the broad realm of private relationships should be capable of solving their own problems if they are left free of state constraint and given the opportunity to do so. Governments should act in a circumscribed manner, always cognizant that the most important features of social and economic life should be individual freedom and responsibility, private property, and free enterprise.

2.3   Socialist Thought and the State

In contrast to conservative thought is **socialism**, a broad set of ideas on the left of the political spectrum (Horowitz, 1996; Johnston, 1996; Bazowski, 1999; Campbell and Christian, 1996; Nelson, 1995). Just as conservatism possesses variations and sub-schools of thought, so the general concept of socialism is subject to internal divisions, as various theorists and political activists have sought to define either the essence of, and/or the most practicable means of, achieving the "socialist" ideal. Any discussion of socialism becomes a study of its various theoretical approaches, their historical origins, and their practical application in the political world. Such a study, entailing such concepts as Marxism, communism, democratic socialism, and social democracy, traces the practical political thought and action of trade unions, communist parties, labour parties, socialist parties, and social democratic parties. The Canadian left has witnessed the interplay of all these elements of the "socialist" experience. Here, I focus on the dominant strain of socialist thought and practice found in Canada, namely, that of Fabian parliamentary socialism (Horowitz, 1996:154-55).

2.3.1   Essential Socialism

At the heart of all socialist thought is the belief that society is best understood in terms of collective, not individual, interests. Rather than viewing the individual as the key feature of social life, socialists view society itself as the central feature of human interaction. While socialist thought grants that individuals can and must possess individual human rights to protect their legal and political interests, it views individuals as most important in society because of their group affiliations. Rather than seeing society composed of a multitude of atomistic, self-referential, and inherently selfish individuals, socialists tend to view society in communal terms. A society is a community, a grouping of collectives, each possessing differing interests, but with a holistic, communal interest associated with "the greatest good of the greatest number." Social life is to be viewed in relation to collective interests and the communal needs and wants of the vast majority of common people who comprise society.

In looking at this or any society, socialists will devote close attention to the nature of the groups comprising that society and the social interrelationships they exhibit. According to socialist thought, all societies must be understood in terms of class and class relations, for all societies possess socio-economic classes, and the interrelationships between these classes define economic and political life. Socialists claim that societies are invariably divided into unequal classes—unequal in numerical size, wealth, influence, and power (Johnston, 1996: 63-67).

The upper class, comprising a small fraction of the total population, includes the wealthiest members of the business and social elite, who own, control, and manage most of the wealth (capital and large businesses) and who dominate the senior ranks of private sector management. From these positions of power, the members of this class direct the working of the economy to their own benefit, and, through their control of business power, they exert great influence over the long-range thinking and operations of the mainstream political parties and governments of the country.

Economically beneath this upper class is a much larger but less powerful middle class. Various analysts have used many means to classify the nature of the "middle class," with membership being defined either by income level (e.g., mid-range), or economic position (e.g., professional, middle management, small/medium business ownership,) or even by self-ascription—a sense of seeing oneself as being within the broad middle ranks of society, reasonably well-to-do, and basically content with one's economic situation. Depending on the definition used, the number of persons in any society that can be considered middle class may vary widely; given the looseness of the definition, the term can encompass all those ranging from the barely moderately wealthy to those just shy of being considered upper class.

Within socialist class analysis, the class comprising the largest number of persons is the working class or the lower class (or the "proletariat," to Marxists), which is also the poorest. The members of this class possess limited wealth, must sell their labour through a variety of low to mid-paying jobs, and are the least educated, least well-connected socially, and least capable of achieving personal success in such a class system. The members of this class struggle to make ends meet while striving to enhance their life position through finding steady employment by working for businesses owned or managed by members of the upper or middle classes (the "bourgeoisie," in Marxist thought). This quest for the stability and security of a good job also motivates working-class interest in such matters as public education and unions.

According to the socialist perspective on society, dominant social relations are always class-based and rooted in economic power. Within society, the vast bulk of economic power, and thus social power and influence, is controlled by the upper class, with some significant proportion held by the upper-middle class, but with the working class remaining mostly underprivileged and impoverished. A social system with such an unequal distribution of wealth and power is considered by socialists to be inherently unfair, unjust, unstable, and undesirable, since the majority of people in society are deprived of equitable access to the wealth, goods, and services they themselves help to produce, while a small socio-economic elite controls and reaps these benefits. Such a system is unstable in that this maldistribution of wealth breeds poverty, ignorance, crime, anger, and disillusionment, all of which can and will fray the fabric of society, resulting in social resentment, unrest, protest, disorder, and perhaps even revolt and revolution.

Given this identification of basic and profound problems afflicting society, the key socialist question becomes: What is to be done? This question, and its answers, give rise to the greatest theoretical and practical political differences among social democrats, democratic socialists, communists, and Marxists (Johnston, 1996: 104-16). The latter two groups are noteworthy for their belief that profound social and economic change to the capitalist system can be derived only through a violent social revolution, overseen by a "dictatorship of the proletariat." Such a revolution is aimed at transforming the social and power relations in society through the abolition of private property and free enterprise, the establishment of radical socialist governments dedicated to the creation and operation of state-controlled command economies, the repression of political opposition to the revolution, and the suppression of individualism into a collective social identity overseen and controlled by the state. All these actions, in radical socialist thought, are necessary means to the end of creating a classless and utopian society.

2.3.2   Fabian Socialism

In contrast to Marxist and communist positions that stress violence, revolution, radicalism, and non-democratic means of action, there is a more moderate, reformist, democratic strain of socialist thought in Canada. This approach stresses that the major problems facing society can be peacefully resolved by society itself if and when the vast majority of working- and lower-middle-class people elect governments committed to acting in their best interests. Through the democratic process, the common people themselves have the potential to win control of the state, thus turning the institutions of government to the development of public policies designed to promote the social and economic welfare of the common people. In this way, a socialist vision of reform and economic progress can be achieved by way of evolutionary rather than revolutionary means through the working of democratic politics and the actions of democratic socialist parties and governments. This approach to socialism, one rooted in the democratic parliamentary tradition of Britain, is best captured under the rubric of Fabianism (named after the Fabian Society, founded in London in 1884 by a number of British socialists, among them the playwright George Bernard Shaw).

Fabian thought has influenced the left in Canada. Its broad approach to socio-economic and political action, however, has never been unidimensional—while Fabian socialists share many beliefs regarding human nature, the nature of society, and the problems inherent in the working of a capitalist society, they themselves have long been divided as to the practical political means to address these problems. Within Fabianism two broad streams—democratic socialism and social democracy—differ on the scope, speed, and degree of reform to be promoted by governments and the extent to which the private sector and the free enterprise system should be subordinated to the public sector and socialist ideals. Democratic socialists and social democrats can agree, however, that the existing social system can and must be fundamentally altered to make it more responsive to the needs of that vast majority of ordinary people comprising the working class and the lower-middle class. The Fabian vision of social reform takes a distinctively collectivist approach to human nature and human obligations. Rather than seeing society as comprised of self-centred, materialistic, and competitive individuals, Fabian thought affirms

- that society should be communal;
- that individuals are social animals;
- that they generally can, will, and should care for one another; and
- that the vast majority of people are compassionate and will seek to establish a society in which all are treated fairly and justly.

Fabian socialists stress that people are inherently cooperative, kind, compassionate, and willing to share and that, while people seek the fulfillment of their basic human needs for sustenance, shelter, health, education, and welfare, they are willing to work together to ensure that all in society can mutually enjoy the material and social benefits of the wealth of society. Fabian thought holds that people can and should demonstrate concern for the common good. As rational beings they recognize that the social and economic interests of the collectivity transcend those of the individual and that the vast majority of people will be prepared to place the interests of the community ahead of those of any one individual or group seeking to advance narrow agendas of materialistic self-interest.

This collectivist, cooperative, and humanitarian approach to social relations leads to a very clear notion of social reform. Since the capitalist socio-economic system is structured with a highly unequal division of wealth substantially benefitting only a small proportion of the total population, while the vast majority comprising the lower and lower-middle classes suffer relative deprivation, this socio-economic system must be transformed to provide for social and economic equality for all the members of society. Because the power and influence of the private sector is enormous in any capitalist system, the most effective means of promoting such social and economic reform is through the use of state power.

2.3.3   Democratic Socialism and Social Democracy: Fabianism, the State, and Public Policy

While Fabians generally agree on the necessity for major social and economic reforms to advance the interests of the vast majority of the population, their own progressive political activity stems from democratic and parliamentary modes of action. A split between Fabian viewpoints occurs when they begin to focus on practical political and governmental means to their ends (Johnston, 1996: 111-16). Exactly how to achieve Fabian socialist goals marks the fault line between democratic socialist and social democratic thought.

Democratic socialists tend to advocate for much deeper and more profound changes to the existing social and economic order than do social democrats. Democratic socialists stress that their approach to policy is in keeping with socialist principles, whereas the social democrats stress that their approach is more cognizant of existing political realities, that social and economic change must be built in a careful, incremental manner.

The differences between these two groups are most pronounced with respect to general economic policy. Democratic socialists tend to stress the need for the existing capitalist economy to be subject to a great degree of state oversight and regulation, or even control and ownership in certain sectors and fields, on the principle that the economy is a collective resource of the entire community, designed to benefit all the members of society, and not a set of private institutions and markets to be manipulated by a small number of entrepreneurs for their own individual and selfish interests. Therefore, the state, as the democratic guardian of the collective interest, should play a leading role in promoting the economic development of the whole society through policies of strict socio-economic regulation, economic nationalism, industrial growth coupled with regional diversification and development, and the equitable sharing of the riches of the economy. While democratic socialists, in contrast to their more radical Marxist and communist critics, will generally accept the continued existence of a market economy founded on the principles of free enterprise, private property, and the basic operating principles of supply and demand, they feel that such an economy must be subjected to substantial state oversight and regulation to ensure that important goals of public policy are met and that the broad interests of society are not sacrificed to the pursuit of private gain. Such oversight and regulation can take many shapes and forms, depending on current exigencies, but classic examples of democratic socialist regulatory ideals have been

- strong labour standards regulation and workers' compensation rules and procedures;
- strict occupational health and safety standards;
- consumer protection legislation;
- competition rules designed to protect against monopolistic corporate behaviour; and
- strict rules and regulations respecting environmental protection, conservation, remediation, and penalties for those guilty of environmental degradation.

democratic Socialist

Social democrats agree in principle with the foregoing theoretical and practical policy goals, but differ from democratic socialists with respect to how these goals are to be achieved; how fast and how hard to push the private sector; how far the role of the state should be expanded into the working of the economy; and how great a burden, both in financial and regulatory terms, the state should impose on the private sector. Social democrats support the long-term objectives of the democratic socialist vision with regard to these matters while suggesting that often a more cautious, less intrusive, and more pragmatic approach to public policy development is required, both to gain public support for such policy goals and for business to become willing to live with them. Social democratic versions of policy undertakings are less sweeping, more controlled and limited, and less burdensome on the private sector while also giving less authority and a more restricted role to the institutions of the state. Of course, democratic socialists will argue with social democrats over these points by insisting that this more restrained social democratic vision of public policy development and programming offers but a pale shadow of what ideal socialist policy should be.

Democratic socialists have advocated for a variety of initiatives to promote economic development in this country through the promotion of state ownership in the economy and the use of extensive subsidies to support either the continued existence or creation of new public or private industrial ventures. Policies of nationalization, Crown corporation growth, state support for industrial incentives, and regulation itself are seen as means of fashioning an economy that is subject to the control and leadership of a democratic government, not just a private market. Through such control and leadership, the economy can be shaped and directed to respond to and meet social and economic goals set by government. Thus, the economic actions of the federal state are not just the promotion of the parts of the national economy that are healthy and vibrant, but the diversification of this economy to meet the economic and social needs of the economically disadvantaged regions of the country. Democratic socialists uphold policies of regional development and industrial diversification, often founded on programs of state subsidies, government decentralization, preferential state contracting with respect to public works, and the promotion of regional equalization payments.

This broad concern for the viability of the Canadian economy, coupled with a desire to promote and maintain a strong state presence in managing the economy, has led democratic socialist thought also to be highly skeptical of greater economic ties to the United States and, in particular, to policies of free trade with the Americans. Free trade policy, first in theory and now in practice, is perceived by many democratic socialist critics as representing a diminishment of Canadian economic capacity and a downgrading of Canadian control over our economy. As more control is seen to have fallen into the hands of American entrepreneurs and the ability of Canadian governments to regulate and intervene in the economy to advance public goals have become dangerously limited, they fear that Canadians are losing their ability to have their economy serve their needs rather than those of multinational corporations (Barlow, 1991; McQuaig, 1999).

While most social democrats agree with the principles of such democratic socialist thought, they disagree on the best practical means to promote these policy objectives (Whitehorn, 1996; Campbell and Christian, 1996:139-50). In advocating more cautious and less intrusive policy means to these ends—means likely to be more compatible with, and supportable by, prevailing public and business opinion—social democrats call for smaller, more restricted, and carefully targeted initiatives.

- Rather than outright nationalization of the entire economy, social democrats support the nationalization of selected elements of it.
- Rather than the nationalization of an entire industrial sector, they advocate the creation of one Crown corporation designed to provide a state presence within that sector.
- Rather than opposition to all free trade initiatives with other nations, and especially the United States, they support the creation of more regulated fair trade initiatives; the drafting of tougher trade treaties providing protection for social, cultural, regional, and environmental interests; and the operation of existing free trade treaties subject to greater government support for Canadian economic interests.

Thus, social democrats favour a series of initiatives that, while progressive (both economically stronger and more responsive to public needs), are nonetheless more compatible with the existing economy, in no way threatening its overall stability. Democratic socialists, however, contest such "practical" reasoning as being "compromised," claiming that such social democratic thought has been too influenced by existing business attitudes to economic development and the privileging of the private over the public sector.

In thinking about economic policy, however, both social democrats and democratic socialists share a common Fabian understanding of the relationship between economic and social policy. In Fabian socialist thought generally, the economy must be understood in social terms—it must be seen as a fundamental element of society, emerging from the shared collective work of society, with its ultimate purpose being to serve the welfare of the entire community. In this sense, economic relations are not divorced from social relations, and the former are to be put towards the service of the latter; the vast wealth generated by the economy must be structured in such a way as to promote the interests of the community; and, in Fabian thought, it is the state that must play the pivotal role in ensuring that economic riches generated by society are equitably shared throughout that society, by all its members.

Such a social approach to economy and wealth distribution leads to a set of Fabian social policies that bring social democrats and democratic socialists closer together, though there are typical differences regarding the scope and depth of desired policy means and ends. Both kinds of Fabians stress the need for the state to channel substantial portions of the economic wealth of society into the provision of necessary health, education, and welfare services available to all members of society. Social democrats and democratic socialists tend to differ, however, with regard to the scope of these policy initiatives, whether, for instance, state-administered and

BOX 2.2
Evolving Socialism

Canadian social democrats and democratic socialists have been striving for years to reinvigorate the left in this country both as an electoral force and as a generator of new policy ideas. Their success over the past two decades has been questionable. What does the NDP need to do to make itself more relevant to Canadians and gain greater parliamentary representation and influence?

Should the NDP move more to the centre of the political spectrum, as did the British Labour Party under Tony Blair, as a means of being perceived as more reasonable and sensible so as to gain greater political support, or would such a move represent a betrayal of socialist values and principles?

Should the NDP accept the broad contours of the socio-economic policy framework established and maintained by the Liberals since 1993? Should the NDP accept NAFTA and globalization as facts of life, as well as the leading role of the private sector as being the key player in the economy? For the NDP to be credible in national politics, does it have to recognize the importance of balanced budgets, further tax cuts, and debt reduction as necessary and desirable financial ends? And does the NDP have to support a greater role for the Canadian military through increased military spending?

Or can the NDP gain greater support by moving to the left? Should the NDP continue to oppose NAFTA, globalization, and deeper trade relations with the United States? Should the NDP support a stronger state role in the economy through greater regulation and even the creation of new Crown corporations to promote Canadian industrial development? Should there be greater state spending on such matters as social welfare, child care, post-secondary education funding, equalization and regional development, and foreign aid?

state-financed medical care should be extended to include all matters of health care, inclusive of pre-natal and early childhood care, eye care, dental care, and long-term seniors care. Democratic socialists are more willing to advance such claims for service extension, while social democrats are more cautious with regard to the economic and political implications of such proposals. Similar tensions and debates also exist with post-secondary education policy and whether all college and university education should be treated similarly to elementary and secondary education, that is, be provided as a right to all students, so that students and their families are freed from direct service charges and tuition fees. This model of post-secondary education, deriving from the Western European experience, is advocated by those with democratic socialist leanings, while social democrats shy away from the costs and changes involved. Social democrats and democratic socialists also share broad agreement on the basic nature of social policy that should be available to all persons in society. Both stress that all citizens should be entitled to fundamental guarantees of welfare provisions (sustenance and housing) should they be in dire need and that all citizens should be entitled to general policies of social security effected through such programs as workers' compensation, disability payments, family allowances, and seniors' pension plans. All such programs are seen by Fabians as ways of sharing the wealth of society and building social equity throughout the community. Other broad equity-providing public services, along Fabian principles, range from state-administered human rights and labour relations systems, through consumer protection systems, to environmental protection and promotion. While some of these matters have clear economic policy orientations, they also have strong social policy implications, highlighting the Fabian interconnectedness of social and economic relations.

The Fabian progressive and activist role for the state in both economic and social policy fields requires governments to deploy substantial amounts of public monies. Because governments must be capable of matching their social and economic ambitions with practical means, it is not surprising to witness a Fabian approach to taxation policy quite distinct from that of their conservative critics. In Fabian socialist thought, taxation policy is not to be feared, but rather is to be seen as "the price of civilization," a necessary element of social life with all taxation, ideally, being "progressive"— the greater the wealth an individual or corporation possesses, the greater the share of taxation that should be paid, since the wealthier are more able to pay a greater amount of tax without being adversely affected. In turn, the revenue generated by the state should be used to fund and advance the whole array of state-led social and economic policies designed to promote the common interests of the general public. In this sense, Fabian thought does not view taxation per se as a social and economic burden to be borne by individuals and corporations with a greater or lesser degree of resentment, but rather as a social obligation, a duty to invest in the common welfare of society, thereby providing the state with the ability to provide necessary and desirable public services throughout society. In this sense, taxation policy cannot and should not be discussed in isolation from the services provided by the workers and the service provided by the state, and there should be a recognition among the public, including the business community, that the provision of high-calibre and effective public services requires that the state itself be well funded. In this sense, all taxation is to be seen as an investment in a better future for all people.

The common denominator to all such Fabian social, economic, and taxation policy initiatives, of course, is the leading and active role to be played by the state. In Fabian socialist thought, governments can and must play a dominant role in social and economic relations, because they are the only institutions that can speak for society as a whole. They are the only bodies designed to represent the public will while being charged with a duty to serve and promote the public interest. They are also the only institutions in society whose policy-making activities carry the force of law, meaning that governments possess a wide legal power to enforce their will over the private sector, making them the only institutions in society that can rival private business in terms of influence and power. Thus, Fabian socialist thought is statist in orientation, with both social democrats and democratic socialists being very comfortable with the prospect of governments playing a leading and decisive role in the social and economic life of society. In sharp contrast to conservative distrust of the state and desire to privilege individual over collective interests, Fabian socialists view the state as a set of institutions that can be and should be instrumental to the promotion of the common good; indeed, they think that governments, as democratically accountable bodies, are the only bodies that can be trusted with representing and advancing the common interests of the general public because they are the *only* bodies that can be *politically* charged with this social responsibility.

Fabian expectations about the public sector and public servants are likewise high. The public sector has a vital role to play in the life of society, and all public service personnel, from senior managers to rank-and-file employees, are considered important contributors to the work of government. All these officials are viewed as having significant roles to play in the development, management, and implementation of policies and programs designed to improve the quality of life for all members of society. The state, to be a progressive force within society and the economy, needs to marshal and direct high intelligence as it turns its collective mind to resolving the great social and economic problems confronting society. To Fabians, this work is a cause, and this cause is momentous, requiring dedication and effort from those who work within government and who manage these public affairs. While such officials are viewed as deserving great public respect, due to the importance of their work, there is also the expectation that they will be committed to the ideals and goals of public service and that they will faithfully and creatively work to further the best interests not only of the government but of the state it serves.

2.4 Modern Liberalism and the State

Standing between the broad ideologies of contemporary conservatism and Fabian socialism is modern **liberalism** (Horowitz, 1996; Johnston, 1996; Nelson, 1995; Bazowski, 1999; Campbell and Christian, 1996). This conception of social and economic relations and the appropriate role of the state in society is one that consciously seeks the middle ground between conservative and Fabian thought, striving to blend certain of the ideas of each of these schools into a coherent, balanced, pragmatic, yet principled understanding of socio-economic life and the purpose of government. Thus, modern liberalism can be seen as a conciliatory approach to political ideas, borrowing from both conservative and Fabian viewpoints, and blending these ideas into a centrist vision of political thought and governmental practice. The virtue of this approach, as proclaimed by liberals, is not only that it is "synthetic"—bringing together the best ideas of the other schools of thought—but also that it is flexible, allowing liberalism to shift either to the left or the right of the political spectrum as social and economic values and priorities ebb and flow with the passing of time and as ideas respecting the appropriate role of government within society also change.

In tandem with conservatism, modern liberalism supports ideas of

- individualism, freedom, and liberty;
- the virtue of competition; and
- the importance of private property and free enterprise.

Together with conservatives, liberals accept and promote the foundational ideas of capitalism and a free market economy:

- that the private sector will be and should be the driving force in the economy;
- that economic leadership within this country should emerge from the private sector and the generally free operation of private markets;
- that private enterprises are the best generators of wealth in society; and
- that the private sector should be relied upon to create and distribute most of the goods and services needed by society.

This overall reliance on the private market comes from a perception that the private sector tends to be far more economical, efficient, and effective in the performance of these general economic tasks than the public sector.

This centrist approach to economics is supported by liberals on ethical grounds in that it prioritizes individuals and their freedoms. Liberalism asserts, as a general principle,

- that the individual is the pre-eminent social unit;

- that societies should be designed to maximize individual freedom, liberty, and well-being; and
- that individuals themselves are best-suited for making decisions respecting their own interests.

In its understanding of society and the economy, modern liberalism is, so far, virtually indistinguishable from contemporary conservatism. Both stress fidelity to the basic principles of capitalism; both support the practical and philosophic arguments in support of private property, individual competition, and free enterprise; and both proclaim the individual as the central element of social life.

But modern liberalism also borrows from the Fabian socialist tradition. Like social democrats, liberals stress that an unregulated capitalist economy will breed systematic economic and social unfairness and inequality to such a high degree that the growing divisions between the wealthy and the poor eventually will become destabilizing to the private economy and to society overall. Modern liberalism contends that while the principles and practices of individualism and free enterprise are basically sound, they need to be balanced with other principles and practices emerging from a more social and collectivist orientation to society. While liberal thought supports the promotion of individual equality of opportunity, it also contends that, in certain circumstances, society must be concerned also with the collective interests of all of its members and their well-being. Thus, with respect to essential needs, such as health, education, welfare, and human rights, governments must be able to assure all people that they will be guaranteed a certain equality of social condition. Such a policy affirms the importance of each and every life within society, recognizes humans' fundamental needs, and assures all individuals that regardless of the vicissitudes of life and the differentiated capacities of people, these needs will always be met; that every individual life will be treated with respect by the state; and that each and every member of society should be, and should feel themselves to be, viable, equal, and constructive participants within society.

2.4.1 Liberalism and Public Policy

Modern liberalism thus conceives of society as requiring a pragmatic yet principled balancing of economic and social interests—a balancing of business principles with social ethical standards in such a way as to maintain the effectiveness of the free market economy while ensuring that the entire society collectively benefits from the working of the economy, that a significant proportion of the wealth generated by the economy is redistributed back into society, and that all individuals irrespective of social class are treated with equal dignity.

In modern liberal thought the state plays a vital role in the working of society and of the economy. While the private sector should be the main driving force of the economy, the state nonetheless has an important role to play managing the general direction of the economy, ensuring that economic growth is coupled with economic stability and social purpose, and promoting certain broad socio-economic goals beneficial to the welfare of the nation overall. Thus, liberal thought countenances a certain degree of state intervention in the economy to advance the national interest. For example, liberals have defended the value of Keynesian economics—macro-economic management by which the state seeks to assure economic growth and stability through an active governmental fiscal policy. In periods when the economy is facing declining growth, lessened business opportunities, possible or real recession, and growing unemployment, Keynesian theory recommends that governments invest in the economy by means of public spending on infrastructure programs, industrial incentives, social welfare projects, and major national and regional economic development plans so as to pump large sums of money into the economy. The strategy is to stabilize economic activity, protect and promote full employment, ward off economic decline, promote consumer confidence and consumer spending, and set the stage for renewed economic growth within the private sector. In theory, once such economic growth is underway, the state can and should rein in its public spending, recoup any public accounts deficits through taxation levied on the growing economy, and leave the private sector economy generally to run itself, subject to certain strategic state oversight and direction. In this manner liberal thought stresses that the state can and should play an important and progressive role in managing a healthy economy beneficial to the interests of both business and the general public.

Such belief in the progressive goals that can be accomplished by the state through intelligent intervention in the economy also leads liberalism to be generally supportive of other state initiatives designed to advance broad economic goals beneficial to what liberals believe to be the national interest. Such initiatives include state support for policies of national economic development, whereby governments promote the creation and elaboration of Canadian-owned and controlled industries operating in sectors deemed by governments to be of strategic significance to the long-term economic (and, therefore, social) best interests of this country. Thus, liberals support state incentives and investments directed at private sector actors active in such fields as resource development, advanced manufacturing, industrial research and development, science and high technology, and, more recently, information technology and management information systems. In seeking to support economic development in these fields, modern liberals have been supportive of state regulation and direct state ownership as means to this end. Liberals have shown themselves to be much more willing than conservatives to regulate the private sector to promote specific approaches to Canadian-centred economic and industrial development and to turn to the formation of Crown corporations as a means of ensuring a Canadian presence in important sectors of the economy and of advancing Canadian national economic interests.

The liberal willingness to use the instruments of the state in this manner is also not restricted to issues of broad national policy. Modern liberalism has also been very attuned to concerns of regional disparities across this country and to calls for specific policies of regional economic development to address these problems. Liberals have justified a vast array of active state interventions in the economy, via grants, loans, subsidies, preferential state contracting, and the creation of regionally oriented Crown corporations to promote regional development. Rather than allowing regional disparities to remain as a "natural" outcome of market forces, liberals regard such disparities as socio-economic creations to be managed, if not rectified, by progressive state policy.

In all such cases of state action, however, with respect to either national or regional economic policy matters, liberals maintain that their initiatives are not designed to replace or even to challenge the legitimate interests of private sector economic actors, but that they complement and enhance the economic working of the private market. In liberal thought the state is not to be seen as a foe of business but as a promoter and defender of the long-term best interests of the private sector, nationally and regionally. But the state does have its own interests just as the country has it own needs, and the role of the state is to ensure that the long-term best interests of the entire country are served. Thus, liberals stress that, while the public and private sectors may witness short-term conflicts of interest, as each advances differing policy approaches, the long-term interests of the two forces share the same concern for a healthy and vibrant private sector economy within a stable and prosperous social system. The state is to ensure that the long-term harmony of interests between the public and private sectors is not lost through short-term conflicts. In this sense, modern liberalism is an ideology of the mixed economy—an economy founded upon the working of the private sector but one in which the public sector has a major part to play in overseeing and aiding the development of the private sector and ensuring that its work benefits society as a whole.

Liberal willingness to use the institutions and powers of the state for national and regional economic development is the platform for a complex attitude to Canadian relations with the United States. While liberal thought stresses the primary importance of the private market, the lead role of the private sector in fashioning economic relations and generating growth and wealth in this society and, thus, the general importance of free trade between countries, the economic size and power of the United States does impact on liberal policy. Recognizing that the national interests of the United States and Canada, both in terms of social and economic policy, are distinct, and acknowledging that Canadian interests can be threatened by the self-interested economic actions of the United States, liberal thought seeks a middle ground between conservative and social democratic policy approaches to Canadian-American relations. The liberals design strategies to regulate the relationship between these two countries, to promote a wide degree of free trade between them, but a free trade managed in such a manner as to defend interests vital to Canadian economic sovereignty, to uphold the primacy of Canadian social policy, and to protect Canadian cultural identity. Liberal thought with respect to the United States is marked by a sensibility that the economic aspects of this international relationship must never be the sole determining forces in structuring Canadian policy and that its social and political aspects must also be accorded high priority in deciding any policy developments pertaining to the Americans. Thus, for liberals, Canadian national interests and Canadian nationalism itself are never to be sacrificed to the narrower interests of free market economics.

This same approach of balancing, of seeking the middle ground of compromise and conciliation, is also found in liberal approaches to social policy. While the existence and promotion of a healthy and vibrant private sector economy is central to liberal thought, so, too, is the idea that such an economy cannot exist without a healthy, vibrant, and stable society committed to principles of fairness, justice, and social equity. The state must see to it that the essential needs of individuals and of society at large are met, to guarantee that these principles are reified.

It was mentioned earlier that modern liberalism stresses that all individuals should be entitled to high quality, publicly provided health care, regardless of one's ability to pay for such care. Access to excellent health care is viewed, by liberals, as a fundamental right of citizenship, to be provided equally to all citizens of the state via the working of public policy. Given this understanding of the social importance of health care and its relationship to individual rights and public duties, it is clear to liberals that health care must be a subject for public administration and public service rather than a commodity to be bought and sold on the private market through the working of the private sector. Liberal thought adopts a similar viewpoint with respect both to general educational and to social welfare policy. All individuals are seen as possessing fundamental rights to state-supported primary, secondary, and post-secondary education, as well as possessing core guarantees that, should they ever fall upon hard economic times, they will be protected through the existence of a social safety net—a series of publicly funded social security programs such as welfare, public pensions, and workers' compensation systems—designed to ensure that all persons will have their most basic material needs to shelter and sustenance met by the state.

All the foregoing forms a moral centre to liberal thought. The assumption by the state of the responsibility to ensure to all members of society that their basic human needs to health care, education, and social security will be attended to by the workings of the public service equates such needs with fundamental rights possessed by all individuals in the society. In this formulation the state possesses a positive duty to defend and promote these rights and to provide all individuals with equal access to the public services designed to meet these social needs. In keeping with this approach to social policy, liberal thought extends similar coverage to such policy matters as environmental protection, human rights protection, and cultural promotion. All individuals and society overall are viewed as having a right to a clean and safe environment, one capable of sustaining and promoting all forms of natural life, and it is the duty of the state to guard this natural environment, to protect its long-term interests, and to take remedial legal action against all those individuals and corporations that harm it. Similarly, the state possesses a positive duty to protect and promote human rights within society by guaranteeing to all individuals

- that they have rights to equal treatment and respect regardless of such socio-economic characteristics as race, religion, ethnic or national origin, gender, physical or mental disability, or other such distinguishing yet inherent individual traits;
- that they have a right to be free from social and economic discrimination on the basis of these characteristics; and,
- if and when such discrimination does occur, that they have access to legal redress via designated law enforcement agencies of the state.

Finally, liberal thought also recognizes the importance of broad cultural protection and promotion within society by stressing that the state has a positive duty to defend and affirm cultural interests deemed to be of core importance to the general society. Thus, it will express support for public policies designed to promote such matters as Canadian nationalism, regional identity, bilingualism and biculturalism, and multiculturalism through such avenues as the promotion of Canadian radio and television broadcasting, film production, and the generation and advancement of Canadian fine arts and letters, academic scholarship, and athletics and sports teams.

Within liberal thought the state is perceived as having a major role to play in promoting and enhancing the social and economic life of the country. But while liberal social policy borrows heavily from Fabian thought in terms of its ethical direction, liberals are keen to point out their differences. Although the state must play an active role in the promotion of social policy, all such actions should be reasonable, moderate, and consistent with the long-term best interests of the private sector while not placing an onerous financial burden upon the private sector. Again, in classic fashion, liberalism seeks the middle ground between conservatism and Fabianism, seeking to balance general private sector interests with broad public policy goals, promoting and advancing necessary social policies, but fashioning and implementing these policies so as not to weaken or threaten the foundations of the private sector economy.

This liberal principle of balance and moderation extends to taxation policy. A relatively activist state in both general economic and social policy fields necessitates significant funding. Liberals support fair individual and corporate taxes in the name of progressiveness, believing that people and corporations in this society should not shy away from making the necessary contributions to the common good. Here, liberal thought follows the social democratic concept of the moral duty of fair taxation. Nevertheless, liberal thinking differs from the Fabian on the question of degree and balance. Liberals will insist that while taxation is necessary and important to the working of a progressive government, taxation rates should be set so as not to impose real burdens on individuals or corporations or to jeopardize the overall success of the private sector. Once again, the principle of moderation arises in the need for governments to be cautious in setting taxation rates, ensuring that the state is receiving only that amount of revenue required to provide necessary public services. But such caution does not negate the use of deficit financing if such activity is necessary in the pursuit of broader economic and social policy goals, provided that such deficit financing is

BOX 2.3
Social Liberals/Business Liberals

Just as there is a range of ideological perspectives among conservatives and socialists, so too are there different strains of liberals.

Those who are more centre-left in their thinking will term themselves "social liberals." They are more concerned with and interested in policy and program matters dealing with social welfare policy, cultural policy, Canadian nationalism, environmental protection and regulation, human rights promotion, and international development and the promotion of peace and security through Canadian foreign policy and multilateralism.

Prime Ministers Pearson and Trudeau were commonly associated with the social liberal side of the Liberal party.

In contrast, those liberals who are more centre-right in their thinking are termed "business liberals." They are more comfortable with and interested in matters respecting economic and industrial policy. Business liberals tend to stress the importance of fighting deficits, promoting balanced budgets, paying down national debt, and promoting a competitive Canadian economy through the support of Canadian businesses. They tend to stress the importance of tax cuts as desirable public policy, as well as close trade and economic relations with the United States and other major trading partners.

Prime Ministers Mackenzie-King, St. Laurent, and Chrétien were commonly associated with the business liberal side of the Liberal party.

While Paul Martin was long viewed as being a "business liberal" when he was finance minister under Prime Minister Chrétien from 1993-2002, how he was defined as prime minister remained a topic of hot debate within the Liberal Party, the federal government, and the country at large. How would you assess Paul Martin's leadership?

carefully planned and managed, including a plan for how these deficits must eventually be repaid, whether through the generation of greater tax revenue and/or the streamlining of public service in the future.

With taxation policy, as with so much else, the terms that locate liberal thinking along the political spectrum are balance and flexibility. Liberalism seeks a balanced approach to the taxation interests of both the private and public sectors while giving governments a flexible range of options for meeting their revenue requirements by stressing that the state should never become a serious financial burden upon the private sector. Both conservative and Fabian socialist critics of liberal thought and action question whether such liberal principles and practices are desirable or achievable, with these debates themselves serving to demonstrate the relative differences in both theoretical and operational approaches to taxation policies and the social and economic role of the state in society.

2.4.2   Liberalism and the State

In striving for the ideological and political middle ground between conservative and Fabian approaches to public policy, liberalism calls upon the state to play a major role in mediating competing economic and social interests by striving to promote and protect the core principles and activities of the private sector while advancing the basic social needs and rights of all citizens. Within the liberal world view, governments are not minor players in the social and economic life of society but integral to the current and future well-being of society and its economy; they have important roles to play while managing and directing the economic life of society and in fulfilling and advancing the major social concerns of people living within this society. Considering the importance of these roles, all public servants are significant and necessary actors to the fulfillment of the governments' policies. In contrast to conservatives' thinking that the public service should be of only secondary or even tertiary importance to the life of society, liberals agree with Fabians that, since the public service is of primary importance in social and economic life, the work of public servants should be respected and even applauded. Liberals think that governments require an expert and professional public service, staffed by well-trained and highly motivated persons who are committed to the economical, efficient, and effective delivery of public services, led by senior managers committed to the goals of good government, the development of progressive and intelligent public policies, and the promotion of public service accountability. Senior management must be expert not only in the inner workings of the state bureaucracy and the ways and means of implementing public policies, they also must be

- sensitive to the broad political dynamics in the larger society confronting the governments;
- aware of the ideological significance of the balancing process inherent in the making of public policies;
- knowledgeable of competing economic and social interests; and
- committed to the general concepts of long-term public interest.

Public sector management is vested with great responsibility within the liberal world view: government is called upon to play an active role in the life of society, and government requires the talent and commitment of a skilled and professional public service dedicated to progressive public sector management.

2.5 Ideas, Policy, and the Role of the State in Practice

Conservative, Fabian socialist, and liberal thought are all fundamental and legitimate elements of the political spectrum in this country. They are "fundamental" in that all three schools of thought have been instrumental in different ways, at different times, and in different parts of the country in shaping the way Canadians understand society, economics, politics, and the role of the state. And they are "legitimate" in that all three schools of thought exist within the realm of democratic thought; each approach is fully consistent with the fundamental democratic principles and practices of parliamentary government, majority rule, respect for minority rights, free and fair elections, respect for human rights and freedoms, and obedience to the rule of law. Each school of thought can also claim a long and distinguished pedigree in Canadian history as having formed a part of the evolving social and political understanding of what it means to be Canadian, of how and why Canadians should interact with one another, and of just what should be the role of the state in serving the social, economic, and government needs of Canadians (Horowitz, 1996).

While all three approaches make up important elements of our political tradition, this does not mean that all three have been equally significant in their impact on how Canadians, and their governments, think and act.

2.5.1 The Triumph of the Liberal Centre

Throughout the twentieth century, modern liberalism has proven itself to be the set of ideas that has been most influential to this country both in relation to political thought and governmental practice. The pre-eminence, even dominance, of liberal values in Canadian politics and government can, in turn, be attributed both to the breadth of the centrist liberal approach and to its flexibility—its willingness to borrow (some critics would say steal) from both the right and left of the political spectrum in order to find a successful blend of political principle with practical results.

Liberalism is very much an **ideology of the centre**, seeking to assume the best and the most reasonable ideas from both conservatism on the right of the political spectrum and Fabian socialism on the left in order to form an effective and coherent set of values and policy approaches. Liberalism can be defended and promoted by its supporters as an ideology of principled compromise and pragmatic wisdom—an approach to politics and government that is representative of, and appealing to, the moderate centre of political life. This political centre has become remarkable for its sound economic management (dedicated to promoting regulated free enterprise, economic growth, and the prospering of a mixed economy), balancing such concerns with support for a wide array of social, environmental, and cultural policies designed to serve the needs of all people.

The political attractiveness of such an approach to government is readily apparent in its ability to appeal across the ideological spectrum, and it is just this attractiveness that the Liberal Party of Canada turned to its electoral advantage in the past century. The Liberal Party adopted modern liberalism (reform liberalism as it was known at the time) at its convention of 1919 and, under the leadership of Mackenzie King, came to be the centrist party *par excellence* (Campbell and Christian, 1996: 77-83; Whitaker, 1977). It claimed the middle ground of Canadian politics and has rarely been pushed from this position since. It has proven itself capable of borrowing from the left or right as circumstances require, but has always been able to envelop these accommodations under a mantle of liberal principle. And, by dominating the centre of the political spectrum, the Liberal Party has likewise been able to dominate federal electoral outcomes, demonstrating through the political and electoral history of this country that most Canadians tend to be centrist in their political and ideological leanings. The Government of Canada was under the leadership of Liberal administrations for 72 of the 100 years of the twentieth century, including 43 of the 49 years between 1935 and 1984, the period during which modern society and the modern liberal state was born. With the vast majority of the Canadian population being moderate and middle-of-the road in their approach to matters of economic and social policy and the role of the state, this centre ground possesses the greatest impact in Canadian elections. Here, generally, is where most votes are to be gained, where most parliamentary seats are to be won, and, thus, where government power is to be achieved. Given this long-standing tendency of the Canadian public towards political moderation, the Canadian electorate has seen fit to make the Liberal Party the most successful federal party over the past century (Whitaker, 1996; Clarkson, 1996), producing generalized support for a mixed economy, general Keynesian macro-economic management, progressive social welfare policy, and moderate taxation regimes that have come to characterize what it means to be Canadian.

The policies, programs, and structures of the federal government in particular over the post-Second World War period reflect all the important elements of the modern liberal state. From the end of the war through the mid-1980s, the country witnessed the vast growth of the state as the governments of Mackenzie King, St. Laurent, Pearson, and Trudeau sought to promote the social and economic well-being of Canadians through the creation of policies and programs designed to improve the Canadian quality of life. The full scope of these initiatives, when seen in total, is quite astonishing. Policies ranged from the introduction of a broad array of programs commonly referred to as the social safety net (family allowances, the Canada Pension Plan, the unemployment insurance system, disability insurance, and federal transfer funding to the provinces in support of provincially administered social welfare programs) to the establishment of the Canadian health care system, which provides all citizens with equal access to state-funded medical services regardless of province of residence or ability to pay. Such activist policies also included federal financial support for the development of a comprehensive post-secondary system of colleges and universities, as well as funding for a variety of programs designed to promote regional development in disadvantaged parts of the country. These regional development initiatives also included a guarantee of federal support for financial equalization payments to the relatively poorer "have-not" provinces to enable them to provide essential public services at a level of quality equal to the national norm for such services.

There was and is much more to the activist state created by these successive Liberal governments. Policies and programs of official bilingualism and biculturalism, dating from 1969, and multiculturalism, dating from 1972, were established both to promote French and English language rights and the cultural interests of more recent immigrant groups. Human rights policies themselves, inclusive of affirmative action and employment equity programs, were also advanced by the Canadian Human Rights Commission, established in 1975. Canadian cultural policy was promoted through such agencies as the CBC, the CRTC, the National Film Board, the Canada Council, and Sport Canada, with these bodies benefitting Canadian cultural interests as diverse as the music and film industries, Canadian amateur hockey, and the National Ballet of Canada.

Under Liberal leadership the federal government also came to play a prominent and growing role in the economic life of the country after the Second World War. Successive Liberal governments practised a variation on Keynesian macro-economic management, pumping public monies into the economy via long-term and ongoing policies of social spending, infrastructure development, and industrial subsidy programs, all with the purpose not only of meeting immediate social and industrial development goals but of priming the private sector with public monies so as to enhance economic activity, job creation, consumer confidence, private sector production, and

---

BOX 2.4
Major Federal Crown Corporations and Regulatory Agencies in the Early 1980s

Air Canada
Atomic Energy Control Board
Atomic Energy of Canada Ltd
Canada Labour Relations Board
Canada Mortgage and Housing
Canada Post
Canadair Ltd.
Canadian Arsenals Ltd.
Canadian Broadcasting Corporation
Canadian Competition Bureau
Canadian Environmental Assessment Board
Canadian Human Rights Commission
Canadian Immigration and Refugee Board
Canadian Mint
Canadian National Railways
Canadian Radio-Television and
   Telecommunications Commission

Canadian Saltfish Corporation
Canadian Transportation Commission
Canadian Wheat Board
Cape Breton Development Corporation
de Havilland
Economic Council of Canada
Eldorado Nuclear
Export Development Corporation
Farm Credit Corporation
Foreign Investment Review Agency
National Energy Board
National Film Board
Pêcheries Canada
Petro-Canada
Science Council of Canada
VIA Canada

---

general economic growth. Major economic infrastructure programs, for example, ranged from the creation of the Trans-Canada Highway system and the Trans-Canada Oil and Gas Pipeline of the 1950s to the steady development of a nationwide airport and air transportation system in the 1960s and 1970s. More specifically, a variety of Crown corporations, regulatory agencies, economic development agencies, think tanks, and state programs were introduced with the purpose of enhancing Canadian economic performance. By the 1980s the number of federal Crown corporations and subsidiaries, regulatory agencies, and other related economic development actors numbered well over 200, as highlighted in Box 2.4.

All such government activity—both social policy and economic policy—increasingly elevated the state in the ordinary life of the country. It meant that the federal government (and eventually most provincial governments) became central to the social and economic working of the country; that the public sector grew in size (organizationally, in numbers of personnel, and financially), scope of activity, and political and economic significance compared to the private sector; and that the cost of maintaining this government and its level of programming also increased, resulting in higher taxation rates or, as was increasingly common from the mid-1970s through the mid-1990s, increasing annual public-sector deficit financing, contributing to a growing national debt. These matters and their impacts will be outlined and assessed in greater detail in the later chapters of this text. The important point to note here is that all such growth was justified by governments at the time as desirable political actions directed towards very real and important social and economic needs, which necessitated an activist and progressive response by the state. It is also worthy of note that such growth by the state over these postwar decades was generally supported by all major political parties at the time, as well as by the general public. Indeed, it has long been argued that the electoral success of the Liberal Party throughout most of the second half of the twentieth century can be attributed to its correctly understanding mainstream Canadian public opinion and its response to the blend of progressive yet prudent, statist yet entrepreneurial, mixed economy and Keynesian, moderate-reform liberal thought adhered to by most Canadians.

2.5.2 The Centre Convergence: Conservative Variations

The political dominance of liberal ideology over these years had significant impact on the party fortunes and orientations of the Liberal Party's main political challengers. The prevailing influence of liberalism and the electoral appeal of the moderate centre in Canadian political life came to exert a profound moderating and centrist pull on both the federal Progressive Conservative and New Democratic parties (Horowitz, 1996: 156-60; Dyck, 1996: 396-98; Campbell and Christian, 1996: 35-51, 131-47). As it became abundantly clear to these parties that most Canadians were more

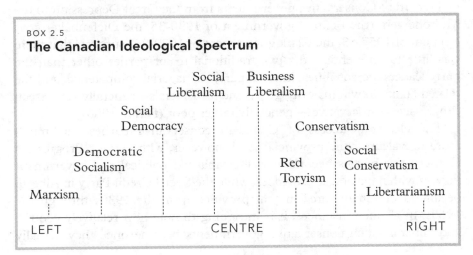

BOX 2.5
The Canadian Ideological Spectrum

or less progressively liberal and centrist in their political orientations, and that the Liberal Party was superbly positioned in the centre of the political spectrum to enable it to reap electoral support and parliamentary majorities from this wide block of public opinion, these other political parties became more centrist themselves in their quest for electoral support.

This dynamic, which can be traced from as early as the 1920s through to the 1980s, resulted in these parties (or their predecessors) becoming more moderate and liberal in their policy positions and—if and when one was able to win power—in governmental actions. The Conservatives refashioned themselves numerous times over these years, even adding "Progressive" to their official title in the 1940s, in a clear effort to signal to Canadians that the party was not reactionary in its economic thinking. In fact, the Conservative Party was never as "conservative" as its name implied; it often endorsed a Red-Tory-inspired direct state action policy in promoting Canadian economic and social development. Examples of such policy outcomes include the National Policy and the construction of the Canadian Pacific Railway under the Macdonald government, the creation of the CBC under the Bennett government, and the maintenance of pre-existing Crown corporations inherited by Conservative governments such as Diefenbaker's. It can be argued that the Progressive Conservative Party was just as Keynesian in macro-economic policy orientation as the Liberal Party from the 1950s through the 1980s. So pronounced was the general policy convergence between the two mainstream federal parties following the Second World War that many analysts and members of the general public often wondered whether there was any real matter of substantive policy or program approach to distinguish them in any meaningful way. The limited record of Conservative governments from the Great Depression to the Mulroney era (the Bennett government of 1930-35, the Diefenbaker government of 1957-63, the Clark government of 1979-80) suggests that there was little to differentiate the two traditional major parties other than the party leaders' personalities, internal party managerial competence, and the related ability to win majority governments: Liberals—generally very great; Progressive Conservatives—generally rather poor (Perlin, 1980).

The electoral success of Canadian conservative parties was much more prevalent at the provincial level, however, with various Progressive Conservative parties becoming well-established political and government powers within particular provinces, while the Social Credit Party in Alberta became a dominant force in that province from the 1930s through the 1960s. In all such instances, it is intriguing to note how relatively centrist and "liberal" such conservative governments became once they actually had to embrace the task of governing while also having to deal with a federal Liberal government increasingly embarked upon progressive and activist state policies. Provincial Progressive Conservative governments in the Maritimes, such as those of Robert Stanfield in Nova Scotia in the 1960s and of Richard Hatfield in New Brunswick in the 1970s and 1980s, were distinctly Red Tory in policy outlook, especially with regard to provincial economic development initiatives, the creation of industrial and transportation infrastructure, and support for new health and social welfare programs subject to federal funding assistance. The Progressive Conservative government of Bill Davis in Ontario over the 1970s and early 1980s was also noted for a variety of progressive social and economic policy initiatives—rent controls, the development of environmental protection policies, and the steady elaboration of human rights protection and enforcement as the multicultural face of the province changed. Even the Progressive Conservative government of Peter Lougheed in Alberta in the 1970s and early 1980s shared a moderate and even reformist mantle, with its support for the creation and elaboration of a national health care system based on substantial federal support of provincially administered hospitals, as well as its own foray into state intervention and direction through the Alberta Heritage Fund (based on oil and gas royalties), whose monies were used to invest in new and emerging primary, secondary, and tertiary industries within the province. While all such moderate, centrist, and even statist policy and program interventions of these governments can be attributed to unique political conditions facing them at these particular times, it should be borne in mind that all had to address public opinion that was essentially moderate, centrist, and generally supportive of the activist federal state. No wonder even Progressive Conservative governments in the provinces came to replicate, albeit in more modest fashions, the development of moderate and centrist interventionist states at the provincial level of government (Dyck, 1996a).

2.5.3   The Centre Convergence: Fabian Variations

A similar political and governmental analysis is applicable to the New Democratic Party (NDP). While this party always espoused a social democratic policy orientation, its political rhetoric has moderated over the decades (Whitehorn, 1996; Morton, 1986; McLeod, 1994). Indeed, the forerunner of the NDP, the Cooperative Commonwealth Federation (CCF), was founded in the depths of the Great Depression with an explicit democratic socialist mandate calling for massive state regulation of the economy, the nationalization of all major economic sectors (including the banks), and the eventual elimination of the capitalist system in Canada through the creation of a socialist order. Armed with such an idealist vision of the left, the CCF was able to make itself a significant player in federal politics over the 1940s and 1950s, becoming the dominant force in Saskatchewan provincial politics. The Saskatchewan CCF, under the leadership of Tommy Douglas, won the provincial election of 1944, inaugurating 20 years of uninterrupted CCF/NDP government in the Prairie province.

Such electoral and governmental success, however, was unmatched anywhere else in the country either at the federal or provincial level. By the mid-1950s the leadership of the CCF recognized that mainstream Canadians, including the vast majority of working-class men and women, were moderate in their ideology and more liberal than socialist in outlook and that if the CCF were to gain electoral success it would have to move more towards the centre of the political spectrum. This the party did in the late 1950s-early 1960s as it amended its party constitution, eliminating the controversial "eradication of capitalism" platform, and stressing the need for all progressive and liberally minded Canadians to come together to help build a country founded upon an active state, but one comprising also a vibrant private sector. As part of this political transformation the party name was changed to the New Democratic Party—a name stressing democracy over socialism.

This shift to the centre was influenced by two significant developments, each of which is a common feature of Canadian politics. Once the CCF won power in Saskatchewan in 1944 and was then called on to govern the province, the party under Premier Douglas proved to be more moderate and centrist in its policy orientation than its own rhetoric had suggested. Capitalism was not abolished in Saskatchewan, nor was the continued viability of the private sector ever threatened by the CCF government, which, in practice, supported a balance of private and public sector leadership in the running of the economy, long before the official platform of the CCF/NDP came to endorse this new political stance. The NDP has won power at differing times in four provinces—British Columbia, Saskatchewan, Manitoba, and Ontario—and in all instances their policy and program positions have been far from radical. Not one of these governments ever sought to "socialize" its province, while, in most instances, each government came under attack from its own party loyalists and supporters for becoming too soft, too moderate, too willing to compromise on social democratic principles in order to maintain, or at least to seek to maintain, current public popularity and political support. The trials and tribulations of the Ontario NDP government of Bob Rae are illustrative of this point (Monahan, 1995).

This observation should not be read as implying that all these governments were limited and compromised in their ability to provide effective social democratic governance. These CCF/NDP governments were among the most progressive and influential provincial governments in Canadian history, with that of Saskatchewan legendary for its pioneering role in social and economic policy:

- first in establishing comprehensive, publicly funded medical care;
- first in establishing provincial human rights legislation;
- first in establishing post-secondary student loan programs; and
- a leader in promoting provincial Crown corporations and regulatory agencies designed to oversee the development and management of key economic sectors.

In all these matters, the CCF/NDP governments of Saskatchewan led the way, not only providing social and economic leadership respected by most people in the province (hence, the historic electoral success of the party) but also demonstrating to Canadians in general, and to other parties and governments in particular, how governments could play a more active and beneficial role in the lives of common Canadians.

2.5.4   Maintaining the Liberal Centre

These were lessons not lost on the federal Liberal Party. Its ability to borrow, adapt, refurbish, reform, reorder, and even steal popular ideas from other mainstream parties, from either the right or, more often, the left, and to turn these ideas into their own policies, platforms, and programs is the second great feature of Canadian political history. The ability to manage this political feat of taking, adapting, and adopting a popular political message while stripping the original political messenger from the message itself is clearly an organizational skill of prime importance, and one finely honed by the federal Liberal Party over decades of practice upon both the CCF/NDP and the Progressive Conservative Party (Wearing, 1981; Clarkson, 1996).

Just as it was clear to the leadership of the CCF/NDP that the party had to move towards the centre if it ever wished to gain electoral success, so, too, did the leadership of the federal Liberals realize, over time, that some of the policy positions advocated by the CCF/NDP—for example,

BOX 2.6
Evolving Liberalism

The Liberal Party of Canada under the leadership of Prime Minister Paul Martin faced, and still faces certain profound questions respecting its strategic direction.

Should the party remain on the centre-right of the political spectrum, as desired by business Liberals, stressing prudent financial management and the need for smaller, more efficient government, or should the government, in renewed fiscal health, return to what many social Liberals would see as its more natural position on the centre-left of the spectrum?

Would the Liberals be wise to promote policies of greater trade integration with our NAFTA allies, especially the United States, as well as encouraging greater industrial efficiency and productivity in Canada? And should this country still be seeking greater reductions in tax rates as well as progress on reducing the national debt? And does this country require greater spending in regards to national defence as well as closer cooperation with the United States on matters of security policy and the "War on Terror"?

Or should the policy stress now be on a reinvestment in social programs? Should there be greater spending on health care, child care, and post-secondary education? Should the federal government seek to promote policy aimed at reducing university and college tuition rates? Is there a need for greater federal spending in relation to supporting the infrastructure of cities, to improving environmental standards and implementing the Kyoto Accord, and to bettering the quality of life of Aboriginal peoples?

And is there some compromise between these business Liberal and social Liberal policy positions that the Liberal Party can cogently articulate?

unemployment insurance, old age pensions, family allowances, welfare entitlements, labour law reform, and national health insurance—had wide and growing popular appeal. If the Liberal Party could champion these causes as their own, reasoned Liberal strategists while reassuring Canadians that any such social and economic reforms would only be introduced in measured, pragmatic, and economically viable ways, then the Liberal Party itself could gain the support of those large numbers of Canadians seeking such progressive policies while maintaining the support of those concerned with social and economic policy prudence. Thus, the Liberals adopted a classic centrist party stance: they presented themselves as the party of sound practical and managerial judgement capable of effectively running a moderate mixed economy while also being open and receptive to new ideas, concerns, principles, and policies currently ascendant in political discourse and gaining widespread popular favour. Thus, they were trusted, by the vast majority of citizens holding middle-of-the-road political tendencies, to offer sound, stable, and prudent social and economic management, in no way dangerous to the economic health or the existing social system.

Furthermore, implicit in this was a promise for the future, that when a broad and growing social consensus for new ways and means of addressing social and economic problems should arise, the state would be prepared and able to address these concerns and to deliver popular and progressive social and economic policy with effective management.

2.6   The Shifting Centre of Canadian Politics and Government

In seeking to understand political parties, governments, and the political undercurrents affecting the nature of public policy development and the working of public sector management, it is important to realize not only that parties can and do shift their positions along the axis of the political spectrum, but that the dominant centre of the axis can itself move left or right as prevailing social attitudes change. The point here is simple, yet profound, in its implications for parties, governments, and the broader public these parties and governments seek to serve.

History has demonstrated that the liberal centre of the Canadian political spectrum has been the predominant ground for building public support. As we have just seen, the success with which the Liberal Party has held this centre ground has led the leading parties of the left and the right to moderate—to "liberalize"—their platforms to further their political and electoral appeal to the majority of voters.

But this is not to suggest that the centre ground is itself permanently anchored in an unchanging moderate liberal environment. In fact, the centre of the political spectrum moves in response to changing social and economic ideas prevalent in society at any given time and so must be defined relatively. Hence comes the interest of most major parties in seeking to dominate such central ground, for it is here, by definition, where the majority of the population resides and, thus, where the majority of votes is to be found. Since the centre is defined in terms of the political values of the majority, then as these understandings respecting the desired nature of society, the economy, and the role of the state change with time, then the nature of the political centre may have to be measured from altered perspectives as well. This process can be seen in the shifting of political platforms and the reinvention of party policy over the past century (Dyck, 1996: 396-97).

In the early decades of the twentieth century the political culture of this country was dominated by conservative, *laissez-faire* principles, supportive of free enterprise, a largely unregulated private sector, and a very small state playing a limited role in the social and economic life of the country.

This was the era of the "night watchman" state, with the role of government assumed by most people, including the two main political parties, to be the provision of basic public security and infrastructure services (policing, national defence, roads, harbours, railways, and sanitation), supported by minimal taxation. A federal income tax system was not introduced in this country until 1918 as a "temporary" wartime exigency. In those years the centre of Canadian politics was essentially what we today think of as the right of the political spectrum, and, notwithstanding the gradual emergence of the Canadian labour, agrarian populist, and socialist movements that would lead to the creation of the CCF in 1933, both Conservative and Liberal parties shared a broadly similar conservative orientation towards the nature of society, the importance of individualism, the sanctity of private property, the virtues of free enterprise, and the wisdom of a limited and restrained public sector. While the Conservatives possessed a Red Tory heritage dating back to the relatively active statist policies of the Macdonald government, the party under Borden was as conservative in its values as was the Liberal Party of Laurier. Significant political differences emerged only in matters of party leadership and policy positions relating to the French-English question, Canadian-American relations, and Canada's position within the British Empire (Campbell and Christian, 1996: 27-33).

A slow alteration in the nature of Canadian political culture rose in the 1920s when the federal Liberal Party came to endorse reform liberalism as its credo. This relative leftward shift by the party can be attributed both to Mackenzie King's own strongly held views as to the philosophic importance and moral virtue of reform liberalism as well as to the Liberals' sense of a political reorientation among a majority of Canadians in favour of a modest centre-left approach to social and economic life. In other words, they sensed that the broad political centre was itself shifting from the solid right towards the soft left.

While this political shift was reflected more in party platform than in Liberal government policies and programs over the 1920s and 1930s, the prolonged period of economic collapse, widespread poverty, and social malaise experienced during the Great Depression reinforced Mackenzie King's support for reform liberalism, while it also created the social conditions for the emergence of a serious and persistent political threat from the left. The CCF became an organized and articulate voice of democratic socialism, and in the 1930s and 1940s it came to be viewed by the Liberals as their greatest long-term threat. Growing public belief in the capable and progressive leadership that could and should be played by the state was only enhanced by the experience of the Second World War (Campbell and Christian, 1996: 77-83). For the six years of this conflict the country operated under a state-directed command economy in which all sectors of society—public, private, and voluntary—worked towards a common goal. The war years not only witnessed the creation of a remarkable Canadian military capacity, but the development of a powerful industrial economy operating at full employment and directed, by the state, to serve a great national crusade. The war years brought increasing wealth and prosperity to the country, the growing unionization of the industrial workforce, and the involvement of women in this workforce. Most importantly, it was the state itself, in the form of the federal government, that emerged from the war years as a major driving force in the life of the country, a force that had demonstrated that it could confront difficult challenges and overcome them through the exercise of firm, competent, and visionary leadership. The federal government had demonstrated through its wartime actions that the immense material resources and wealth of the nation could be used to achieve large ends when strategically directed to common goals. For many Liberals the war demonstrated that Keynesianism worked, that the economy could be subject to successful macro-economic management, and that the state could deploy public resources to address serious social problems such as unemployment, poverty, hunger, lack of shelter, lack of education, and lack of hope.

The end of the war marked the beginning of modern Canada and the rise of the modern Canadian state. The government of Mackenzie King, in fact, heralded this new state through certain policy initiatives launched during the war or shortly thereafter:

- a national unemployment insurance system (1940);
- family allowance payments (1945); and
- a national labour relations system recognizing the legality of trade and industrial unions, unionization, and free collective bargaining between union and management (1944).

These initiatives formed the prelude to the amazing growth of the federal state in Canada after the war. Between 1945 and 1984 the federal government was controlled by the Liberal Party for 33 of 39 years, and, despite the Progressive Conservative governments of John Diefenbaker and Joe Clark, the Liberals came to be popularly viewed as the "Natural Governing Party." During these years successive Liberal governments under St. Laurent, Pearson, and Trudeau built the modern, mixed-economy, welfare state that has defined Canadian politics and government and that has

---

BOX 2.7
Governments in Power and Prime Ministers Since 1900

1900–1911	Liberal	Wilfrid Laurier
1911–1917	Conservative	Robert Borden
1917–1920	Unionist*	Robert Borden
1920–1921	Conservative	Arthur Meighen
1921–1926	Liberal	William Lyon Mackenzie King
1926	Conservative	Arthur Meighen
1926–1930	Liberal	William Lyon Mackenzie King
1930–1935	Conservative	R.B. Bennett
1935–1948	Liberal	William Lyon Mackenzie King
1948–1957	Liberal	Louis St. Laurent
1957–1963	Progressive Conservative	John Diefenbaker
1963–1968	Liberal	Lester Pearson
1968–1979	Liberal	Pierre Trudeau
1979–1980	Progressive Conservative	Joe Clark
1980–1984	Liberal	Pierre Trudeau
1984	Liberal	John Turner
1984–1993	Progressive Conservative	Brian Mulroney
1993	Progressive Conservative	Kim Campbell
1993–2003	Liberal	Jean Chrétien
2003–	Liberal	Paul Martin

* Conservative–Liberal wartime coalition

---

become highly influential and imitated, to various degrees, by all the provincial governments in the country. In a period of time marked by a seemingly ever-growing economy, steady industrialization, increasing trade and commerce, and an ever-wealthier society with a constantly growing middle class, the federal and provincial governments possessed budgetary surpluses and seemed to have the capacity for understanding, addressing, and resolving almost any social and economic problem through the application of state power. Indeed, it was Pierre Trudeau who best captured this sense of optimism, purpose, and capability when, in the federal election of 1968, he stated that the prime objective of his Liberal government would be nothing less than the creation of the "Just Society" (Campbell and Christian, 1996: 86-93).

To understand the phenomenal growth of the state, both federally and provincially, during these years, it is important to know that all such growth in policies, programs, and institutions was generally met with great favour by the general public. While the growth of the public sector clearly benefitted the interests of those directly employed within governments (as will be addressed later in this text), the establishment of the modern liberal state cannot be understood simply as a response to the institutional self-interest of state-centred senior bureaucrats and political leaders. Rather, each new policy initiative, program, department, Crown corporation, and regulatory agency was established to meet an existing social or economic problem or weakness. Governments were being confronted constantly by various political parties, interest groups, business groups, and community groups bringing forward demands that they address such problems and weaknesses through the exercise of some form of state power. At times such interests reflected centre-left political opinion, which led, for instance, to the establishment of the Canadian health care system in the 1960s; at other times, those seeking state action were the politically centre-right and right-wing elements of the Canadian business community. As Bruce Doern (1978) has argued, it is a myth that business interests are, and always have been, hostile to direct state intervention in the economy. At times such interests actively call for and support state intervention, especially with regard to taxation and regulatory policy, if such intervention will organizationally and economically benefit them. Take, for example, the perpetual support by the major chartered Canadian banks for federal banking regulations that restrict the entry of new banks—new challengers and hence new competition—into the Canadian banking sector; or the support by major petro-chemical corporations for taxation and investment policies beneficial to the major players in this field; or the historic support by many corporations for direct and indirect subsidization policies and programs designed to enhance their economic activity, employment rates, and profitability. The growth of the state in this period, then, is not to be viewed solely as a response to political pressures arising from the centre-left of the political spectrum; the centre-right, and Canadian business in particular, has been a powerful advocate for activist public policies enhancing their self-interest.

2.6.1   The Centre Shift Rightward: The Mulroney Government

While the centre of political opinion in Canada, as throughout the western world, was clearly grounded in the terrain of modern liberalism throughout the first three decades following the Second World War, by the late 1970s a change in opinion became apparent. By the mid-1970s the national economy began to experience serious problems of "stagflation"—an unhealthy combination of inflation and stagnant economic growth. The results were increasing unemployment, declining growth and productivity, increasing labour unrest, rising consumer prices, and declining consumer and business confidence as fears of recession came to replace any sense of economic optimism. These growing economic fears engendered concerns for the ability of individuals to succeed in providing basic necessities for themselves, let alone to attain "the good life," and for the ability of governments to manage the economy and lead society to a brighter future. This led to a growing disenchantment with government and, in the late 1970s and early 1980s, to an increasing criticism from the right of the political spectrum not only that government had failed in its attempt to lead the economy but that, more pointedly, the idea that any government could or should engage in the macro-economic management of the economy was fallacious. Keynesianism was attacked by conservative critics, who also steadily complained that government was not a solution to these growing economic and social tensions but was, in fact, a major cause of the problems in the first place. "Less, not more, government" became the conservative mantra, with the concomitant position being that more business-friendly, private sector-oriented policies would promote economic growth. From this viewpoint the desired government was one that would rein in a bloated and incompetent state, "freeing enterprise" to get on with the task of building a strong and viable economy (Woolstencroft, 1996).

Central to this neo-conservative vision was fervent criticism of the growth of government during the postwar era, of the expansionist role of the state in the economy and society, and of the growing reliance by both federal and provincial governments of all political stripes on deficit financing as a means of maintaining social and economic programming. Such recourse to steady deficit spending, as inaugurated by the federal government in 1971, was viewed by conservatives not only as a sign of fiscal folly but of the proven inability of the public sector to lead an economy and manage its own affairs with business-like efficiency and prudence. By 1984 the federal government had run 13 consecutive deficit budgets, with the annual deficit for 1983-84 reaching $32.4 billion; each annual deficit added to the accumulated national debt, which by 1984-85 had reached almost $200 billion. Increasingly, conservatives reacted against such financial practices, stressing that deficits should be eliminated, that the debt should be paid down, and that, to achieve these ends, the role of the state in the economy and society should be drastically reduced.

By the early 1980s conservatives in Canada were buoyed by the electoral successes of their counterparts in Britain and the United States. Both

BOX 2.8
The Canadian Political Spectrum

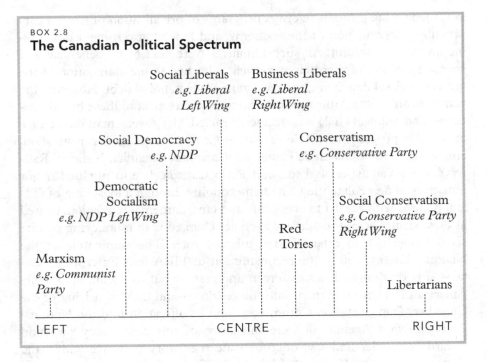

Prime Minister Margaret Thatcher and President Ronald Reagan preached a return to traditional conservative values associated with individual responsibility and initiative, free enterprise, the need to protect private property, the importance of competition, the key role to be played by the private sector, and the need to radically diminish the size and scope of the public sector so as to regain control over public finances while advancing the interests of business. The re-emergence of conservative thought to a level of great prominence and influence in Canadian political life, however, was relatively slow and marked by some ironic twists. While the last Trudeau government of 1980-84 was marked by confusion and lack of direction in the energy sector, leading to dramatic policy reversals with the National Energy Policy (NEP), the major sign of a pending rightward shift came in 1984 with the federal election victory of Brian Mulroney and the Progressive Conservative Party.

This new Progressive Conservative government came into power promising to restore economic confidence in the country through the traditional conservative policies of free enterprise, individualism, competition, and support of the private sector. As a fundamental part of this conservative reorientation, it pledged itself to reduce the role of the federal government in Canadian life through rigorous programs of privatization of Crown corporations, deregulation of the economy, and federal government downsizing and fiscal restraint. All such initiatives were held to be beneficial and necessary in and of themselves, as well as leading to the elimination of the growing federal deficit and the reduction of the national debt. However, the actual record of the Mulroney government with respect to these broad economic and political goals was decidedly mixed. His government did engage in a major program of whole or partial Crown corporation privatization, among them Air Canada, de Havilland, Canadair, Canadian National Railways, Canadian Arsenals Ltd., and Petro Canada. It also pursued major initiatives to deregulate the Canadian economy through a loosening of federal policies with regard to economic and environmental regulation, as well as downsizing federal regulatory agencies charged with monitoring private sector adherence to established regulatory rules. The elimination of the National Energy Policy, the reconstitution of FIRA into Enterprise Canada—a body designed not to screen and restrict but to encourage mainly American foreign investment into the country—and the downsizing of the Canadian Transportation Commission and its alteration into the National Transportation Agency all were indicative of this new policy direction towards a smaller and less onerous state regulatory presence within the Canadian economy (Gollner and Salée, 1988).

Of course, the greatest move towards the fundamental reordering of the Canadian economy and the role of both federal and provincial governments was the ratification of the Canada-United States Free Trade Agreement on 1 January 1989, following some three years of difficult bilateral negotiations and fractious political debate. This free trade agreement, later expanded in the early 1990s to include Mexico in NAFTA, endorsed market economics, the lead role of the private sector in the economy, and economic efficiency and corporate profitability as key goals of society, while it condemned as generally deleterious the impact of government regulation on the economy (Walker, 1993; Belous and Lemco, 1995). These agreements defend and promote the interests of private sector entrepreneurialism and trade while controlling and restricting the range of economic and social policy instruments and actions available to all governments to regulate the economy and establish national or subnational (provincial/state) economic support programs. The push for free trade was part of a broader conservative policy agenda, furthered by conservative political actors on both sides of the border, which succeeded in institutionalizing this pro-market, free enterprise, less government agenda throughout all of North America. Given the decidedly ideological orientation of free trade policy, and the real and potential limitations that such policy implies for specific government initiatives and the general role of the state in society and the economy, it is no surprise that the free trade issue dominated the life of this country in the late 1980s and early 1990s and that the federal election of 1988—the infamous Free Trade Election—was one of the most bitterly fought and divisive election campaigns in Canadian history.

While privatization, deregulation, and free trade policy stand as exemplars of the Mulroney government's conservative vision, the "conservative" record of his government, however, is debatable. Many conservative critics of the Mulroney government—notably Preston Manning, Stockwell Day, and those who would eventually rally to the Reform Party—claimed that this government was not conservative enough, not sufficiently true to conservative principles and practices, and that, in fact, it was still excessively liberal-centrist in many of its orientations.

In reviewing the history of the Mulroney administration, it is clear that it maintained and defended a set of policies and programs integral to the nature and working of the modern liberal state, many of them inherited from the preceding Trudeau government. Such policies and programs included the Canada Health Act, the Unemployment Insurance and Canada Pension Plan systems, federal-provincial Canada Assistance Plan program funding, equalization payments to poorer provinces, a vast array of industrial and agricultural subsidy programs, a variety of regional development initiatives (including the creation of the Atlantic Canada Opportunities Agency and Western Diversification), and a number of other policy initiatives. While the Mulroney government can be seen as much more right-wing in policy orientation compared to the Trudeau administration, it nonetheless remained a party of the centre-right by maintaining many of the features of the welfare and activist state built up by successive Liberal governments. Indeed, the evidence of substantial fidelity to a relatively centre-right federal program and public sector management policy can be seen in the revenue and expenditure pattern of the Mulroney administration. Despite rhetoric supporting major tax and spending cuts and deficit reduction (see Chapter 7), the years of the Mulroney government imposed an increasing tax burden on most Canadians, especially those with middle-class incomes. This enhanced tax burden was epitomized to most Canadians by the introduction, in 1991, of the much-despised federal Goods and Services Tax, the GST. As critics such as McQuaig (1996) argue, the evidence of the Mulroney government's conservative orientation with respect to taxation policy was its increasing reliance on individual income tax and consumption taxes, such as the GST, to provide public sector revenues, coupled with a sharply decreasing proportion of total federal revenues accounted for by corporate taxation. Such a shift in taxation policy clearly privileged corporate Canada and upper-income Canadians at the expense of lower- and middle-class Canadians.

It was in the field of federal expenditure policy, however, that the centrist tendency in the Mulroney government was most pronounced. Far from constricting government spending, as conventional conservative thought would advocate, the fiscal record of the Mulroney government was one of ever-increasing federal spending, higher annual deficits and debt loads, and a greater reliance on public borrowing to meet expenditure requirements. In 1985-86, the first full year of the Mulroney government, total federal budgetary expenditures stood at $109.8 billion, with an annual deficit for that year of $33.4 billion; by 1992-93, its last year, total federal budgetary spending stood at $159.3 billion, with a deficit of $39.0 billion. Thus, not-withstanding its public pronouncements respecting the need for the government to be more economical and efficient in its undertakings, for the public service to be more frugal and to be able to do more with less, and for Canadians overall to be more self-sufficient and to not look to government as a solution to so many of society's problems, this Progressive Conservative government was consistently unwilling to put into practice the harsh medicine of rigorous and persistent conservative fiscal restraint policy.

This tactic ultimately paid the Progressive Conservative Party no political dividend. To many conservative-minded Canadians, the disconnection between conservative principles and rhetoric on one hand, and the centrist, traditional liberal fiscal approach of the Mulroney government on the other, simply demonstrated that the Progressive Conservatives were no longer to be trusted with advancing a conservative agenda in Ottawa. This position was most strongly advocated by Preston Manning and the emergent Reform Party. To many liberal and social democratic-minded Canadians, however, the policy legacy of the Mulroney government—its conservative advocacy of privatization, deregulation, and free trade—suggested that Canadian politics, government, and society were becoming increasingly subject to American values and government practices. These people distrusted almost every move of the Mulroney government, and they disparaged any claim made by Mulroney that his government was one of the moderate centre-right. The political result of such a decline in Progressive Conservative support from both the right and centre-left of the political spectrum was the electoral rout of the party in the federal election of 1993.

2.6.2 The Centre Shift Rightward: The Chrétien Government

It is ironic that the profound shift to the right by the federal government in the 1990s was undertaken by the Liberal government of Jean Chrétien, but this irony fades somewhat when one appreciates the political context within which this government found itself (Campbell and Christian, 1996: 103-107; Dobrowolsky, 2000; Clarkson, 1996).

In the general election of 1993, the Liberal Party campaigned on a rather vague platform of centre-left Liberal platitudes as enunciated by their Red Book:

- to restore honesty and accountability to public life;
- to promote the social and economic well-being of all Canadians, not just a privileged few;
- to protect the Canadian social welfare system, including the creation of a national daycare program;
- to reinvest in public infrastructure;
- to eliminate the GST and replace it with a fairer consumption tax;
- to reopen and renegotiate the terms and conditions of free trade with the Americans to better promote Canadian national interests; and
- to promote governmental fiscal stability and deficit reduction by encouraging a growing economy and undertaking cautious cutbacks in areas of obvious government waste and mismanagement.

In particular reference to the federal deficit, the Red Book committed a new Liberal government to reduce the deficit to 3 per cent of gross domestic product, roughly $25 billion. Once in power, though, this centre-left agenda was quickly displaced by one that was increasingly conservative in orientation, leading the government to move decisively to the centre-right in its policies and programs.

Chrétien's new government quickly came to sense that the ideological centre of Canadian politics was continuing to shift further to the right as most Canadians expressed continued and growing fear (as documented through both government and privately commissioned public opinion polling) that the federal deficit, debt, and size of government were the major problems facing the country and that these problems had to be resolved before any new socio-economic reform projects could be advanced. Such expressions of conservative opinion among the general public were, in turn, often encouraged and advanced by a host of other political actors and forces existing within the realm of public policy discussion, actors such as the national and regional media; business advocacy organizations such as the C.D. Howe Institute, the Business Conference on National Issues, the Canadian Manufacturing Association, the Canadian Confederation of Independent Business, and a collection of other smaller, more specialized business support groups; and the Reform Party and the remains of the Progressive Conservative Party. Among the broader forces felt by the Chrétien government were those of the major American bond-rating agencies instrumental in setting the credit-worthiness of the Canadian federal government, the fear of a fiscal collapse of the government if it could not gain access to borrowed monies at a reasonable rate of interest, and the general pressure of mainstream business influence and conservative thought with respect to policy options in the face of such dire fiscal difficulties.

In this political environment of high federal deficits and debt, of a still large state presence in the economy, and of a strong rightward orientation in public opinion with regard to politics and government, it is no surprise that the Liberal government under the leadership of Jean Chrétien and his finance minister, Paul Martin, made the elimination of the deficit their number one priority in their first term of office. Martin had always been on the right wing of the Liberal Party, more a "**business liberal**" than a "**social liberal**," and had always stressed the need for prudent fiscal management in the affairs of the federal government. In the 1990s, this future prime minister became the second-most powerful figure within the government, after the prime minister himself, and his views on the necessity for deep and persistent budget cuts aimed at eliminating the federal deficit altogether came to represent the government's overall approach to financial management. As Martin famously remarked in 1995, "We are in hock up to our eyeballs," and, in reference to the budgetary target of reducing the deficit to $25 from $42 billion, over three years, "It is a target we will meet come hell or high water" (Greenspon and Wilson-Smith, 1997: 203-04).

In essence, the Liberal government moved to take the rhetoric of the previous Progressive Conservative government and turn it into policy and program reality. Whereas the Mulroney government had been perceived as merely paying "lip service" to fiscal restraint, the Chrétien government was committed to actually restoring fiscal prudence to Ottawa by practising aggressive budgetary reduction designed to result in steady deficit reduction and elimination. Ultimately this policy resulted in balanced and then surplus budgets. This policy approach allowed the government to express its sober concern for the deficit/debt crisis facing the country and to brag about its rigid fidelity to tough financial management as the means for resolving this problem while also eventually gaining it fiscal manoeuvering room to proceed with policies of debt reduction, tax cuts, new socio-economic spending programs, or a combination of all three. In the short term, the Liberals moved to the right of the political spectrum as the centre of Canadian politics continued its rightward shift. This allowed them to continue to lay claim to the centre ground of political life as the party and government that could be trusted to serve the interests of most Canadians in continuing to provide intelligent and balanced, yet restrained and prudent approaches to policy and program development, coupled with fiscal restraint. Once the deficit had been overcome and if and when the political centre began to move back towards the centre-left, they would be well-positioned to deal with this development.

The Chrétien government was true to its word in eliminating annual federal deficits and in beginning to reduce the size of the national debt. This they achieved through a variety of measures designed to increase federal revenues, to decrease governmental expenditures, to restructure the size and scope of the federal government, and to transform public-sector management while also benefitting from strong growth in the national economy over the latter years of the 1990s. Over the past decade, however, we witnessed profound changes in the way the federal government operated: how it related to citizens, the private sector, and other governments (provincial, municipal, and the United States); how it organized and managed itself; and how it exercised its power in a changing social and economic environment. We witnessed an enhanced revenue-generating capacity of the federal government, inclusive of the retention of the GST while also observing a major program of public service and program spending reductions. We have seen major exercises in budget-cutting, including unilateral downloads to the provinces, program reviews, increased privatization and deregulation, public sector commercialization, and a generalized thrust to provide a more business-oriented and corporate approach to the running of government. The Chrétien government over the latter 1990s presided over a major reorientation in the way the federal government works, what it does, and how it relates to society. These changes have been momentous, and the analysis of them forms much of the remaining chapters of this book.

All such changes and reforms, moreover, dramatically affected the nature and role of public sector management. As the federal government undertook the process of downsizing and retrenchment, the structure and mission of the federal public service was subject to great change, change that caused and still causes much unease and debate both within the public service and among those who take an interest in the life of the public service. As Canadian society generally, and its federal government in particular, swung to the right in the 1990s, we generally observed a downsized policy and program role for the federal government and all of its provincial counterparts. The implications for these public sectors was that they experienced serious cutbacks to financial and personnel resources only to hear further calls to do more with less. Generalized policies of restraint, privatization, and deregulation also led governments to strip departments and agencies of particular roles they had long administered as essential public services; in this sense, some restraint policies called for the public sector to do *less with less*. Other policies of restraint demanded that public sectors interact and interrelate with the private sector in more innovative and supportive ways, promoting the private sector as the principal motor of economic growth in the country, while also borrowing practices and attitudes from the realm of private business for use in the management of public sector services so as to enhance the economy, efficiency, and effectiveness of public service delivery.

All such changes posed considerable challenges to the public sector and elicited great debate as to what should be the best management practices of the public sector and how the public sector should interrelate with citizens, the private business sector, and the Canadian public. Moreover, these matters remain at the forefront of political debate regarding the future of this country and the future policy and program direction of its governments.

2.7   Ideas, Policy, and the Future Role of the State: The Martin Government

In recent years political debate has begun that will shape the course of Canadian politics and the Canadian state for years to come. As the federal and now most provincial governments have proven themselves capable of resolving, in one manner or another, the political and administrative problems surrounding budgetary deficits, they are entering an era of political choice, an era in which governments can and likely will realize balanced budgets and, at times, substantial annual budget surpluses. It is noteworthy that the federal government has consistently posted budgetary surpluses since 1997, with all federal parties committed to running government with balanced budgets. And while most provinces have balanced, or have come very close to balancing, their annual budgets, the province of Alberta has reached the milestone of eliminating its provincial debt as of 2004. The political choice that all governments face now becomes one of how to allocate the billions of dollars of increased revenue that they can accumulate. Indeed, the federal government alone, in 2000, predicted that accumulated budgetary surpluses would approach $150 billion by 2005. Such a forecast enabled it to initiate a $100 billion tax cut over these years while also reinvesting some $23 billion into the national health care system. This renewed fiscal strength of the federal government also gave it far more flexibility in addressing the aftermath of the 9/11 terrorist attacks against the United States. Whereas the 1990s was a period marked by the politics and administration of fiscal restraint and policy and program retrenchment, the first decade of the twenty-first century has been marked by a new beginning for political and government leadership. But who will lead and in what direction? And what will be the political and ideological orientation that most Canadians will want their leaders and governments to adopt?

These questions will shape political discourse and governmental activity in this country for the next decade. We have already observed the emerging contours of this debate, however, at the federal level, and these contours are painted in distinctly ideological shades.

Once the Liberal government of Jean Chrétien tamed the deficit, a new era of balanced budgets and surpluses opened new opportunities for the Liberals to redefine who they are, what they believe in, where they believe the Canadian government should be leading the Canadian people, and to what ends. With the retirement of Prime Minister Chrétien in the fall of 2003 and the establishment of a Liberal ministry under the leadership of Paul Martin, the governing party faced two basic options. One was to stay the course, believing that the political centre ground of Canadian politics would remain to the centre-right of the ideological spectrum. This would mean that the Martin Liberal government should position itself as a more conservative Liberal government, one that would continue

- to stress the need for tax cuts;
- to pay down the national debt;
- to support "business-friendly" economic and regulatory policies;
- to enhance Canada's national defence and security and intelligence capabilities;
- to maintain a restrained, less interventionist state presence in the country; and,
- at the same time, to promote the necessity of supporting core social and economic policies such as national health care, employment insurance, regional equalization, regional development policies, and substantial federal transfers to the provinces with respect to health, post-secondary education, and social assistance programs.

This position advocated by the "right-wing camp" within the Liberal government is one that saw the past decade as a historic turning-point in the history of the country and the party, with the party and government now moving to entrench the rightward shift of the country as the new orthodoxy of the Liberal Party.

In contrast to this position is the option of supporting a policy and program shift to the centre-left of the ideological spectrum, in the belief that the centre of Canadian political thought will itself be moving more centre-left in future years as more Canadians tire of conservative-dominated socio-economic policies and seek to reinvigorate and reconstitute the priorities of the modern liberal state that was once characteristic of Canadian political and governmental life. With strong public accounts as well as a painfully learned recognition of the types of problems that can ensue from both excessive public spending and ill-designed taxation regimes, those on the centre-left of the Liberal Party already have traced out a vision of a new, more activist, and progressive Liberal government, one that

- reinvests in and guarantees the continued existence of the Canadian health care system;
- re-establishes secure funding to the provinces in support of health, education, and welfare programs;
- actively maintains and promotes programs of equalization and regional development; and
- aggressively advances new policies and programs designed to address such problems and serve such diverse social and economic needs as child welfare protection and promotion, technological innovation, support for Canadian research and development, industrial competitiveness and export capability, health care funding to include pharma-care and geriatric home-care, the promoting of Aboriginal self-government and just land claims settlements, reinvesting in and upgrading national transportation and public works infrastructure, enhancing Canadian foreign aid, and refurbishing and re-equipping the Canadian military to meet both old and new national and international commitments.

The government of Paul Martin and the federal Liberal party thus confronted a fundamental policy choice that will define its vision of national leadership for years to come. And perhaps in typical liberal fashion, the Martin government moved cautiously in dealing with these policy choices, seeking to find the reasonable middle ground that would distinguish the

BOX 2.9
Paul Martin and Minority Government

On 28 June 2004 the Liberal Party under the leadership of Paul Martin was returned to power in the thirty-eighth Canadian General Election, but only with a minority government. The party standings were:

	House of Commons Seats	% Popular Vote
Liberals	135	36.7
Conservatives	99	29.6
Bloc Québécois	54	12.4 (48.8 in Quebec)
NDP	19	15.7
Independent	1	
Total	308	

Any minority government will pose unique challenges and difficulties to a prime minister and his/her cabinet and senior advisors, and this one was no exception. In a minority government situation the governing party does not possess the capacity to pass legislation and survive votes of non-confidence on its own; rather, it will require the support of one or more of the opposition parties, giving these parties an exceptional influence in the life of Parliament and the government seldom witnessed when a governing party has a majority.

So how would the prime minister proceed? The price of Conservative support would be general restrictions on federal spending, increased tax cuts to individuals and corporations, the abolition of the national gun registry, greater support for NAFTA and globalization, and greater support for national defence spending and closer military and diplomatic relations with the United States, including intercontinental missile defence.

The price of NDP and Bloc Québécois support would be the virtual opposite of Conservative policy. These parties wanted greater reinvestment in health, education, and social-environmental policies; a rejection of increased tax cuts, especially to wealthy Canadians and corporations; the maintenance of the gun registry; greater support for national (or Quebec's) economic self-interest; limited increased spending in national defence, with such money going more to peacekeeping initiatives than war-fighting capabilities; and resistance to closer military and diplomatic ties to the United States.

Governing is all about making choices amid competing policy options with finite financial and human resources. How well did Prime Minister Martin exercise policy and program choice in this set of circumstances? What accounted for his choices, and could he have chosen better?

political centre in Canadian politics for the next decade or two. In the fall of 2004, former Prime Minister Martin signed a health policy accord with all other first ministers that would witness a transfusion of $75 billion in federal funds over ten years into provincial health care systems. His government also stressed the need to reinvest in cities, to better promote post-secondary education, to better protect the environment through the implementation of the Kyoto Accord, and to provide significantly stronger funding to the Canadian military. But all of these new initiatives were to be achieved within a framework and commitment to maintaining balanced budgets and providing tax relief when necessary and convenient. All in all, it was a classic appeal to the political centre.

In seeking to counter the political appeal of the federal Liberal party and their hold on power since 1993, the forces of the Canadian right were fundamentally reorganized in 2003-04. The Progressive Conservative Party and the Canadian Alliance (formerly the Reform Party) merged into the Conservative Party of Canada and, under the leadership of Stephen Harper, has sought to establish itself as a voice of "true conservatism" while positioning itself as a government-in-waiting. It advocates such "common sense" policies and programs as

- deeper tax cuts across the board;
- the deployment of the bulk of the federal surplus to federal debt reduction;
- the continued diminishing of the role of the federal government through more downsizing, privatization, and deregulation;
- the downplaying of federal social-welfare policy while supporting traditional family values;
- the transfer to the provinces of major responsibilities for health, education, and social assistance policy;
- the support for more private sector models of health care delivery;
- the elimination of federal regional development policies and programs; and
- the restraint of federal human rights, bilingualism and biculturalism, and multiculturalism policies.

The two major policy fields requiring additional federal spending in light of the threat of international terrorism, of course, are national defence and security and intelligence. Such a plan of action, if implemented by a future Conservative government, would have an immense effect on the existing nature and role of the federal government, marking a further restrained and limited state presence in the social and economic life of the country. The creation of the Conservative Party and the demise of the Progressive Conservative Party leaves as an open question whether Red Tories can find a home in the new party or whether they might gravitate elsewhere.

As conservatives seek to establish a viable and electable alternative to the Liberals on the right of the political spectrum, the NDP, in turn, has clearly positioned itself to the left, stressing the need for much greater social policy activism while recognizing the need to promote fiscal prudence and economic growth largely founded on the operation of the private sector. New Democrats have always been torn between fidelity to the principles of social democracy and the practicalities of winning power from a centrist-minded public, and the early years of this century will indicate whether their party becomes more of a principled social movement or a pragmatic parliamentary opponent capable of posing an effective challenge to the Liberals from the centre-left. Every party competing for national power (excluding analysis of the Bloc Québécois) is trying to gauge, and striving to influence, the broad structure of Canadian public opinion with regard to ideology, the ideal role of the state, and the general sets of social and economic policies and programs that resonate best with the majority of Canadians.

Regardless of the eventual outcome of these political debates, ensuing elections, and the rise and fall of parties and governments, two points remain fundamental. One is that ideological beliefs have been and continue to be important to the political evolution of this country and the work that is expected of Canadian governments. While the broad centre of Canadian political thought is dominated by liberal values, this centre is far from static, being susceptible to influence from both the right and the left. In the past we have seen Canadian governments tending to a policy and program approach consistent with moderate liberal centrist understandings of the desired role of the state. But we have also seen the broad centre of the political spectrum shift in reaction to changing social and political beliefs respecting the role of the state, with these shifts having considerable impact upon the structure of governments, their policy and program undertakings, and the degree to which they are active in the social and economic life of this country. The second point follows from this first. The role of the state is central to all political and ideological discourse in this country, and, regardless of the party actually forming the government, certain issues will always dominate this ongoing national debate:

- the nature of the ideal state and the degree to which the current state, in practice, meets this ideal;
- the organization of government, its responsiveness to the public, and the degree to which bureaucratic authority is made subject to democratic control;
- the working of government departments, agencies, and Crown corporations, and the ability of these organizations to deliver mandated public policies in economical, efficient, effective, ethical, and accountable manners; and
- the quality of government leadership exhibited both by politicians and by senior public servants.

All of these points attest to the importance of public sector management in the routine life of Canadian governments. The effective management of the state is critical to whatever any government seeks to accomplish in terms of policy and programs; therefore, a close study of the evolution, nature, and current dynamics of Canadian public sector management will be at the forefront as we review and assess the inner workings of the Canadian government in the following chapters.

Key Terms

business liberals: Those persons on the right wing of the Liberal party who stress the primacy of economic policy concerns and fiscal prudence over more social policy considerations. Business liberals are likely to express interest in balanced budgets, tax cuts, debt repayment policy, and industrial development and trade policy.

conservatism: An ideology stressing the importance of individualism, liberty, freedom, equality of opportunity, private property, capitalism, free enterprise, and business interests. Conservative thought stresses that the state should play a generally limited and circumscribed role in the life of society.

democratic socialists: Left-wing socialists, who stress that a party such as the NDP should be much more radical and forthright in demanding fundamental reform to the nature of socio-economic life in this country. Democratic socialists call for a greater state presence in the regulation of society and the economy as well as state ownership of leading national industries. Democratic socialists also tend to view the NDP more as a social movement than as a competitive political party, with the role of the movement being to promote and advocate for socialist principles and values.

ideology of the centre: The political idea that most people in Canada are moderate in their political thinking, seeking a reasonable balance and blending of the policy ideas associated with conservatism, socialism, and liberalism. Also, the idea that most people in Canada seek a mixed economy in which the state has an important role to play in promoting and leading socio-economic development in this country, but with these actions being undertaken in tandem with respect for the important role that the private sector also plays. In addition, the idea that most people are centrist and moderate in their political thinking, meaning that the party that can dominate the middle ground in Canadian politics will be the party that can reap most votes in Canadian elections, thus being able to win power.

liberalism: An ideology stressing the need to balance and mediate the competing claims of conservatism and socialism. Liberalism places stress on the importance of individualism, freedom, equality of opportunity, private property and the importance of the private sector while also stressing that these values and their policy offshoots have to be balanced with concern for the collective well-being of society, equality of condition with respect to certain fundamental matters of social policy, and the need to have a substantial state so as to regulate the working of the economy so as to promote broad national or provincial interests.

Red Toryism: An ideological variation of conservatism stressing the importance of tradition, the maintenance of Canada's historic link to Britain and the British monarchy, and the importance of a Canadian national collective identity that can and will require the active protection and promotion of the state.

social conservatives: Conservatives who tend to place a greater emphasis on the importance of social policy and moral issues, usually with a grounding in religious beliefs, as opposed to those conservatives more interested in economic policies and matters of business. While most conservatives believe in a limited role for the state in the socio-economic life of the country, social conservatives stress that the state has a vital role to play in regulating and prohibiting matters relating to pornography, abortion, same-sex marriage, and lewdness in mass culture, while regulating and promoting such matters relating to family values, faith-based welfare policies, and school prayer.

social democrats: Those persons who are right-wing socialists, stressing that a party such as the NDP should be more moderate and practical in its socio-economic policy positions so as to better appeal to the broad centre of the Canadian political spectrum. Social democrats assert that the NDP needs to accommodate itself to the existence of the private sector and must be willing and able to work with the private sector in matters of economic policy. Social democrats in the NDP also stress that the party must see itself as a political party with a credible message for Canadian electors rather than as a visionary movement appealing only to democratic socialists.

social liberals: Those persons on the left-wing of the Liberal party who stress the primacy of social policy concerns over the concerns of business and economic policy. Social liberals are likely to express interest in social welfare policy, human rights, environmental policy, international development, and Aboriginal rights.

socialism: An ideology stressing the importance of social collectivism, class consciousness, the socio-economic interests of common working-class and middle-class people, the concept of equality of condition and freedom from want, and concern for the gross inequalities in wealth and power found through the working of a capitalist society and economy. Socialists stress that profound social and economic reform to the problems found in modern capitalist societies can only be achieved through active and progressive public policies designed by the state, under the leadership of socialist governments, for the benefit of common people.

References and Suggested Reading

Barlow, Maude, and Bruce Campbell. 1991. *Take Back the Nation*. Toronto: Key Porter Books.

Bazowski, Raymond. 1999. "Contrasting Ideologies in Canada: What's Left? What's Right?" In James Bickerton and Alain-G. Gagnon, eds., *Canadian Politics*. Peterborough, ON: Broadview Press. 79-108.

Belous, Richard S., and Jonathan Lemco. 1995. "The NAFTA Development Model of Combining High- and Low-Wage Areas: An Introduction." In Richard S. Belous and Jonathan Lemco, eds., *NAFTA as Model of Development: The Benefits and Costs of Merging High- and Low-Wage Areas*. Albany, NY: State University of New York Press. 1-20.

Campbell, Colin, and William Christian. 1996. *Parties, Leaders, and Ideologies in Canada*. Toronto: McGraw-Hill Ryerson.

Clarkson, Stephen. 1996. "The Liberal Party of Canada: Pragmatism versus Principle." In Hugh G. Thorburn, ed., *Party Politics in Canada*. Scarborough, ON: Prentice-Hall. 262-79.

Delacourt, Susan. 2003. *Juggernaut: Paul Martin's Campaign for Chrétien's Crown*. Toronto: McClelland and Stewart.

Dobrowolsky, Alexandra. 2000. "Political Parties: Teletubby Politics, The Third Way, and Democratic Challenge(r)s." In Michael Whittington and Glen Williams, eds., *Canadian Politics in the 21st Century*. Toronto: Nelson. 131-58.

Doern, G. Bruce. 1978. "Introduction: The Regulatory Process in Canada." In Bruce Doern, ed., *The Regulatory Process in Canada*. Toronto: Macmillan of Canada. 1-33.

Dyck, Rand. 1996a. *Canadian Politics: Critical Approaches*. 2nd ed. Toronto: Nelson.

—. 1996b. *Provincial Politics in Canada: Towards the Turn of the Century*. 3rd ed. Scarborough, ON: Prentice-Hall Canada.

Gollner, Andrew B., and Daniel Salée, eds. 1988. *Canada Under Mulroney: An End of Term Report*. Montreal: Véhicule Press.

Gray, John. 2003. *Paul Martin: The Power of Ambition*. Toronto: Key Porter Books.

Greenspon, Edward, and Anthony Wilson-Smith. 1997. *Double Vision: The Inside Story of the Liberals in Power*. Toronto: Seal Books.

Horowitz, Gad. 1996. "Conservatism, Liberalism and Socialism in Canada: An Interpretation." In Hugh G. Thorburn, ed., *Party Politics in Canada*. 7th ed. Scarborough, ON: Prentice-Hall Canada. 146-62.

Johnston, Larry. 1996. *Ideologies: An Analytic and Contextual Approach*. Peterborough, ON: Broadview Press.

McLeod, Ian. 1994. *Under Siege: The Federal NDP in the Nineties.* Toronto: Lorimer.

McQuaig, Linda. 1995. *Shooting the Hippo: Death by Deficit and Other Canadian Myths.* Toronto: Penguin Books.

—. 1999. *The Cult of Impotence: Selling the Myth of Powerlessness in the Global Economy.* Toronto: Penguin Books.

Monahan, Patrick. 1995. *Storming the Pink Palace: The NDP in Power, A Cautionary Tale.* Toronto: Lester Publishing.

Morton, Desmond. 1986. *The New Democrats 1961-1986: The Politics of Change.* Toronto: Copp Clark Pitman.

Nelson, Ralph. 1995. "Ideologies." In Robert M. Krause and R.H. Wagenberg, eds., *Introductory Readings in Canadian Government and Politics.* 2nd ed. Toronto: Copp Clark. 25-40.

Perlin, George. 1980. *The Tory Syndrome: Leadership Politics in the Progressive Conservative Party.* Montreal: McGill-Queen's University Press.

Walker, Michael A. 1993. "Free Trade and the Future of North America." In A.R. Riggs and Tom Velk, eds., *Beyond NAFTA: An Economic, Political and Sociological Perspective.* Vancouver: Fraser Institute. 13-21.

Wearing, Joseph. 1981. *The L-Shaped Party: The Liberal Party of Canada 1958-1980.* Toronto: McGraw-Hill Ryerson.

Whitaker, Reginald. 1977. *The Government Party: Organizing and Financing the Liberal Party of Canada 1930-1958.* Toronto: University of Toronto Press.

—. 1996. "Party and State in the Liberal Era." In Hugh G. Thorburn, ed., *Party Politics in Canada.* 7th ed. Scarborough, ON: Prentice-Hall. 249-61.

Whitehorn, Alan. 1996. "Audrey McLaughlan and the Decline of the Federal NDP." In Hugh G. Thorburn, ed., *Party Politics in Canada.* 7th ed. Scarborough, ON: Prentice Hall, 315-35.

Woolstencroft, Peter. 1996. "The Progressive Conservative Party." In Hugh G. Thorburn. ed., *Party Politics in Canada.* 7th ed. Scarborough, ON: Prentice Hall Canada, 280-305.

Related Web Sites

POLITICAL PARTY SITES
  <http://www.liberal.ca>
  <http://www.conservative.ca>
  <http://www.ndp.ca>
  <http://www.blocquebecois.org>

POLITICAL INFORMATION SITES
  <http://www.canoe.ca>
  <http://www.library.ubc.ca/poli>
  <http://www.thehilltimes.ca>
  <http://www.journalismnet.com/canada>

CHAPTER 3

Institutions of Governance: The Environment of Public Sector Management

As the foregoing chapters have illustrated, government plays a major part in the life of this society and is the focal point of significant debates regarding the appropriate role of the state in Canadian politics. Differing parties bring many contrasting viewpoints to this debate, and a major reassessment of the desired place, function, and purpose of the federal government in this country is already underway. Regardless of these broader policy developments, however, one fundamental political truth remains: the state in general, and the federal government in particular, will continue to be vital components in Canadian social and economic life, and any party seeking to exercise federal political power in this country will have to master the often complex and confusing intricacies of the executive institutions of the federal government.

At the apex of power in the federal government stand certain pre-eminent decision-making authorities: the **prime minister**, **cabinet**, government departments, the senior management of the public service, and—to the uninitiated—an often bewildering variety of cabinet committees and central agencies, all mandated with the task of providing executive leadership to the federal government and, thereby, to the Canadian people. These government authorities perform the executive tasks demanded of any managerial body: strategic priority-setting, policy-making, policy and program direction and implementation, the promotion of sound management of all such policies and programs, and the creation of accountability structures by which those who exercise power are held responsible for their actions. But this management system is a public system at the head of a democratic government and therefore must also ensure that ultimate responsibility for government policy and program decision-making is borne by democratically elected representatives of the people.

These obligations impose important responsibilities and challenges for those living and working within these central executive authorities, as well as for those seeking to understand this executive and its power relations. How is the executive command system of the federal government organized? Who are the pivotal actors? What is the mechanism of this system? Has this system been able to provide Canadian governments with sound managerial capacity, especially in relation to priority-setting, program implementation, and ongoing policy and program review and analysis? And what of power relations within this executive? What are, and what should be, the roles of elected cabinet ministers relative to non-elected senior public sector managers? Do non-elected officials exercise too much power in this system, and can a more effective balance between the roles and responsibilities of politicians and bureaucrats be found? Finally, what is the nature of the power relationship between ministers and the prime minister? What is the nature of prime ministerial authority, how has it been changing and evolving in recent decades, and what are we to make of the increasing centralization of executive power in the hands of the prime minister?

While much of the analysis in the following two chapters pertains necessarily to the organization of the institutions of government, the dynamic centre is the power relations within the federal executive, the evolution of the executive structure over the past five decades—especially in the Trudeau, Mulroney, Chrétien, and Martin governments—and the current command system of decision-making found in the Harper **ministry**.

3.1   The Prime Minister and Cabinet: The Political Executive

The cabinet is the central executive decision-making body of the federal state and, standing at its head, leading and directing it, is a minister paramount above all others—the prime minister. This official, the head of government, is the single most influential person in the federal state; thus, all analyses of Canadian government come to revolve around the composition and exercise of prime ministerial authority.

Given the significance of the prime minister and cabinet to the working of Canadian government and politics, it is perhaps surprising to find that these institutions and their roles and responsibilities are nowhere codified within the formal, written constitution (Monahan, 1997: ch.3). Rather, the office of prime minister and the organization of cabinet exist within the realm of constitutional conventions, the informal, non-codified yet immensely strong traditions that flesh out the skeletal constitutional text. Within the Constitution Act, 1867, formal executive power in and over Canada is vested in Her Majesty the Queen, with this power being officially exercised by the governor general. The Constitution Act, 1867 also provides for the establishment of the Queen's Privy Council, to be appointed by the governor general, to "aid and advise" that official in the exercise of executive duties, while also stipulating that the exercise of all general powers by the governor general "shall be construed as the Governor General acting by and with the Advice of the Queen's Privy Council for Canada" (Constitution Act, 1867, Section 13).

In the formal language of the Constitution Act, 1867, the **Privy Council** is thus designated as the body that will exercise *de facto* ("in fact," whether or not recognized legally) executive authority in the country as opposed to the *de jure* ("by right," fully legal) executive power of the Crown. This is in keeping with the traditions and practices of British parliamentary democracy, and it is to the Privy Council and its conventions and usages that we look to understand the emergence of real political power in this country. In formal constitutional law, the Privy Council is the advisory body to the governor general, but important constitutional conventions have grown up around the exercise of Crown powers and those of the Privy Council. In making current appointments to the Privy Council, the governor general draws from the ranks of the party commanding the confidence of the House of Commons. This is not a matter of law but of convention, is based on the only sensible course of action available, and takes place with almost the same force of expectation as if it were law. The leader of this governing party becomes the prime minister, *primus inter pares*—the "first among equals"—within the Privy Council. Appointment to the Privy Council is thus contingent upon one's party winning an election, gaining either a majority, or at least a plurality, of the seats in the House of Commons. Such a democratic victory entitles that winning party to form a government by assuming command of the Privy Council that will "aid and advise" the governor general in the exercise of all executive authority within the ambit of the federal state. A further constitutional convention then stipulates that, in the exercise of such executive power, the governor general shall generally follow the "advice" of the Privy Council as "orders," thus making the Privy Council itself, and not the governor general, the effective executive authority in the state.

Appointments to the Privy Council are lifelong, an honourary testament to the importance of that person in the public life of the country. With life-long appointments, however, the full membership of the Privy Council naturally becomes quite large. As of 2005 the full Privy Council consisted of some 325 members. This, of course, is a wholly unworkable number of persons to act as an executive advisory body, especially one whose size and membership makes it susceptible to political dissension. Thus, the convention became that only those privy councillors selected from the current Parliament should act as the *de facto* advisors of the governor general, forming the real executive within the country. This stipulation distinguishes current from past privy councillors, with the current members comprising an executive committee—a cabinet—of the full Privy Council. The cabinet, chaired by the prime minister, exercises full executive authority in and over the federal state.

The formal appointment process of the cabinet bears scrutiny for what it tells us both about the powers of the prime minister and about the political demands placed upon him or her in establishing a broadly representative executive governing authority (Jackson and Jackson, 1998: 265-72; Aucoin, 1999: 112-17). Following an election, the governor general calls on the leader of the winning party to form a government. The governor general appoints this person to the Privy Council and bestows upon him or her the title of "Right Honourable," at which point he or she becomes prime minister. The prime minister will then "advise" (that is, "order") the governor general to make other appointments to the Privy Council, as a cabinet to assist in the exercise of government power. These appointees to the Privy Council usually are appointed as ministers of the Crown, being made responsible for the leadership and oversight of a department (referred to as a "portfolio"), and they are given the title "the Honourable." The prime minister can also "recommend" the appointment to the Privy Council of ministers of state. These ministers of state act as junior ministers, not administering department portfolios of their own but serving as assistants to other senior ministers. The senior ministers, along with the prime minister, comprise the cabinet proper. If ministers of state are appointed to the Privy Council, they will not be full members of cabinet and will not be full participants in cabinet meetings. Rather, they will comprise a part of what is known as the governing ministry, with the cabinet itself remaining the executive authority within the ministry (Aucoin, 1999: 113). Once sworn into office, the cabinet becomes the power centre of the federal government, exercising full executive authority throughout the federal state and the country overall. At the apex of this power system, stands the prime minister.

3.1.1 The Prime Minister

While the cabinet is the heart of the Canadian government, dominant executive authority is found not so much in the cabinet as in the office of the prime minister. Contrary to the traditional aphorism that the prime minister is but *primus inter pares*, the reality of power relations within any cabinet is such that the prime minister rules the cabinet, thus making any claim to equality with other cabinet colleagues to be one of polite but hollow pretense. As Rand Dyck (1996: 480-83) has argued, the enormous authority of the prime minister within cabinet can be observed through a variety of powers, privileges, and responsibilities that can be reduced to six points.

he governing party. The political
nated. To get where he or she is,
ership in his or her party and has
, as any opposition leader would
party membership, influenced its
ideological message, and inspired
g plurality of Canadian voters to
, the party leader/prime minister
rty politics, those most cherished
lectoral success. Thus, the prime
" upon the party; he or she will
he party such that members of the
ucus in particular, want to follow
vision for the country, and want to
nts" assisting an inspirational and
most fundamental characteristic
g a committed and enthusiastic
by simple virtue of having gained
access to the office in the first place.

[handwritten note: • each week come prepared with 2 questions from the readings.]

2. *It is the exclusive power of the prime minister to select a cabinet.* As mentioned above, the prime minister alone possesses the privilege of instructing the governor general whom to appoint to the cabinet, so the prime minister alone is the architect of cabinet composition. In selecting a cabinet, a prime minister's actions will be influenced by certain constitutional conventions and political understandings, but the very power of choice, of picking and choosing from among many ministerial hopefuls, gives a prime minister extraordinary influence over the elected party members—the caucus—and

---

BOX 3.1
The Prime Minister's Key Powers and Responsibilities

- Head of government.
- Governing party leader.
- Selection and leadership of cabinet.
- Key government policy-maker.
- Chief architect of government structure.
- Appointment of senior executive and judicial officials.
- Special relationship to the Clerk of the Privy Council.
- Special relationship to governor general.
- Key government leader in Parliament.
- Chief communicator of the government.
- Chief international representative of the country.

---

cabinet. The prime minister alone will decide who from among the parliamentary caucus will gain a seat at the cabinet table, and, in so doing, the prime minister alone shapes the substance and style of the cabinet. The cabinet so chosen will, in turn, become a reflection of the prime minister's goals, ambitions, and desires for the party and government, as well as being a statement of his or her appreciation for who among the caucus is best able to serve the party and government. Cabinet membership reflects a prime minister's understanding of who within caucus are most capable of undertaking the onerous tasks of ministry, who are most experienced in political leadership, who are most loyal and deserving of such promotion, and who are the rising stars within the party who will become the leaders of the party and the inheritors of the current prime minister's legacy. And, finally, the prime minister's cabinet appointments must also be understood in a negative sense, as a power of dismissal. If and when the prime minister ever becomes dissatisfied with the performance of a minister, the prime minister alone has the full and final power to ask for the resignation of the minister or to dismiss the minister in the event he or she refuses to resign. Just as the prime minister has ultimate authority in deciding who gets into cabinet, so, too, does he or she have final decision-making power with respect to how long any minister remains in cabinet. All ministers serve "at the pleasure" of the prime minister, and all know that their continuation in office is contingent on their maintaining his or her trust and support.

3. *The prime minister is also the chief architect of the very structure of the government and of what will be the decision-making system of the cabinet.* It is the

prime minister who determines how many government departments there will be, what will be the scope and nature of these portfolios, and whether new departments should be created or old ones disbanded or amalgamated into other existing departments. The prime minister is instrumental in deciding the future of regulatory agencies and Crown corporations, whether new ones should be established or existing ones modified, privatized, or abolished. Beyond such general matters of government structure, the prime minister is responsible for the organization of cabinet and the systems to be used in determining policy and making government decisions. Each prime minister brings his or her own style to the routine working of cabinet administration but, in the past 45 years, certain major developments aiming to enhance and improve the quality and accountability of cabinet decision-making have fundamentally transformed the nature and working of cabinet. In studying the working of cabinets past and present, one must become conversant with the roles and interplay of a seemingly byzantine system of cabinet committees and central agencies designed to coordinate and assist in the process of determining policy priorities, and one must also come to understand the relative power relations between senior public servants, senior political advisors, ministers, and the prime minister. Any such study, for any period of Canadian political history ranging from the government of Macdonald to that of Harper, reveals a fundamental political truth: the prime minister is the predominant figure in every government—always the cabinet-maker, always the head of the cabinet, always the chair of the most important committees of cabinet, and always the chief policy-maker within cabinet and the government. Because each prime minister brings to government that personal knowledge, those ideals, and that vision of what a good government should be, his or her influence is so pronounced that we come quite reasonably to speak of "Trudeau's government," "Mulroney's administration," or "Harper's ministry."

4. *The prime minister is vested with wide authority to make appointments within the government and to other state institutions*. While the power to appoint cabinet ministers tends to be the most readily apparent appointment power, the prime minister has the power to appoint the governor general and the lieutenant-governors in the provinces; the members of the Senate; the judges of the Supreme Court of Canada, the Federal Court of Canada, and the superior courts of the provinces; and all Canadian ambassadors abroad. But, possibly more important than such high-profile appointments as these, the prime minister also has full discretionary power to appoint persons to the most senior ranks of the federal public service: the heads

of federal regulatory agencies and Crown corporations and those who will serve as deputy ministers—the senior public service heads—within each government department. Finally, the prime minister alone has the power to appoint the most senior public servants within the country—the Clerk of the Privy Council and the Secretary to Cabinet, the official head of the Public Service of Canada. In these latter government appointments, as compared to the vice-regal, legislative, and judicial appointments, the prime minister has the greatest capacity to directly shape and control the government's policy and program orientation, to set its ideological and managerial tenor, and to order its administrative working.

5. *A prime minister's power is related to his or her special role in Parliament and the liaison he or she has with the governor general.* As head of government as well as head of the governing party, the prime minister is also the central player in the House of Commons. The prime minister sets the tone of Parliament, and, in the daily Question Period, it will ordinarily be the prime minister who will be the target of most opposition attacks just as it will be the prime minister who will be looked to, by the governing party, as the chief advocate and defender of government policy. Although the prime minister does not attend most of the routine debates in the House of Commons due to time constraints, it is the proposed legislation emanating from the cabinet that sets the agenda for the House of Commons, and it is the prime minister's expectation of party loyalty and discipline that influences all government backbenchers (those of the party not holding cabinet positions) routinely to support government policy and to vote according to the wishes of the prime minister and cabinet. Should any government backbencher break ranks with this "party discipline" and for any reason vote against the government's proposed legislation, suffice it to say that the prime minister has an ample array of political weapons with which to punish such an act of disloyalty: private or public reprimand and rebuke, loss of party privileges, expulsion from caucus, or even expulsion from the party altogether. Such actions are, of course, rare, since most government backbenchers are eager to demonstrate their loyalty to their party and its government not only due to their ideological commitment to its party positions, but also as a means of illustrating their ability to serve the party, thereby attracting the attention of the prime minister and senior advisors with respect to future cabinet appointments.

The parliamentary influence of the prime minister is also observed with respect to the his or her relationship to the governor general. It is the prime minister alone who officially "advises" the governor general with respect to the exercise of executive powers, and, in real terms, this power is most felt in reference to the dissolution of Parliament and the calling of a general election. It is the prime minister who, as a general constitutional rule, possesses the real power to order the termination of a parliamentary sitting and the issuance of writs for new elections. As is often said of politics, "timing is everything" and here we observe the prime minister in sole control of one of the most important political and governmental tools—the timing of the next election.

6. *The prime minister is the chief communicator for the government, both at home and abroad.* Within the world of international relations the prime minister is the primary diplomat of the country, the decision-maker with regard to Canadian foreign policy, and represents Canada at major bilateral meetings with the American president, at annual meetings of the Group of Eight, at meetings of the Commonwealth and the Francophonie, and at some events at the United Nations. On the national stage, the prime minister acts as the chief "public relations officer" of the government, rightly viewed by the government, the opposition parties, the media, and the general public as the leading figure of power in the government, with the attendant responsibility for carrying the message of the government throughout the country. The prime minister is the ultimate link between the government and the national media as it engages in the process of news coverage and journalistic analysis. Thus, he or she is expected to engage in press conferences, parliamentary "scrums," and routine interviews with the media, all as a means of communicating, advancing, and defending the message of the government to the public.

In an era marked by the decline of political party organizations, the growing concentration of party power in the hands of party leaders, and the overwhelming influence of television in political life, the leadership role of the prime minister cannot be underestimated. He or she becomes the living embodiment of their government, and this is very much how modern prime ministers wish to be perceived by the public. They are the driving force of the government, the central actor on the political stage, giving direction and meaning to the work of government. They see themselves as the "great communicators" for their governments and seek to establish a special rapport with the people of Canada through successful use of the media. Indeed, the very fact that a party leader is now prime minister is proof of such a rapport with the necessary percentage of the Canadian public, and prime ministers will always seek to maintain that relationship. Since the Trudeau years, this act of interrelationship with the Canadian public has come to be a very personal one—a connection between the prime minister as a person and the general public. A prime minister seeks to maintain and strengthen such a bond of trust. When prime ministers can maintain the trust of their parties and followers, their political and electoral capacities are formidable indeed, not only over the country and opposition parties in general but, even more so, over their own party and government. When prime ministers begin to lose such public trust and loyalty, the beginning of the end of their political careers is at hand.

3.1.2 The Prime Minister and Cabinet Selection

The power of the prime minister within the government, the parliamentary process, and the Canadian nation is vast. Any prime minister is the heart and soul, intellect and muscle, of any government. But the prime minister needs the assistance of ministers, so **cabinet selection** is the first focus of the position's powers. Although the prime minister is solely responsible for the selection of **cabinet ministers**, several constitutional conventions and political usages have developed governing and structuring this exercise of prime ministerial authority.

In appointing a cabinet every prime minister must address certain realities (Dyck, 1996: 485-90; Aucoin, 1995: 175-78; Jackson and Jackson, 1998: 269-73). The first constraint on the prime minister's power is that, as a general rule, all cabinet ministers must be selected from among those members of the governing party holding seats within Parliament. This derives from the principles and practices of responsible government, stipulating that the exercise of government power ultimately should be the preserve of democratically elected politicians answerable and accountable for their actions before Parliament. In this sense, the prime minister and cabinet are first and foremost Members of Parliament (MPs), elected representatives of the people, leading the party that commands the confidence of the House of Commons, and they have a right to power only for as long as their government can maintain majority support on the floor of the Commons. An understanding of the constitutional basis for the cabinet explains not only the democratic foundations of cabinet government but also the significance of party discipline to the continued life of any government—it is all-important.

Because the prime minister must generally select members of cabinet from those with seats in Parliament, a common sense rule follows, that he or she will look to the party caucus as the main source of cabinet material. From 1867 on, this has been the general practice for obvious constitutional and political reasons. Cabinet ministers selected from the governing party's ranks in the House of Commons possess the merits of having won democratic election and of being, or becoming, the leading members of the governing party. As MPs, they also sit within the Commons, leading the governing party from the front benches, and directly answerable to the opposition parties for their exercise of power. Selecting cabinet ministers from the governing ranks of the House of Commons satisfies the requirements of responsible government.

But there can be exceptions. A cabinet minister does not *necessarily* have to come from the House of Commons, meaning that a person does not necessarily have to be democratically elected to be eligible for cabinet service. A prime minister may appoint a member of the Senate to cabinet and may even, on rare occasions, appoint an "ordinary" citizen as a minister. Both instances, however, are out of the ordinary, exceptions to the "Commons' rule." In the first case, a prime minister will usually appoint one member from the government party in the Senate to the cabinet as the government's Senate representative. While this Senate appointee is usually viewed as holding an honourary position in cabinet, there are times when such a senator rises to regional prominence. This occurs when the governing party does not have any MPs elected from a certain province or even region, yet the prime minister is intent on realizing some form of representation in cabinet from that province or region. In such circumstances the prime minister is expected to "reach into the Senate" for a party loyalist coming from the part of the country in question. In the aftermath of the federal election of 1997, for example, the Liberal Party was left without a single seat in the province of Nova Scotia. In this case, Prime Minister Chrétien appointed Liberal Senator Al Graham to the cabinet as both the government representative in the Senate and as the cabinet representative for Nova Scotia. In the second, even rarer, case a prime minister may appoint a non-MP to cabinet, an "ordinary citizen" who has not been elected. This person, however, is invariably someone of whom the prime minister thinks very highly, someone with strong party and policy credentials, and someone whom the prime minister wishes to see in his or her cabinet for immediate political reasons. However, it is understood that the person so appointed must undertake to win a seat in the House of Commons as quickly as possible, and, should this quest for electoral legitimacy prove unsuccessful, constitutional convention dictates that the appointee must promptly resign from cabinet. In 1996 Stéphane Dion entered cabinet in this fashion as a new representative from Québec, later winning his Montreal seat in a by-election.

In looking at the more general political usages respecting cabinet selection, certain basic understandings and rules can be observed from Canadian political history. In selecting cabinet ministers, all prime ministers have been motivated by concerns of party and cabinet politics, provincial representation, socio-demographic representativeness, and individual talent.

With regard to the first point, prime ministers usually see wisdom in appointing veteran MPs to cabinet, especially those with previous cabinet experience. Knowledge is a form of power, and all prime ministers will seek to be the beneficiary of the collective experience of those with past knowledge in the running of government. Prime ministers will also tend to appoint to cabinet those caucus members viewed by the party as being the senior leaders of caucus, including those MPs who ran for the party leadership but lost. As Dyck (1996: 487) asserts, prime ministers often find it more advantageous to have party leadership rivals, both past and present, inside cabinet and thus subject to the constraints of cabinet loyalty and confidentiality than on the outside, where they are freer to criticize the prime minister and his or her leadership. Thus, it is no surprise that Jean Chrétien named Paul Martin to the post of Minister of Finance in 1993 and kept him there throughout his first two terms in office.

As Susan Delacourt and John Gray have written, however, the relationship between Chrétien as prime minister and Martin as finance minister increasingly soured over their years in power. This dynamic was fueled by Martin's surging ambition to succeed Chrétien as party leader and prime minister, as well as by Chrétien's growing distrust of Martin's political instincts, his ego, and the internal party "machine" that Martin was using to gain control of the grassroots organizations of the Liberal party. These tensions eventually led to Martin's being removed from the Chrétien ministry in 2002 (Delacourt, 2003; Gray, 2003). It is noteworthy that when Martin did succeed Chrétien as party leader and prime minister in December 2003 and announced his own cabinet, none of those Liberals who had challenged him for the leadership of the party over the past year—John Manly, Alan Rock, or Sheila Copps—were included in his ministry. Martin clearly wanted only "Martin loyalists" in his cabinet, yet this rebuff of the "Chrétienite" wing of the party was noted by members of the party as well as by the media, leading some to wonder about the ability or interest of the new prime minister and his senior advisors in healing the internal rifts that the "battle of the succession" had opened.

All prime ministers are also concerned with the ideological composition of their cabinet in relation to the relative diversity of political opinion within the party. Just as all Canadian federal political parties have left, centre, and

---

BOX 3.2
Key Prime Ministerial Considerations in Appointing Cabinet Ministers

- Ministers should hold seats in the House of Commons.
- Ministers should reflect the ideological diversity of the governing party.
- Ministers should reflect the country's provincial and regional diversity.
- Provincial representation in cabinet should be proportionate to the province's share of overall population.
- Cabinet membership should reflect the French-Canadian/English-Canadian reality of the country.
- Cabinet membership should be sensitive to the equitable representation of women.
- Cabinet membership should be sensitive to the equitable representation of ethnic, visible, and other minorities.
- Cabinet membership should be sensitive to the equitable representation of religious groups found in Canada.
- Cabinet membership should be based on merit.

---

right wings, relatively speaking, so too will prime ministers tend to want such ideological diversity reflected in the cabinet to make it broadly representative of the sweep of opinion found within the party. Each prime minister, however, will fashion such representativeness to achieve the balance of opinion most desirable and effective in developing and implementing his or her public policy.

Beyond internal party ideological representation is the ideal that every province and each major region of the country should be given some sense of "balanced" representation in cabinet. This principle, recognizing the fact of federalism and the importance of provinces and regionalism in the governance of the Canadian state, has come to be a defining feature of federal cabinet composition. All prime ministers in Canadian history have sought equitable and balanced regional representation in cabinet, with adherence to this principle constrained only by the availability of caucus members from each province. In an ideal world, the prime minister wants a strong caucus deriving from all ten provinces, with each province being home to a goodly number of government MPs. The prime minister then can appoint a cabinet with representation from each province, with the more populous provinces having a proportionately greater cabinet representation. Ontario tends to have the most, followed closely by Quebec. British Columbia and Alberta follow, if numbers permit, with mid-range numbers of cabinet ministers, while the less populous provinces usually find themselves with one to two ministers each. A prime minister's task, of course, is made much more difficult when the caucus is not representative of all provinces. At certain times a governing party may have few or no elected members from some provinces and scant caucus representation across whole regions, as was the case of the Trudeau Liberals and the West in the late 1970s and early 1980s, of the Clark Progressive Conservatives and Quebec in 1979, and of the Chrétien and Martin Liberals and those parts of the West other than Manitoba from 1993. At times like these cabinets simply cannot be regionally representative of the country, because the governing party itself is not so regionally representative.

Another important political dynamic is that concern for provincial or regional representation can, at times, come to outweigh or even overwhelm concern for political knowledge and experience in cabinet selection. Simply put, if a province returns only one government MP, that person, regardless of education, background, and experience, is virtually guaranteed a seat in cabinet thanks to the representational principle. At the same time, if another province has returned a large contingent of government MPs, such as Ontario's returning 100 Liberal members from 103 ridings in 2000, the vast majority of these MPs have no realistic hope of ever getting into cabinet, as they must compete with the more experienced members of their provincial caucus for a finite and relatively small number of cabinet positions for that province. Those caucus members from the larger province, disadvantaged by the working of this representational logic, may then begin to look to the single caucus member from the other province, now holding a cabinet position, with quiet resentment. The left-out members may feel, with some justification, that each of them, individually, is better suited for the job than the cabinet member, who holds the position only by virtue of province of origin. There are two basic lessons to be derived from this. One is the importance of regional representation in cabinet composition. The other is that cabinet selection often breeds resentment and rivalry between the "ins" and the "outs," between those fortunate enough to have a cabinet position and the many more government caucus members who, for various reasons, have not been selected to government office, yet who jealously yearn for elevation to the commanding heights of executive power. It is a fallacy that government parties always unite loyally behind their cabinet. While the government demands that such a display of unity and loyalty be the public face of the party, more often than not, behind closed doors, the governing party is marked by divisions and rivalries between caucus members and certain ministers. And while most caucus members usually can be counted on to demonstrate loyalty to the prime minister, such a display of loyalty and support will not be extended equally to all other members of cabinet.

Although provincial and regional representation is the major consideration in cabinet composition, other concerns respecting socio-demographic representation have also become significant. All prime ministers traditionally have sought a proportional balance in cabinet between francophones and anglophones, with the former receiving around one-third of cabinet seats to the latter's two-thirds. Prime ministers will also strive for regional balance within these groups, seeking to appoint a certain number of French-Canadians coming from outside Quebec (Acadians or Franco-Ontarians, for example), as well as at least one English-Canadian coming from Quebec (Irwin Cotler, for example). The other traditional demographic consideration in cabinet formation dating from the time of Confederation is that of religious balance. Prime ministers establish a rough balance between Roman Catholics and Protestants while also seeking a similar sub-balance between the various major Protestant denominations. Over the past century, as religious tolerance has grown within the country, the Jewish community has been represented in cabinet whenever possible. Since the appointment of Herb Gray to the Trudeau cabinet in 1969, Jews have traditionally held between one and two cabinet seats (Dyck, 1996: 489).

In more recent decades, prime ministers have moved to accommodate concern for gender equality and multiculturalism in their cabinets. A woman first entered the federal cabinet in 1957 when Ellen Fairclough was appointed to the Diefenbaker government, and since then the representation of women in cabinet has slowly grown to the point that in the past two decades they have accounted for roughly 15 to 20 per cent of the cabinet total. Although these figures are far from depicting gender equality, they nevertheless constitute a major change in the social face of modern cabinets compared to their predecessors of 50 and more years ago. Similar slow and evolutionary changes are also to be observed with respect to the representation of ethnic and visible minorities. Whereas such persons never found their way into the cabinets of Macdonald, Laurier, or Mackenzie-King because they simply were not represented in most political parties or government caucuses, this also slowly began to change after the Second World War. Members of European ethnic groups other than French or English began to enter cabinets in the 1950s and 1960s, and since then such non-visible minority representation has come to be taken for granted in federal cabinets. The same cannot be said about visible minorities, and this is an area where prime ministers can still engage in groundbreaking work to make cabinet much more representative of Canadian society.

While prime ministers are constrained in their ministerial appointment-making by both long-established and newly developing expectations of representation, they must balance such demands with considerations of individual capabilities, demonstrated merit, and fitness for responsibilities to come. All prime ministers want strong cabinets, staffed by persons holding a combination of intelligence, training, experience, determination, social vision, and political acumen. A cabinet appointment is an entré into the elite ranks of government, a call to be part of the select few who will be responsible for the executive leadership of the country. For most politicians, it is what they have dreamed about, and for the vast majority of those privileged to "get the call," the cabinet appointment will be the pinnacle of their political career. Given the magnitude of the decision, all prime ministers treat the appointment process with great care and concern, and though the exigencies of provincial/regional or socio-demographic representation may necessitate the appointment of someone who may not possess the educational background or demonstrated political experience of other appointees, such decisions usually take place in the light of other mitigating factors and do tend to be the exceptions to the rule. Prime ministers need and want exceptionally talented cabinet ministers and will work hard to fashion and maintain such a team.

Finally, if it is very difficult for a government MP to get into cabinet, it is even more difficult to stay there. Cabinet ministers must perform well, and, regardless of the various circumstances leading to any one person's appointment, if that minister proves himself or herself incapable of fulfilling the tasks of a minister or comes to be viewed by the prime minister to be more of a detriment than an asset to the government, such a person will not last long within cabinet. With the prime minister's sole power to appoint comes also the sole power to remove a "failing" minister and to replace that person with another aspiring caucus member eager to enter the limelight. And all ministers know this; they are all aware that they serve "at the pleasure" of the prime minister and that there are many caucus colleagues closely watching their ministerial performance. So long as they can demonstrate sound ministerial leadership, their position is assured, and they can even rise within the senior ranks of the party and government. But should they seriously falter, weakening the political capital of both the government and the party, they will find themselves subject to deep criticism within their own caucus and will lose in the scramble of others claiming to be better able to serve the government and the prime minister.

3.1.3 The Prime Minister and Cabinet Size

As mentioned above with respect to prime ministerial powers, the prime minister not only possesses sole authority over cabinet appointments, but also has leading authority regarding the size of his or her cabinet and its organizational structure (Dyck, 1996: 491-94; Aucoin, 1999: 117-19; Archer, Gibbins, Knopff, and Pal, 1999: 238-44). The sizes of cabinets have varied greatly since Confederation with the general trend over the last half-century being one of a steady increase until the 1990s. In 1867, the first cabinet of John A. Macdonald numbered 13 departments and ministers, and subsequent cabinets stood around this number until the 1920s. The decades from 1920 to 1960 saw the slow emergence of the progressive liberal state (Chapter 2); as the role of the state evolved and expanded, so did the size of the federal government, including a steady increase in the numbers, roles, and responsibilities of government departments. By 1960 the number of departments and ministers stood around 20, which increased to about 30 ministers under Trudeau. This growth continued under the Mulroney government, with his cabinet in the mid-1980s reaching an all-time high of 40 ministers. The trend began to reverse itself in the 1990s with the short-lived government of Kim Campbell, who reduced her cabinet to 24 ministers as a demonstration of her government's commitment to downsizing the public sector and financial restraint. With his advent to power in 1993, Jean Chrétien maintained this smaller and supposedly more efficient cabinet while launching a significant alteration of central government administration. Whereas in the past all ministers were full members of cabinet, after 1993 Chrétien followed the British model of ministry organization with two types of ministers: department ministers and secretaries of state. In 1993 Chrétien appointed 22 ministers to head the departments of government, with these ministers comprising the full cabinet; he also appointed eight secretaries of state to assist certain of these department ministers in their duties. These secretaries of state are ministers of the Crown sworn into the Privy Council and bound by all the rules of cabinet collective responsibility (to be outlined below), but they are not full ministers in that they do not possess department portfolios, they are not entitled to attend all cabinet meetings, and they receive neither the full salary or staff support of full ministers. In total, the Chrétien ministry numbered 30, with 22 in cabinet proper. In 1997, this ministry grew to 37 members—29 full ministers and eight secretaries of state. When Paul Martin became prime minister in December 2003 he maintained the ministry form of cabinet organization, although he altered some of the nomenclature. As of 2005 the Martin ministry had

37 members—28 full cabinet ministers, seven ministers of state (formerly known as secretaries of state), and the two leaders of the government in the Senate and House of Commons. This Martin ministry and its cabinet system is assessed in greater detail in Chapter 4.

3.1.4   Cabinet Ministers: Roles and Responsibilities I

When appointed to cabinet, full ministers are given one or more departments (also called "portfolios") to manage. As the political heads of these departments, they are officially responsible and accountable to the government, to Parliament, and to the Canadian people for all policy and administrative decisions and actions of that department or departments and of all the regulatory agencies and Crown corporations reporting to these departments (Archer, Gibbins, Knopff, and Pal, 1999: 241-43; Jackson and Jackson, 1998: 272-74).

Within the British parliamentary tradition, ministerial responsibility involves two distinct yet related concepts. First, **individual ministerial responsibility**, as noted above, means that the minister

- is individually responsible for the running of his or her department(s);
- is ultimately responsible, before Parliament, for the policy and program development of the department(s); and
- is accountable for all decisions made by the department(s) while he or she is in charge.

Thus, if need be, the minister is expected to stand in the House of Commons and answer any and all questions from the opposition parties regarding the operation of the department(s) and to explain and defend the actions of the department(s) before the media. And, if and when allegations of gross ministerial or departmental incompetence and/or corruption are brought to light, which cannot be explained or defended satisfactorily, the minister will be expected to resign so that parliamentary and public trust in the government can be rebuilt.

The second form of ministerial responsibility, much less understood by the public, is that of **collective ministerial responsibility**. This necessitates that all ministers collectively support all decisions and actions of cabinet. As members of cabinet, ministers are not just the heads of particular departments with a responsibility to bring discreet departmental concerns, policy issues, and proposed legislation to cabinet for discussion and, hopefully, approval, they are collectively responsible for the executive

BOX 3.2
Federal Government Departments: 1867; 1984; 1997

1867 First Macdonald Ministry	*1984* First Mulroney Ministry	*1997* Second Chrétien Ministry
Justice	Veterans Affairs	Agriculture and Agri-Food
Militia and Defence	External Affairs	Canadian Heritage
Privy Council	Employment and Immigration	Citizenship and Immigration
Secretary of State	Justice and Attorney General	Environment
Secretary of State for	Public Works	Finance
Provinces	Transport	Fisheries and Oceans
Finance	Solicitor General	Foreign Affairs and
Receiver General	Health and Welfare	International Trade
Customs	Fisheries and Oceans	Health
Inland Revenue	Regional Industrial Expansion	Human Resources
Public Works	Agriculture	Development
Post Office	Indian Affairs and Northern	Indian Affairs and Northern
Agriculture	Development	Development
Marine and Fisheries	Treasury Board	Industry
	National Revenue	Justice
Source: J.E. Hodgetts,	Finance	Labour
1973: 89.	Defence	National Defence
	Multiculturalism	National Revenue
	Supply and Services	Natural Resources
	Fitness and Amateur Sport	Public Works and
	Science and Technology	Government Services
	Labour	Solicitor General
	Secretary of State	Transport
	Tourism	Treasury Board
	Energy, Mines, and Resources	Veterans Affairs
	Small Business	
	Environment	Source: R. J. Jackson and D.
	Youth	Jackson, 1998: 345.
	Consumer and Corporate Affairs	
	International Trade	
	Mines	
	Communications	
	Forestry	
	External Relations	
	Source: Landes, 1987: 104.	

governance of the country as a whole. All ministers thus bear formal common responsibility for the development of government policy, the approval of draft legislation, the adoption of orders-in-council, and the management of the nation's finances and public personnel systems. In a spirit of "all for one and one for all," each cabinet minister is expected to share an interest in government policy and program developments beyond those in his or her own portfolio, to engage in all full cabinet discussions and debates on a host of issues, and to provide considered judgement on the merits and demerits of general cabinet business. While individual ministers are meant to be the key players and advocates with respect to their own individual department portfolios, their skills and abilities are engaged also in the general development of government policies and programs (Kernaghan, 2002: 104-06).

Cabinet, then, as a decision-making body, must be understood in collective terms. Individual ministers may propose department policy and program initiatives to cabinet, but cabinet, either as a whole or through its subcommittees, has the right and duty to assess and dispose of these matters as it deems fit. While these cabinet discussions can take many forms, they are meant to be an exercise in collective decision-making under the leadership of the prime minister. The prime minister controls the agenda of full cabinet meetings or the meetings of key cabinet committees and usually seeks the input of all members with respect to agenda items. Cabinet discussions are meant to be full and frank analyses of

- policy and program options;
- the desired course of government action;
- the weaknesses, problems, and dangers confronting the government; and
- the best ways and means of overcoming these difficulties.

All members of cabinet will be expected to participate fully in cabinet deliberations, to express their viewpoints strongly, and to debate the pros and cons of proposed actions in an environment of mutual respect and confidentiality. It follows from this that all cabinet deliberations are strictly confidential, meaning that members are never to divulge the substance of cabinet debates. Such secrecy is meant to ensure not only that individual ministers and senior officials can speak their minds freely, but that the cabinet as a whole can discuss a whole range of options and can move back and forth on proposed courses of action, assessing their policy and political

---

BOX 3.4
Ministerial Responsibilities

Individual ministerial responsibility:
- Every minister is individually responsible to Parliament for the operation of his/her department.
- Every minister must answer to Parliament for the policy and program developments in her/his department.
- Every minister must explain and defend the actions of his/her department to Parliament.
- Every minister must be prepared to resign if gross ministerial or departmental incompetence is found to have occurred on her/his watch.

Collective ministerial responsibility:
- All ministers bear common responsibility for the final approval of government policy.
- All ministers are expected to support government legislation in Parliament.
- All ministers are expected to promote and defend all government policies and programs in public.
- If a minister cannot, in good faith, promote and defend government policy, she or he will be expected to resign from cabinet.

---

strengths and weaknesses prior to formal decisions being made without fear of publicity constraining their deliberations and actions.

3.1.5   Cabinet Decision-Making: An Overview

While the substance of cabinet discussions are secret, we do derive something of their style from the memoirs and reminiscences of past ministers and prime ministers. Cabinet documents are not subject to Freedom of Information rules and regulations (see Chapter 11); they are kept confidential for a period of 30 years. What is offered here is a brief overview of the basic format of cabinet decision-making dating back some 50 years; Chapter 4 offers a much more detailed review of the development of cabinet decision-making systems over the past 20 years. This will lead to a critical assessment, based upon the leading research of Donald Savoie (1999), of the decision-making systems found within the Martin government. But before such a detailed assessment and critique is undertaken, it is helpful to understand the working of the cabinet of past governments (Dyck, 1996: 497-98; Jackson and Jackson, 1998: 274-77; Bakvis and MacDonald, 1993: 53-57).

In structuring the deliberations of cabinets, most prime ministers have preferred a wide-open discussion on the merits and demerits of policy and program proposals with all possible governmental, political, and socio-economic considerations being canvassed. Prime ministers in the past have tended to encourage a free-flowing discussion of policy options in which all ministers could offer their advice and concerns. It has also been quite common for prime ministers to play a passive role in such discussions, often sitting back and listening to the discussion and debate as ministers address the strengths and weaknesses and the political and administrative pros and cons of a policy matter. In such scenarios, prime ministerial intervention comes in two versions: either towards the end of a discussion when the prime minister will summarize the salient points of consideration and his or her sense of the emerging consensus around the table, or in the midst of the debate when the prime minister will stress his or her interest in the cabinet achieving a desired outcome. As Savoie (1999: 84-86) has written of the cabinet meetings of the Trudeau government, the discussion often resembled a university seminar. Of course, not all ministers are equal in the eyes of the prime minister or other ministers on account of any combination of background, past experience, length of service in cabinet, knowledge of the given policy field and policy position, or general intellectual sophistication, so prime ministers and other ministers give differential weight to the value of particular ministers' opinions. In cabinet discussions, however, it has been extremely rare for deliberations to result in a formal vote. Prime ministers have routinely sought a consensus on the matter under discussion, and such a consensus has usually emerged over time—sometimes quickly, at other times, more slowly. The reticence to hold votes can be easily comprehended: no prime minister has ever wanted to see the emergence of a minority bloc in cabinet challenged and defeated by a majority bloc; such a development would run counter to the ideal of the cabinet as a body of collective responsibility acting as one unified executive force. The concept of collective ministerial responsibility, according to which all ministers must support all of the decisions and actions of cabinet, means that all prime ministers want their cabinets to achieve consensus on most policy matters. Furthermore, this practice leads all ministers to feel themselves a positive part of all decisions taken by cabinet. A system of cabinet voting also runs the risk of establishing a false equality between ministers when, in reality, all ministers are not politically equal, particularly the prime minister. For these reasons no prime minister has or ever would accept a voting procedure; hence, the quest for cabinet consensus under firm prime ministerial leadership, which, as a general rule, has been routinely achieved.

BOX 3.5

The Harper Cabinet, 2006: Who's Who (in order of precedence)

Stephen Harper, Prime Minister

Robert Nicholson, Leader of the Government in the House of Commons and Minister for Democratic Reform

David Emerson, Minister of International Trade and Minister for the Pacific Gateway and the Vancouver-Whistler Olympics

Jean-Pierre Blackburn, Minister of Labour and Minister of the Economic Development Agency of Canada for the Regions of Quebec

Gregory Thompson, Minister of Veterans Affairs

Marjory LeBreton, Leader of the Government in the Senate

Monte Solberg, Minister of Citizenship and Immigration

Chuck Strahl, Minister of Agriculture and Agri-Food and Minister for the Canadian Wheat Board

Gary Lunn, Minister of Natural Resources

Peter MacKay, Minister of Foreign Affairs and Minister of the Atlantic Canada Opportunities Agency

Loyola Hearn, Minister of Fisheries and Oceans

Stockwell Day, Minister of Public Safety

Carol Skelton, Minister of National Revenue and Minister of Western Economic Diversification

Vic Toews, Minister of Justice and Attorney General of Canada

Rona Ambrose, Minister of the Environment

Michael Chong, President of the Queen's Privy Council for Canada, Minister of Intergovernmental Affairs and Minister of Sport

Diane Finley, Minister of Human Resources and Social Development

Gordon O'Connor, Minister of National Defence

Bev Oda, Minister of Canadian Heritage and Status of Women

Jim Prentice, Minister of Indian Affairs and Northern Development and Federal Interlocutor for Métis and Non-Status Indians

John Baird, President of the Treasury Board

Maxime Bernier, Minister of Industry

Lawrence Cannon, Minister of Transport, Infrastructure and Communities

Tony Clement, Minister of Health and Minister for the Federal Economic Development Initiative for Northern Ontario

James Flaherty, Minister of Finance

Josée Verner, Minister of International Cooperation and Minister for La Francophonie and Official Languages

Michael Fortier, Minister of Public Works and Government Services

Cabinet Make-Up

Atlantic Canada – 3
Quebec – 5
Ontario – 9
Manitoba – 1
Saskatchewan – 1
Alberta – 4
B.C. – 4

Women – 6 of 27

Once a cabinet decision has been made on a given matter, a consensus with which the prime minister is comfortable, the practical working of the principle of collective responsibility necessitates that all members of cabinet fully support the decision. Regardless of any one minister's relative criticism or opposition to the proposed course of action within the sanctity of the cabinet room, once the matter has been approved by full cabinet all ministers are expected to close ranks, to endorse the decision as their own, and to present a unified government face to Parliament and the country. Such a display of unity has always been viewed as politically necessary, since the opposition and media would pounce on any hint of cabinet division as a sign of weakness in the government and evidence that it was unsure of the direction in which it wished to lead the country. It has also been a necessity for the obvious reason that it signals to the entire public service that the executive is strong, that it knows its collective mind, and that it is committed to the policy and program means and ends that it is advancing. Should any individual minister, however, for whatever reason of principle or practice, feel unable to consent to and support the cabinet decision so reached, that minister is expected to resign from cabinet. Although cabinet resignations are rare and most ministers routinely and fully support the decisions of cabinet, the fact that they have occasionally happened shows all the more clearly the collective nature of cabinet decision-making.

3.1.6   Cabinet Ministers: Roles and Responsibilities II

Ministerial roles and responsibilities cannot be understood without a view also to the important and time-consuming expectations borne by ministers beyond their department and cabinet responsibilities (Savoie, 1999: 240-48; Tardi, 2002: 283-85). Being appointed a minister of the Crown in no way diminishes other pre-existing duties and expectations. On the contrary, a ministerial appointment heightens the demands placed on such a member of the government caucus. Beyond the ministerial responsibilities, both individual and collective, of a member of cabinet, a minister remains an MP and a caucus member and becomes a much more significant actor within the governing party. The minister must continue to bear all the duties and expectations of an MP: he or she must be prepared to take part in Question Period, parliamentary debates, and parliamentary committee meetings, especially in relation to his or her department responsibilities, as well as continuing with all routine constituency work, fulfilling the role of a local representative for the "home" riding and being an "ombudsperson" for constituents seeking assistance in dealing with the federal bureaucracy.

> BOX 3.6
> ## Cabinet Ministers' Duties
>
> - To fulfill one's individual ministerial responsibilities.
> - To fulfill one's collective ministerial responsibilities.
> - To fulfill one's responsibilities as an MP.
> - To fulfill one's responsibilities as a member of the governing caucus.
> - To fulfill one's responsibilities as a member of the party.

All ministers know, or should know, that they have to maintain close and personal connections with their constituents to assure local electors that, notwithstanding their larger national government responsibilities, they remember where they came from, whom they directly represent in Parliament, and whose support they need in the next election so as to remain in Parliament.

Beyond this continuing and important role as an MP, by virtue of being in cabinet ministers acquire yet other responsibilities. Ministers remain members of the government caucus and are expected to maintain a close and open relationship to caucus, being available to discuss government policy and administrative matters with caucus members, thereby maintaining and building backbench support and awareness of the activities of government. The development and nurturing of this liaison is significant to the long-term success of any minister, especially if he or she will be seeking promotion to more important cabinet positions involving even more advanced and demanding leadership requirements. Ministers who ignore this caucus reality do so at their own political peril.

All ministers, by virtue of their appointments, become leading figures within the party overall. They are seen as primary or secondary leaders of the party depending on their portfolios and experience in government, as loyal lieutenants to the prime minister, and some as future leaders of the party. Ministers will definitely be perceived as leading spokespersons within cabinet for their home province and region, with some recognizing that their very presence in cabinet is attributable to their being perceived as "provincial" representatives. Other ministers may be perceived also, depending on their socio-economic backgrounds, as the representatives of the concerns of women, visible and ethnic minorities, religious minorities, the handicapped, or Aboriginal Canadians. In whatever role the minister is viewed by him or herself, by the prime minister and cabinet, and by the party, so the minister must effectively perform this role not only within the government but also within the party. In practice this means the minister must attend a wide variety of caucus and party meetings and events designed to promote everything from regional concerns and policy interests to the policy and program ambitions of those social groups the minister is deemed to represent.

This recitation of roles and responsibilities suggests the crushing workload that ministers face. Their departmental duties and the exercise of their individual and collective ministerial duties alone could consume all their time. As has long been recognized by ministers, they could devote 24 hours a day, seven days a week, to their portfolios and still not accomplish all they wish. And yet, they have other pressing and important demands on their time: from constituents, from Parliament, from caucus, and from the party. In this environment of many and often competing obligations, time itself becomes the most precious commodity within the grasp of a minister, some utilizing this resource better than others.

Ministers are also human beings with personal and family lives. These, too, must be nurtured and promoted if an individual is to maintain a healthy personal psychological balance, strong friendships, and stable and happy relationships with loved ones. The time required to meet these basic yet profound goals, however, is time that must be taken from other demands. The personal life of the minister thus competes with the public life, and all ministers struggle to strike the appropriate balance. Most yearn for more time with family and friends, cherishing downtime away from the glare and heat of public responsibilities. And, at worst, as Steve Paikin has documented, the demands of public life can lead to such stress-related problems as the alienation of friendships, marriage partners, and family members, leading to marriage breakdowns and the self-destructive behaviour associated with alcohol and drug abuse (Paikin, 2003). When thinking of ministers, reflect on the multiple stresses associated with their work, the time demands they face, and the sacrifices that must be made as private lives are reconfigured by public duties.

3.2 Government Departments and Crown Agencies: The Bureaucratic Executive

Central to government organization in this country are two main types of institutions: **departments** and **Crown agencies**. The former are better known, but the latter are also very significant as we shall see (Jackson and Jackson, 1998: 343-46; Dyck, 1996: 509-13, 521-25; Tardi, 2002: 285-87).

Government departments, each headed by a minister, fulfill the chief roles of public administration and public sector management. As a prime minister and cabinet make decisions regarding desirable public policy for the country, addressing such matters as what, how, where, and when existing programs should be modified and new policies initiated, they look primarily to the departments for providing the means to these ends. Departments are the workhorses of government, and each has four generic functions:

- program administration;
- policy development;
- research, analysis, and record-keeping; and
- general liaison and communication.

First, a department engages in the delivery of government programs within its field of jurisdiction. When a new policy is developed by a government, usually the pertinent department is given responsibility for transforming the policy into a program: the series of discrete operational tasks and goals that link the department (i.e., the government) to those whom the policy is designed to serve. Thus, departments act as the operational "conveyor belts" of government activity, taking government policies and seeing that they are applied within society. Departments do not deal only with new policies and programs deriving from the current government, however. While these matters are an important part of their work, most of the programs they implement are those deriving from the policy initiatives of past governments.

When any new government comes into power, with many new ideas regarding policies and programs, it does not inherit a bureaucratic vacuum but, rather, a full-fledged system of policies and programs addressing the whole breadth of government activity in that field, with all existing administrative divisions fully engaged in the ongoing tasks of routine program administration. Any new government has the right, of course, to study, alter, and reform the already functioning policies and programs of the departments it inherits, but it is rare for any new government to fundamentally transform *all* the policy and program activities of existing departments. On the one hand, such a task would be absolutely enormous, entailing change and disruption of monumental proportions to the routine workings of government; on the other hand, such a task would be administratively and politically undesirable, indeed, foolish, for the reason that all government programs exist for certain reasons and they all have established beneficiaries grown accustomed to these particular state services; moreover, in most instances, existing department programs are valuable in that they serve long-recognized public needs.

Within any government then, the influence of past decisions, past government policy outcomes, and past program developments are present from the outset as departments continue the routine implementation and delivery of programs that most people expect to see continued. In fact, the vast majority of any government's work involves the implementation of programs devised and promulgated by previous governments. In this sense all governments are incrementalist, rooting their current program administration in the policy decisions of the past. This means that there are policy decisions and programs that the current government can accept and continue without any substantial policy analysis or administrative review. The Mulroney government inherited the Trudeau government's policies and programs respecting bilingualism and biculturalism, program funding and equalization payment to the provinces, health care, regional development policy, immigration and citizenship policy, human rights policy, and agricultural subsidization policy, just as the Chrétien government inherited the Mulroney government's policies and programs in foreign and defence policy, environmental policy, income security policy, health care policy, the GST, and free trade. And, in turn, despite Paul Martin's desire to be different from Jean Chrétien, his government inherited the policy and program legacy of the Chrétien ministry respecting balanced budgets, a smaller government, and concern for the need to reinvest in public services, as well as such controversial issues as the national gun registry, same-sex marriage, and governmental ethics. This dynamic of political and administrative inheritance underscores the longevity of particular policy and program understandings and the ideological beliefs that sustain them. As centrist liberal ideas and values have dominated in the role of the Canadian state for most of the twentieth century, so, too, have they come to dominate the nature and working of governments, becoming the entrenched reality of routine policy and program administration within which all subsequent governments must begin their work.

The influence of pre-existing policies and programs within departments does not preclude governments and departments from pursuing new ways of conducting government business. The other vital function of departments is policy development. Each department becomes expert in the process of policy and program implementation within its field, including

- the operational strengths and weaknesses of existing policies and programs;

BOX 3.7
Key Functions of Departments

- Delivery of departmental programs and services.
- Promotion of departmental research and policy analysis.
- Maintenance of departmental records.
- Promotion of departmental communication and liaison with other related interests.
- Adherence to all financial management rules and regulations.
- Adherence to all human resources rules and regulations.
- Training of departmental staff.

- the continuing needs of the department's clients, be they individual citizens, interest groups, or business corporations; and
- the potential for further state action to enhance government effectiveness in that field.

As department officials, from "front-line" field office workers to middle-level managers, gain such knowledge, this information is communicated up the chain of command to senior management and senior policy advisors. These officials then have the responsibility of taking such accumulated knowledge and digesting it, assessing it, studying it, and developing either reforms and modifications to existing policies and programs—the "fine-tuning" of current practices—or the creation of wholly new policies and programs designed to address new and pressing concerns they deem important. It is not unusual to witness significant modifications to most department policies and programs as departments refine their work with respect to such specific matters as, for example, discerning more optimal means of delivering regional development policy, of maintaining an effective military, of promoting social welfare policy, or of promoting economic development and fair systems of taxation.

This process of policy and program reform/adjustment/renewal/creation will, of course, be closely tied to the leadership interests of the department's minister. Each minister comes to a department with certain ideas as to how the department can perform its government role more effectively and how department policy can be strengthened. Every minister will want to work closely with senior department management to assess the strengths and weaknesses of existing department policies and programs and how they can be improved. Of course, there is no guarantee that a minister and senior staff will see "eye to eye" with regard to either the assessment of ongoing departmental activities or the choice of desired program and policy reforms. At times departmental interests in certain reforms will be seen by ministers as essentially administrative and technical in nature and, thus, of insufficient political interest to merit deep ministerial attention. At other times senior staff and a minister may disagree over the very substance of reform proposals; for example, senior staff may question the managerial, administrative, and policy wisdom of certain policy and program options advanced by a minister. Although each minister is the formal head of his or her department, the power and influence relations between ministers and their senior department managers are usually very complex and require sophisticated methods of interaction. And ministers do not always get their way.

Flowing from both their program administration and policy development roles, all departments possess important duties pertaining to ongoing record-keeping, research, and analysis while also maintaining the "institutional memory" of the department and its actions and non-actions. Departments are complex bureaucratic entities active within a government and political world where, to quote Max Weber, "knowledge is power." To gain knowledge about their activities and to forge knowledge that will enable them to better deliver programs and develop policies, all departments gather and maintain information regarding their activities—records of their policy and program initiatives and records of all their departmental studies, previous and ongoing—for the assessment of department activities and all possible future courses of action to enhance departmental effectiveness. Furthermore, departments routinely study, research, analyze, and record the activities of other departments with similar portfolios in other governments, both in this country and abroad. Thus, the federal Department of Environment maintains close contacts with provincial environmental departments, sharing information with them, watching and assessing what they do in addressing environmental concerns and problems, and sharing and learning "best practices" in the administration of environmental policies and programs. Likewise, the Department of National Defence maintains close contacts with its counterparts in other countries, especially those of our NATO allies, interrelating with them, analyzing their defence strategies, and developing Canadian military training, organization, and equipment to dovetail with their needs. Through all such study, analysis, and record-keeping, one can appreciate how these bureaucracies come to be associated with flurries of documents and papers flowing back and forth and accumulating in department files. Indeed, one of the important functions of departments is maintenance of such records for current and future officials and ministers.

No department can function effectively without detailed knowledge of its field of operation, whether knowledge of current administrative practices, technical improvements, or strategic policy options, or the past records of such matters and of action undertaken or not undertaken. Every department keeps the institutional memory for its portfolio, for it is the department itself that will be looked to by the government, cabinet, and prime minister as the body with most expertise in its field. The department must know itself; its field of operation; the challenges, difficulties, and opportunities it confronts; its strengths and weaknesses; and the various options it has to "do things differently" should it so wish. The department must encompass its past expertise and know why its field has evolved as it has, why certain policies and programs were advanced and implemented as government initiatives, and to what ends and effects, as well as knowing why other policy and program options were rejected. Understanding "non-actions" is often as important and instructive as comprehending the logic of actions taken, because "non-actions"—initiatives contemplated but eventually rejected—illustrate assessments of costs and benefits and strengths and weaknesses, all of which are crucial to understanding how, administratively, and why, politically, a department currently operates as it does. And, should a new government and a new minister seek to do something new, it is unlikely that the department has not already considered and assessed the "new" option proposal at some point in the near or distant past, meaning that the current minister and senior management can access a body of existing information and knowledge from which to begin the process of review, assessment, and policy development.

Closely tied to this role of record-keeping, research, and analysis is the fourth function of departments, namely, communication and liaison with others interested in its work. These others range from a host of governmental and non-governmental organizations; to department clientele, policy and program stakeholders, parliamentary actors, and the media; to ordinary citizens. Departments must communicate with those concerned with their policies and programs about almost everything they do. Such communication can involve the provision of information and services to citizens (clients) entitled to a department service, or liaison with business and other public interest groups concerned with the work of the department, or providing information to MPs or the media following the activities of the department. Departments liaise closely with such parliamentary officials as the members of the Office of the Auditor General, the Office of the Official Languages Commissioner, and the Office of the Privacy Commissioner. And, as noted above, all departments are expected to maintain very close lines of communication with other departments of the federal government whose work may touch on theirs, with related provincial government departments sharing the same or related portfolio field, with related departments of foreign governments, and with all the cabinet committees and central agencies of the federal government to be introduced in the next chapter.

The primary goals of any department with regard to communication are:

- to gain information relevant to its duties;
- to maintain close lines of communication with department clients and those concerned with departmental policy development and program delivery;
- to promote rigorous feedback channels with such clients and other interests enabling department officials to become aware of, and to quickly respond to, emerging policy and program problems;
- to establish and manage effective liaison with all important government and parliamentary actors active within the federal state; and
- to establish and maintain such links with other relevant actors within other governments, both domestic and foreign.

To accomplish all this, department members are expected to possess excellent communication skills, enabling them to collect, accumulate, and synthesize information and to channel this intelligence to all those inside and outside of the government who need such information.

3.2.1 Department Structure: A Functional Typology

In assessing departments and seeking to explain their organizational rationale, numerous authors have developed more-or-less intricate typologies of departmental organization; one can choose from the works of Jackson and Jackson (1998: 344), Kernaghan and Siegel (1999: 203-07), and Inwood (2004: 129-33). However, in establishing a sleeker and simpler outline of the general function of departments and their forms, one observes them falling into two broad categories—service departments or support departments—based on their roles and relationships either to the government in particular or the public in general. The majority are best understood as being "line" or "operational" **service departments**, because their primary responsibility is to

---

BOX 3.8

**Departmental Structure:
A Functional Typology of Departments, 2005**

Service Departments	Support Departments
Agriculture and Agri-Food	Finance
Canadian Heritage	Foreign Affairs
Citizenship and Immigration	Health
Environment	Intergovernmental Affairs
Fisheries and Oceans	International Trade
Human Resources and Skills Development	Justice
Indian Affairs and Northern Development	National Defence
Industry	National Revenue
Labour and Housing	Public Works and Government
Natural Resources	Services
Social Development	
Transport	
Veterans Affairs	

---

provide services directly to the public or to specific client groups within the public. The Department of Agriculture and Agri-Food provides programs and funding in aid of Canadian farmers and the food production industry, just as the Department of Fisheries and Oceans' mandate is to support the Canadian fishing industry through financial measures that assist fishers, to regulate fish stocks and fishing practices, and to license and oversee those involved in the fishery. Citizenship and Immigration, Indian Affairs and Northern Development, and Industry, Human Resources and Skills Development all provide a wide variety of services to many constituencies of Canadians, from the landing, reception, and integration of new Canadians into this country; the maintenance, along with First Nations' governments, of social and economic services guaranteed by treaties to Aboriginal peoples; various forms of financial support, training, and business advice to Canadian entrepreneurs; and the provision of training for jobs and skills development for all Canadians. Program implementation and delivery frequently require department offices to be dispersed across the country's vast geography. Most Canadians are familiar with such offices if they have sought anything from the government, from postage stamps to employment insurance benefits, from job-training programs to small business development loans. But these departments, though the largest and most popularly known, are not necessarily the most influential within government.

In contrast to the "line" service departments are those with a primary responsibility for providing policy and program assistance more to the government itself than to the general public. These departments, fewer than their "line" counterparts, are the **support departments**; they include such diverse bodies as Public Works and Government Services, Finance, Foreign Affairs and International Trade, Justice, Health, Intergovernmental Relations, and National Defence. These departments provide either administrative or policy services, or some combination of the two, to the government itself. Foreign Affairs and International Trade, for example, has the gargantuan task of providing the government with all those services dealing with Canada's relations with the broader world, extending from diplomatic and consular work abroad to intelligence gathering and from representing and supporting Canadian state interests in differing countries to promoting Canadian international trade, commerce, and investment. Public Works and Government Services provides, maintains, and disposes of all government properties and goods and services—from pens, paper, and office equipment to automobiles, trucks, and civilian aircraft needed by other government departments and their officials. Other support departments such as Finance, Health, and Justice supply the government with information, intelligence, and policy options within their specific policy fields. When the government, and specifically the cabinet, needs detailed information on the nature of the Canadian economy and on the track record of success or failure of budgetary matters and economic policies, it turns to the Department of Finance. Likewise, when it needs advice and information about the Canadian health care system, the nature and working of health care programming in the provinces, and the degree of provincial compliance with the standards of the Canada Health Act, it turns to the Department of Health. It is these departments, not their service counterparts, that play a most powerful role as the information and intelligence linkages between the social, economic, and political life of Canada and the policy-makers in the federal government (Tardi, 2002: 295-97).

It is interesting that, in 1999, the ranking of these service departments was significantly altered when the federal government transformed Revenue Canada, traditionally the service department responsible for taxation, customs and tariff policy, and tax collection, into a special operating agency of the federal government now known as the Canada Customs and Revenue Agency. This agency is no longer a government department, and the more than 40,000 employees who work for this agency are officially no longer employed by the Treasury Board, meaning that they are no longer classed as members of the Public Service of Canada. The federal government can and will assert that it has "reduced" the size of the Public Service of Canada by some 40,000 employees when, in fact, these officials are still employed by the government but within an agency that acts as its own employer. This innovation is evidence both of the degree to which department forms are subject to change and also of the political considerations inherent in reforming the structure of the federal government.

Most support departments differ from their service counterparts, furthermore, in that they are much smaller institutions, with fewer staff and smaller operating budgets, and with each department geographically tied to the nation's capital. This is especially true of Finance, Foreign Affairs and International Trade, Health, and Justice, but less so of Public Works and Government Services. The latter two, while headquartered in the capital region, have larger staffs than the other support departments, forcing them to spread out somewhat. The one exception to all this, of course, is the Department of National Defence. While this department is clearly a government support department, in that it is mandated to provide the government with military support if and when requested and its personnel, generally, do not provide services directly to the Canadian public, it is neither relatively small, nor inexpensive, nor geographically concentrated. Rather, the Department of National Defence, with a personnel complement of some 65,000 persons, is the largest department, by staff, in the federal government, with these personnel dispersed across military bases throughout the country as well as on active service overseas. And, given its unique equipment and facilities requirements, it possesses one of the largest budgets of any department in the government.

3.2.2 Department Structure: Hierarchy, Size, and Magnitude

All departments, regardless of category, are hierarchical and pyramidal, as can be seen in Box 3.9. They are multi-layered bureaucracies with an operational base much larger than their middle-management layer of directors and directors-general and an even smaller number of senior managers—associate deputy ministers and assistant deputy ministers—who comprise the leading administrative and policy actors within the department headquarters in Ottawa. At the apex of department power and authority stands the minister and, just below him or her, the deputy minister—the most senior public servant within the department. This hierarchical structure is common throughout all governments both in this country and abroad. The institutional form is valuable both for its ability to provide a clear line of managerial command and control down through the various layers of the

BOX 3.9
Departmental Hierarchy

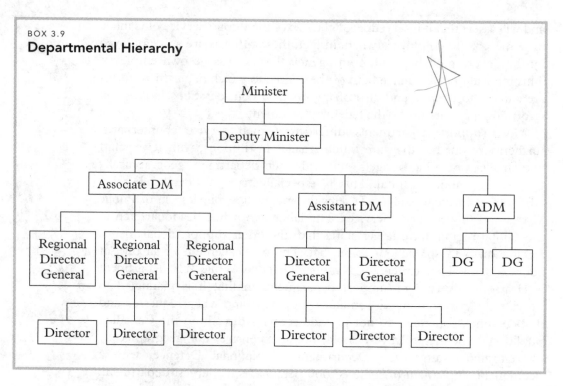

department and for its ability, in theory, to provide a clear line of information flow up through the hierarchy from field-level operations and regional offices to senior management in the headquarters. Of course, Canadian government history is replete with examples of such lines of communication breaking down for various reasons, leading to a variety of smaller or larger governmental and political problems (Chapters 5 and 8). Despite periodic problems with the operation of the departmental system of management, no government has sought to fundamentally transform this system of organizing government work.

In understanding departments, it is useful to consider size and operational magnitude. While some departments, such as the policy support departments, can be relatively small in terms of total numbers of staff and with their employees highly concentrated in the national capital region, most line-operational service departments share neither of these traits. Most service departments, given their function of providing operational services directly to the public, of necessity possess large numbers of staff and junior and middle managers spread across the country in many regional and local offices. Departments such as Agriculture and Agri-Food and Human

Resources and Skills Development employ thousands of public servants, most of whom work in offices found in all the major and in many minor urban locations across the country. Other departments, such as Fisheries and Oceans and Citizenship and Immigration also employ thousands of persons, with their field-level employees dispersed in more territorially specific parts of the country—the east and west coasts for Fisheries and Oceans and the major urban centres and international entry points for Citizenship and Immigration. Likewise, officials with the departments of Environment, Industry, and Transport are dispersed across the country, as are most of the service personnel of the Department of National Defence.

This general geographic dispersion of most of the staff employed with service departments, as well as National Defence, is one of the key challenges confronting senior management who are called upon to show leadership, maintain effective communications, and command and control large numbers of staff and middle and junior management spread over a country the size of a continent. Though the advent of modern means of telecommunications has clearly enhanced the ability of senior management to remain "in touch" with developments in the regions, the tension posed by such territorial dispersion is one that is always of concern to both field staff and management and the officials in office headquarters in Ottawa-Hull. Often both groups lament communication breakdowns between themselves and the inability of the "other side" to fully comprehend and appreciate the organizational and administrative difficulties faced by "their side."

Adding to the management challenges of communication and intra-departmental understanding is the sheer magnitude of ordinary departmental decision-making. Any service department operates dozens of separate programs providing services to an extensive number of individuals, interest groups, and/or businesses within its purview. In any given day, week, or month, such a department will be interacting with thousands of citizens/clients, with department officials making literally hundreds to thousands of decisions regarding

- entitlements to services;
- the nature of services owing to any given citizen, group, or corporation;
- the delivery or non-delivery of services;
- the possible obligations owed by such citizens, groups, or corporations to the department; and
- the assessment of future needs for services.

Service departments thus interact with citizens/clients on a routine basis, with department staff and junior management making most decisions regarding the application of department programs flowing from policy directions they receive from program supervisors and more senior management. Senior management routinely address a host of matters: the fine-tuning of department programming, the assessment of program and policy strengths and weaknesses, departmental administrative and managerial capabilities, new policy initiatives, and the ongoing financial and personnel management issues that require constant attention for the department to function properly. In short, senior management is occupied with scores of pressing matters requiring countless decisions on a daily basis. And this is the case also with the support departments. Though these do not possess the scale of matters that their service counterparts must address, they are nevertheless occupied with program delivery for their government clients, with senior management having to address all the concerns common to the economical, efficient, and effective management of any department.

Any department is thereby awash in decision-making. As mentioned above, government departments are complex bureaucracies involved in the most important functions of government: program delivery, policy-making, records-keeping, research and analysis, and communications. The proper management of all of these matters requires the staff and management of departments to make vast numbers of decisions, from the most bureaucratically routine to the most politically significant. The departments are, both in theory and practice, the key actors for linking a government to the country it serves, and the decision-making within departments constitutes a significant proportion of the substance of public sector management within this country.

3.3   The Bureaucratic Executive: Crown Agencies

Distinct from government departments is a second set of government institutions known as Crown agencies (Kernaghan and Siegel, 1999: chs. 9-10; Inwood, 2004: ch. 5; Wiseman and Whorley, 2002: 382-96). These are organizations such as Crown corporations, regulatory agencies, and other unique service institutions specifically designed to develop and implement special policies and programs that call for the host institution to be substantially independent in its routine operations from the government of the day. There are some 400 federal (and an even larger number of provincial) Crown agencies in this country active in a wide variety of policy fields as outlined in Chapter 2. Federal Crown corporations such as

Canada Post, the CBC, VIA Rail, and the Canadian Wheat Board tend to be the more publicly known, but regulatory agencies such as the CRTC, the Canadian Labour Relations Board, the National Transportation Board, and the Immigration and Refugee Board are also major agencies, while special agencies such as Elections Canada, the Public Service Commission, and the Royal Canadian Mounted Police also deserve mention. All such Crown corporations, regulatory agencies, and special agencies share certain common organizational characteristics in that

- they are all institutions designed to be relatively independent of government;
- they are not organized as regular government departments; and
- they are not subject to the regular departmental systems of account-ability, financial management, and personnel administration, as we shall see in subsequent chapters.

All such agencies exist as unique institutions possessing special commercial, legal, or administrative relationships to the government and the public.

3.3.1   Crown Corporations

Crown corporations are designed either to provide commercial services to Canadians and/or to interact with Canadian citizens and businesses in a corporate-like fashion. Historic Crown corporations, such as Air Canada, Canadian National Railways (CN), and Petro-Canada, were specifically designed to enter a given field of commercial activity—air transportation, rail transportation, and oil and gas exploration, refining, and marketing, respectively—and to promote the public interest by providing services to the public, with such service delivery often coming into direct competition with existing private sector service providers. Such competition can still be observed through CBC-TV's relationship to CTV and CanWest Global. Other corporations may not have a direct commercial and competitive mandate such as this, but will be expected to act in a cost-effective and "business-like" manner either in the management of a state monopoly, such as Atomic Energy of Canada Ltd., Canada Post, or the Royal Canadian Mint, or in the delivery of special services to individual citizens or business ventures. Examples of current Crown corporations involved in the latter functions are the National Film Board (NFB), the Export Development Corporation, the Farm Credit Corporation, the Federal Business Development Bank (FBDB), and the St. Lawrence Seaway Authority, as well as such

---

BOX 3.10
Major Federal Crown Corporations and Major Federal Privatizations

Major Crown Corporations—2006	Major Privatizations—1980s-1990s
Canada Post Corporation	Canada Communications Group
Canadian Broadcasting Corporation	Canadian Arsenals
Atomic Energy of Canada	Canadian National Railway
VIA Rail Canada Inc.	CN Subsidiaries: CN Hotels; CPCN
National Film Board	Telecommunications (CN half);
National Gallery of Canada	Northwestel Inc; Terra Nova
National Arts Centre Corporation	Telecommunication
National Capital Commission	Air Canada
Canada Mortgage and Housing	Eldorado Nuclear
Marine Atlantic Inc.	Fishery Products International
Bank of Canada	Teleglobe Canada
Royal Canadian Mint	Telesat
Federal Business Development	Northern Canada Power Commission
Bank of Canada	Northern Transportation Company
Export Development Corporation	De Havilland Aircraft Inc.
St. Lawrence Seaway Authority	Canadair
Canadian Wheat Board	Petro-Canada
Farm Credit Corporation	Canada Development Corporation
Atlantic Canada Opportunities Agency	
Western Canada Development	

---

regional development corporations as the Atlantic Canada Opportunities Agency (ACOA) and Western Canada Development.

Governments usually have a number of motives for establishing Crown corporations. One is, obviously, for the state to play an important role in the management of a particular field of commercial activity deemed by the government to be of national significance. This activity can derive from a number of motivations:

- to defend traditional forms of economic activity and service delivery (the Cape Breton Development Corporation and the Canadian Wheat Board);
- to promote new industrial and commercial activity (Petro-Canada, ACOA, Western Canada Development, FBDB, CBC); and
- to ensure the delivery of important services nationwide (Air Canada, CN, and VIA Rail).

From a government promoting Canadian economic nationalism, we have CN, Air Canada, Petro-Canada, and de Havilland. From governments promoting and defending Canadian culture we have the CBC, NFB, and National Gallery of Canada.

Once a government has decided to enter a particular field of commercial or entrepreneurial activity, what are the advantages that distinguish the Crown corporation? A Crown corporation is operationally independent from the routine financial and personnel management rules and regulations normally associated with government departments. This means that the corporation can engage in its own hiring and personnel management practices free from the more restrictive and controlled practices of regular departments (Chapter 8). It can engage in business undertakings, commercial transactions, and financial management free from the complex systems of department budgeting (see Chapter 6). Its board of directors may not be selected from the ranks of the "permanent" public service but from those in the private sector or in the general community who have an interest in the mission of the corporation. The operational heads of Crown corporations, therefore, will not be permanent public servants, such as deputy ministers, but will be men and women generally drawn from outside the ranks of government and appointed by the prime minister and cabinet to serve for varying terms (three, five, or seven years) as members of the corporation's board of directors. Once appointed, such a board is then free to hire senior management, again from outside the ranks of the permanent public service, ideally bringing in people with managerial and operational experience and expertise in the corporation's field of activity. Thus, the CBC can be staffed by persons knowledgeable in radio and television broadcasting, for example, while the Canadian Wheat Board is provided with management skilled in the details of agricultural economics, supply management, and international grain marketing.

Operational independence is also vitally important to the policy and program development function of Crown corporations, which exist "at arm's length" from the government of the day so that the government's political interests do not interfere with the professional managerial judgement of senior corporation leadership. For example, it has long been recognized that the decision-making of the CBC, especially in relation to news and public affairs broadcasting, should not be subject to either direct or even indirect influence by the government. The very credibility of the CBC as a public broadcaster hinges upon its ability to be, and to be seen to be, by the Canadian public as an independent actor insofar as its broadcasting initiatives are concerned. Similar interests respecting operational autonomy are also witnessed in such Crown corporations as diverse as the FBDB, VIA Rail, and Canada Post. In these and other instances the basic concern is the same: corporate decision-making should be based on the best judgement of those managers and directors hired to fulfill the mandate of the Crown corporation, not on the partisan political interests of the government. However, such an arm's-length relationship can also insulate the government from political controversies. In certain instances where decision-making by a Crown corporation elicits divisive commentary and public criticism, such as when Canada Post raises postal rates or when VIA Rail reduces levels of passenger rail service, the government will be quite content to state that the matter is an operational decision fully within the jurisdiction of the corporation and that it is inappropriate for the government to intervene in the working of the corporation. This being said, however, one should also be aware of those circumstances when cabinet ministers might sense some political advantage to be gained by trying to influence a Crown corporation with respect to some matter. Such incidents do happen, often to the consternation of Crown corporation senior management, revealing that the actual operational independence of these institutions is, in certain respects, contingent on ministerial self-denial when it comes to administrative interference in routine operations and on not-too-close opposition party and media scrutiny of their routine work.

The formal and informal relationships between Crown corporations and the government are quite special. While all Crown corporations are established by government legislation approved by Parliament, this legislation providing each corporation with its broad policy mandate, the routine exercise of this mandate will be left to the management and staff of each corporation itself. Furthermore, no corporation is directly responsible to any one minister, but each is expected to report annually to Parliament on its work. In certain instances, such as with the CBC, ACOA, and Western Canadian Development, the corporation receives annual contributions from the government to fund its programs in whole or in part. In other instances, as with Canada Post, VIA Rail, and, historically with Petro-Canada, Air Canada, and CN, the corporation is financially self-sufficient, deriving its operational revenue from the sale of services.

As mentioned in the preceding chapter, over the past two decades the major policy initiative confronting most Crown corporations has been **privatization** (Kernaghan and Siegel, 1999: ch. 8; Inwood, 2004: ch. 5). This refers to the undertaking by which governments divest themselves of Crown corporations, selling them to private investors. Privatization may take many forms, ranging from the wholesale purchase of a Crown corporation by one private business venture (e.g., de Havilland was purchased by Boeing and later resold to Bombardier and Teleglobe Canada was sold to Memotec) to the divestiture of a Crown corporation by offering publicly traded shares (e.g., Air Canada, Petro-Canada, CN). In this latter instance, which is the more common practice, the government sponsoring the privatization can impose sale restrictions on the proportion of the privatized corporation that any one purchaser can control while also restricting the amount of shares that can be held by non-Canadian interests. Through such share offerings, governments can also retain some minority stock interest in the privatized corporation, as has been the case with Air Canada and Petro-Canada, though most governments following this option tend to stress that their minority interests will be "non-voting" with regard to shareholder decision-making.

As I have said, the policy of privatization is controversial. Advocates of privatization, usually representing a right-of-centre ideological perspective, make both practical and philosophical arguments in favour of the approach. Stress is placed on evidence that many Crown corporations are uneconomic and inefficient, tending to waste public monies. Supporters of privatization also argue the importance of raising public revenues through the sale process, with such revenues at times reaching into the billions of dollars. These monies can then be earmarked for national deficit and/or debt reduction. Finally, and perhaps most importantly, advocates of privatization argue that governments simply should not be in the business of owning and operating commercial enterprises. They assert that such business activity is best undertaken by the private sector operating under the discipline of the profit motive, that the state should not be competing with the private sector, and that government can best assist in promoting a climate of free enterprise and market economics by dismantling Crown corporations.

Critics of privatization challenge all these points, also through a variety of practical and philosophical arguments. Defenders of Crown corporations, tending to represent a left-of-centre ideological perspective, stress that many Crown corporations are, and have been, economical and efficient, often generating substantial profits for the state (as was the case with Petro-Canada and as is the case with Canada Post and such provincial Crown corporations as power utilities and liquor distribution corporations) and that where Crown corporations have failed to achieve profitability, as with de Havilland, Canadair, and the Cape Breton Development Corporation, often political interference with the corporation and the establishment and maintenance of weak management systems go far in explaining their poor performance. Advocates point out

- that Crown corporations were established for valid public policy reasons;
- that they were and are designed to provide important services that the private sector either would not or could not offer to the country overall, or to particular regions of the country; and
- that the CBC, the NFB, CN, Air Canada, VIA Rail, and Petro-Canada played, and either are still playing or should still be playing, vital roles in promoting Canadian nationhood by strengthening Canadian culture, advancing Canadian nationalism, and defending Canadian national economic sovereignty.

Defenders of Crown corporations argue that privatization is, at best, a simplistic way of raising public revenues to deal with deficit and debt problems, being akin to "selling off the family heirlooms to pay the mortgage." Critics call attention to the curious dynamic that potential private sector investors only wish to purchase profitable or potentially profitable Crown corporations, thus posing the question of why a government should divest itself of such attractive assets. Of course, the move to privatization is motivated by conservative thought, just as the support of a continued state presence in the economy via the role of Crown corporations is motivated by reform liberal or Fabian socialist viewpoints respecting the desired role of the state in society.

As mentioned in the previous chapter, the 1980s and 1990s were a period marked by a general rightward shift in the broad centre ground of Canadian politics: the election of the Progressive Conservatives under Brian Mulroney in 1984 and the election of a rather "conservative" Liberal government under Jean Chrétien in 1993. During these years there were privatizations of a substantial number of federal Crown corporations, including such major ones as Air Canada, Canadair, de Havilland, Eldorado Nuclear, Teleglobe Canada, Petro-Canada, and CN. While the CBC was not part of this privatization wave, it remains a subject of privatization speculation; the Canadian Alliance party suggested, during the federal election of 2000, that CBC-TV be considered for divestiture. This privatization wave, however, may now be subsiding because of the declining pressure of deficits and debts as a driving force for privatization, as well as of a slow realignment in public opinion in favour of keeping the existing Crown corporations, especially the CBC and NFB, as important defenders of Canadian national interests. Since 2004, the Martin government did not make Crown corporation privatization a high priority on its policy agenda. Of course, this declining government interest in privatization may also be related to the fact that most major Crown corporations have already been auctioned off by past Progressive Conservative and Liberal governments.

3.3.2   Regulatory Agencies

Regulatory agencies are the second main type of Crown agency found in this country (Kernaghan and Siegel, 1999: ch. 10). Although regulatory agencies share certain of the organizational features found in Crown corporations—namely, a quasi-independence from the government and separate systems for appointments and financial and personnel management—they are significantly different.

Whereas Crown corporations are engaged in some specific commercial or economic transactions with individuals or other businesses, regulatory agencies are involved in the development and implementation of general forms of economic and social regulation across various and wide fields of activity as prescribed by law. Regulation itself refers to rules and standards developed either by government agencies or departments and generally approved by Parliament and designed to govern the actions of all individuals, groups, and businesses active within a given field of socio-economic activity. As highlighted in Chapter 1, state regulation can encompass everything from occupational health and safety standards, product quality and safety standards, occupational and professional licensing requirements, and environmental protection standards, to the regulation of labour relations and the protection of human rights entitlements. Such government regulation can be generally perceived as falling into three broad types: economic, social, and environmental regulation.

Economic regulation deals with such matters as price and tariff setting and oversight, product supply management, market entry and conditions of service, product content, and methods of production. Federal regulatory agencies such as Investment Canada, the National Energy Board (NEB), the National Transportation Board, and the Tariff Board engage in such economic regulation, addressing such things as the desirability of mega-corporate mergers involving foreign companies, the construction of oil and gas pipelines and the nature of their distribution networks, the restriction and punishment of "economic dumping" by foreign firms into the Canadian marketplace, and the maintenance of service standards and price competition in the transportation industry. Social regulation deals with such matters as labour standards, health and safety provisions, protection of human rights entitlements, and the promotion of Canadian culture. For example, the Canadian Labour Relations Board, the Canadian Food

---

BOX 3.11

Major Federal Regulatory Agencies—2006

Canadian Dairy Commission
Canadian Environmental Assessment Agency
Canadian Food Inspection Agency
Canadian Human Rights Commission
Canadian International Trade Tribunal
Canadian Nuclear Safety Commission
Canadian Radio-television and Telecommunications Commission
Canadian Transportation Agency
Immigration and Refugee Board of Canada
Indian Claims Commission
National Energy Board
National Parole Board
Pension Appeals Board
Privacy Commission of Canada
Public Service Staff Relations Board
Security Intelligence Review Committee
Standards Council of Canada
Transportation Safety Board of Canada

Inspection Agency, the Canadian Human Rights Commission, and the CRTC are active in promoting, respectively, such matters as the collective bargaining and industrial dispute resolution system for those firms subject to federal labour law, food production quality control, adherence to and respect for federal human rights law, and advancing Canadian content regulations within the sphere of television and radio broadcasting. The social regulation activities of all these agencies have distinct economic overtones for affected businesses, illustrating that in practice there is no simple demarcation between economic and social regulation. CRTC terms and conditions pertaining to television and radio broadcast licence renewals, for example, have a social impact on the promotion of Canadian broadcast content, but this social impact carries a distinct financial obligation borne by the licence-holders to utilize and create Canadian programming material while limiting, in a relative sense, the use of already existing and less expensive foreign content (usually American). To defenders of such regulatory initiatives, however, these costs are the costs of doing business in the field in this country, one that carries with it important social obligations. They also point out that Canadian content regulation has the intended desirable effect of promoting the economic activity of producers of Canadian radio and television content, namely, artists, actors, performers, writers, and the whole gamut of people involved in radio and television production.

A similar logic applies in environmental regulation. The Canadian Environmental Assessment Agency is required to conduct comprehensive reviews of all major economic development projects within federal spheres of jurisdiction that might have environmental consequences. The agency is called upon to study the environmental impact of such initiatives, for example, as natural gas pipeline construction in Nova Scotia and New Brunswick (in conjunction with hearings of the NEB), fish habitat restoration projects in coastal British Columbia and Yukon, ski development projects in national parks across the country, and low-level military jet flight-training in Labrador. While all such decision-making regarding the appraisal, modification, approval, or disapproval of planned developments will have direct impact on the quality of the environment, such decisions have immediate and long-term economic consequences for those interested in the business side of these ventures. Again, this illustrates the interconnectedness of the environmental, economic, and social spheres; the importance of these activities to Canadians; and the difficulty of the tasks confronting regulatory bodies seeking to advance the public interest through their work.

As with Crown corporations, regulatory agencies possess special "arm's length" relationships from the government, yet in these cases relative autonomy is called for not out of any corporate interest but on account of the special legal roles they fulfill. Regulatory agencies are mandated to develop and implement regulatory standards upon all actors (individuals, groups, corporations, and even other federal government bodies) in their field of jurisdiction. In other words, the CRTC regulates the CBC equally with CTV and CanWest Global, while the Canadian Human Rights Commission has jurisdiction over all employers and employees subject to federal regulation in Canada, including all members of the federal public service. In fulfilling their work, all regulatory agencies are quasi-judicial entities in that their decision-making has legal authority. They are called upon to apply legal provisions found in their enabling statutes to circumstances they confront on a case-by-case basis and to make decisions as to whether certain actions of various individuals, groups, corporations, or government bodies are in conformity with established regulatory rules and practices as understood and applied by the agencies. The final decisions of these agencies carry with them the force of law, enabling some actors to legally continue with their desired courses of action while requiring others to desist, to accept the finding of the agency, and to make their behaviour or practices conform to the law as expressed by the agency.

Given the legal nature of this work, the special position of these agencies becomes clear. They require a quasi-independent status to be able to undertake their regulatory decision-making free from any political intervention or interference from the government of the day. Their need for operational autonomy from the government arises not only out of a sense of their own professionalism but because of the legal obligations they carry; they must be free from any real or perceived bias emanating from the organizational link between the government and the agency. While governments possess the power to establish agencies and their mandates, to alter and amend these mandates through legislative action, to appoint the boards of directors or commissions of these agencies, and, on special occasions, to issue policy directives to these agencies, they are nonetheless forbidden from interfering with agencies, that is, from intervening with agencies outside of normal hearing procedures with respect to the handling of any given case. In fact, any such intervention in a given case is illegal and subject to punishment. (See the chapter on Administrative Law on the Thinking Government web site.) As mentioned with respect to Crown corporations, however, it is important to bear in mind that such insulation of an agency from the government not only benefits the professional legal operation of the agency but can also relieve pressure from a government by enabling its ministers to claim that certain "hot" political issues—such as pay equity disputes, environmental disputes, or broadcast licensing matters—are, in fact, legal issues properly disputed before regulatory agencies and thus beyond the realm of ministerial action. In many of these instances, governments are quite happy to transfer responsibility for decision-making from themselves to other duly constituted authorities.

Just as Crown corporations have been at the centre of much political debate over the past two decades with respect to privatization, certain regulatory agencies have also been subject to controversy respecting deregulation. Both of these policy dynamics evolve from the same rightward shift in political discourse during these years. Deregulation refers to a government's move to diminish or eliminate particular regulatory provisions governing a certain field of activity that was hitherto subject to government regulation. It is perceived by its generally right-of-centre advocates as a means, once again, of promoting free enterprise, enhancing the working of the private sector, and lessening the administrative and economic burden borne by private firms subject to regulation. In contrast to these perspectives, deregulation is seen by its generally left-of-centre critics as an ideologically motivated attack on the role of the state, leading to a weakening of the public interest with respect to economic, social, and environmental policy.

However, while there has been some substantial deregulation of economic activities at the federal level from both the Mulroney and Chrétien governments, the overall relative impact of such deregulation has been much less than the overall impact of privatization over the same time period. In the 1980s and 1990s, most major federal Crown corporations in this country were privatized; the same cannot be said of most major federal regulatory agencies and deregulation. Where deregulation has been felt most is in

- the economic fields of oil and gas production, pricing, and export;
- foreign investment screening;
- the administration of financial services; and
- the elimination of restrictions on competition in the transportation industry, inclusive of air, rail, and trucking industries.

Despite these significant examples of deregulation, however, the regulatory scope of the federal state remains substantial indeed. In terms of economic policy, bodies such as the Atomic Energy Control Board, the Canadian Labour Relations Board, the NEB, Investment Canada, the National Transportation Board, and the Canadian Tariff Board remain intact, while the major social and environmental policy agencies previously mentioned also remain in place. Thus, regulatory policy remains a major part of the state presence in this country, and the work of these regulatory agencies is a major component of the public sector management system of the federal government. Indeed, rather than viewing deregulation as a major threat to the regulatory role of the state, it can be argued that systematic budget-cutting, underfunding of regulatory agencies, and the downloading of certain regulatory responsibilities to other levels of governments and to the private sector has posed a greater threat to the pre-existing federal regulatory system than any direct initiative of deregulation. This theme will be addressed more fully in Chapter 7.

3.3.3   Special Agencies

Special agencies that also fall under the general rubric of Crown agencies (Jackson and Jackson, 1998: 347) include quite a few unique public bodies that provide special services either to the government in particular, or to the public in general, or to both. These bodies are not departments, nor Crown corporations, nor regulatory agencies, but are such permanent entities as Elections Canada, the Public Service Commission of Canada, the Office of the Official Languages Commissioner, Statistics Canada, the National Archives, the RCMP, and the Canadian Security Intelligence Service. All these agencies provide special services to the government of Canada and to the Canadian public, services either so unique or politically or legally sensitive as to require a status of quasi-independence from the government. With respect to temporary bodies, one can include in the list such organizations as royal commissions and special policy task forces. All such agencies play an important role in the broad process of government, with the permanent special agencies being, within their own fields of jurisdiction, vital elements in the delivery of public services.

3.4   Bureaucracy and Accountability

Departments, Crown corporations, regulatory agencies, and special agencies comprise the principle institutions of the federal public service. These are the bodies that governments rely on for the delivery of most policies and programs; thus, these organizations are the key links not only between the government and the public but also between the elected executive and the professional bureaucracy. Given the importance of these institutions and these linkages, questions inevitably arise about the degree to which they and the officials working within them are accountable both to the government and the general public. Crown agencies exist as quasi-independent administrative actors, specifically designed to be substantially autonomous from government with respect to their routine operations. Yet these agencies are state institutions, possessing mandates from government to develop and implement public policies. Within these parameters, how are they to be responsible and accountable for their actions? Government departments are the workhorses of government, vested under the authority of ministers of the Crown and falling under the collective political control of the prime minister and cabinet; nonetheless, they are often massive bureaucracies administering large sets of detailed and complex policies and programs. In what manner and to what degree can elected ministers and cabinets subject these institutions to effective political and managerial control, such that ultimate administrative power and authority rests in the hands of elected and, thus, democratically responsible public officials rather than in the hands of unelected public servants? These questions go to the heart of power relations in government and the complex interrelationship between democracy and bureaucracy (see Chapters 4 and 12). In Chapter 4, we will examine the relationship between ministers and departments, displaying the intricate power relations within senior department management and the complex interplay between senior department officials and their political "masters." How have prime ministers in the past 45 years dealt with these relationships and related tensions through the development of cabinet decision-making systems? Let us turn to each of the Trudeau, Mulroney, Chrétien, and Martin cabinet systems to discover some surprising and perhaps disturbing insights into power relations in contemporary Ottawa.

Key Terms

cabinet: The collection of ministers selected by the prime minister to provide ministerial leadership to government departments and agencies as well as providing advice to the prime minister on the development of government policies and programs.

cabinet minister: A person, usually an MP of the governing party, selected by the prime minister to be the political head of a government department and to participate in the decision-making of the government overall. Ministers must exercise their duties in accordance with the rules of individual ministerial responsibility and collective cabinet responsibility.

cabinet selection: The process by which a prime minister constructs a cabinet. A prime minister will take various factors into consideration when selecting given persons to cabinet posts, with the formal appointment to cabinet being given by the governor general.

collective ministerial responsibility: The duty of a minister to be part of the prime minister's executive team responsible for providing overall political leadership for the federal government. All ministers will be expected to participate in the setting of strategic policy direction as well as supporting all of the strategic and tactical initiatives of the government

Crown agencies: The term given to the collective whole of Crown corporations and regulatory agencies in order to distinguish these governmental institutions from government departments.

Crown corporations: Those institutions of government established to exist in a quasi-independent status from the government of the day so as to enable them to engage in commercial activities. Crown corporations are not departments and thus are not headed by a minister but rather by a board of directors appointed by the government.

departments: The leading institutions through which a government organizes its policy and program activities and through which it delivers services either to the public or to other governmental institutions. Every department is headed by a cabinet minister who is the political leader of the institution, the linchpin between the department and the cabinet and Parliament.

individual ministerial responsibility: The duty of a minister to be individually responsible and answerable to Parliament for the policy and program undertakings of his or her department. The minister, as legal head of a department, must bear full responsibility for the successes and failures of that department.

ministry: The term given to the collective whole comprised of the prime minister, his/her cabinet ministers, and ministers of state without portfolios.

prime minister: The leader of the governing party in Parliament and thus the head of government. The prime minister possesses the key leadership role in the federal system as the head of the cabinet and is responsible for the strategic policy and program direction of the government.

privatization: The government policy of divesting itself of Crown corporations by selling such corporations to private sector owners. Privatization may occur through the outright sale of a Crown corporation to a single private buyer or through share offerings to multiple investors on the stock market.

Privy Council: The formal, constitutionally mandated advisory council to the governor general with respect to the exercise of executive power in the federal government. The Privy Council per se is an honourary body whose executive cabinet consists of the prime minister of the day and his/her ministers, thus giving them key governmental authority.

regulatory agencies: Those institutions of government established to exist in a quasi-independent status from the government of the day so as to enable them to engage in socio-economic regulation. Regulatory agencies apply legal rules of conduct with respect to a given field of activity to individuals, corporations, and other institutions of government.

service departments: The majority of departments of the federal government, whose key policy and program responsibilities are to provide services directly to citizens, corporations, interest groups, and other clients. As distinct from support departments.

special agencies: A small set of federal government institutions that are designed to operate in a quasi-independent status from the government of the day so as to provide a unique service to the government or Canadians generally; this service delivery necessitates such quasi-independent status and agency leadership designed on a board of directors or commissioner model.

support departments: The minority of departments of the federal government, whose key policy and program responsibilities are to provide organizational and operational support to the government itself, its institutions, and its policy and program capacity. As distinct from service departments.

References and Suggested Reading

Adie, Robert F., and Paul G. Thomas. 1987. *Canadian Public Administration: Problematical Perspectives*. 2nd ed. Scarborough, ON: Prentice-Hall Canada.

Archer, Keith, Roger Gibbins, Rainer Knopff, and Leslie A. Pal. 1999. *Parameters of Power: Canada's Political Institutions*. 2nd ed. Toronto: Nelson.

Aucoin, Peter. 1995. "The Prime Minister and Cabinet." In Robert M. Krause and R.H. Wagenberg, eds., *Introductory Readings in Canadian Government and Politics*. 2nd ed. Toronto: Copp Clark. 169-92.

—. 1999. "Prime Minister and Cabinet: Power at the Apex." In James Bickerton and Alain-G. Gagnon, eds., *Canadian Politics*. 3rd ed. Peterborough, ON: Broadview Press. 109-28.

Bakvis, Herman, and David MacDonald. 1993. "The Canadian Cabinet: Organization, Decision-Rules, and Policy Impact." In Michael M. Atkinson, ed., *Governing Canada: Institutions and Public Policy.* Toronto: Harcourt Brace Jovanovich Canada. 47-80.

Delacourt, Susan. 2003. *Juggernaut: Paul Martin's Campaign for Chrétien's Crown.* Toronto: McClelland and Stewart.

Dyck, Rand. 1996. *Canadian Politics: Critical Approaches.* 2nd ed. Toronto: Nelson.

Gray, John. 2003. *Paul Martin: The Power of Ambition.* Toronto: Key Porter.

Hodgetts, J.E. 1973. *The Canadian Public Service: A Physiology of Government 1867-1970.* Toronto: University of Toronto Press.

Inwood, Gregory J. 2004. *Understanding Canadian Public Administration: An Introduction to Theory and Practice.* 2nd ed. Scarborough, ON: Prentice-Hall Allyn and Bacon Canada.

Jackson, Robert J., and Doreen Jackson. 1998. *Politics in Canada: Culture, Institutions, Behaviour and Public Policy.* 4th ed. Scarborough, ON: Prentice-Hall.

Kernaghan, Kenneth, and David Siegel. 1999. *Public Administration in Canada: A Text.* 4th ed. Toronto: Nelson.

—. 2002. "East Block and Westminster: Conventions, Values and Public Service." In Christopher Dunn, ed., *The Handbook of Canadian Public Administration.* Toronto: Oxford University Press.

Landes, Ronald G. 1987. *The Canadian Polity: A Comparative Introduction.* 2nd ed. Scarborough, ON: Prentice-Hall Canada.

Monahan, Patrick. 1997. *Constitutional Law.* Toronto: Irwin Law.

Paikin, Steve. 2003. *The Dark Side: The Personal Price of Political Life.* Toronto: Viking Canada.

Savoie, Donald J. 1999. *Governing from the Centre: The Concentration of Power in Canadian Politics.* Toronto: University of Toronto Press.

Tardi, Gregory. 2002. "Departments and Other Institutions of Government." In Christopher Dunn, ed., *The Handbook of Canadian Public Administration.* Toronto: Oxford University Press.

Whittington, Michael S. 2000. "The Prime Minister, Cabinet, and the Executive Power in Canada." In Michael Whittington and Glen Williams, eds., *Canadian Politics in the 21st Century.* Toronto: Nelson. 31-54.

Wiseman, Nelson, and David Whorley. 2002. "Lessons on the Centrality of Politics from Canadian Crown Enterprises." In Christopher Dunn, ed., *The Handbook of Canadian Public Administration.* Toronto: Oxford University Press.

Related Web Sites

GENERAL CANADIAN GOVERNMENT
<http://www.canada.gc.ca>

PRIME MINISTER'S OFFICE
<http://www.pm.gc.ca>

PRIVY COUNCIL OFFICE
<http://www.pco-bcp.gc.ca>

CHAPTER 4
Ministers, Deputy Ministers, and Cabinet Decision-Making Systems

The previous chapter introduced the main institutions of federal governance, outlining the functions of such political actors as the prime minister, ministers and cabinets, and bureaucratic entities like departments and Crown agencies. Although it offered critical analysis of the power relations between these various actors, its purpose was to define the main players and institutions constituting the heart of the executive system in Ottawa. As suggested at the end of Chapter 3, the power relations between these actors is of great importance not only to those involved "in the system" but to those of the general public interested in decision-making within the federal government. We turn now to the nature of these power relations and questions of political authority, ministerial responsibility, governmental accountability, and central executive control.

4.1   Ministers and Deputy Ministers: The Tension Between Democracy and Bureaucracy

We have seen that departments are very large and complex organizations, staffed by hundreds if not thousands of employees, administering dozens upon dozens of programs, and making thousands upon thousands of decisions large and small in the delivering of programs and the making of government policies. Departments are the central administrative entities of any government and, at the head of every department, stands a minister. The minister is the formal leader of the department bearing individual responsibility for all actions and decisions taken by it. As a democratically elected Member of Parliament (MP) and member of cabinet, the minister also performs a leading role in the working of the democratic system. The principles of responsible government determine that only the party having won a majority, or at least a plurality, of parliamentary seats at the most recent general election can form a government and that, as a general rule, only MPs representing the governing party can become cabinet ministers. Thus, the control of executive power, in general, is vested in the party that has won a commanding number of seats in Parliament. Concomitant to this, the exercise of executive power within each department is constitutionally placed within the hands of an MP who will be individually responsible to Parliament and, through himself or herself, to the Canadian people he or she represents in Parliament. Thus, in accordance with constitutional theory, the vast power and authority of the federal bureaucracy is subject to the democratic control of the elected members of cabinet, with these officials themselves being subject to the oversight of Parliament.

Despite the formal logic of these constitutional relationships, a practical problem lurks within this system of duties and responsibilities, and this problem has been at the centre of government organizational reform initiatives dominating the inner workings of Ottawa for the better part of five decades. Simply put, can ministers really be expected to bear full responsibility for everything their departments do? Should ministers be responsible for any and all policy and administrative decisions taken by their department officials, including even the many standard and routine operations within the department, of which the minister may be wholly unaware? Is this the level of responsibility that should be expected of ministers, or is this an impossible and unrealistic burden for them to carry? If the latter, who assumes this burden? And if this duty falls upon the shoulders of senior managers within the departments, how are these duties to be understood, what are the appropriate roles of senior management, and how does this new power relationship between ministers and senior managers accord with the democratic principles of responsible government and accountability?

4.1.1 The Deputy Minister: Roles and Responsibilities

Those in the senior ranks of government understand that no one minister can possibly hope to actually oversee and run a department on his or her own. On the one hand, such an undertaking would call for a superhuman effort by ministers both in devoting the time and effort to master the numerous workings of any department and in taking responsibility for the operational decision-making of the department and its many programs. And all such actions, of course, are in addition to all of the other responsibilities borne by cabinet ministers as outlined in Chapter 3. On the other hand, such an undertaking assumes that the minister is actually expert in public administration, public sector management, and the intricate details of the policy field in which the department operates. In both instances, to assume that either condition is realistically viable or even desirable is to be overly idealistic and to challenge conventional wisdom respecting the appropriate role of the minister.

Rather than viewing a minister as the actual "hands-on" supervisor of a department and so involved in its routine management, it is better and more accurate to see him or her as the political head of the department: the most senior official, responsible to cabinet and Parliament for its policy development and evolution as well as for its general program implementation (Dyck, 1996: 489-91; Savoie, 1999: ch. 8). In this sense, which is clearly what prime ministers have long understood to be the proper role of the minister, the person appointed as minister is expected to be neither an operational manager nor the main expert in department policy. These roles can be, and are, played by other senior officials. The minister plays the role of the "gifted generalist," the political leader who charts the overall direction of the department in keeping with the general strategic direction of the government overall and who acts as a liaison between the bureaucratic reality of the department and the political centre of the government. To use a common metaphor, the proper role of the minister is to work at "steering, not rowing" the department.

Evident, then, is the necessity for every department to be provided with a number of senior officials whose responsibilities are to fulfill the routine operational, managerial, and policy analysis roles needed by any complex organization. Within every department these responsibilities are met by senior management, and the most important of these senior managers is the department **deputy minister**. Whereas the minister is the political head of the department, the deputy minister is, in every sense of the term, the administrative head of the organization and the chief manager of the department, who is responsible to the minister and prime minister for

- the economical, efficient, and effective administration of its policies and programs;
- the review, assessment, and development of new policy initiatives;

BOX 4.1
The Deputy Minister—Roles and Responsibilities

- Administrative head/chief manager of department
- Responsible to prime minister for efficient and effective operation of department
- Chief policy advisor to minister
- Responsible to minister for departmental financial management
- Responsible to minister for departmental personnel management
- Responsible to minister for departmental legal obligations
- Chief communicator for department
- Liaison with other departments, central agencies, institutions, and interest groups
- Maintenance of rapport with clerk of the privy council regarding operation of the department
- New policy and program development and implementation
- Effective implementation of existing and ongoing department policies and programs
- Responsible for leadership, motivation, and strategic direction within department

- the effective operation of the department's liaison and communication function; and
- the routine attention to the department's ongoing needs for financial, personnel, and legal administration.

Thus, it is the deputy minister, and not the minister, who is in command of the routine implementation of departmental duties and who is responsible to the minister for ensuring that the department is able to fulfill its many duties to all those interested and affected by its work. The deputy minister, and not the minister, is the official expert in department affairs, public sector management, and all aspects of policy-making with respect to the department and its portfolio (Dyck, 1996: 511-12; Kernaghan and Siegel, 1999: 210-12, 412-17, Bourgault, 2002: 431-34).

In fulfilling these roles deputy ministers are assisted by other senior managers just one or two steps beneath them in the department hierarchy. These associate and assistant deputy ministers (both are sometimes referred to as ADMs) are in charge of one of the main functional divisions within a department—operations, finance, personnel, or policy—and typically are expert in their particular fields of jurisdiction. **Associate deputy** ministers are more senior than assistant deputies; departments usually have one or two working closely with the deputy minister on policy and operational matters affecting the entire department. Beneath the level of associate, departments have a number of **assistant deputy ministers** who support the work of the deputy minister and associate deputy ministers. Assistant deputy ministers, who can number from seven to ten in large departments, have specialized policy, operational, or administrative portfolios within a department, making these officials the head specialists for each of the functional subgroups of the department. All such ADMs, however, are routinely assisted by a variety of other senior managers serving under them whose duties are to manage the standard work of their given branches and to supervise program directors, staff, and all regional offices distributed across the country.

Within this hierarchical web of interrelationships, the deputy minister stands in direct command and control of a set of officials forming the executive heart of the department. It is these senior managers and their middle-management colleagues who oversee the work of policy and program implementation within the department and address matters that form the daily, weekly, and monthly routine of department life. These are the officials who also manage the problematic issues and tensions that invariably arise as general directives are applied to specific cases and as particular program entitlements or duties have to be interpreted, understood, and delivered to those affected by the work of the department, be they clients, corporations, or citizens. And within this bureaucratic world it is the deputy minister who

- orchestrates these managers and their staffs;
- leads them;
- provides them with direction, support, and inspiration; and
- ensures they have all the required resources—financial, personnel, and legal—for them to do their jobs effectively.

The deputy minister stands at the apex not only of a large operational bureaucracy but at the top of a powerful information-gathering and intelligence-formulating apparatus. Within a bureaucratic system in which knowledge is very often power, he or she is placed in a position both to receive information, intelligence, and advice from senior staff with respect to the policy and program working of the department and to transmit directives, suggestions, and advice back down to these officials and their staff with respect to their duties and the obligations of the department. Thus, the deputy minister and his or her senior staff stand at points of pivotal importance to the working of their department. Because they are responsible for the actual running of the organization, all deputies possess a close and important relationship to their ministers.

While each deputy minister is operationally responsible to his or her minister, it is important to remember that he or she is not appointed by the minister but rather holds his or her position "at the pleasure of the prime minister." It is the prime minister, acting with the advice of the **Clerk of the Privy Council**, who appoints deputies, usually from the ranks of associate or assistant deputy ministers; who shifts them from portfolio to portfolio; and who, if necessary, removes them from office. It is to be noted here that in overseeing the work of his or her deputies the prime minister will act in concert with the clerk of the Privy Council, who—as the head of the public service—acts as the linchpin between the political world of the cabinet and the administrative spheres of departments. A deputy is removed from office when a prime minister, usually newly elected, deems such a move to be necessary to ensure the smooth implementation of a government's policy agenda while assuring the minister in question that the most senior administrative ranks of the department are committed to working with him or her in pursuit of the governing party's policies and programs.

The practical effects of this appointment process are fourfold (Inwood: 2004: 141-44, Bourgault, 2002: 435-37).

1. *Deputy ministers are appointed from the ranks of the professional public service.* They are senior public servants who have had decades of experience working within various branches of the government, gaining promotion through the ranks of management, and possessing and exercising ever greater responsibilities through their duties. To be appointed deputy minister is, to virtually every public sector manager, the pinnacle of one's career, the crowning professional reward following years of hard work and faithful government service. The career path necessary to obtain such an appointment means that most deputies will be in their fifties when they receive their first appointment to the deputy ranks. Once a person is appointed, he or she is eligible for lateral transfers from one department to another, meaning that some deputies will have extensive experience in a number of departments during their years of deputy service. Most deputies, however, remain in one department for an average of five to six years, meaning that within that department the deputy will have much longer continuity of service than the minister, who serves in any one department for an average of three to four years. This time differential comes to be

BOX 4.2

The Clerk of the Privy Council—Roles and Responsibilities

- Deputy minister to the prime minister
- Secretary of the cabinet
- Head of the Public Service of Canada
- Provide non-partisan advice to the prime minister and cabinet about the administrative activity of the federal government
- Provide non-partisan advice to the prime minister and cabinet about the merits and demerits of existing and proposed policies and programs of the federal government
- Provide non-partisan advice to the prime minister on the appointment, promotion, demotion, or removal of department deputy ministers and other senior officials
- Provide advice to deputy ministers on the operations of their departments
- Report to the prime minister on the operational effectiveness of the Public Service of Canada
- Work with senior officials in promoting ongoing organizational reform and renewal of the Public Service of Canada
- Is the principal spokesperson, advocate, and defender of the institutional interests of the Public Service of Canada

quite important in assessing the power relations between ministers and their deputies.

2. *Being a career member of the public service, the deputy minister will be the non-partisan head of the department,* bringing to it professional judgement gained from years of practical managerial experience as to how the department can best be managed, how programs can best be implemented and administered, and how policy can best be developed. As deputy ministers are the senior managerial and administrative heads of departments, they bring to their work the virtues of neutral bureaucratic expertise and the independent wisdom of the professional public servant.

3. Since the appointment is by the discretion of the prime minister, *the deputy minister is ultimately responsible to the prime minister for the overall exercise of his or her duties.* While the deputy directly serves a minister, he or she nevertheless owes a primary responsibility to the prime minister, who wants to know that the department minister in particular, and the cabinet in general, can be assured that a department is administered economically,

efficiently, and effectively. The deputy is the person both to assure the prime minister that the department is professionally sound and capable of serving and advancing the policy and program agenda of the government and to guarantee that the department and its senior management faithfully serve and protect the interests of the minister.

4. Finally, the nature of the prime ministerial appointment also implies that in the performance of the deputy's duty, *the deputy minister is relatively insulated from the power and authority of the minister*. The deputy serves the minister, is responsible to the minister, and is formally subordinate to the minister, yet is not subject to the minister. The point here is nuanced, but significant. Rather than being subject to the control of the minister, the deputy minister is a professional colleague—administrator for, but also advisor to, the minister, enabling and assisting the minister in "steering" the complex administrative apparatus of the department.

The relationship between ministers and their deputies is of crucial importance in the power relations in any government, and these relationships are complex. The deputy minister's general duty is to serve the minister not only by attending to the routine management of the department but also by providing expert, non-partisan, and professional advice with respect to the overall running of the department, its strategic direction, and the merits and demerits of new policy and program initiatives. It is here, in relation to the policy role of the department, that the relations between the deputy and the minister become most intricate. The deputy is well-versed in the policy environment confronting the department and is called upon by the minister to provide expert opinion on the strengths and weaknesses of current department policies, to assess policy reform proposals from all interested parties and groups (including those of the minister and the governing party), and to propose and assess new policy initiatives emanating from senior department managers. In fulfilling these tasks the deputy minister must walk a fine line between professional and non-partisan policy analysis and advice, with a close eye both to the best administrative and managerial interests of the department and its policy responsibilities and to committed policy advocacy related to the political interests of the governing party. Deputies will tend to stress the former role while being fully cognizant of the need to carefully embrace the latter position once a departmental and ministerial consensus has emerged respecting a given policy and program approach. These opinions are based on

- their professional experience as to the nature of the department's portfolio;
- its proper role, capabilities and limitations;
- the ability of particular policies and programs to attain desired ends given specified means; and
- the capacity of the department to efficiently and effectively implement new policy proposals with existing or newly established means.

In providing all such advice to the minister the deputy is to be free to offer full and frank commentary on the administrative, legal, and even broad political (as distinct from partisan) merits and demerits of policy proposals as well as on the organizational ways and means of achieving desired policy ends. Deputies need to be critical analysts of any and all new policy ideas coming from any source, including the minister.

And yet, the deputy minister also is expected

- to serve the minister;
- to assist in the development of new policy and program undertakings desired by the minister, the cabinet, and the prime minister; and
- to help facilitate the development of government policy while maintaining a professional managerial sensibility in the general process of policy development.

The striking of this balance between the administrative and political sides of policy development is never easy, calling for great sensitivity on behalf of ministers and their deputies. The main dynamic here is that both sets of actors need one another, each bringing special skills, capabilities, and yet limitations to the decision-making process. The minister is always a key player, being the political head of the department and having a vital interest in the development of new policy and program initiatives supporting and promoting overall government priorities as well as his or her own policy agenda. This points bears close attention. In thinking of the relationship between a minister and his or her deputy and senior department management, it is important to remember that a minister will come to his or her portfolio with a clear but limited set of objectives. Most ministers will realize that they will be in their portfolio for three to four years and that during this time they will be fortunate to secure one or two new major policy or program initiatives. Ministers are, therefore, very careful in selecting the matters they will pursue as their policy initiatives and take a highly strategic approach to their role within their departments (Savoie, 1999: 240–48). It follows from this that ministers tend to refrain from becoming involved in the day-to-day administrative working of their departments, correctly sensing that they have neither the time, expertise, nor interest in addressing the plethora of routine matters. Leaving these matters to senior department officials liberates the minister to concentrate on strategic initiatives.

Nevertheless, for assistance with these matters, too, the minister must turn to the deputy. The deputy minister can bring expertise and wisdom to bear on all of these matters and is expected, even required, to advise the minister, however unwelcome some of the advice may be. The deputy, likewise, is expected to be equally critical and dispassionate with respect to policy initiatives emerging from other sources, including the department itself. In fulfilling his or her role as the chief department policy advisor to the minister, a deputy never properly serves his or her minister by being a "Yes" person. They must give fully detailed and critical advice to their ministers, meaning that they must be free at all times to challenge a minister's expression of facts and opinions and to say "no" to a minister, with due respect, asking for a reconsideration of a proposed matter on either theoretical, operational, legal, or managerial grounds. Here is where the deputy's personal and professional insulation from the minister defines their relationship.

All deputies know that their duty is to turn the minister's policy ideas into policy statements and viable programs. While this duty calls for the application of professional wisdom and expertise, it also calls for flexibility in serving a variety of political masters over time. Differing parties, as they come to power, bring differing political and ideological perspectives on the role of the state and the nature of policy, and their ministers take these "new" ideas and turn them into policy and program reality. In this process, deputies play a very significant advisory role, regardless of the party in power and regardless of the policy approach of the new government. Thus, deputy ministers, in their role as non-partisan and professional department managers, are expected to provide their best policy and managerial advice to ministers of any political perspective, be they Liberals, Conservatives, or New Democrats. The role of the deputy is always to aid the minister—advancing what the deputy considers to be sound advice towards fulfilling the aims and desires of the minister while also apprising the minister of any administrative, operational, or legal constraints on department action. This entails assessing the variety of options facing the department, outlining the strengths and weaknesses of each, and recommending to the minister a course of action that best marries the minister's aims with the best interests of the department in the considered, professional judgement of its senior staff.

What ministers expect of their senior managers is, in sum,

- to oversee the routine administrative work of the department;
- to implement established policies and programs in ways that are economical, efficient, and effective; and
- to deal with small problems before they become bigger administrative and political problems.

In this sense, as Robert Adie and Paul Thomas (1987: 166-67) have written, deputies understand that their first duty to their minister is to keep him or her "out of trouble" by managing the department well; by maintaining effective and positive communications with all actors interested in the work of the department; and by quickly, smoothly, and, hopefully quietly solving departmental problems as they first arise. No minister wants to deal with big and difficult administrative problems, and no deputy would relish having to admit that internal departmental administrative malfunctioning had become so pronounced as to require ministerial attention—inevitably at the expense of the minister's own strategic policy agenda.

Second, ministers expect their senior managers to assist them in the development, cabinet approval, and departmental implementation of their policy agenda, by which a minister's political leadership will be judged. Senior officials have a vitally important role to play in this process, and the success or failure of a minister also reflects on the professional success or failure of senior officials themselves. Deputies in particular have two very important yet difficult sets of interests to balance. As chief department administrators they must provide sound management for the operation of their departments, and as chief policy advisors to their ministers they must provide professional and non-partisan policy advice, while, at the same time, they are committed to assisting their ministers in fulfilling their policy and program objectives. It is a task that requires the skills of a capable administrator, negotiator, listener, policy analyst, politician, communications expert, and diplomat. It is far from an easy task, but one that brings great professional satisfaction to those fortunate enough to attain such responsibilities.

While a symbiotic relationship exists between a minister and his or her deputy, the final decision-making authority with respect to all policy matters, of course, lies with the minister. All deputies are aware of this reality, recognizing that though their role in the department policy-making process is substantial, it is, ultimately, advisory. The minister is the official finally accountable to Parliament and the Canadian people for the exercise of ministerial authority.

BOX 4.3
Deputy Ministers' Workload

Deputy ministers have very busy lives. A recent 2004 survey by the Canada School of Public Service indicated that they work an average of almost 69 hours per week. The typical Monday to Friday workday is usually 12 hours long, and most deputies spend an additional eight hours or more each week in evening meetings or weekend work.

Deputy ministers consider this an acceptable and necessary work schedule given their responsibilities, the complexity of their duties, and the demands on their time.

As Donald Savoie has written of deputy ministers in *Breaking the Bargain: Public Servants, Ministers, and Parliament,* "...they spend on average one hour out of every three on interdepartmental issues. Typically they allocate nearly twice as much time to meetings with their peers as on matters involving their own ministers. They are at the very centre of departmental activities and are always trying to accommodate 'the urgent,' the 'important,' and the 'unforseen.' Planning is always left wanting." (Savoie, 2003: 139).

Time Spent Working by Deputy Ministers

Hours/Week	Number of Deputy Ministers
Less than 60 hours:	0
From 60-64 hours:	8
From 65-69 hours:	7
From 70-74 hours:	6
From 75-79 hours:	3
From 80-84 hours:	1
From 85-90 hours:	2
Over 100 hours:	1
Average:	68.6 hours

Source: Canada School of Public Service, *The Contemporary Role and Challenges of Deputy Ministers in the Government of Canada,* 2004.

The politics of the minister/deputy relationship deserve a further comment. Even though deputy ministers are members of the public service, sworn to provide professional and neutral service to any and all ministers, there are times when a minister and a deputy simply cannot co-exist within the same department due to real or perceived differences of understanding of policy and administrative approaches or desired policy ends. In such circumstances, it will be the deputy who must give way. As mentioned earlier, such events usually occur with the election of a new government, when a new cabinet is established and new ministers representing a hitherto opposition perspective come into power and gain control of each department. In such circumstances a new prime minister and/or new ministers simply may not trust some of the deputy ministers they inherit, believing them to be too closely associated to the policy and program initiatives of the former government that they were elected to change. In these instances, the new prime minister, acting with the advice of the clerk of the Privy Council, may reassign a "questionable" deputy to a different portfolio or other senior position in the government or may dismiss the deputy altogether from the public service. In certain cases deputies themselves know that a new government harbours questions about their political perspectives and their perceived loyalty to the new administration, or they question the policy wisdom of a new government; in these cases, it is common for such deputies to offer their resignations to the incoming prime minister.

In such periods of political transition from one government to the next it is interesting to note that, although some deputies are reassigned by a new prime minister and some may resign on their own accord or be removed from government service, in most transitions the vast majority of deputies remain in their pre-existing department positions. There have been no real "bloodbaths" among deputies during transition periods in Canadian federal politics. On the contrary, most newly elected governments recognize that they need the professional experience of most of the existing deputies to assist them in understanding and appreciating the practical difficulties of managing a government and its departments and that the new government can benefit greatly from the advice of these most senior of public servants. In 1984, the newly elected Mulroney government maintained most of the deputies it inherited from the Trudeau government, just as the newly elected Chrétien government in 1993 retained the majority of deputies it inherited from the Mulroney government. In turn, when Paul Martin succeeded Jean Chrétien as prime minister in December 2003, he likewise maintained the deputy ministers of his predecessor, many of whom he had worked with while serving as finance minister under Chrétien. This tendency is also common within most provincial governments, with certain exceptions (Inwood, 2004: 141-42; Dyck, 1996a: 455) It speaks volumes for the professional integrity and loyalty exhibited by deputy ministers in the performance of their duties.

4.2   Ministers, Deputy Ministers, and Senior Management: The Authority Dilemma

The relationship between ministers, deputy ministers, and other senior department management is complex. While ministers are the political heads of departments and the responsible officials accountable to Parliament and the Canadian public for the policy and administrative actions of departments, most of the managerial oversight and direction of departments is vested in deputy ministers, who are, in turn, assisted by a variety of associate and assistant deputy ministers and other senior management officials. These are the public servants who deal with and manage the routine administrative and program implementation work of the department as well as all ordinary research, policy and program analysis, and departmental communication and liaison functions. And, as outlined above, the deputy ministers and relevant assistant and associate deputy ministers have a major role to play in the policy-advisory and policy-making function of the department. Given this bureaucratic reality of the pre-eminence of senior managers within the leadership of a department in general, and of the leading role of the deputy minister in particular, certain fundamental and troubling questions arise regarding the nature of government and the role of elected ministers in the decision-making process. In blunt terms, does the predominance of senior management officials—all of whom are permanent public servants—within the operational life of departments mean that these essential institutions of government are more subject to the influence and control of unelected bureaucrats than to elected politicians? Considering the major contributions that deputy ministers and their senior aides make to program administration and policy development, does this combination of departmental longevity, administrative knowledge, and policy and program expertise overshadow the roles of elected ministers? Can policy generalists—the ministers—really be expected to control and direct the work of policy experts—the deputy ministers—or will the opinions of the ministers come to reflect the beliefs of the deputies as the expert opinion and knowledge of the latter overwhelm and "re-educate" the generalist understandings of the elected ministers? Does the senior public service necessarily cause a problem of democratic control and accountability in government? Can the concepts and interests of bureaucracy and democracy be appropriately balanced and managed so that the actors involved know their legitimate roles, including their limitations?

4.2.1   Organizing Government Power: The Departmentalized Cabinet

This tension between the concepts of bureaucracy and democracy has long been a feature of Canadian government life, influencing the structure of cabinet decision-making systems for the better part of the last half-century. The current cabinet decision-making system, with its unique sets of institutions and processes, has evolved from this historical process, so it is helpful to review how the modern cabinet and its "system" has come to be.

For most of the twentieth century, Canadian prime ministers (as well as premiers) ran their governments through what J. Stephan Dupré (1987) has termed a **departmentalized cabinet system**. This refers to a system of cabinet organization and decision-making in which each minister was officially responsible for his or her own department, its administration, and policy development and in which each department functioned on its own, without formal organizational linkages to any other department. Policy-making within the department was largely incremental, a series of small and discrete step-by-step initiatives designed to address new concerns and opportunities as they arose while remaining committed to past practices and undertakings. Within this system there was little long-range planning, as each department only addressed matters it considered important on a case-by-case basis, learning by experience what types of policy and program initiatives best suited its interests and the needs of its clientele. Cabinet itself possessed few, if any, policy coordinating institutions enabling its members to develop a coherent and systematic approach to policy and program development across the entire government; the prime minister himself and his closest advisors were the only cabinet members who were informed of all pending initiatives, with the prime minister alone being responsible for the coordination, planning, timing, and introduction of new government undertakings and related decision-making. Ministers and their departments were fairly autonomous actors within the overall governmental process, each developing policies and programs with little collective centralized oversight from cabinet. In this system the flow of government authority with respect to policy-making could be described as "bottom-up," in that departments and their senior officials were the key players in new policy and program development. Full cabinet met to discuss and approve new initiatives, but in such a system of devolved departmental authority, each minister and department was usually accorded the widest possible latitude in all such initiatives because the sponsoring minister and department were viewed in any case as the lead players possessing the bureaucratic expertise in the policy field under discussion. So long as a minister could gain the support of the prime minister in a new undertaking, full cabinet approval was virtually a certainty (Dyck, 1996: 491-94, Dunn, 2002: 311-12, 316-318).

Such a system of cabinet organization and functioning placed great authority in the hands of the prime minister, of course, as always is the case in any parliamentary system of government, but it is also noteworthy that this departmentalized system of organization led, at some times, to the emergence of strong ministers and, at all times, to the emergence of deputy ministers as major participants in the policy-making process.

The relative autonomy associated with this decision-making system allowed a cabinet minister who was exceptionally talented, hard-working, administratively capable, and politically savvy to become very influential within the government. Provided that the minister's ideas and initiatives

BOX 4.4
Departmentalized Cabinet System

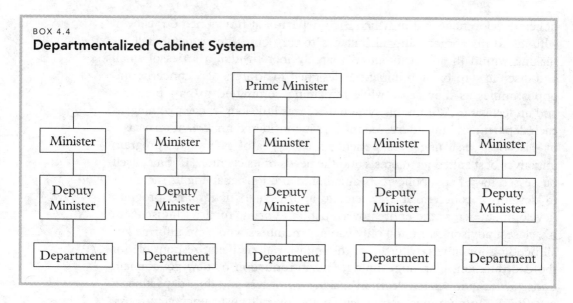

had the support of the prime minister, such a leader could forge ahead with policy development within the ministry without much consultation with cabinet colleagues. Some ministers who served in the same portfolio over an extended period of time became virtually synonymous with the department and its policy field, extending even greater credibility and authority in their spheres of influence. In the governments of Mackenzie King and St. Laurent, for example, Jimmy Gardiner of Saskatchewan served as Minister of Agriculture for 22 years, while C.D. Howe, from Ontario, became closely tied to the fields of finance and industry, gaining the epithet "Minister of Everything" (Bakvis and MacDonald, 1993: 53). Such strong ministers often carved out responsibilities for themselves as regional ministers, becoming the lead cabinet representatives for their region, dispensing patronage and benefits to the party faithful, and providing the communication link between the needs and wants of that region and the prime minister and cabinet. Such a minister was Ernest Lapointe, who became Mackenzie King's Quebec lieutenant, serving him faithfully from 1921 to 1941 while also acting as the chief advocate for Quebec's interests in cabinet. With his death in 1941 this role devolved upon Louis St. Laurent.

But not all ministers would or could be strong figures within cabinet; such leadership talent is rare and the competition for ministerial pre-eminence is always fierce. To go even further, it can be argued that most ministers in the era of the departmentalized cabinet were not strong ministers even within their own departments. Those who were of ordinary talent, drive, and capabilities became ordinary and competent ministers but not major and authoritative figures in the history of their departments. For those who possessed less than average skills in relation to their other cabinet colleagues, their ministerial tenures were considered weak and problematic. In all instances, however, the figures who rose to prominence in the working of the departmentalized cabinet were the deputy ministers. In a system of substantial departmental autonomy, the senior managerial head of any department clearly became one of the two most important persons within the department, and, should the minister himself or herself be less than a commanding figure, the deputy minister rose to be, *de facto*, the most important person in the department, informally eclipsing the *de jure* authority and prestige of the minister.

A deputy who spent his or her entire public service career within one department progressively climbing through the decades into more senior management (as was not uncommon during this time) became an expert in the life of that department, intimately knowledgeable about its programs and clientele, its interests, and its policy field. Such a person became, quite naturally, not only the most worthwhile person with whom to speak regarding the current and future administrative and policy work of the department but also the most influential advisor to each and every minister served. Should the minister be strong, the deputy would help the minister to become even stronger in his or her policy initiatives while also assuming the burden of managing routine administrative work. Should the minister be less capable, the deputy would routinely be left in charge not only of the ordinary managerial work of the department but of policy advice, ideas, and undertakings. Regardless of the situation, deputy ministers came to be such pivotal bureaucratic actors in the governmental decision-making system that, by the end of the Second World War, observers of the federal government were referring to them as "**mandarins**" after the mandarins of Imperial China, who were the formal bureaucratic and often the informal political "power behind the throne." It was just this influence and power, however, that increasingly led to questions in the 1960s regarding the democratic legitimacy of such a bureaucratic system and the ways and means by which the decision-making authority of democratically elected politicians could be enhanced over public servants (Bakvis and MacDonald, 1993: 54-55; Dyck, 1996: 491-92).

4.2.2 Organizing Government Power: The Institutionalized Cabinet

The origins of the modern **institutionalized cabinet** can be traced to the 1960s and the government of Lester Pearson (Dupré, 1987: 236-58; Dunn, 2002: 318-321). Upon coming to power in 1963 Pearson sought to reform the unstructured and "chaotic" cabinet procedures of the Diefenbaker era (Van Loon and Whittington, 1987: 473) with a new approach to executive action that offered greater systematization to cabinet decision-making, while, at the same time, it enhanced the relative power of elected ministers *vis-à-vis* unelected senior officials, including deputies (Bakvis and MacDonald, 1993: 54-57; Thomas, 1999: 132-38). Pearson inaugurated a permanent system of "standing" cabinet committees, staffed by ministers themselves, with each committee given responsibility for developing "recommendations" for government action with respect to a broad jurisdictional field of activity, this field spanning the portfolios of a number of related departments. Full cabinet, in turn, met to discuss these policy and program recommendations and endorsed those they collectively desired as government initiatives. And, as a central coordinating committee of cabinet, Pearson established the **Priorities and Planning Committee** (P&P), a body, as the name implies, designed to be the lead voice in establishing and articulating the general policy agenda of the government. Given its central role in this new cabinet structure, P&P was the only cabinet committee chaired by the prime minister himself, with its remaining membership drawn from the chairs of all other cabinet committees as well as other ministers chosen by the prime minister. As such, P&P came to be seen by many as an "inner cabinet."

This new structure of cabinet organization was endorsed, strengthened, and deepened by Pierre Trudeau, and his system of cabinet institutions was largely embraced and maintained by the government of Brian Mulroney. This full-fledged institutionalized cabinet, as it came to be called during the Trudeau years, was a complex amalgam of cabinet committees and advisory bodies known as central agencies. The purpose of such an involved cabinet structure, as Bakvis and MacDonald (1993: 55) have argued, was to enhance the ability of cabinet to "optimize" the use of its time and resources so as to address issues and problems in a more "professional" and "technocratic" way, resulting in decisions that would be more "coordinated" and "informed and rational" than ever before. The system was also designed to establish a process of decision-making in which ministers possessed the institutional means for being the primary actors of government, with the cabinet collectively in command and control of a bureaucratic network capable of giving ministers and the prime minister the full range of information, options, and advice necessary to enable them to make sound policy and program determinations. The incremental approach to decision-making associated with the departmentalized cabinet system was to be transcended by a rationalistic approach, one placing great stress on "top-down," centralized, and systematic decision-making.

Through the creation of **central agencies** independent and separate from government departments, moreover, ministers were provided with a variety of sources of information, intelligence, and policy advice on government matters so that individually and collectively they were no longer "beholden" to the possibly narrow and institutionally self-serving views of senior department officials. The creation of multiple cabinet support agencies was explicitly understood by Trudeau as establishing a system of decision-making marked by a plurality of advisory bodies and voices capable of providing "countervailing" advice to cabinet. The cabinet, through either its committees or its deliberations in full, was then in the commanding position of assessing a variety of informed positions and approaches to the same topic, of reviewing the strengths and weaknesses of differing options, and, finally, of exercising choice on the option understood by cabinet as best meeting its policy and program aims.

This system of decision-making, as refined by Trudeau and inherited by Mulroney, was desired for the premium it placed on rationality (Aucoin, 1986). The end products of this process were expected to be policies and programs characterized by their logic, their consistency to established government priorities, and their sound practical design. This process made decision-making rigorously systematic, dispassionate, and intelligent. Key government priorities and goals were established at the outset of the process, and then programs were sought to fulfill these desired ends. And in assessing such means-ends relationships, all possible program options were subjected to detailed analysis involving strengths and weaknesses, costs and benefits, with only the most logical, well-founded, substantial, and competent option surviving such systematic scrutiny. The outcome of such a decision-making process naturally was, according to its advocates, policies and programs noted not only for their substantive rationality but also by their procedurally systematic and logical pedigree. In comparison to the ad hoc, bottom-up, incremental decision-making associated with the departmentalized system of cabinet organization, this new approach to the inner workings of cabinet was viewed by its early promoters as nothing short of revolutionary, the coupling of human intelligence and ingenuity to the technocratic processes of bureaucracy. As we will see, however, the best laid plans of rational planners often did not transpire as planned.

4.3   The Institutionalized Cabinet: A Detailed Review

While the cabinet structures of the Trudeau, Clark, Turner, Mulroney, Campbell, Chrétien, and Martin governments all differ, they all are characterized as institutionalized cabinets. The following is an overview of the nature and working of such a cabinet system.

4.3.1   Cabinet Committees

Within the institutionalized cabinet system, departments were grouped together into spheres of shared policy and program interests, with the ministers of these "sister" departments becoming the members of a given **cabinet committee**. Thus, departments with broad social policy interests (health, labour, human resources, and environment, for example) were grouped together under a cabinet committee on social development, while departments with broad economic policy interests (finance, industry, trade and commerce, transportation, and regional development) were united under a cabinet committee on economic development. Similar subdivisions were formed with respect to foreign and defence policy, security and intelligence, government operations and public works, communications, the environment, and treasury policy. Most portfolios required the minister to sit on more than one cabinet committee. For example, the Minister of Foreign Affairs sat on the committees for both foreign and defence policy and security and intelligence; the Minister of Citizenship and Immigration sat on the committees for social development, communications, and government operations. Commonly, a number of other cabinet committees existed, such as legislation and house planning, public service, and special committee of council (to deal with order-in-council appointments). Each prime minister had full discretion to add, delete, or reconfigure cabinet committees, as he or she saw the need for greater or fewer or newer committees and committee portfolios—hence, the creation of a committee on national unity and constitutional reform during the latter Trudeau and Mulroney years and the creation of committees on operations and expenditure review during the Mulroney government's second term in office. During this second term, Mulroney presided over a cabinet of 40 ministers allocated into some 15 separate committees. The composition of this cabinet committee structure as of 1986 is shown in Box 4.5.

Regardless of their fields of interest, all cabinet committees shared certain basic roles. First and foremost they provided a forum where ministers with complementary portfolios, and ministers alone, came together to

BOX 4.5

Institutionalized Cabinet System—circa 1986

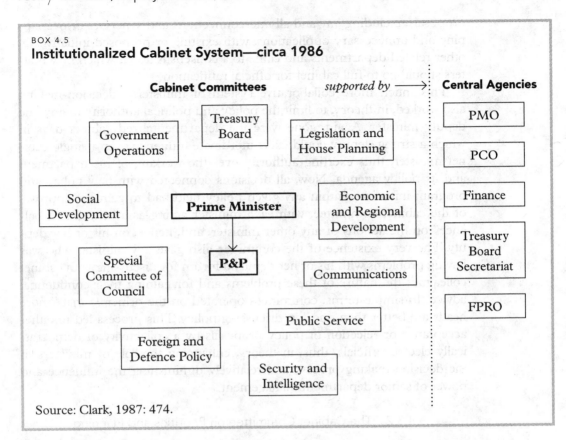

Source: Clark, 1987: 474.

discuss policy and program concerns and developments of interest to all of them. As time progressed, the committees also became a locus of discussions with respect to department budget allocations under the working of the Policy and Expenditure Management System (PEMS), outlined in greater detail in Chapter 6. As a forum of ministers, each committee not only enabled its members to address new policy initiatives but to discuss the strengths and weaknesses of all government actions and programs within the committee's jurisdiction and the ways to address problem areas. In this way, policy and program administration and development came to have a greater collectivist orientation. Gone were the days of the departmentalized cabinet in which a policy initiative emanating from a single department could eventually become law with only the most cursory attention by other ministers. Now, all ministers with related policy and program interests were enabled and expected to discuss and debate new initiatives from "sister" departments. They assessed the relative strengths and weaknesses of new proposals, including any and all interconnections and synergies or overlapping and unnecessary duplications, with existing or proposed initiatives in other related departments and came to a consensus about which new matters should go to full cabinet for official ratification.

This much more collaborative system of ministerial decision-making also worked, in theory, to limit the policy and political authority of any one deputy minister. Again, gone were the departmentalized cabinet days in which a strong deputy could exert inordinate influence over a single cabinet minister, thus exerting authority over the working of his department and its policy agenda. Now, all decisions connected with new policy and program initiatives within any given policy field had to gain the approval of the cabinet committee, with each minister acting as a "check and balance" on the actions of any other minister, and, hence, on his or her deputy. The very existence of the committee also gave any minister who was having problems with his or her deputy a forum for discussing with cabinet colleagues the nature of these problems and for gaining their confidential advice. In simple terms, committees operated on the principle that "more heads are better than one," in discussing policy. This process led to either acceptance or rejection of policy proposals by a collectivity of democratically elected officials, thus, in theory, enhancing the role of ministers in the decision-making process and relatively diminishing the influence and power of senior department management.

4.3.2 The Cabinet Committee on Priorities and Planning

The P&P became the leading committee within cabinet from the mid-1960s through the early 1990s (Van Loon and Whittington, 1987: 472-81). It was the one committee chaired by the prime minister as a matter of course, and its members consisted of all the chairpersons of all other cabinet committees, the minister of finance, and such other senior ministers designated to serve on P&P by the prime minister. During the Trudeau and Mulroney years this committee came to be the central decision-making body of cabinet, possessing these six main functions:

- setting long-range government priorities;
- dealing with short-term political crises;
- establishing broad goals and objectives for the other standing committees of cabinet;
- reviewing all decisions made by the standing committees and resolving any policy or program disputes arising from these committees;

- setting budgetary parameters for committees and departments to live within under the working of the Policy and Expenditure Management System (PEMS); and
- establishing policy and program initiatives in the name of the full cabinet.

With the heightened executive leadership role afforded by P&P and with the more specialized and targeted executive decision-making provided by the standing committees, it became increasingly the case during these years that full cabinet was less and less the central decision-making body of the government. Rather than full cabinet meeting regularly to review matters and make final decisions, it met only to ratify decisions respecting priorities, policies, and programs already established by relevant standing committees and approved by P&P.

4.3.3 Central Agencies

While the establishment and working of cabinet committees are vital elements of the institutionalized cabinet system, they are but half of the system. Alongside the cabinet committees there came to exist a set of advisory bodies to cabinet designed to provide the cabinet in general, or the prime minister in particular, with detailed information, intelligence, and expert opinion and advice regarding any and all matters (Thomas, 1999; Whitaker, 1995). Though certain of the central agencies, such as the Privy Council Office, long predated the Trudeau cabinet, it was during the early years of that government that the central agency system as we now know it came into existence. Within this advisory system, which remains largely intact to this day, four central agencies rose to prominence, each with its own composition and unique role to play in the cabinet decision-making system: the Prime Minister's Office, the Privy Council Office, the Department of Finance, and the Treasury Board.

4.3.3.1 THE PRIME MINISTER'S OFFICE

The **Prime Minister's Office** (PMO) is, as the name suggests, a set of officials specifically mandated to serve the administrative, policy, and political needs of the prime minister. The members of the PMO are the prime minister's personal staff, appointed directly by, and entirely responsible to, the prime minister. Thus, they are political appointees, serving at the pleasure of the prime minister, and are not members of the permanent public service. The staff complement of the PMO varies in size. Under Trudeau it numbered

BOX 4.6

The Stephen Harper PMO, 2006: Senior Officials' Who's Who (An Early Look)

Stephen Harper	Prime Minister
Ray Novack	Executive Assistant to the Prime Minister
Ian Brodie	Chief of Staff
Patrick Muttart	Deputy Chief of Staff
William Stairs	Director of Communications
Darren Cunningham	Manager, Parliamentary Communications
Mark Cameron	Manager of Policy
Bruce Carson	Senior Policy Advisor
Michel Lalonde	Senior Policy Researcher
Dave Penner	Director of Appointment
Carolyn Stewart Olsen	Press Secretary

At the time of writing (early February, 2006) this was the likely shape of the Harper PMO. Source: *The Hill Times*, Monday, January 30, 2006, p. 11, *The Globe and Mail*, Tuesday, February 14, 2006, p. A4.

around 100 persons, and it peaked at roughly 120 under Mulroney in 1985-86. In seeking a relatively downsized government, Chrétien held his PMO to 63 during his first term, raising it to 83 by the end of his second (Thomas, 1999: 133, 140). Paul Martin aimed for an even leaner staff complement; as of 2005 there were 73 persons working in the Martin PMO.

The senior ranks of the PMO usually consist of a chief of staff, a senior policy advisor, a research director, a director of communications, and a director of operations. All of these persons are hand-picked for these positions by the prime minister and usually are long-time friends and political colleagues—persons whom the prime minister knows and trusts, whose political opinions and instincts are dependable, and who are committed to furthering the political work and vision of the prime minister. Not surprisingly, most of these people served as chief election campaign strategists in the most recent election. They helped orchestrate the election of the prime minister and are, therefore, personal advisors and confidants the prime minister continues to want and need.

The PMO is designed to provide routine administrative assistance to the prime minister as well as to offer policy advice. It deals with such matters as correspondence, media communications and relations, advice on partisan appointments, the organizing of public appearances, and the drafting of speeches. Above and beyond immediate business, however, the senior members of the PMO look to the future and to maintaining the prime minister in office. They provide him or her with advice of a directly political and partisan nature:

- how the prime minister should address the leading issues of the day;
- what types of actions and decisions the prime minister should be making, or not making;
- how the prime minister should be relating to other ministers and caucus members;
- how the prime minister should be dealing with the various opposition leaders and their parties;
- how the prime minister should be relating to the media and how the prime minister is perceived by the media;
- what type of message and image the prime minister should be sending to the general Canadian public as well as to various major interest groups; and
- who the prime minister should be meeting with, talking to, and dealing with in the pursuit of his or her policy agenda.

In this sense, as Paul Thomas has written, the PMO plays the role of a "political switchboard," plugging the prime minister into a host of communication linkages with the caucus and party, other government officials, the media, and the vast array of interest groups concerned with government policy (Thomas, 1999: 141) And always, at the head of this "switchboard" are the senior officials of the PMO, the trusted confidants, advising the prime minister on the political merits and demerits of everything he or she is doing, and on what is required, in direct partisan terms, to fulfill the political goals for government, to beat off the opposition, and to position his or her government and party for a return to power at the next general election.

4.3.3.2 THE PRIVY COUNCIL OFFICE

In contrast to the PMO's explicitly political and partisan role as a central agency, the **Privy Council Office** (PCO) is an administrative support and policy advisory agency to the entire cabinet, designed to give the prime minister and cabinet expert and non-partisan advice on the management of cabinet decision-making and government operations (Savoie, 1999: ch.5). Also, in contrast to the PMO, the PCO is an office of the public service, staffed by career public servants, and its head, the clerk of the Privy Council and secretary to Cabinet, is the most senior public servant in the country and official head of the Public Service of Canada. This person is appointed by the prime minister and, as a rule, is drawn from the ranks of senior department deputies. For a deputy minister to be appointed clerk is to reach the pinnacle of a career within the public service.

Given its role as a general service support agency to cabinet, the PCO undertakes a number of important duties. First and above all, it provides logistical support to cabinet and all cabinet committees—developing agendas, organizing meetings, preparing informational material and analytical briefing notes for ministers, taking and circulating minutes, and disseminating cabinet and committee decisions. Throughout the government, the PCO also possesses a policy review and analysis function, providing ministers and the prime minister with assessments of current policies and programs and analyses of new policy and program options. Beyond these matters, the PCO has a general responsibility for overseeing the "machinery of government and the appointment of senior public service personnel" (Dyck, 1996: 495). In 1993, the PCO was additionally given jurisdiction for overseeing and providing advice to the cabinet with respect to federal-provincial relations when the Federal-Provincial Relations Office was reincorporated into the PCO.

The Privy Council Office usually employs in the range of 150 to 175 public servants, with these officials divided into such general offices as operations, plans and consultations, management priorities, and senior personnel secretariat. It is also divided into specific policy branches: foreign and defence policy, security and intelligence, Aboriginal affairs, economic and regional development policy, social development policy, regulatory affairs and orders-in-council, legislation and house planning and counsel, machinery of government, and financial planning and analysis. From this brief listing of offices and branches one can observe that the PCO is designed to address policy and program matters spanning the full range of government responsibilities, with the various members of the PCO expected to provide expert, professional, and non-partisan advice to ministers and the prime minister respecting the nature of specific government undertakings, their managerial strengths and weaknesses, and the desirability and viability of possible reform options. The officials in these offices and branches, though small in number, are nevertheless some of the most influential public servants in the country, standing, as they do, at one of the nerve centres of federal government decision-making.

The head of this organization, the Clerk of the Privy Council and Secretary to Cabinet, oversees one of the most important organizations in the federal government and bears three major and interrelated responsibilities: deputy minister to the prime minister, secretary to the cabinet, and head of the federal public service. In his first role, the clerk meets daily with the prime minister to review ongoing administrative and policy matters and to offer non-partisan advice on the running of government, the development of government policies, the administrative requirements for implementing such policies and attendant programs, and the organization and operation of government decision-making systems themselves. The clerk plays a vital role in assisting the prime minister in

- structuring cabinet committees;
- structuring and restructuring department portfolios and functions;
- offering advice on senior public service appointments; and,
- in particular, tendering advice on all matters affecting the appointment, promotion, demotion, and even removal of department deputy ministers.

The clerk as head of the public service is intimately involved in all major reform initiatives designed to improve the overall operational efficiency and effectiveness of the public service and its management. Chapter 10 highlights a number of such contemporary reform undertakings.

As Secretary to the Cabinet, the clerk assists its ministers in the organization and working of its committees as well as of full cabinet meetings, assuring

- that the cabinet and its committees receive all relevant briefing materials, policy and program analyses, and administrative-operational reviews;
- that ministers are privy to the relevant information available for the making of executive decisions; and
- that the paper-flow into and out of cabinet and its committees is conducted in a detailed, accurate, efficient, and secure manner, always cognizant that all cabinet meetings, reviews, and discussions are strictly confidential.

Finally, as head of the public service, the clerk is responsible to the prime minister for the overall functioning of the administrative operations of the federal government ensuring:

- that departments are well organized and staffed;
- that their senior management are competent to undertake the roles and responsibilities assigned to them; and

BOX 4.7
Key Roles and Responsibilities of Central Agencies

PMO

Policy advice to the prime minister
Research advice to the prime minister
Communications advice to the prime
 minister
Operational advice to the prime minister
Scheduling advice to the prime minister
Media advice to the prime minister
Partisan advice to the prime minister

PCO

Policy advice to prime minister and cabinet
Research advice to prime minister and
 cabinet
Logistical support to cabinet
Executive leadership of public service
Federal/provincial relations advice to prime
 minister
Operational support for public service
Non-partisan, professional advice to
 cabinet

Finance

Economic policy advice to prime minister and
 cabinet
Development of annual budget
Tax policy advice to prime minister and
 cabinet
Budget coordination with departments
Policy advice to prime minister and cabinet on:
  International trade
  NAFTA
  Debt repayment

TBS

Management of public service
Financial management support to departments
Accountability oversight for departments
Personnel management support for
 departments
Official employer of the public service

- that the employees working within departments are trained, motivated, and prepared to undertake their duties in the federal bureaucracy.

The clerk also assists the prime minister in making senior executive appointments to federal Crown corporations and regulatory agencies, and, though the clerk and PCO will respect the operational autonomy of these Crown agencies, as explained in the previous chapter, the clerk will maintain a "watching brief" over the actions of all such agencies, reporting to the prime minister on their strengths and weaknesses; the managerial and political environments they face; and the need for senior agency executive appointments, legislative review, and, in rare instances, policy directives to agency boards of directors.

4.3.3.3   THE DEPARTMENT OF FINANCE

While the **Department of Finance** is, in fact, a regular government department under the category of central support departments, it also acts as a central agency to cabinet within its role as macro-economic policy advisor to the prime minister and cabinet on all policy and program matters touching upon the economy and government revenues and expenses—meaning virtually everything the government does (Savoie, 1999: ch. 6). As Greg Inwood (2004: 133-34) asserts, this department's jurisdictional role over the economy and in the provision of general government financial management makes it in many respects "the most powerful actor in the federal government," elevating its minister second only to the prime minister in political significance and government power.

Finance has a number of major responsibilities, any one of which would make it a major player in government but, when combined, make it a heavyweight in the world of power politics. First, it is this department that provides the prime minister and cabinet with most of its macro-economic information respecting the health of the Canadian economy and the effects of government activity in general, and taxation policies in particular, both real and proposed, on the viability of the economy and the private sector. Secondly, this department and its minister has full responsibility, in very close consultation with the prime minister, for the development of the government's annual budget. Officials from Finance provide advice to the prime minister and other relevant cabinet ministers regarding taxation policy, predicted multi-year revenue streams, and desirable government expenditure parameters. In consultation with the most senior political leadership of the government and various senior officials in the other departments, Finance crafts a budget

- that establishes federal tax policy (general increases, decreases, or marginal modifications) for both corporate and personal taxation rates;
- that addresses deficit and debt management; and
- that provides a multi-year government revenue stream and broad fiscal framework for the management of this revenue by the government— deficit and/or debt reduction, existing program funding, taxation reductions, and/or new program development.

As the providers of economic policy advice and budget-making (detailed in Chapters 6 and 7), Finance is a coordinating hub in the government; its officials must relate with senior officials from every other department both to gain information—their existing expenditure requirements and their desired spending goals—and to instill in the senior leadership of every other department the government's view of the fiscal climate, its revenue and expenditure policy, and the expenditure parameters for departments' programs. Through this policy coordinating activity, Finance can then bring significant influence to bear on the development of social, cultural, and environmental policies and their economic consequences.

Third, beyond its macro-economic and financial management duties, Finance provides advice to the cabinet concerning:

- international trade and tariff policy, including the management of foreign trade treaties such as the NAFTA;
- foreign borrowing and debt repayment issues;
- the overseeing of the national debt; and
- balance of payments and foreign exchange matters.

Finance fulfills all these roles and wields the enormous power and influence it does through some 600 public servants. These officials, the self-perceived "guardians" of sound financial management, form an elite within the federal bureaucracy, as much feared as respected by those other public servants and ministers from other departments who must interact with them. As Inwood (2004: 134) suggests, such is the authority of those who control "the purse strings."

4.3.3.4 THE TREASURY BOARD

Whereas Finance provides macro-economic advice to the prime minister and cabinet for the management of government revenues and expenses, the Treasury Board (TB) and its administrative arm, the **Treasury Board Secretariat** (TBS), provide micro-economic advice to cabinet pertaining to all internal government expenditure and personnel management (Savoie, 1999: ch. 7).

The TB is a department of government headed by a cabinet minister titled the President of the Treasury Board. The TB includes other cabinet ministers, such as the minister of finance, but its secretariat, the TBS, is its operational heart. The TBS, staffed by some 800 public servants, reviews and analyzes in detail the annual budgets of all departments to ensure that they fall within the broad spending parameters set by Finance. Department budgets are screened by TBS for compliance with government priorities and spending targets and have to receive TBS approval prior to ratification. TBS stays in close touch with senior department management as "guardians" of the public purse, seeking to contain current and future department spending to the ratified limits, while department managements typically seek to obtain as much latitude as possible with respect to existing and new spending so as to expand department goals and activities.

The second major responsibility of the TBS is to oversee the general management of public personnel policy in the federal government. As of 1967, the TB became the official "employer" of government personnel, bearing responsibility for representing the employer in all matters of collective bargaining and grievance management. The TB also manages salaries, salary scales, job classifications, employee training, and long-range recruitment patterns within the public service, as well as promoting the "merit principle" within all personnel management decision-making.

4.4   The Institutionalized Cabinet: "Making a Mesh of Things"

In Paul Thomas's wry assessment of the working of the institutionalized cabinet system, the phrase "making a mesh of things" carries with it both descriptive and analytical insight (Thomas, 1999). During the Trudeau and Mulroney years, the institutionalized cabinet system created a mesh of interrelating roles and responsibilities held by quite a range of political and bureaucratic decision-makers, all bringing distinct sets of ideas, positions, and professional viewpoints to the process of policy and program decision-making. It clearly made the working of the federal government, at the most senior levels, much more layered, multi-faceted, pluralistic, involved, and complex than anything that had gone before. Such complexity, however, brought with it other dynamics less desirable to the government and its managerial process, and Thomas's quip captured these dynamics in the pun on "mesh = mess." While an institutionalized system of cabinet organization is never, in theory, designed to make decision-making simpler, serious questions began to arise during the 1970s and 1980s as to whether the "mesh" of committees, agencies, and departments, of competing advisors and institutions, of rules and responsibilities, had rendered government decision-making too difficult, too complex, too time-consuming, and thus too problematic as a way to organize the most important function of government—namely, making policy and program decisions in an intelligent yet expeditious manner. Serious questions arose as to whether the institutionalized cabinet system had the effect, as planned, of enhancing the policy-making role of elected ministers while diminishing the political influence and power of their deputy ministers.

4.4.1 The Institutionalized Cabinet:
Decision-Making in Practice, the Formal View

It is difficult to encapsulate the nature of cabinet decision-making from the late 1960s through the early 1990s as all governments during this time period sought to "fine-tune" the institutionalized system to better meet their policy and program goals. The Trudeau government was not averse to modifying the process of cabinet decision-making, and the Mulroney government likewise engaged in a variety of changes to the structures and processes of cabinet during its nine-year tenure in office, including increasing the number of ministers to 40 and significantly expanding the number of cabinet committees. Some significant alterations to the institutionalized system were also wrought by the short-lived governments of Joe Clark and Kim Campbell (Jackson and Jackson, 1998: 274-75; Kernaghan and Siegel, 1999: 396-98), but despite marginal changes to the system, certain basic elements and processes were common to the decision-making of all these cabinets during these years.

At the heart of the strategic decision-making process, the P&P, chaired by the prime minister, established the policies and priorities of the government while also overseeing and approving the work of all other cabinet committees. P&P set the broad agenda of the government, settling on the three to five major issues to be embraced by the prime minister and cabinet as the defining objectives of the government in a term of office. In establishing this agenda, P&P was closely assisted by the PCO and the Department of Finance, with the latter providing P&P with detailed economic forecasts and multi-year revenue and expenditure assessments within which all government policies and programs were expected to live. In all such priority-setting, of course, the prime minister was in daily contact with his senior advisors in the PMO.

Once the prime minister and P&P had agreed on an agenda for the government and had also agreed to multi-year revenue and expenditure projections, this information was relayed, with the assistance of the PCO, throughout the communication channels of the senior executive to cabinet committees, other central agencies, and all departments and their political and administrative heads. With this information in hand, the general process of operational policy and program decision-making began, or more precisely, continued, with this activity being largely centred within the departments.

Each department was responsible for the initiation of new policies and programs within its sphere of jurisdiction as well as the management of pre-existing department undertakings. As a department developed new initiatives that would require legislative enactment or amendment and the expenditure of "new" monies, its deputy minister and other senior department officials were expected to consult widely and liberally with all other government actors in any way concerned or affected by the new initiative. Thus, senior department managers routinely communicated with officials from "sister" departments (with relevant deputy ministers remaining in very close contact), as well as with officials in PCO, Finance, TBS, and even the PMO, if needed. This, of course, was in addition to all the department communications and consultations with client groups, officials from concerned interest groups, and members of the general public.

Once the senior officials from the department had resolved on a particular new policy and course of action for a program, having received sufficient support (or at least non-obstruction) from officials from other departments and central agencies and approval for the plan from their own minister, the deputy minister, in consultation with senior advisors and the minister, produced a **Memorandum to Cabinet** that would become the focal point of the minister's liaison with his or her cabinet colleagues and officials from central agencies. Each Memorandum contained a Ministerial Recommendation, an Analysis section, and a Communications Plan:

- The *Recommendation* was normally a short summation of the policy issue and the cabinet decision anticipated by the sponsoring minister.
- The *Analysis* entailed background relevant to the policy, the nature of the problem being addressed, and the ways this problem would be broached by the new policy and related programs. It addressed the strengths and weaknesses of the proposed initiative as well as other options for dealing with the problem and the positive or negative impacts the proposed policy and other options would have on targeted groups in particular, society overall, and any province or region it directly affected. The Analysis outlined and assessed the direct and indirect political implications of the proposal—for example, the relationship of the proposal to general government policy priorities as set by P&P, existing government commitments, and past party promises—and projected costs, sources of funding, and any new personnel requirements arising from the implementation of the new policy. The Analysis then stressed either the new initiative's conformity to pre-established spending guidelines set by Finance and the TB or the strong reasons for revising such guidelines to allow the

proposed initiative to proceed. Its discussion also contained material outlining the positions taken by other concerned departments and central agencies for or against the proposal.

- The *Communications Plan* outlined how the minister intended to present the new policy to the public, how the department would begin the process of program implementation, and how it would engage in ongoing consultations with affected individuals, corporations, interest groups, and the media.

In short, the Memorandum to Cabinet was designed to "provide ministers with a full range of realistic options, the advantages and disadvantages of each, and their financial and policy implications" (Dyck, 1996: 498; Jackson and Jackson, 1998: 276).

Once produced and approved by the minister, the Memorandum was transmitted to the PCO for distribution to the members of the relevant cabinet committee having jurisdiction over the department and its broad policy field. The PCO provided briefing notes on the proposal to all the members of the relevant committee as well as to the prime minister and PMO. These briefing notes contained detailed assessments of the strengths and weaknesses of the proposal from officials within the PCO as well as from Finance and the TBS. The cabinet committee then met to discuss the matter and make a decision for or against the proposal. At this meeting the sponsoring minister advanced and defended his or her Memorandum, speaking to the strengths of its policy and program design and seeking to diminish any concerns about, or criticisms of, the proposal. Cabinet committees were designed to allow ministers to come together and to engage in full and frank discussions of shared policy matters and to develop courses of action all committee members and their respective departments could support. Such meetings could become testy affairs as ministers debated among themselves the theoretical, practical, administrative, and political value of a proposal. And, as Jackson and Jackson (1998: 277) have observed, any minister's chance of getting a Memorandum through cabinet committee was contingent on gaining central agency support and in demonstrating to committee colleagues that the new initiative would not threaten funding to other initiatives desired by other committee members.

Following the committee discussion, which could extend over a number of meetings, a decision would be made for or against the Memorandum, at which point the committee decision would be written up by committee staff provided by the PCO, as a Committee Report. Should the proposal be rejected, the Committee Report would explain why, and the proposal would be sent back down to the sponsoring department, with a suggestion that the department reconsider and rework its plans in keeping with the analysis found in the Report. Should the proposal be accepted, however, the Report would be sent on to full cabinet for ratification. If the committee vote in favour of the proposal was unanimous, the Report would record this and usually full cabinet would endorse it without discussion. Within the Mulroney administration, P&P routinely endorsed such Committee Reports without referral to full cabinet. If and when a Report was not unanimously endorsed, however, full cabinet debated the issue, with the PCO and the PMO briefing the prime minister on how best to deal with the matter. In these full cabinet meetings objections of Finance and the TBS were well-represented by their respective ministers. Once the cabinet had resolved a matter, one way or the other, to the satisfaction of the prime minister, the outcome was drafted as a Record of Decision and transmitted to the relevant department.

4.4.2 Institutionalized Cabinet Decision-Making: The Prime Ministerial Prerogative

What has just been outlined as the formal decision-making process for the cabinets from the late 1960s through the early 1990s remains a good basic description of decision-making within the Chrétien and Martin cabinets in the early years of the twenty-first century, with some modifications and revisions that will be mentioned below. However, there has always been a shadow decision-making process operating alongside, and in competition to, this formal process. This is prime ministerial direction, or what Tom Axworthy (1988), a former principal secretary to Trudeau, has called the **strategic prime ministership**. Just as any one minister must make strategic choices of the few policy matters for ministerial attention, so, too, a prime minister will target a select number of policy items for the government's policy agenda. According to Bakvis and MacDonald (1993: 64-65), a prime minister and government usually have three policy matters that become the strategic focus of the government over a four-year term of office. The prime minister and his or her senior ministers and advisors (P&P, PMO, PCO, Finance, TBS) devote most of their attention to these priority matters, delegating to individual ministers and their departments responsibility for overseeing all the routine administrative work of government, as well as all other policy and program development matters not considered by the prime minister to be of high priority status. Once again, senior officials in the departments are expected to manage the routine activities of departments, keeping their ministers, and thus the government, out of trouble, and thereby enabling the prime minister and his or her inner circle of senior ministers and staff to devote themselves to major strategic initiatives—during the Trudeau years: bilingualism and biculturalism, wage and price controls, constitutional reform, national unity, and national energy policy; under Mulroney: regional development, free trade, privatization and deregulation, constitutional policy, tax reform, and deficit reduction.

Moreover, when a prime minister became personally interested in a policy and program matter, believing it to be one of vital interest to his or her government and its policy priorities, he or she would assume control and direction above any minister and department and would fast-track the policy through P&P and full cabinet, with the relevant minister and senior department officials assuming supporting roles. In such circumstances the prime minister was invariably supported by officials from the PCO and the PMO, in close consultation with the minister of finance and his senior officials. Policy matters handled in this manner were far from routine, touching usually upon political and socio-economic issues viewed by the prime minister and senior advisors as of the greatest importance to the country.

Deferring for the moment the cabinet decision-making system of the Chrétien and Martin governments, let us first examine the strengths and weaknesses of the institutionalized cabinet system during the Trudeau and Mulroney years.

4.4.3 Institutionalized Cabinet Decision-Making: A Critical Analysis

The institutionalized system of cabinet decision-making did achieve a number of the goals of its proponents. The complex web of organizational interrelationships created by the system was much more structured, systematic, and rationalistic in contrast to the departmentalized system of cabinet decision-making. This much more formalized and process-oriented system of decision-making was one that demanded and received a great deal of bureaucratic networking as policies and programs were initiated, assessed, accepted, and developed. And through such networking, the system called for and received much greater input from a much wider field of analysts and advisors than had any decision-making system hitherto. Prime Minister Trudeau wanted to create a cabinet system marked by a plurality of different policy and program viewpoints from among his senior bureaucratic advisors, and this he achieved. The expanded and vital roles played by central agencies clearly altered the bureaucratic power relations that had dominated Ottawa prior to the 1960s, with deputy ministers as a group

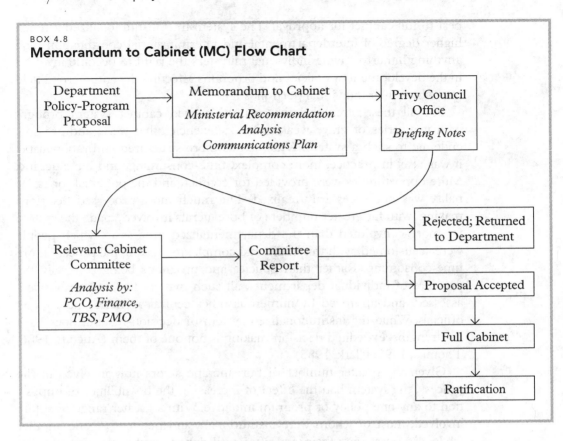

BOX 4.8
Memorandum to Cabinet (MC) Flow Chart

witnessing the decline of their relative power and influence in the face of the new institutionalized process.

This change was the effect of the greater plurality of advisory sources that ministers, individually or collectively, could draw upon in their policy and program deliberations. However, this is not to suggest that deputy ministers and their officials have become less than important figures in the policy-making process and the life of departments: far from it, as we shall see.

Shifting focus to the elected ministers, we see that the institutionalized system had the effect of sharpening the policy-planning role of cabinet, at least among those senior ministers sitting within P&P, while also enhancing the ability of individual ministers to play greater policy and program development roles within their own cabinet committees. The cabinet committee system provided all ministers with a set of venues where they could review, assess, discuss, and develop new policies and programs arising from their own and related departments, recommending those initiatives considered best to full cabinet for approval. The system thus institutionalized a much higher degree of interdepartmental and interministerial coordination than anything hitherto, giving individual ministers the right to become involved in the development of policies and programs affecting the entire broad field into which their individual portfolios fell.

For all these strengths, the institutionalized cabinet system brought with it a series of grave weaknesses, deficiencies that were, and are still, endemic to such a system. While it was more structured and rationalistic, it was also, in practice, more complex, time-consuming, and bureaucratic. More opportunities were provided for conflict, and the potential for rationality was not necessarily realized. The much more processed decision-making, with far greater numbers of bureaucrats involved, made the system far more convoluted than the departmentalized process to which people were accustomed, with this additional complexity making the process more time-consuming. Rather than policies and programs being primarily the preserve of individual departments, all such matters had to be reviewed, assessed, and approved by numerous other central agencies and cabinet officials. While the institutionalized system of decision-making does have its strengths, expedited decision-making is not one of them (Aucoin, 1986; Thomas, 1999; Clark, 1985).

Given the greater number of bureaucratic actors now involved in the process, the system had the effect of increasing the possibilities of opposition to any one policy or program initiative. With a greater range of actors involved, most of whom were institutionally independent of one another while also possessing their own often well-defined and competing ideas as to what was desirable public policy and program development, the system tended to promote conflict as much as consensus. Departments always had competed with one another for scarce financial and personnel resources with which to launch and maintain policies and programs and had competed for power, authority, and prestige within Ottawa's bureaucratic world. They continued to compete among themselves, but the new structure threw them into competition with other central agencies from which they also needed support. And a number of these agencies, such as Finance and TBS, perceived their organizational roles, in part, as being "guardians of the public purse," seeking increasingly to constrain policy and program spending and to direct such spending along lines they, rather than the departments, desired. In requiring all policy and program initiatives emanating from departments to receive scrutiny and eventual endorsement from central agencies prior to ratification by cabinet, the institutionalized system did not create a completely impossible system, but it did result in one in which every department faced a far greater number of challenges, difficulties, and potential conflict prior to the approval of any departmental initiative.

The rationalist "mesh" necessitated that any new initiative be subjected to analyses, reviews, assessments, and critical scrutiny by other departments, other ministers, cabinet committees, and central agencies. Each of these others could object to the initiative, in whole or in part, if they believed that it neither met a pressing national or regional interest nor served the best interests of their own bureaucratic needs. Bureaucrats can be very parochial and self-serving, jealously guarding their own interests at the expense of the favoured policies and programs of others. As Hartle (1976) has written, the power relations between these competitive interests can be viewed as a game, with each player seeking to advance its own promotion, power, money, and greater financial and personnel resources over those of the other players. From this perspective bureaucratic competition is the norm, and all players are acutely aware of the constraints and difficulties imposed upon them by the structured interrelationships that the institutionalized system imposed on them. Successful policy and program development—winning the game—necessitates that a department navigate these webs of competing interests, defend departmental initiatives, and build the political, ministerial, and bureaucratic allegiances required to obtain the approvals necessary to turn an initiative into a ratified policy or program.

To proponents of the institutionalized system, of course, these changed dynamics were eminently reasonable and positive developments; departments were now compelled to address a more complex web of bureaucratic assessors and interests; and ministers had the benefit of a more complete analysis of the merits and demerits of such initiatives, policy, and program alternatives. In theory, initiatives that could withstand such scrutiny would be highly meritorious and desirable as government policies and programs, while those that could not meet these tests should quite rightly have their weaknesses identified early, being sent back to the sponsoring department for reassessment and reworking. In practice, however, the clear lines of such logic often became blurred by departmental and political in-fighting, and contests not only between departments and central agencies, but even between central agencies. Players built allegiances with like-minded players as they engaged in sparring with other bureaucratic challengers; contenders sought to build the political and bureaucratic bases of support they believed would strengthen their positions for eventual victory. In such a playground, senior department officials and especially deputy ministers, became vital to the success of future departmental initiatives, so that such officials became engaged in a complex realm of organizational diplomacy, liaison, negotiation, competition, and struggle for administrative and political advantage in the never-ending process of bureaucratic politics and policy and program decision-making.

In casting this realm of bureaucratic politics into a game mould, it is important to notice that policy and program disputes exist not only between departments, and between departments and central agencies, but among the central agencies themselves. Agencies might at times differ bitterly regarding either or both the general and the more specific agenda that the government should be following. The widely representative central agencies serving as policy and program advisory bodies to the prime minister and cabinet, with each agency institutionally independent from every other, should be expected to produce such differences of opinion. Indeed, from a pluralist perspective, such differences of opinion were to be welcomed. Trudeau, for example, consistently desired debate around the strengths and weaknesses of differing policy and program options. However, sharp and prolonged divisions of opinion among senior advisory bodies can cause problems, and the divisiveness inculcated by the institutionalized system clearly came to hurt the policy-making of the Trudeau government in the 1970s. As Richard French (1984) has shown, during these years there were three principal planning systems competing for dominance within the federal government: a policy planning system founded upon the PCO and P&P, a financial policy planning system based on the work of the Department of Finance, and a policy evaluation system rooted in the work of the TBS. The bureaucratic competition, conflict, and in-fighting among these central agencies served more to hinder than to help the policy-making capacity of the government, thus becoming a contributory factor to the policy drift associated with the Trudeau government between 1974-79.

In considering the practical working of the institutionalized cabinet systems during the Trudeau and Mulroney eras, it is also instructive to examine studies of how the decision-making systems of these governments actually evolved. The writing of such authors as French (1984), Hartle (1976), Savoie (1990, 1999), Bakvis and MacDonald (1993), and Aucoin (1999) do not make comforting reading for true believers in government rationalism. All these analysts reveal that, notwithstanding the pretensions to rationality, the cabinet systems of these years were marked more by departmental and agency competition, general in-fighting, and old-fashioned claims of personal and organizational self-interest than by any dispassionate analysis of policy options. As French and Hartle have asserted, any hope of rational decision-making in the Trudeau government was quickly lost in the bruising world of bureaucratic politics in which each minister, senior official, department, and agency was motivated to defend its own interests, to maximize its strengths and benefits, and to enhance its ability to gain desired ends, be these re-election or promotion or greater resources, prestige, and power. The "near-death" experience of the Trudeau government in 1972, when it was reduced to a minority, also had the effect of souring Trudeau and his senior ministers on their own claims to rationality and what such a formal system could offer a government immersed in the real-world tasks of governing.

As Savoie and Bakvis and MacDonald have also shown, the Trudeau government came to be characterized by a two-tiered system of policy-making. With respect to policy matters of direct concern to the prime minister, the practice of strategic prime ministership prevailed, with the prime minister and his senior advisors devoting close control, management, and rigorous analysis to those select matters of utmost national and governmental importance. All other policy matters, however, were left to the routine working of the system, with this process becoming marked more by administrative competition and struggle—over such seemingly mundane yet politically significant matters as budget allocations for special projects desired by departments and their ministers—than by any concern for the long-term best interests of the country. In referring to the ministers involved in such parochial and self-serving actions as "process participants," Savoie (1990: 193-94) writes:

> Policy content, political ideology, government organization, management issues—and even government programs themselves—are all of limited interest to the process participants.... Projects are what matters, and the more the better. They will look to their own departments to come up with specific projects for their own ridings or for the regions for which they are responsible.

In commenting on this approach to policy-making, in which concern for project development (designed to maximize ministerial profile and electability), department budget, and personnel capacity came to outweigh most others, Bakvis and MacDonald (1993: 66) were struck by the haphazard and uncoordinated nature of decision-making emerging from a system designed to produce just the opposite type of outcome. Looking at the actual means by which cabinet ministers in the Trudeau and Mulroney governments engaged in decision-making, these authors found that the process tended "to be fluid and often chaotic," because deals were "often consummated outside the formal confines of committees" as ministers worked among themselves to reach arrangements of mutual benefit prior to official cabinet committee meetings. Far from the cabinet system being highly formal and rationalistic, these authors observed a decision-making system that was in general highly idiosyncratic and personal, very much contingent on the capabilities and power of individual ministers and their senior department staff to secure their objectives, as well as on the drive and determination of senior officials in central agencies to resist and restrict such gains by department challengers. Despite a highly structured system of decision-making designed to encourage rational discourse and systematic policy outcomes, the reality was characterized by political in-fighting, power politics, and bureaucratic self-interest. Rather than a supposedly objective system of decision-making founded on the technocratic processes of cost-benefit analyses and rational choice, they observed one bound to the all-too-human characteristics of subjectivity and personal politics. In short, the former organizational ideals could not displace the latter governmental realities.

Assessing the working of the Mulroney government, these authors find similar dynamics. Bakvis and MacDonald stress that Mulroney, like Trudeau, followed the practice of strategic prime ministership, but, unlike his predecessor, he was even more willing to engage in the routine management of particular departmental issues and to encourage a more informal, brokerage-style of cabinet decision-making. As Aucoin found, Mulroney was much less enamoured of rationalistic processes than Trudeau, preferring one-on-one dealings between ministers and their staffs and, often, the complete bypassing of formal cabinet committee discussions. Under Mulroney, ministers, departments, and central agencies were expected to be deal-makers, much like the prime minister himself, and a premium was placed on the ability of system participants to negotiate mutually acceptable policy and program agreements. Cabinet committees became opportunities for recording already established policy and program understandings, with P&P just endorsing these policy decisions.

These analysts observe a discrepancy between the formal, surface nature of the supposedly systematic and rationalistic policy-making process and the much more informal undercurrents of this process, with decision-making proving to be much more conflicted and disorganized than it appeared to the public. The relationship between the Mulroney government and central agencies, as Aucoin explains, was initially one in which the government distrusted the PCO, fearing it was excessively influenced by past Liberal appointments. In the early years of the Mulroney administration, according to Aucoin's outlines, the prime minister tended to rely heavily on the PMO for policy and program advice, coming only slowly to trust the PCO as he was able to appoint and promote more of its senior ranks. The Mulroney government never experienced this sort of policy tension with its central agencies, but this was also because the PCO was allowed a less strategic policy-making role, this being assigned to the senior officials in PMO. Finance came to dominate the realm of economic policy and general government fiscal direction, with the TBS holding a much more focused and limited role in overseeing and directing internal government financial management. In comparison to the Trudeau years, most of these central agencies played a more circumscribed part in strategic planning, with the noted exception being the PMO—the agency staffed with senior personnel hand-picked by the prime minister himself. In keeping with Mulroney's desire for substantial personal control over vital policy interests and to restrain ever-increasing government spending, he created in his second term two new cabinet committees—the Operations Committee and the Expenditure Review Committee, the former to be chaired by the deputy prime minister and to address newly arising and urgent matters facing the government, and the latter to be chaired by the prime minister himself and to engage in deficit reduction initiatives and the downsizing of government programs.

In reflecting on the cabinet decision-making systems found in both the Trudeau and Mulroney governments, it is interesting to observe how these institutionalized systems quickly lost any pretense of being rational processes geared to the production of truly rational policy and program outcomes. In both instances, the processes of rational decision-making either collapsed under their own weight, as with the Trudeau government, or were never warmly embraced in the first place, as was the case with the Mulroney government (Aucoin, 1986). And in both instances, while each government claimed its actions were "rational," in fact each tried to provide optimal management to routine policy and program matters while devoting careful and systematic attention to only a select number of strategic policy items of particular interest to the prime minister. What we have observed is not so much rationalism but a hybrid of departmental incrementalism with an overlay of strategic prime ministership.

Although the ability of the institutionalized cabinet system to generate rational decision-making was hopelessly overblown by its early advocates, what of the other great claim of its proponents: that the system would diminish the influence of unelected bureaucratic mandarins, thereby enhancing the policy decision-making role of elected ministers? On this matter, results were decidedly mixed. Putting into operation the institution-alized system did result in ministers having greater opportunity to engage in collective policy and program decision-making through the work of cabinet committees. And, in this process of decision-making, ministers did have available to them much more detailed information and expert advice coming from a wider variety of professional and independent bureaucratic sources. Under the institutionalized system, a minister could become much better informed and generally have a larger impact on policy-making than under the old departmentalized system.

But, as Van Loon and Whittington (1987: 494-95), among others, have argued, the institutionalized system has not diminished the overall influ-ence of senior public servants—unelected bureaucrats—within the process of government decision-making. While the creation of cabinet committees and the increased role of central agencies has diminished the relative influ-ence and power of any individual deputy minister, most of the central agen-cies themselves (excepting the PMO) are staffed by career public servants whose duty is to offer policy and program advice to the prime minister and all other ministers. Thus, the historic influence and power of one set of senior officials—the deputy ministers—has simply been "checked and balanced" by another set of senior officials—the "guardians" in the central agencies. One can speak of a diminishment of overall authority by depu-ties, but one cannot claim that senior public servants, in general, are any less influential on the working of the system. Rather, it can be argued that within the logic of the institutionalized system, elected ministers are just as dependent on the information, intelligence, and advice deriving from senior unelected officials, but now they at least have a plethora of compet-ing bureaucratic sources for such advice.

In assessing these power relations, it is important not to minimize the continuing influence of deputy ministers and other senior department management. These officials, and especially the deputy ministers, still remain the kingpins of the departments, with the departments themselves remaining the primary developers and implementers of all government pol-icies and programs. These officials still comprise the heart of departmental power and, though they may no longer possess the same degree of power relative to their predecessors prior to the 1960s, they remain, nonetheless, among the major players in government. Ministers still need to work closely with their senior department staff if they are to achieve success within their department portfolios, and officials from central agencies must work effec-tively with their departmental counterparts if strategic goals of the govern-ment are to be effectively implemented.

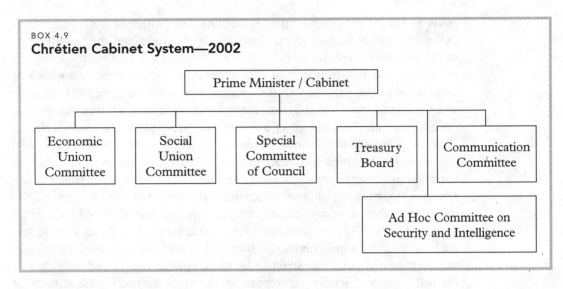

BOX 4.9
Chrétien Cabinet System—2002

4.5   The Chrétien Government: The Command Mode

In the 1990s such major changes to the cabinet decision-making system were made that, while most of the basic forms of the institutionalized system remain, we should now refer, as Aucoin (1999) and Savoie (1999) argue, to a **command mode** of decision-making. These changes began under the short tenure of Prime Minister Kim Campbell, as she sought to distinguish her government from that of Brian Mulroney by stressing a more efficient system of decision-making. She reduced the number of cabinet ministers from 40 to 24, downsized the number of cabinet committees from 11 to five, and established an Operations Committee of cabinet in lieu of P&P. When Jean Chrétien became prime minister in 1993, he maintained most of this smaller cabinet form, acquiescing in the shift towards a lighter, more efficient, and less complex system of government decision-making. In 1993, Chrétien appointed 22 cabinet ministers, but also named eight secretaries of state for a ministry of 31, including himself. He also established only four cabinet committees—Economic Union, Social Union, Special Committee of Council, and Treasury Board—for the review and assessment of emerging policies and programs. The other central agencies saw their numbers of staff reduced in the overall effort to produce a smaller, less costly, yet more nimble government. With all these organizational changes, Prime Minister Chrétien also abolished the short-lived Operations Committee while giving it no replacement, meaning that the smaller full cabinet of 22 ministers was, in theory, the leading strategic policy priority and planning body of the new government in lieu of either the Operations Committee or P&P. In 1997, at the advent of his second term, Chrétien slightly modified the composition of cabinet, increasing its membership to 29 ministers and eight secretaries of state, for a full ministry of 38, while also adding a communications committee to the existing cabinet committees. Following the 9/11 terrorist attacks against the United States, the cabinet committee system was altered once again with the addition of a committee on security and intelligence.

In comparison to the much larger and much more institutionally and procedurally complex Trudeau and Mulroney cabinet systems, that of Chrétien was significantly smaller, simpler, and, in theory, much more sensitive to ministerial and departmental initiatives, suggesting to the uninitiated that it is somewhat akin to the departmentalized system of the pre-1960s. With the absence of a central strategic cabinet committee, such as P&P or Operations, the former hierarchical structure of cabinet was replaced by one appearing to be more egalitarian, as each member of the full cabinet officially participates in the main decision-making body of the government. In 1993 Chrétien also established a new system of financial management—the Expenditure Management System—intended to enhance the economy and efficiency of government operations while also providing departments themselves with much greater operational autonomy for developing and implementing policies and programs of their own. In assessing all these changes to "streamline" the cabinet decision-making system, Aucoin (1999: 126) stressed that the prime minister "expects his cabinet ministers to manage their portfolio responsibilities using their own individual statutory authority; they are to refrain from bringing issues to cabinet for collective decisions that they themselves can resolve."

This relative emphasis on departmental autonomy should not be mistaken for a return to a departmentalized system of decision-making benefitting strong ministers at the expense of power centralized in the prime minister and his key advisors. Far from it. As Savoie (1999: 1-8) demonstrated in his incisive study of contemporary power relations in Ottawa, the Chrétien government witnessed a centralization of authority with respect to strategic priority-setting and policy-making to such a degree that one can speak of "court government"—decision-making on key strategic matters being effectively monopolized by the prime minister, a few select ministers, and a coterie of senior advisors.

Savoie was quick to point out that this centralization of power in the position of the prime minister had been evolving throughout the Trudeau and Mulroney years, with Chrétien merely accentuating a long-developing trend. However, this tendency towards a concentration of power "at the centre" was aided and abetted over the 1990s by the politics of deficit reduction. While prime ministers and ministers of finance have always been the two most powerful figures within any government, the perceived deficit and debt crisis that the Chrétien government inherited in 1993 was one that enabled the prime minister and his minister of finance, Paul Martin, to assume both strategic and operational control over the vast apparatus of the federal government. As deficit reduction policy and government down-sizing came to be the key strategic concerns of the Chrétien government during its first two terms, this policy direction had the necessary side-effect of giving these two effective control of all government budgetary policy; this development, in turn, short-circuited the routine process of departmental policy and program decision-making and department-agency competition. In a government environment in which most new departmental initiatives came to focus on budgetary cutbacks and related program service reduc-tions, the scope of departmental activity was significantly delimited and channelled by those in command of the new budgetary process—namely, the Department of Finance, the minister of finance, and the prime minis-ter. The end result was one of power and authority gravitating to the stellar member of the system in Ottawa, with the departmental "planets" relegated to distinctly secondary positions, a dynamic we have already observed in the working of the institutionalized system of decision-making.

Savoie's research showed how the slowly evolving division of labour between routine administrative/policy program matters and strategic pol-icy and program management and development was well maintained by the Chrétien government. The former routine matters were left to the line departments, their ministers, and staff, with any new initiatives requiring cabinet approval handled, formally, in the traditional manner of Memoranda to Cabinet, relevant cabinet committee review, central agency analysis, and eventually full cabinet approval or rejection. This process of cabinet deci-sion-making, of course, was also one informally marked by the bureaucratic politics and department-agency competition and in-fighting commonly associated with the institutionalized system. The latter strategic matters, however, those policy and program matters viewed by the prime minister and his senior advisors to be of vital national importance, were adopted by these forces of "the centre" as their prerogative and are managed in any way they deem appropriate. In addressing the role of the prime minister in Chrétien's system of power politics, Savoie (1999: 57) wrote that,

> There is one individual, however, who can at any time upset the collective versus individual responsibilities and, with no

advance notice, take an issue that would properly belong to a minister and her department and bring it to the centre. The Prime Minister can intervene in any issue—big or small—if he feels that his judgment is required.... The important point here ... is that the Prime Minister can intervene in a departmental matter when and where he pleases.

In making such decisions, any prime minister will be motivated by a number of strategic considerations leading him or her to believe that the policy or program matter in question is of such importance as to require centralized oversight. Once this decision is made, however, and the matter falls within the orbit of the prime minister, he or she will virtually always get his way with respect to the matter.

Savoie's opinion by the late 1990s was that a number of troubling dynamics were coming to characterize the working of the federal government. One was the relative decline of cabinet as an effective strategic decision-making body. He stressed that whereas cabinet had been a decision-making body under Pearson and like a university seminar under Trudeau, it had degenerated under Mulroney and Chrétien into a mere prime ministerial focus group (Savoie, 1999: 3). While this somewhat cynical attitude fails to recognize the important business cabinet takes care of in matters of routine administration and policy, Savoie was undoubtedly correct about the growing importance of strategic prime ministership. In the most significant policy and program issues confronting his government, Chrétien repeatedly demonstrated that he was *le boss*, in firm control of priority determination and government direction, and that he would brook little dissent from his desired courses of action.

The practical extent of prime ministerial control over core government decision-making will be canvassed in greater detail with respect to financial management and budgetary politics, but it is fair to say that we have witnessed a concentration of power at "the centre" of government unlike anything we have seen hitherto in a centralization of authority unprecedented among most western democracies. Savoie (1999: 362) could find few factors that mitigate the prime ministerial strength.

4.6 The Martin Government: Command Mode II

When he became prime minister in December 2003, Paul Martin built upon the cabinet system he inherited from Jean Chrétien while seeking to distinguish his form of leadership from that of his predecessor. Martin

BOX 4.10
Martin Cabinet System, 2005

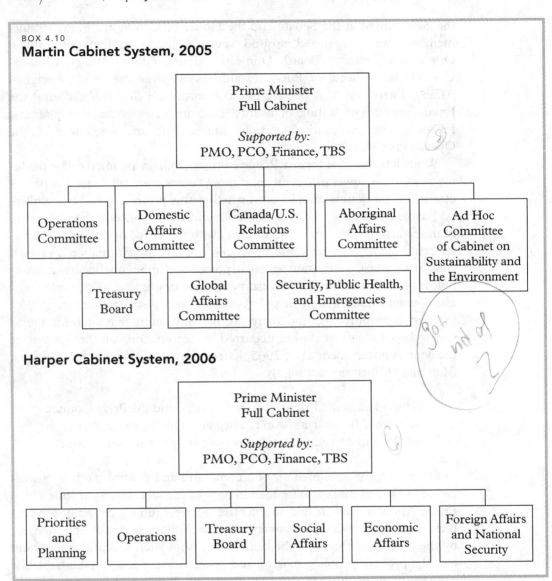

Harper Cabinet System, 2006

came to the prime ministership promising greater democratization in the functioning of government, greater participation in policy-making by MPs, and greater transparency in the working of the executive. Whether his government will be capable of achieving these goals remains a subject of great political speculation. As of 2005 the Martin cabinet consisted of 37 members—28 full ministers, seven ministers of state, and the leaders of the government in the Senate and the House of Commons. These cabinet members were organized around seven standing cabinet committees: Operations, Treasury Board, Domestic Affairs, Global Affairs, Canada-U.S. Relations, Security, Public Health and Emergencies, and Aboriginal Affairs. There was also one ad hoc committee on Sustainability and the Environment. The setting of overall government priorities and planning remained the prerogative of full cabinet, with the assistance of the Operations committee.

While it is true that former Prime Minister Martin assumed office pledging to exercise power differently and more "democratically" than his predecessor, strong doubts existed as to whether this promise could be fulfilled. As Savoie has argued, there has been an enormous concentration of power in the hands of "the centre" in Ottawa, with the office of the prime minister being the key recipient and beneficiary of this transformation. For Paul Martin to consciously transfer such power and influence to other stakeholders—cabinet ministers, government MPs, opposition MPs, senior officials—would mark a shift in policy-making and power politics in Ottawa of seismic proportions. And there are no indications that such an alteration in how Ottawa works has occurred. In commenting on the working of the Martin government as of 2005, Jeffrey Simpson wrote in the *Globe and Mail* that "[d]ecisions are highly

> centralized in the Prime Minister's Office and the Privy Council because Mr. Martin won't delegate. The Prime Minister is involved in everything, including minutiae" (Simpson, 2005).

Of course, the continuation of a command and control mode of governance in Ottawa must also be seen in light of the fact that, as of June 2004, Prime Minister Martin had to exercise power within a minority government situation in which his government could be defeated at any moment by the combined forces of the opposition. With such precariousness built into the process of policy-making and governance, it is understandable for a prime minister to want to be in control of all facets of key policy-making and program development. This is simply in keeping with the logic of the strategic prime ministership long found in Ottawa, even if this means a move away from a promise of more participatory government. But what of the longer term?

As we move out of the era of budgetary restraint, one of the important questions to be addressed concerning the evolution of the cabinet decision-making system is whether the advent of budget surpluses will alter and restrict this concentration of power "at the centre." As the government's coffers fill and it is seen by all participants in the policy-making process as having greater fiscal capacity to exert its influence in the country, this may weaken the relative ability of the prime minister and minister of finance to exert overwhelming control in the life of the government. As the government develops the capacity to do more with respect to social, economic, cultural, environmental, and foreign and defence policy, responsible ministers for these policy matters and their departments may come to be stronger players in the process of policy-making and program implementation. We may then witness a return to a more familiar balance of interests between the forces of the centre and departments, thereby enhancing the relative position of cabinet as a decision-making body. But all this remains, at the moment, speculation. Savoie's analysis of power relations in contemporary Ottawa remains sobering, and there is no evidence that any relative enhancement of routine ministerial and departmental authority can begin to impact the strategic powers of the prime minister in his role as *le boss*.

4.7   The Harper Government

In January 2006, the Conservatives, under the leadership of Stephen Harper, defeated the Paul Martin Liberals, winning a minority government. Harper came to power promising a leaner administration committed to promoting greater accountability and ethics in government while also devoted to securing tax relief for individuals and corporations and enhancing health care choices.

The cabinet established by Prime Minister Harper was noticeably smaller, numbering only 27 ministers compared to 39 in the previous Liberal government. At the time of writing, this Conservative government is just at the start of its life, and Harper will face a number of challenges: Will he devolve power and influence to Parliament as a means of addressing the "democratic deficit" or will he maintain centralized power in his PMO? Will he govern from the centre of the Canadian political spectrum or will he seek to move the policy agenda of the country to the right? Will he devolve greater fiscal capacity and policy influence to the provinces or will he work to maintain a strong central government? And how successful will he be in setting a policy direction for the country while managing a precarious minority government? Having attained the summit of Canadian politics and government, this prime minister faces the acid test of leading a very complex country.

Key Terms

assistant deputy minister (ADM): One of the most senior executive officials responsible for providing administrative leadership for a department. Assistant deputy ministers are ranked below associate deputy ministers, with the assistants usually responsible for a particular functional portfolio within the department, e.g., ADM Finance, ADM Human Resources.

associate deputy minister: One of the most senior executive officials responsible for providing administrative leadership for a department. Associate deputy ministers rank immediately below the deputy minister to whom they are responsible for providing system-wide support and assistance.

cabinet committees: The functional groupings into which a prime minister will divide his/her cabinet ministers so as to assist in the conduct and development of policy and program decision-making. As of 2006 the Paul Martin cabinet included seven full cabinet committees: Operations, Treasury Board, Domestic Affairs, Global Affairs, Canada-U.S. Relations, Security and Intelligence, and Aboriginal Affairs.

central agencies: In an institutionalized cabinet system the prime minister and cabinet will be assisted by a number of specialized support agencies designed to provide expert policy advice and program assistance to the cabinet. The key central agencies of the Canadian government are the Prime Minister's Office, the Privy Council Office, the Department of Finance, and the Treasury Board Secretariat.

Clerk of the Privy Council: The highest ranking public servant in the federal public service. The clerk is also Secretary to Cabinet and, as such, acts as the deputy minister to the prime minister. The clerk is also the official head of the Public Service of Canada. The clerk's position and role is non-partisan, whose function is to provide expert advice to the prime minister and cabinet with respect to the operational dynamics of policy-making and program implementation within the federal public service. The clerk also supervises departmental deputy ministers and will advise the prime minister on matters respecting deputy minister promotions, transfers, and removals.

command mode: A term used to describe the ever increasing centralization of decision-making power and authority in the hands of the prime minister and his/her key advisors with respect to policy and program matters. The command mode is related to the strategic prime ministership.

Department of Finance: One of the key support departments in the federal government and also a central agency of great power and authority. The Department of Finance is responsible for setting the annual federal budget as well as providing the prime minister and cabinet with advice on macro-economic policy, trade, and taxation matters.

departmentalized cabinet system: A system of cabinet organization dominant in Ottawa prior to the 1960s. The departmentalized cabinet system was noted for its lack of central agencies and cabinet committees. Policy-making in this system was largely decentralized to each department, working under the leadership of the minister and prime minister. Deputy ministers possessed great relative power in this system.

deputy minister: The administrative head of a department. Deputy ministers are appointed by the prime minister and serve as the most senior public servant in charge of a department. The deputy's role is to be the chief executive officer of the department, responsible for the routine administrative working of the department while also working with the responsible minister on policy and program development.

institutionalized cabinet system: The system of cabinet organization prevalent in Ottawa from the 1960s on. Institutionalized cabinet systems are noted for the presence of often intricate systems of cabinet committees supported by an array of central agencies. Institutionalized cabinet systems are designed to provide for more rational and systematic policy-making by requiring such policy-making to arise from a decision-making system that requires much greater planning, prioritization, and programming based upon consensus gathering from a plurality of cabinet committees and central agencies. Such a system is designed to heighten the influence of elected ministers in decision-making by lessening the political/administrative influence of any one senior unelected official.

mandarins: The term frequently given to deputy ministers in the departmentalized cabinet system in reference to their seemingly omnipresent power and authority in the actual running of government.

Memorandum to Cabinet: The formal document containing a policy proposal arising from a department and that requires discussion and ratification by cabinet in order to become government policy. A Memorandum will contain three elements: the policy Recommendation, the Analysis of the proposed policy, and a Communications Plan for the policy.

Priorities and Planning Committee (P&P): The key cabinet committee in the Trudeau and Mulroney era institutionalized cabinets. P&P was the overarching cabinet committee, chaired by the prime minister, with the mandate of coordinating all other cabinet committees and setting the strategic policy direction of the government. P&P was disbanded by Chrétien in 1993, with its strategic policy-making role reverting to full cabinet under the leadership of the prime minister. As of 2005 Paul Martin had maintained this Chrétien innovation.

Prime Minister's Office (PMO): A central agency providing direct policy-making and operational/administrative/communications support to the prime minister. The PMO is a wholly partisan body with its employees directly chosen by the prime minister. The senior officials of the PMO, all un-elected advisors to the prime minister, rank among the most influential persons in the government.

Privy Council Office (PCO): A central agency providing direct policy-making and operational/administrative support to the prime minister, the cabinet, and its committees. The PCO is a non-partisan institution of government, staffed by public servants, with a function to serve as a key policy and program transmission link between the political executive and the administrative organs of the federal government. The head of the PCO is the Clerk of the Privy Council

Office and the Secretary to Cabinet. The clerk is the official head of the federal public service.

strategic prime ministership: The term given to the policy dynamic of a prime minister setting the strategic direction of a government by selecting four to six key policy and program aims as being the most important matters of policy-making and program implementation that will define his/her four- to five-year term in office. These matters will be "brought to the centre" for prime ministerial leadership and direction, while all other more routine matters of policy and administration will be left to ordinary ministers and departments for routine management.

Treasury Board Secretariat (TBS): A central agency providing policy and program advice to the prime minister, cabinet, and all government departments and agencies with respect to internal matters of financial management, human resources management, and accountability. The Treasury Board also acts as the official employer of the federal government with respect to collective bargaining, and the TBS is responsible for providing administrative support for this function.

References and Suggested Reading

Adie, Robert F., and Paul G. Thomas. 1987. *Canadian Public Administration: Problematical Perspectives*. 2nd ed. Scarborough, ON: Prentice-Hall Canada.

Anderson, G. 1996. "The New Focus on the Policy Capacity of the Federal Government." *Canadian Public Administration* 39: 469-88.

Archer, Keith, Roger Gibbins, Rainer Knopff, and Leslie A. Pal. 1999. *Parameters of Power: Canada's Political Institutions*. 2nd ed. Toronto: Nelson.

Aucoin, Peter. 1986. "Organizational Change in the Machinery of Canadian Government: From Rational Management to Brokerage Politics." *Canadian Journal of Political Science* 19 (March): 3-27.

—. 1995. "The Prime Minister and Cabinet." In Robert M. Krause and R.H. Wagenberg, eds., *Introductory Readings in Canadian Government and Politics*. 2nd ed. Toronto: Copp Clark. 169-92.

—. 1999. "Prime Minister and Cabinet: Power at the Apex." In James Bickerton and Alain-G. Gagnon, eds., *Canadian Politics*. 3rd ed. Peterborough, ON: Broadview Press. 109-28.

Axworthy, Tom. 1988. "Of Secretaries to Princes." *Canadian Public Administration* 31: 247-64.

Bakvis, Herman, and David MacDonald. 1993. "The Canadian Cabinet: Organization, Decision-Making Rules, and Policy Impact." In Michael M. Atkinson, ed., *Governing Canada: Institutions and Public Policy*. Toronto: Harcourt Brace Jovanovich Canada. 47-80.

Bourgault, Jacques. 2002. "The Role of Deputy Ministers in Canadian Government." In Christopher Dunn, ed., *The Handbook of Canadian Public Administration*. Toronto: Oxford University Press. 430-49.

Brooks, Stephen. 1993. *Public Policy in Canada: An Introduction*. 2nd ed. Toronto: McClelland and Stewart.

Campbell, Colin. 1983. *Governments Under Stress: Political Executives and Key Bureaucrats in Washington, London and Ottawa.* Toronto: University of Toronto Press.

Campbell, Colin, and George Szablowski. 1979. *The Superbureaucrats: Structure and Behaviour in Central Agencies.* Toronto: Macmillan.

Clark, Ian D. 1985. "Recent Changes in the Cabinet Decision-Making System in Ottawa." *Canadian Public Administration* 28: 185-201.

—. 1987. "Recent Changes in the Cabinet Decision-Making System," PCO Mimeo (1986). In Richard J. Van Loon and Michael S. Whittington, eds., *The Canadian Political System: Environment, Structure and Process.* 4th ed. Toronto: McGraw-Hill Ryerson. 474.

Delacourt, Susan. 2003. *Juggernaut: Paul Martin's Campaign for Chrétien's Crown.* Toronto: McClelland and Stewart.

Doern, G. Bruce, and Richard W. Phidd. 1992. *Canadian Public Policy.* 2nd ed. Toronto: Methuen.

Dunn, Christopher. 2002. "The Central Executive in Canadian Government: Searching for the Holy Grail." In Christopher Dunn, ed., *The Handbook of Canadian Public Administration.* Toronto: Oxford University Press. 305-40.

Dupré, J.S. 1987. "The Workability of Executive Federalism in Canada." In H. Bakvis and W. Chandler, eds., *Federalism and the Role of the State.* Toronto: University of Toronto Press.

Dyck, Rand. 1996a. *Canadian Politics: Critical Approaches.* 2nd. ed. Toronto: Nelson.

—. 1996b. *Provincial Politics in Canada: Towards the Turn of the Century.* 3rd ed. Scarborough, ON: Prentice-Hall.

French, Richard. 1984. *How Ottawa Decides: Planning and Industrial Policy Making, 1968-1984.* 2nd ed. Toronto: James Lorimer.

Gray, John. 2003. *Paul Martin: The Power of Ambition.* Toronto: Key Porter Books.

Hartle, D.G. 1976. *A Theory of the Expenditure Budgetary Process.* Toronto: University of Toronto Press.

Inwood, Gregory J. 2004. *Understanding Canadian Public Administration: An Introduction to Theory and Practice.* 2nd ed. Scarborough, ON: Prentice-Hall Allyn and Bacon Canada.

Jackson, Robert J., and Doreen Jackson. 1998. *Politics in Canada: Culture, Institutions, Behaviour and Public Policy.* 4th ed. Scarborough, ON: Prentice-Hall.

Kernaghan, Kenneth, and David Siegel. 1999. *Public Administration in Canada: A Text.* 4th ed. Toronto: Nelson.

Monahan, Patrick. 1997. *Constitutional Law.* Toronto: Irwin Law.

Savoie, Donald J. 1990. *The Politics of Public Spending in Canada.* Toronto: University of Toronto Press.

—. 1999. *Governing from the Centre: The Concentration of Power in Canadian Politics.* Toronto: University of Toronto Press.

—. 2003. *Breaking the Bargain: Public Servants, Ministers, and Parliament.* Toronto: University of Toronto Press.

Simpson, Jeffrey. 2005. "What's Happened to Paul Martin?" *The Globe and Mail,* 11 February 2005: A13.

Thomas, Paul G. 1999. "The Role of Central Agencies: Making a Mesh of Things." In James Bickerton and Alain-G. Gagnon, eds., *Canadian Politics.* 2nd ed. Peterborough, ON: Broadview Press. 129-48.

Van Loon, Richard J., and Michael S. Whittington. 1987. *The Canadian Political System: Environment, Structure and Process.* 4th ed. Toronto: McGraw-Hill Ryerson.

Whitaker, Reginald A. 1995. "Politicians and Bureaucrats in the Policy Process." In Michael S. Whittington and Glen Williams, eds., *Canadian Politics in the 1990s.* 4th ed. Toronto: Nelson. 424-40.

Whittington, Michael S. 2000. "The Prime Minister, Cabinet, and the Executive Power in Canada." In Michael S. Whittington and Glen Williams, eds., *Canadian Politics in the 21st Century.* Toronto: Nelson. 31-54.

Related Web Sites

GENERAL CANADIAN GOVERNMENT
<http://www.canada.gc.ca>

PRIME MINISTER'S OFFICE
<http://www.pm.gc.ca>

PRIVY COUNCIL OFFICE
<http://www.pco-bcp.gc.ca>

TREASURY BOARD SECRETARIAT
<http://www.tbs-sct.gc.ca>

DEPARTMENT OF FINANCE
<http://www.fin.gc.ca>

CHAPTER 5
Theory of Organizational Design and Management Decision-Making

Thus far we have examined a number of concepts related to the nature and working of government in this society. We have assessed the breadth and depth of the state presence, its omnipresent impact on most facets of socio-economic and cultural life in Canada, and the major ideological views on the ideal role of government in the state. We have explored the structure of the federal government, the roles of the main political and bureaucratic managers within the government, and the complex power relations that exist between them. We have seen that the policy fields in which governments operate are many, substantial, and important to the lives of Canadians, whether or not they are aware of it. We have a general idea of the contributions of a succession of governments to the development of the modern Canadian state, and we are aware that most Canadians have supported the basic values, as well as the practical public policy concepts, underlying this evolution. We have also seen that a large and complex governmental apparatus has developed over the latter half of the last century to implement the policies associated with this state, and that this bureaucracy is an essential feature of the government, providing the political executive with the institutional means of developing and transforming policy ideas into program achievements.

No government can exist without bureaucracy, and, equally, no bureaucracy can function without management. Governments that set expansive public policy objectives for themselves require the services of large numbers of educated, trained, and directed public servants, organized into a multiplicity of public institutions, whose duty is to execute the will of elected ministers, to serve and advance their policy and program objectives, and, in the largest sense, to promote the interests of society. To meet the obligations of such a vast undertaking demands effective organization and utilization of human potential, material resources, and legal expertise and the channelling of these resources so as to best meet the needs and goals of the government.

This chapter, and the five that follow, will concentrate on the management function in government, with particular focus on the history, evolution, and current dynamics of management within the federal government. They will address such matters as

- the history and evolution of both financial and personnel management within the federal government;
- how the federal government and other provincial governments have dealt with the problems of deficit elimination and debt control;
- how the federal government has addressed concerns for the development of a representative, responsive, and equitable public service; and
- how governments and public services have sought to develop policies and programs designed to promote the ethical behaviour of all those working within the public sector.

As an introduction to these topics, this chapter will be devoted to a theoretical review of management—its meaning and the schools of thought concerned with organizational design and managerial decision-making, especially in relation to the public sector.

We will assess the important functions of management and the two broad conceptual models that dominate thought about organizational structure, the role of management, and the ideal flow of bureaucratic influence and power. We will also look at theories of decision-making and the major techniques associated with such action and assess the motivations of the actors involved.

One of our themes is the significant difference between the values and operational dynamics of the public sector compared to the private sector. This distinction must always be kept in mind when thinking about public sector management—that the public sector is a more demanding environment for management than is the private sector. Such a proposition, of course, is counterintuitive to people brought up with a rather cynical view of the work of governments, so we will explore the complexities of management within the public sector. Another theme is the tension between **structural-mechanistic** and **organic-humanistic** approaches to management, with each school of thought having great influence on how we think about public administration and the working of governments. The structural-mechanistic approach that had dominated the field has, in the past half-century, waned in the face of pressure from the organic-humanistic approach. The strengths of this latter way of looking at management will be recorded and assessed, but so too will its weaknesses, with the result that we will see that the structural-mechanistic approach remains very useful in helping us to understand the inner workings of management. Finally, we examine the tension between rationalist and incrementalist forms of management. These and other forms of managerial decision-making will be reviewed and analyzed to highlight the many perceived problems with incremental decision-making and the long-standing managerial drive to promote rationalism in all decision-making. Yet, at the same time, we will note the many problems with rationalism and the equally long-standing pervasiveness of incrementalism as an important and viable means of conducting management.

The aim is to provide an overview of a quite complex field of management theory. Many of the theoretical concepts addressed here, however, will be encountered again in subsequent chapters as we turn from theory to practice and as we continue to review the actual process of management within government.

5.1   The Functions of Management

What does management do? Many analysts have used this question as a starting point for studies in organization theory and practice, and, regardless of whether one is looking at public sector or private sector organizations, certain management functions are common to any bureaucracy. In his studies of French management in the early twentieth century, Henri Fayol (1971) documented five functions common to managers in all organizations: planning, organizing, commanding, coordinating, and controlling. This list was later elaborated and expanded by the American organizational theorist Luther Gulick (1937). Management within the American federal government, according to Gulick, was constituted under seven headings: Planning, Organizing, Staffing, Directing, Coordinating, Reporting, and

Budgeting (**POSDCORB**). These activities not only constituted management within the government, but delineated administrative responsibilities essential to the success of any bureaucratic organization. As Robert B. Denhardt (1999: 286) has stressed, the elements of the acronym provide a checklist to managers "about what they should be doing."

1. *Planning*
   - involves both the assessment of an organization's present condition, goals, and directions—its current strengths, weaknesses, opportunities, and threats (modern SWOT analysis)—and its future aims and ends.
   - is that vital management undertaking of "knowing where you are" and "where you want to get to" and how to effectively move from the former to the latter state. An organization that neglects planning will tend to flounder in the present, devoting too much attention to the routine administration of current policies and programs and not enough consideration to overall objectives, the capacity of current undertakings to achieve general organizational goals, and the development of ways and means to improve the organization's ability to better realize such goals in the future.
   - includes understanding the organization's *raison d'être*, its current effectiveness in achieving organizational goals, and developing awareness of its operational environment.
   - enables the organization to respond to changes in its environment, to address weaknesses in its current operational behaviour, and to develop new and better policies and programs that will also promote the interests of the organization into the future.

2. *Organizing*
   - refers to a collection of managerial activities related to the structuring of the bureaucratic entity.
   - begins with the establishment of a particular organizational design and the defining of roles and responsibilities to be followed by management and staff.
   - involves such matters as deciding on the nature of an organization's hierarchy—whether it is steep or shallow, centralized or decentralized; whether the flow of information, authority, and influence within

BOX 5.1
Gulick's Functions of Management

Planning
Organizing
Staffing
Directing
Coordinating
Reporting
Budgeting

the organization is more "top-down" or "bottom-up," or some form of differential balancing of the two; and whether the general power relations within the organization between management and staff, and even among management itself, are more authoritarian or egalitarian.

- involves thinking about the fundamental goals and responsibilities of an organization and creating the bureaucratic structure to fulfill and meet those goals and responsibilities in the most economical, efficient, and effective manner possible.
- is intimately related to personnel management: the responsibility for organization depends not only on the operational "architecture" of an organization, but also on the design of jobs and the duties and reporting relationships that management and staff will assume within the functioning organizational entity.

3. *Staffing*
- is Gulick's term for the vital management tasks related to personnel within an organization.
- is the "acquiring, training and developing of personnel to conduct the organization's activities" (Denhardt, 1999: 286).
- deals with such matters as the hiring and promotion of management and staff as well as the unpleasant realities of the disciplining and, if need be, their demotion and firing.
- deals with the complexities of assessing and managing human beings and the management of human wants and needs, likes and dislikes, feelings, attitudes, and expectations, with all the potential for interpersonal disagreement and conflict that human interaction implies.
- entails effective personnel management with organizational communication, employee motivation, the resolution of interpersonal conflict, and the promotion of sound managerial-workforce interaction (see Chapters 8 and 9).

4. *Directing*
- is one of the natural outcomes of managerial-workforce interaction. Management must direct staff towards the realization of organizational ends, but they must also do more. They must direct the use of all other resources—material, financial, and legal—towards the achievement of institutional goals.
- "is often the most dynamic and most visible management function. It includes the three critical management activities: leading, motivating and changing things when necessary" (Denhardt, 1999: 286).

- engages the pivotal managerial function of decision-making. Management is called upon to make decisions all the time; to determine how the current operations of the organization relate to its overall objectives; and to decide how to utilize organizational resources so as to promote and achieve these organizational goals, economically, efficiently, and effectively.
- is a vital component of good leadership and, as we shall see, effective leadership proves to be the most important of all managerial undertakings (Chapter 12).

5. *Coordinating*
- recognizes the bureaucratic complexity of most organizations and the need for management to ensure that people's interests, responsibilities, and needs and the organization's other resources and functions all are recognized, understood, and integrated towards the development and implementation of the organization's objectives—which in government means policies and programs.
- refers to "bringing things together," or "making a mesh of things," in Paul Thomas's phrase (Thomas, 1999), to ensure that the necessary actors and resources interrelate in a timely and productive manner, thereby facilitating the realization of organizational ends.

6. *Reporting*
- addresses the managerial requirement of dealing with information and communicating information throughout the organization and beyond. As institutions deal with a complex operational environment, they gain knowledge and intelligence about that environment, and such information is crucially important in helping it to understand its current operational strengths, weaknesses, opportunities, and threats and its future needs, goals, and options.
- is a primary responsibility of management, since sound information management is critical to effective management.
- to be effective, takes information, turns it into organizational intelligence, and then disseminates this to all who need to be aware of it.
- can flow internally and downward to subordinate managers and staff; can flow upward to superordinate managers and political leaders; or can flow externally and laterally to other organizations and parties outside of the bureaucracy but interested in the work of the organization. Regardless of the direction and ultimate receiver, reporting and information management is an essential aspect of management.

7. *Budgeting*

- refers to the managing of money.
- is crucial because all organizations run on money. The "securing, planning for, and managing of organizational funds" is one of the most important elements of management, and, as we shall observe in Chapter 7, financial management considerations, especially in relation to deficit and debt control, can rise to overwhelm all other organizational interests.
- effectively is always important to the well-being of any organization and, therefore, is always part of the routine operational procedures of the organization, requiring significant attention to the raising, handling, and distribution of money within and beyond the organization.
- may become the overarching issue of organizational significance, dominating even the leadership work of management.

Gulick's list of management functions quickly became a classic within the field of organizational theory, with POSDCORB the thumbnail explication of management roles and responsibilities. While this list is instructive, it is not definitive, and numerous other organizational theorists have reformulated and elaborated it, using Gulick's technique of managerial taxonomy to search for more precise understandings of management functions. Garry Yukl (1998: ch. 2) highlights a number of these reinterpretations of Gulick in his work on organizational leadership, devoting special attention to the analysis of Henry Mintzberg. Mintzberg's review of management roles (1973: 92-93) identifies ten concepts that echo Gulick's findings, but he also emphasizes the importance of leadership and crisis management. In this taxonomy, Mintzberg divides management functions into three fields:

1. Information-processing roles: monitoring information, disseminating information, and acting as a spokesperson for the organization.

2. Decision-making roles: involving the manager in: policy and program development and administration, resource allocation, negotiation between interested actors, and conflict resolution—what Mintzberg calls the "disturbance handler role."

3. Interpersonal roles: performing as a figurehead for the organization, liaising with other bodies in its broad operational environment, and providing leadership for the institution.

BOX 5.2
Mintzberg's Functions of Management

Information Processing Roles:
- Monitoring information
- Disseminating information
- Acting as a spokesperson for the organization

Decision-Making Roles:
- Policy and program development and administration
- Resources allocation
- Negotiation between interested actors
- Handling disturbances

Interpersonal Roles:
- Figurehead for the organization
- Liaison officer for the organization and other bodies
- Leader within the organization

Mintzberg sees the leadership role as pervading all others. Leadership is the management role that unites all the others in a coherent direction to integrate, coordinate, and focus all management responsibilities and actions towards the realization of basic organizational goals. It is the single most important managerial function within an organization because it rises or falls, progresses or regresses, achieves or fails its desired ends contingent upon the quality of managerial leadership it possesses.

Among the leadership qualities Mintzberg highlights is skill in the handling of crises, the "disturbance handler role" (Yukl, 1998: 25). Managers are called on to deal with unforeseen problems posing a threat to the effectiveness of the organization in pursuing its given tasks. All organizations face such problems sooner or later, and the ability of the manager to resolve crises and address difficulties calmly and expeditiously while preserving and promoting the long-term operational goals of the organization is of paramount significance. Mintzberg suggests, furthermore, that crises should be seen as learning opportunities; presenting management with a difficult environment, they provide an opportunity to review and rethink operational behaviour, to reconsider and redesign the organizational means by which they seek to achieve desired ends, and even to re-evaluate and renew the very ends of the organization itself. All organizations, if they are to be successful over the long term, need constantly to adapt to the operational environment as it changes and evolves. Successful adaptation requires the manager to seize opportunities for creative action to resolve difficulties while maintaining the best of the organization's operational and managerial heritage.

5.2 The Special Environment of Public Sector Management

The roles of management are many, complex, and important. Organizations of any considerable size become intricate, comprising a wide variety of human, material, and intellectual components, often with a multiplicity of internal interests and power dynamics that may not always be directed to the same organizational goals. A fundamental objective of management is to define, organize, coordinate, and direct an organization towards the realization of established organizational ends. Though this proves an involved task in any institution, consider the heightened complexity of management within the public sector (Inwood, 2004: 9-14).

Managers within the public sector confront a policy and program environment of byzantine complexity. It is an environment in which organizations routinely possess multiple goals, which are as often attached to sweeping concepts of socio-economic, cultural, and political well-being as they are to more circumscribed concepts of economical and efficient administration. These organizations have convoluted reporting relationships with a multiplicity of "superiors," not all of whom will agree even about the fundamental policy purpose of the organization. Managers themselves serve a range of interests and responsibilities that may at times compete, because the environment demands not only administrative skills but is so highly politicized that political manoeuvring is omnipresent. In fact, the evaluation of achievement or failure is as likely to be stated in political terms as in terms of administrative goals. In contrast to what many in the private sector believe, the public sector environment is much more complex than that usually found in the private sector. That great managerial challenges are found within the public sector is readily discerned through a comparison of the operational environments of the two sectors.

Notwithstanding the difficulties of effectively fulfilling basic management functions in any organizational environment, management within the private sector is always necessarily geared to the demands of profitability. All activities of the staff and management of a private organization are directed towards making a profitable return on investment. This focus on the "bottom line" comes to be the ultimate test of the private organization's worthiness: Is it making money? And this becomes the guiding vision of private sector management—to pursue the functions of management to realize this fundamental business goal. This goal, in turn, is easily verifiable through a review of an organization's budget, balance sheets, and financial statements. Acceptable profit margins indicate overall organizational, and hence managerial, success, while losses are a clear indication of managerial failure leading to organizational decline. The "profit margin" thus constitutes an "acid test" of private sector managerial capability. Those organizations that can pass this test will continue to exist and prosper, with their management relatively secure in their positions and actions; those that fail, however, will witness the demise of their existing management, as owners and boards of directors seek managers capable of achieving profitable organizational performance; if business success remains elusive, such failing organizations will sooner or later die.

Contrast this to the operational environment of public sector management. While concerns for economy and efficiency have increasingly become significant considerations for government, government organizations (with the exception of most Crown corporations) simply do not possess the same "bottom line" as private corporations. The primary purpose of most government organizations is not to realize a profit but to provide a public service. They are not engaged in commercial activities involving the production and sale of a product but in the provision of goods and services designed to meet public needs and interests as defined by an elected government that is accountable through Parliament or a provincial legislature to the public. One role of public sector organizations is to assist in the development of policies and programs designed to provide operational form to the plans and vision of a prime minister or premier and cabinet. An equally important purpose, however, is to serve the long-term interests of the general public through the fair, competent, and professional implementation and administration of all pre-existing and new government policies and programs. Public sector organizations serve not only the interests of the government in power but the interests of the public in its need for sound and accountable public services.

In fulfilling these roles, profitability is rarely if ever a factor, nor would most Canadians want commercial considerations to come into play with the provision of most public services. For example, the administration of justice, the enforcement of law, and the operation of the courts are not activities designed to be measured in terms of profitability, and the same generally holds true for the delivery of other public services ranging from health care, education, and social assistance to such matters as environmental protection, cultural promotion, and national defence. While

BOX 5.3
Key Private Sector / Public Sector Differences

	Private Sector	Public Sector
Purpose	business enterprise	provision of public services
Goals	simple/economic	complex/economic/social/political
Service targets	customers/clients	citizens
Criteria of success	profitability	effective implementation of services
Measurement of success	financial/objective	political/subjective
Accountability owed	to owners/shareholders	to elected leaders/citizens
Operational environment	marketplace/realm of business/private	government/realm of politics/public
Focus of management	one-dimensional	multi-dimensional
Skills of management	business-oriented	program/policy-oriented

most people expect policies and resulting programs to be administered efficiently, most do not presume that the state should be generating profits from these activities nor do most want public sector managers to approach their duties with such attitudes in mind. Rather, these are policy and program undertakings established with the view of providing needed services to citizens while also promoting the collective good of society. The provision of publicly administered education and health care policy, for example, has come to be perceived as a collective good, an entitlement held by all citizens and designed to enhance both individual and collective security, just as environmental and defence policies are seen as state requirements aimed at serving the well-being of the entire society. Such policies are viewed as constituting collective duties that the state owes to all the members of society rather than being conditional services that may or may not be provided to individuals on a commercial basis, with the state seeking to maximize profits through its actions. Of course, there is much current debate respecting the commercialization of health care and educational policy, which would result in the creation of two-tiered health care and education systems whereby those with greater wealth would be entitled to purchase differential and, arguably, superior forms of these sorts of services than would otherwise be provided to most citizens (see Chapter 11). The very vehemence of the debate surrounding these proposals is indicative of the degree to which most Canadians hold these policy fields to be essential public services divorced from the commercial realm.

In the absence of a clear profit-and-loss method for measuring operational success, most public sector managers undertake their work in a less straightforward environment of performance measurement, but one which has a vital managerial motive nonetheless. In the government environment the profit motive has been replaced by a motive to seek the most effective allocation of finite financial and human resources to enhance desirable results. Political and administrative value judgements about success or failure are much more prevalent than any simple accounting of money. People measure and assess not only such quantitative matters as the amount of resources deployed and the numbers of goods and services produced or delivered, but also the qualitative benefits derived from such actions. How does one determine the success of a government program? How does one assess the merit of a program providing a necessary public service where the program itself is not designed to make money? Once one breaks from the simple profitability standard of performance measurement found in the private sector, one enters a complex world of differential opinions respecting the identification of ends, the appreciation of means, and the evaluation of the degree to which particular means have successfully, efficiently, or effectively led to the attainment of particular ends.

How does one measure quality? How does one assess, for example, the merits and demerits of the administration of the Canada Health Act? Does one look at the amount of money currently spent on health care and the medical facilities, staff, and patient care that such spending supports? Or does one look at the pattern of such spending support over the past decade, comparing the responses of appropriately sampled staff and patients against the decline in funding over the mid-1990s? Does one look at the new and developing medical procedures available to Canadians and their increasing life-spans? Or does one look to the quality of life of Canadians? If so, how does one measure "quality of life"?

Evaluation of the success of a government policy also might be made from beyond the system. For example, how does Canadian medical services' coverage compare with that of the United States, Britain, or the Scandinavian countries? Where in the spectrum of systems of publicly and privately administered health care in North America do Canadian health services fall? Should we focus on the fact that, in Canada, all citizens possess a right to advanced standards of medical care regardless of ability to pay, or should the focus of attention be on lengthening waiting lists and the number of physicians leaving the country to relocate to the United States?

Each question offers a legitimate field of enquiry for assessing the merits and demerits of health care policy in this country. How any particular person or group answers these questions (or whether they attempt to answer some of them at all) will be highly contingent upon the political and ideological orientation of that person or group, their perspectives on the role of the state in society, and their understanding of what an ideal health care system should be. Moreover, how any public sector manager working within the health care system answers these questions is contingent upon the policy and program direction and leadership of senior management, the minister, the cabinet, and the prime minister. Organizational performance measurement is as much a political act as an administrative assessment; all managerial actions are assessed and evaluated in light of the policy objectives of the particular government. And the nature of program evaluation complexity highlighted here in relation to health care policy is duplicated in every other policy field where public services are provided outside of a "for profit" mode of program delivery.

None of the foregoing is to suggest, however, that program evaluation does not occur in the public sector or that any form of program evaluation will be acceptable to the public sector. This is not the case. The reality is that, rather than there being just one essential form of evaluation as in the private sector, within the public sector there can and will be various ways of measuring and assessing the work of a policy or program, with some methodologies designed to direct more attention to the quantitative policy or program delivery and others meant to emphasize qualitative assessments. As there are a variety of approaches to performance evaluation, so too there are differences in the nature and quality of such evaluations, with some more comprehensive, more detailed, more oriented to policy matters, or more concerned with program administration and implementation than others. Future chapters will devote greater attention to matters of program evaluation and the attempts by governments to improve their evaluation methodologies, but a basic fact remains. In all instances, organizational performance evaluation within the public sector continues to be, at heart, a political act, bound as much—if not more—to the subjective analyses of qualitative conditions than to the objective review of quantitative conditions.

5.2.1   Privacy and Publicity

A number of other differences between private and public sector management merit attention. Within the private sector, management takes place within a largely "private" sphere of activity. Absent any legal requirements for openness or public disclosure of decision-making, managers in the private sector operate in a largely confidential and obscure environment. Their workplaces are private property, and they can and usually do insist on their rights to conduct management functions in private, "behind closed doors." Contrast this with the public sector, where management is engaged in "public" service and is accountable to senior departmental officials, who are accountable to elected ministers, a cabinet, and the prime minister or premier, who are, in turn, accountable to a Parliament or legislature, which is accountable to the general public. This system of public service, founded on public policies and funded by public monies, naturally engages the public's interest in the work of public sector management in the administration of their rights and interests. And as this system is the outgrowth of public policies developed by an elected government and enshrined in law, public sector management is administratively and/or legally obligated to be open and accountable to a great many other public officials. The accountability relationships extend to central agencies and the auditor general in relation to financial management; the Public Service Commission, the Public Service Staff Relations Board, the Office of the Official Languages Commissioner, and the Canadian Human Rights Commission with respect to personnel policy; and the Canadian courts in regard to all matters of administrative law. Furthermore, government decision-making carried out in the public interest is subject to the freedom of information legislation that allows members of the public, usually the media, to gain access to government files and reports. The logic behind such openness and reporting relationships is that the public service is *public*, designed to provide services to the public; its actions are subject to scrutiny, commentary, and oversight by government players and central agencies, members of Parliament or legislatures and their officers, the courts, the media, and the general public. Compare this level of openness and scrutiny to the closed and secretive decision-making that is routine within the private sector.

Think, too, of the differences between **citizens** and **consumers/clients**. The private sector deals with people who are consumers or clients in a strictly commercial setting. Transactions between consumers/clients and the private organization occur when the organization provides goods or services for a particular fee. But if the would-be consumer or client cannot afford the product, then he or she has no right to it, and the private organization will refuse to engage in any form of transaction. Now, while certain Crown corporations such as Canada Post and VIA Rail do

> BOX 5.4
> ## The Special Obligations of the Public Service
>
> - To deal with people as citizens.
> - To respect the rights of citizens.
> - To treat all citizens equally.
> - To professionally implement and administer public policy.
> - To serve the political executive in developing public policy.
> - To uphold the law.
> - To serve and promote the best interests and traditions of the public service.
> - To serve and promote the public interest.

engage in commercial forms of relationship with consumers/clients, most government organizations—departments, regulatory agencies, and some Crown corporations—deal with people as citizens. As citizens, we are equal members of society bearing rights or entitlements to particular government services simply by virtue of citizenship. For example, as citizens we all

- possess rights to elementary and secondary school education and to extensive forms of state-provided medical care as provided by federal and provincial health care legislation;
- have equal rights to legal protections as enshrined in the Criminal Code and human rights acts and occupational health and safety protections found in federal and provincial product standards and labour codes;
- have entitlements and expectations to such public policies as environmental protection, social welfare provision, the security of Canada's international borders, and the maintenance of the country's national defence.

Specific groups of Canadians—children, parents, or pensioners; farm producers, fishers, or forestry workers; the unemployed, those seeking job skills retraining, or students seeking student loans—may also have entitlements to specific federal or provincial program assistance depending upon the nature of specific policies and legislation.

In all relationships between the government and its citizens, the government has a legal obligation to treat all citizens equally whether as individuals that make up the general public or as a specific group, to provide for the legitimate needs and interests of all citizens as mandated by law, and to refrain from illegally discriminating against individuals. For example, a bureaucratic decision to refuse a citizen necessary medical care, law enforcement protection, or public education because that citizen or his or her family is poor and could not otherwise afford the service, would constitute blatant discrimination and a breach of the law. In this respect, the public sector is fundamentally different from the private sector. Whereas the private sector deals solely with business transactions between sellers and buyers, the public sector deals with a much broader array of policy concerns ranging from citizens' rights, entitlements, and duties as defined by law, to the regulation, maintenance, and promotion of "Peace, Order and Good Government."

In reflecting on this complicated public sector environment, it is also necessary to consider the full range of actors and forces that public sector managers must actually serve. While their private sector counterparts also face a range of actors and forces among their customers/clients along with whatever legal obligations are borne by the enterprise, they function within a more clearly defined and circumscribed operational environment: their essential duty is to render service to their superiors, with these superiors in turn tied to a chain of command leading either to an owner or board of directors. Public sector managers, in contrast, confront a multifaceted environment containing a number of differing "superiors." They have formal reporting and accountability relationships with their immediate departmental or agency superiors, and these officials report up the chain of command to a deputy minister. From this perspective, public sector managers not only have a duty to serve their organization and its senior management through the effective development, implementation, and administration of organizational policies and programs, but informally they serve a number of other interests. All managers possess a general duty to serve the organizational interests of their minister, with this relationship becoming more intricate and sophisticated the higher up the organizational pyramid one moves. Senior departmental managers are often closely involved with ministers in the formulation of policy and the resolution of program implementation difficulties, and the most senior of departmental executives—assistant deputy ministers, associate deputy ministers, and deputy ministers—interact with their ministers on a close and continuing basis. Deputy ministers themselves, as administrative heads of departments, are in daily contact with their minister, briefing him or her on policy and program developments within the department, helping the minister to deal with issues and problems emerging from the portfolio, and working with the minister on new project undertakings. Deputy ministers also work with ministers on the ways and means of defending and promoting both the department's interests and those of the minister within the broader context of the working of the bureaucracy, the operations of cabinet, the interests of the prime minister, and the necessities of dealing with Parliament and the media. From this perspective, deputy ministers are as closely involved in the political life of their minister, within the Ottawa environment, as they are in the routine operation of their department, with the general understanding being that these two facets of managerial life are reverse sides of the same bureaucratic coin.

This blending of broad political duties with the more standard administrative ones is just one of the special features of public sector management, especially at the most senior levels. Just as managers possess a duty to serve their minister, they are also called upon to report to and to serve other administrative actors within the government system. As noted earlier, senior managers do not report only to their immediate departmental or agency superiors; they are asked to report to and/or interact with central agencies, the Public Service Commission, the Public Service Staff Relations Board, the Human Rights Commission, and such officers of Parliament as the auditor general and the commissioner of official languages. Senior management may also be called upon to report directly to committees of Parliament with respect to the administrative working of departments and agencies. Deputy ministers are appointed directly by the prime minister, with their duty being not only to serve their minister but also to serve the prime minister through their management of departmental responsibilities. They thus have a dual accountability role, possessing two masters while also maintaining a close operational liaison with the Clerk of the Privy Council who is the head of the public service.

There remain three other duties held by all members of the public service:

1. *The duty to uphold the law.* All actions and powers of the public service are prescribed by law, all policy and program activities are mandated by law, and all public servants bear a duty to preserve and promote the law in all their undertakings. Public servants thus have a duty to the law, and under no circumstances are they to counsel any other—subordinate or superior—to violate the law.

2. *The duty to abide by and promote the best interests and traditions of the public service* as an institution with its own values, principles, expectations, and interests relating to the profession of public service. Members

of the public service, and especially its managerial leadership, are expected to understand and support these concepts; to embody and operationalize these values, principles, and expectations through their work; and always to undertake their duties in such a manner as to bring credit to the profession of public service.

3. *The duty to serve the public interest at the broadest and simplest levels.* As public sector management is directed towards the goal of public service, all state officials are charged to undertake their functions so as to promote the best interests of the public as defined by law and understood through the professional judgement of managers themselves. Public servants work in a different sort of relation with the general public from commercial employees in that the basic rationale for their work is to support the public interest; to recognize, affirm, and defend the legal rights of citizens; and to work in order to improve the quality of life within this society.

Far from the materialistic self-interest that lies at the heart of the private sector, at the centre of the concept of public service are noble aspirations of collective duty and assistance to others.

5.3 The Politics/Administration Dichotomy

At the highest level of public sector management, administrative and political considerations become intrinsically interrelated (Whitaker, 1995). In contrast to those organizational theorists who insist there should be a clear division, or dichotomy, between the world of politics and the world of administration, we can see already that such a demarcation between these concepts, especially at the most senior and strategically important level of managerial decision-making, is impossible. Rather than living in a simple world where political leaders—elected ministers—design policies and programs, and managers and public service staff implement and administer them, we live in a complex world where senior political and administrative leaders interact and work together in an intricately involved manner. The politicians certainly do bring political ideas, visions, and goals into the policy-making process, but administrators are far from mere administrative technicians. Rather, senior managers play important roles in the development, review, analysis, and reform of policies and programs, working closely with ministers to fashion viable government approaches to the policy and program needs of society. In this work, the demarcation between that which is purely "political" and that which is essentially "administrative" becomes hopelessly blurred, as each point of view serves the other. Hence, the elastic nature of the terms "political" and "administrative" in relation to the development and implementation of public policy.

5.4   Management Functions and Organizational Design

The functions of management are all crucially important to the success of any organization. The complexity of the public sector environment, moreover, heightens the difficulty of the management role. To appreciate the nature of management and its work, however, it is necessary to understand the organization being managed. All bureaucracies, be they public or private, are founded upon organizations, and these organizations can be designed and operated in a number of different manners. Over the past century two broad models of organizational design have emerged from both the theory and practice of bureaucratic activity, and both these models, in their own ways, have proven highly influential in the structural nature and operational working of public sector management in this country. The first model is the "structural-mechanistic" approach to organization, supporting and promoting a more hierarchical, authoritarian, centralized, top-down command and control approach to management; the second is the "organic-humanistic" approach, stressing more the importance of people over structure and promoting a more de-hierarchical, egalitarian, decentralized, top-down and bottom-up participatory approach to management in which managers and employees work together in the development of ways and means to achieve organizational goals.

5.5   The Structural-Mechanistic Model

5.5.1   Max Weber

Organizational theory had its origins in the late nineteenth and early twentieth centuries, when ways of looking at and thinking about bureaucracies were explored by such authors as Max Weber (1946), Frederick W. Taylor (1967), and Luther Gulick and Lyndall Urwick (1969). Among these classical theorists of bureaucracy it was Weber (1864-1920), a German sociologist, who contributed most to our modern understanding of the concept of bureaucracy. According to Weber, the term "**bureaucracy**," a composite of the French word for office and the Greek word for power, should be seen as a strictly neutral noun. Bureaucracy is a system of organization in which power and influence is held by officials in particular offices, with each office mandated a role or duty for achieving ends set by the rulers or overseers of the organization, with the work of all offices orchestrated by these leaders to serve the broader goals and interests of the organization in total. A bureaucracy is found in any complex organization of an appreciable size, either in the private or public sector. While the term "bureaucracy" has acquired many negative connotations, the term, as used by Weber, is descriptive, not pejorative. A properly constituted bureaucracy within any organization, Weber stressed, would express eight principles:

- a hierarchical structure,
- a unity of command,
- a specialization of labour,
- employment and promotion based on merit,
- positions based on full-time employment,
- decisions founded on impersonal rules,
- work recorded and maintained in written files, and
- a clear distinction between bureaucratic work responsibilities and the private interests of any particular employee.

These principles invite greater elaboration.

1. *Hierarchical structure.* Weber suggested the structure of any bureaucracy must be hierarchical, its components arranged in a series of "superior-subordinate relationships" based on a formal chain of command between managers and employees. Each component within the **hierarchy** has its head official, who reports directly to the head of the next most superior office, and so on up the chain of command to the very top of the organization and its most superior officer.

2. *Unity of command.* The chain of command allows speedy and effective transmission of orders and directions from top management down throughout the hierarchy and for the passing of information, reports, and advice from subordinates to superiors up from the lower echelons of the organization. The hierarchy and chain of command is designed to maintain strict control and managerial leadership over the administrative working and policy direction of the organization while also facilitating communication and accountability throughout the organization. Within the chain of command all subordinate managers know precisely what their duties are, and they receive all necessary instructions and directives from their superiors. They know exactly what they are responsible for, to whom such responsibility

is owed (their immediate superior), and the consequences of any failure to perform required duties. If this understanding of bureaucracy sounds highly militaristic, that is because it is—Weber was greatly influenced by the structure and organization of the Imperial German Army.

3. *Specialization of labour.* Within this hierarchy labour is "specialized"— broken down into particular jobs with clearly defined roles, responsibilities, and requirements. Once such work duties have been determined, particular officials, either managers or employees, are assigned to these particular jobs in accordance with their education, training, skills, experience, and capabilities. These officials then devote all their labour to their assigned tasks, becoming specialized in their roles, which leads to their work being performed in the most efficient way possible, which produces the most effective results.

4. *Employment and promotion based on merit.* Closely associated with the specialization of labour is the principle of merit. All officials, whether management or staff, are to gain and maintain their positions solely on the basis of objective professional merit. Officials are appointed to the bureaucracy on account of their education, training, skills, or experience in reference to particular bureaucratic duties. Once appointed, the maintenance of one's position and promotion to higher positions of importance within the hierarchy are contingent on demonstrated merit—the enhancement of one's education and training and the successful undertaking of one's given duties and responsibilities.

5. *Full-time employment.* The concern here is more for the institution than for the person, which is to say that officials in the bureaucracy should have no other occupational or professional obligations or factors that may affect or interfere with the performance of their bureaucratic duties. Bureaucratic officials are expected to devote all their occupational attention to their own bureaucratic jobs; their profession of service belongs to the organization as a whole.

The foregoing organizational principles were designed to create a professional bureaucracy capable of engaging in and achieving the efficient and effective administration of organizational goals. To obtain these ends, Weber added three principles of ideal bureaucracy:

6. *Decisions founded on impersonal rules.* Rather than decision-making based on personal likes and dislikes, whims, biases, or the self-interest of particular

individual officials, all bureaucratic decision-making should be founded on pre-existing rules designed by management for the furtherance of the long-term goals of the organization. By adhering to such pre-established rules of action, officials use their bureaucratic power and influence not only for their own interests but for the interests of the organization. Furthermore, such reliance on pre-existing rules is designed to promote objectivity, consistency, regularity, and uniformity in decision-making. By adhering to pre-set rules established to apply to a particular fact-situation, officials can ensure that all like-cases are treated in a like-manner, meaning that all persons having to deal with the bureaucracy are receiving the equal, fair, and objective treatment determined and desired by those senior managers who have established the rules of bureaucratic action. The fair and equal application of set rules also signals to management that their aims respecting the treatment of given cases and the application of desired policies are being consistently implemented across the breadth of the organization, so that the actions of the bureaucracy and its officials reflect the professional policy and program objectives of the senior leaders of the organization and not the arbitrary and subjective interests of particular subordinates.

7. *Work recorded and maintained in written files.* Closely related to the principle of impersonal rules is the maintenance and use of written records. Because bureaucratic decision-making is founded on pre-existing rules, such rules need to be codified, promulgated, and formally delineated in all official decisions. Codification and promulgation is required so that all officials and interested parties can know what bureaucratic rules apply to a given situation. Formal explication of all organizational actions and the rules used with regard to any given decision assists both the bureaucracy and its "clients" with rule application. By maintaining detailed written records of all decision-making, and by documenting all cases that have come before them, officials can learn more about the nature of the issue or problem being addressed and the claims for service being brought to the bureaucracy, the relevant rule or rules that such claims fall under, the applicable bureaucratic decision for the given case, and the resultant action taken by officials in dealing with the matter. Such a written record can be useful to the organization in a number of ways.

- When field-level officials document their actions, they are demonstrating how they properly and fairly have applied pre-existing rules to a given case. This produces a verification that is important to organizational accountability.

- Such records can also be used, however, to identify problems and failures with the application of rules, identifying those officials who misunderstood and/or misapplied the rules either through deliberate misconduct or errors in interpretive judgement.
- Written records provide the opportunity for review and analysis as part of the accountability function, enabling more senior management to maintain oversight of decisions made; to determine whether they are in need of correction; and to assess whether officials further down the chain of command are in need of some form of education, training, advice, supervision, or discipline.
- The written record also provides senior managers with an overview of the operational decision-making of the organization, the types and volume of cases with which it deals, and the nature of ensuing bureaucratic decision-making.
- Such records can be used by senior management in reviewing the work of the organization leading to new decision-making for staffing and job growth, greater employee training, the redesign and fine-tuning of existing rules, and the development of wholly new policies and rules to better address new situations and concerns.
- Finally, the use of written records, by any bureaucracy, is very important to all those who must interact with it. Written records explain how and why certain decisions were made as they were, or demonstrate why other alternatives were not considered or not pursued. If and when a person or group wishes to challenge a given bureaucratic decision, moreover, on the possible grounds that the decision was in violation of pre-existing rules, that the rules themselves were not fairly and properly applied, or that the rules themselves failed to properly and justly deal with a given circumstance, then the written record of bureaucratic actions taken, along with knowledge of the formal rules designed to guide such actions, is vital to the launching of a specific appeal of the decision or the initiation of a broader policy protest.

8. *A clear distinction between bureaucratic employment and the private interests of any given employee.* The power, responsibilities, and privileges associated with a bureaucracy are to be understood as residing in the bureaucratic positions themselves and not in the particular persons who may currently hold those positions. No particular official ever "owns" his or her position, and he or she cannot pass it on to whomsoever he or she likes. The position, rather, is held by the organization; the organization's leadership decides who will occupy it and undertake its associated responsibilities for a given

period of time. It follows from this definition that bureaucratic employment is a form of professional service, with all employees—management and staff—organized into a system of full-time, permanent employment that provides them with job security while also ensuring the organization that its employees are dedicated to the work of the organization and do not have obligations to other occupational "forces." In keeping with this logic, all employees should be well-remunerated for their work, with it being further understood that no employee is to use his or her office and its powers and responsibilities to secure private gain in any way. The selling of office (influence peddling), bribery, and conflicts of interest are improper behaviours that should be prohibited by managerial superiors on the grounds that they corrupt the bureaucratic professionalism, efficiency, effectiveness, and rationality of the organization.

5.5.1.1 WEBERIAN BUREAUCRACY: AN OVERVIEW

While Weber sought to elucidate what bureaucracy was, and how and why organizations were bureaucratically structured, he also stressed that bureaucracy in its ideal form of features and principles was the single best means of achieving the organizational ends of professionalism, efficiency, effectiveness, and rationality. According to Weber, these were the most important considerations of any organization regardless of its specific goals, be they commercial, philanthropic, or governmental. The ultimate role of management in any organization was to attain its goals in the best fashion possible, and "bureaucracy" was the ideal means to this end. "Experience tends to universally show," wrote Weber, "that the purely bureaucratic type of administration ... is ... capable of attaining the highest degree of efficiency and is in this sense formally the most rational known means of carrying out imperative control over human beings" (Denhardt, 1999: 291).

A number of points in the Weberian approach to bureaucracy and its impact on the evolution of organizational thought and practice, especially in relation to public sector management, merit consideration. The most obvious is how prevalent Weber's bureaucratic features and principles are in the structures of organizations. As a rule, government organizations are hierarchical (Chapter 3), with formal managerial and accountability systems based on linear chains of command. The concepts of specialization of labour and the merit principle have also become essential organizing principles of personnel management (Chapter 8). The importance of records of all decisions based on pre-existing and codified rules has also become a fundamental component of bureaucracy, especially important for the legal dimensions of rule application and dispute resolution (see the Administrative Law chapter on the Thinking Government web site).

Weberian concern for bureaucratic professionalism and the clear differentiation between bureaucratic obligations and private interests has always been a topic of concern for those interested in the well-ordered functioning of organizations; we will explore this matter further in Chapter 11 when looking at government ethics. Weber's assessment of bureaucracy identifies components of bureaucratic organization design and functioning that are as significant now as they were a century ago.

Weber's understanding of bureaucracy, however, also helps us to understand the emergence of the pejorative connotation of the term. Although his use of the term is neutral, the establishment of large bureaucracies designed to work along Weberian lines has led to organizational systems that many people find difficult to deal with and easy to criticize. Problems with bureaucracy include the following:

- Organizations of large and complex hierarchies can be difficult to comprehend and intimidating to those affected by or having to cope with bureaucratic decision-making.
- The very size of certain institutions may result in many people feeling estranged from them, with the organizations being viewed as populated by "nameless, faceless bureaucrats" whose real life is far removed from that of the people whom their decisions affect.
- Although bureaucratic decision-making may be based on the application of pre-established impersonal rules, these rules can be drafted in such a general manner that the nuances and special considerations of any one real case may be lost or ignored by decision-makers. The result is that persons who believe their "cases" are special and unique, either because they are genuinely unusual or simply because they uniquely apply to their concerns, will see their "special" case treated in a routine matter by a large bureaucratic organization that deals with all like cases in a like manner.
- The bureaucratic ideal of consistency, uniformity, and fairness can result in affected individuals feeling that bureaucracy is simply a large organization of "rule-bound" officials applying standardized yet ill-designed and rigid approaches to decision-making and problem-solving in a thoughtless and regimented manner in which the unique concerns and individual characteristics germane to a particular case become lost through the appeal to standard operating procedures.

Prob's with bureacracy

- The bureaucratic ideal of written documentation and maintenance of records can result in criticisms that an organization is "awash" in paper, that decision-making becomes "bogged down" in paperwork, that documents come to matter more than people, and that excessive reliance on formal paper records detracts from officials seeing the "human" side of the case before them.
- The Weberian principle designed to make decision-making more efficient, fair, and rational can lead to criticisms that an organization is distant, remote, intimidating, rule-bound, confusing, short-sighted, stupid, delay-ridden, and obsessed with "red tape"—in other words, "bureaucratic" in the pejorative sense.

Final reflections on Weber must be directed to his basic analytical focus. His approach to studying organizations was highly structural and systematic. He conceptualized bureaucracy as an hierarchical organization subject to the will of a centralized and decisive managerial authority exercised through a clear and distinct chain of command. The fundamental purpose of bureaucracy, moreover, was instrumental rational administration, that is, the creation of a system through which the organization could achieve its goals in the most economical, efficient, and effective manner conceivable. These considerations become the chief concerns of management seeking to develop and implement the ways and means necessary to utilize the organizational instruments at their disposal in the most intelligent, highly refined, and productive manner possible. The realization of such operational and instrumental competency was viewed as the hallmark of rationality—organizational ends conceptually and systematically correlated to the best-crafted and efficiently implemented means of achieving these ends. Weber explained all the features and principles of his ideal bureaucracy in terms of their being the most rational means to the end purpose of the organization. Specialization, the merit principle, impersonal rules, written records, and the separation of official from private interests all served the broader objective of a bureaucratic structure that would realize predetermined ends. From this perspective, a bureaucracy is analogous to an elaborate and complex machine, or a military organization, designed and controlled by management and their superiors to exercise some form of power in society and, by so doing, to serve the ends of those superiors. The machine is a structured system of means-ends relationships, subject to the commanding will of a unified managerial presence, and, when effectively led, can produce phenomenal organizational results. The actual ends of the "machine" however, and their moral worth, were subjects that Weber refrained from exploring, asserting that these were subjective matters more suited to political and philosophical analysis than objective organizational assessment.

5.5.2 Frederick W. Taylor

While Weber's work offered a classic statement of the mechanistic approach to organizations and the importance of formal, hierarchical structures, Frederick. W. Taylor (1856-1915) presented a systematic analysis of desirable mechanistic operating practices within an organization (Taylor, 1967). As a "time and motion" specialist, Taylor approached the study of management from exactly the opposite viewpoint from Weber. Whereas Weber focused on broad macro-institutional dynamics, Taylor was interested in the micro-management of industrial employees and the development of ways by which the work of employees could be made more efficient, therefore more productive, therefore more profitable. Like Weber, however, Taylor also adopted a mechanistic view of organizations, seeing all such institutions as equivalent to machines, with employees the necessary components and adjuncts of these machines. According to Taylor, the role of management was to ensure that the organizational machine ran as smoothly and efficiently as possible and that individual workers were used by management in the most efficient and productive manner conceivable. This approach was called "**scientific management**": the reduction of management to clearly defined, objective, and systematic principles and practices through which organizational behaviour could be rendered most rational—rationality conceived in terms of means-ends relationships *à la* Weber. As a part of this quest for **rationality**, Taylor placed great stress on the duty of management to review carefully every job performed by an employee. Through such a review, and using the techniques of scientific management, a manager could break down the functions of every job into its different component elements to study and determine how each was undertaken and how it could be improved upon and made more "rational," which would lead ultimately to the discovery of the "one best way" by which a given employee should, and therefore must, perform a given task. This technique of job analysis, in turn, invited managers to analyze the entire work process for which they were responsible; to devise ways by which all such work could be made more economical, efficient, and speedier; and to decide how the work of any one individual employee could be consistently and systematically measured and evaluated in light of pre-established rational expectations of efficiency. Through such comparative evaluations, employees who exceeded expectations could be financially rewarded, while those falling below set expectations could be better trained, or warned, or otherwise disciplined.

Taylor's approach to management complements Weber's in that both seek organizational rationality through the development of structures and operating procedures calculated to result in the identification and promotion of the most economical, efficient, and effective means to realize managerial and organizational ends. When we look at the running of an organization from a Taylorist perspective, we see that a number of his attitudinal dynamics are significant. One is that Taylor viewed all employees as essentially poorly educated, lazy, and uninterested in the life and work of the organization that employed them, seeking, at best, to get the most pay from the employer while performing the barest minimum of work. The role of management was to closely study and supervise all employees, selecting them in light of physical or mental attributes for particular jobs, and then working them like machines to gain the maximum amount of efficient productivity while paying them accordingly. In contrast to this negative view of workers, Taylor saw management personnel as the enlightened members of any organization, those who were to understand, learn from, and practise the principles of scientific management, and who were to possess the duty of organizing and running their institution along eminently rational lines.

5.5.3   Luther Gulick and Lyndall Urwick

In contrast to Taylor's focus on the micro-management and organization of worker activity, the American public administration analysts Luther Gulick and Lyndall Urwick, in the 1930s and 1940s, redirected attention to the broad dynamics of the institution, seeking to establish a "science of administration" by identifying, analyzing, and defining administrative truths common to the design and working of all organizations (Gulick and Urwick, 1969). They were most concerned with developing systematic knowledge respecting such basic managerial matters as institutional design, **span of control**, the effectiveness of command systems, the nature of departmentalization, the functioning of management, and the politics/administration dichotomy.

In their work on organizational theory, Gulick and Urwick stressed the importance of hierarchical organization but noted that there were many forms by which a bureaucracy could be organized based on the desired span of control of superiors. Span of control determines the pattern of reporting relationships between a superior and his or her immediate subordinates. It can be narrower or wider, with each articulation producing strengths and weaknesses in the organization as well as defining its organizational structure, as shown in Box 5.5.

An organization based on a narrow span of control

- is much more hierarchical than one founded on a broad span.
- involves greater levels of middle management linking the top echelons of the organization to its field offices and line workers. The benefit of such an organizational structure lies in the ability of a superior to more closely observe and understand the actions of a smaller number of subordinates than is the case with a wider span.
- allows for the greater ability of a supervisor to direct and supervise the actions of immediate subordinates and to oversee the quality of their actions.

The main drawback of a narrow span of control, however, is that it accentuates the hierarchical nature of the organization, placing more bureaucratic layers between the top and bottom of the institutional pyramid. This makes effective formal communication throughout the organization more complicated and time-consuming, because all communication within the organization is designed to flow through proper channels, moving step-by-step through the various levels of responsible officials. A communication flow within an extended hierarchy, travelling either up or down, must pass through many hands, increasing the possibility that messages and their meanings can become modified, distorted, or even repressed through the process of interpretation and transmission at each managerial level.

Communication problems can lead to the development of informal channels of communication whereby officials bypass particular layers of management in their message-sending in an effort to expedite the flow of communication, or to avoid the involvement of particular officials in the communication flow, or to combine these two strategies, with the result that communication patterns become highly idiosyncratic. This pattern may result in particular messages moving more quickly through the system and some forms of communication and information being made more readily available to particular managerial actors, but such informality in management action violates the principle of unity of command. Through such behaviour, superiors may not necessarily be informed of the communications activities of their subordinates, and subordinates may not necessarily receive information and instructions from their immediate superiors. Managerial action and decision-making based on such informal patterns of communication tend to result in certain officials and their understandings

BOX 5.5
Narrow Span of Control

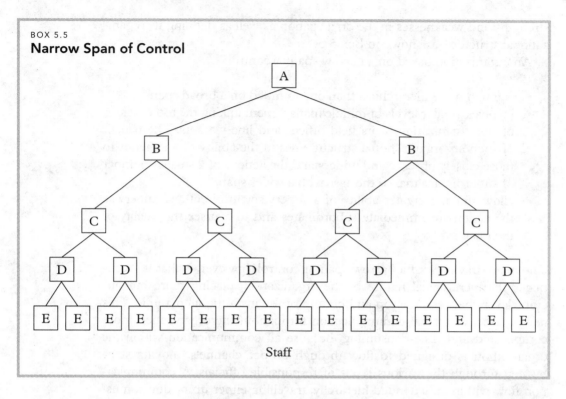

Staff

and opinions being overlooked, usually resulting in the build-up of animosity between officials and distrust of an organizational decision-making process that will come to be viewed as more arbitrary than rational.

The alternative to a narrow span of control is a broad span. As highlighted in Box 5.6, a broad span of control flattens the hierarchy by removing layers of middle management. This has the benefit of aiding effective formal communication within the organization because there are fewer steps that messages need to travel between the top and the bottom. In this way, senior management can be more directly linked to the lower echelons and can be much better apprized of the state of affairs in their organization than is the case with a narrow span. The problem with a broader span of control, however, is the stress that it places on superiors. Rather than supervising a smaller number of subordinates, as in the narrow span of control, they are now called upon to oversee, control, and direct a much larger number of officials beneath them, officials who are engaged in a greater range of organizational activities. The elimination of middle-management ranks places greater expectations and responsibilities on senior managers, because these officials supervise a much more complicated work environment. As Gulick and Urwick noted, this wider span of control can lead to management failures and breakdowns as senior officials become overburdened by their additional responsibilities.

The solution to all these problems, of course and as Gulick and Urwick argued, was to delineate a viable compromise between a narrow and wide span of control, one that maximized the benefits of effective command while also promoting good patterns of communication. Gulick and Urwick

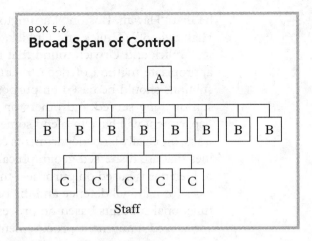

BOX 5.6
Broad Span of Control

Staff

stressed that no set "span of control rule" can be equally applicable across all organizations because certain organizations, and their management, function better with a narrower span of control and others with a broader one. They suggested that the appropriate span of control for an organization would be contingent on such variables as the nature of the work supervised, the educational and training standards of subordinates, the extent of geographical decentralization of the organization, and the organizational history and general stability of the institution. While Gulick and Urwick thus failed to discover a scientific rule for devising an appropriate span of control, they consistently argued that their study of the concept highlighted principles and considerations that could and should form the basis of any systematic managerial approach to organizational design.

This concern for devoting systematic attention to management problems also led Gulick and Urwick to address the issue of **departmentalization**. How should government departments and subunits be organized, and what should be the defining principles of organization? They stressed four concepts that dominate considerations of departmental organization: purpose, process, persons or things served, and place. "Purpose" refers to the function of a department or subunit—what it is conceived to do or provide— while "process" refers to the means to be taken to achieve desired ends. Thus, departments or subunits can be organized, for example, around the purposes of "furnishing water, controlling crime, or conducting education," or around the processes of "engineering, medicine, carpentry, stenography, statistics, or accounting." Or, they can be organized around the persons or things served, such as "immigrants, veterans, Indians, forests, mines, parks, orphans, farmers, automobiles or the poor," or around the place of service, be that "Hawaii, Boston, Washington, the Dust Bowl, Alabama, or Central High School" (Gulick and Urwick, 1969: 15).

Gulick and Urwick found that there was no firm rule for selecting the appropriate method of departmentalization. Some departments and their subunits should be based on purpose, others on process; some on the person or thing served and others on place. In many instances, moreover, a department will have to blend some or all of these features through its subunits, especially large departments of a federal government with responsibilities that are dispersed geographically. For example, Canada's Department of Defence is based on purpose—the provision and support of military services for national defence and the promotion of strategic interests—but has functional subunits based on process, such as land, air, and naval services; specialized equipment procurement; legal and medical services; and officer training systems. These departments, furthermore, are also highly influenced by considerations of place, with operational elements of each being largely decentralized across the country and abroad. In determining the appropriate form of departmentalization and the desired blending of organizational requirements for any one institution, Gulick and Urwick emphasized the importance of administrative and managerial judgement rendered in light of the knowledge of organizational functions and attributes and the desired role of the institution.

Concern for departmentalization also leads Gulick and Urwick to devote attention to the concepts of line and staff functions as considerations in organizational design.

- *A line function* is one in which officials provide a service directly to the general public or to a particular client group within the public.
- In contrast to this, *a staff function* is one in which given officials, possessing a specialized skill or mandate, provide services not to the general public per se, but either to officials engaged in line functions or to the government as a whole. Classic examples of the staff function are the provision of legal support, personnel and financial management support, and policy and planning support to those engaged in line undertakings.

This distinction between line and staff functions is common within particular departments, and most government departments possess specific sub-offices devoted to the provision of the staff support functions listed above. In fact, departments themselves can be classified as either line or staff, depending on the general nature of their activities and whether they provide services directly to the public or to specialized client groups or to the government as a whole. You will recall just such distinctions from Chapter 3 where current federal departments were differentiated into "service" or "support" roles, the former engaged in classic line functions and the latter providing general staff and government-wide support services.

As Gulick and Urwick sought to develop a "science of administration," Gulick devoted special consideration to the delineation of the essential functions of management. This endeavour resulted in his famous acronym POSDCORB that we reviewed at the beginning of this chapter, where we noted the continuing value of this taxonomy. Gulick and Urwick also stressed the importance of the politics/administration dichotomy, which emerged from the writings of Woodrow Wilson, who argued that matters of a purely political and partisan nature should be clearly separated from matters of management and administration. The former is the focus of passion, argument, and political/ideological debate concerning matters of government leadership and policy ends, while the latter is the preserve of systematic rationality aimed at developing and operating the best means to achieve desired policy ends. The logic of the dichotomy, as understood by Gulick and Urwick, was that matters of policy definitely shaped the purposes of state action, but that the actual design and implementation of policy and the operationalization of governmental activity were to be state undertakings subject to the dispassionate, reasoned, and professional wisdom emerging from the "science of administration."

As we have already noticed, however, the politics/administration dichotomy cannot withstand critical scrutiny either as a description of, or prescription for, bureaucratic activity. And, as we will see, much of the work of Gulick and Urwick was subjected to serious criticism by authors challenging their claims that there can be a "science of administration" or that organizations can or should be understood from a structural-mechanistic viewpoint. Even Gulick and Urwick themselves came to realize that they were stressing the importance of systematic review and analysis of organizational phenomena and the use of considered managerial judgement more than scientific truths in the making of decisions. But this does not diminish the general importance of their contribution to the study of organizations. Quite the contrary. In speaking of their intellectual legacy, Kernaghan and Siegel (1999: 54) have written:

> Gulick and Urwick contributed to the theory of organizational behaviour by synthesizing and disseminating other people's ideas. Nevertheless, these two men made a valuable contribution

---

BOX 5.7
**Key Concepts of the Structural-Mechanistic
Approach to Understanding Organizations**

1. Organizations are to be understood in structural terms.
2. Hierarchy is the best means of organizing a bureaucracy.
3. The logic of an organization is to achieve ends in the most economical, efficient, and effective means possible.
4. Institutional rationality is to be understood in instrumental means-ends relationships.
5. Management in an organization should possess a command and control relationship within the organization.
6. Power within an organization should flow from the top down.
7. Senior management is the "driver" of the organization.
8. Ordinary employees are expected to faithfully execute the orders of management.

---

both by forcing people to think about management in a systematic manner, and in beginning to set out certain principles—many of which are still seen as beneficial guides to action today.

A further appraisal of the structural-mechanistic model is to be found on the Thinking Government web site under the Chapter 5 link.

5.6 The Organic-Humanistic Model: Early Studies

Even as the structural-mechanistic model dominated thought and practice in organizational management in the early decades of the twentieth century, it became the subject of criticism by analysts seeking a better, more accurate approach to understanding how organizations work and how and why people within them behave as they do. One of the first of these was Mary Parker Follett (1868-1933), whose studies of organizations led her to question the command-and-control approach to power (Follett, 1951, 1965). Rather than viewing power as operating in a linear and downward-flowing fashion, Follett argued that a better way to understand power in organizations is to see it as flowing in a circular manner, like a current, both up and down the organizational hierarchy. Power, according to Follett, can be exercised downward upon subordinates, but their reactions to this exercise of power, both positive and negative, will flow back up the hierarchy, and these reactions influence those who wield formal power. Hostile employee reactions to the exercise of managerial authority will weaken an organization's ability to realize its goals, while supportive reactions will enhance such goal achievement. Thus, Follett recognized a distinction between the formal power held by management and the informal power possessed by employees and utilized by them through their reactions to formal power. The sound exercise of management power, so Follett believed, was to be found in management using its authority and making decisions in such a manner as to motivate employees and elicit positive reactions to management actions. From this perspective, the exercise of power is part of a human and interactive process, with the reaction of subordinates to such power being just as important as the objectives and methods of those superiors initiating executive decisions.

This interest in the sociological and psychological aspect of organizational life was heightened by the Hawthorne Studies of the 1920s (Mayo, 1960; Roethlisberger and Dickson, 1964). These experiments into worker behaviour and the ways and means of inducing greater productivity, all undertaken in the spirit of scientific management, led researchers such as Elton Mayo to argue that organizational behaviour could not be understood in simplistic terms of incentive and power. Employee reaction to management efficiency initiatives was complex, but the main factor in explaining employee behaviour was the existence of "informal groups" of employees and their attitudes to work. The Hawthorne Studies broke ground in identifying factors of organizational life existing outside of the formal parameters of the structural-mechanistic model. The discovery of informal groupings within organizations—that is, the tendency of employees, and even managers, to band together with similarly situated and like-minded colleagues for mutual comradeship, socialization, support, and defence—fundamentally challenged pre-existing understandings and assumptions of organizational behaviour and called into question both the relevance and effectiveness of many of the "truths" of scientific management. The existence of informal groups within organizations also led a new wave of organizational theorists to devote attention more to informal interpersonal relations within organizations, especially those between superiors and subordinates, than to the formal structures of power relations. If informal group relations were the dominant factor in explaining employee activity, as the Hawthorne Studies indicated, then the whole realm of informal organizational dynamics merited the greatest attention.

5.6.1 Chester Barnard

One early writer on the informal group and management was Chester Barnard (1886-1961), who said that effective management and organizational success was contingent on clear and open communication between employees and management and on management recognizing and progressively responding to the complex nature of employee attitudes to organizations (Barnard, 1962). The role of management, according to Barnard, was to encourage employees to identify psychologically with the basic goals of the organization, thus ensuring that, in the informal life of the organization and its various communication patterns, employees would still sympathize with and support the interests of the organization and would encourage others to have positive attitudes towards it and its objectives. The ways to induce such employee loyalty, he argued, were not only monetary rewards but such newly emerging concepts in personnel relations as the provision of good working conditions, the encouragement of employees' pride in their work, and the promotion of organizational unity. By promoting a sensibility of shared purpose, management conveyed the idea that the organization comprised both management and workers, superiors and subordinates, and that all had a necessary place in the organization, all had special roles to play, and that the success of the whole was contingent upon all working together towards the common goals of the organization. As these organizational objectives were met and the interests of the organization were served, so too would the interests of all those comprising the organization be served, be they management or workers, with all mutually benefitting from the success of the organization.

Barnard's work, first published in 1938, was a "how to" managerial approach to employee motivation, and marked a uniquely different interpretation of the role of management from that promoted by Taylor and his disciples of scientific management. The stress on the importance of employer-employee cooperation and the need for management to reach out to employees and to respond to both their material and psychological needs set the stage for Abraham Maslow's famous work on motivation.

5.6.2 Abraham Maslow

Abraham Maslow (1970) was interested in the nature of motivation in the workplace, believing that this concept was much more complex than the structural-mechanistic model would suggest. He thought that financial reward or fear of discipline or job loss were not the only motivational factors affecting workers. Through his studies, Maslow developed a hierarchy of human needs, asserting that all workers, and indeed all people, are motivated by five successive needs, ranging from the most basic and material to the most complex and philosophical, intangible yet profoundly significant. This hierarchy of needs, from the most basic to the highest order, consists of:

- physiological needs for food, shelter, clothing, sex, and sleep;
- safety needs for security, stability, and freedom from fear;
- human needs for belonging and love, for friendship and membership and involvement in a community;
- the need for esteem through achievement, competence, independence, prestige, and status; and
- the need for self-actualization, self-fulfillment, and the attainment of fundamental goals in life.

Maslow argued that all people possess these needs, which are inherent in human beings; that all people want to, and need to, satisfy these needs in their own ways; that many aspects of these needs are present in the thoughts and concerns of employees within a workplace; and that, as the more basic needs are attended to, individuals then seek the satisfaction of the higher order needs. This approach to workplace motivation presented a more intricate and involved explanation of employee expectations than anything devised by Taylor. Maslow averred that all five needs come into play within the workplace, that differing employees have differing needs, and that the same person can have differing needs at differing times. Therefore, the role of management in developing appropriate methods of addressing employee motivation is very complicated; one-dimensional approaches to such motivation will always fail to respond to the complexity of human needs. On the other hand, however, the more management is able to satisfy not only the basic human needs but also the more advanced ones, the greater the likelihood of employee satisfaction with their work, and, hence, the greater the likelihood of harmony between the interests of labour and management and the greater the productivity of workers. The attainment of such levels of satisfaction, however, require a fundamental shift in the way that management traditionally viewed employees and their role in the productive life of the organization. Rather than viewing them merely as adjuncts to machines, as "cogs in wheels," Maslow emphasized that enlightened management should perceive workers as complex human beings with complex needs and recognize that these needs include a fundamental desire to work,

BOX 5.8
Maslow's Hierarchy of Needs

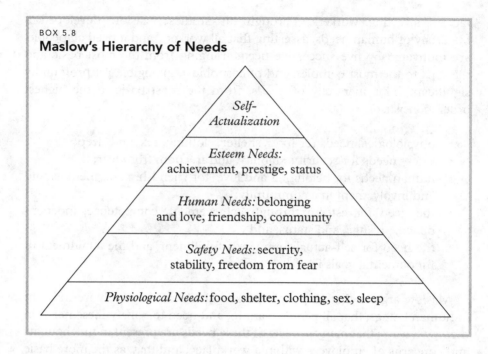

to be active participants in their workplace, to be valued for their contribution to the organization within which they work, and to be allowed to contribute productively to this organization. The questions for management, then, become how to satisfy these needs and reap the rewards of contented and productive employees.

5.6.3   Douglas McGregor

Maslow's ideas respecting motivation and the need to develop a more complex and enlightened approach to understanding organizations and management in turn inspired Douglas McGregor to study management theory and develop a two-pronged typology of management styles, which he termed "Theory X" and "Theory Y" (McGregor, 1960). In McGregor's view, Theory X refers to the traditional structural-mechanistic approach to management and its assumptions respecting employees. In Theory X, employees are assumed to be lazy, of limited education and interests, disinclined to work, and motivated solely to gain as much income for as little work as possible. Therefore, all workers must be coerced to work, must be closely supervised and controlled, and must be disciplined when they misbehave, as certainly they will. It follows that most employees will be irresponsible; uninterested in the life and goals of the organization where they work; passive; and in need of strong managerial control, direction, and leadership if they are to achieve anything of productive worth to the organization. The basic psychological profile emerging from Theory X is that employees are like poorly brought-up children, in need of a strong military-style parent/manager who will provide order, discipline, and purpose to their lives.

In contrast to this, Theory Y is the emerging organic-humanistic approach to organizations and management. Theory Y suggests that work is natural to human beings; that human beings are inquisitive and creative creatures who actually want to work and who want to be engaged in productive, meaningful, and rewarding labour; and that, under the right circumstances and conditions, work can be very satisfying. Given these beliefs, McGregor suggested that workers should not need to be coerced to work if management properly makes the workplace and the work-process a fulfilling and progressive experience. If these conditions are met, if workers are engaged in productive, meaningful, and rewarding work, and if management interacts with them as skilled participants and colleagues in the work-process rather than as lazy children expected to behave as machines, then employees will respond to their work with enthusiasm and creativity. As McGregor argued, most workers subject to traditional mechanistic approaches to management possess enormous amounts of unrecognized and unused skills, knowledge, experience, and potential. This is a human resource going to waste; it is also a resource that can be and should be identified and developed by intelligent management as just that—a resource to be used to the advantage of the organization. One of the vital skills for management, according to McGregor, is to understand its employees, to recognize its workforce as a pool of talent ready and willing to be utilized in the service of organizational goals, to be willing to interact with its workforce more as partners and colleagues than as masters and servants, and to encourage the participation of employees in the development and operation of the workplace. Through the writing of McGregor, as with Maslow before him, we observe the emergence of the concept of participatory management as a new, progressive, and exciting method of organizing workplaces in a way that recognizes and affirms the talents of employees, the desire for mutual employer/employee respect and recognition, and the productive potential of cooperative work.

5.6.4   Herbert Simon

While Follett, Mayo, Barnard, Maslow, and McGregor, among others, were challenging traditional attitudes towards the formal organization and the nature of employees and their motivations, Herbert Simon was vigorously criticizing much of the work of Gulick and Urwick and other structural-ist writers seeking to develop a "science of administration" (Simon, 1957). Simon attacked the belief that matters of administration could be reduced to scientific rules, stressing that organizations, administration, and manage-ment were inherently human creations and undertakings and, as such, were far more subjective than objective in their working. In demonstrating this point, he spoke of the "Proverbs of Administration." Rather than demon-strating a science of administration, writers such as Gulick and Urwick had advanced principles of organizational design and assessments of particular organizational options that were often simplistic, contradictory, and in no way scientific in the sense of relating to objective, verifiable, and repeat-able truths. The classic example of this, so Simon argued, was Gulick and Urwick's notion that administrative efficiency and effective command can be enhanced through the development of an organization based on a nar-row span of control. This principle runs counter to the other principle advanced by these same authors that administrative efficiency and effective command also can be enhanced through the flattening of organizational hierarchy and a minimizing of middle-management levels.

As Simon vigorously asserted, however, it is impossible to have a nar-row span of control co-existing with a broad span of control; as we have already seen in the discussion on Gulick and Urwick, such principles in and of themselves are mutually exclusive, each approach to span of control bringing with it strengths and weaknesses. A management choice has to be made as to which form of control is to be followed in any particular case, this decision being based on the considered judgement, by management, of the credits and debits of each form in relation to the organization being managed. Even Gulick and Urwick came to admit that such an exercise of judgement was required, but Simon then countered that a "true" science of administration would not require that sort of a judgement at all nor allow for the emergence of such a problem in the first place. That the necessity for an exercise of human judgement as to the appropriate span of control should arise—rather than a universal, firm, and unequivocal application of a hard scientific rule—was proof to Simon that the so-called "science of administration" was not a science at all but, at best, an elaborate listing of principles, all of which required further human interpretation. This conclusion, according to Simon, did not belittle the work of Gulick and Urwick with respect to the systematic study of organizational design and working, but simply affirmed the importance of devoting critical social science interpretational techniques and assessments to the study and evaluation of organizations and the functions of management. These matters are, at heart, human creations and activities, and must be subjected to humanistic rather than mechanistic forms of analysis.

5.6.5   Chris Argyris

In keeping with the work of McGregor, Chris Argyris (1957, 1964) asserted that formal organizational structures and traditional management practices were inconsistent with human nature and thus contradictory to the long-term interests of organizations. Individual human development, Argyris concluded, routinely passes through a number of stages, moving from simpler to more involved and complex forms of understanding and life behaviour. These stages, occurring from infancy to adulthood, flow from passivity to activity, from dependence to independence, from limited to greater ranges of interests and behaviours, from shorter to longer time perspectives, from smaller to greater individual undertakings, from a position of subordination to positions of equality or superordination, and from a lack of awareness to greater awareness. Moving along each dimension contributes to what Argyris believed to be a healthy adult personality.

Such normal development, however, is spurned by traditional management theory. Rather than expecting employees to grow with their work and to develop greater involvement in, and responsibility for, their actions in the workplace, the scientific management form of leadership expected workers to be unmotivated, passive, submissive, and limited in all their attitudes to work and the organization within which they were employed. This approach to management, Argyris suggested, failed to understand human nature and thus failed to recognize the potential of workers in helping to build an organization. Such an approach, moreover, was one much more likely to result in labour-management conflict and personnel problems, as employees either challenge the application of managerial control and/or revert to subterfuge and opposition to management goals through passive resistance informed, communicated, and supported through the dynamics of the informal group. A far better approach to management, Argyris argued, was to understand human personality; to recognize its potential for growth, development, and creative action; and to "fuse" these qualities with the objectives of the organization. Rather than viewing employees as problematic children to be controlled and ordered, enlightened management should view their employees as creative individuals, human assets that can and will bring operational vigour and intellectual dynamism to any organization, if they are properly encouraged and allowed to effectively participate in the life of the organization. In this perspective, the role of management is to recognize that its human resources are just as valuable, if not more so, than its other material and financial resources and that these human resources deserve development and involvement in the operational life of the organization, ultimately resulting in the progressive mobilization of employee talent in the service of the long-term interests of the organization. With Argyris as with McGregor, we observe the beginning of the concept of participatory management.

5.6.6   Peter Drucker

Much of the analytical thrust of the organic-humanistic model of understanding organizations leads to support for the concept of **participatory management**. Two of the pioneering studies on the theory and practice of participatory modes of decision-making and goal achievement within organizations were published by K. Lewin, R. Lippitt, and R.K. White in 1939 and by L. Coch and J.R.P. French in 1948. The best-known and most influential advocate of participatory management, however, is Peter Drucker (1954). In his studies, Drucker challenged some of the most basic suppositions of Weber and the structuralist understanding of organizations. Rather than viewing hierarchy and specialization as necessary and desirable features of organizations, supportive of efficient, effective, and rational management, Drucker claimed that these very concepts can and do lead to organizational problems and failures. As we have already observed, if organizations place emphasis on narrow spans of control between superiors and subordinates, they will become increasingly hierarchical, with resulting problems of weakened communication flows, a greater distance between field-level workers and top management, a lessened ability of senior management to fully comprehend major actions occurring within the organization, and the creation of an organizational structure that becomes increasingly difficult to understand and direct. An over-emphasis on specialization, moreover, can lead to subunits of an organization becoming excessively focused on their own particular work and interests to the detriment of the broader needs and interests of the organization overall. Specialization can threaten organizational unity, with various specialized subunits coming to think and act in very individualistic ways. It can also threaten

BOX 5.9
Key Concepts of the Organic-Humanistic Approach to Understanding Organizations

1. Organizations are complex living entities, populated by human beings.
2. Organizations possess formal and informal lines of communications.
3. All organizations will possess informal groupings of people.
4. People in an organization possess complex motivations.
5. Employees in an organization are the best resource of the organization.
6. Management should structure its actions to maximize the innate potential of its human resources.
7. Hierarchies should be shallow, allowing for ease of communication within the organization.
8. Power and influence should flow both top-down and bottom-up in the organization.
9. Participatory management is an ideal form of organizational managerial behaviour.

the unity of the management of the organization when generalist managers come to believe, or are led to believe by a highly specialized subunit, that it is so specialized and unique that only its specialized managers can effectively supervise and direct its actions. To the extent that these managerial dynamics come to exist within an organization, that organization is losing managerial direction and common organizational purpose.

In addressing these problems, Drucker argued that management constantly needs to direct attention to the life and operations of the organization overall and, in doing so, promote the highest degree of communication possible within the organization. Through such wide communication, both downwards and upwards, management can make use of all of its personnel resources in understanding the organization, in assessing its strengths and weaknesses and its potentials and opportunities, and in setting its goals and overseeing its operations. In keeping with authors such as Mayo, McGregor, and Argyris, Drucker stressed that management should actively embrace its employees, seeking to decentralize the exercise of power within the organization by involving them in decision-making related to their work, thereby enabling management to learn and benefit from their workplace experience. As power is decentralized and as employees are brought into the decision-making process, management can gain a wealth of knowledge about

- how the organization actually operates at both the formal and, more importantly, the informal, level;
- how its operations could be improved and streamlined;
- how its field-level actions, service delivery, and rapport with its external environment—consumers, clients, others—could be enhanced; and
- how its actual product or service could be bettered.

Such participation would also bring yet other appreciable benefits to the organization and its management. By involving affected staff in the decision-making process, Drucker asserted, such employees would be more likely to accept and support final operational decisions rendered by management; through being involved in new decision-making from the very outset, affected employees would more likely "buy into" new operational approaches and goals, giving these new initiatives a far greater degree of formal and informal support than would otherwise be the case with usual management decisions made in the usual top-down manner. This form of participatory decision-making

- would educate employees in the operational working and strategic direction of the organization in its entirety;
- enhance the problem-solving and analytical skills of both employees and middle managers;
- promote the managerial capabilities of middle managers, because they have to master a more complicated yet rewarding form of decision-making; and
- facilitate conflict resolution and team-building within the organization.

As Drucker argued, effective participation would not only improve both the quality of managerial and staff actions, but would actually reduce the incidence of problems arising within the organization because better decision-making leads to better communications and operations, resulting in a more smoothly flowing, efficient, effective, rational and, ultimately, happier organization. The exercise of decentralized power through participatory modes of decision-making in contrast to authoritarian modes of decision-making founded upon centralized power was thus, to Drucker, the key to organizational success.

Such support for systems of participatory management, however, has not gone unchallenged. As Inwood (2004: 67-9) has argued, the process of actually engaging in participatory forms of consultation and decision-making can be very disruptive to the routine operations of an organization, and it may raise expectations among employees of inclusiveness and efficacy which cannot be realized by managers. Participatory management, in theory, is meant to devolve and decentralize managerial decision-making—rather than being top-down, decision-making and, hence, operational power is an amalgam of top-down/bottom-up relationships, whereby both managers and employees share in the making of decisions. But there are a number of significant problems here. Is the central motivation behind the establishment of participatory management the desire to enhance the workplace experience and role of employees, or to promote the interests of management by enhancing employee productivity? While these two motivations may not be mutually exclusive in all circumstances, they can be in certain instances. This raises the question as to whether the interests of employees can be blended and merged with the interests of management so that a viable form of co-management can emerge. But is this what management truly wants? Is management prepared to relinquish some significant degree of its managerial and decision-making role to its employees? In other words, does participatory management result in a sharing of power to the extent that management has lost a substantial degree of its command-and-control authority? If, on the other hand, participatory management simply results in consultation between staff and management, with management retaining full right to make managerial decisions as it deems appropriate, will this participatory management gain the approval and active support of employees?

This tension between power and authority within the organization is central to any analysis of participatory management within any given institution. It carries particular relevance to public sector organizations because of the additional issue of accountability. Simply put, if public sector organizations are designed to facilitate and serve public policy as promoted by ministers and a prime minister (or premier) and cabinet, who are responsible to legislative bodies and the public, is participatory management a threat to democratically elected government? Is accountability in a democratic system compromised if certain of the decision-makers—namely, the unelected employees—are not accountable for their actions in a chain of command? If ministers and senior managers must always be accountable for the policy and program actions of their departments and agencies, is there any viable justification for them to devolve decision-making authority on subordinates, even if such devolution appears to be operationally effective? These questions become critical to the actual implementation of

BOX 5.10
The Role of Management I

Structural-Mechanistic Model

According to Weber: The chief concern of management seeking to develop and implement the ways and means necessary to utilize the organizational instruments at their disposal in the most intelligent, highly refined, and productive manner possible is instrumental rational administration, that is, the creation of a system through which the organization may achieve its goals in the most economical, efficient, and effective manner conceivable.

According to Taylor: The role of management is to ensure that the organizational machine runs as smoothly and efficiently as possible and that individual workers are used and worked by management in the most efficient and productive manner conceivable.

According to Gulick: Management should be concerned with: Planning, Organizing, Staffing, Directing, Coordinating, Reporting, and Budgeting (**POSDCORB**) in the most efficient way possible, based on the narrow or broad span of control within an organization.

Organic-Humanistic Model

According to Follett: The sound exercise of management power is to be found in management using its authority and making decisions in such a manner as to motivate employees and elicit positive reactions to management actions.

According to Barnard: The role of management is to encourage employees to identify psychologically with the basic goals of the organization, thus ensuring that, in the informal life of the organization and its various communication patterns, employees sympathize with and support the interests of the organization and encourage others to have positive attitudes towards it and its objectives.

According to Maslow: The role of management in developing appropriate methods of addressing employee motivation is very complicated; one-dimensional approaches to such motivation will always fail to respond to the complexity of human needs. On the other hand, however, the more management is able to satisfy not only the basic human needs but also the more advanced ones, the greater the likelihood of employee satisfaction with their work, and, hence, the greater the likelihood of harmony between the interests of labour and management and the greater the productivity of workers.

According to McGregor: One of the vital skills for management is to understand its employees, to recognize its workforce as a pool of talent ready and willing to be utilized in the service of organizational goals, to be willing to interact with its workforce more as partners and colleagues than as masters and servants, and to encourage the participation of employees in the development and operation of the workplace.

According to Argyris: The role of management is to recognize that its human resources are just as valuable, if not more so, than its other material and financial resources and that these human resources deserve development and involvement in the operational life of the organization, ultimately resulting in the progressive mobilization of employee talent in the service of the long-term interests of the organization.

According to Drucker: Management should actively embrace its employees, seeking to decentralize the exercise of power within the organization by involving them in decision-making related to their work, thereby enabling management to learn and benefit from their workplace experience.

participatory management initiatives within the public sector, and the history of such initiatives has not been kind to their advocates (Chapters 8 and 10). A further appraisal of the organic-humanistic model is to be found on the Thinking Government web site under the Chapter 5 link.

5.7   Managerial Decision-Making: Approaches, Techniques, and Motivations

This chapter thus far has devoted attention to the functions of management and organizational theory. We have reviewed the major roles and responsibilities of management and the two main models of organizational design and operation that have emerged from the extensive literature on the nature and working of bureaucracy. A related field of study involves analysis of the various approaches by which management engages in decision-making. Regardless of the organizational nature of an institution—be it steeply hierarchical or not; centralized or decentralized; rooted in a top-down, authoritarian, command-and-control model of management or in a more top-down/bottom-up, egalitarian, participative form of management—managerial decision-making can vary, depending on the techniques and motivations by which management addresses its policy and program environment. There are a number of different approaches by which management can structure its decision-making and through which one can outline and assess the nature of this decision-making; some of these approaches are more normative, explaining how managerial decision-making *should* be exercised, while others are more descriptive, suggesting how such decision-making *actually* occurs. Thus, some approaches deal more with the *techniques* of making decisions, while others focus attention on the *motivations* behind the process. In all instances, however, decision-making approaches will involve such factors as

- how management seeks to understand and organize information and knowledge;
- how it understands its own interests and aims in decision-making; and
- what it views to be the most reasonable, effective, and viable means to the realization of pre-established ends.

Managers make choices as to how they will organize policy and program decision-making, and a variety of approaches help us understand the choices management makes. In this section and the one following, we will review seven of these approaches, which provide the focal point for the major descriptive and analytical schools of thought regarding decision-making as found in the literature on organizational theory.

5.7.1 Incrementalism

As Charles E. Lindblom (1959, 1968) persistently maintained, **incrementalism** is the oldest and most traditional form of managerial decision-making. This term refers to a technique by which decision-makers base their actions on both existing organizational policies and practices and past methods of addressing problems. The essential logic of incrementalism is that managers should and do accept the existing policies and programs of their organization as the basis of the work of the institution. They inherit most of their policy and program responsibilities from past decisions, and their duty is to maintain the smooth implementation of these institutional initiatives into the future.

Thus, most of the work of management is the maintenance of the status quo and the "managing" of present issues and problems to provide institutional consistency, the broad policies and objectives having been set by organizational leaders in the past. Even when problems and difficulties inevitably arise in the working of the status quo, however, the incrementalist technique still dominates. When managers are confronted with problems in need of resolution, Lindblom said, they should engage in the most traditional and simplest form of decision-making, namely, finding the easiest, simplest, and quickest solution to solve the problem at hand while expending the least amount of time, effort, and concern and while also maintaining the greatest degree of consistency and fidelity to existing policy and program operations of the organization. Such an approach to decision-making asserts that managers should deal with operational problems on a serial, incremental basis as they present themselves, with the process of problem resolution being both evolutionary and as elementary as possible.

Rather than being called upon to engage in great and complicated studies of problems and their underlying causes and being expected to plan ways and means for addressing these problems "from scratch," managers should be encouraged to rely on the past wisdom of their organization, its tradition for dealing with problems, and the understanding that whatever is done to address a current problem must be consistent with the operational context of the existing organization. Hence, Lindblom suggested two kinds of reforms: simple reforms that would represent only positive improvements to organizational action and marginal, incremental reforms to existing policies and practices. Change and reform are a necessary feature of managerial

---

BOX 5.11
Incrementalism: Key Concepts

- Current decisions should be rooted to past decisions.
- Decision-making should be as simple and easy as possible.
- Management should look for easy and "doable" solutions to problems.
- Reform works best if done in small, successive, incremental stages.
- Management should base proposed reforms on successful past reforms.

---

action if an organization is to successfully respond to, and adapt to, its own changing environment, but, for Lindblom, the key to such successful change is a process

- easily understandable by management and staff;
- quickly "doable," without the need for a great investment of time and resources or the development of new and complicated skills by management and staff; and
- institutionally viable in practice, meeting the goals and objectives for which they have been designed.

In other words, he advocated change that is simple rather than complex, easy rather than difficult, evolutionary rather than "revolutionary" in terms of its effect on the organizational culture of affected institutions and their management and staff.

To achieve these ends, so Lindblom argued, reforms and changes work best when they come in small, successive steps; marginal, incremental changes are much more likely to be viable and successful than massive, wholesale changes, due to both their simplicity of design and consistency with pre-established and well-understood aims and practices of the organization. As has often been said of incrementalism, it is, at best, the "science of muddling through."

In advancing this approach to managerial decision-making, Lindblom asserted that it is both descriptive and normative:

- *descriptive* in that it illustrates how most managers in organizations actually make decisions, and
- *normative* in that it defines how decisions ought to be made.

Lindblom argued that incrementalist practices are found in all organizations and that where they are ignored, in favour of more rationalistic techniques of decision-making, they tend to reappear. The strength of incrementalism, both descriptively and prescriptively is in its simplicity. The greatest virtue of incrementalist decision-making is that it tends to be the easiest, most straightforward, and comprehensible form of decision-making; this, Lindblom and others claimed, makes it the most effective form. In dealing with the questions of what is the basic role of management and how managers should engage in the process of management, the incrementalist response is simply

- that management involves doing what management has done in the past;
- that management is about maintaining and promoting pre-established and ongoing organizational responsibilities and programs in keeping with existing policies and set goals; and
- that when problems arise and reforms must be undertaken, the role of management is to engage in this process of change in a simple, incremental, yet considered fashion.

Rather than calling on managers to engage in highly complex forms of intellectual review, analysis, and problem-solving, as found in rationalistic techniques of decision-making, an incrementalist approach enables managers to make marginal adjustments to existing policies and programs in order to resolve current problems and satisfy existing needs for reform, but without having to reinvent and re-engineer the entire policy and program structure of the organization. In other words, managers are enabled to deal with problems and opportunities for change, in an easy, circumscribed, and doable manner, without devoting enormous amounts of time and effort to the process of change. They are then given more time to do what they arguably do best—manage and maintain the existing work of the organization.

While incrementalism clearly has the virtue of simplicity and fidelity to past ways of thinking and acting, such attitudes are viewed by some of its critics as its major flaws. Amitai Etzioni (1967) contends that operational simplicity can mean that more complex problems and sophisticated solutions are ignored in the quest for the easiest "fix." There may be times when difficult problems and challenges call for new and elaborate policy and program alternatives, yet the logic of incrementalism militates against such options being given serious consideration. In this sense, incrementalism can be seen as successive decision-making that is essentially unplanned. It makes management reactive instead of proactive. Rather than showing creative leadership designed to set the organizational agenda and take command of the organizational environment, management relying on incrementalist techniques becomes passive and disengaged from future planning. The basic role of management is to deal with problems once they have arisen, rather than to forestall such problems in the first place.

Incrementalism's stress on past practices, moreover, is also a subject of criticism. By emphasizing that current and future policy and program decisions should conform to past practices, Etzioni suggests that an incrementalist approach tends to be backward-looking rather than forward-looking. Such an approach, by its very logic, moves away from or even against progressive thought and action, while it benefits those interests, both within government and in society, that have been well-served by past forms of policy-making and program implementation. Social reform groups seeking major changes to the nature and form of government action in order to redress past injustices, for example, will find little comfort when a government addresses their concerns and their perceived problems in an incrementalist fashion.

Lindblom's valorization of the importance and prevalence of marginal policy and program reforms within the life of any organization is also open to serious dispute. As Kernaghan and Siegel (1999: 132-33) assert, while Lindblom is correct in holding that most organizational decisions can be seen as effecting simple, marginal variations on past forms of action, a number of institutional decisions, including some of the most important ones affecting the life of an organization or government, cannot be explained by incrementalist logic. These decisions are those that result in something entirely new—for example, the creation of the CBC, the National Film Board, and Petro-Canada as federal Crown corporations, or the establishment of workers' compensation, labour relations, collective bargaining, publicly funded medical insurance, or official bilingualism. Decisions of this sort may not be the most common organizational and governmental decisions, but they can be among the most significant that any organization makes, as it develops wholly new and innovative means to address current and perceived difficulties and opportunities. If incrementalism fails to effectively explain decision-making in these circumstances, as Kernaghan and Siegel suggest, the interpretative value of the technique can be seriously called into question.

5.7.2 Rationalism

Rationalism refers to a technique of managerial decision-making that emerged in the United States in the 1950s, primarily centred around the American defence establishment and designed to be a comprehensively logical and systematic alternative to incremental decision-making. In contrast to managerial decision-making as basically reactive and relatively unplanned, rational techniques of decision-making enable management to engage in sophisticated policy planning, program analysis, and decision implementation. At the core of rationalism is the belief that, unlike incrementalism, the main focus of management should be the future and development of policies and programs designed to maximize organizational goals with the minimum of cost, effort, and other institutional drawbacks. The rationalist technique of decision-making, as expounded by James R. Anderson (1984), begins with planning. Rather than simply basing current and future actions on past practices, managers are encouraged

- to analyze their organization;
- to conceptualize its goals, values, and objectives;
- to determine what the organization should be achieving in the future; and
- to clarify and prioritize all organizational objectives in rank order.

Managers must not only know what the essential operational purpose of their organization is, but how this purpose can be served through a variety of ends and how to establish priorities among these ends to achieve these goals. Once such basic planning has been undertaken and organizational ends have been determined and ranked, managers can identify and analyze all possible operational means that could be pursued by the organization towards the realization of these ends. Through this work, management identifies all the various policy and program options that the organization either confronts or possesses. Once all such options have been delineated, the task of management is to analyze systematically and logically each and every option in order to assess its strengths and weaknesses, costs and benefits, and potential and limitations, as the rational method for choosing a given policy or program to serve the set end. As a result of such analysis, all enumerated policy and program options will be ranked and prioritized in light of their capability to realize organizational goals; the logical result of this ranking process is the identification of the one option that best meets the needs, and the ends, of the organization while presenting it with

> BOX 5.12
> ## Rationalism: Key Concepts
>
> - Decision-making should be based on planning, analysis, and critical thinking.
> - Planning requires the setting of clear objectives, goals, and ends.
> - Objectives, goals, and ends must be prioritized according to needs.
> - Once priorities are set, all means to achieve desired ends must be identified and analyzed.
> - Ends-means analysis necessitates cost-benefit analysis.
> - All program means to achieve desired policy ends must be assessed and prioritized according to greatest success in achieving desired ends.
> - Those program means best able to maximize desired end results are to be the preferred courses of action for management.
> - All program implementation is to be monitored and assessed to determine whether program means are achieving policy ends, or whether further means-ends refinement is needed.

the fewest negative consequences. This becomes the preferred operational course of action to be implemented by management.

Once a policy option has been implemented, however, the rationalist process does not come to an end. Program activity must be constantly reviewed and analyzed, with management actively measuring the degree to which the given undertaking—the program so means selected—is actually meeting the goals and ends for which it was designed and chosen. Through such measurement, management is presented with a steady flow of information that it can use to either fine-tune the existing program to better serve organizational ends or to revisit the entire issue of ends and means, policy options, costs and benefits, and informed choice in the selection of a better means to the institution's objectives. The basic goal of such an operational technique is to provide management with the fullest range of knowledge, information, and intelligence regarding its organization, goals, and the various methods available to fulfill these goals in the most economical, efficient, and effective manner possible.

This technique of decision-making was much applauded by most policy analysts when it first appeared. Rather than decisions based upon past practices and easiest marginal actions, organizational decisions were to be based on the best techniques of systematic and logical analysis geared to the discovery of the best means for achieving set goals. Rationalism was to provide management with a technique through which it could both maximize the realization of policy and program objectives while achieving these ends in the most instrumentally rational ways possible. Future chapters will examine the influence of rational planning within Canadian governments, both federal and provincial, and the practical problems they encountered, but some of the basic limitations of this technique can be summarized quickly.

Despite the seeming reasonableness and desirability of systematic planning, analysis, and policy and program prioritization, each one of these subject matters is highly contentious and hotly debated. Planning necessitates the setting of goals—yet what happens when disputes arise as to what an organization's goals are or should be? What if an organization has multiple goals, with differing actors within the organization stressing the rationality and importance of opposing goals? How should these contending goals be prioritized, and what happens when differing organizational actors set different priorities for the same organization? The problem here becomes even more difficult when a government is called upon to rank, order, and prioritize its general policy objectives. What is the first priority of a government? Economic development? Social development? The preservation of law and order? The promotion of health care? National unity? Environmental protection? Is it ever possible for a government to prioritize these matters, and, if so, how would this decision-making be undertaken? Moreover, how much time, effort, and divisive debate would ensue? Would such decision-making be based on objectively rational considerations of goals and objectives, or would it become inherently subjective? Can there be such a dynamic as objective decision-making respecting government priorities and activities, or is all such analysis and review of government action and resultant decision-making necessarily subjective, more the realm of value judgements than value-free objective reasoning? Can there be such objective reasoning?

Such fundamental concerns for the identification of goals foreshadow the problems associated with policy and program analysis. Can one rationally engage in cost-benefit analysis of government activities, especially those with broad socio-economic, cultural, and political overtones? And does one have to rationally assess all government activities and all possible options for new and different ways of addressing these activities? Or does one have to rationally assess just those policy options that are simply contrary to prevailing political and ideological understandings of sound and moral policy? Is the sinking of foreign fishing vessels, for example, a policy option worthy of considered attention in the assessment of policy means towards preserving Canadian fish stocks? Furthermore, how does one rationally measure all the costs and benefits of all policy options associated with such matters as tax policy, health care spending, defence policy, environmental policy, or immigration policy? On a practical scale, the amount of work involved in such an analytical effort for any one of these tasks would be enormous, very complicated, and hugely time-consuming. Such undertakings, moreover, pose very difficult conceptual problems. Can one engage in a quantitative analysis of qualitative considerations, concerns, and goals? If so, how does one quantify qualitative conditions, and can one gain broad analytical support and consensus for one's efforts? If not, how are resulting disputes to be rationally resolved? How does one quantify, for example, the importance of a clean environment, and how does one engage in a cost-benefit analysis that can both quantify the impact of economic activity, both pro and con, on human beings and their environment and assess the quality—merits and demerits—of environmental protection policies and programs that, as yet, may not exist in fully implemented forms? Can one engage in a rational, quantitative analysis of prospective policies and programs and anticipated costs and benefits? If one seeks, however, to engage fully in qualitative analyses of qualitative conditions, fully embracing the importance and necessity for value judgements in decision-making, is such decision-making any longer purely "rational"? What happens when differing analysts produce differing cost-benefit analyses applying to the same matter as a result of differing value judgements? How does one rationally resolve these disputes?

The problems highlighted here, in short, focus critical attention on the central premise of rationalism—that the assessment of organizational goals and operations are amenable to pseudo-scientific measurement and analysis that will result in clear and objective assessments of organizational aims and priorities. But is this proposition tenable? And if it were attempted, would the practice of rational decision-making be beneficial to an organization, enabling its management to engage in thoughtful, considered evaluations of organizational ends, means, objectives, and opportunities, or would it be a recipe for debate, rancour, and discord, tearing at the fabric of management? Critics of rationalism, such as Lindblom, have asserted that despite the superficial appeal of the concept's logic, its ability to deliver what it promises—systematic thought, rational planning, and policy and program prioritization—is hopelessly flawed by the complex nature of organizations, their inability to gain consensus on organizational goals or on cost-benefit analyses of policy and program options, and the sheer difficulty of trying to do rational planning in the "real world." Contrary to making management easier and better, Lindblom suggests that rationalism leads to confusion, disagreement, and much time-consuming analysis that actually detracts from the decision-making capacity of any given organization. Rather than leading to concerted and intelligent action, rationalism can lead to "analysis paralysis" and unending series of reviews, assessments, studies, and counter-studies seeking to measure the immeasurable and gain agreements where agreement is virtually impossible, all leading to frustration and failure. Hence, Lindblom's observation that the best technique of managerial decision-making should be the easiest and most viable form of decision-making, this technique being, in his viewpoint, incrementalism.

5.7.3   Bounded Rationalism

As rationalism came under attack both for its perceived theoretical and practical limitations, a number of other managerial decision-making techniques were advanced to synthesize some of the best elements and aims of both rationalism and incrementalism into a better system of action. Herbert Simon (1957) argued in favour of what he termed "**bounded rationalism**." In this technique of decision-making, while management should strive for the basic ideals of rationalism in their decision-making—careful planning, goal identification, the systematic analysis of ends and means, and the attempt to engage in prioritization—all such actions must be understood as occurring and being circumscribed within certain pre-existing bounds of reality. These "bounds," or "givens," relate to such matters as

- the history of the organization;
- the political and socio-economic environment within which the organization must function;
- the existing range of policies and programs that might be acceptable to its policy environment as well as to the existing government of the day; and
- other matters such as existing legal and constitutional frameworks for governmental action, limited financial and personnel resources, and limited time for policy-making.

All these givens, as Simon argued, establish an operational framework within which any public sector bureaucracy must undertake its actions, meaning that no bureaucracy has perfect freedom to engage in the type of unrestricted policy analysis suggested by rationalism in its purest form. Government bodies must function within pre-established legal and constitutional orders; a tradition of past practices and past understandings of desired and acceptable policy and program initiatives, as well as current recognition that certain policy options are simply non-starters unworthy of any consideration; and a finite world of financial and personnel resources and time. It is highly unlikely that, for example, a department of industry or of economic development found in either the current federal or any provincial government, and mandated the task of reviewing and reporting on possible ways and means of promoting economic well-being, would or should devote any significant amount of time and effort addressing the policy options of wholesale nationalization and state control of the economy. Such options are unacceptable ideologically to any government in this country and thus unworthy of any attention. For similar reasons, it is unlikely that the current federal Department of Intergovernmental Relations would ever devote serious attention to assessing the merits of Quebec separation. Such matters are simply beyond the scope of prevailing ideological and political viability, meaning that time devoted to a comprehensive and rational analysis of these options would be, in effect, time wasted. Simon was very clear in stressing that all managerial decision-making has to occur within the bounds of reason and practicability, and, like Lindblom, he was concerned that such decision-making had to be of such a character as to be manageable and doable in the real world, with people working under real-world constraints.

Simon asked that management engage in decision-making in a rational manner but with the scope and expectations of decision-making no longer geared to a comprehensive review of all goals, options, and cost-benefit analyses designed to lead to the identification and prioritization of the best policy and program means to desired ends. In contrast to this quest for a rational ideal, Simon suggested that decision-makers should concentrate on the quest for the most optimal policy or program designed to address the needs of the given organization within given constraints while posing the minimum degree of difficulty to the organization in terms of planning, analysis, consensus-building, consistency to past practices and ideals, and program implementation. Rather than seeking the best, most rational solution derived from all possible options, bounded rationality calls for decision-makers to determine the most satisfactory option in light of the organizational and operational constraints under which the organization and its management must function. In searching for such optimal policy and program options, however, managers have to engage in careful, thoughtful policy analysis in keeping with the basic principles of rationalist inquiry. The basic aim of management is still to engage in planning, to set priorities, and to assess, as well as possible, means-ends relationships through the use of cost-benefit analyses and all other methods of modern management, but with the scope of the task much reduced in terms of the depth of analysis expected and required.

5.7.4 Mixed Scanning

As a technique of managerial decision-making, bounded rationalism offers a more practical method of action, though one that is far less ambitious. It seeks to integrate the best long-range planning objectives of rationalism while being cognizant of the factors of organizational history, past practices, and the real practical and ideological limitations that constrain the actions of any organization. A different method of synthesizing these factors was that proffered by Amitai Etzioni (1967). In his analysis of decision-making techniques, he stressed that organizations and governments generally make two types of decisions—fundamental and incremental. Etzioni agreed with Lindblom that the vast majority of organizational and government decisions are incremental, constituting marginal successive changes to ongoing policies and programs, with the objective of improving the work of the organization or government overall without the need for major wholesale change or reform of existing priorities or practices. These types of decisions, however, do not constitute the full range of decisions made by these bodies. There are times, as Etzioni suggested, when governments and organizations make fundamental reforms to their operations or develop wholly new policies, programs, and institutions designed to achieve newly established objectives and priorities. There are also times, as Mintzberg has noted, when governments or organizations engage in crisis management and quickly develop new methods and approaches for dealing with problems. New initiatives such as these cannot be explained in incrementalist terms but are to be understood as emerging from a technique of decision-making in which decision-makers engage in a form of highly defined yet circumscribed rationalism. Rather than engaging in rationalist analysis of all matters affecting a government or specific organization, they will direct systematic and highly detailed attention to the one policy or program matter in question, leaving all other matters to be managed in the traditional and easier incremental fashion. But for the subject matter under review, decision-makers will be broadly rationalistic in

- studying the problems confronted by existing policy and programs;
- reviewing desired policy and program objectives;

- assessing the various policy and program options that exist as reasonable and viable objects for consideration given ideological and practical constraints; and
- engaging in a considered review of the various strengths and weaknesses, costs and benefits of the various options under scrutiny.

Etzioni recognized that all such decision-making would be both complicated and contentious, eliciting great debate among those within governments in general, within affected organizations in particular, and among interested observers outside of governments. This type of debate and controversy is endemic to any form of rational decision-making, as we have observed, but when governments or organizations engage in fundamental decision-making and apply rationalist techniques to a narrow range of important matters, they will brace themselves for these considerations and difficulties on the grounds that such decision-making, on a limited or circumscribed scale, will result in superior program reform. Governments generally and commercial organizations consistently seek the best of incrementalism and rationalism, scanning their environments, activities, needs, and objectives to determine which matters require only simple, incremental attention and which others require the more detailed, sophisticated, yet complex and more difficult rationalistic technique. We will observe examples of mixed scanning in the chapters below, indicative of the practicality of this method.

5.8 Managerial Decision-Making: Theoretical Approaches

Incrementalism, rationalism, bounded rationalism, and mixed scanning represent methods of decision-making widely found in practice or strongly advocated and promoted in policy-making theory. Each of these techniques has its theoretical supporters, all stressing that their preferred method offers a normative foundation for managerial decision-making. Each is *prescriptive*, claiming to be an ideal form of decision-making, while advocates of incrementalism, bounded rationalism, and mixed scanning also argue that these methods are *descriptive* of how much decision-making is actually performed in government. These techniques of decision-making, however, do not stand alone within management theory. There are a number of other approaches offering more descriptive and analytical appraisals of how and why governments, management, and bureaucracies act as they do, especially probing the underlying motivations of decision-makers. These other approaches include public choice theory, bureaucratic politics theory, and policy networks theory, with the major decisional motivations being, respectively, individual self-interest, institutional self-interest, and group self-interest.

5.8.1 Public Choice Theory

Public choice theory, in its fullest iteration, refers to "the economic study of non-market decision-making, or simply the application of economics to political science" (Kernaghan and Siegel, 1999: 134). This theory, promoted by such authors as Anthony Downs (1957), Albert Breton (1974), and Douglas Hartle (1976), assumes that all actors involved in broadly political decision-making are motivated by considerations of material self-interest and act in rational, systematic, and self-serving ways to maximize their own interests or utility. While public choice theory seeks to explain *all* decision-making occurring within the public sector, inclusive of the actions of politicians, lobbyists, and voters through such a framework, much public choice theory is directly related to public sector managerial decision-making. Public choice theory posits that all politicians and public servants—staff and, more importantly, managers—possess the same materialistic and individualistic motivations as all other people. They are driven to promote and advance their own material self-interest, and they seek to achieve this goal through the use and manipulation of public policy and public goods. This becomes the technique of decision-making. A politician will advocate policies and programs that will secure his or her electoral victory, and, once elected, he or she will continue to defend and promote these initiatives and others that are viewed as being crucial to continued electoral success. And through such success, each elected representative gains access to the benefits of office—a state income, a generous pension plan, travel allowances, offices, and staff. And, if one is so fortunate as to rise to the ranks of cabinet, one gains even more of these material benefits as well as the personally satisfying attributes of power and prestige.

With respect to public sector managers, the basic materialistic logic is much the same. Public choice theory holds that managers exercise their power and influence not to serve the public interest but to maximize their own private interests. This goal can be achieved in a number of ways, but always with the technique of decision-making using public policies and programs towards the promotion of individual self-interest. Public choice theory stresses that all managers make decisions and advocate for policies and programs designed to benefit their superiors—both more senior managers and ministers—thereby benefitting not just the interests of these superiors but, more strategically, raising their own profile in the eyes of these more powerful actors and, consequently, raising their own employment promotion potential into the bargain. All managers act in ways to support policies and programs that will enhance the mandate, staff, and budget of their given institutional domain, be that an office, section, branch, division, or entire department. Organizational growth is sought by all managers, according to this approach, because through growth managers raise their own responsibilities and powers and, consequently, their access to greater organizational wealth, perquisites of office, and personal income. What is often referred to as "empire-building" is thus perceived by public choice theorists as a fully logical outcome of the materialistic drive found in all managers. All such officials strive to gain more and more access to, and control over, public wealth and power through the exercise of their public (but privately motivated) duties.

Such an understanding of deeply rooted, self-regarding managerial action turns the concept of public service on its head, and it is this feature of public choice theory and its underlying motivational foundation that its critics most fervently attack. Many analysts argue that while individual self-interest may always be a motivation helping to explain some bureaucratic decision-making, it is simple-minded in the extreme to assert that the drive to maximize individual self-interest explains all such decision-making. To believe this is to believe that public servants have no other motivations than selfish materialistic ones, that no public servant is motivated by beliefs in public service or a sense of duty to country, a desire to serve the interests of his or her home institution and its public, or a belief in the progressive role of the state. Public choice theorists would hold that all these explanations of individual managerial behaviour are essentially bogus, nice platitudes designed to conceal baser human instincts. Critics of public choice theory hold that often such nobler sentiments do serve to explain, in part, the behaviour of public servants, including senior managers, and that such sentiments are and should be at the very centre of the ethos of the public service.

5.8.2   Bureaucratic Politics Theory

Rather than seeing individual self-interest as the basic explanatory factor of managerial decision-making, **bureaucratic politics theory** holds that institutional self-interest is the key to this matter, with all managers directing their decision-making in order to promote the long-term best interests of their home institution. According to this understanding of decision-making, most forcefully presented by Graham Allison (1971), all governments are composed of a variety of differing departments and agencies, each with its own policy and program aims and objectives, and each working to advance its own institutional interests. The same holds true with respect to all subunits within departments and agencies. As decisions have to be made, managers act to serve not only the long-term best interests of their organization overall, but that of their own particular branch or office within the broader organization. Managerial decision-making is thus contingent upon one's position and location within the broader organization, and this matter of position colours any given manager's approach to what is in the best interests of the organization, or, in Allison's famous aphorism: "Where you stand depends on where you sit"(Allison, 1971: 176).

The internal logic of this understanding of decision-making, of course, is that far from any government being a uniform entity with a common orientation to the "public interest" and the types of policies and programs best suited to promoting this interest, every government represents a vast amalgam of institutions and organizations, all possessing different interests, different understandings of public policy, and different preferred ways and means of policy and program development and implementation. Actual decision-making is then a grand competition between these various institutions and organizations as they vie for power and influence within government in order to secure their preferred approaches and options for policy and program development. Consequently, all bureaucratic units and subunits are engaged in a complex system of bargaining between themselves, with each seeking to develop policy and administer programs that each sees to be not only in the broad public interest, but also in its own institutional self-interest. Operational decision-making will eventually emerge from such interplay and competition, as senior bureaucratic and political leaders with particular organizations, or senior political and bureaucratic leaders within a government, make choices between various contending forces, but with all of these leaders, in turn, seeking to serve and promote the best interests of their own "home" institutions. In all such decision-making, certain actors will inevitably be more powerful and influential than others due to a variety of factors ranging from:

- material considerations of size;
- financial and personnel strength and institutional capacity;
- institutional reputation;
- the historic role and responsibility of any given institution;

- the quality of the policies and programs advanced by the particular bureaucratic units; their congruency with prevailing political and ideological understandings of needed policies and programs; and
- the ability of the manager to set and maintain a broad strategic direction while also successfully engaging in the tactics of "playing the game" by working well with "allies," by coping well with "competitors," and by building operational coalitions of key actors in the decision-making process supportive of the interests of the given institutional actor.

In many instances, ultimate decision-making will represent a compromise position between desired policy and program objectives and initiatives agreed to by differing actors; at other times, and under differing circumstances, decision-making will reflect the victory of one or more actors and the defeat of others.

5.8.3   Policy Network Theory

A final understanding of managerial decision-making is that of **policy network theory**. According to Paul Pross's (1986) appraisal of decision-making, every policy field is one in which a plurality of institutions, groups, interests, and individuals compete with one another in an attempt to advance their own self-interest. Through such competition, all such persons closely interact with those government departments and/or agencies that have decision-making jurisdiction within a given policy field, seeking to have these government actors support the preferred policy and program approaches of the given actor. These departments and agencies, in turn, possess an organizational duty to engage with all these other actors in such a way as to manage the policy field that is of shared interest to all and to develop policies and programs that will serve the broad public interest in that policy field. Every policy field is seen as a complex network of private and public actors and interests with forces interacting with one another and competing with one another in the quest for desirable policies and programs. And the key role of lead public sector actors within each field, within each network, is to distill the public interest from the various private and other public interests with which they are confronted, as well as from their own considered judgement as to what the public interest is, and should be, in relation to the policy field in question.

Such policy networks can be complex, making this decision-making by lead government actors quite challenging. The other actors in any policy

BOX 5.13
The Role of Management II

Incrementalism: In dealing with the questions of what is the basic role of management and how managers should engage in the process of management, the incrementalist response is simply that management involves doing what management has done in the past; that management is about maintaining and promoting pre-established and ongoing organizational responsibilities and programs in keeping with existing policies and set goals; and that when problems arise and reforms must be undertaken, the role of management is to engage in this process of change in a simple, incremental, yet considered fashion.

Rationalism: The main focus of management should be the future and development of policies and programs designed to maximize organizational goals with the minimum of cost, effort, and other institutional drawbacks. Management identifies all the various policy and program options that the organization either confronts or possesses. Once all such options have been delineated, the task of management is to analyze systematically and logically each and every option in order to assess its strengths and weaknesses, costs and benefits, and potential and limitations, as the rational method for choosing a given policy or program to serve the set end.

Bounded rationalism: While management should strive for the basic ideals of rationalism in their decision-making—careful planning, goal identification, the systematic analysis of ends and means, and the attempt to engage in prioritization—all such actions must be understood as occurring and being circumscribed within certain pre-existing bounds of reality. Rather than seeking the best, most rational solution derived from all possible options, bounded rationality calls for management to determine the most satisfactory option in light of the organizational and operational constraints under which the organization and its management must function.

Mixed scanning: Rather than engaging in rationalist analysis of all matters affecting a government or specific organization, management will direct systematic and highly detailed attention to the one policy or program matter in question, leaving all other matters

network can range from other government bodies (federal, provincial, municipal, or international) to interest groups, business groups and individual corporations, and individual citizens. The policy network for the federal Department of Health, for example, includes provincial departments of health; hospitals and hospital associations; federal and provincial associations representing physicians, surgeons, and nurses; associations representing pharmaceutical producers; and, of course, the direct consumers of health care, all citizens concerned with the state of health care policy in the country.

In making policy and program decisions with respect to the "network," managers in lead government institutions are expected to act in a manner designed to promote the long-term best interests of all actors within the policy community, as they perceive this, while they are engaged in a to be managed in the traditional and easier incremental fashion. But for the subject matter under review, decision-makers will be broadly rationalistic in studying the problems confronted by existing policy and programs; reviewing desired policy and program objectives; assessing the various policy and program options that exist as reasonable and viable objects for consideration given ideological and practical constraints; and engaging in a considered review of the various strengths and weaknesses, costs and benefits of the various options under scrutiny.

Public choice theory: Public sector managers exercise their power and influence not to serve the public interest but to maximize their own private interests. Managers make decisions and advocate for policies and programs designed to benefit their superiors—both more senior managers and ministers—thereby benefitting not just the interests of these superiors but, more strategically, raising their own profile in the eyes of these more powerful actors and, consequently, raising their own employment promotion potential into the bargain. Managers act in ways to support policies and programs that will enhance the mandate, staff, and budget of their given institutional domain, be that an office, section, branch, division, or entire department.

Bureaucratic policy theory: Managers act to serve not only the long-term best interests of their organization overall, but that of their own particular branch or office within the broader organization. Managerial decision-making is thus contingent upon one's position and location within the broader organization, and this matter of position colours any given manager's approach to what is in the best interests of the organization, or, in Allison's famous aphorism: "Where you stand depends on where you sit"(Allison, 1971: 176).

Policy network theory: Managers in lead government institutions are expected to act in a manner designed to promote the long-term best interests of all actors within the policy community, as they perceive this, while they are engaged in a complex process of liaison, communication, "networking," discussions, and debate with all interested actors—other government bodies (federal, provincial, municipal, or international), interest groups, business groups and individual corporations, and individual citizens.

complex process of liaison, communication, "networking," discussions, and debate with all interested actors. Not all actors will be considered equal, however, and not all opinions, analysis, proposals, and demands will be accorded equal weight. The policy network is perceived as a series of concentric circles, with the lead government department or agency occupying the central ground, surrounded by a variety of other actors, with some closer—being deemed more important and thus more influential to government decision-makers and, therefore, possessing a more intimate operational relationship to the government actor—and others more distant, being deemed less important or influential. As with the bureaucratic politics approach to decision-making, the factors deciding closeness to, and influence with, a government actor within the policy network can be many and varied, ranging from institutional connections and intergovernmental relationships with the lead governing actor, through the socio-economic power of differing groups, their political relationships with the government of the day, the perceived political and ideological legitimacy of the positions and proposals advanced by differing groups, their professional respectability, and their ability to mobilize public opinion and media support behind their causes.

Within this pluralistic world of competing interests and groups, managers are called upon to cope with a complex environment. They are expected to relate to these differing actors; to canvas their viewpoints, concerns, and expectations for current programs and the development of new policies; and to communicate their own governmental and organizational appraisal of how well existing programs and policies are being implemented. They are also called upon to convey to all interested groups and interests the constraints under which the government must operate, the policy and program objectives of the leading government institution in the network, and the realistic expectations of what this institution can deliver in terms of improved program administration and policy development. All such communication calls for analytical capacity as well as diplomatic skill, with governing actors expected both to manage the network and its pre-existing sets of program activities and administrative actions and also provide leadership for new policy initiatives. Governing actors are expected to maintain and serve pre-established programs designed to promote the existing interests and needs of the policy network and its constituent elements while also developing new policies and programs calculated to satisfy the long-term interests of the policy network, thus serving the broader public interest. Such managerial decision-making within a pluralistic operational environment is never easy. Government actors must be the agents of sound management, visionary leadership, and effective compromise, as they seek to balance, mediate, and serve a variety of particular group and individual interests that are, in themselves, competing and contending.

5.9 Managerial Decision-Making: Reflections on a Complex Reality

This chapter has presented a brief overview of the leading concepts and approaches in management theory. As we have seen, there are a number of ways of thinking about management, of how organizations should be structured, and how management should approach its operational and leadership responsibilities. We have considered two models of organizational theory and management—the structural-mechanistic model and the organic-humanistic model—and how the nature of organization, and the role of management within the organization, is perceived and understood quite differently within each model. The former assumes that organizations should be hierarchical, with a management style founded on a top-down, authoritarian, more centralized, command-and-control approach to decision-making and the exercise of managerial power within the organization. The latter calls for organizations to be less hierarchical, with a management style oriented towards a top-down/bottom-up, egalitarian, decentralized, participatory approach to decision-making and the utilization of power within the organization. These two models of organizational theory and design have greatly structured thought and practice pertaining to management in this country, and we will observe the interplay of these models, and their constituent ideas, on Canadian public sector management in future chapters. Indeed, we have already seen the impact of the centralized command-and-control approach on the exercise of executive power within the Canadian cabinet and the role of the prime minister (Chapter 4). However, the federal government, in recent decades, has undertaken a variety of initiatives aimed at making its management systems more open and participatory, more facilitative of multidirectional communication patterns, more empowering of managers and staff, and better able to develop organizational goals that link all members of organizations behind shared and common purposes. Such seemingly noble initiatives have often failed to become entrenched in the real-world working of the federal bureaucracy, however, leaving some commentators wondering if they have been but cynical ploys to manipulate public opinion. We will review a good number of these initiatives, highlighting their operational history, and assessing the degree of their successes and failures. Through such analyses we will perceive not only strong formal interest in the organic-humanistic model of organizational design and management but the continuing strength of elements of the older, more traditional structural-mechanistic model, at least in terms of the "realpolitik" of governmental decision-making.

The foregoing pages have also illustrated four major techniques of management: incrementalism, rationalism, bounded rationalism, and mixed scanning. These techniques provide interesting frameworks for thinking about how governments make policy; how managers approach their decision-making tasks; the types of considerations that structure their thinking; and the means by which they actually engage in priority-setting, the determination of necessary actions, and the actual mechanisms of decision-making. As will also be demonstrated in subsequent chapters, all four techniques of management help to explain the actions of governments and their management at differing times, though the push for policy and program rationalism has always experienced great problems of legitimacy as rationalistic initiatives confront major practical obstacles to their effective implementation and working. Thus, we will see the continuing importance of incrementalism as a fundamental aspect of managerial decision-making and the role of mixed scanning not only as a viable technique of management but as a relatively helpful explanation for real-world government and managerial action. The appeal to management of a rational technique is strong, however, and despite the many failures of actual rationalistic undertakings, the interest in rationalism, or at least bounded rationalism, as a desired technique of decision-making continues.

We have reviewed three major motivational understandings of managerial decision-making: public choice theory, bureaucratic politics theory, and policy networks theory. Each of these approaches to decision-making offer differing insights into the theory and practice of management, each probing a different aspect of bureaucratic motivation and action—individual self-interest, institutional self-interest, and the broader public interest. We will see intriguing examples of actual bureaucratic decision-making and government action where each one of these understandings can help to explain policy and program outcomes. Rather than thinking of these three approaches as self-contained and mutually exclusive theoretical devices, it is better to perceive them as offering different but related explanations of the complexities of bureaucratic motivation at different times, under differing circumstances. Each approach may offer distinctive insights into the making of particular managerial decisions under scrutiny.

We have at our disposal a complex series of theoretical models, techniques, and approaches for understanding government and managerial decision-making. And these concepts can interrelate in differing manners. Each of the four techniques of management is equally applicable to the role of management as explicated by either of the two models of organizational design. Managers operating under a hierarchical, top-down, command-and-control orientation to management may pursue their goals either through incrementalist or rationalist techniques, for example, just as managers working through de-hierarchicalized, participative orientations may seek to attain these ends through techniques of bounded rationalism or mixed scanning. Each of the motivational approaches to management, moreover, is also equally applicable for explaining decision-making in either of the two organizational models as well as on the four major decision-making techniques. In other words, government organizations, institutional design and working, and managerial decision-making are complex, eliciting a variety of intellectual methods for analyzing their realities. This simply under-scores the importance of the study of organizational and managerial theory. Given the vast scale of government action and the complicated nature of government and managerial decision-making, it is likely that no one theory will ever offer a comprehensive understanding and explanation of govern-ment bureaucracy, but these theoretical approaches and techniques help to explain how and why governments and their managements act as they do.

The chapters that follow turn to the broad contours of public sector management as found primarily within the federal government. Chap-ters 6 and 7 review and assess major developments in the field of financial management, while Chapters 8 and 9 do likewise with personnel manage-ment. Chapter 10 deals with certain contemporary issues in management reform, with resulting debates and controversy. Chapter 11 is concerned with accountability, responsibility, and ethics, while Chapter 12 concludes with reflections on the ethics and challenges of leadership.

Key Terms

bounded rationalism: A theory of management seeking to find a middle ground between the theories of incrementalism and rationalism. Bounded rationalism, as advanced by Herbert Simon, suggests that policy-makers should strive for the most rationalistic means to achieve desired ends within the constraints of pre-existing systems of organizations and limitations of time and knowledge.

bureaucratic politics theory: A theory of management stressing that the actions of actors in the policy-making/program administration process are to be best understood as being conditioned and influenced by the interests, traditions, and values of the organizations in which any given actor works.

bureaucracy: In its classical Weberian understanding, bureaucracy refers to gov-ernment through the power of office-holders. A classical bureaucracy is founded upon hierarchy, unity of command, specialization of labour, merit, permanent employment, impersonal rules, written records, and professionalism.

citizens: In relation to public sector management the concept of citizenship is important in that citizens usually have equal rights to public services, with gov-ernment institutions bearing a legal obligation to provide citizens with high-cali-bre services without any cash-transaction nexus.

consumers/clients: In relation to public sector management the concept of con-sumers/clients is important in that consumers/clients are distinguished from citi-zens, since they are usually understood as relating to service providers through a cash-transaction nexus. Consumers/clients do not necessarily possess a right to public services.

departmentalization: In organizational theory the concept that there are a number of ways and means by which organizational departments can be organized depending on function, location, and clientele, and on the nature of span of control.

hierarchy: The concept that an organization should be constructed and managed in a pyramid structure, with managerial authority concentrated at the apex of the organization and with power flowing top-down.

incrementalism: A theory of management holding that decision-making is best done through small, measured steps, rooted to past actions and behaviours, with the goal of making improvements to already existing systems of organization.

organic-humanistic model: A school of thought holding that organizations are best understood as being living entities, populated by human beings who have multiple and complex motivations, with the role of management being to understand the human dynamics of the organization, its people and modes of communication, and to participate with employees in developing policy and programs.

participatory management: In organizational theory a concept holding that a desired form of management is one in which managers interact with employees, seeking the input and knowledge of employees in the development of policy and programs so as to ensure that policies and programs are well designed and implemented while also encouraging employees to take a deep interest in the life of the organization.

policy network theory: A way of understanding managerial decision-making by viewing every policy field as a network of public and private institutional actors and interest groups, all interacting and competing with one another as each advances its own self-interest.

POSDCORB: An acronym developed by Luther Gulick to highlight the key functions of management: Planning, Organizing, Staffing, Directing, Coordinating, Reporting, and Budgeting.

public choice theory: A theory of management stressing that the actions of politicians, public servants, and interest groups in the policy-making/program administration process are to be understood in terms of economic and material self-interest.

rationalism: A theory of management holding that decision-making is best undertaken through comprehensive planning, prioritization, ends-means assessments, cost-benefit analysis, and performance measurement.

rationality: In public sector management the concept that organizational behaviour should be rooted to ends-means relationships whereby the goal of management is to achieve desired ends through utilization of the most economical, efficient, and effective means possible.

scientific management: An approach to organizational theory championed by Frederick Taylor in which the role of management is to reduce work to clearly defined and objective practices and methods, so that these practices and methods can be constantly made more economical, efficient, and effective.

span of control: In organizational theory the concept that a superior can only exercise effective control and direction over a limited number of subordinates. Organizations can be structured with a relatively wide span of control or a narrow span of control, depending on the functions of the organization.

structural-mechanistic method: A school of thought holding that organizations are best understood as being analogous to machines, with a definite hierarchical structure, where the task of management is to design and operate the organizational machine so as to maximize productive output.

References and Suggested Reading

Allison, Graham. 1971. *Essence of Decision: Explaining the Cuban Missile Crisis.* Boston, MA: Little, Brown.

Anderson, James R. 1984. *Public Policy-Making.* New York: Holt, Rinehart and Winston.

Argyris, Chris. 1957. *Personality and Organization: The Conflict Between System and the Individual.* New York: Harper and Row.

—. 1964. *Integrating the Individual and the Organization.* New York: John Wiley and Sons.

Barnard, Chester. 1962. *The Functions of the Executive.* Cambridge, MA.: Harvard University Press.

Breton, Albert. 1974. *The Economic Theory of Representative Government.* Chicago, IL: Aldine.

Coch, L., and J.R.P. French, Jr. 1948. "Overcoming Resistance to Change." *Human Relations* 1: 512-32.

Denhardt, Robert B., with Joseph W. Grubbs. 1999. *Public Administration: An Action Orientation.* 3rd ed. Fort Worth, TX: Harcourt Brace College Publishers.

Downs, Anthony. 1957. *An Economic Theory of Democracy.* New York: Harper and Row.

Drucker, Peter F. 1954. *The Practice of Management.* New York: Harper and Row.

Etzioni, Amitai. 1967. "Mixed-Scanning: A 'Third' Approach to Decision-Making." *Public Administration Review* 27: 385-92.

Fayol, Henri. 1971. *General and Industrial Management.* Trans. Constance Storrs. London: Pitman.

Follett, Mary Parker. 1951. *Creative Experience.* New York: Peter Smith.

—. 1965. *The New State.* Gloucester, MA: Peter Smith.

Gulick, Luther. 1937. "Notes on the Theory of Organization." In Luther Gulick and L. Urwick, eds., *Papers on the Science of Administration.* New York: Institute of Public Administration. 1-46.

Gulick, Luther, and L. Urwick, eds. 1969. *Papers on the Science of Administration.* New York: Augustus M. Kelley.

Hartle, Douglas G. 1976. *A Theory of the Expenditure Budgetary Process.* Toronto: University of Toronto Press.

Inwood, Gregory J. 2004. *Understanding Canadian Public Administration: An Introduction to Theory and Practice.* 2nd ed. Scarborough, ON: Prentice-Hall Allyn Bacon.

Kernaghan, Kenneth, and David Siegel. 1999. *Public Administration in Canada: A Text.* 4th ed. Toronto: Nelson.

Lewin, K., R. Lippitt, and R.K. White. 1939. "Patterns of Aggressive Behaviour in Experimentally Created Social Climates." *Journal of Social Psychology* 10: 271-301.

Lindblom, Charles E. 1959. "The Science of Muddling-Through." *Public Administration Review* 19: 79-88.

—. 1968. *The Policy-Making Process*. Englewood Cliffs, NJ: Prentice-Hall.

Maslow, Abraham H. 1970. *Motivation and Personality*. New York: Harper and Row.

Mayo, Elton. 1960. *The Human Problems of an Industrial Civilization*. New York: Viking Press.

McGregor, Douglas. 1960. *The Human Side of Enterprise*. New York: McGraw-Hill.

Mintzberg, Henry. 1973. *The Nature of Managerial Work*. New York: Harper and Row.

Pross, A. Paul. 1986. *Group Politics and Public Policy*. Toronto: Oxford University Press.

Roethlisberger, F.J., and William J. Dickson. 1964. *Management and the Worker*. Cambridge, MA: Harvard University Press.

Simon, Herbert. 1957. *Administrative Behaviour*. 2nd ed. New York: Free Press.

Thomas, Paul G. 1999. "The Role of Central Agencies: Making a Mesh of Things." In James Bickerton and Alain-G. Gagnon, eds., *Canadian Politics*. 2nd ed. Peterborough, ON: Broadview Press. 129-48.

Turner, Frederick Winslow. 1967. *The Principles of Scientific Management*. New York: W.W. Norton.

Weber, Max. 1946. *From Max Weber: Essays in Sociology*. Ed and trans. H.H. Gerth and C. Wright Mills. New York: Oxford University Press.

Whitaker, Reginald A. 1995. "Politicians and Bureaucrats in the Policy Process." In Michael S. Whittington and Glen Williams, eds., *Canadian Politics in the 1990s*. 4th ed. Toronto: Nelson. 424-40.

Yukl, Garry. 1998. *Leadership in Organizations*. 4th ed. Upper Saddle River, NJ: Prentice-Hall.

CHAPTER 6
Public Sector Financial Management

As we saw in Chapters 1 and 2, Canadian governments have enormous responsibilities that involve them in most facets of life within this society. One practical truth flows from this: governments live on money—large amounts of cash, income, securities, and credit. Governments could not function without billions upon billions of dollars to sustain their public policy and program management activities, so matters of revenue generation and expenditure management are among the most important and controversial aspects of public sector management.

For the better part of three decades, macro-financial management concerns have dominated the Canadian political landscape as the federal and all provincial governments have wrestled with budgetary deficits, the ways and means to eliminate them, and the policy options created through running budgetary surpluses. Over the last two decades of the twentieth century, all governments became more conscious of prudent financial management and the need to live within their means. By the 1990s all governments, regardless of political affiliation, had come to prioritize deficit reduction leading to deficit elimination, subordinating all government activities to this overarching policy objective. We then experienced the politics and administration of fiscal restraint and deficit-cutting:

- public sector budget cutbacks;
- program and service reductions;
- public sector employment downsizing;
- privatization;

- deregulation;
- the downloading and offloading of government services; and,
- concomitant with such restraint policies, the greater use of consumption taxes and the enhanced role of user fees for many government services.

Through these initiatives, however, most Canadian governments (and especially, for our purposes, the federal government) have shown that deficits can be reduced and even eliminated and that progress can be made on public debt reduction. Indeed, the government of Alberta in 2005 even demonstrated that not only annual deficits but even a general debt can be eliminated, provided that a government has the revenue from a growing economy and the political desire to prioritize aggressive debt repayment. Governments can become much leaner and much more economical and efficient organizations than they had been in the past, and they have shown that they can alter themselves and evolve in response to both internal and external demands for change. In this sense, governments, and especially the federal government, have proven themselves to be adaptable and, some would say, creative, capable of substantial reform in the face of major challenges.

All such actions, though, reflect distinct policy choices and bear with them policy and program consequences. There is more than one way to eliminate a deficit and balance a budget (Chapter 7), and, depending on the method followed, one may observe greater or lesser tax increases; greater or lesser reductions in government services; and greater or lesser reliance on downsizing, public sector cutbacks, privatization, deregulation, and the use of user fees. Furthermore, the consequences of these various methods can be quite distinct. Depending on one's political and ideological perspective, policies of financial restraint may lead to better, more economical, efficient, and effective government or they may lead to worse, more limited, and ineffective government that does a disservice to the public interest. Or, we may find ourselves somewhere in the middle, experiencing a smaller, less costly government that runs annual surpluses yet also realizing that such a government has fewer resources and thus less capability for performing the range of tasks many people expect. Whether the issue is environmental standards and drinking water quality arising from the Walkerton scandal, or the quality of public health protection and SARS, or national defence and the appropriate level of funding for the Canadian military, or university tuition fees policy and the quality of post-secondary education funding, there is a direct linkage between budgetary decision-making and the quality of public services available to Canadians.

Such concerns bring into sharp relief current policy choices facing Canadian governments and the Canadian public now that, through one way or another, public sector deficits have been largely eliminated, and these governments are now anticipating, if not already reaping, large and growing annual budgetary surpluses. The policy choices are stark and politically divisive. Should such surpluses be reinvested into public services and government programs that have been subjected to deep cutbacks over the past decade? Or should they be returned to individual citizens in the form of general taxation reductions? Or should they be devoted to the reduction of the national debt? Or should there be some blending of these three options? This debate currently affects policy discussion across all governments in this country and is one that has come to dominate policy analysis at the federal level both within the government and among all federal parties.

This chapter and the next will consider these matters of budgetary politics and administration as we probe the inner workings of financial management within the federal government. Chapter 7 will focus on the politics and management of deficits, the manner by which the federal government eliminated the federal deficit in the 1990s, and the policy and administrative choices we now face in an era of budgetary surpluses; this chapter will highlight and assess the broader, deeper, and more general aspects of routine financial management across government organizations with particular attention devoted to the historical development of contemporary financial management systems.

All governments face criticism for their management of public monies, and all governments have been tarred with a certain image: that of bloated, inefficient, incompetent organizations, which waste hundreds of millions, if not billions, of hard-earned dollars taken from Canadian taxpayers. While this image is much more myth than reality, as will be illustrated below, the image remains potent due to the unfortunate examples of mismanagement *cause célèbres* that attract media and, hence, political attention. The federal sponsorship scandal that dogged the last years of the Chrétien government and rocked the Martin government in 2005 is but a notable case in point. In any one year, the annual report of the auditor general will reveal numerous examples of questionable government and managerial behaviour ranging from sloppy accounting practices, to weak managerial oversight, to poorly designed and administered programs. The reports of the auditor general routinely highlight problems with the financial management of departments and agencies, stressing the need for the government in general, and senior public sector management in particular, to devote greater care and concern to the accountability of all government policies and programs.

Accountability in government—the public duty to be responsible for all actions undertaken by government and to perform government duties with due regard to prudence, law, social responsiveness, and the managerial concepts of economy, efficiency, and effectiveness—has become one of the organizing principles of modern democratic government; it has important financial management implications as well. All governments, all departments and agencies, and all public sector managers are called to exercise their authority over public monies in accountable manners. Public sector financial management is thus best viewed as a form of trusteeship, with these officials—ministers and managers—the trustees of the public, bearing a duty to manage government financial resources in the most responsible ways possible.

As we study the financial management aspect of the public service, notice the programmatic tension between incrementalist and rationalist approaches to financial management, the continuing quest for rationalist methods of financial administration despite their many limitations, and the inner workings of rationalistic budget-making and auditing systems. The dynamics of budgeting are inherently political, and the best-laid plans of "rational" budgeting will often founder in the complex world of public sector financial management. But we will begin by assessing the current scope and nature of federal government spending.

6.1   The Nature of Government Spending

Tables 6.1 through 6.11 (see at the end of this chapter) come from the Fiscal Reference Tables published annually by the Department of Finance. These tables review the basic financial indicators of the federal government as of 2004-05. Total federal expenditures for 2004-05 totalled $196.7 billion. To support this expenditure, total revenues numbered $198.4 billion, resulting in a budget surplus of $1.6 billion. This surplus, however, was only the eighth since 1970, all eight having been recorded since 1997. By way of contrast, in 1993, the year in which the Liberal Party of Canada reclaimed federal power under the leadership of Jean Chrétien, the federal government possessed total revenues of $120.2 billion and made total expenditures of $159.3 billion, resulting in a deficit of $39.0 billion. While this deficit figure was the highest ever recorded for any one year, the fact that the federal government was operating in a deficit mode was hardly news; the federal government had been running deficits consistently since 1970, with each deficit having to be covered by federal borrowing. This annual borrowing persistently added to the federal debt. Whereas the federal debt stood at $20.3 billion in 1970, by 1980 it was at $91.9 billion, by 1990 it stood at $377.6 billion, and as of 2004-05 it registered $499.8 billion. This latest figure, however, did mark a significant decline in the federal debt since 1996. In that year, the debt hit an all-time high of $562.8 billion. Since then, the deficit reduction strategies of the Liberal government have shaved some $63 billion off the federal debt. In 2003-04, the federal government paid down $9.0 billion on its debt.

On the revenue side, as of 2004-05, 54 per cent of total federal revenues were gained through personal taxation, which included the payment of employment insurance premiums; 21.6 per cent came from indirect taxation and the GST; and 15.1 per cent was derived from corporate taxation. By contrast, in 1992-93, the last full year of the Mulroney Progressive Conservative government, personal taxation accounted for 62.0 per cent of total revenues, while indirect taxation provided 22.3 per cent and corporate taxation 5.9 per cent of this total.

In viewing how this money is spent, one can see in the Fiscal Reference Tables for 2005 that the single largest spending object, consuming 38.6 per cent of total spending, was Finance expenditures, including debt financing charges and social policy transfers (health, social assistance, and post-secondary education funding) to the provinces. Public debt charges alone accounted for 17.3 per cent of all federal spending. Total federal spending on direct programs other than national defence accounted for 32.6 per cent. Major transfers to persons (such as old age security, family allowance, and employment insurance benefits) accounted for 21.7 per cent of budgetary expenditures. Fiscal arrangements and transfer payments to the provinces consumed 21.3 per cent of federal spending, and defence obligations a further 7.1 per cent.

As one can see from the tables, certain basic longitudinal dynamics can be discerned. Over the past 15 years the proportion of total revenue accounted for by personal taxation (personal taxation and employment insurance premiums) increased through the early 1990s, reaching a peak of 62 per cent in 1992-93. Since then the figure has declined marginally to 54 per cent in 2004-05. Over the same time period, the percentage of total federal revenues deriving from corporate taxation has more than doubled, increasing from 5.9 per cent of the total in 1992-93 to 15.1 per cent in 2004-05. These figures, however, reflect more the surging growth in the Canadian economy over these years and the increasing business and commercial activity in the country than they do actual increases in corporate taxation rates. Also, while both total revenues and expenditures have tended to increase over the past three decades, with the latter outpacing the former, thus leading to annual deficits and a growing federal debt, the past decade or so has known dramatic fiscal swings. In the early 1990s, federal revenues actually declined as a result of recession, while total expenditures grew and then hovered around the high $150 billion range. In the mid-1990s, however, because of a concerted effort to restrain and eliminate the deficit, federal revenue growth had been elevated to the $150 billion range, again mainly due to a growing national economy, while total program expenditures were contained and reduced to a low of $102.2 billion in 1996-97. The overall result of all these developments, however, was the elimination of the federal deficit by 1997-98 and the beginning of a gradual paying down of the accumulated federal debt. As we entered the new century, the pace of growth in the economy experienced in the last years of the 1990s has slowed, leading the prime minister and the minister of finance to warn that the size of future surpluses may be significantly smaller than the $20.1 billion recorded in 2000-01. Nonetheless, the federal government under the prime ministership of Paul Martin was committed to maintaining some form of government surplus, so that Canadians were confronted with strategic policy questions about the best course of action for using it. As we will see below, these questions and this issue will help to frame Canadian politics and the practice of government for years to come.

Two lessons, moreover, can be derived from all of these figures and dynamics:

1. The scope of federal financial management is truly enormous. The federal government is the single largest economic actor within Canada, and the impact of its financial decision-making is felt by each and every Canadian.

2. Government decisions about financial management can result in discernible changes in budgetary policy that can have a demonstrable impact on the entire Canadian society.

Current political concerns—such as the impact of deficit reduction, the social and economic consequences of government cutbacks, the fraying of the social safety net, the perceived declining relevance of government, the fiscal choices confronting governments with respect to current budget surpluses, and the future role of the state in the post-deficit era—reflect the ongoing importance of government financial management and the policy choices, trade-offs, and options that it embodies.

6.2   The Traditional Elements of Financial Management

The financial management considerations of governments involve two separate but related processes: revenue and expenditure.

6.2.1   The Revenue Process

The revenue process concerns the ways and means by which money is raised to sustain the operations of governments. As observed from the data presented, general revenue sources can include individual and corporate taxation, service charges, fees and duties, and borrowing. The preparation of the federal annual revenue budget is the foremost responsibility of the prime minister and the minister of finance. In Chapter 4, we noted that these two actors have always been the dominant figures in government budgetary planning, and, with the current command approach to leadership exhibited by prime ministers Chrétien and Martin and their finance ministers, the authority and influence of these leaders has been even more elevated within official Ottawa. Assisting these officials in their duties are the departments of Finance and Customs and Revenue. Officials in these institutions, under the close leadership of their ministers, develop a government-wide economic policy outlook, a fiscal plan, and specific revenue-raising proposals designed to facilitate government functions while staying true to broad government economic and fiscal objectives. The officials develop these plans in close consultation with the prime minister and the minister of finance, the plenary cabinet and cabinet committees, and the leading central agencies—the Treasury Board Secretariat (TBS), the Privy Council Office (PCO), and the Prime Minister's Office (PMO). Consultations also extend to senior officials from other departments and even other provincial governments, and it is now common for the Department of Finance to hold pre-budget hearings with leading interest groups representing business, labour, and social interests. The focal point of all such work is the presentation of the annual budget by the minister of finance to the House of Commons, usually in late February or early March (Strick, 1999: 89-91).

The **revenue budget** attracts most popular and media attention because it has a direct impact on almost everybody in its taxation component and also because of the budget speech's theatrical presentation. But regardless of revenue's "popularity," the financial management process that is of greatest importance to those who either work within governments or who are concerned with the organizational working of governments is the expenditure process (Doern, Maslove, and Prince, 1988).

6.2.2   The Expenditure Process

The development of the **expenditure budget** involves officials from every department and agency in the setting of institutional goals and financial requirements. In turn, cabinet committees assess and analyze these studies and requests, and in this work they are assisted by further studies, reviews, and financial management plans and evaluations prepared by Finance, the PCO, and the TBS. The development of the annual federal expenditure budget, presented to Parliament in the form of massive Main Estimates (the Blue Book), is a process that is awesome in its breadth and complexity and terribly important for its impact upon government.

The **Main Estimates** directly outline the levels, purposes, and objectives of public spending within each department and agency, thereby providing both a reference for measuring total government and department spending and for assessing specific spending priorities. The Main Estimates provide the starting point of a chain by which governments can be held to account for the quantity and quality of their spending activities in reference either to specific departments, agencies, programs, or branches, or with reference to government-wide trends.

This chain of accountability historically was tied to Parliament, as the ultimate "guardian of the public purse," but it now extends far beyond the floor of the House of Commons. Parliamentary debates on the revenue and expenditure budgets have always tended to be more symbolic than substantive given the influence of the governing party during times of majority governments. The main actors in the financial management accountability process are usually found outside of the House of Commons itself. They are government departments, cabinet committees and central agencies; the auditor general; the Public Accounts Committee of Parliament; and political parties, interest groups, and the media. Their respective roles will be considered in more detail below.

6.3   Approaches in Expenditure Budgeting

All expenditure budgets have a number of purposes. On one basic level they are statements and guidelines in regard to how, when, where, why, and in what amounts a government will spend its revenue (Adie and Thomas, 1987: 252-53). In this respect a budget acts as a list of financial intent, allowing administrative and political superiors to exercise some control over departments and agencies by insisting that set expenditure levels not be exceeded. On a deeper level, though, a budget can and should act as a management tool, allowing senior managers to assess and evaluate the degree of economy, efficiency, and effectiveness found within any organization. By reviewing the changing quantity of financial resources expended by an organization and relating this to other changing quantitative and qualitative phenomena—such as greater organizational output, greater service delivery, or enhanced client or citizen satisfaction with government services—managers can gain important knowledge about how well their organization is meeting its objectives. Good budgetary analysis can inform managers about procedures that enhance employee efficiency and program effectiveness while also highlighting activities that are less economical and efficient. It can allow managers and their political superiors to set new tactical and strategic directions for the future, as well as determine how well their organizational priorities are being met and whether existing undertakings can be modified, improved, or eliminated in order to free up monetary resources for new priorities and initiatives. In this respect a budget acts as an ongoing management information device designed to provide organizational intelligence to the leaders of any given bureaucracy.

The ideal budget will contain certain aspects of these three elements: control, management information, and planning. In practice, however, the ideal is often not realized. As will be seen, there were two major forms of public sector budgeting practised by Canadian governments until the mid-1990s, only one of which consciously sought to achieve the ideal—with limited success. It is important to study these forms because they constitute the heritage of financial management through which current budgetary policies, understandings, and practices have evolved. And they also offer important lessons as to what types of financial management practices work well in the real world of decision-making and what types do not. Much of what follows will be a study in failed or weak financial management initiatives, especially in relation to budgetary rationalism. It is important to study these failures for what one can learn from them and to observe how current practices emerged out of them.

6.3.1 Budgetary Incrementalism

The traditional form of expenditure budget-making found in all Canadian governments until the 1960s was that of the **incremental "line-item" budget** (Kernaghan and Siegel, 1999: 621-24). This approach to budgeting is so named because the ultimate budget document is a line-by-line list of objects of expenditure to be paid for by a given department or agency or office over a specific year (see Box 6.1). As you can see, the budget lists

BOX 6.1
Hypothetical Line-Item Budget

Federal Court of Canada—Regional Office

Item	2006 (Budget)	2005 (Actual)
Salaries (Regular)	$415,000	$404,000
Salaries (Overtime)	24,000	20,500
Employee Benefits	67,000	65,000
Office Equipment	33,500	28,700
Office Supplies	15,100	12,500
Facility Rent	90,900	87,700
Cleaning Services	38,000	36,000
Security Services	51,000	49,000
Travel	5,000	5,000
Library	35,000	33,600
Miscellaneous	5,000	5,000
Totals	$779,500	$747,000

specific objects—such as salaries, benefits, equipment, rent, travel, and vehicles—and a comparison of expenditure levels for these items in light of the previous year's expenses. This form of budget is quite rudimentary and, thus, simple to create. In order to create the budget for the upcoming year, a budget manager need only take the previous year's budget totals for each item and marginally adjust them to take account of such factors as inflation, contractual obligations, change in service levels, and alterations in populations served. Such marginal adjustments to an established base result in only incremental change to the overall budget, where the basic activities of the organization are accepted as given. In such a process the only question is the degree to which funding levels for established objects of expenditure will either increase or decrease.

This approach to budgeting has both the benefits and problems associated with simplicity. On the positive side:

- A line-item budget is relatively easy to draft. Managers know that their next year's budget will simply be a revision of their last budget; its shape and form and content will remain basically unchanged.
- This acceptance of the existing roles and purposes of established organizations leads managers to be unconcerned with justifying and

defending the purposes and interests of their organization within the broader spectrum of general government activities.

- An incremental approach preserves the status quo, meaning that all established organizational actors are guaranteed that they and their basic programs and policies will persist into the future. They need not engage in the difficult politics and decision-making attached to the assessment and negotiation of trade-offs in broad government policy and spending priorities.

- The process is not abnormally difficult or time-consuming. Middle-level managers with a solid understanding of their branches can easily draft such a budget, and senior managers and their political superiors can readily understand them (Henry, 1995: 210-11).

It should be noted that a line-item budget tends to be "bottom-up" rather than "top-down" within any organization. Given the detailed concern for items of expenditure, their changing costs, and service level alterations, this is a type of budget most easily and readily prepared by middle managers, as they are the ones most familiar with the routine financial and operational workings of their organizations and their changing incremental needs. These managers establish their budgetary requests and submit them up the bureaucratic hierarchy for approval from senior management. This system is inherently decentralized, placing the bulk of budgetary decision-making power in the hands of the middle managers sprinkled throughout any organization. It is not surprising that this form of budgeting has been highly praised by these very same officials!

On the negative side, however, such simplicity brings certain drawbacks:

- The very rudimentary nature of the line-item budget means that it is of limited value as a management or planning tool.

- Given the scant nature of the information provided, senior managers and political superiors have limited ability to assess and evaluate the quality of the bureaucratic work being sustained. Senior officials will know how much money is being spent on what items and the nature of incremental change over the past year, but that is all.

- The budget itself provides neither information to allow for studies of how efficiently resources are being used nor information to measure the longitudinal effectiveness of government programs over time or comparatively across program fields.

- Senior managers are not provided with information allowing them to evaluate and fine-tune organizational operations or to systematically plan for future policy and program improvements.
- The line-item budget is essentially a backward-looking document. In planning for next year's budget, managers look to the past for guidance, not to future goals and priorities.
- At best, the line-item budget allows senior officials to exert some control over the spending habits of middle managers in that overspending on an item can be readily observed. But this is clearly of limited benefit.

The very "bottom-up," simple, incremental features in the line-item budget guarantee that it is of restricted value for those concerned with centralized program evaluation and policy development both within any organization in particular or the entire government in general. Of course, this is a condition deemed highly favourable by middle managers, since it enhances their influence and power within their organizations (Brown-John, LeBlond, and Marson, 1988).

6.3.2   Performance Budgeting

A variation on the line-item budget, developed in the late 1960s and designed to provide somewhat greater managerial and planning information to senior officials, is the **performance budget** (Henry, 1995: 211-12). In this form of budgeting, efficiency evaluations are built into the process by determining a relationship between financial inputs and service outputs. Middle managers are asked not only to provide a line-item listing of expenditures but also, where possible, to provide a quantitative listing of services provided through such expenditures over the past year. Thus, a relationship can be drawn between money spent and services rendered: How many documents were prepared or phone calls answered per secretary? How many workers' compensation claims were handled per claims officer? How many restaurant investigations were conducted per board of health officer?

Through this approach to budgeting the limited nature of the line-item budget can be overcome to a degree.

- Performance budgeting allows for the development of efficiency evaluations, since the efficiency of a given operation can be measured over time, and general efficiency ratings of differing operations can be compared one to another—a fire department, for example, could demonstrate greater efficiency gains than a court office.

- Information of this sort can then be used by senior managers, policy analysts, and political leaders in evaluating the various claims for budgetary support made by differing organizations; more efficient organizations can be rewarded while the less efficient can be informed that their operational performance needs to be improved before they will gain increased funding.
- Similarly, such performance budgeting techniques enable senior managers to pinpoint those middle managers who are adept at gaining efficiency improvements compared to those who are not; the former can then be favoured over the latter.

Despite all these benefits, however, performance budgeting also has weaknesses:

- It is still, essentially, an incrementalist device and can only be applied to those services that are easily quantifiable: letters written, calls answered, investigations undertaken. But not all public services are easily quantifiable, and important distinctions must be made between quantitative and qualitative values. International diplomacy or intelligence-gathering or policy analysis do not necessarily lend themselves to fast and ready quantitative evaluation. They are services that are ongoing, part of a web of activities any one part of which may be quite unimportant in isolation but which are necessary components of a broader whole.
- Quantitative analysis of particular administrative processes—documents prepared, calls answered, meetings held—reveals nothing about the quality of such works. Are good documents prepared? Do callers receive sound, helpful information? Do meetings help to promote communication and solve problems? These are all qualitative considerations that require careful, qualitative analysis, analysis in which people may reasonably disagree as to the merits of a given undertaking.
- Quantitative analysis may provide certain crude efficiency indicators, which may be valuable in certain narrow respects, but as a general management tool and planning device, performance budgeting results in more frustration than satisfaction.

By the late 1960s, management and policy analysts in this country and abroad were looking towards radically new methods of public sector expenditure budgeting that would bring management and planning concerns to the fore.

6.3.3 Budgetary Rationalism

The development of program budgeting systems can be traced to the American Defence Department in the 1950s and 1960s. Given the problems and weaknesses associated with incremental line-item and performance budgeting, there was a concerted effort to develop a new system of budgeting—program budgeting—that would link, in a systematic fashion, monetary inputs to policy and program outputs. The aim was to establish a budgetary system that was organizationally holistic and rational, allowing senior administrative and political leaders to fully comprehend the operational working of any organization while also allowing for comprehensive, rational policy prioritization and planning at the level of both the individual organization and the government overall (Henry, 1995: 212-13).

By the mid-1960s this approach swept through public administration circles in the western world as the new, rational way to do public sector expenditure budgeting. Within Canada, **budgetary rationalism** was first embraced in a systematic fashion by the federal Liberal government of Pierre Trudeau. In 1969 his government introduced a new system of program budgeting known as Planning-Programming-Budgeting Systems (PPBS), which was to dominate federal financial management thinking for the better part of a decade (French, 1984: 34-37). Since then, subsequent governments have struggled with the operationalization of program budgeting, leading to a number of program budget variations being propagated, implemented, and either discarded or modified. The history of federal financial management over the past four decades is a story of by-and-large failed attempts to develop a workable system of rational program budgeting. Over this time period, a number of major program budgeting changes were initiated, none of which have lived up to expectations. We can discern in them the many problems associated with rational planning and the longevity and continued importance of the much maligned but nevertheless persistent approach of incremental budgeting.

6.3.3.1 PLANNING-PROGRAMMING-BUDGETING SYSTEMS

The development of PPBS was a conscious effort by senior administrative and political leaders in the federal government to operationalize rationalism in the budget-making process by linking strategic thought to organizational activity to actual spending decisions. As the name suggests, budgetary decision-making was to be predicated on strategic planning through which the government would begin the process of funding government activity by establishing policy priorities and objectives. Having established and ranked such desires and ends according to comparative importance, the process moved on to conceptualizing and assessing the operational ways and means by which such ends could be achieved. This is the programming component of the system. Once desired programs had been structured, prioritized, and accepted by the government, appropriate multi-year funding levels for particular programs were established to allow them to meet the planned goals the whole system was designed to facilitate.

A Treasury Board guide (1969: 8) neatly summarized the six essential concepts of PPBS:

- setting specific objectives;
- systematic analysis to clarify objectives and to assess alternative ways of meeting them;
- framing budgetary proposals in terms of proposals directed towards the achievement of objectives;
- projection of the costs of these programs a number of years into the future;
- formalization of plans of achievement year by year for each program; and
- an information system for each program to supply data for the monitoring of achievement of program goals and for the reassessment of the program objectives and the appropriateness of the program itself.

Box 6.2 provides a hypothetical example of the typical end-product of a program budget. Note how, in a few words, the budget seeks to present information describing a program, its objectives, and priorities. The financial data are presented in three groups:

- The "A" budget reflects funding levels of all existing and approved programs, with account taken of cost-of-living and service-level fluctuations. These figures provide information on the policy and program status quo and what its preservation would cost.
- The "B" budget reflects claims for new undertakings and what their financial implications will be. It was always assumed in this approach that most critical attention would fall on the assessment

of'' "B" budget items, as they represent new initiatives and financial obligations to meet new policy objectives.

- The "X" budget represents those items that are considered to be of lowest priority to the sponsoring department and that could be eliminated without major harm occurring to the general priorities of the department. The "X" budget never gained much support from program managers who prepared PPBS budgets. Few were ever inclined to admit that existing programs in their departments were expendable. During the 1970s when PPBS was seriously practised by the federal government, moreover, growing government spending habits had the effect of rendering the "X" budget exercise of little value. Only through growing concern for restraint and cutbacks in the 1990s was interest regained in the "X" budget concept among budget planners.

Finally, the sample budget displays a concern for certain performance measures. Information highlighting achievements and the value of the program is provided. This material is designed to assist senior managers and political leaders in assessing the worthiness of the entire program and of the request for "B" budget enhancement.

This PPBS approach to budgeting marked a radical transformation from earlier incremental approaches. Now there was an explicit recognition that the entire budget process must link strategic planning and prioritization with operational management concerns while still maintaining a focus on budgetary controls. Thus, PPBS sought to achieve all three of the ideal goals of budgeting. There was also an explicit recognition of the importance of comparative analysis, cost-benefit analysis, and performance measurement in assessing programs and developing budget proposals. The development of program budgeting marked the development of program analysis as a key component in financial management. PPBS and all other program budget approaches were founded on the position that priorities and objectives could be programmed and that the quantitative and qualitative worth of programs could be assessed, evaluated, and ranked. Better performing programs could be identified and supported, and weaker programs could be subjected to appropriate criticism and restraint. Through the operation of the entire system, the government could enhance the realization of policy priorities while inculcating in managers the need to stress the importance of planning, critical analysis, and efficient and effective program implementation and evaluation (French, 1984: 36-41).

BOX 6.2

Hypothetical Program Budget

Federal Court of Canada—Regional Office

Program Description: The provision of local court facilities and services for those bringing cases under the Federal Court Act. This regional office offers a full range of managerial and administrative support services for the judiciary, Crown and private counsel, and interested citizens.

Budget Requests: Budget Year 2006

A-Base Request: To maintain existing services respecting management and administrative support for the court. Totals provide funding for three management and seven administrative positions, standing office equipment and supplies (see attached list), facility rental and related costs (see attached list).

Budget 2006	Estimated 2005	Actual 2004	Actual 2003
$779, 500	$747,000	$741,000	$739,000

B-Budget Request: Permission to hire one additional junior manager and one staff person to engage in development and implementation of new case-flow management system to expedite case-flow. Through such an initiative the current pace of litigation delay could be reduced from six to three months, a 50-per-cent improvement. Such management reforms have received endorsement by the Canadian Judicial Council, the Canadian Bar Association, and the jurisprudence of the Supreme Court of Canada. (See attached report.) This initiative also conforms with established best-practices policy of the Federal Court of Canada.

Requested	Forecast		
2006	2007	2008	2009
$90,000	$92,000	$94,500	$97,000

X-Budget Report: The Office is currently understaffed and under-resourced, placing a great strain on existing management and personnel. Resulting X-Budget capabilities are restricted to travel and miscellaneous reductions of $1500.

Possible	Forecast		
2006	2007	2008	2009
$1500	$0	$0	$0

PPBS in theory had much to commend it but, in practice, it ran into a vortex of problems, many of its own making. On the positive side, program budgeting sought the benefits of rationalism. Government officials were encouraged to think systematically about what they were doing and to think about financial management in a comprehensive, holistic, and analytical manner. Rather than treating a budget as a simple listing of objects of expenditures that will incrementally change over time, program budgeting demanded that officials think about governmental ends and means, priorities, objectives, methods, and analysis. In short, PPBS sought to encourage clear, rational, future-oriented thinking by government officials.

But the theory could not withstand its meeting with reality. For all its theoretical virtues, PPBS confronted certain major practical problems endemic to rationalist policy approaches. One set of problems centred on the practical difficulties of actually doing "rational" planning and analysis (French, 1984: 79-85). PPBS called for the setting and ranking of government priorities; this was easier said than done. At the department or agency level, differing officials within the organization have differing perspectives as to what should be the organization's top priorities. Remember that the determination of priorities will condition subsequent program and spending decisions. Therefore, it was in the organizational self-interest of all managers to have their interests and responsibilities ranked high. Given this approach to the issue, within any institution a multiplicity of perspectives as to the institution's key priorities and objectives can be found. For example, what would be the top priorities of the Department of National Defence? Military preparedness? The defence of Canadian territory? Fulfilment of NATO commitments? International peacekeeping? Regional development and institutional support for Canadian armaments and technology manufacturers? The development of a viable militia? Differing officials within the department could validly support each of these positions as being most important and necessary, not to mention being congruent with their personal organizational ambitions. And even among those who stressed military preparedness, there would be the question of how. Through support of the army? Or the navy? Or the air force? In a world of limited financial resources, prioritization here was so contentious as to be virtually impossible. Officials from each service could and would develop perfectly rational plans as to why their branch of the service should be given priority treatment. And, of course, each such plan would be roundly attacked as being misinformed and misguided by those supporting a different set of priorities.

The problems set out here in simple terms offer a glimpse of the internecine bureaucratic battling that one encounters every time priority-setting becomes a part of the work of an organization. And the problems experienced within any given department or agency are magnified when attention turns to the entire government as an institution. Through PPBS, the cabinet itself was called upon to prioritize general government objectives so as to facilitate desirable funding allocations to each department and its agencies. But what were the key priorities of the government? Economic growth? Social justice? Job creation? Fiscal responsibility? Constitutional reform? International harmony? Environmental protection? Support for women's interests? Support for children's interests? Support for business interests? Support for labour interests? Support for First Nations' interests? Such a list could go on and on.

The difficulty here is that *each one* of these matters could have been among the key priorities of the government and, perhaps, according to one's ideological perspective, should have been. Thus, the upper echelons of government were confronted with the problems of prioritization that had been generated in every department. Which objectives were more important than others, thereby deserving greater financial support? Here, each department and each cabinet minister advocated the importance of his or her own particular policy and program interests. Finance historically has supported the goals of stable economic growth and fiscal prudence; the old Department of Health and Welfare long supported the development of an expansive and expensive social safety net; the Department of the Environment advocated environmental consciousness and the enforcement of environmental regulations, while the departments of Agriculture, Fisheries and Oceans, Industry and Trade, and Regional Economic Expansion, for example, all advocated economic policy priorities rooted in their organizational mandates.

Given such differing positions on government priorities, all of them thoroughly researched and forcefully presented, the federal government experienced great difficulties in systematically establishing and ranking priorities. Actually, the government treated the task as both impossible and unnecessary, since, in the 1970s and 1980s, there was always some money to be expended on each objective. But by stressing that all government objectives were priorities, the concept of prioritization lost its impact. Budgetary decision-making and resource allocation were subject then not to the process of rational allocation but to the power of those departments and ministers capable of exercising greater influence within the centralized decision-making institutions of the government. These power relations (canvassed in Chapter 4) led authors such as French (1984) and Hartle (1976) to refer to the policy-making approaches of the 1970s as "chaotic," governed more by bureaucratic power politics than any form of rational discussion and analysis. In the current era of fiscal restraint, interest in prioritization has been revived, but still the difficulties in accomplishing prioritization persist, leading governments to turn to simpler and blunter methods of exacting cutbacks (see Chapter 7).

As if prioritization and ranking did not pose difficulties enough, PPBS also experienced great problems respecting the measurement and analysis of program activities and the assessment of future needs. How does one measure the effectiveness of a government program? Any program will have a multiplicity of objectives, all calling for differing forms of evaluation. For example, how does one determine the success of federal regional development programs? By the amount of money spent? By the numbers of jobs created? By the economic activity generated? By the entrepreneurialism promoted? By an analysis of demonstrated economic outcomes in comparison to opportunity costs? By the communities and ways of life that are preserved? By the ability of the governing party to gain re-election in the affected ridings? All such factors can be elements of an evaluation, depending on the analytical perspective of the evaluator. And, depending on the factors of evaluation chosen, the outcome of any one analysis can be diametrically opposed to that of another, even when they are evaluating the same program.

The issue of planning also posed a major problem to PPBS. The system called for long-range planning involving multi-year forecasting of economic and political trends, financial considerations, and alterations in service level demands. But all such planning is prone to breakdown due to the unpredictability of economic developments and human behaviour. Unexpected general economic slowdowns can render the most detailed five-year financial plan a piece of junk, and unexpected political developments can leave a hitherto sound strategic plan in tatters. Defence departments throughout all NATO countries are still adjusting to the unprecedented shock of the collapse of their prime enemy and their basic *raison d'être*—the Soviet Union. Political conditions can change rapidly, with the result that multi-year or five-year planning is akin to crystal-ball gazing. Just compare the changes in general attitude to border and airline security between September 10, 2001 and September 12, 2001.

Beyond all these planning problems, PPBS encountered another set of difficulties stemming from the changed bureaucratic power relations inaugurated by the system. In contrast to incrementalist budget systems, PPBS shifted decision-making power into the hands of senior policy analysts and managers within departments and central agencies (Kernaghan and Siegel,

1999: 628-29). It was these persons, and not middle managers, who now dominated the budget process, which called for central planning and decision-making that only such senior officials could provide. This concentration of centralized power resulted in most middle-ranking department officials viewing the new system with a leery eye; clearly, they were losing authority and prestige to their departmental overseers and to the rising elite in the central agencies, and this did not bode well for amicable cooperation between these actors.

The greatest power shift was that involving central agencies. In the new world of centralized planning and programming, institutions such as the PCO, the TBS, and Finance came to play major roles, since they were called upon to develop their own advisory positions on the strategic priorities of the government as well as providing, to cabinet and cabinet committees, detailed critical appraisals of the worthiness of department and agency plans and proposals. Whereas under the old departmentalized system of policy decision-making, department budgets had been subjected to little external review, now such review was gruelling, with ministers coming to rely very heavily upon the analysis and advice provided to them by those in the central agencies. As a result, these agencies actively carved out a niche for themselves within the corridors of power in Ottawa—they claimed that, in contrast to the departments, they were independent "actors," not beholden to any particular policy or program initiative and not subject to the influence of any particular interest group, and that their appraisals of departmental and governmental priorities and programs were more sound because they were operationally removed from program delivery.

There was a certain degree of truth in this contention, much to the chagrin of department officials, and this understanding was not lost on cabinet ministers. On the other hand, as French (1984: ch. 2) has pointed out, the central agencies themselves came to be identified with particular policy approaches and preferred priorities, such that department counterclaims of central agencies' biases contained a degree of truth. Of course, all the institutional actors in the system eventually became identified with particular approaches to department and general government priorities and programs so that no one institution could rightfully make any legitimate claim to being an independent and impartial participant in the system. As Hartle (1976: ch. 1) has observed, by the time the system was fully operationalized, the upper echelons of the federal government resembled a "jungle" of bureaucratic warfare, motivated by institutional self-interest, in which every actor fought every other actor for preferential standing in the battle for priority status and access to financial resources.

The new system consciously established competing sources of power and called upon all actors to interact with one another in the preparation of priorities, objectives, programs, and budget requests. Thus, it required an enormous amount of analysis:

- Budget-makers were asked not only to think about next year's needs but needs for the next five years.
- Department managers had to assess and situate their program activities in light of the strategic policy priorities of the entire department.
- Policy analysts with central agencies were expected to conceptualize policy priorities for the entire government and to evaluate and plan departmental strategic initiatives accordingly.
- Departmental actors had to closely analyze their own work while being acutely aware of the analyses of central agencies and of other departments.
- Central agencies had to develop their own analytical frameworks for policies and programs in light of departmental analyses of these same matters and in light of previous departmental criticisms of earlier central agency analyses.

Analysis became the buzzword of the system, eventually becoming one of its great problems. In short, PPBS became prone to *analysis paralysis*, a debilitating condition arising from too many senior officials throughout the government spending more and more time doing analyses of what the government should be doing, rather than getting on with the job of governing (Adie and Thomas, 1987: 267-68).

In calling for rational analysis of all priorities, objectives, policies, and programs, PPBS became a system that required superhuman strength to operate. Not surprisingly, few superhumans were found in the government, with the result that the highly complex system of planning and budget decision-making became prone to breakdown and failure. Such was the case with PPBS. Because of all the difficulties mentioned here, this budgeting system began to lose support in the federal government throughout the 1970s. By 1978 it was dead in the water (French, 1984: 148). Many factors help to explain this failure, but a simple truth should not be overlooked. For any bureaucratic undertaking to survive, it must possess the virtue of simplicity, so that those living and working within the system view it as an aid in helping them undertake and improve upon their work. If and when the system becomes so cumbersome and demanding that it dominates and frustrates the organizational life of the actors it was meant to serve, it is dysfunctional and needs to be replaced.

6.3.4   Modified Rationalism

Considering the problems associated with PPBS, its demise was not unexpected. Although support for the system waned, such was not the case for the concept of budgetary rationalism. Senior bureaucratic and political leaders both in Ottawa and the provinces were still attracted to a rationalistic approach to budget-making for its perceived ability to promote the values of prioritization, planning, critical analysis, and systematic program development. After all, these are all integral elements of the management process, and any organization ignores these matters to its peril. Moreover, in bureaucracies predicated on the belief that knowledge is power, there was the understandable human belief that reasonable, well-educated human beings could overcome the difficulties with rational planning in a rational manner, leaving the benefits of rationalism intact. So, while PPBS disappeared into bureaucratic history, the federal government experimented with other forms of rational budget systems.

6.3.4.1   THE POLICY AND EXPENDITURE MANAGEMENT SYSTEM (PEMS)

Although by the late 1970s senior officials in the federal government were recognizing the failure of PPBS, there was still substantial interest in the development of a planning and budgeting system that would provide a rationalist approach to policy and financial decision-making. Despite all of the difficulties associated with PPBS, Management by Objectives (MBO), Operational Performance Measurement Systems (OPMS), and the then fledgling Zero-Based Budgeting system (ZBB) (material on these can be found on the Thinking Government web site), senior officials and policy analysts recognized that there was theoretical and practical value in planning, in thinking about priorities, in setting objectives, in working on measures of program effectiveness, and in making budgetary decisions upon such informed judgements. There was a clear reluctance in Ottawa officialdom to reject rationalism outright, as this was viewed as tantamount to an acceptance of incrementalism with all of its problems of short-term, backward-looking, non-analytical organizational thought. So, despite the problems with PPBS, in 1979 a new policy and budgetary planning system was inaugurated in Ottawa by the Progressive Conservative government of Joe Clark: The Policy and Expenditure Management System (**PEMS**). It has been subjected to many alterations over the past 15 years, and though it has been superseded by the Chrétien government's Expenditure Management System, its structural logic still exerts influence over the current system of financial management within Ottawa (Adie and Thomas, 1987: ·268-74; Inwood, 2004: 327-28).

Like PPBS, PEMS was a financial management system designed to integrate planning, programming, and budget allocation. PEMS took the basic budgeting structure of PPBS—multi-year planning, policy prioritization, program budgeting—and sought to give it new life by more closely linking political and administrative decision-making. PEMS sought to enhance the role of ministers in financial management by decentralizing (relatively) budgetary decision-making down to cabinet committees. The cabinet committee system endured many changes during the life of PEMS but Box 4.5 from Chapter 4 shows what the system looked like in 1986.

There were three basic and interrelated elements to PEMS, with the entire system operating over a five-year horizon.

1. In each year the government would revise its *Multi-Year Fiscal Plan*. The preparation of this plan was the responsibility of the Department of Finance, emphasizing its central role in the entire process. It provided a detailed assessment of the contemporary revenue and expenditure position of the government as well as forecasting it for the next four years and established broad revenue targets of the government in keeping with Finance's analysis of the health of the national economy. In conjunction with the Treasury Board, Finance would plan the allocation of such revenue among departmental sectors for program delivery. In developing the Multi-Year Fiscal Plan Finance had to take account of broad government priorities set by the Priorities and Planning (P&P) committee of cabinet and of sectoral priorities set by the other specific cabinet committees. Finance also had to address the issue of the appropriate level of deficit financing to be entered into and the consequent degree of restraint necessary to maintain the financial health of the government itself. Once prepared, this Multi-Year Fiscal Plan was presented to P&P for review, revision, and eventual acceptance.

2. Once approved, the Fiscal Plan served as the foundation for allocating funding levels to the various sectoral committees of cabinet in order to support established and new programs ("A" and "B" budgets). These committees, comprising the ministers of the departments making up the given sector, had as their responsibility the allocation of their sector's fund among its departments and programs. Each policy sector received its total funding in what was known as an *Envelope*. This Envelope—a funding level—was

comprised of a Reference Level for funding approved programs and a Policy Reserve for funding new initiatives or enhancing established programs. There was also a small Operating Reserve to be used to fund special projects during emergency or unforeseen circumstances. The distribution of these funds was at the discretion of those sitting on the cabinet committee. In this manner, financial management was decentralized to responsible ministers.

3. Each separate department had a role to play in the planning and budgeting process through the preparation of a number of departmental plans designed to assist themselves and other actors in making the whole system work. Each department was to prepare a Strategic Overview, later termed a *Ministerial Strategic Memorandum.* This document, prepared for the use of the prime minister and P&P, provided a review of departmental objectives in light of general government priorities, an assessment of alternative means of pursuing departmental goals, an assessment of new policy options contemplated by the department, and a review of program evaluations and actions taken to enhance program performance. This information was used by P&P in evaluating each department's position within broad government planning, and a compendium of these plans and reviews, prepared by PCO, was used in formulating Finance's Multi-Year Fiscal Plan.

Apart from these documents each department had to prepare two operational plans: a Multi-Year Operational Plan (MYOP) and a Budget Year Operational Plan (BYOP). The MYOP was an assessment of a department's long-term planning over three years. This document usually contained material dealing with long-range priorities and objectives, an assessment of how existing programs fit such priorities, and a review of benefits derived from existing programs. The BYOP was a more detailed plan. It contained a list of financial resources available to the department, the operational goals to be undertaken through such funding, and an evaluation plan to assess the performance quality of department programs. Both these plans were prepared in consultation with the TBS and required its approval prior to being authorized as official departmental planning devices (Adie and Thomas, 1987: 274-76).

While PEMS proved to be a more long-lived financial management system than PPBS, it too suffered from the now familiar defects of rationalism. Planning and policy prioritization proved extremely difficult, both in times of growing government expenditures and in more recent times of fiscal restraint. In both instances, the decision-making process was characterized by intense bureaucratic in-fighting, as departments and central agencies fought to advance or protect their own institutional self-interest. A further problem with the planning process, one that cast doubt on the whole concept of rational planning, was that only some 5 per cent of total federal expenditures were usually accounted for in "B" budgets. Thus, the whole complex planning process for the development of new priorities and initiatives and the determination of relevant funding levels only affected around 5 per cent of government spending. Roughly 95 per cent of total federal expenditure was accounted for in the "A" budgets for established programs deeply embedded in the legal and political structures of Canadian life. Such programs, however, were not subject to detailed annual scrutiny, as this was deemed an inefficient use of time, meaning that their ongoing approval was a given, much like the situation found in incremental budgeting. Criticisms eventually arose as to whether the sophisticated and involved planning process of PEMS was necessary and desirable in light of the very limited extent of budgetary allocations affected by its decision-making (Adie and Thomas, 1987: 277-79).

The issue of program evaluation also proved to be an ongoing problem for all the same reasons observed with earlier rationalist initiatives. However, under PEMS the evaluation debate now extended into cabinet committees and between such committees and central agencies, as all these actors sought to advance their own interests by either supporting or attacking particular evaluations. Rather than facilitating the planning process, the development and analysis of evaluations had the effect of rendering the system more complex and divisive.

This issue reveals a deeper problem associated with PEMS. As can be observed, the whole process involved an enormous amount of organizational work. The system demanded and bred plans, meetings, analyses, memorandums, reviews, evaluations, and discussions leading to further plans, meetings, analyses, and so on. While decisions were made eventually, the process was extremely complex and cumbersome, making it very time-consuming. As is commonly accepted, time is the most precious commodity for senior managers and ministers, so many of the leading officials within the federal government developed a critical perspective on the amount of time required to get anything done. And a further common criticism was that the budget-making process never stopped. With multi-year planning and annual revisions to Strategic Plans, MYOPs, and BYOPs, budget preparation was a continuing cyclical affair that, quite literally, never ended. Administrative overload and creeping analysis paralysis clouded the end result (Inwood, 2004: 328).

A final predictable point respecting PEMS was the substantial role played by both Finance and the TBS in the system. In setting the annual Fiscal Plan, in consultation with P&P and the TBS, Finance possessed great authority to influence government priorities and to establish the framework of sectoral funding to be provided for in the estimates and sent to the cabinet committees through the Envelopes. Many officials came to resent and fear the centralized power of Finance as well as its generally "conservative" approach to fiscal policy, program development, and general government restraint. Finance gained the reputation as the institution in Ottawa that would always say "No." The TBS, likewise, came in for criticism from departments, since all department planning and program development documents required TBS scrutiny and approval prior to submission to relevant cabinet committees and P&P. TBS was positioned to exert great influence over program development and evaluation undertaken by departments. Not surprisingly, this authority was also resented and feared by many within departments as representing centralized control over departments by officials possessing a loyalty other than to the department itself.

It is important to bear in mind that as PEMS was operationalized in the 1980s it was never static. The system was highly complex, and this complexity itself resulted in it being modified, at various times, in an attempt to "fine-tune" and simplify its operation. In the late 1980s the Envelope disbursements were eliminated in favour of "Reference Levels" for departments and specific programs. Over this same time period, and in response to department criticisms of over-centralization, there was a steady relaxation of central control over financial resources within a department's budget, meaning that departments could juggle their monies to address emerging policy concerns without having to gain prior central agency approval. This reform, however, occurred at the same time that Policy Reserves—"B" budgets—were shrinking to virtually nothing on account of general financial restraint policies mandated by Finance. In this environment almost any new departmental initiative had to be funded solely out of reallocated monies already found in the department's "A" budget (Inwood, 2004: 328).

By far the single greatest change to PEMS over the late 1980s and early 1990s was the reform of the cabinet committee system and consequent decision-making process. During Mulroney's second term in office the number of cabinet committees increased from 10 to 14. Also, with the membership of P&P expanding to almost equal that of full cabinet, a new Operations Committee, chaired by the prime minister and comprising other senior ministers, became the real agenda-setting body. Coupled to this initiative was a new Expenditure Review Committee, likewise chaired by the prime minister, which had the duty of scrutinizing all program activities in light of needs for financial restraint. As Donald Savoie has stressed, while these Mulroney reforms served to marginally enhance the power of individual departments with respect to discretionary spending, their greater impact was to extend the financial management authority of the prime minister and his inner circle (Savoie, 1999: 40-41).

6.3.4.2 PEMS: PROBLEMS AND LIMITATIONS

By the early 1990s the problems and limitations of PEMS were obvious to everyone. It was a complex, difficult, divisive, and time-consuming budgetary process offering few redeeming attributes. Though financial management and budgetary planning clearly required a systematic and rationalistic approach, such an approach could not and did not result in actual policy and program outcomes being either systematic or rational. Rather, as French (1984), Hartle (1976), Savoie (1999), and Bakvis and Macdonald (1993) argued, such outcomes were more easily explained as the result of power politics, bureaucratic in-fighting, and organizational self-interest than by any appeal to the rationality of the system. Rather than observing a rationalist system of financial management that was actually performing as intended, we observed a system that was performing in more and more incrementalist fashions, with individual budgetary actors—ministers, deputy ministers, departments, agencies, and their officials—making isolated, step-by-step deals to secure their own institutional aims and personal self-interest.

By the advent of the 1990s a further problem with PEMS was readily apparent. Notwithstanding its claim to offer a rational and top-down form of control over all public spending, PEMS was clearly proving itself incapable of providing the government with a method of controlling the increase in public spending and the growing budgetary deficit. All through the 1980s and the operationalization of the PEMS system, federal spending had outpaced revenue generation, resulting in an increasing federal deficit. In 1980, for example, the deficit stood at $14.5 billion on total federal spending of $63.4 billion. By 1985, Prime Minister Mulroney's first full year in office, the deficit was at $33.3 billion based on $109.8 billion in total spending. By 1993, the year Mulroney resigned, the deficit stood at $39.0 billion, with total federal expenditures of $159.3 billion. While the Progressive Conservatives had come to power in 1984 promising fiscally conservative rule, and while the Mulroney government had long advocated the importance of prudent financial management, the need for government to live within its means, and the significance of deficit reduction, it consistently failed to deliver on these very important policy pledges. Consequently, PEMS was implicated in this failure.

6.3.5   Budget Systems: An Appraisal

It is interesting that all rationalist systems of financial management were originally designed in periods of growing economic and fiscal prosperity to supply governments with supposedly rational ways and means for managing growth. They were not designed with the purpose of enabling governments to manage the difficult and painful tasks of restraining programs, restricting spending, and cutting deficits. To meet these new goals, governments—especially the federal government—had to turn to a different form of financial management.

It is also instructive that, despite some two decades of concerted efforts to develop an effective and viable system of rational financial management, by the early 1990s not one system had succeeded in actually providing the federal government with a comprehensively rationalistic means of sound budget-making and financial management. This was not the end of the quest for budgetary rationalism, however, as the next chapter will demonstrate, but the numerous theoretical and practical problems associated with rationalism were cause for concern. In practice, much of the routine administrative work within departments and agencies associated with the development and operating of organizational budgets remained essentially incremental, notwithstanding the formally rationalistic framework within which such decision-making was structured. While departments and agencies were supposedly using rationalistic methods of budget-making, in practice these methods tended to collapse under their own weight and difficulty. Middle and senior managers had to "muddle through" as best they could, using the previous year's budget as a guide to what they wanted and expected to achieve for the next year, assuming that their "A" base was sacrosanct and that any alteration to their existing financial requirements would be, for better or worse, only "incremental."

The persistence of this approach to budget-making in the "real world" of bureaucratic politics, despite its many apparent limitations, gives one pause. Apparently, the importance of simplicity, understandability, and manageability in bureaucratic decision-making should not be underestimated. Furthermore, it seems that abstract rationalism conceived in ideal terms and conditions cannot cope with the inherently political nature of budgetary decision-making in the complex world of government with its many competing visions, vested interests, institutional actors, and pre-established understandings as to what is desirable, just, and necessary. Efforts to reduce political and managerial decision-making into nice, neat rationalist forms simply belie the complex and complicated world of government, a world in which the instrumental values of rationalist thought are only one of the many considerations that go into the development and operationalizing of public policies and programs. These are lessons that should not be lost on those interested in the theory and practice of government.

6.4   Budget-Making Tactics

Before leaving this study of incrementalist and rationalist financial management systems it is worthwhile to briefly consider another analytical perspective on the nature and working of expenditure budget-making. So far, this chapter has adopted a macro-analytical perspective on budget-making. A different and equally interesting approach is a micro-analytical review of budget-making tactics used by actors within bureaucratic settings. As French (1984) and Hartle (1976), among others, have explicitly argued, public sector budget-making can be viewed as a "game," with different "players" assuming different roles as they play for the big stakes of money, power, position, and prestige within the world of government policies, programs, and bureaucratic interests. The American political scientist Aaron Wildavsky (1964, 1992) adopted this approach to understanding budgetary decision-making in the United States, and he devoted much attention to the tactical relationships between budgetary actors. The following borrows from his work to give a sense of the tactical "jungle" that exists within the senior managerial ranks of government when budget-making is underway (Wildavsky, 1992: ch.3).

According to Wildavsky, the budget process can be viewed as a struggle or a game between contending governmental forces. On one side are the **spenders**, government departments and agencies intent on developing and running programs to serve citizen and "client" needs while at the same time enhancing the power and prestige of the enacting institution, its senior management, and minister. On the other side are the **guardians**, central agencies such as Finance, the TBS, and the PCO, mandated the task of controlling government spending to ensure that policy and program aims are obtained through the most economical and efficient use of government resources while ensuring that all government spending follows key governmental priorities and is closely scrutinized. In this ongoing struggle between the "spenders" and the "guardians," each side has employed various tactics to achieve its ends.

6.4.1   Spenders' Tactics

1. *Inflate the budget.* This tactic is quite universal. Since spenders know that guardians will be scrutinizing their budget, looking for "fat," they build in "fat" in the hope that not all the surplus requests will be cut. Also, there is the hope that in focusing their attention on the obvious "fat," the guardians might overlook less obvious funding enhancements.

2. *Spend now, save later.* This is an ingenious tactic that may not be a deception. Spenders can argue that certain new programs requiring funding support now will eventually result in greater government savings in other fields later. For example, more money in nursing and preventative health care now can result in less spent on physicians' services and hospitalization later; more spent on regional development now may mean less spent on unemployment and welfare costs later.

3. *Mobilize interest groups.* If spenders know that a new program will be difficult to fund, it will be in their best interests to alert interest groups that will benefit from the new program. These groups can then lobby the government for the new program, at once placing pressure on the government to take action while enhancing the profile and perceived political awareness of the spending department. This tactic is extremely common, especially in relation to business groups.

4. *The thin edge of the wedge.* This is another classic tactic. If spenders realize that it will be difficult to get a complex new program funded, it will be to their advantage to get at least an initial part of the program started. Once a program has begun, the department can encourage clients to make use of it, and as public demand for the program grows, the department can return to the guardians in future years requesting additional funding to support an "established" and successful initiative.

5. *Crisis initiatives: or, it's an ill wind that blows no one good.* Spenders know that crises, real or perceived, can become the catalysts for new programs and more money. The September 2001 terrorist attacks against the United States resulted in greater funding for the Canadian military and enhanced security at Canadian airports and border checkpoints, while the Quebec constitutional issue has eased the ability of federal economic development projects for Quebec to gain approval.

6. *Attack popular programs.* If spenders are confronted with the absolute necessity to cut programs, it may be in their best long-term interests to cut one of their most desirable, as opposed to least desirable, programs. By slashing a popular program, the spending department can anger its clients and then suggest to them that to save the program they need to lobby the government. In confronting cutbacks in Ontario, the provincial Ministry of the Attorney General announced that the number of Crown attorneys would have to be reduced, resulting in longer delays in criminal proceedings with the likelihood of more cases being dismissed for excessive delay. Needless to say, this proposal elicited public outrage at the cuts and demands for more funding for the courts.

7. *The end run.* A final tactic, rarely used but brazen when seen, is for the spender to simply ignore the financial management rules of process, to promise a new program, and to start spending money on it. The department and minister then confront their colleagues with a *fait accompli* in the hope that public support for the initiative will prevent the guardians and the general cabinet and prime minister from killing it. Ron Irwin, Minister of Indian Affairs and Northern Development, took such action in 1994, when he promised major new funding to improve water and sewage services on northern Manitoba Indian reserves without prior central agency approvals. In making this announcement, he was gambling that he would gain the support of Aboriginal communities, generally favourable public opinion and media support, and, most importantly, prime ministerial backing for what he perceived of as both a needed and politically desirable social policy action. In all of this, the minister's suppositions were borne out, and his commitment was accepted as government policy. Such unilateral actions are very risky, however, and thus rare. The cost of failure can extend from repudiation and public embarrassment to demotion or dismissal from cabinet.

6.4.2 Guardians' Tactics

1. *Set the rules.* Officials in central agencies can seek to thwart department overspending by establishing systematic rules and procedures in respect to all funding requests. The whole history of rational financial management is a reflection, in part, of senior guardians seeking to establish systems that militate against end runs, crisis initiatives, or cases of special pleading. Indeed, according to a somewhat perverse logic, the slower and more complex the process of budgetary approval the better, as these difficulties may have the effect of wearing down the enthusiasm of spenders.

2. *Demand documentation.* A traditional means by which guardians can slow down and even stop spenders' actions is to require studies and analyses for all spenders' plans. If spenders claim that a program can save money in the long run, guardians will demand to see the studies and statistics to bear out this claim. If and when such documentation is forthcoming, it can be subjected to rigorous analysis, and, if guardians are unconvinced by the research, this can become a justification for denying the requested funds.

3. *Broad consultation and investigation.* Just as spenders can manipulate groups to advance their interests, so too can central agencies. If guardians are confronted with policy analysis from certain influential groups, they can seek contrary opinion from other affected groups and departments. No program will ever have unanimous support, and, if central agencies are suspicious of the merits of an initiative, broad consultation will likely elicit contrary opinions that can become the basis for a rejection of the proposed policy.

4. *Know thine opponent.* As central agencies must deal regularly with departments, it is in their interests to recruit, as analysts, officials who have previously worked in departments. In this way, the guardians receive intelligence from those who were formerly spenders, meaning that those in central agencies are well aware of the types of tactics used by departments. Of course, this is a two-way street, with departments also recruiting former central agency officials for the same purposes.

5. *Just say no.* A final tactic available to all guardians is simply to reject department requests for additional funding and to confront the spenders with budget reductions that they must absorb. This has become an increasingly popular tactic in recent years for guardians, the prime minister, and the minister of finance.

6.5 Post-Budget Analysis: The Audit Function

All the foregoing macro- and micro-policy analysis has devoted attention to the creation of the expenditure budget. But this is only one part of the budgetary process. An equally important element, and a vitally important component of the accountability process in government, deals with the review of budgetary decision-making and program performance once the budget has been established. When the expenditure budget has been approved by cabinet and passed through Parliament in the form of the Main Estimates for all departments and agencies, these institutions then receive their appropriations for the upcoming year. These monies fund established programs and any new initiatives for which the department or agency has received authorization. Once funds have been allocated and expended, we enter the second and much less known stage of public sector financial management—the audit function. A number of institutions have important auditing roles to play, but the most important are operating departments and agencies, the Office of the Auditor General, and the Public Accounts Committee of Parliament.

6.5.1 Auditing

Auditing is a management process in which actual expenses incurred are measured and evaluated in light of pre-established criteria for such expenses. Public sector audits

- are usually conducted on an annual basis;
- have traditionally provided a rather narrow financial accounting of monies spent;
- provide a detailed listing of expenditures in a given department or agency;
- the legal authority for such spending;
- a comparison of expenses incurred in relation to those planned; and
- any findings of irregularities between planned and actual expenditures.

This is known as an "attest and compliance" audit. It is designed to allow any interested party—manager, politician, citizen—to know the financial position of the given institution, its recent history of financial undertakings, and whether such undertakings have conformed to its financial mandate as planned by the government and approved by Parliament (Kernaghan and Siegel, 1999: 651).

In the past 20 years this traditional approach to auditing has been augmented by additional managerial concerns (Sutherland, 1980). As interest in sound management and financial restraint has grown, the audit process has been expanded to measure and assess the qualities of economy, efficiency, and effectiveness found within government programs. On the proposition that all government spending is but a means to a public policy end, public sector audits should not only measure dollars expended, but also such matters as whether such expenses were made in the most economical fashion possible, whether program means were designed to make the most efficient use of government resources, and whether government programs were effectively meeting the goals that they were established to achieve. This approach to auditing, with its constant reference to the "Three E's"— economy, efficiency, and effectiveness—is known as *comprehensive auditing*, and it has become the dominant, although controversial, approach to auditing found in governments across Canada.

6.5.2   The Departmental Audit Process

As departments and agencies possess most responsibility for spending money, they also have a primary responsibility for conducting audits of their financial activities. Departments are responsible for keeping accurate records of all their financial transactions as well as for collecting data on their achievement of departmental objectives: whether programs were implemented with due regard to economy and efficiency and whether programs worked to effectively meet departmental goals. All such information is integral to the management process and is designed to be used not simply to exercise financial control over middle managers but to enable them to undertake departmental responsibilities in the most optimal fashion.

6.5.3   The Office of the Auditor General

While departments and agencies have an important role in the audit process, the most important institutional actors in this field are the federal **auditor general** and provincial auditors general (Sinclair, 1979). At both the federal and provincial levels, auditors general act as parliamentary "watchdogs," with the duty of carefully scrutinizing all government financial activities and providing advice and criticism about the findings. At the federal level, the auditor general is an Officer of Parliament. He or she is nominated by the prime minister but officially appointed by Parliament to a fixed term of ten years service or until the appointee reaches the age of 65. Once appointed, the auditor general possesses the same quality of tenure as a federal judge, giving him or her the extraordinary independence required by someone who will oversee probing audits of the government itself.

The Office of the Auditor General is responsible for auditing

- most federal institutions, including all departments and agencies;
- some 50 Crown corporations;

BOX 6.3

The Auditor General of Canada: Roles and Responsibilities

- Auditing the Public Accounts of all federal departments and most federal Crown corporations and regulatory agencies
- Auditing the Public Accounts of the federal territories of Nunavut, the Northwest Territories, and Yukon
- Reporting to the government and to Parliament respecting the economy, efficiency, and effectiveness of federal government programs
- Providing advice to federal government departments and Crown agencies as to how their economy, efficiency, effectiveness, and operational managerial capacity can be improved
- Identifying problems within the financial management of federal government policies and programs, thereby providing Parliament credible, empirical information enabling Members of Parliament to hold the government to account
- Promoting "Best Practices" within government departments and Crown agencies in respect to financial management
- Ensuring that all government financial undertakings are ultimately reviewed, scrutinized, and assessed and this information made public, so that the Canadian people can be made aware of the state of financial management within the federal government
- Acting as a "Watchdog" for Parliament, and by extension the media and the public, regarding the quality and control of public spending

- the public accounts of Yukon, Northwest Territories, and Nunavut; and
- all government-wide financial policies such as centralized purchasing, communications, and payroll management.

In fulfilling this duty the auditor general issues a number of reports to Parliament each year regarding the quality of financial management found in the government for the financial year just past—that is, the previous year's accounts. These reports usually are tabled quarterly and provide critical insight into the financial working of specific departments and Crown agencies and their programs. They offer recommendations about how financial management practices in these bodies can be improved, also listing department and agency responses to these recommendations. All such documentation becomes important not only to the government but also to the opposition parties in Parliament and to the national media. They become the subject of parliamentary questions and debate, with the media typically looking to highlight examples of wasteful government spending. In seeking to understand government financial management, however, it is always important to read the reports themselves to gain a sense of the broad dynamics of the quality of such management. Contrary to much popular opinion, these reports generally reveal that the calibre of financial management and spending control and oversight in the federal government is quite high. All government programs are subject to close audit scrutiny, and, as a general rule, most government spending in any one year meets the audit requirements of the auditor general. Of course, with government spending approaching $200 billion, there will always be exceptions to this rule, and it is these exceptions, the minority of cases revealing problematic spending and control practices, that elicit critical commentary by the auditor general. And it is these cases, most recently illustrated by the sponsorship scandal, that attract media and parliamentary attention (see Box 6.4).

In fulfilling their responsibilities, auditors general traditionally undertook only the basic attest and compliance audit; they reported on whether or not the government's financial books were in order and whether all transactions were undertaken with proper authority. By the 1970s, however, the worth of this type of audit was being questioned by public policy and management analysts, who stressed that critical analysis respecting the economy, efficiency, and effectiveness of government activities should also become a part of the auditing function. In 1977, under the leadership of federal Auditor General James J. Macdonell, and following a series of damning indictments of federal financial mismanagement, the Office of the Auditor General was given legal authority to engage in **comprehensive auditing**. This approach is officially defined (Canadian Comprehensive Auditing Foundation, 1985: 8) as:

> An examination that provides an objective and constructive assessment of the extent to which financial, human, and physical resources are managed with due regard to economy, efficiency and effectiveness, and, accountability relationships are served.
>
> The comprehensive audit examines both financial and management controls, including information systems and reporting practices, and recommends improvements where appropriate.

As the federal Office of the Auditor General and its provincial counterparts have moved to implement such comprehensive auditing, they have become embroiled in operational and political controversies. These stem from the nature of the concept itself. First, though measuring economy can be fairly straightforward, the same cannot be said for measuring efficiency or effectiveness. As Kernaghan and Siegel (1999: 651) have said, "Efficiency and effectiveness, like beauty, are frequently in the eye of the beholder." Federal regional development programs, for example, routinely

---

BOX 6.4
The Auditor General and the Sponsorship Scandal

While most government programs are awarded passing grades in Auditor General Reports, auditors can be highly critical of certain programs that they find questionable, with these critical findings having the potential to cause acute political problems for a government. A telling example of this is found in the history of the sponsorship scandal of 2004-05.

As mentioned in Chapter 1, in the wake of the 1995 Quebec referendum the federal government under the leadership of Prime Minister Jean Chrétien established a Sponsorship Program designed to raise the profile of the federal government and federalism overall in the province of Quebec through the spending of federal monies on the promotion of arts, culture, and sporting events in that province. Between 1996 and 2003 some $250 million was spent on such events. As these years unfolded, however, there were growing rumours from Quebec that the program was increasingly characterized by financial malpractice, abuse of process, and outright corruption and criminal fraud.

In her 2002 Report, Auditor General Sheila Fraser recommended the RCMP investigate the Sponsorship Program on the grounds that, according to preliminary findings, it seemed that federal bureaucrats broke "just about every rule in the book" in dealing with certain Quebec advertising agencies.

In her 2004 Report the auditor general found that the Sponsorship Program was the subject of rampant financial abuses. Fraser asserted that senior government officials running this program had wasted money and shown gross disregard for proper financial management rules in the handling of public money. She found that more than $100 million had been paid to various advertising agencies with Liberal Party connections; most of this money had been obtained for little or no work.

"I think," Ms. Fraser said to the media, "this is such a blatant misuse of public funds that it is shocking. I am actually appalled by what we've found. I am deeply disturbed that such practices were allowed to happen in the first place. I don't think anybody can take this lightly" (CBC News 2004).

Following the release of this report in February 2004, Prime Minister Paul Martin called a public inquiry, under the direction of Justice John Gomery, to investigate the sponsorship scandal. Testimony before the Gomery inquiry implicated the federal Liberal party and government in Quebec in the waste of public money and the creation of kickback schemes whereby federal money paid to advertising agencies was illegally paid back to various officials in the party. These allegations served to undermine both the credibility of the Liberal government of Paul Martin as well as the cause of federalism within Quebec. By 2005 findings such as these had shaken the Martin government to its core, severely weakening its standing in public opinion, and emboldening a hitherto divided and seemingly weak opposition.

And all these developments could be traced back to the work of the auditor general and her officials.

have been attacked by the more conservative-minded for being both wasteful and an inefficient use of federal funds while failing to solve the problems of regional underdevelopment, thus being ineffective. But such programs have been equally defended and advanced by persons of all political stripes for a variety of reasons. They may prove themselves to be effective over the short term in promoting job creation, and, over the long term, they may be valuable in generating industrial and commercial activity in economically depressed parts of the country, thus promoting needed economic development, industrial diversification, employment opportunity, and greater wealth. Such long-run policy outcomes, in turn, justify the merits of spending on the program as an efficient use of resources in the support of broad government objectives. The key evaluation question becomes contingent upon time. Does one evaluate efficiency and effectiveness over a one-year time horizon? Or five years? Or ten years or more? Depending on the approach taken, conclusions can be diametrically opposed.

In the 1880s Prime Minister John A. Macdonald was viciously attacked for building the CPR at great public expense, almost bankrupting the young country. At the time, many viewed Macdonald's "National Dream" as an act of stupidity, proof of his poor leadership and wanton disregard for financial prudence. Ten years after his death in 1891, though, the railway had become instrumental in binding the country across the continent and an integral part of Canada's growing economy. Since then its construction has been recognized as one of the greatest examples of political leadership in Canadian history.

Also, the effectiveness issue raises the old problem of program evaluation and the sorting out of program objectives. What is the objective of enhanced spending on employment equity policy and the Canadian Human Rights Commission? To enhance human rights in general? To enhance the rights of groups previously discriminated against? To promote certain jobs and a certain institution within the federal government? To promote a symbolic "feel good" sense among Canadians? Or to make the government look good in public opinion leading up to an election? Differing analysts and differing auditors could approach this issue from any one of these perspectives, resulting in many differing interpretations of program effectiveness and desirability. It is quite conceivable that, through such an exercise, the Office of the Auditor General and the government could come to quite divergent perspectives on the quality and worthiness of such a program. Which opinion should then prevail? That of an unelected senior bureaucrat or that of the elected government?

A second problem arises from these operational difficulties. The Office of the Auditor General has tended, in the past decade, to find itself in more political disputes with governments over its role in evaluating government programs. While disputes over the integrity of regional development programs have been common, the single greatest controversy erupted in relation to a Trudeau government decision to allow Petro-Canada to purchase Petrofina in the early 1980s with the use of $1.7 billion in public funds. The federal government maintained that this undertaking was a sound investment, necessary to strengthening Petro-Canada and securing Canadian influence in the petroleum industry. But the Office of the Auditor General questioned whether due regard for economy and efficiency had been followed by the government and Petro-Canada in this initiative. In order to probe these concerns, the auditor general requested access to all relevant documents pertaining to the sale, only to be told that the core planning and operational papers were cabinet documents protected by the rule of cabinet confidentiality. Nevertheless, the auditor general demanded to see these documents in order to pass judgement on the quality of the original decision. The government refused.

As this dispute dragged on, the Mulroney government came to power; yet, despite their loathing of the old Trudeau government, even they refused to hand over the documents on the grounds that cabinet decisions on matters of national policy should be free from scrutiny by the auditor general. The auditor general, in turn, brought a legal challenge to the government, claiming that he had the legal right to review all relevant documentation pertaining to any investigation by his office. The government still contested this claim, and the case eventually proceeded to the Supreme Court of Canada. In 1988, the court ruled in favour of the government, stressing that the auditor general had no legal right to obtain and scrutinize confidential cabinet documents. The court held that the appropriate course of action for the auditor general in such cases is to make mention in the annual report of such denial of access and to let Parliament decide what an appropriate response should be. The government was quite satisfied with this decision, but the Office of the Auditor General viewed it as a serious setback to its ability to carry out audits of major undertakings (Auditor General of Canada, 1989: 23-27).

This case was very important in drawing to public attention the type of controversies that can erupt between governments and the Office of the Auditor General when the focus of audits extends to the matters of comprehensive auditing. By seeking to analyze and evaluate the Three E's, auditors general can move into some very delicate political territory and into direct conflict with the government of the day. Such conflicts pose a dilemma: What body should ultimately assess the economy, efficiency, and effectiveness of governments? The government itself? The auditor general? Or Parliament? All three institutions have important roles to play in the auditing process, requiring that an appropriate balance be struck between them. The difficulty observed in the past, and still found today, is in striking that appropriate balance.

6.5.4   The Public Accounts Committee and Parliament

The work of the **Public Accounts Committee** (PAC) closes the financial management accountability loop to Parliament. A permanent committee of the House of Commons, the PAC has the duty of reviewing and analyzing the annual reports of the auditor general and providing reform recommendations to the government. The PAC is unique among parliamentary committees in that, by tradition, it is chaired by a member of the Official Opposition. This has the effect of ensuring that the agenda of the committee is not under the control of the governing party. The committee's actual independence is limited, however, since, as with any parliamentary committee, membership is based on party standings in the House of Commons. The effect of this rule is that in a time of majority government, the committee will be dominated by members of the governing party. When party discipline is factored into this dynamic, it is clear that the PAC is far from being the same type of independent watchdog as the auditor general. This political reality becomes the PAC's greatest disability; nevertheless, it has a significant role to play (Kernaghan and Siegel, 1999: 656).

Simply by existing as an official conduit through which the auditor general's report must pass, the PAC provides the auditor general with a platform upon which the report can be discussed and publicized. Likewise, the committee's proceedings and its report to Parliament provide the chair and opposition members of the committee with the opportunity to scrutinize and criticize government financial management, often calling senior managers to appear before it to answer questions about their operational undertakings. Such events can garner media attention if a story is considered "juicy" enough, and prolonged media coverage of the auditor general's report and related PAC hearings can result both in great publicity of administrative problems and great discomfiture for those deemed responsible for them. One need only think of the Human Resources Development Canada transitional jobs funding and accounting scandal of 2000 (Geddes, 2000) to see the veracity of this claim. In this case the department was severely criticized by the auditor general, the media, and the opposition parties for devoting hundreds of millions of dollars for job training initiatives but with limited department supervision and accounting for the money spent. Jane Stewart, the minister responsible, and her senior department staff had to endure scathing criticism and ridicule, and, as the minister repeatedly proclaimed to the PAC, the House of Commons, and to the media, her department would never again allow such sloppy managerial and auditing practices to exist.

The eventual report of the PAC to Parliament stands as an official appraisal of government management to be referred to later in debate and election campaigning by the opposition parties. Thus, even though the governing party knows that in routine times of majority government it can control the final decisions of the PAC, the process itself is one that the governing party must treat with care and that senior managers must always treat with respect. No senior official wishes to be castigated by anyone from the PAC as being less than competent and uncooperative. Once the final report of the PAC is tabled in Parliament, the accountability loop is closed, and Parliament is at liberty to do with the report and its recommendations as it pleases.

6.5.5   The Audit System: An Appraisal

The auditing process as outlined here leaves many people with a sense of unease. Effective auditing is an essential requirement of any financial management system, yet one can identify numerous problems with the manner in which the process actually works. The very concept of comprehensive auditing is problematic, resulting in auditors general becoming enmeshed in some very controversial and political issues of evaluation and interpretation. The Office of the Auditor General nevertheless has wide and independent power to audit the financial activities of the government and to assess the degree to which government spending is in accordance with the principles of economy, efficiency, and effectiveness. But the auditor general only has power to review and to report to Parliament; he or she has no executive authority to order that reforms be made to government operations. Only the government itself can "reform" itself, and it is formally answerable only to Parliament. And yet it is here that the impact of the auditor general's reporting to Parliament via the PAC is diminished because this body, and the broader institution of Parliament itself, is a politicized body, subject to the influence of party discipline and, most of the time, to the political realities of a majority government.

All this has led to a common complaint that the audit process in general is a sham, much sound and fury that ultimately results in very little: auditors general reports are duly presented to Parliament and just as duly talked about and then shelved, to collect dust. This attitude, however, fails to appreciate the real significance of the auditing process and the institutions of the Office of the Auditor General and the PAC. Because they exist and because all governments must submit themselves to the auditing process, all governments and their political and administrative leaderships must devote attention to financial management. They must be concerned with the quality of economy, efficiency, and effectiveness in government operations, because they know these matters will be the focus of attention of audits and audit reports. Any auditor general's greatest power is the power of publicity and the ability to air problems with financial management and governmental accountability to Parliament, the political parties, the media, and the general public. No government wants to be the subject of intense and critical opposition and media scrutiny respecting its ability to manage public finances, thus there is a strong and ingrained instinct for governments to conduct their management of public monies in such a manner as to avoid such critical commentary. And most of the time, as auditors general report, most government financial management activities are in keeping with desired principles of accountability. Notwithstanding all the difficulties of doing comprehensive audits, the most important fact is that they are done.

6.6   Eliminating the Deficit, Managing Surpluses

In the enduring interplay between spenders and guardians no one side is always dominant though, as we have seen in Chapter 4, the prime minister and minister of finance will always be lead players in the "game" regardless of other considerations. The power of these respective forces, however, ebb and flow with changing economic conditions, interest group pressures and media interest, the quality of ministerial and bureaucratic leadership, and the prevailing political climate. In this way, the interplay of micro-level budgetary tactics and activities can and will affect the long-term development and success of macro-level financial management planning. Over the 1990s, however, the prevailing political climate took a definite turn to the centre-right of the ideological spectrum, with the result that the federal government came under increasing pressure, from both within and without, to tackle the growing problem of the federal fiscal imbalance, the shortfall between revenues and expenses, and, consequently, the ever-growing federal deficit. As fiscal restraint and deficit reduction came to be key policy priorities, the government adopted several approaches to financial management. One general approach was a direct descendent of PEMS and, as such, was imbued with a rationalistic sentiment. The other, a more specialized approach to deficit reduction and program cutbacks, was unlike anything Ottawa had ever seen. It is to the politics and administration of deficit fighting and the new era of budget surpluses and policy choices that we now turn.

Key Terms

accountability: The public duty borne by all governments and public servants to be responsible for actions undertaken by government and to perform government duties with due regard to prudence, law, social responsiveness, and the managerial concepts of economy, efficiency, and effectiveness.

auditing: The management process by which actual expenses incurred are measured and evaluated in light of pre-established criteria for such expenses.

Auditor General of Canada: An Officer of Parliament appointed to a ten-year term of office and given the responsibility of conducting comprehensive audits of all federal departments and agencies, some 50 Crown corporations, and the northern territories. While most reports of the auditor general find that most government programs are implemented in appropriate manners, critical reports can become major political headaches for the government of the day.

budgetary rationalism: A system of budgeting in which program spending is systematically linked to program planning, prioritization, development, and evaluation. Rational systems of budgeting seek to base all expenditures upon elaborate plans regarding program development where all programs have been subjected to critical cost-benefit analysis and priority-setting. Budgetary rationalism emerged in Canada in the 1960s and has remained a potent force in financial management thinking ever since. PPBS and PEMS are variations on budgetary rationalism.

comprehensive auditing: A form of auditing whereby auditors assess government programs in light of the criteria of program economy, efficiency, effectiveness, and accountability.

expenditure budget: That part of the general federal budget designed to illustrate those policies and programs upon which the federal government will spend its money. The expenditure budget highlights how and where and why and to what desired goals the federal government will expend public monies.

guardians: In budget-making tactical thinking guardians are those officials in central agencies, such as Finance and Treasury Board, whose responsibility is to ensure that all government departmental budgets are as prudent as possible and that all government spending is subject to strict control and scrutiny.

incremental line-item budget: A system of budgeting whereby budgets are constructed incrementally based upon the previous year's budget. In setting a budget through this approach, managers simply take the previous year's budget as a reference point and incrementally alter it to take account of marginal changes with respect to the costs of running its programs. This is a very simple form of budgeting that was officially transcended by rational budgeting. Yet incremental budgeting as a way of thinking and acting has great staying power.

Main Estimates: The complete listing of all government spending, by department and program, for an entire budgetary year and selected future years. The Main Estimates are presented to the House of Commons following the annual budget presentation by the Minister of Finance.

performance budget: A system of budgeting that is intermediary between incremental and rational budgeting. In a performance budget an incremental-style budget is embellished with the addition of efficiency evaluations whereby budgeted program expenditures are correlated to services provided as a result of such spending.

PEMS: The Policy and Expenditure Management System. This was the federal government's macro-system of financial management dating from 1979 through 1993. PEMS was a rational form of financial management that was based upon the earlier PPBS system. PEMS sought to promote rational planning, prioritization, and program management coupled with greater financial controls exercised by departments and their ministers. In 1994 newly elected Prime Minister Jean Chrétien replaced the PEMS system with the Expenditure Management System (dealt with in Chapter 7).

PPBS: The Planning-Programming-Budgeting System. This was the federal government's macro-system of financial management dating from 1969 to 1979. PPBS was designed to be a fully comprehensive system of rational budgeting marked by extensive planning, prioritization, cost-benefit analysis, elaborate multi-year programming and budgeting, and intricate operational measurement systems. PPBS necessitated enormous time and effort to be expended in the development of budgets, with this work becoming an ongoing dynamic in government departments. While support for PPBS waned by the end of the 1970s, interest in maintaining a rational approach to budgeting remained.

Public Accounts Committee (PAC): A permanent committee of the House of Commons and one always chaired, by tradition, by a member of the Official Opposition party. The PAC has the duty of overseeing the financial management of the federal government and to do this the PAC closely reviews the reports of the Auditor General, conducting investigations when it deems them necessary.

revenue budget: That part of the general federal budget designed to illustrate the tax, duties, tariffs, user fees, sales of goods and properties, and other income-generating measures taken by the federal government in a given year.

spenders: In budget-making tactical thinking "spenders" are those officials in line departments and agencies who are primarily interested in increasing the flow of monies into their institutions so as to enhance the program work of these institutions and, correspondingly, to enhance their own power, prestige, importance, and workforce.

References and Suggested Reading

Adie, Robert F., and Paul G. Thomas. 1987. *Canadian Public Administration: Problematical Perspectives*. 2nd ed. Scarborough, ON: Prentice-Hall Canada.

Auditor General of Canada. 1989. *Report of the Auditor General of Canada to the House of Commons, Fiscal Year Ended 31 March 1989*. Ottawa: Minister of Supply and Services.

Bakvis, Herman, and David MacDonald. 1993. "The Canadian Cabinet: Organization, Decision-Rules, and Policy Impact." In Michael M. Atkinson, ed., *Governing Canada: Institutions and Public Policy*. Toronto: Harcourt Brace Jovanovich Canada. 47-80.

Brown-John, C. Lloyd, André LeBlond, and D. Brian Marson. 1988. *Public Financial Management: A Canadian Text*. Scarborough, ON: Nelson Canada.

CBC News. 2004. "Auditor General Gives Details of 'Scandalous' Sponsorship Program." Available at: <http://www.cbc.ca/stories/2004/02/10/fraser_report>.

Canadian Comprehensive Auditing Foundation. 1985. *Comprehensive Auditing in Canada: The Provincial Legislative Audit Perspective*. Ottawa: Canadian Comprehensive Auditing Foundation.

Doern, G. Bruce, Allan M. Maslove, and Michael J. Prince. 1988. *Public Budgeting in Canada*. Ottawa: Carleton University Press.

Finance (Department of). 2005. Fiscal Reference Tables. Ottawa: Department of Finance Canada.

French, Richard D. 1984. *How Ottawa Decides: Planning and Industrial Policy Making 1968-1984*. 2nd ed. Toronto: James Lorimer.

Geddes, John. 2000. "Saving Ms. Stewart." *Maclean's* 14 February: 17-21.

Hartle, Douglas G. 1976. *A Theory of the Expenditure Budgetary Process*. Toronto: University of Toronto Press.

Henry, Nicholas. 1995. *Public Administration and Public Affairs*. 6th ed. Englewood Cliffs, NJ: Prentice-Hall.

Inwood, Gregory J. 2004. *Understanding Canadian Public Administration: An Introduction to Theory and Practice*. 2nd ed. Toronto: Pearson Prentice-Hall.

Kernaghan, Kenneth, and David Siegel. 1999. *Public Administration in Canada: A Text*. 4th ed. Toronto: Nelson Canada.

Savoie, Donald J. 1999. *Governing from the Centre: The Concentration of Power in Canadian Politics*. Toronto: University of Toronto Press.

Sinclair, Sonya. 1979. *Cordial but not Cosy*. Toronto: McClelland and Stewart.

Strick, John C. 1999. *The Public Sector in Canada: Programs, Finance and Policy*. Toronto: Thompson Educational Publishing.

Sutherland, Sharon. 1980. "On the Audit Trail of the Auditor General: Parliament's Servant, 1973-1980." *Canadian Public Administration* 23: 616-44.

—. 1986. "The Politics of Audit: The Federal Office of the Auditor General in Comparative Perspective." *Canadian Public Administration* 29: 118-48.

Treasury Board of Canada. 1969. *Planning-Programming-Budgeting Guide*. Ottawa: Queen's Printer.

Westmacott, Martin W., and Hugh P. Mellon, eds. 1999. *Public Administration and Policy: Governing in Challenging Times*. Scarborough, ON: Prentice-Hall Allyn and Bacon Canada.

Wildavsky, Aaron. 1964. *The Politics of the Budgetary Process*. Boston, MA: Little Brown.

—. 1992. *The New Politics of the Budgetary Process*. 2nd ed. New York: HarperCollins.

Related Web Sites

AUDITOR GENERAL OF CANADA
<http://www.oag-bvg.gc.ca>

DEPARTMENT OF FINANCE
<http://www.fin.gc.ca>

TREASURY BOARD SECRETARIAT
<http://www.tbs-sct.gc.ca>

TABLE 6.1
Fiscal Transactions (millions of dollars)

Year	Budgetary revenues	Program spending	Operating surplus or deficit (-)	Public debt charges	Budgetary surplus or deficit (-)	Accumulated deficit	Non-budgetary transactions	Financial requirements (-) / source
1961-62	6,468	6,630	-162	832	-994	14,825	332	-662
1962-63	6,662	6,595	67	915	-848	15,673	-667	-1,515
1963-64	7,099	7,304	-205	993	-1,198	16,871	903	-295
1964-65	8,220	7,542	678	1,050	-372	17,243	-5	-377
1965-66	9,063	7,933	1,130	1,110	20	17,223	-78	-58
1966-67	9,860	9,164	696	1,182	-486	17,708	72	-414
1967-68	10,745	10,501	244	1,286	-1,042	18,750	491	-551
1968-69	12,047	11,250	797	1,464	-667	19,417	-1,192	-1,859
1969-70	14,399	12,566	1,833	1,694	139	19,277	-302	-163
1970-71	14,982	14,111	871	1,887	-1,016	20,293	-1,302	-2,318
1971-72	16,619	16,295	324	2,110	-1,786	22,079	-257	-2,043
1972-73	19,205	18,807	398	2,300	-1,902	23,980	514	-1,388
1973-74	22,430	22,076	354	2,565	-2,211	26,191	893	-1,318
1974-75	29,251	28,238	1,013	3,238	-2,225	28,416	720	-1,505
1975-76	31,657	33,892	-2,235	3,970	-6,205	34,620	1,444	-4,761
1976-77	34,408	36,596	-2,188	4,708	-6,896	41,517	2,621	-4,275
1977-78	34,626	39,974	-5,348	5,531	-10,879	52,396	2,749	-8,130
1978-79	36,974	42,980	-6,006	7,024	-13,030	65,425	-19	-13,049
1979-80	42,029	45,502	-3,473	8,494	-11,967	77,392	3,891	-8,076
1980-81	48,867	52,765	-3,898	10,658	-14,556	91,948	5,632	-8,924
1981-82	60,307	60,867	-560	15,114	-15,674	107,622	6,334	-9,340
1982-83	60,662	72,808	-12,146	16,903	-29,049	136,671	2,636	-26,413
1983-84	63,952	75,885	-11,933	20,430	-32,363	157,252	7,857	-24,506
1984-85	70,683	82,963	-12,280	24,887	-37,167	194,419	6,795	-30,372
1985-86	76,430	82,162	-5,732	27,657	-33,389	227,808	3,765	-29,624
1986-87	85,311	86,435	-1,124	28,718	-29,842	257,650	2,334	-27,508
1987-88	95,562	93,356	2,206	31,223	-29,017	286,667	3,734	-25,283
1988-89	103,748	96,163	7,585	35,532	-27,947	314,614	2,755	-25,192
1989-90	112,930	100,827	12,103	41,246	-29,143	343,757	10,561	-18,582
1990-91	116,326	105,191	11,135	45,034	-33,899	377,656	5,615	-28,284
1991-92	122,842	111,300	11,542	43,861	-32,319	409,975	2,542	-29,777
1992-93	120,287	117,974	2,313	41,332	-39,019	448,994	10,270	-28,749
1993-94	116,040	114,471	1,569	40,099	-38,530	487,524	6,147	-32,383
1994-95	122,486	114,933	7,553	44,185	-36,632	524,156	8,831	-27,801
1995-96	131,397	111,996	19,401	49,407	-30,006	554,162	9,071	-20,935
1996-97	140,853	102,260	38,593	47,281	-8,688	562,850	2,464	-6,224
1997-98	152,116	106,864	45,252	43,120	2,132	560,718	8,956	11,088
1998-99	156,146	109,995	46,151	43,303	2,847	557,871	2,329	5,176
1999-00	166,112	109,583	56,529	43,384	13,145	544,726	-5,293	7,852
2000-01	182,748	118,694	64,054	43,892	20,162	524,564	-8,859	11,303
2001-02	171,688	125,018	46,670	39,651	7,019	517,545	-7,356	-337
2002-03	177,832	133,593	44,239	37,270	6,970	510,576	631	7,601
2003-04	186,207	141,355	44,852	35,769	9,083	501,493	-2,838	6,245
2004-05	198,420	162,672	35,748	34,118	1,630	499,863	3,190	4,820

Due to a break in the series following the introduction of full accrual accounting, data from 1983-84 are not directly comparable with earlier years.

Source: Finance, 2005: 9.

TABLE 6.2
Fiscal Transactions (per cent of GDP)

Year	Budgetary revenues	Program spending	Operating surplus or deficit (-)	Public debt charges	Budgetary surplus or deficit (-)	Accumulated deficit	Non-budgetary transactions	Financial requirements (-) / source
1961-62	15.7	16.1	-0.4	2.0	-2.4	36.0	0.8	-1.6
1962-63	14.9	14.8	0.2	2.0	-1.9	35.1	-1.5	-3.4
1963-64	14.8	15.2	-0.4	2.1	-2.5	35.2	1.9	-0.6
1964-65	15.6	14.4	1.3	2.0	-0.7	32.8	0.0	-0.7
1965-66	15.6	13.7	2.0	1.9	0.0	29.7	-0.1	-0.1
1966-67	15.2	14.1	1.1	1.8	-0.7	27.3	0.1	-0.6
1967-68	15.4	15.1	0.3	1.8	-1.5	26.9	0.7	-0.8
1968-69	15.8	14.8	1.0	1.9	-0.9	25.5	-1.6	-2.4
1969-70	17.2	15.0	2.2	2.0	0.2	23.0	-0.4	-0.2
1970-71	16.6	15.6	1.0	2.1	-1.1	22.5	-1.4	-2.6
1971-72	16.9	16.6	0.3	2.1	-1.8	22.4	-0.3	-2.1
1972-73	17.5	17.1	0.4	2.1	-1.7	21.8	0.5	-1.3
1973-74	17.4	17.1	0.3	2.0	-1.7	20.3	0.7	-1.0
1974-75	19.0	18.3	0.7	2.1	-1.4	18.4	0.5	-1.0
1975-76	18.2	19.5	-1.3	2.3	-3.6	19.9	0.8	-2.7
1976-77	17.2	18.3	-1.1	2.4	-3.4	20.8	1.3	-2.1
1977-78	15.7	18.1	-2.4	2.5	-4.9	23.7	1.2	-3.7
1978-79	15.1	17.6	-2.5	2.9	-5.3	26.7	0.0	-5.3
1979-80	15.0	16.3	-1.2	3.0	-4.3	27.7	1.4	-2.9
1980-81	15.5	16.8	-1.2	3.4	-4.6	29.2	1.8	-2.8
1981-82	16.7	16.9	-0.2	4.2	-4.3	29.9	1.8	-2.6
1982-83	16.0	19.2	-3.2	4.4	-7.6	36.0	0.7	-7.0
1983-84	15.5	18.4	-2.9	5.0	-7.9	38.2	1.9	-6.0
1984-85	15.7	18.5	-2.7	5.5	-8.3	43.2	1.5	-6.8
1985-86	15.7	16.9	-1.2	5.7	-6.9	46.9	0.8	-6.1
1986-87	16.6	16.9	-0.2	5.6	-5.8	50.3	0.5	-5.4
1987-88	17.1	16.7	0.4	5.6	-5.2	51.3	0.7	-4.5
1988-89	16.9	15.7	1.2	5.8	-4.6	51.3	0.4	-4.1
1989-90	17.2	15.3	1.8	6.3	-4.4	52.3	1.6	-2.8
1990-91	17.1	15.5	1.6	6.6	-5.0	55.5	0.8	-4.2
1991-92	17.9	16.2	1.7	6.4	-4.7	59.8	0.4	-4.3
1992-93	17.2	16.8	0.3	5.9	-5.6	64.1	1.5	-4.1
1993-94	16.0	15.7	0.2	5.5	-5.3	67.0	0.8	-4.5
1994-95	15.9	14.9	1.0	5.7	-4.8	68.0	1.1	-3.6
1995-96	16.2	13.8	2.4	6.1	-3.7	68.4	1.1	-2.6
1996-97	16.8	12.2	4.6	5.6	-1.0	67.3	0.3	-0.7
1997-98	17.2	12.1	5.1	4.9	0.2	63.5	1.0	1.3
1998-99	17.1	12.0	5.0	4.7	0.3	61.0	0.3	0.6
1999-00	16.9	11.2	5.8	4.4	1.3	55.4	-0.5	0.8
2000-01	17.0	11.0	5.9	4.1	1.9	48.7	-0.8	1.0
2001-02	15.5	11.3	4.2	3.6	0.6	46.7	-0.7	0.0
2002-03	15.4	11.5	3.8	3.2	0.6	44.1	0.1	0.7
2003-04	15.3	11.6	3.7	2.9	0.7	41.1	-0.2	0.5
2004-05	15.4	12.6	2.8	2.6	0.1	38.7	0.2	0.4

Due to a break in the series following the introduction of full accrual accounting, data from 1983-84 are not directly comparable with earlier years.

Source: Finance, 2005: 10.

TABLE 6.3
Budgetary revenues (millions of dollars)

Year	Tax revenues					Employment insurance premiums	Other revenues	Total budgetary revenues
	Personal income tax	Corporate income tax	Other income tax	Excise taxes and duties	Total tax revenues			
1961-62	2,052	1,302	197	2,204	5,755	278	435	6,468
1962-63	2,018	1,298	216	2,395	5,927	285	450	6,662
1963-64	2,168	1,375	216	2,525	6,284	296	519	7,099
1964-65	2,535	1,669	233	2,890	7,327	310	583	8,220
1965-66	2,637	1,759	278	3,344	8,018	327	718	9,063
1966-67	3,050	1,743	305	3,628	8,726	343	791	9,860
1967-68	3,650	1,821	323	3,718	9,512	346	887	10,745
1968-69	4,334	2,213	318	3,747	10,612	432	1,003	12,047
1969-70	5,588	2,839	349	4,009	12,785	490	1,124	14,399
1970-71	6,395	2,426	378	4,060	13,259	493	1,230	14,982
1971-72	7,227	2,396	420	4,637	14,680	569	1,370	16,619
1972-73	8,378	2,920	353	5,272	16,923	745	1,537	19,205
1973-74	9,226	3,710	338	6,355	19,629	1,001	1,800	22,430
1974-75	11,710	4,836	434	8,506	25,486	1,585	2,180	29,251
1975-76	12,709	5,748	493	8,143	27,093	2,039	2,525	31,657
1976-77	14,634	5,363	521	8,637	29,155	2,470	2,783	34,408
1977-78	13,988	5,280	569	9,123	28,960	2,537	3,129	34,626
1978-79	14,656	5,654	645	9,697	30,652	2,783	3,539	36,974
1979-80	16,808	6,951	883	10,215	34,857	2,778	4,394	42,029
1980-81	19,837	8,106	966	11,661	40,570	3,303	4,994	48,867
1981-82	24,046	8,118	1,138	15,843	49,145	4,753	6,409	60,307
1982-83	26,330	7,139	1,130	15,776	50,375	4,900	5,387	60,662
1983-84	26,530	7,174	908	16,215	50,827	7,229	5,896	63,952
1984-85	28,455	9,234	1,021	18,177	56,887	7,676	6,120	70,683
1985-86	32,238	9,068	1,053	19,491	61,850	8,630	5,950	76,430
1986-87	36,733	9,732	1,355	21,049	68,869	9,667	6,775	85,311
1987-88	42,422	10,710	1,162	22,941	77,235	10,602	7,725	95,562
1988-89	45,456	11,549	1,578	25,771	84,354	11,107	8,287	103,748
1989-90	50,584	12,820	1,361	28,155	92,920	10,727	9,283	112,930
1990-91	56,201	11,545	1,372	24,067	93,185	12,551	10,590	116,326
1991-92	59,687	9,215	1,261	27,308	97,471	15,338	10,033	122,842
1992-93	56,975	7,095	1,191	26,771	92,032	17,576	10,679	120,287
1993-94	49,977	9,098	1,533	26,940	87,548	19,298	9,194	116,040
1994-95	55,326	10,969	1,700	27,457	95,452	18,293	8,741	122,486
1995-96	58,834	15,372	1,882	27,251	103,339	19,089	8,969	131,397
1996-97	62,557	16,235	2,671	29,204	110,667	19,949	10,237	140,853
1997-98	69,597	21,179	1,999	31,146	123,921	19,242	8,953	152,116
1998-99	72,179	21,213	2,208	31,717	127,317	19,064	9,765	156,146
1999-00	79,070	22,115	2,646	33,298	137,129	18,628	10,355	166,112
2000-01	85,879	28,293	2,982	35,769	152,923	18,655	11,170	182,748
2001-02	79,501	24,242	2,925	37,133	143,801	17,637	10,250	171,688
2002-03	81,707	22,222	3,291	41,357	148,577	17,870	11,385	177,832
2003-04	84,895	27,431	3,142	41,365	156,833	17,546	11,828	186,207
2004-05	89,833	29,956	3,560	42,857	166,206	17,307	14,907	198,420

Due to a break in the series following the introduction of full accrual accounting, data from 1983-84 are not directly comparable with earlier years.

Source: Finance, 2005: 11.

TABLE 6.4
Budgetary revenues (per cent of GDP)

| Year | Tax revenues | | | | | Employment insurance premiums | Other revenues | Total budgetary revenues |
	Personal income tax	Corporate income tax	Other income tax	Excise taxes and duties	Total tax revenues			
1961-62	5.0	3.2	0.5	5.4	14.0	0.7	1.1	15.7
1962-63	4.5	2.9	0.5	5.4	13.3	0.6	1.0	14.9
1963-64	4.5	2.9	0.5	5.3	13.1	0.6	1.1	14.8
1964-65	4.8	3.2	0.4	5.5	13.9	0.6	1.1	15.6
1965-66	4.6	3.0	0.5	5.8	13.8	0.6	1.2	15.6
1966-67	4.7	2.7	0.5	5.6	13.5	0.5	1.2	15.2
1967-68	5.2	2.6	0.5	5.3	13.6	0.5	1.3	15.4
1968-69	5.7	2.9	0.4	4.9	13.9	0.6	1.3	15.8
1969-70	6.7	3.4	0.4	4.8	15.3	0.6	1.3	17.2
1970-71	7.1	2.7	0.4	4.5	14.7	0.5	1.4	16.6
1971-72	7.3	2.4	0.4	4.7	14.9	0.6	1.4	16.9
1972-73	7.6	2.7	0.3	4.8	15.4	0.7	1.4	17.5
1973-74	7.2	2.9	0.3	4.9	15.2	0.8	1.4	17.4
1974-75	7.6	3.1	0.3	5.5	16.5	1.0	1.4	19.0
1975-76	7.3	3.3	0.3	4.7	15.6	1.2	1.5	18.2
1976-77	7.3	2.7	0.3	4.3	14.6	1.2	1.4	17.2
1977-78	6.3	2.4	0.3	4.1	13.1	1.1	1.4	15.7
1978-79	6.0	2.3	0.3	4.0	12.5	1.1	1.4	15.1
1979-80	6.0	2.5	0.3	3.7	12.5	1.0	1.6	15.0
1980-81	6.3	2.6	0.3	3.7	12.9	1.1	1.6	15.5
1981-82	6.7	2.3	0.3	4.4	13.6	1.3	1.8	16.7
1982-83	6.9	1.9	0.3	4.2	13.3	1.3	1.4	16.0
1983-84	6.4	1.7	0.2	3.9	12.4	1.8	1.4	15.5
1984-85	6.3	2.1	0.2	4.0	12.7	1.7	1.4	15.7
1985-86	6.6	1.9	0.2	4.0	12.7	1.8	1.2	15.7
1986-87	7.2	1.9	0.3	4.1	13.4	1.9	1.3	16.6
1987-88	7.6	1.9	0.2	4.1	13.8	1.9	1.4	17.1
1988-89	7.4	1.9	0.3	4.2	13.8	1.8	1.4	16.9
1989-90	7.7	1.9	0.2	4.3	14.1	1.6	1.4	17.2
1990-91	8.3	1.7	0.2	3.5	13.7	1.8	1.6	17.1
1991-92	8.7	1.3	0.2	4.0	14.2	2.2	1.5	17.9
1992-93	8.1	1.0	0.2	3.8	13.1	2.5	1.5	17.2
1993-94	6.9	1.3	0.2	3.7	12.0	2.7	1.3	16.0
1994-95	7.2	1.4	0.2	3.6	12.4	2.4	1.1	15.9
1995-96	7.3	1.9	0.2	3.4	12.8	2.4	1.1	16.2
1996-97	7.5	1.9	0.3	3.5	13.2	2.4	1.2	16.8
1997-98	7.9	2.4	0.2	3.5	14.0	2.2	1.0	17.2
1998-99	7.9	2.3	0.2	3.5	13.9	2.1	1.1	17.1
1999-00	8.0	2.3	0.3	3.4	14.0	1.9	1.1	16.9
2000-01	8.0	2.6	0.3	3.3	14.2	1.7	1.0	17.0
2001-02	7.2	2.2	0.3	3.4	13.0	1.6	0.9	15.5
2002-03	7.1	1.9	0.3	3.6	12.8	1.5	1.0	15.4
2003-04	7.0	2.3	0.3	3.4	12.9	1.4	1.0	15.3
2004-05	7.0	2.3	0.3	3.3	12.9	1.3	1.2	15.4

Due to a break in the series following the introduction of full accrual accounting, data from 1983-84 are not directly comparable with earlier years.

Source: Finance, 2005: 12.

TABLE 6.5

Budgetary revenues (per cent of total)

	Tax revenues					Employment insurance premiums	Other revenues	Total budgetary revenues
Year	Personal income tax	Corporate income tax	Other income tax	Excise taxes and duties	Total tax revenues			
1961-62	31.7	20.1	3.0	34.1	89.0	4.3	6.7	100.0
1962-63	30.3	19.5	3.2	36.0	89.0	4.3	6.8	100.0
1963-64	30.5	19.4	3.0	35.6	88.5	4.2	7.3	100.0
1964-65	30.8	20.3	2.8	35.2	89.1	3.8	7.1	100.0
1965-66	29.1	19.4	3.1	36.9	88.5	3.6	7.9	100.0
1966-67	30.9	17.7	3.1	36.8	88.5	3.5	8.0	100.0
1967-68	34.0	16.9	3.0	34.6	88.5	3.2	8.3	100.0
1968-69	36.0	18.4	2.6	31.1	88.1	3.6	8.3	100.0
1969-70	38.8	19.7	2.4	27.8	88.8	3.4	7.8	100.0
1970-71	42.7	16.2	2.5	27.1	88.5	3.3	8.2	100.0
1971-72	43.5	14.4	2.5	27.9	88.3	3.4	8.2	100.0
1972-73	43.6	15.2	1.8	27.5	88.1	3.9	8.0	100.0
1973-74	41.1	16.5	1.5	28.3	87.5	4.5	8.0	100.0
1974-75	40.0	16.5	1.5	29.1	87.1	5.4	7.5	100.0
1975-76	40.1	18.2	1.6	25.7	85.6	6.4	8.0	100.0
1976-77	42.5	15.6	1.5	25.1	84.7	7.2	8.1	100.0
1977-78	40.4	15.2	1.6	26.3	83.6	7.3	9.0	100.0
1978-79	39.6	15.3	1.7	26.2	82.9	7.5	9.6	100.0
1979-80	40.0	16.5	2.1	24.3	82.9	6.6	10.5	100.0
1980-81	40.6	16.6	2.0	23.9	83.0	6.8	10.2	100.0
1981-82	39.9	13.5	1.9	26.3	81.5	7.9	10.6	100.0
1982-83	43.4	11.8	1.9	26.0	83.0	8.1	8.9	100.0
1983-84	41.5	11.2	1.4	25.4	79.5	11.3	9.2	100.0
1984-85	40.3	13.1	1.4	25.7	80.5	10.9	8.7	100.0
1985-86	42.2	11.9	1.4	25.5	80.9	11.3	7.8	100.0
1986-87	43.1	11.4	1.6	24.7	80.7	11.3	7.9	100.0
1987-88	44.4	11.2	1.2	24.0	80.8	11.1	8.1	100.0
1988-89	43.8	11.1	1.5	24.8	81.3	10.7	8.0	100.0
1989-90	44.8	11.4	1.2	24.9	82.3	9.5	8.2	100.0
1990-91	48.3	9.9	1.2	20.7	80.1	10.8	9.1	100.0
1991-92	48.6	7.5	1.0	22.2	79.3	12.5	8.2	100.0
1992-93	47.4	5.9	1.0	22.3	76.5	14.6	8.9	100.0
1993-94	43.1	7.8	1.3	23.2	75.4	16.6	7.9	100.0
1994-95	45.2	9.0	1.4	22.4	77.9	14.9	7.1	100.0
1995-96	44.8	11.7	1.4	20.7	78.6	14.5	6.8	100.0
1996-97	44.4	11.5	1.9	20.7	78.6	14.2	7.3	100.0
1997-98	45.8	13.9	1.3	20.5	81.5	12.6	5.9	100.0
1998-99	46.2	13.6	1.4	20.3	81.5	12.2	6.3	100.0
1999-00	47.6	13.3	1.6	20.0	82.6	11.2	6.2	100.0
2000-01	47.0	15.5	1.6	19.6	83.7	10.2	6.1	100.0
2001-02	46.3	14.1	1.7	21.6	83.8	10.3	6.0	100.0
2002-03	45.9	12.5	1.9	23.3	83.5	10.0	6.4	100.0
2003-04	45.6	14.7	1.7	22.2	84.2	9.4	6.4	100.0
2004-05	45.3	15.1	1.8	21.6	83.8	8.7	7.5	100.0

Due to a break in the series following the introduction of full accrual accounting, data from 1983-84 are not directly comparable with earlier years.

Source: Finance, 2005: 13.

TABLE 6.6
Excise taxes and duties (millions of dollars)

Year	Goods and services tax	Sales tax	Customs import duties	Energy taxes	Other	Total excise taxes and duties
1961-62	–	1,045	534	–	625	2,204
1962-63	–	1,108	645	–	642	2,395
1963-64	–	1,278	581	–	666	2,525
1964-65	–	1,588	622	–	680	2,890
1965-66	–	1,917	685	–	742	3,344
1966-67	–	2,073	778	–	777	3,628
1967-68	–	2,146	746	–	826	3,718
1968-69	–	2,098	762	–	887	3,747
1969-70	–	2,294	818	–	897	4,009
1970-71	–	2,281	815	–	964	4,060
1971-72	–	2,653	989	–	995	4,637
1972-73	–	3,052	1,182	–	1,038	5,272
1973-74	–	3,590	1,384	287	1,094	6,355
1974-75	–	3,866	1,809	1,669	1,162	8,506
1975-76	–	3,515	1,887	1,488	1,253	8,143
1976-77	–	3,929	2,097	1,261	1,350	8,637
1977-78	–	4,427	2,312	1,030	1,354	9,123
1978-79	–	4,729	2,747	844	1,377	9,697
1979-80	–	4,651	2,996	1,171	1,397	10,215
1980-81	–	5,355	3,185	1,509	1,612	11,661
1981-82	–	6,148	3,435	4,521	1,739	15,843
1982-83	–	5,842	2,828	5,147	1,959	15,776
1983-84	–	6,561	3,376	4,168	2,110	16,215
1984-85	–	7,592	3,794	4,479	2,312	18,177
1985-86	–	9,345	3,971	3,348	2,827	19,491
1986-87	–	11,972	4,187	1,965	2,925	21,049
1987-88	–	12,927	4,385	2,603	3,026	22,941
1988-89	–	15,645	4,521	2,646	2,959	25,771
1989-90	–	17,672	4,587	2,471	3,425	28,155
1990-91	3,110	10,053	4,001	3,192	3,711	24,067
1991-92	15,311	–	3,999	3,441	4,557	27,308
1992-93	15,420	–	3,811	3,437	4,103	26,771
1993-94	15,939	–	3,652	3,640	3,709	26,940
1994-95	17,062	–	3,575	3,824	2,996	27,457
1995-96	16,880	–	2,969	4,404	2,998	27,251
1996-97	18,159	–	2,676	4,467	3,902	29,204
1997-98	19,717	–	2,766	4,638	4,025	31,146
1998-99	20,936	–	2,359	4,716	3,706	31,717
1999-00	23,121	–	2,105	4,757	3,315	33,298
2000-01	24,759	–	2,784	4,792	3,434	35,769
2001-02	25,292	–	3,040	4,848	3,953	37,133
2002-03	28,248	–	3,278	4,935	4,896	41,357
2003-04	28,286	–	2,887	4,952	5,240	41,365
2004-05	29,758	–	3,091	5,054	4,954	42,857

Due to a break in the series following the introduction of full accrual accounting, data from 1983-84 are not directly comparable with earlier years.

Source: Finance, 2005: 14.

TABLE 6.7
Budgetary Expenses (millions of dollars)

Year	Major transfers to persons	Major transfers to other levels of government	National defence	Other	Total program expenses	Public debt charges	Total expenses
1961-62	1,601	642	1,626	2,761	6,630	832	7,462
1962-63	1,669	737	1,575	2,614	6,595	915	7,510
1963-64	1,712	798	1,684	3,110	7,304	993	8,297
1964-65	1,793	918	1,536	3,295	7,542	1,050	8,592
1965-66	1,823	841	1,548	3,721	7,933	1,110	9,043
1966-67	1,983	1,016	1,640	4,525	9,164	1,182	10,346
1967-68	2,385	1,464	1,754	4,898	10,501	1,286	11,787
1968-69	2,612	1,813	1,761	5,064	11,250	1,464	12,714
1969-70	2,888	2,237	1,789	5,652	12,566	1,694	14,260
1970-71	3,281	2,954	1,818	6,058	14,111	1,887	15,998
1971-72	3,942	3,610	1,862	6,881	16,295	2,110	18,405
1972-73	5,153	4,134	1,937	7,583	18,807	2,300	21,107
1973-74	6,042	4,585	2,224	9,225	22,076	2,565	24,641
1974-75	7,620	5,884	2,526	12,208	28,238	3,238	31,476
1975-76	9,233	6,874	2,966	14,819	33,892	3,970	37,862
1976-77	9,873	8,399	3,373	14,951	36,596	4,708	41,304
1977-78	11,104	8,512	3,776	16,582	39,974	5,531	45,505
1978-79	12,030	9,551	4,096	17,303	42,980	7,024	50,004
1979-80	11,967	10,601	4,377	18,557	45,502	8,494	53,996
1980-81	13,793	11,578	5,063	22,331	52,765	10,658	63,423
1981-82	16,051	13,088	5,672	26,056	60,867	15,114	75,981
1982-83	21,697	14,177	6,599	30,335	72,808	16,903	89,711
1983-84	22,514	17,125	6,897	29,349	75,885	20,430	96,315
1984-85	23,888	18,548	7,641	32,886	82,963	24,887	107,850
1985-86	25,062	18,879	8,114	30,107	82,162	27,657	109,819
1986-87	26,423	19,569	8,866	31,577	86,435	28,718	115,153
1987-88	27,400	20,518	9,403	36,035	93,356	31,223	124,579
1988-89	28,780	22,145	9,940	35,298	96,163	35,532	131,695
1989-90	30,501	23,417	10,635	36,274	100,827	41,246	142,073
1990-91	34,343	22,928	10,976	36,944	105,191	45,034	150,225
1991-92	38,900	24,865	10,421	37,114	111,300	43,861	155,161
1992-93	39,646	26,544	10,408	41,376	117,974	41,332	159,306
1993-94	37,211	26,947	10,771	39,542	114,471	40,099	154,570
1994-95	34,958	26,313	10,210	43,452	114,933	44,185	159,118
1995-96	33,906	26,076	9,459	42,555	111,996	49,407	161,403
1996-97	33,587	22,162	8,417	38,094	102,260	47,281	149,541
1997-98	33,600	20,504	8,726	44,034	106,864	43,120	149,984
1998-99	34,169	25,523	8,964	41,339	109,995	43,303	153,298
1999-00	34,157	23,243	9,740	42,443	109,583	43,384	152,967
2000-01	36,571	24,724	9,305	48,094	118,694	43,892	162,586
2001-02	38,409	26,616	10,032	49,961	125,018	39,651	164,669
2002-03	40,188	30,645	11,332	51,428	133,593	37,270	170,863
2003-04	41,960	29,392	12,449	57,554	141,355	35,769	177,124
2004-05	42,619	41,955	13,924	64,174	162,672	34,118	196,790

Due to a break in the series following the introduction of full accrual accounting, data from 1983-84 are not directly comparable with earlier years.

Source: Finance, 2005: 15.

TABLE 6.8
Budgetary Expenses (per cent of GDP)

Year	Major transfers to persons	Major transfers to other levels of government	National defence	Other	Total program expenses	Public debt charges	Total expenses
1961-62	3.9	1.6	3.9	6.7	16.1	2.0	18.1
1962-63	3.7	1.7	3.5	5.9	14.8	2.0	16.8
1963-64	3.6	1.7	3.5	6.5	15.2	2.1	17.3
1964-65	3.4	1.7	2.9	6.3	14.4	2.0	16.4
1965-66	3.1	1.5	2.7	6.4	13.7	1.9	15.6
1966-67	3.1	1.6	2.5	7.0	14.1	1.8	16.0
1967-68	3.4	2.1	2.5	7.0	15.1	1.8	16.9
1968-69	3.4	2.4	2.3	6.7	14.8	1.9	16.7
1969-70	3.4	2.7	2.1	6.7	15.0	2.0	17.0
1970-71	3.6	3.3	2.0	6.7	15.6	2.1	17.7
1971-72	4.0	3.7	1.9	7.0	16.6	2.1	18.7
1972-73	4.7	3.8	1.8	6.9	17.1	2.1	19.2
1973-74	4.7	3.6	1.7	7.2	17.1	2.0	19.1
1974-75	4.9	3.8	1.6	7.9	18.3	2.1	20.4
1975-76	5.3	4.0	1.7	8.5	19.5	2.3	21.8
1976-77	4.9	4.2	1.7	7.5	18.3	2.4	20.7
1977-78	5.0	3.9	1.7	7.5	18.1	2.5	20.6
1978-79	4.9	3.9	1.7	7.1	17.6	2.9	20.4
1979-80	4.3	3.8	1.6	6.6	16.3	3.0	19.3
1980-81	4.4	3.7	1.6	7.1	16.8	3.4	20.2
1981-82	4.5	3.6	1.6	7.2	16.9	4.2	21.1
1982-83	5.7	3.7	1.7	8.0	19.2	4.4	23.6
1983-84	5.5	4.2	1.7	7.1	18.4	5.0	23.4
1984-85	5.3	4.1	1.7	7.3	18.5	5.5	24.0
1985-86	5.2	3.9	1.7	6.2	16.9	5.7	22.6
1986-87	5.2	3.8	1.7	6.2	16.9	5.6	22.5
1987-88	4.9	3.7	1.7	6.4	16.7	5.6	22.3
1988-89	4.7	3.6	1.6	5.8	15.7	5.8	21.5
1989-90	4.6	3.6	1.6	5.5	15.3	6.3	21.6
1990-91	5.1	3.4	1.6	5.4	15.5	6.6	22.1
1991-92	5.7	3.6	1.5	5.4	16.2	6.4	22.6
1992-93	5.7	3.8	1.5	5.9	16.8	5.9	22.7
1993-94	5.1	3.7	1.5	5.4	15.7	5.5	21.3
1994-95	4.5	3.4	1.3	5.6	14.9	5.7	20.6
1995-96	4.2	3.2	1.2	5.3	13.8	6.1	19.9
1996-97	4.0	2.6	1.0	4.6	12.2	5.6	17.9
1997-98	3.8	2.3	1.0	5.0	12.1	4.9	17.0
1998-99	3.7	2.8	1.0	4.5	12.0	4.7	16.8
1999-00	3.5	2.4	1.0	4.3	11.2	4.4	15.6
2000-01	3.4	2.3	0.9	4.5	11.0	4.1	15.1
2001-02	3.5	2.4	0.9	4.5	11.3	3.6	14.9
2002-03	3.5	2.6	1.0	4.4	11.5	3.2	14.8
2003-04	3.4	2.4	1.0	4.7	11.6	2.9	14.5
2004-05	3.3	3.3	1.1	5.0	12.6	2.6	15.3

Due to a break in the series following the introduction of full accrual accounting, data from 1983-84 are not directly comparable with earlier years.

Source: Finance, 2005: 16.

TABLE 6.9

Budgetary Expenses (per cent of total)

Year	Major transfers to persons	Major transfers to other levels of government	National defence	Other	Total program expenses	Public debt charges	Total expenses
1961-62	21.5	8.6	21.8	37.0	88.9	11.1	100.0
1962-63	22.2	9.8	21.0	34.8	87.8	12.2	100.0
1963-64	20.6	9.6	20.3	37.5	88.0	12.0	100.0
1964-65	20.9	10.7	17.9	38.3	87.8	12.2	100.0
1965-66	20.2	9.3	17.1	41.1	87.7	12.3	100.0
1966-67	19.2	9.8	15.9	43.7	88.6	11.4	100.0
1967-68	20.2	12.4	14.9	41.6	89.1	10.9	100.0
1968-69	20.5	14.3	13.9	39.8	88.5	11.5	100.0
1969-70	20.3	15.7	12.5	39.6	88.1	11.9	100.0
1970-71	20.5	18.5	11.4	37.9	88.2	11.8	100.0
1971-72	21.4	19.6	10.1	37.4	88.5	11.5	100.0
1972-73	24.4	19.6	9.2	35.9	89.1	10.9	100.0
1973-74	24.5	18.6	9.0	37.4	89.6	10.4	100.0
1974-75	24.2	18.7	8.0	38.8	89.7	10.3	100.0
1975-76	24.4	18.2	7.8	39.1	89.5	10.5	100.0
1976-77	23.9	20.3	8.2	36.2	88.6	11.4	100.0
1977-78	24.4	18.7	8.3	36.4	87.8	12.2	100.0
1978-79	24.1	19.1	8.2	34.6	86.0	14.0	100.0
1979-80	22.2	19.6	8.1	34.4	84.3	15.7	100.0
1980-81	21.7	18.3	8.0	35.2	83.2	16.8	100.0
1981-82	21.1	17.2	7.5	34.3	80.1	19.9	100.0
1983-84	23.4	17.8	7.2	30.5	78.8	21.2	100.0
1984-85	22.1	17.2	7.1	30.5	76.9	23.1	100.0
1985-86	22.8	17.2	7.4	27.4	74.8	25.2	100.0
1986-87	22.9	17.0	7.7	27.4	75.1	24.9	100.0
1987-88	22.0	16.5	7.5	28.9	74.9	25.1	100.0
1988-89	21.9	16.8	7.5	26.8	73.0	27.0	100.0
1989-90	21.5	16.5	7.5	25.5	71.0	29.0	100.0
1990-91	22.9	15.3	7.3	24.6	70.0	30.0	100.0
1991-92	25.1	16.0	6.7	23.9	71.7	28.3	100.0
1992-93	24.9	16.7	6.5	26.0	74.1	25.9	100.0
1993-94	24.1	17.4	7.0	25.6	74.1	25.9	100.0
1994-95	22.0	16.5	6.4	27.3	72.2	27.8	100.0
1995-96	21.0	16.2	5.9	26.4	69.4	30.6	100.0
1996-97	22.5	14.8	5.6	25.5	68.4	31.6	100.0
1997-98	22.4	13.7	5.8	29.4	71.3	28.7	100.0
1998-99	22.3	16.6	5.8	27.0	71.8	28.2	100.0
1999-00	22.3	15.2	6.4	27.7	71.6	28.4	100.0
2000-01	22.5	15.2	5.7	29.6	73.0	27.0	100.0
2001-02	23.3	16.2	6.1	30.3	75.9	24.1	100.0
2002-03	23.5	17.9	6.6	30.1	78.2	21.8	100.0
2003-04	23.7	16.6	7.0	32.5	79.8	20.2	100.0
2004-05	21.7	21.3	7.1	32.6	82.7	17.3	100.0

Due to a break in the series following the introduction of full accrual accounting, data from 1983-84 are not directly comparable with earlier years.

Source: Finance, 2005: 17.

TABLE 6.10
Major Transfers to Persons

Year	Old age security benefits	Family allowance benefits	Employment insurance benefits	Relief for heating expenses	Total
1961-62	625	521	455		1,601
1962-63	734	532	403		1,669
1963-64	808	538	366		1,712
1964-65	885	573	335		1,793
1965-66	927	598	298		1,823
1966-67	1,073	603	307		1,983
1967-68	1,388	608	389		2,385
1968-69	1,541	612	459		2,612
1969-70	1,731	615	542		2,888
1970-71	1,907	616	758		3,281
1971-72	2,205	614	1,123		3,942
1972-73	2,524	608	2,021		5,153
1973-74	3,035	993	2,014		6,042
1974-75	3,445	1,824	2,351		7,620
1975-76	3,934	1,958	3,341		9,233
1976-77	4,437	1,980	3,456		9,873
1977-78	4,861	2,122	4,121		11,104
1978-79	5,491	2,093	4,446		12,030
1979-80	6,320	1,725	3,922		11,967
1980-81	7,418	1,851	4,524		13,793
1981-82	8,585	2,020	5,446		16,051
1982-83	9,643	2,231	9,823		21,697
1983-84	10,406	2,326	9,782		22,514
1984-85	11,418	2,418	10,052		23,888
1985-86	12,525	2,501	10,036		25,062
1986-87	13,445	2,534	10,444		26,423
1987-88	14,349	2,564	10,487		27,400
1988-89	15,202	2,606	10,972		28,780
1989-90	16,154	2,653	11,694		30,501
1990-91	17,039	2,639	14,665		34,343
1991-92	18,168	2,606	18,126		38,900
1992-93	18,758	1,823	19,065		39,646
1993-94	19,578	7	17,626		37,211
1994-95	20,143	-	14,815		34,958
1995-96	20,430	-	13,476		33,906
1996-97	21,207	-	12,380		33,587
1997-98	21,758	-	11,842		33,600
1998-99	22,285	-	11,884		34,169
1999-00	22,856	-	11,301		34,157
2000-01	23,668	-	11,444	1,459	36,571
2001-02	24,641	-	13,726	42	38,409
2002-03	25,692	-	14,496		40,188
2003-04	26,902	-	15,058		41,960
2004-05	27,871	-	14,748		42,619

Due to a break in the series following the introduction of full accrual accounting, data from 1983-84 are not directly comparable with earlier years.

Source: Finance, 2005: 18.

TABLE 6.11

Major Transfers to Other Levels of Government (millions of dollars)

Year	Canada Health and Social Transfer[1]	Fiscal transfers	Insurance and medical care	Education support	Canada Assistance Plan	Other	Alternative Payments for Standing Programs	Total
1961-62		196	283	19	144			642
1962-63		215	336	26	160			737
1963-64		207	392	27	172			798
1964-65		276	433	27	182			918
1965-66		306	354	28	153			841
1966-67		371	384	71	190			1,016
1967-68		578	435	108	343			1,464
1968-69		615	588	227	383			1,813
1969-70		734	806	301	396			2,237
1970-71		959	1,088	388	519			2,954
1971-72		1,136	1,400	450	624			3,610
1972-73		1,326	1,649	481	678			4,134
1973-74		1,633	1,749	485	718			4,585
1974-75		2,323	2,121	504	936			5,884
1975-76		2,511	2,549	535	1,279			6,874
1976-77		3,252	3,008	649	1,490			8,399
1977-78		3,206	2,814	1,096	1,396			8,512
1978-79		3,175	3,488	1,365	1,523			9,551
1979-80		3,575	3,858	1,515	1,653			10,601
1980-81		4,055	3,982	1,600	1,941			11,578
1981-82		4,879	4,283	1,628	2,298			13,088
1982-83		5,753	4,060	1,532	2,832			14,177
1983-84		6,208	5,564	2,065	3,288			17,125
1984-85		6,208	6,330	2,265	3,745			18,548
1985-86		6,286	6,400	2,277	3,916			18,879
1986-87		6,679	6,607	2,232	4,051			19,569
1987-88		7,472	6,558	2,242	4,246			20,518
1988-89		8,684	6,678	2,227	4,556			22,145
1989-90		9,582	6,663	2,166	5,006			23,417
1990-91		9,245	6,033	1,862	5,788			22,928
1991-92		9,935	6,689	2,142	6,099			24,865
1992-93		8,664	8,307	2,887	6,686			26,544
1993-94		10,101	7,232	2,378	7,236			26,947
1994-95		8,870	7,691	2,486	7,266			26,313
1995-96		9,405	7,115	2,365	7,191			26,076
1996-97	14,911	9,418	-217	-41	105		-2,014	22,162
1997-98	12,421	10,000	162	5	24		-2,108	20,504
1998-99	16,018	11,645	2		8		-2,150	25,523
1999-00	14,891	10,721			56		-2,425	23,243
2000-01	13,500	12,684				1,000	-2,460	24,724
2001-02	17,300	11,978					-2,662	26,616
2002-03	21,100	10,366				1,500	-2,321	30,645
2003-04	22,341	9,351				400	-2,700	29,392
2004-05	23,781	12,863				8,057	-2,746	41,955

Due to a break in the series following the introduction of full accrual accounting, data from 1983-84 are not directly comparable with earlier years.

[1] In 1996-97, the Canada Health and Social Transfer (CHST) was introduced to replace the Canada Assistance Plan, Education support and Insurance and medical care. Starting in April 2004, the CHST has been divided into Canada Health Transfer and Canada Social Transfer.

Source: Finance, 2005: 19.

CHAPTER 7
Dealing with Deficits and Managing Surpluses

In its budget of 2005 the Liberal minority government led by Prime Minister Paul Martin went on what some media commentators suggested was a spending spree. The government promised $12.8 billion over five years for the Canadian military, the biggest increase in defence spending in two decades. A further $5 billion was directed to an early learning and child care initiative, while another $5 billion was earmarked for the promotion of environmental protection and sustainable development. An additional $5 billion of gas tax revenue was to be devoted to urban development and the upgrading of municipal infrastructure nationwide. And there was much more. An increase of $3.4 billion over five years for international aid; a $2.7 billion increase over five years for guaranteed income supplement benefits for seniors; $735 million for Aboriginal health care systems; $688 million for arts and heritage promotion; $500 million for global peace and security initiatives; $398 million for immigration settlement and integration programs; $375 million over five years for federal research granting agencies; and the list goes on. This spending, moreover, was in addition to previously announced plans from 2004 to reinvest upwards of $41 billion on health care over ten years and $33 billion on equalization funding for the provinces over the same time period.

And yet, to counter criticism that the government had blown the lid on spending, Finance Minister Ralph Goodale was quick to stress that the government was maintaining a balanced budget and that, indeed, this budget would be the eighth consecutive surplus budget registered by the federal government since 1997, a record not witnessed since Confederation. Canada was the only Group of Seven (G-7) country to record a budget surplus in 2004 and was projected to be the only G-7 country with surpluses for 2005 and 2006. The 2005 budget also called for reductions in corporate income taxes as well as reductions in the accumulated national debt. The prime minister was happy to assert that Canada possessed the strongest financial posture of any major industrialized country in the world, enabling him to feel confident in his spending plan.

How times have changed in Ottawa over the past decade! Whereas most Canadians are now getting used to surplus federal budgets and ambitious plans for new government spending and/or policies of tax cuts and debt repayments, just over a decade ago such a world of fiscal strength seemed nearly impossible to even contemplate. In the early 1990s the federal government was awash in deficits and debt, as indeed most G-7 countries still are today, and to many observers it seemed that this state of affairs would carry on well into the future. By the early 1990s the federal government had been running deficits for over 30 years, and it appeared that it was financially and politically impossible for any government to reverse this situation. But the seemingly impossible did happen. If the federal government today has the fiscal freedom to choose among any number of policies and programs and to provide them with viable funding, then this operational freedom was purchased through hard decisions made in the 1990s.

The 1990s were remarkable in the history of the federal government and its system of financial management. The decade began with the Progressive Conservative government of Brian Mulroney facing a budgetary deficit of $29.1 billion on total spending of $142.0 billion; it ended with the Liberal government of Jean Chrétien boasting of a budgetary surplus of $13.1 billion on total program spending of $152.9 billion. Whereas at the beginning of the decade government deficits had seemed like a permanent fixture of public finance, impervious to change despite years of budgetary reform attempts by the Mulroney government, by the middle of the decade this perception was dramatically different. When the Liberals came to power in 1993 they inherited not only a substantial deficit and debt problem but also a public attitude towards government finances that was more and more willing to accept harsh medicine to reduce the deficit. This government also inherited a Department of Finance that was increasingly adamant that the best means to secure significant deficit reduction was through strong cut-backs in program spending and the size of government.

As we will observe in the following narrative and analytical case study in deficit fighting and managing new surpluses, the Chrétien government quickly came to accept the policy position advocated by Finance; by so doing, it backtracked on earlier commitments made by the Liberal Party in their *Red Book*, published during their victorious election campaign of 1993. The narrative will devote attention to the **"command" mode of government** exercised by the prime minister and his finance minister and the drastic and often imperious manner by which the "forces of the centre" engaged in systematic yet essentially incrementalist budget-cutting.

While the experience of deficit elimination during these years says much about rationalist and incrementalist approaches to financial management, the effects of such actions now present the Canadian government (and all other provincial governments that have gone through similar dynamics) with certain major challenges. The federal deficit has been tamed but at a substantial cost. The size and impact of the federal government in Canadian social and economic life has been significantly reduced. Most federal programs experienced deep cutbacks in the 1990s, leading many Canadians to wonder and worry about the quality and sustainability of federal commitments to such policies as health, education, social assistance, environmental protection, economic development, regulatory protection, infrastructure maintenance, national defence, and the promotion of Canadian culture. Major cutbacks to the federal public service itself also led to doubts about the ability of the federal government to effectively monitor its own work, to promote the public interest and accountability, and to maintain a viable public sector workforce with a healthy state of morale.

All these matters will be addressed below, as will broader questions respecting the use which should now be made of by the current government of healthy revenue streams, balanced budgets, and some substantial government surpluses. Should such monies be reinvested back into public services and programs that have experienced cutbacks in the past decade? Or should they be used to fund tax cuts to individuals or corporations? Or to pay down the accumulated federal debt? Balanced budgets, if not growing surpluses, place the Canadian government in the midst of an ideological debate unlike any that existed in the 1990s, with this debate likely to dominate Canadian politics for the decade to come. A more profound issue is whether the management style portrayed through this deficit elimination period—that of a command-and-control, highly centralized, top-down form of decision-making—will continue to characterize the actions of the federal government in the new post-deficit period. Or is this form of decision-making more associated with crisis management? Now that the crisis has been resolved, will we witness a return to a more "normal" form of budgetary decision-making, and if so, what will be the nature of this "norm"?

7.1   The Deficit and the Mulroney Government

In the fall of 1993, Jean Chrétien won his first federal election as leader of the Liberal Party of Canada. His party easily defeated the incumbent Progressive Conservatives, led by the ill-starred Kim Campbell, as they were rent both by the rise of the nationalist Bloc Québécois in Quebec and the populist right-wing Reform Party in Western Canada. The Progressive Conservative Party also faced great and widespread public antipathy towards the former prime minister, Brian Mulroney, and his legacy in office (Forbes, 1996). Privatization, deregulation, the failed Meech Lake Accord, Free Trade, the Goods and Services Tax (GST), and the failed Charlottetown Accord had all had the effect, to varying degrees, of dissipating public support for the Mulroney government. Indeed, by 1992, many Canadians spoke of Brian Mulroney in terms of contempt bordering on hatred, with his government registering record low public opinion ratings. As public support for the Mulroney government eroded, precipitating his retirement from public life in the spring of 1993, one other issue dogged his administration and would be a part of his legacy inherited by any new government—namely, the federal deficit.

As we noted, in 1984-85, Prime Minister Mulroney's first full year in power, the annual federal deficit stood at $37.1 billion on total program spending of $107.8 billion. The net public debt (the accumulated deficit) totalled a record $194.4 billion. In his first Economic and Fiscal Statement published on 8 November 1984, Minister of Finance Michael Wilson reiterated Mulroney's commitment that fiscal restraint, prudent financial management, and deficit reduction were to be central features on the agenda of the newly elected Progressive Conservative government: "We have set for ourselves four challenges: first, to put our own fiscal house in order so that we can limit, and ultimately reverse, the massive buildup in public debt and the damaging impact this has on confidence and growth" (Maslove and Moore, 1998: 23). As these authors and others, such as Carmichael (1988), have written, however, the record of the Mulroney government with respect to deficit reduction policy never matched its rhetoric. Despite repeated public statements concerning the importance of fiscal restraint and deficit-cutting, the Progressive Conservatives, in 1984, "did not enter office with a clear set of targets and/or proposals for cutting the deficit" (Carmichael, 1988: 229). It was not until 1986 that this government established medium-term fiscal targets designed to stabilize the deficit by reducing it to a level whereby the net growth in annual federal debt "no longer exceeded the growth of the economy, that is, the growth of GDP" (Carmichael, 1998: 231).

The logic of this position accentuated the relationship between annual deficits and the growth of the national debt. Because annual deficits existed, the consequent revenue shortfall had to be made up by government borrowing on both domestic and foreign money markets. As deficits increased, the government became more and more indebted to a variety of major financial lenders. And, as with any debtor, the government was called upon to pay annual carrying charges—interest payments—to its creditors for the right to maintain the debt and its ability to borrow in future. The fiscal solvency of any government (as with any individual or private corporation) was measured by its ability to carry such a debt by maintaining steady interest payments. The tension here for any government, however, was two-fold.

1. First, annual interest payments on the accumulated debt took the place of spending public monies on other social and economic priorities and programs. By 1985, public debt charges totalled 25.2 per cent of total federal budgetary expenditures (Fiscal Reference Tables, 2005); thus, a quarter of all federal spending was necessarily diverted to past and current deficits, with much of this money, ranging into the tens of billions of dollars annually, being sent abroad to foreign financial interests.

2. Second was the "whip-saw" effect. As the deficit increased, it increased the net public debt, resulting in increased interest charges, resulting in even more public monies having to be diverted away from program spending and towards interest payments. In 1975, for example, public debt charges had accounted for only 10.5 per cent of total federal spending when the deficit stood at $6.2 billion. By 1985 debt servicing charges had more than doubled, while the annual deficit had grown six-fold (Federal Financial Reference Tables, 2000).

The problem the Mulroney government then faced was this: if the deficit and debt continued to grow at this rate, and if the rate of growth of the debt exceeded the rate of growth of the economy, as was the case in the mid-

1980s, the ability of the government to sustain its overall financial management of the country would be thrown into jeopardy. Absent a fundamental
change either in the economy or in the government's practice of financial
management, the country would eventually "hit the wall," the euphemistic
term used to describe the moment when lenders would refuse to continue
to lend to a government and would actually recall their loans. Such an event
would confront a government with the possibility of bankruptcy.

Thus, the Mulroney government initiated in 1986 a stabilization plan
aimed at ensuring that the national debt, in relative terms, would begin to
decline in proportion to the growth of the economy. To achieve this goal,
the plan called for a reduction in the annual deficit by some $16 billion by
1990-91, resulting in an annual deficit of only some $22 billion by that year
(Carmichael, 1988: 231). But even this modest goal proved unattainable.
While the deficit did decline in the mid-1980s from $37.1 billion in 1984-
85 to $27.9 billion in 1988-89, this was the lowest it ever reached under the
Mulroney government. By 1990-91 the deficit had risen to $33.8 billion
(double the 1986 forecast), and by 1992-93 it had "ballooned" to $39 bil-
lion. In explaining this glaring failure both in deficit reduction policy and
in the ability to match words to deeds, Carmichael (1988: 232) argued that
economic problems arising in the mid- to late 1980s quickly came to diso-
rient the federal government's deficit reduction plans. The collapse of both
oil and grain prices during these years had the double effect of reducing
federal taxation and royalty revenues while also increasing federal expenditures through economic adjustment and support payments to Western
farmers. In 1986 alone, subsidies to prairie grain producers via the Special
Grains Program cost the federal treasury some $1 billion. The recession of
the early 1990s only exacerbated the fiscal problems of a declining economy and rising interest rates. The former weakened federal revenue generation just at the time when public demands for increased social welfare
services and economic development spending were increasing. In 1992-93,
for example, federal budgetary revenue actually declined by some $2 bil-
lion compared to the previous year, while total program spending increased
by some $7 billion. Higher interest rates also had the inescapable effect of
increasing debt servicing charges at the very moment the deficit was already
increasing. The Mulroney government thus faced the combined problems
of weakened revenues, higher debt financing costs, and increased expenditures at the same time as it was officially committed to fighting the deficit.

Apart from these economic and fiscal problems, however, Maslove and
Moore (1998) claim that the Mulroney government also faced definite
political limitations—some of their own making. Despite this government's

rhetoric concerning the importance of deficit reduction and widespread support for this policy option among the business community, the Canadian public generally remained ambivalent on the issue. Public opinion polling undertaken by Angus Reid between 1988 and 1992 revealed that no more than 13 per cent of respondents ever believed deficit reduction should have been a high priority policy item of the federal government (Maslove and Moore, 1998: 32-33). This general lack of concern, coupled with a growing public hostility to the Mulroney government and its alleged overly close ties to the business community, resulted in a political climate that was not conducive to dramatic deficit-cutting. In observing the actions of the federal government during these years, Maslove and Moore mention that only in its final year in office did the Mulroney government succeed in actually reducing program expenditures in nominal dollars. In all the other years dating from 1984, program spending in any one year had always been successively greater than the year before, notwithstanding government rhetoric on the need to restrain spending. Whereas total federal program spending had stood at $82.9 billion in 1984-85, by 1992-93 it totalled $117.9 billion, falling marginally to $114.4 billion in 1993-94.

This suggests that the Mulroney government was confronted by a souring of public opinion that simply did not see the importance of the deficit issue or did not trust the Mulroney government with its resolution. In turn, the government itself was obviously reluctant to show aggressive leadership and make the hard program spending restrictions required by a serious deficit reduction strategy. Indeed, the only major initiative taken by the government over these years to reform the state of its fiscal management was on the revenue side of the equation. The introduction of the GST in 1990 was designed not only to make the tax system fairer by replacing an indirect manufacturers' sales tax with a direct, and thus publicly visible, general sales tax, but to enhance federal revenues by extending the scope of the tax (Maslove and Moore, 1998). Under the GST, most consumer transactions were, and are, taxed at a uniform rate, the implication being that, as the economy grew and consumer spending increased, so too would federal sales tax revenue. By 1993-94, revenues from the GST amounted to some $15.9 billion, whereas in 1990-91, the last year of the old manufacturers' sales tax, total revenues had amounted to only $10.0 billion. As Prime Minister Mulroney suggested in introducing the GST, this reformed system of taxation was to play an important role in eventually improving and balancing the fiscal condition of the federal government. The attainment of this goal, however, was not to be accomplished by Mulroney and the Progressive Conservatives.

7.2 The Deficit and the Liberal *Red Book*

When the Liberal Party came to power in the fall of 1993, they inherited a federal government with a $38.5 billion deficit and a total accumulated debt of $487.5 billion (Fiscal Reference Tables, 2005). Service charges on this debt alone accounted for 25.9 per cent of all federal expenditures. And, according to Department of Finance projections prepared for the new government on current revenue and expenditure patterns, the deficit was expected to rise to $46 billion and beyond. To some senior officials in Finance, if the country was not yet "hitting the wall," it was getting dangerously close to "the abyss" (Greenspon and Wilson-Smith, 1997: 53-54).

The newly elected government had a deficit plan, however, that was part of a three-pronged approach to broad socio-economic and financial management. As outlined in the Liberal Party platform document "Creating Opportunity: The Liberal Plan for Canada," better known as the **Red Book**, the Liberal government was committed to promoting economic growth, the preservation of social and cultural programs, and the reduction of the deficit (Liberal Party of Canada, 1993). The *Red Book* promised

- to promote economic development through a $6-billion, two-year, public works infrastructure program designed to provide needed upgrades to roads, bridges, and sewers while also stimulating the economy and providing thousands of much needed jobs;
- to replace the GST with a fairer tax (although one that would be revenue neutral, i.e., generating the same revenues for the federal government as the GST);
- to promote the creation of technology partnerships and innovation funds as a means of supporting the "New Economy" and enhancing international trade;
- to defend the Canadian social welfare safety net;
- to work with Canadians in helping them gain job skills;
- to provide income security and assist with welfare benefits to those in need;
- to maintain the integrity of the Canadian health care system;
- to establish a national daycare system for Canadian families and children, but only when general economic growth exceeded 3 per cent;
- to provide consistent and stable funding for the CBC; and
- to maintain a modest approach to deficit management. The Liberal Party stressed that the deficit could and should be reduced, within three years, to the point where it was equivalent to 3 per cent of GDP,

or, in real terms, to some $25 billion. A deficit of this magnitude was considered quite manageable by the newly elected Chrétien team.

Nowhere in the *Red Book* did the Liberal Party speak in favour of massive program spending reductions, or of major job cuts to the public service, or of planning to reduce the deficit to zero within any given time-frame. It also should be noted that Paul Martin was one of the key players in the Liberal Party who was called upon by Chrétien to help draft the *Red Book*, especially its provisions respecting financial management and the deficit (Savoie, 1999: 78).

As evinced by the results of the 1993 election, the Liberal platform resonated well with a plurality of Canadian voters. In many respects, as Greenspon and Wilson-Smith (1997: 7-8) assert, the *Red Book* was a classic example of a Liberal appeal to the broad centre of the Canadian political spectrum, a long-standing dynamic (see Chapter 2). It offered to the Canadian public a balanced approach to socio-economic management, one that recognized the importance of job creation, the preservation of social and cultural programs, and the need to impose a substantial degree of discipline over the deficit. But deficit-fighting was not the be-all and end-all of the government; rather, the deficit was to be managed with a sense of proportion and balance such that the means taken to address the deficit problem would not impinge upon other vital social and economic priorities. The liberal logic of the *Red Book* was that the state had a major role to play in maintaining and directing the social and economic well-being of the country while also working to ensure that the deficit would not grow out of control. By establishing a target for the deficit to be no more than 3 per cent of GDP within three years, and then keeping it at this proportionate level, the Liberals accepted that fiscal restraint was a necessary component of sound financial management, but that the deficit had to be seen in holistic terms.

As Linda McQuaig (1995: ch. 2) has written with respect to the logic of the *Red Book*, a deficit is not necessarily a problem to any government so long as it is stable, the rate of growth of the economy is higher than its growth rate, and interest rates are set at reasonable levels so as to stabilize and minimize debt servicing charges. Provided that these fundamentals of economic and fiscal management are established and maintained, a deficit can be tolerated and will actually decline over time, as economic growth rates outpace the deficit, resulting in growing revenues that can be used for further deficit reduction. From this perspective, any government can grow out of a deficit without having to engage in massive and painful budget cutbacks in program spending. The *Red Book* implicitly endorsed this way of thinking; it offered an approach to managing the deficit that did not explicitly call for large cuts in federal programs, the downsizing of the federal public service, or the reduction of the role of the state. The Liberal method of deficit management promised to be different from a more conservative approach to deficit reduction, with the Liberal approach founded more on fiscal balance, economic growth, and the progressive role of the state.

7.3   The Deficit and the Early Days of the Chrétien Government

Among the first decisions taken by Jean Chrétien as the newly elected prime minister was to appoint Paul Martin, his former leadership rival, as minister of finance. As Donald Savoie (1999) has written, these two positions are always the two most powerful and influential within any government, and, in the years to come, the entire history not only of the deficit but of the Liberal government would revolve around these two men.

At the outset of its new life, the government consciously supported the principles and statements enunciated in the *Red Book*. However, as Martin settled into work at the Department of Finance, the first of a series of adjustments in his thinking, and eventually in the thinking of the prime minister, began to occur. Finance has always been the leader in setting budgetary policy and the broad contours of macro-financial management, and, thus, this department had primary responsibility for developing deficit reduction policy. As a variety of analysts as diverse as Feehan (1995), McQuaig (1995), Maslove and Moore (1998), and Greenspon and Wilson-Smith (1997) have documented, the senior leadership in Finance found much to object to in the *Red Book*.

The problem with the *Red Book*'s deficit policy was that it failed to appreciate the severity of the deficit, the growing problem of debt financing, and the need for government program spending to decline if the deficit was to be tamed. The minister of finance initially disagreed with such an analysis. As Greenspon and Wilson-Smith (1997:ch. 4) document, in his first months in office, Martin argued with his officials in defence of the *Red Book*'s logic that the government could stabilize the deficit and actually grow out of it by developing policies to stimulate the economy, create jobs, increase business and commercial activity, and, consequently, enhance the tax base of governmental revenues. During early 1994, however, the minister slowly but increasingly came to agree with the more conservative thinking that was predominant in his department. A number of factors help to explain this turnaround in his opinions.

At the outset of Martin's term, he and the Liberal government were startled by the magnitude of the deficit they had inherited from the previous government. The last Conservative budget presented in April 1993 had forecast a deficit of $32.6 billion for 1993-94. By November 1993, the first month of the Liberal government, Finance projected that the actual deficit for that year would run between $44 and $46 billion. As it turned out, the final deficit for 1993-94 was $38.5 billion, but the experience of witnessing a $6 billion overrun on the deficit was clearly a shock to the new minister (Greenspon and Wilson-Smith, 1997: 65). As the Liberal government was just beginning the process of governing, it had to recognize that it was $6 billion further behind than had been anticipated, meaning that its 3 per cent deficit target would be tougher to meet than expected.

The evolution in Martin's thinking continued throughout 1994 as he, and the prime minister, observed the deficit in relation to the debt; they came to believe that the latter was even more dangerous to the country than the former. Even as the government was initiating a modest program of spending restraint as outlined in its first budget in the spring of 1994, the nature of debt servicing charges and interest rates began to overwhelm its thinking in terms of gradual deficit reduction. In 1994, interest rates increased by 2 per cent. On an accumulated debt that then stood at $524 billion, this resulted in a $4.1 billion increase in debt servicing charges in one year, leading to total debt charges of $44.1 billion in that year, or 25 per cent of total expenditures. Moreover, the $38.5 billion deficit from the previous year added another $4 billion in interest charges for future years. In a position paper prepared for the minister, senior Finance officials calculated that, with anticipated future interest rates, even should the government run a balanced operating budget—revenues equal to expenditures, excluding interest charges—for the next five years, debt servicing charges would increase from $38 billion to $60 billion. In such circumstances, the logic of the *Red Book* appeared to be "a bad joke" (Greenspon and Wilson-Smith, 1997: 56). What were considered, at best, noble sentiments ran squarely against a call for far more dramatic action against both the deficit and the debt. "Martin now saw clearly," Greenspon and Wilson-Smith write (1997: 203), "that the debt, most of it compound interest, with no socially redeeming value, stood between him and his activist impulses. Moreover, the hope he had expressed early in the term of government that Canada, with a lower inflation rate than the United States, should enjoy the benefits of lower interest rates would remain unattainable so long as investors demanded a higher premium to compensate for the risks posed by the debt."

The experience of his first budget, delivered in the spring of 1994, and the general business and media reaction to it, also came as a shock to Martin. In this budget—billed as a moderate way to address the triple needs of economic growth, social fairness, and deficit control, as enunciated in the *Red Book*—he announced a series of modest tax increases and $3.7 billion in spending cutbacks to such program fields as national defence, foreign aid, subsidies to businesses, unemployment insurance, and government operations. The verdict of the business community and the national media, however, was negative, stressing that the new government had failed to appreciate the magnitude of the fiscal problem facing the country and that its deficit reduction initiatives were not much better than those attempted by the previous Mulroney government (Savoie, 1999: 73). Martin was learning that modest approaches to deficit reduction would not gain the support of the business community, either at home or abroad, or of the mainstream national media. And, as he was informed by senior policy officials in his department, public opinion polling and focus group work indicated that the Canadian public in general, and leading business interest groups in particular, were increasingly predisposed to approve aggressive government action on deficit reduction (Savoie, 1999: 173).

By the fall of 1994, Martin was convinced of the need for a major and concerted attack against the deficit as a means not only of reducing but actually eliminating the deficit altogether. He stressed that such a hard line on the deficit was ultimately justified as a means to the end of stopping the growth of the debt and, over time, of witnessing its gradual decline. As a further stimulus to this new way of thinking, one totally different from that of the *Red Book*, he had also become committed to the belief that high deficits and high debt fundamentally hampered the national economy and the growth of Canadian productivity and technological innovation. Prior to entering office, he had believed and argued that the deficit and growing debt was a result of a sluggish economy mismanaged by the Mulroney government. The preferred solution to this problem, as reflected in the *Red Book*, was to stimulate the economy while exercising modest restraint on the deficit. As the economy grew, so would government revenues, thereby resulting in a slow but steady decline in the deficit and debt, thereby resulting in a stronger, more viable and productive economy. But now, after a year in power, the finance minister had come to echo the mainstream sentiments of his department. Rather than being viewed as an effect of poor economic performance, the deficit was seen as its general cause, producing an economic climate not conducive to growth and development.

Greenspon and Wilson-Smith (1997: 204) quote Martin's address to the parliamentary Finance Committee in October, 1994:

> How do we improve productivity? To my mind and to all of our minds, the answer is clear. We must improve our skills. We must do better at innovation. We must provide a welcoming climate for investment. We must remove the disincentives we have created for both business and individuals—disincentives that encourage dependence and stand in the way of opportunity. Finally, we must get our fiscal house in order.

As Martin's thinking with respect to the deficit was changing over 1994, so too was that of the prime minister. Whereas Chrétien had initially supported the three-pronged logic of the *Red Book*, by mid-1994, he, too, was coming to see a need for major action on deficit reduction as a means to promoting sound fiscal management and long-term productivity, expansion, and economic growth. As Greenspon and Wilson-Smith (1997: 25-26) argue, this rather restrained approach to fiscal and economic policy, one very much in keeping with orthodox economic thinking coming from the private sector, was very much in keeping with the prime minister's temperament. Chrétien had always been a "pragmatist," as these authors suggest, one who avoided grand plans and attempts at comprehensive rationality in favour of small-scale, incremental initiatives designed to produce quick, tangible, workable, and desirable results. In this sense, Chrétien had always been much more interested in matters of sound routine management than "the vision thing," and, by mid-1994, sound routine management had come to be seen by him, and his inner circle, as requiring substantial deficit reduction. In a speech on 18 September 1994, in Québec City, he spoke about the future work of his government. He affirmed the importance of promoting economic growth, of creating jobs and economic opportunity, and of promoting industrial innovation and productivity, and he re-affirmed his government's commitment to reduce the deficit to 3 per cent of GDP. In this speech there was "a quote from John Maynard Keynes himself. It stated that periods of economic expansion were the ideal times to tame deficits. 'So now is the time.' Chrétien stated" (Greenspon and Wilson-Smith,1997: 202).

In coming to this realization both the minister of finance and the prime minister were themselves influenced by two external yet related stimuli: one more specific, the other more general. The specific matter was the Mexican currency crisis that began in December 1994. The Mexican economy teetered near collapse, afflicted by a combination of high public sector deficits and debt and international investor reluctance to maintain loans to the Mexican government. Only significant International Monetary Fund intervention to stabilize the peso and the announcement of firm commitments from the Mexican government to undertake massive fiscal restructuring including major public sector spending cutbacks ended this crisis. The problems in Mexico were felt in Canada, with the *Wall Street Journal* describing the Canadian dollar as a "basket case." As Donald Savoie has written, senior officials in the department of Finance as well as increasing numbers of cabinet ministers came to see the financial position of the federal government in increasingly bleak terms. Something dramatic would have to be done to restore confidence in the ability of the federal government to take care of its own finances (Savoie,1999: 177-78).

The second more general anti-deficit stimulus affecting Chrétien and Martin during this time, and in subsequent years, was general public opinion polling that consistently revealed that the mainstream Canadian public was, indeed, very fearful of continued high deficits and debt and that it was willing to tolerate, even wanted, governments to take strong and concerted actions to bring down and even eliminate deficits. As noted earlier, whereas in Mulroney's second term in office only some 13 per cent of poll respondents ever believed deficit reduction to be a high priority for the federal government, by early 1995 similar polling suggested that 48 per cent of Canadians now believed deficit reduction to be a high priority worthy of major government action (Maslove and Moore, 1998: 33) In this sense, the Chrétien government enjoyed a level of public tolerance and even support for "harsh fiscal medicine" unlike anything the Mulroney government ever experienced. And Chrétien and Martin did not miss their opportunity.

7.4 The Prime Minister and Finance: Attacking the Deficit

A special professional relationship between Jean Chrétien and Paul Martin endured throughout their years of deficit fighting. The two came to think and act as one, with the finance minister being the lead actor in developing and executing expenditure restraint policy, while the prime minister supported and defended his actions, even fending off other ministerial challengers if need be. There was thus a distinct *modus operandi* between the two: Martin was in command of all operational matters respecting the government's financial management, while Chrétien offered and provided full strategic and tactical support emanating from the power of the prime ministership (Savoie, 1999: 171) What Savoie refers to as "the centre" of government was moving into the deficit battle.

7.4.1   The Expenditure Management System (EMS)

In understanding the Chrétien government's policy on financial management, two major initiatives deserve notice, as does the operational style of the main policy players. As can be surmised from the foregoing, this operational style was that of the "command mode," as discussed in Chapter 4. Throughout 1994, the Department of Finance and the Treasury Board Secretariat (TBS), in conjunction with the Privy Council Office (PCO), worked on redesigning the overall system of government financial management and expenditure control. The result was the introduction and putting into operation of the **Expenditure Management System** (EMS) in February 1995. This was the latest variation in the long history of rationalist financial management systems. As with the Policy and Expenditure System (PEMS), its immediate precursor, EMS was designed to provide the government with a general system of financial management, linking together in a systematic method the demands of planning, programming, budgeting, and subsequent evaluation. Through the working of EMS, departments were given greater relative latitude in the development and implementation of policy and program priorities, while central authorities were enabled to exercise greater financial controls over the entire workings of the government. Though EMS and PEMS share much in common, they differ most in their grand strategic orientation. Whereas PEMS was designed as a system to generally oversee the growth of government undertakings in light of key priorities, the basic objective of EMS was to reduce and restrain government spending. In the words of the TBS (Treasury Board, 1995: 2) itself: "The Expenditure Management System requires the ongoing review of programs and spending to reduce expenditures and identify opportunities for reallocation to higher priority programs.... The Expenditure Management System will support ministers in dealing with the difficult fiscal situation the country faces and help the transition to quality services and affordable government."

As with PEMS, EMS centres around certain undertakings. The Department of Finance, in consultation with cabinet committees and TBS, is responsible for the preparation of a Budget Plan establishing multi-year funding targets for all departments and agencies, in keeping with broad government priorities for program services and financial restraint. Departments and agencies receive their funding levels directly and are responsible for program delivery. Unlike PEMS, however, EMS makes no provision for any Policy Reserve; there are no "B" budgets. Should a department wish to undertake a new policy and program initiative, it has to be funded out of its established Reference Level of funding. Any such reallocation, moreover, will require the advice, review, and support of both the TBS, for its financial implications, and the cabinet, for all policy implications. In this respect, a substantial degree of centralized control has been applied to departments, notwithstanding the official assertion of greater departmental autonomy. The TBS, moreover, maintains a small Contingency and Operating Reserves, to be used in extraordinary or emergency situations when unanticipated government spending is required.

The other new initiative with EMS is that the department planning process has been significantly altered. Multi-Year Operational Plans (MYOPs) and Budget Year Operational Plans (BYOPs) are now things of the past, replaced by a Departmental Business Plan. These plans offer a three-year perspective on a department's priorities and objectives in light of its existing level of funding. They provide an overview of strategies and actions anticipated by the department, its goals and program targets, and an outline of management approaches and performance measures designed to assess the quality of program delivery. They also contain information on current program performance and anticipated performance enhancements, allowing for informed appraisals of the effectiveness of departmental activities. The plans are developed in consultation with the TBS and are integrated into the TBS's new system of **Managing for Results** (MFR). Through MFR, the TBS is mandated

- to review all departmental Business Plans;
- to assess them for clarity, viability, accuracy, and efficacy; and
- to assess the competency with which departments are measuring their performance and the degree to which they are achieving the results they have set for themselves.

The self-proclaimed role of the TBS, however, is not to be that of a meddling superior but of a supportive facilitator, working with departments to "enhance management and resource flexibility." Performance measurement, a classic goal of budgetary rationalism, is at the heart of MFR, and as the TBS (Treasury Board, 2000: ch. 1) asserts, all departments and their managers must be committed to this goal. Through MFR, all managers "...are expected to define results, ensure that their attention is continually directed towards results achievement, measure performance regularly and

BOX 7.1
The Expenditure Management System

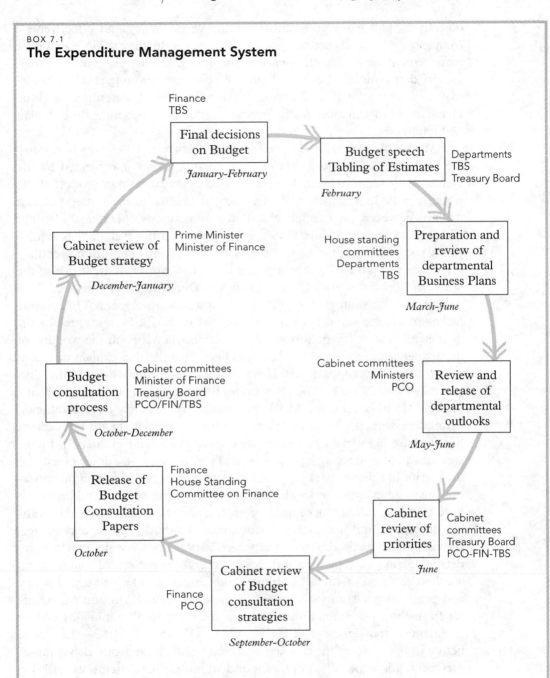

Finance
TBS

Final decisions on Budget

January-February

Budget speech Tabling of Estimates

Departments
TBS
Treasury Board

February

Prime Minister
Minister of Finance

Cabinet review of Budget strategy

December-January

House standing committees
Departments
TBS

Preparation and review of departmental Business Plans

March-June

Cabinet committees
Minister of Finance
Treasury Board
PCO/FIN/TBS

Budget consultation process

October-December

Cabinet committees
Ministers
PCO

Review and release of departmental outlooks

May-June

Finance
House Standing
Committee on Finance

Release of Budget Consultation Papers

October

Cabinet review of priorities

Cabinet committees
Treasury Board
PCO-FIN-TBS

June

Finance
PCO

Cabinet review of Budget consultation strategies

September-October

Source: Treasury Board of Canada, 1995: 8.

objectively, and learn and adjust to improve efficiency and effectiveness. Managers at all levels are accountable for the results they achieve to higher management, to ministers, to Parliament, and to Canadians." All TBS analyses of departmental Business Plans, of course, become part of the information used by the TBS in consultations with cabinet committees and the Department of Finance for the preparation of the upcoming Budget Plan and Estimates.

EMS has been in official operation since February 1995, which was also the beginning of several years of deep spending cuts inaugurated by the system of Program Review to be discussed below, so any evaluation of the working of EMS in a period of "normalcy" can only be preliminary; certain matters, however, can be highlighted. In evaluating the operational worth of EMS, Maslove and Moore (1998: 34) argued that the system "has significantly contributed to the government's ability to control program spending. It has done so largely by consolidating budgetary power in the hands of the 'guardian' central agencies, particularly the Department of Finance." This was exactly the strategic intention of the system's developers. While Savoie makes much the same point in his analysis of EMS, he also stresses the greater role called for performance evaluation, via MFR, in the working of departments and the need for departments to identify and explain ways and means to assess program performance in all their submissions to the TBS (Savoie, 1999: 221-22). This very point, however, points to basic problems facing EMS in general and MFR in particular. As with any of their rationalist predecessors, they face the classic problems associated with rationalism: how to gain agreement on planning, prioritization, and evaluation. Public servants and politicians, departments and central agencies, differ greatly on the merits and demerits of particular approaches to planning and prioritization, just as they argue as to whether or not particular policies and programs have met and fulfilled acceptable performance standards. Even the drafting of desired and acceptable performance standards can be a challenge, risking simple platitudes and overgeneralization on one side, or excessive detail focusing on repetitive and easily achievable operational standards on another, or sharp divisions of opinion and disagreement about broad policy and program goals on yet another. In these respects, EMS and MFR suffer from the same limitations as any of the supposedly rationalist system of financial management—PEMS, PPBS, OPMS, or MBO—that came before it. It also faces the problems of complexity, paperwork, debate, disagreement, and time consumption found within earlier systems, as differing bureaucratic and political actors with vested self-interests seek, as always, to engage in the eternal struggle to advance their own goals and interests.

BOX 7.2

Roles in the Expenditure Management System

Budget consultations

CABINET
· Review Budget strategies, policy priorities and fiscal targets

PARLIAMENT
· House Standing committees review and report on Estimates and departmental Outlooks
· Standing Committee on Finance reviews and reports on Budget Consultation Papers

THE PUBLIC
· Provide input to individual ministers and the Minister of Finance on the Budget
· Comment on proposed spending plans to parliamentary standing committees

POLICY COMMITTEES OF CABINET
· Formulate strategic sector priorities for input into the Budget and expenditure planning processes
· Oversee the design and implementation of new programs
· Develop reallocation packages to fund any significant new initiatives

EXPENDITURE MANAGEMENT SYSTEM

DEPARTMENTS AND AGENCIES
· Deliver effective and efficient programs and services
· Develop departmental Business Plans and release Outlooks that reflect Budget decisions
· Prepare departmental Estimates, including Part III

PRIVY COUNCIL OFFICE
· Focus on overall government and prime ministerial priorities and the integrity and functioning of the system
· Provide support to Cabinet and its committees

FINANCE MINISTER / DEPARTMENT
· Set the fiscal framework
· Focus on the economic outlook, macro-economic management, tax and fiscal policy, expenditure management at the macro level with primary emphasis on major statutory programs and debt management
· Prepare Budget Consultation Papers and the Budget documents

TREASURY BOARD / SECRETARIAT
· Account for expenditures, including Main Estimates
· Help develop reallocation options
· Review departmental Business Plans
· Focus primarily on all expenditures other than major statutory expenditures and public debt and manage the Operating Reserve

Cabinet decision-making process

Service to the public and value for money

Expenditure and Budget planning and coordination

Source: Treasury Board of Canada, 1995: 10.

It is these very limitations, and the nature of the bureaucratic politics they illuminate, that led the central players in the Chrétien government to question the ability of EMS to furnish, on its own, the means to fully address the deficit problem. While EMS could perform the basic function of providing the government with a more streamlined general system of financial planning and management, Chrétien and Martin doubted its ability to enable the government to engage in substantial, consistent, and persistent spending cutbacks to ongoing government programs. To achieve this goal the government needed a special instrument of financial management, and this they constructed through the process of Program Review.

7.4.2   Program Review

Program Review had its origins in the Liberal government's first budget of 1994. Prior to its delivery, senior officials in the Department of Finance had made presentations to Martin suggesting that, even with the modest economic growth and low inflation they were forecasting, the national economy could never generate such revenues as to enable the federal government to reduce the deficit substantially, neither to the 3 per cent of GDP target nor even lower levels. In short, the argument that it was possible to grow out of the deficit was flatly rejected by the senior echelons of the department as patently unfeasible. They also argued against major increases in taxation, stressing that the country was suffering from tax fatigue bordering on tax revolt (Savoie, 1999: 173-74). While a growing economy could and would produce additional revenues to be used for deficit reduction, the opinion of the department was that movement on the revenue side of the financial management equation would be insufficient to significantly address the deficit. The logical conclusion was that serious reduction in the deficit could only be achieved through major reductions in program spending. Martin accepted this approach in principle by early 1994, and, in announcing "a review of all departmental spending in the 1994 Budget," he inaugurated the most far-reaching exercise in government cutbacks in Canadian history.

By May 1994, the policy had been given a structure. Martin and Chrétien agreed that the Program Review exercise would assess all government spending with the exception of major transfers to persons, such as unemployment insurance benefits and seniors' pensions, and major transfers to governments, such as Established Programs Financing and the Canada Assistance Plan. It was also agreed that the exercise would be "designed and managed ... by three central agencies of the federal government: the

BOX 7.3
The Six Tests of Program Review

Public Interest Test

Does the program area or activity continue to serve a public interest?

Role of Government Test

Is there a legitimate and necessary role for government in this program or activity?

Federalism Test

Is the current role of the federal government appropriate, or is the program a candidate for realignment with the provinces?

Partnership Test

What activities or programs should or could be transferred in whole or in part to the private or voluntary sector?

Efficiency Test

If the program or activity continues, how could its efficiency be improved?

Affordability Test

Is the resultant package of programs and activities affordable within the fiscal restraint? If not, what programs or activities should be abandoned?

Source: Canada, Privy Council Office, 1994.

Privy Council Office, the Department of Finance, and the Treasury Board Secretariat" (Savoie, 1999: 174). The operational work of Program Review would be overseen by a Steering Committee of Deputy Ministers (SCDM), headed by the Clerk of the Privy Council and Secretary to Cabinet, and numbering among its members the deputy minister of finance, the secretary of the Treasury Board, the deputy secretary (plans) of the Privy Council Office, and three deputy ministers from operational-line departments. In providing for political leadership for the exercise, the prime minister established a Coordinating Group of Ministers (CGM) to be chaired by Marcel Massé, which included Paul Martin; Treasury Board President Art Eggleton; the three cabinet committee chairpersons, Sheila Copps, André Ouellet, and Herb Gray; and three other ministers, Brian Tobin, Anne McLellan, and Sergio Marchi. As Savoie is quick to stress, however, this group was established only as an informal committee to advise the prime minister and the minister of finance on the Program Review initiative: "The Prime Minister was steadfast in his opposition to the proliferation of formal cabinet committees and it was he who decided that the committee be ad hoc. Accordingly, the papers submitted to the group did not go through the formal cabinet document process" (Savoie, 1999: 174).

In its initial design, Program Review was intended as a short-term process, whereby most programs of the government would be scrutinized by responsible departments and agencies, as well as by the central agencies, in order to assess their needs, organization, economy, efficiency, and effectiveness. What was required was a quick experiment in rationalist program evaluation. It was anticipated that improved and more economical ways of delivering services could be identified. As highlighted in Box 7.3, Program Review had six tests and related purposes. By working through these guidelines, the actors in the process were to develop program reforms and cost-saving measures that would eventually find their way into government reorganizations and budget reductions.

There was much fanfare in Ottawa over 1994 with respect to this supposedly wholesale reappraisal of the nature and working of the federal government. Many senior officials from departments and central agencies reported that they took the process very seriously, since it was among the first institutional reform initiatives of the new government. But, as Paquet and Shepherd (1996: 47-54) and certain senior officials have since reported, Program Review never lived up to expectations. It did not launch a profound reassessment of the role of government in society, of the status and functioning of the federal government in particular, or of the ways and means by which the work of government could be more economically, efficiently, and effectively delivered. Rather, as Paquet and Shepherd assert, Program Review was reduced to an ad hoc and incrementalist-style budget-cutting exercise in which Finance and to a lesser extent the TBS were the dominant players. Rather than seeking a fundamental review and rationalist "reinvention" of government itself, something the senior officials of these agencies likely looked upon as being hopelessly naive, the key guardians in charge of the process came to see it as a device to execute and obtain the deficit targets set by Finance. At the very outset of the process, Finance had established the total amount of spending cutbacks that had to be achieved by the government in order to meet its deficit target commitments. By mid-1994, this overall reduction figure was placed at $10 billion dollars for the first year of Program Review, with the process expected to run for three years, each year anticipating a similar, general spending reduction target. Once this general target was set, Finance scrutinized the operating budget of each department, assigning "notional" spending cutback expectations that were to form the basis of planning decisions within each department (Savoie, 1999: 175-77).

With budget-cutting becoming the goal of the process, any pretence to administrative rationality and systematic planning in refashioning the very foundations of government and public sector management was quickly lost. In his study of Program Review, Arthur Kroeger wrote that the budget-cutting process was essentially "rough and ready," with Finance officials playing the lead role by stipulating the percentage cutbacks that each department would have to endure. In reviewing the work of Finance officials in establishing these cutback reference levels, Kroeger asserted that it was widely understood by participants in the process that the work of Finance, while supposedly rational, was utterly unscientific. Reductions were simply grouped into three categories: large, being 25 per cent; substantial at 15 per cent; and token at 5 per cent. In explaining why this "rough and ready" approach was adopted, Kroeger lamented that there was no real alternative because there was no time for proper policy evaluations (Savoie, 1999: 177).

Savoie's research confirms these findings. He reports that senior officials in Finance accepted that expenditure reductions were "urgently needed" across the board, and that they had to act with dispatch. As one official explained:

> We were under the gun, there is no question about that. We did not have the luxury to wait twelve months for an elaborate study to tell us that expenditure cuts were required or where we should make cuts. We knew two things for certain—we knew that we needed to cut spending and we knew that we had to do it quickly. (Savoie, 1999: 177)

Through the summer and fall of 1994, the Program Review exercise played itself out, with Finance coming to exert a dominant pressure in all decision-making. Despite the claim that the process was intended to be participatory among all affected actors, with departments reviewing and assessing their own needs and abilities to realize spending reductions in light of the "notional" targets set by Finance, Ottawa insiders understood that Finance, in reality, dictated the funding level reductions that departments would have to absorb, with the "notional" figures becoming real demands. Affected departments were left to tailor and cut their programs to fit their new reduced expenditure levels.

As it became clear to all concerned that Program Review had become, in essence, an "ad hoc" budget-cutting exercise dominated by Finance, a number of other departments and their ministers sought to evade the discipline of the review process by appealing directly to the prime minister— the tactical "end-run." Savoie's view of these efforts is revealing: at the last cabinet meeting before the summer break in June, 1994, the prime minister made all his cabinet colleagues aware that he stood firmly behind his finance minister and that, together, they would meet the deficit targets set by Finance (Savoie, 1999: 179). There was to be "no light" between the prime minister and his minister of finance.

This reality, as well as the degree of control exercised by the "forces of the centre" over the Program Review process, was nowhere better illustrated than in the history of the Department of Industry's attempt to escape from the dictates of Finance. Industry was targeted by Finance for a "large" funding reduction, and John Manley, then its minister, appealed directly to Chrétien, objecting to the planned cutbacks and stressing that such a reduction would be a "major political mistake" for the government.

> It became, in the words of one Finance official, "[a] game of political chicken and see who would blink first. We knew that this was a critical moment in the exercise, and if we were forced to back down on this one, there was no telling where the exercise would end up. We stood firm. The Prime Minister supported us completely and Industry had no choice but to play ball. *Cuts to its budget would be made with or without the involvement of the Minister of Industry and his officials.*" (Savoie, 1999: 179-80, italics added)

This is a remarkable admission by any standard—testimony to the centralization of power in Ottawa with respect to strategic policy matters and the, at times, limited powers not only of line departments but also of their ministers. Thus, Program Review had gone from a planned exercise in rationalist restraint in government to a process of systematic and, in effect, unilateral yet incrementalistic cutbacks to most departments, with all essential decision-making vested in the hands of a few guardians. And the two most important actors here were, without doubt, the minister of finance and the prime minister.

By late 1994, however, it became obvious to these figures and their senior advisors in Finance that the Program Review process, as initially conceived, was on course to fall far short of the $10 billion in expenditure savings targets set in the spring. This realization, coupled with the pressure of the Mexican currency crisis, resulted in what some considered almost a panic by January 1995 (Savoie, 1999: 180). During this time, the Program Review exercise was revamped, with Finance directing the entire process and issuing new orders to departments with revised and deeper cutback levels. The Department of Defence was now targeted for deep cuts, as was Human Resources Development Canada. This latter decision had the effect of not only derailing a major social policy review orchestrated by Lloyd Axworthy but once again demonstrated the centralized power of Finance. It was during this time period, moreover, in speaking on national television with respect to the absolute necessity of the government's meeting its set deficit reduction target that Martin made his famous declaration, "It is a target we will meet come hell or high water" (Greenspon and Wilson-Smith, 1997: 203-04).

The 1995 budget marked the first official effects of Program Review, and it is from here that one can discern the unmistakable trend towards full deficit elimination within two years. This budget hit Ottawa and the country like a bombshell, as was clearly Martin's intent, and its reverberations, both positive and negative, are still being felt. Beginning in 1995:

- 45,000 positions were eliminated from the Public Service of Canada and the military.
- The Department of National Defence budget sustained massive cuts of a further $1 billion over three years.
- The Department of Foreign Affairs and International Trade lost $500 million in foreign aid.
- The Department of Human Resources Development Canada felt the single greatest blow with a reduction of $1.8 billion in expenditures and 5,000 staff positions over three years.
- In percentage terms, every department budget, save Indian Affairs and Northern Development, was reduced, and most of these reductions were substantial. Transportation was slashed by some 50 per cent, while Industry and Natural Resources were slashed by 40 per cent each.
- A host of other departments, such as Fisheries and Oceans, Environment, Agriculture, Heritage, and Human Resources Development, were decimated by 20 to 40 per cent.
- With respect to specific programs, such spending reductions resulted in the elimination, for example, of freight rate assistance and transportation subsidies for Western farmers and major restrictions to most agricultural and industrial subsidy programs affecting undertakings as diverse as the Cape Breton coal industry, the Quebec aircraft parts industry, the Ontario electronics industry, and the British Columbia forestry industry.
- Major changes were introduced to the unemployment insurance program. It was renamed Employment Insurance, its benefits programs were reduced, and its eligibility requirements were raised, especially in relation to part-time, seasonal, and frequent claimants.
- Transfer payments to the provinces with respect to health, social assistance, and post-secondary education also were reformulated.

The federal government unilaterally disbanded both the Established Programs Financing (EPF) system and the Canada Assistance Plan (CAP), replacing them with the new Canada Health and Social Transfer (CHST); it then downsized the federal commitment to the social programs covered by the CHST by $4.5 billion, though provinces were given greater latitude in how they could spend the reduced funding they received for their health, welfare, and university and college systems (Savoie, 1999: 181; Inwood, 2004: 314-16).

In total, the 1995 budget brought forth plans for a total of $29 billion in expenditure reductions over three years, though it is important to realize that many of these announced cuts were to anticipated future spending rather than to actual current expenditures. In real terms, program spending was reduced to $111.9 billion, or 13.8 per cent of GDP, down from $114.9 billion from the year before. This new GDP percentage figure, however, was the lowest level of program spending since 1965 and, before that year, the lowest level since 1950. The deficit for 1995-96 stood at $30.0 billion, down $6.6 billion, or 22 per cent from the year before and down $9 billion from when the Chrétien government first assumed office. While this 1995-96 deficit figure amounted to 3.7 per cent of GDP, it was down from 4.8 per cent the year before and was forecast to be under 3 per cent by 1996-97. Indeed, in June 1995, the federal cabinet, at Martin's urging, approved a reduction in the deficit target from 3 per cent of GDP to 2 per cent by 1997-98, with Finance anticipating a deficit of $17 billion by that year (Savoie, 1999: 181).

Program Review continued beyond 1995, though it never had the same impact as in 1994 and 1995. Phase Two of the exercise was conducted over 1995 and 1996, and though defence, foreign aid, and social housing programs were specifically targeted for major cutbacks, all departments were expected to endure further reductions of 3.5 per cent over the previous year. In comparison to Phase One, these reduction targets were considered modest and were much easier to meet. Most departments achieved these new economies through recourse to user fees, cost recovery initiatives, and contracting out of services (Savoie, 1999: 181). Following the 1996 budget, which saw program spending fall to $102.2 billion, or 12.2 per cent of GDP, and the deficit reduced to $8.6 billion, or 1.0 per cent of GDP, Program Review was officially transferred to the TBS (Savoie, 1999: 182). Here it was to become part of the standard operating procedure of the TBS; in effect, it was disestablished, having served its purpose for the Department of Finance, its minister, and the prime minister.

BOX 7.4
Changes in Federal Departments Spending 1997/98 Relative to 1994/95

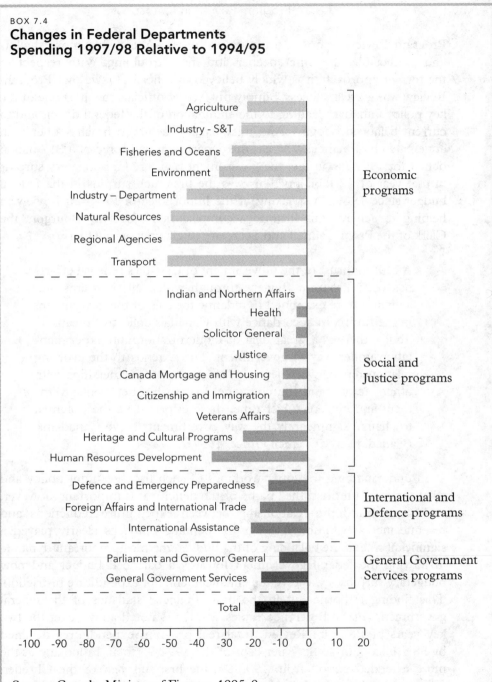

Source: Canada, Minister of Finance, 1995: 9.

7.4.3 Program Review in Retrospect

Program Review is open to two types of assessment, one more shallow and predictable, the other deeper and more troubling. With respect to the former approach, it is widely believed in official Ottawa that Program Review was a great success. Simply put, senior officials saw it as one of the key policy initiatives leading to the elimination of the federal deficit and to current balanced budgets. And this goal was achieved much sooner than anticipated by Finance. Whereas the department had forecast a $17 billion deficit for 1997-98, in fact the government registered a budgetary surplus in that year of $2.1 billion. This was the first such surplus in the federal budget since 1969. In speaking of the importance of Program Review in helping to achieve this historic accomplishment, Jocelyne Bourgon, the Clerk of the Privy Council and Secretary to Cabinet, wrote that :

> A central thrust of the Government of Canada's renewal efforts has been Program Review, through which all programs and activities were examined to redefine the role of the government in the future, in accordance with Canada's collective means.... Today, there is a great deal of modernization and experimentation under way in government. This extends to the evolving relationship between levels of government, partnerships with other sectors, and the changing relationship between government and citizens. Over time, these efforts have the potential to change significantly the way governments serve Canadians. (Canada, Privy Council Office, 1997)

In understanding the inner workings of such fiscal restraint policy and what the media termed the "battle of the deficit," it is important, however, to bear in mind the relationship between expenditure reductions and revenue increases. Though program spending cutbacks clearly played a significant role in the balancing of the budget, the most important dynamic in moving the federal government towards a balanced budget and now budgetary surpluses was revenue enhancement, not expenditure restriction. This finding is borne out in the basic financial statistics of the federal government (Fiscal Reference Tables, 2001). As noted above, over the two key years of Program Review, total real program expenditures declined by $8.1 billion, or some 7 per cent of the 1994-95 total. In looking at the more extended period from 1993-94, the first full year of the Chrétien government, through 1999-2000, total program spending declined by only

$4.9 billion, or some 4.2 per cent. Although these reductions were and are important, they pale in comparison to the changes on the revenue side of the financial management equation. In 1993-94, total federal budgetary revenue stood at $116.0 billion. Over the mid-1990s and the broad period covered by Program Review, total revenues increased from $122.4 billion in 1994-95 to $152.1 billion by 1997-98, the first year of a balanced budget. During this time, federal revenues had grown by 29.7 billion or by some 24 per cent over the 1994-95 figure. In looking at the two crucial years of Program Review, federal revenues increased by $20.8 billion, or 17 per cent of the 1994-95 total. And in the extended period from 1993-94 to 1999-2000, total budgetary revenues increased by $50.1 billion, or some 43 per cent.

An important component of such enhanced revenues, moreover, was the federal government's Employment Insurance (EI) fund. As eligibility requirements were made more restrictive and benefits less substantial, the fund began to grow and generate a surplus of its own. By 1995-96, for example, EI premiums payable to the federal government amounted to $18.5 billion, rising to $19.3 billion by 1998-99. Over these years, Finance made use of this EI surplus for deficit reduction payments, allocating a total of $25.7 billion to this end (Finance Canada, 2000: Table 3; Hale, 2000: 71-72). It is here, in this increased revenue stream, including especially the EI surplus, that one finds the main answer to the problem of the deficit. Thus, the essential logic of the *Red Book* was correct all along: the most effective means for dealing with a deficit was through the promotion of economic growth and consequent revenue enhancement, not program spending cutbacks.

While a variety of academic studies have confirmed the obvious importance of Program Review in enabling the federal government to reduce program expenditures, ultimately contributing to deficit elimination (Armit and Bourgault, 1996), a number of other critical analysts have raised serious issues about its exercise and consequences. As Paquet and Shepherd (1996) argued in their study, contrary to the rosy picture painted by Bourgon, Program Review essentially failed to transform the way government is planned and organized and how public services are established, administered, and implemented. Despite the Six Questions of Program Review, calling upon all departments and agencies to initiate a rationalist discourse on the future orientation and purpose of public services in their policy field, the process in effect became a highly centralized form of top-down budget-cutting by executive dictate. This position was aptly summarized by a senior federal official interviewed by these authors:

From my perspective, the Federal Program Review, while producing dramatic results in terms of dollars or job cuts, was primarily a scramble for cash, and did not represent a "redesign" or "re-invention" of government, as has been claimed by some. Federal departments cut what could be cut, and little real attention was paid to the six starting criteria. There was little or no attempt made to examine the structure and process of government on a horizontal basis, to lessen the pressures which require departments to incur such enormous overhead costs (e.g., the massive impact of bloated Central Agencies and their multiple controls and demands on departments, the costs of the unwieldy, obsolete and ineffective personnel system ... and the unduly centralized and control-oriented financial and administrative systems).

There is little evidence that the Program Review was either strategic or guided by any overall notion of where this will take the Federal role. (Paquet and Shepherd, 1996: 52)

This attitude lends support to the findings of Savoie mentioned above, to the effect that much of the real decision-making emanating from Finance with respect to departmental spending level reductions was "utterly unscientific" and "rough and ready," due to there being "no time for elaborate evaluation studies." It is true that some departments did approach the exercise with a genuine desire to engage the Six Questions and to restructure their operations so as to render them more economical, efficient, and effective, as a number of analysts such as Skogstad (1998), Bakvis (1998), and Lindquist (1998) have suggested. Nonetheless, these efforts ran on a more basic central imperative: the need to make drastic spending cuts in a very short period of time. As Savoie has argued, and as Paquet and Shepherd (1996) and Inwood (2004: 316) have endorsed, this latter imperative overwhelmed any pretence of rational planning. Rather than witnessing a form of systematic, rational, and participatory financial management, we observe a highly centralized, command-and-control management system operating in a "crisis atmosphere." In Phase One of Program Review, the key decision-making was increasingly ad hoc, with the Department of Finance setting and then resetting broad departmental cutback targets essentially designed to meet not departmental concerns but the even broader financial restraint needs and targets of the government overall. In Phase Two, this level of unplanned, ad hoc decision-making was replaced by across-the-board budgetary reductions for all departments—all departments were expected to reduce operational program spending by uniform increments without any reference to long-range planning and strategic prioritization. In short, decisions were made, departmental budgets were almost universally subject to significant reductions, and the federal government was able to lay the foundation for full deficit elimination within two years of the inauguration of Program Review, but the means to achieve this end can hardly be seen as "rationalist."

7.4.4   The Balanced Budget in Retrospect

The federal government balanced its budget in 1997-98, registering a $2.1 billion surplus. Since then, it has consistently produced balanced budgets and some substantial surpluses. In 1998-99, the annual surplus was $2.8 billion, ballooning to $20.1 billion in 2000-01. Over the first five years of the twenty-first century, total federal surpluses were anticipated to be in the $100-120 billion range, enabling the federal government to initiate a $100 billion tax cut for these years in its 2000 budget. Even with this tax reduction, the largest tax cut in Canadian history, the federal government still ran budgetary surpluses through the first years of the new century. In 2001-02, the final surplus for the year stood at $7.0 billion, and in 2003-04, the registered final surplus was $9.0 billion. All of these final year-end surpluses were allocated directly to the national debt. In fact, the fiscal health of the federal government was so good over the early years of the new century that, in 2004, the Martin government brought forth spending commitments in health totalling $41 billion over ten years while also increasing federal support for equalization policy by $33 billion. The 2005 budget, in turn, called for $41.2 billion in new spending over five years, with the bulk of this money being directed to the policy fields of national defence, the environment, cities, child care, seniors' care, and Aboriginal concerns. Despite this spending initiative, one very much influenced by the dynamics of a prime minister facing a minority Parliament, the Martin government in 2005 still recorded a surplus of $1.6 billion.

The federal deficit, as a persistent problem, is clearly over, yet certain interesting policy and management questions arise. What were and are the governmental consequences of such major cutbacks to public services over the mid-1990s? Were such deep program spending cuts necessary in order to eliminate the deficit, as Finance long argued, or were other less drastic and less harmful policy options available? And finally, what are we to make of the government's future policy and program options respecting how to best utilize current and future revenue streams? If and when surpluses can be attained, should these monies be used for tax cuts or should they be reinvested into public services?

7.5 The Consequences of Restraint

Beyond balanced budgets and the potential for growing surpluses, Program Review and the battle of the deficit have left after-effects in the federal government and the country overall. A number of authors such as Greenspon and Wilson-Smith (1997), Armit and Bourgault (1996), and Sandford Borins (1995a, 1995b) applaud the government for eliminating the deficit, for bringing "sound fiscal management" to the federal government, and for helping to restructure government by promoting the theory and practice of the New Public Management (NPM). This approach to government stresses the need for governments to be smaller and leaner, much more concerned with matters of economy and efficiency, and willing to borrow from and work with the private sector in developing new ways to provide services to the public. In this sense, the NPM calls for governments to "reinvent" themselves along private sector lines: to stress the values of privatization, deregulation, downloading, and off-loading of public service responsibilities and to stress the importance and the necessity of "doing more with less." Much more will be said of the NPM in Chapter 10.

In contrast to these analysts, however, many other commentators have been quick to point out the limitations, problems, and deleterious consequences of Program Review and its impact of "shrinking the state." As the foregoing discussion has demonstrated, Program Review had a significant impact on every federal department save Indian Affairs and Northern Development. In 1995-96 alone, total program spending declined by $3.0 billion compared to the previous year; in 1996-97, a further $9.7 billion was removed from such spending (Department of Finance, 2000). But this was the end of the total expenditure cutbacks. In 1997-98, total program spending rose by $4.6 billion, and such spending has been rising substantially every year since then. In 2000-01, total program spending amounted to $118.6 billion, rising to $162.6 billion in 2004-05, an increase of $44 billion, or 37 per cent, in these years alone.

By the end of the twentieth century, however, as both Savoie (1999) and McQuaig (1998) asserted, the billions in Program Review expenditure cutbacks have resulted in total federal program spending, measured in relation to GDP, equivalent to early 1950s levels, a time period predating the development of the modern liberal social welfare state. Is such restraint compatible with a progressive state? Can the government maintain the quality of public services that most Canadians have come to expect? And are most Canadians willing to see a substantially smaller federal government with a more limited role in the social, economic, political, and even military life of this country?

In assessing the practical consequences of government downsizing, a number of authors have been quite critical of its effects on the public service and its abilities to deliver quality programs to the Canadian public. In the aftermath of Program Review, most public attention was directed to matters of broad social policy and health care. As mentioned above, the 1995 budget amalgamated the EPF system and the CAP into one unified federal transfer program, the Canada Health and Social Transfer, and then unilaterally cut the amount of funding for this CHST program by $4.5 billion, or roughly 30 per cent, over three years. Provincial governments complained bitterly of this treatment, claiming the federal government was acting in a manner inconsistent with stable federal-provincial relations and sound social welfare program support, but they were all left facing major reductions in funding for such matters as health care facilities and services, post-secondary college and university systems, and social services and welfare systems. These governments, in turn, passed on these reductions to the affected program areas, institutions, or municipal governments. The overall result, as argued by authors such as Maslove (1996), Prince (1999), Haddow (1999), Bach and Phillips (1998), and Shields and Evans (1998), has been

- budget cutbacks,
- service reductions,
- health care delays and growing patient waiting lists,
- generally increasing post-secondary tuition fees, larger university and college class sizes,
- ever-increasing service fees,
- decline in social assistance payments,
- the growing deterioration of most institutional facilities and public buildings,
- the growing problem of homelessness and the rise in food banks,
- growing concern about the inadequacy of childcare policy,
- growing concern about the widening division between rich and poor in this society, and
- an increasing sense that the quality of public services in this country has significantly declined in the past decade.

Indeed, such public sentiments were generally confirmed by public opinion polling undertaken by *Maclean's* in the fall of 2000. Fully 61 per cent of respondents reported that the general quality of health care in this country had substantially declined in the past two decades, while 46 per cent said the same of the public education system (*Maclean's*, 25 December /1 January 2001: 58-60).

Similar concerns were echoed for environmental policy. As a result of the 1995 budget, the Department of Environment experienced a 32 per cent reduction in its budget over three years, resulting in a loss of roughly one-quarter of its staff. The ironic feature of these spending cuts, as Glen Toner (1996) has commented, is that they came at the same time as the department was facing greater roles and responsibilities with respect to environmental protection and regulation; the promotion of sustainable development; conservation; and the development of policy and program- ming for climate change, bio-diversity, and endangered species. Thus, in a very serious way, the department has been called upon to do more with less. Questions remain, as a consequence, as to whether it can meet stated policy goals with such diminished resources, or whether it can only do less with less. In particular, environmental lobby groups have been very critical of reduced environmental inspection programs and the trend to off-load such responsibilities to provincial governments, which, in turn, off-load them onto local governments or turn them over to voluntary private sec- tor oversight (Toner, 1996: 124-25). It was just such a web of diminished resources and responsibilities and downloaded, downsized, and privatized services that were at the heart of the investigation into water quality arising from the Walkerton, Ontario, public health scandal. And, to confirm such general public concerns, the *Maclean's* survey mentioned above (2001: 54) also reported that fully 49 per cent of respondents claimed that the quality of the Canadian environment and environmental protection has substan- tially declined in the past two decades.

Such a list of departmental spending cuts, program reductions, service limitations, and declining public confidence in public service delivery could be extended to almost every department and agency of the federal govern- ment. Only a few more examples will be given here. The Department of Transport witnessed

- program spending cuts of roughly 50 per cent, resulting in the elimi- nation of most transportation subsidies for rail carriers;
- a diminished role for VIA Rail;

- the transfer of most national airports to local authorities; the privatization of the national air traffic control system;
- the increasing use of user fees at airports and harbours;
- the amalgamation of the Canadian Coast Guard with the Department of Fisheries and Oceans; and
- the sale of roughly half of all formerly federally operated ports (Bakvis, 1998).

The Department of National Defence experienced budget cuts of some 15 per cent, which had the effect of

- forcing base closures;
- postponing the replacement of antiquated naval helicopters;
- reducing the size of the regular military to about 60,000 service personnel; and
- placing 25 per cent of the Air Force's CF-18 fleet into "flyable storage" (Sjolander, 1996; Cox and Sjolander, 1999).

As Sjolander, among others, has explained, these cutbacks lead to serious questions not only regarding the military's ability ever to engage in combat, should that be deemed necessary, but also its ability to sustain the level and degree of peacekeeping operations for which it has become internationally renowned in the past three decades. These criticisms were forcefully echoed by the federal auditor general in her 2000 Report (Auditor General, Annual Report, 2000), calling into question not only this country's peacekeeping capabilities, but its capacity to provide an effective response to new concerns respecting national defence and international security arising from 9/11.

Finally, as mentioned above, Human Resources Development Canada (HRDC) lost $1.8 billion in program spending and 5,000 staff positions as a result of Program Review, or about 35 per cent of its total. Such shrinkage in its departmental capacity resulted in major cutbacks to its programming, including the level of benefits available via EI and a reduction in spending for such programs as the Transitional Jobs Funds and the Canada Student Loans Plan (Bakvis, 1998: 96-97). Not to be overlooked here is the fact that staff reductions within HRDC hit its middle management quite hard, resulting in a loss of managerial oversight and ongoing program direction, auditing, review, and redirection. These matters avalanched into the public scandal that enveloped the department and its minister, Jane Stewart, throughout 2000. As charges of corruption and incompetence were levelled at Stewart and the prime minister, as the opposition parties and the media pursued the "Billion Dollar Boondoggle," it became clear that many of the administrative and managerial problems experienced by HRDC could be traced to Program Review and the deep cuts that it had to endure to its operational and managerial capacity. It is arguably the case that these cutbacks weakened the ability of the department to maintain a close and consistent overview and internal department audit control over its elaborate and far-flung system of program spending. In this case, the program spending cutbacks so enthusiastically promoted by the Liberal government in the mid-1990s came to haunt them by the end of the decade.

7.6 Dealing with Deficits: The Mainstream Approach and Other Options

The federal government was not alone in facing a severe deficit and debt problem in the early and mid-1990s. To a greater or lesser degree, every provincial government in the country faced a similar problem, and most provincial governments dealt with their fiscal problems in the same manner as the federal government. Regardless of whether or not every province engaged in a formal process of program review, they all undertook a common deficit reduction methodology—a command mode of deep program spending cuts to most departments and agencies of the government, with the process firmly in the hands of central powers within the executive, namely, the premier, his or her finance minister, and key senior officials in the premier's office and the provincial department of finance. As Premier Ralph Klein was oft-quoted, it was necessary to "cut hard and cut fast" in order to get the operational and political "pain" over with as quickly as possible. He also stressed that such deep cuts had to apply to all departments, so that the administrative suffering was experienced across the government, with no one department or agency left in a position to raise a claim of special status for its own programming. His minister of finance was empowered to say "no" across the board, confident that this position would be resolutely endorsed by the premier (Mansell, 1997: 44-46; Dyck, 1996: 554-56). This approach to deficit reduction was followed in Alberta and New Brunswick in the early years of the 1990s, and it was its success that influenced the thinking of Jean Chrétien and Paul Martin in the mid-1990s. In turn, it was adopted by Mike Harris in Ontario following 1995; by the Parti Québécois government of Lucien Bouchard in the late 1990s; and by the governments of Newfoundland and Labrador, Prince Edward Island, and Manitoba during these years. The Progressive

Conservative government of Nova Scotia embraced deep spending cuts in 1999 with the introduction of its own system of program review, following years of ineffective financial management by the previous Liberal government. The same is now true in British Columbia. Even the NDP government of Saskatchewan, under the leadership of Roy Romanow, engaged in a process of major program spending reductions across many levels of governmental activity, inclusive of health care policy, as that province successfully eliminated deficits run up by years of mismanagement by the previous Progressive Conservative government (Dyck, 1996: 482-85).

And yet, the Saskatchewan experience was different. The NDP government did not engage in wholesale program spending cutbacks, and, in the early 1990s, expenditures in the fields of welfare and social services actually increased despite the general public service reduction policy. A further difference was a strong reliance by the Romanow government on taxation increases as a means of deficit reduction. By the mid-1990s, Saskatchewan had the highest provincial tax rates in the country, based upon a 9 per cent provincial sales tax, a 10 per cent income surtax, and a variety of progressively graduated corporate taxes. Though the tax rates were controversial, especially in comparison to the neighbouring province of Alberta with its lack of a provincial sales tax, the revenue generated by such taxation in Saskatchewan enabled the province to eliminate a $1.6 billion deficit within five years without having to engage in the deep and broad spending cuts found in the other provinces and the federal government (Dyck, 1996: 482-85). In demonstrating this relatively different manner for dealing with a deficit, the Romanow NDP government gave a practical face to the theoretical arguments advanced by such authors as McQuaig (1995; 1998) and Fortin and Osberg (1996).

As McQuiag (1998) has written, public sector deficits were never the gross problems that conventional wisdom claimed them to be. Such deficits, moreover, could have been managed, reduced, and eliminated in much more responsible ways than by massive cutbacks to socio-economic programs and the diminishment of the role of the state in society. There are two key components to this alternative way of thinking.

1. First, the high deficits of the early 1990s were a reflection of the equally high interest rates of that period; if these interest rates had been reduced, so McQuaig argues (1998: ch. 3), the rise in deficits would have been softened and governments' abilities to pay servicing charges and even to reduce deficits would have been enhanced.

2. The second and more crucial part of the argument is that deficit reduction and eventual elimination could have been achieved more easily and reasonably by policies of general economic growth than by public sector program spending cutbacks. Any jurisdiction can grow out of a deficit providing that government spending is controlled and the economy is growing; government revenues will increase because this economic growth will generate greater commercial activity, job creation, and wealth, and, hence, greater corporate, tariff, sales, and income tax receipts.

Provided that all these economic fundamentals are in place, a deficit will eventually fade into insignificance as a natural by-product of a vibrant economy. This approach to the deficit was widely shared by social democratic analysts such as Fortin and Osberg (1996), the left-wing Centre for Policy Alternatives (1998), most opinion leaders in the NDP, and even by certain figures from the mainstream business community (McQuaig, 1998: 63-82). A 1994 Goldman-Sachs report on the Canadian economy and the deficit accepted this alternative approach for dealing with the deficit (McQuaig, 1998: 95-96), and, as mentioned at the outset of this chapter, the policy position advanced here was the one generally endorsed by the Liberal *Red Book* on 1993—that with prudent financial management and a strong economy, the government could grow its way out of the deficit.

The Chrétien government repudiated this policy approach, as documented above, due to pressure from its own Department of Finance, the mainstream media, the conventional wisdom of the North American business community, and the assessment by Chrétien and Martin themselves that a policy of deep program spending reductions was the best political and fiscal means by which to eliminate the deficit. It is important to recognize, however, that an alternative approach was present, that it had some significant intellectual and political credentials, and that it was practised, to a degree, in Saskatchewan.

One element of the alternative approach bears reiteration, however, because it was present in all federal and provincial deficit elimination initiatives. This is economic growth and related increases in government revenues. As McQuaig (1998), Fortin and Osberg (1996), and the Centre for Policy Alternatives (1998) long asserted, economic growth is the best means of deficit elimination; to a great extent, this has proven to be true. Though the federal government and most provinces engaged in policies of deep program spending cutbacks, the revenue side of the financial equation was the most decisive in the unexpectedly speedy elimination of deficits. As noted above, with respect to the federal government, over the main period covered by Program Review, total budgetary revenue increased by $29.7 billion between 1994-95 and 1997-98, or by some 24 per cent, while, over the same time period, total real program expenditures declined by $12.7 billion, or by some 11 per cent. The comparative dynamic here is even more pronounced when one looks at the first seven years of the Chrétien government. Between 1993-94 and 1999-2000, total budgetary revenue increased by $50.1 billion, or some 30 per cent, while total program spending declined by only $4.9 billion, or 4.2 per cent (Fiscal Reference Tables, 2001). This increase in revenue, which was vital to deficit elimination, was the result not of major tax increases by the federal government, though both personal and corporate taxes did increase over this period while EI premiums remained roughly steady, but of a growing economy generating greater taxable wealth. The overall significance of the government's increased wealth due both to substantial economic growth and changed EI policy was clearly observable in the mistaken deficit forecasts of the latter 1990s, when greater than anticipated revenues from a booming national economy and the EI surplus enabled the government to balance the budget some two years ahead of schedule. In retrospect, then, the proponents of the alternative approach to deficit reduction have been vindicated, in part: the elimination of the deficit was contingent on economic growth. While interest rate policy, general tax increases, and program spending reductions can all be a part of a deficit elimination strategy, the most important element contributing to deficit reduction in this country, at both the federal and provincial levels, has been that of general economic growth. The reality of this finding, however, throws into question the presumed necessity of deep spending cuts and the use to which current and future surpluses should now be put.

7.7   Looking to the Future: Planning with Surpluses

In looking back at the 1990s and the issue of the financial management of public sector deficits, a number of matters stand in sharp relief. One is that, contrary to the more moderate approach to deficit reduction advocated by McQuaig and others, and even at one time by Paul Martin himself, all governments in this country were convinced that deficits posed a major threat to their fiscal viability. They came to believe that deficits had to be eliminated quickly, that major program spending cutbacks had to be a central part of this process, and that the best means to this end was a form of crisis management in which key, effective decision-making power was vested in the hands of a few major government actors. Only Saskatchewan differed, to a significant degree, from this *modus operandi*, yet even there the similarities between the actions of the Romanow government and other Canadian governments are noticeable.

In essence, most Canadian governments followed a similar, rather conservative approach to deficit elimination, with this approach gaining the reputation of conventional wisdom by the mid- to late 1990s:

- fixate on the deficit,
- gain and maintain public opinion favourable to sharp program spending cuts,
- concentrate executive power,
- form firm alliances between the head of government and his or her finance minister,
- target almost all program spending,
- set firm reduction targets,
- do not waver from these targets,
- cut hard and cut fast, and
- execute all such spending cutbacks in a general period of economic growth and prosperity so that increased government revenues accentuate the progress made in expenditure reductions.

One can be critical of this approach to deficit elimination, however, on a number of grounds. Was such an approach, with an overt emphasis on program spending reductions, necessary when increasing revenues from economic growth could and would have solved the deficit problem without the need for deep and painful public service spending cuts? Were projected budgetary surpluses in the order of over $100 billion, for 2000-2005, as outlined in the 2000 budget, not suggestive that the many cutbacks to socio-economic programming were largely unnecessary, in fact throwing federal financial management "out of balance" since such large surpluses indicated that federal public services were drastically underfinanced? Has the quality of federal public services, and the very institutional capacity of the federal public service, appreciably declined in the past decade due to such budgetary cutback policy, and is this not reason now to support a generalized "reinvestment" in the public service and its role? Was the move, as outlined in the 2000 budget, to spend the bulk of this surplus on individual and corporate tax cuts wise? Or could that money have been better spent on public services, including not only health and educational funding, but also national defence? And what should be future budgetary priorities: Further tax cuts? Debt repayments? Program reinvestment? And

BOX 7.5
Budget Planning and Minority Government

When a governing party fails to possess a majority of the seats in Parliament, the government is referred to as a "minority government" and the political and administrative environment it faces is far more complex than when the governing party controls a majority of parliamentary seats. Note the following dynamics:

- The government always risks defeat on a vote of non-confidence.
- The government will require the support of one or more opposition parties to sustain government legislation.
- The opposition parties will demand active consultation and involvement in the revision of governmental legislation as it passes through parliamentary debate and committee review.
- The annual budget will have to be crafted so as to accommodate a variety of opposition party interests as well as promoting the government's policy agenda.
- Budget items will be analyzed and prioritized by the government not only in keeping with broad policy objectives but also how popular each item would be in general popular opinion should an election have to be fought over the budget.
- The relative strength or weakness of the governing party in controlling the parliamentary agenda will be contingent on that party's strength in the public opinion polls.
- The actions of all party leaders and leading figures in the government and opposition parties will be scrutinized even more closely than normal by the media.
- The political dynamics of minority governments can make for heated debate, rapidly changing policy developments, shifting political alliances, and short-term policy-making.

is the concentration of executive power within Ottawa to fewer and fewer hands beneficial and desirable? Can and should actions be taken to try to limit and reverse this centralization dynamic?

However one thinks about these questions, one point is clear. The general approach to deficit policy witnessed in this country from the mid-1990s to the first years of this new century clearly works to reduce and eliminate deficits. What was once considered a major and seemingly intractable problem afflicting all governments was virtually eliminated in most jurisdictions save Ontario and British Columbia by 2005, a remarkably short period of time. Following the advent of the 1995 federal budget, the federal deficit was reduced to zero within two years. Thus, deficit elimination proved itself to be far from a nearly impossible task; rather, it was a realistically achievable goal, provided that leadership was applied persistently to this end. In this sense, the story of the deficit is a story not of governmental incapacity and limitation, but of the ability of governments to confront problems, to make hard policy choices among competing options, and to address these challenges in effective and expeditious manners. Again, one may disagree with the means chosen, but one cannot argue that governments are incapable of solving hard problems.

The approach to the financial management of deficits demonstrated here, however, was and is far from rationalistic. Though the system of Program Review followed by the federal government was claimed by its developers and agents to be a process that would bring rationalism and systematic coherence to the management of the deficit, these claims were unsupportable, as we have observed. Rather than offering a rational means of budget-cutting, the system of Program Review came to be a power-play by guardians seeking a simple objective. And this objective was not the redesign of the federal state through a rational discourse on the appropriate roles and responsibilities of the differing orders of government leading to the identification of financial efficiencies, but simple cost-cutting and public service downsizing. As Savoie's work has shown, even key players within the process admitted to the "unscientific" nature of their work, and these conclusions have been confirmed by a variety of academic analysts. Far from being an exercise in rationalism, Program Review was a blend of crisis management, centralized command-and-control *diktat*, and simple incrementalist budget-cutting. It achieved what it was designed to accomplish, but, contrary to its official advocates, it was not a victory for a more rational approach to financial management.

Moreover, it is somewhat ironic that, at the federal level, it was a Liberal government that pursued such a conservative approach to deficit elimination. The Chrétien government proved itself far more effective in deficit elimination than the previous Mulroney government; thus, it can lay claim, according to such diverse critics as the NDP and the *Globe and Mail*, to being one of the most conservative governments in Canadian history over the past 50 years. As Savoie (1999) has illustrated, federal program spending as a percentage of GDP is now down to 1950 levels. As McQuaig (1998) suggests, we have gone "back to the future," to an era of smaller government, greater reliance on the private sector and individualism, a diminished role for the state, and a system of public policy in which the government perceives itself as a limited actor with limited capabilities and limited abilities to fund pre-existing or new policy and program initiatives. Though such a critique is viewed by many as unfair to existing governments in this country and their undertakings to address current socio-economic problems, the criticism directs attention to the very real policy choices that the federal government faces, as do the provincial governments, in the new era of public sector budgetary surpluses.

7.8 Budget Priorities, the Martin Government, and its Critics

With regard to the question of how Canadian governments in general, and the federal government in particular, can best make use of the monies available to them through balanced budgets and even surpluses, we hear a great diversity of opinion among both political parties and interested observers. These differences, of course, mirror the different ideological perspectives concerning the desired role of the state and appropriate public policy directions that we examined in Chapter 2. We are currently in the midst of a significant debate on the future role of government and the policy priorities that should govern the work of the state.

Directing attention just to the federal level of government, in the early years of this century one can discern three broad groups advancing distinct policy approaches for utilizing the increased fiscal flexibility afforded by balanced budgets and surpluses expected throughout the next decade.

Those on the centre-left of the ideological spectrum argue that the bulk of such surpluses should be "reinvested" back into society in the form of increased government program spending in such fields as health, education, social assistance, and in the plethora of other socio-economic activities undertaken by the federal government, ranging from regional and industrial development, job skills training, and infrastructure redevelopment, to cultural promotion and environmental protection. The advocates of this position, such as the NDP, the Centre for Policy Alternatives, the Canadian Labour Congress, and certain members of the left wing of the federal Liberal Party, stress that such an approach is only fair and just. They argue that most federal programs were deeply affected by Program Review, that most programs suffered serious cutbacks during the effort to eliminate the deficit, and that most of the many socio-economic programs and services offered by the federal government have been severely and negatively affected by these cutbacks. Since most Canadians have suffered from the deterioration in the quantity and quality of such federal public services, therefore, now that stable and healthy levels of funding are once again available to the federal government, the first priority of the government should be the restoration, refurbishment, and reform of all government programs that suffered through the cutbacks of the 1990s. While some of the advocates of this position, such as the federal NDP, also argue that a certain portion of the surplus should be earmarked for tax relief and national defence, this is only a secondary consideration. The first priority is the revitalization of public services and an active role for the federal government in the delivery of those services.

In contrast to this statist approach to new budgetary priorities is that of the right wing of the political spectrum. The Canadian Conservative Party, as well as most of the Canadian business community, stress that the federal surplus should be used either for providing major tax cuts to individuals and corporations, or for paying down the accumulated national debt which still stands at $501 billion as of 2003-04, or for some combination of the two. The Conservative Party tends to place greater emphasis on the tax reduction option, sensing this to be more politically popular to the Canadian middle class than the debt reduction initiative—although they are not unmindful of the importance of overall debt reduction—while many business analysts representing the Canadian financial sector favour the debt reduction option. Economic actors such as the major chartered banks view this option as working to enhance the long-run financial health of the federal government and, by extension, of promoting the long-range economic viability of Canadian society. The Canadian Conservative Party, along with most private sector business opinion, has little appetite for renewed and enhanced program spending across the board. While both argue in favour of much greater spending on national defence and for enhanced funding on health care, they remain vehemently opposed to major spending initiatives aimed at restoring social programs to the levels they were prior to Program Review. To the Conservatives, those past levels of program spending were largely responsible for the deficit and debt problem that the country confronted, and no responsible party should countenance a return to such undesirable levels of government expenditure and consequent state involvement in society.

Those on the centre-left, of course, disagree with this analysis, arguing that the deficit was not the result of excessive social spending by government but the logical outcome of a combination of enhanced program spending, diminished generation of government revenue attached to inordinately low corporate and individual taxation rates, and unacceptably high interest rate levels. As these policy dynamics co-existed through the late

1970s and 1980s, the deficit and debt rose to prominence as public policy problems. But the deficit was *not caused* by social spending, as authors such as Wolfe (1986) and McQuaig (1998) stress, or else major deficit problems would have arisen in the 1950s and 1960s at the very inception of the modern liberal welfare state. Given this observation, those on the centre-left remain committed to the belief that enhanced program spending is now both acceptable and required as a result of budgetary surpluses and that it should be devoted to restoring the public programs that have constituted much of the socio-economic fabric of this country.

In the midst of these broad, contending approaches to future fiscal management and public policy orientation stands the federal Liberal Party. This party, the one that oversaw the elimination of the deficit, the ratcheting down of the federal state presence in Canadian society, and the diminishment of federal public services was in the position, over the turn of the century, of determining the shape of the post-deficit federal government. It was presented with clear and distinct policy choices between left and right, between collectivist and individualist, between pro-business and pro-government approaches to public policy, public sector management, and the role of the state. And, in keeping with traditional centrist liberal ideological thought, it is noteworthy that the Martin government stressed publicly that it would follow what it identified as an even-handed, balanced, and centrist approach to future fiscal policy development. With the demise of the deficit in the late 1990s, both Prime Minister Chrétien and his successor, Paul Martin, asserted in turn that, as a matter of general policy, the federal surplus would be reallocated on a balanced and moderate basis: a substantial portion of the surplus would be earmarked for new program spending to reinvest in needed public services, while another significant part of the surplus would be directed to a combination of tax cuts and debt reduction. To Martin, such an approach had the benefit of simplicity as well as being consistent with general liberal values of moderation and balance in socio-economic policy. The government could appeal to both its right and left wings, as well as to the broader left and right wings of Canadian society as a whole, offering each side important validation of its preferred approach to public policy while stressing that the needs and concerns of each always have to be listened to, respected, and acted upon. Through this approach, the Liberal government claimed to be addressing the major economic, tax, and fiscal needs of the country while also demonstrating reasonable care for the preservation and quality enhancement of important public services and concern for those who rely upon strong federal programming. In typical liberal fashion, the Liberal Party laid claim to the centre ground of

Canadian politics, choosing a moderate set of social and economic policies appealing to the broad mass of the Canadian public, and, by so doing, hoping to position itself to reap the electoral rewards of being the dominant force of the centre.

Concerns respecting ethics, alleged corruption, accountability, and government wrongdoing emerging from the sponsorship scandal, however, increasingly dogged the Liberal governments of Jean Chrétien and his successor Paul Martin over 2002 and 2003, leading to the Liberals, under the leadership of Martin, losing their majority government in the federal election of June 2004. Confronted with a minority Parliament, the first in a quarter century (since the Joe Clark Progressive Conservative minority government of 1979-80), Prime Minister Martin became more "liberal" in his government's spending. Budget 2005 was a classic appeal to the liberal centre, giving most everyone something which they desired. The success or failure of the Martin government would be determined by factors other than the public reaction to this budget, though it was what he wanted to use as an indicator of his government's policy vision.

With this budget, many conservative critics of the Liberal government voiced the complaint that the prudent and frugal side of Paul Martin that had long been in evidence during his tenure as finance minister had been lost by his desire to curry favour with the electorate as he faced a minority Parliament. When, in the spring of 2005, the federal Conservative Party and the Bloc Québécois threatened to vote non-confidence in the government, thereby precipitating an election, Prime Minister Martin sought the support of the NDP as a means of surviving a series of confidence votes in the House of Commons surrounding the government's budget. Box 7.6 highlights the nature of the agreement struck between the governing Liberals and the NDP.

A final issue worthy of note here is that of the nature of executive decision-making portrayed in this narrative. Is the command-and-control, highly centralized, top-down form of decision-making we have seen in action with regard to deficit elimination a type of decision-making unique to deficit-fighting—i.e., a form of crisis management that will now be superceded by a more "normal" form of executive decision-making? Or has the command-and-control mode become the standard operating procedure for central strategic decision-making in Ottawa? It is still too early to make any definite ruling on this matter but Savoie's findings, quoted here and in Chapter 4, as to how power is exercised in Ottawa, offer a chilling exposition on the power of the strategic prime ministership. This concentration of power at the centre has been an evolving dynamic of political life within

Ottawa for over three decades, long predating any sense of overwhelming concern and "crisis" having to do with the deficit.

BOX 7.6

The 2005 Liberal-NDP Budget Deal: Minority Government Politics

With the Liberal minority government facing the prospect of defeat at the hands of the Conservatives and Bloc Québécois in the spring of 2005, Prime Minister Paul Martin felt he had no alterative but to seek the support of the NDP if his government were to survive budget confidence votes in the House of Commons.

On April 26, 2005, the governing Liberals and the NDP reached an agreement on additional budgetary items that that would become part of the government's overall budget for 2005-06 and 2006-07. This deal would have the effect of boosting federal spending in social policy fields over these years by some $4.6 billion.

The key details of this agreement were as follows:

- $1.6 billion for affordable housing construction, including Aboriginal housing.
- A $1.5 billion increase in transfers to provinces for post-secondary tuition reduction.
- $900 million for the environment, with 1 per cent more of the federal gas tax allocated to public transportation.
- $500 million more in foreign aid to help bring Canada closer to meeting a commitment of allocating 0.7 per cent of GDP to foreign aid.
- $100 million for a pension protection fund for workers.

The tax cuts found in the original 2005 budget directed to small and medium-sized businesses would remain, but tax cuts for larger firms would be deferred. The reduction of the general corporate tax rate from 21 per cent in 2008 to 19 per cent by 2010, at a cost of roughly $3 billion, would be maintained by the government.

The Conservative Party denounced this agreement as being anti-business and harmful to the fiscal health of the country though the government defended its spending plans by asserting that even with this additional $4.6 billion in spending over two years it would still be running healthy surpluses.

The most important lesson to be learned from this series of events is to appreciate how flexible a minority government can be when it is faced with the necessity of building support from across the House of Commons so as to enable it to survive budget confidence votes. Faced with the prospect of defeat and an early return to the polls, the Martin government sought out the NDP in order to "make a deal."

At the end of the day, the Liberals could claim that their new budget was more responsive to the needs of Canadians while also being fiscally responsible in that the government remained in a budgetary surplus position. The NDP could also claim that their stance in these negotiations had improved the level of public funding for a variety of important social policy fields, notably affordable housing, environmental protection, foreign aid, and tuition policy reform.

On June 23, 2005, this amended budget plan was approved by the House of Commons by a vote of 152-147.

It is entirely possible that the type of power relations documented in this chapter will become the norm for how strategic policy matters are dealt with by the political "centre" within the federal government. Indeed, the former Martin government can be seen as being as tightly controlling and dominated by the "forces of the centre" as were both the Chrétien and Mulroney governments, and this is unlikely to be a simple dynamic associated with a minority government. The latter chapters of this text will return to this issue and what the future contours of power relations in Ottawa might look like.

As we confront the future, the basic outline of the ongoing national debate respecting socio-economic policy is readily apparent and predictable. Those on the left stress the need for greater social spending as well as enhanced defence and security measures; those on the right argue in favour of greater taxation and debt relief on top of greater spending on the military; and the Liberal Party asserts that it seeks to strike a fair and honourable balance between these contending viewpoints. The ongoing public discourse here showcases two extremely important realities. One is the never-ending significance of competing ideas and ideologies in the evaluation of public policy, public sector management, and the work of governments. The other is the importance of government, public policy, and public sector management to the life of this country. The elimination of the deficit and the "re-establishment" of fiscal stability to the federal government has opened up a new phase in the continuing argument about the "true" work of the federal government in this society. And the federal government is carving out a new role for itself through its actions.

Regardless of how one views the merits or demerits of such actions, it is clear that the federal government is redefining its role and the relationship that the federal public service will have with Canadian society. As has always been the case, the work of the government—its ability to develop, implement, and administer policies and programs—is contingent not only upon sound financial management, but on progressive personnel administration. People matter as much as money in the working of government. In the next chapters we will review and assess the history, concerns, and current dynamics of public service personnel management.

Key Terms

command mode of government: A system of executive management in which all policy and program matters deemed to be of key strategic importance to the prime minister are fully subject to the oversight, control, and decision-making influence of the prime minister, the minister of finance, and their key central agency advisors. While this approach to executive management is usually associated with Prime Ministers Chrétien and Martin, its antecedents can be traced to the governments of Pierre Trudeau and Brian Mulroney.

Expenditure Management System (EMS): The current system of financial management found in the federal government. EMS is the latest version of rationalistic financial management planning in Ottawa, being an offshoot of the Policy and Expenditure Management System (PEMS) dating from 1979. EMS seeks to provide a framework for rationalistic policy and program planning, prioritization, programming, and expenditure control.

Managing for Results (MFR): The performance measurement system that is an adjunct component of EMS. MFR is operationalized by the Treasury Board Secretariat (TBS) with the TBS being mandated to review and assess all department business plans to ensure their conformity with the principles, practices and goals of EMS.

Program Review: The major review and assessment of all federal policies and programs that was initiated by the Chrétien government in 1994. Program Review was designed to be a rationalistic analysis and prioritization of all government spending initiatives designed to highlight policies and programs that were expendable. In reality, Program Review became an incrementalist exercise in rough and ready budget-cutting.

Red Book: The federal Liberal Party of Canada platform document for the 1993 federal election. Also known as "Creating Opportunity: The Liberal Plan for Canada," this document was largely written by Paul Martin. It presented a classic liberal-centrist approach to policy development in which rigorous deficit-fighting and program cutting was not part of the plan.

References and Suggested Reading

Armit, Armelita, and Jacques Bourgault, eds. 1996. *Hard Choices or No Choices: Assessing Program Review*. Toronto: Institute of Public Administration of Canada.

Bach, Sandra, and Susan D. Phillips. 1998. "Constructing a New Social Union: Child Care Beyond Infancy." In Gene Swimmer, ed., *How Ottawa Spends 1997-98: Seeing Red; A Liberal Report Card*. Ottawa: Carleton University Press.

Bakvis, Herman. 1998. "Transport Canada and Program Review." In Peter Aucoin and Donald J. Savoie, eds., *Managing Strategic Change: Learning from Program Review*. Ottawa: Canadian Centre for Management Development.

Borins, Sandford F. 1995a. "Public Sector Innovation: The Implications of New Forms of Organization and Work." In B. Guy Peters and Donald J. Savoie, eds., *Governance in a Changing Environment*. Montreal and Kingston: Canadian Centre for Management Development.

—. 1995b. "The New Public Management is Here to Stay." *Canadian Public Administration* 38: 122-32.

Canada, Minister of Finance. 1999. *Budget in Brief: Supply and Services*. Ottawa: Department of Finance.

Canada, Privy Council Office. 1994. *Program Review and Getting Government Right.* Ottawa: Department of Finance.

Canada, Privy Council Office. 1997. *Fourth Annual Report to the Prime Minister on the Public Service of Canada.* Privy Council Office.

Canadian Centre for Policy Alternatives. *Alternative Federal Budget Papers 1998.* Ottawa: Canadian Centre for Policy Alternatives and Choices: A Coalition for Social Justice.

Carmichael, Edward A. 1988. "The Mulroney Government and the Deficit." In Andrew B. Gollner and Daniel Salée, eds., *Canada Under Mulroney: An End of Term Report.* Montreal: Véhicule Press.

Cox, Wayne S., and Claire Turenne Sjolander. 1999. "Damage Control: The Politics of National Defence." In Leslie A. Pal, ed., *How Ottawa Spends 1998-99: Balancing Act: The Post-Deficit Mandate.* Toronto: Oxford University Press.

Department of Finance. 2001. *Fiscal Reference Tables.*

Dyck, Rand. 1996. *Provincial Politics in Canada: Toward the Turn of the Century.* 2nd ed. Scarborough, ON: Prentice-Hall Canada.

Feehan, James P. 1995. "The Federal Debt." In Susan D. Phillips, ed., *How Ottawa Spends 1995-1996: Mid-Life Crisis.* Ottawa: Carleton University Press. 31-58.

Forbes, H.D. 1996. "Interpreting the 1993 Election." In Hugh G. Thorburn, ed., *Party Politics in Canada.* 7th ed. Scarborough, ON: Prentice-Hall Canada. 557-77.

Greenspon, Edward, and Anthony Wilson-Smith. 1997. *Double Vision: The Inside Story of the Liberals in Power.* Toronto: Seal Books.

Haddow, Rodney. 1999. "How Ottawa Shrivels: Ottawa's Declining Role in Active Labour Market Policy." In Leslie A. Pal, ed., *How Ottawa Spends 1998-99: Balancing Act: The Post Deficit Mandate.* Toronto: Oxford University Press.

Hale, Geoffrey E. 2000. "Managing the Fiscal Dividend: The Politics of Selective Activism." In Leslie A. Pal, ed., *How Ottawa Spends 2000-2001: Past Imperfect, Future Tense.* Toronto: Oxford University Press.

Inwood, Gregory J. 2004. *Understanding Canadian Public Administration: An Introduction to Theory and Practice.* 2nd ed. Scarborough, ON: Prentice-Hall Allyn and Bacon Canada.

Liberal Party of Canada. 1993. *Creating Opportunity: The Liberal Plan for Canada.* Ottawa: Liberal Party of Canada.

Lindquist, Evert A. 1998. "Business Planning Comes to Ottawa: Critical Issues and Future Directions." In Peter Aucoin and Donald J. Savoie, eds., *Managing Strategic Change: Learning from Program Review.* Ottawa: Canadian Centre for Management Development.

Maclean's, 25 December 2000/1 January 2001. "We Are Canadian."

Mansell, Robert L. 1997. "Fiscal Restructuring in Alberta: An Overview." In Christopher Bruce, Ronald Kneebone, and Keith McKenzie, eds., *A Government Reinvented: A Study of Alberta's Deficit Elimination Program.* Toronto: Oxford University Press. 16-73.

Maslove, Allan M. 1996. "The Canada Health and Social Transfer: Forcing Issues." In Gene Swimmer, ed., *How Ottawa Spends 1996-97: Life Under the Knife.* Ottawa: Carleton University Press. 283-302.

Maslove, Allan M., and Kevin Moore. 1998. "From Red Books to Blue Books: Repairing Ottawa's Fiscal House." In Gene Swimmer, ed., *How Ottawa Spends 1997-98: Seeing Red; A Liberal Report Card*. Ottawa: Carleton University Press.

McQuaig, Linda. 1995. *Shooting the Hippo: Death by Deficit and Other Canadian Myths*. Toronto: Penguin Books.

—. 1998. *The Cult of Impotence: Selling the Myth of Powerlessness in the Global Economy*. Toronto: Penguin Books.

Osberg, Lars, and Pierre Fortin. 1996. *Unnecessary Debts*. Toronto: James Lorimer and Co.

Paquet, Gilles, and Robert Shepherd. 1996. "The Program Review Process: A Deconstruction." In Gene Swimmer, ed., *How Ottawa Spends 1996-97: Life Under the Knife*. Ottawa: Carleton University Press. 39-72.

Prince, Michael J. 1999. "From Health and Welfare to Stealth and Farewell: Federal Social Policy, 1980-2000." In Leslie A. Pal, ed., *How Ottawa Spends 1999-2000: Shape Shifting, Canadian Governance Toward the 21st Century*. Toronto: Oxford University Press.

Savoie, Donald J. 1999. *Governing from the Centre: The Concentration of Power in Canadian Politics*. Toronto: University of Toronto Press.

Shields, John, and B. Mitchell Evans. 1998. *Shrinking the State: Globalization and Public Administration "Reform."* Halifax: Fernwood Publishing.

Sjolander, Claire Turenne. 1996. "Cashing In on the Peace Dividend: National Defence in the Post-Cold War World." In Gene Swimmer, ed., *How Ottawa Spends 1996-97: Life Under the Knife*. Ottawa: Carleton University Press, 253-82.

Skogstad, Grace. 1998. "Agriculture and Agri-Food Canada: Program Review I and II." In Peter Aucoin and Donald J. Savoie, eds., *Managing Strategic Change: Learning from Program Review*. Ottawa: Canadian Centre for Management Development.

Toner, Glen. 1996. "Environment Canada's Continuing Roller Coaster Ride." In Gene Swimmer, ed., *How Ottawa Spends 1996-97: Life Under the Knife*. Ottawa: Carleton University Press, 99-132.

Treasury Board of Canada. 1995. *The Expenditure Management System of the Government of Canada*. Ottawa: Minister of Supply and Services.

Treasury Board of Canada. 2000. *Managing For Results*. Ottawa: Minister of Supply and Services.

Wolfe, David A. 1986. "The Politics of the Deficit." In G. Bruce Doern, ed., *The Politics of Economic Policy*. Royal Commission on the Economic Union and Development Prospects for Canada. Vol. 40. Toronto: University of Toronto Press.

Related Web Sites

DEPARTMENT OF FINANCE
<http://www.fin.gc.ca>

PRIVY COUNCIL OFFICE
<http://www.pco-bcp.gc.ca>

TREASURY BOARD SECRETARIAT
<http://www.tbs-sct.gc.ca>

CHAPTER 8
Public Sector Human Resources Management

As mentioned in Chapter 1, government and the effects of government are found everywhere within Canadian society. Canadian governments provide a myriad of public services as they fulfill public policy needs, and the provision of these services requires large, professional, and permanent bureaucracies. As federal, provincial, and municipal governments address policy matters ranging from defence and tax collection through the provision of social welfare and judicial administration to public education and sanitation, governments need the services of hundreds of thousands of "employees" to make desired public policies a living reality.

From the broadest definition of "public servant," Canadian governments make use of a kaleidoscope of differing types of workers: from CF-18 pilots to national park wardens; from lawyers to nurses and teachers; from fire-fighters and customs guards to policy analysts, economists, scientists, secretaries, regulatory inspectors, diplomats, historians, social workers, and managers. And the list goes on and on. Just as there is no part of life that is unaffected by the state, so too the servants of the state are all around us, in one occupation or another. This chapter and the next will probe the general nature of public sector human resources management. Some of the findings here may be surprising to some readers as we assess such dynamics as the size of government, employment shifts, the representativeness of the federal public service, and public sector pay levels. We will examine such traditional issues in public sector human resource management as the concept and problems of patronage, the development of the merit principle, and the enactment of this principle at the federal level through the work of the **Public Service Commission**. (Additional material on the development and elaboration of the merit principle across the provincial governments can be found on the Thinking Government web site.) Finally, we will assess contemporary personnel policy initiatives at the federal level to renew and revitalize the Public Service of Canada following the years of downsizing and budget cutbacks of the 1990s. As we enter this new century, the issue of public service recruitment and renewal is fast becoming one of the most important topics within the federal government as well as many of its provincial counterparts. Years of cutbacks have left these governments understaffed, and now, with emerging budgetary surpluses and renewed demands for improved services, these governments are quickly coming to realize that initiatives to enhance policy and program capacity and action also demand that they renew and rebuild their human resources.

8.1   Public Sector Employment Statistics

Employment in the public sector is enormous, and the federal government is the single largest employer in Canada, notwithstanding past public sector cutbacks. The public sector in this country, as defined by Statistics Canada, is divided into two major components: governments and government business enterprises.

1. The "government" component is comprised of the three levels of government—federal, provincial, and municipal—and all their departments, agencies, boards, and commissions. Also included here are all health and social service institutions, including hospitals, public school systems, and all post-secondary educational institutions; cultural facilities; and all federal and provincial regulatory agencies.

2. The "government business enterprise" component consists of all public enterprises—Crown corporations—controlled by governments and engaged in the provision and sale of commercial goods and services. Such bodies include, for example, the CBC, Canada Post, the Canadian Wheat Board, the Enterprise Cape Breton Corporation, Hydro Québec, and SaskEnergy.

As Box 8.1 shows, as of 2004, total public sector employment within Canada accounted for roughly 2.9 million persons. This figure includes

BOX 8.1
Total Canadian Public Sector Employment, 2001-2004 (persons)

	2001	2002	2003	2004
Total Public Sector	2,813,604	2,846,936	2,908,710	2,934,263
Total Government	2,547,264	2,583,036	2,641,470	2,669,304
Federal government*	351,331	359,477	366,428	366,654
Provincial and territorial government	340,378	336,536	349,747	348,083
Health and social service institutions — provincial and territorial	696,321	714,988	738,525	744,570
Post-secondary educational institutions	277,030	284,685	294,441	301,556
Local governments	341,564	344,502	360,980	365,329
Local school boards	540,639	542,848	531,348	543,112
Government business enterprises	266,340	263,901	267,240	264,958
Federal Crown Corporations	89,131	88,429	88,366	87,911
Provincial and territorial Crown corporations	128,047	125,185	127,292	123,988
Local business enterprises	49,162	50,287	51,582	53,060

* Federal government includes reservists and full-time military personnel

Source: Adapted from Statistics Canada, CANSIM, Public Sector Employment, Wages and Salaries, 183-0002, 2005-08-24.

everyone working within the broad public sector at the federal, provincial, and municipal level, and also including everyone working within health and social service institutions, the publicly funded educational sector, and everyone working with a federal or provincial Crown corporation. Of this 2.9 million figure, around 366,000 were in federal government employment, around 1.4 million were in provincial or territorial government service, and around 908,000 were in municipal government employment. Another 265,000 were in government business enterprises throughout all three levels of government.

These figures reveal the enormous presence the public sector has in this country and the importance of governments both as providers of public services and as employers offering an enormous range of job opportunities here and abroad. One can also observe from Box 8.1 the slow but steady growth in all fields of public sector employment across this country from 2001 to 2004. Following years of restraint and reduction in the size of the state and of the general public sector over the 1980s and 1990s, we are now witnessing a resurgence in public sector employment as governments, and especially the federal government, begin to rebuild themselves in order to possess the skilled personnel needed to develop and implement policies and programs as desired by the Canadian public.

When one turns to look specifically at the current federal public service, as listed in Box 8.2, some intriguing dynamics can be observed. The Treasury Board defined the total population of the public service in March 2003 as 163,314, but the Treasury Board's "universe" of the federal public service is different from that of Statistics Canada in that it omits members of the military and officers of the RCMP. The Treasury Board's figures capture those traditionally understood as "bureaucrats" or as working for traditional federal "bureaucratic" institutions, namely, departments, agencies, boards, and commissions.

As Box 8.2 indicates, total employment in the federal public service declined over the 1990s, falling from a high of 224,640 in 1994 to 141,253 in 2000. The year 1995 was a pivotal one in this trend; that year the Program Review exercise announced a planned reduction of the federal public service by 45,000 full-time positions. In reality, between 1995 and 1999 a total of 39,444 indeterminate and seasonal positions were eliminated, marking a 18.1 per cent decrease in such positions, though some 3,000 term and casual positions were added over this same time period. In 1999 Revenue Canada was replaced by the Canada Customs and Revenue Agency (CCRA), which was not defined as a regular department or agency for the purposes of federal employment statistics. The roughly 37,000 employees of the old Revenue Canada who now find themselves employed by the CCRA are no longer officially employed by the Treasury Board, meaning that they are no longer contained in Treasury Board statistics, thus allowing the government to record a seemingly large drop in the "official" size of the federal public service in 1999. This drop is more apparent than real. The employees currently working within the CCRA are government employees in the broader sense—they remain public servants working within a very important arm of the federal government, and their salaries are still derived through general tax revenues. The change was cosmetic, designed more to make the federal public service appear smaller than it truly is than to substantially alter the composition of the government. Of course, the impetus

BOX 8.2
Representation of Designated Groups in the Federal Public Service

PSSRA I-I, Indeterminate, Terms of Three Months or More, and Seasonal Employees

As at March 31,	All Employees	Women		Aboriginal Peoples		Persons with Disabilities		Persons in a Visible Minority Group	
	#	#	%	#	%	#	%	#	%
2003	163,314	86,162	52.8	6,426	3.9	9,155	5.6	12,058	7.4
2002	157,510	82,663	52.5	5,980	3.8	8,331	5.3	10,772	6.8
2001	149,339	77,785	52.1	5,316	3.6	7,621	5.1	9,143	6.1
2000*	141,253	72,549	51.4	4,639	3.3	6,687	4.7	7,764	5.5
(Revenue Canada excluded)									
1999	178,340	91,856	51.5	5,124	2.9	8,137	4.6	10,557	5.9
(Revenue Canada included)									
1998	179,831	90,801	50.5	4,770	2.7	6,943	3.9	9,260	5.1
1997	186,378	92,281	49.5	4,551	2.4	6,227	3.3	8,690	4.7
1996	201,009	96,794	48.2	4,665	2.3	6,291	3.1	8,981	4.5
1995	217,784	103,191	47.4	4,783	2.2	6,935	3.2	8,914	4.1
1994	224,640	105,621	47.0	4,492	2.0	6,623	2.9	8,566	3.8
1993	221,114	102,015	46.1	4,441	2.0	6,755	3.1	8,462	3.8
Workforce Availability 1996 Census		48.7		1.7		4.8		8.7	

* Revenue Canada became Canada Customs and Revenue Agency on November 1, 1999.

Note: The data in this and other tables in this report cover employees identified for the purpose of employment equity in the regulations to the Employment Equity Act. The estimates of workforce availability are based on information from the 1996 Census of Canada and the 1991 post-Census Health and Activity Limitation Survey. They include only those occupations in the Canadian workforce that correspond to occupational groups in the federal Public Service.

Source: Canada, Treasury Board of Canada, 2003: 30.

behind such a change was largely that of appealing to the voices of government restraint and restructuring, aiming to demonstrate that the federal government is becoming a leaner and more efficient organization. Much more will be said later about these employment reduction programs and their implications for the public service.

It is also noteworthy that in the year 2001 employment in the public service actually increased compared to the previous year, a development not witnessed since 1994. Between 2001 and 2003 employment in the federal public service increased by 13,975, or 9.3 per cent. This upswing indicates both that the federal government possessed a balanced budget and that senior management recognized that while the lean years of the 1990s may have been necessary in order to bring fiscal balance back to the federal government, the deep staffing cuts of those years were detrimental to the federal public service, with this service now in need of reinvestment in relation to both funding of programs and the hiring of new employees to facilitate those programs.

As Box 8.3 highlights, the federal public service, as it stood in 2003, was composed of six occupational categories: executive, scientific and professional, administrative and foreign service, technical, administrative support, and operational. The executive category had the smallest population, with a total of 4,209, while the largest category was that of administration and foreign service at 67,389. It is interesting to note the gender and age variations both between and within all six categories. While women comprise 83.1 per cent of the administrative support category and 59.1 per cent of administration and foreign service, they account for only 40.3 per cent of the scientific and professional category and only 33.8 per cent of the executive ranks. Thus, while women account for 52.8 per cent of the total federal public service, the statistics reveal them to be generally congregated in the traditional female occupational categories. But this picture is improving. When one looks at age bands, one can see that younger women are making headway in those occupational categories traditionally dominated by men. Though women constitute only 33.8 per cent of the total executive category, they constitute almost half of all executives between the ages of 35 and 39 and roughly 40 per cent of all executives between the ages of 40 and 49. As time goes on, these women will filter into the most senior executive positions where they are grossly underrepresented. This dynamic of more women being found in the lower age bands compared to the higher is observed in every occupational category save that of administrative support, where women already dominate. Thus, over time, the gender imbalance within the public service will be lessened. How this is being achieved

BOX 8.3

Distribution of Federal Public Service Employees by Designated Group According to Occupational Category and Age Group (as at March 31, 2003)

PSSRA I-I, Indeterminate, Terms of Three Months or More, and Seasonal Employees

Occupational Category	Age Group	All Employees #	Women #	Women %	Aboriginal Peoples #	Aboriginal Peoples %	Persons with Disabilities #	Persons with Disabilities %	Persons in a Visible Minority Group #	Persons in a Visible Minority Group %
Executive	25-29	3	3	100.0	1	33.3	0	0.0	0	0.0
	30-34	49	16	32.7	3	6.1	0	0.0	3	6.1
	35-39	206	98	47.6	9	4.4	3	1.5	16	7.8
	40-44	557	247	44.3	22	3.9	26	4.7	37	6.6
	45-49	926	392	42.3	31	3.3	32	3.5	29	3.1
	50-54	1,431	499	34.9	32	2.2	81	5.7	50	3.5
	55-59	838	145	17.3	11	1.3	39	4.7	31	3.7
	60-64	175	22	12.6	4	2.3	8	4.6	8	4.6
	65-69	23	2	8.7	1	4.3	4	17.4	3	13.0
	70+	1	0	0.0	0	0.0	0	0.0	0	0.0
	Total	4,209	1,424	33.8	114	2.7	193	4.6	177	4.2
Scientific and Professional	20-24	230	141	61.3	5	2.2	4	1.7	36	15.7
	25-29	2,147	1,195	55.7	63	2.9	35	1.6	289	13.5
	30-34	2,843	1,448	50.9	85	3.0	58	2.0	358	12.6
	35-39	3,237	1,490	46.0	94	2.9	93	2.9	375	11.6
	40-44	3,635	1,539	42.3	89	2.4	123	3.4	385	10.6
	45-49	3,752	1,439	38.4	78	2.1	170	4.5	335	8.9
	50-54	3,678	1,195	32.5	73	2.0	186	5.1	316	8.6
	55-59	2,256	578	25.6	40	1.8	114	5.1	272	12.1
	60-64	866	155	17.9	12	1.4	38	4.4	194	22.4
	65-69	186	28	15.1	2	1.1	8	4.3	61	32.8
	70+	50	4	8.0	0	0.0	2	4.0	12	24.0
	Total	22,880	9,212	40.3	541	2.4	831	3.6	2,633	11.5

BOX 8.3 CONTINUED
Distribution of Federal Public Service Employees by Designated Group According to Occupational Category and Age Group

Occupational Category	Age Group	All Employees #	Women #	Women %	Aboriginal Peoples #	Aboriginal Peoples %	Persons with Disabilities #	Persons with Disabilities %	Persons in a Visible Minority Group #	Persons in a Visible Minority Group %
Administrative and Foreign Service	16-19	1	1	100.0	0	0.0	0	0.0	0	0.0
	20-24	1,368	781	57.1	46	3.4	13	1.0	152	11.1
	25-29	5,657	3,289	58.1	212	3.7	133	2.4	742	13.1
	30-34	6,975	4,031	57.8	390	5.6	202	2.9	756	10.8
	35-39	8,851	5,335	60.3	452	5.1	363	4.1	845	9.5
	40-44	11,647	7,529	64.6	457	3.9	659	5.7	774	6.6
	45-49	13,505	8,660	64.1	521	3.9	922	6.8	621	4.6
	50-54	12,698	7,000	55.1	398	3.1	1,078	8.5	550	4.3
	55-59	5,280	2,564	48.6	166	3.1	463	8.8	346	6.6
	60-64	1,222	550	45.0	42	3.4	121	9.9	143	11.7
	65-69	151	50	33.1	6	4.0	5	3.3	19	12.6
	70+	34	8	23.5	0	0.0	4	11.8	3	8.8
	Total	67,389	39,798	59.1	2,690	4.0	3,963	5.9	4,951	7.3
Technical	16-19	13	2	15.4	0	0.0	0	0.0	0	0.0
	20-24	405	201	49.6	14	3.5	7	1.7	17	4.2
	25-29	1,403	746	53.2	52	3.7	27	1.9	89	6.3
	30-34	1,613	729	45.2	74	4.6	34	2.1	104	6.4
	35-39	2,107	776	36.8	67	3.2	68	3.2	118	5.6
	40-44	3,094	934	30.2	88	2.8	113	3.7	152	4.9
	45-49	3,498	981	28.0	94	2.7	194	5.5	131	3.7
	50-54	3,203	733	22.9	71	2.2	198	6.2	124	3.9
	55-59	1,640	271	16.5	30	1.8	88	5.4	87	5.3
	60-64	478	68	14.2	9	1.9	24	5.0	43	9.0
	65-69	90	4	4.4	3	3.3	5	5.6	15	16.7
	70+	13	0	0.0	0	0.0	1	7.7	0	0.0
	Total	17,557	5,445	31.0	502	2.9	759	4.3	880	5.0

BOX 8.3 CONTINUED
Distribution of Federal Public Service Employees by Designated Group According to Occupational Category and Age Group

Occupational Category	Age Group	All Employees #	Women #	Women %	Aboriginal Peoples #	Aboriginal Peoples %	Persons with Disabilities #	Persons with Disabilities %	Persons in a Visible Minority Group #	Persons in a Visible Minority Group %
Administrative Support	16-19	43	29	67.4	2	4.7	0	0.0	1	2.3
	20-24	1,146	912	79.6	69	6.0	23	2.0	92	8.0
	25-29	2,580	2,041	79.1	166	6.4	79	3.1	373	14.5
	30-34	3,029	2,426	80.1	227	7.5	149	4.9	368	12.1
	35-39	4,086	3,395	83.1	265	6.5	249	6.1	358	8.8
	40-44	5,838	5,048	86.5	289	5.0	434	7.4	389	6.7
	45-49	6,500	5,435	83.6	278	4.3	561	8.6	374	5.8
	50-54	5,552	4,541	81.8	208	3.7	590	10.6	361	6.5
	55-59	2,790	2,387	85.6	79	2.8	296	10.6	261	9.4
	60-64	854	723	84.7	26	3.0	102	11.9	130	15.2
	65-69	140	114	81.4	3	2.1	14	10.0	29	20.7
	70+	28	23	82.1	0	0.0	2	7.1	5	17.9
	Total	32,586	27,074	83.1	1,612	4.9	2,499	7.7	2,741	8.4
Operation	16-19	8	2	25.0	0	0.0	0	0.0	0	0.0
	20-24	401	126	31.4	36	9.0	8	2.0	34	8.5
	25-29	1,236	377	30.5	109	8.8	31	2.5	82	6.6
	30-34	1,759	481	27.3	167	9.5	46	2.6	86	4.9
	35-39	2,119	467	22.0	158	7.5	81	3.8	78	3.7
	40-44	3,277	585	17.9	145	4.4	128	3.9	86	2.6
	45-49	3,962	495	12.5	163	4.1	240	6.1	101	2.5
	50-54	3,341	342	10.2	97	2.9	217	6.5	119	3.6
	55-59	1,909	230	12.0	63	3.3	115	6.0	64	3.4
	60-64	584	87	14.9	25	4.3	34	5.8	22	3.8
	65-69	82	14	17.1	3	3.7	8	9.8	4	4.9
	70+	15	3	20.0	1	6.7	2	13.3	0	0.0
	Total	18,693	3,209	17.2	967	5.2	910	4.9	676	3.6

BOX 8.3 CONTINUED
Distribution of Federal Public Service Employees by Designated Group According to Occupational Category and Age Group

Occupational Category	Age Group	All Employees #	Women #	Women %	Aboriginal Peoples #	Aboriginal Peoples %	Persons with Disabilities #	Persons with Disabilities %	Persons in a Visible Minority Group #	Persons in a Visible Minority Group %
Federal Public Service	16-19	65	34	52.3	2	3.1	0	0.0	1	1.5
	20-24	3,550	2,161	60.9	170	4.8	55	1.5	331	9.3
	25-29	13,026	7,651	58.7	603	4.6	305	2.3	1,575	12.1
	30-34	16,268	9,131	56.1	946	5.8	489	3.0	1,675	10.3
	35-39	20,606	11,561	56.1	1,045	5.1	857	4.2	1,790	8.7
	40-44	28,048	15,882	56.6	1,090	3.9	1,483	5.3	1,823	6.5
	45-49	32,143	17,402	54.1	1,165	3.6	2,119	6.6	1,591	4.9
	50-54	29,903	14,310	47.9	879	2.9	2,350	7.9	1,520	5.1
	55-59	14,713	6,175	42.0	389	2.6	1,115	7.6	1,061	7.2
	60-64	4,179	1,605	38.4	118	2.8	327	7.8	540	12.9
	65-69	672	212	31.5	18	2.7	44	6.5	131	19.5
	70+	141	38	27.0	1	0.7	11	7.8	20	14.2
	Total	163,314	86,162	52.8	6,426	3.9	9,155	5.6	12,058	7.4

Source: Canada, Treasury Board of Canada, 2003: 35.

and whether such change is being attained in a just manner will be assessed more fully in the next chapter as will be other matters relating to employment equity and the representation of Aboriginal peoples, persons with disabilities, and persons in a visible minority group.

Box 8.4 provides information on the annual salaries of public servants. These figures deserve careful attention. Contrary to popular opinion, most public servants do not make great "bags" of money. Here we see a salary breakdown and cumulative percentage listing, which indicates the total proportion of all employees earning up to a given amount of income. Thirty-six per cent of all full-time indeterminate employees—those holding terms of three months or more—and seasonal employees earned less than $45,000 per year in 2003. Just over two-thirds (67.6 per cent) of all such employees earned less than $60,000 per year. In contrast, only 10 per

BOX 8.4

Distribution of Federal Public Service Employees by Designated Group and Salary Band (as at March 31, 2003)

PSSRA I-I, Indeterminate, Terms of Three Months or More, and Seasonal Employees

Salary Ban	All Employees #	All Employees C%	Women #	Women %	Women C%	Aboriginal Peoples #	Aboriginal Peoples %	Aboriginal Peoples C%	Persons with Disabilities #	Persons with Disabilities %	Persons with Disabilities C%	Persons in a Visible Minority Group #	Persons in a Visible Minority Group %	Persons in a Visible Minority Group C%
≦19,999	116	0.1	42	36.2	0.0	2	1.7	0.0	0	0.0	0.0	0	0.0	0.0
20,000-24,999	15	0.1	8	53.3	0.1	5	33.3	0.1	4	26.7	0.0	1	6.7	0.0
25,000-29,999	1,294	0.9	780	60.3	1.0	58	4.5	1.0	69	5.3	0.8	53	4.1	0.4
30,000-34,999	6,004	4.5	2,980	49.6	4.4	343	5.7	6.3	406	6.8	5.2	441	7.3	4.1
35,000-39,999	26,776	20.9	18,882	70.5	26.3	1,385	5.2	27.9	1,849	6.9	25.4	2,036	7.6	21.0
40,000-44,999	24,512	36.0	16,071	65.6	45.0	1,068	4.4	44.5	1,403	5.7	40.8	1,974	8.1	37.4
45,000-49,999	20,620	48.6	12,185	59.1	59.1	865	4.2	58.0	1,241	6.0	54.3	1,385	6.7	48.8
50,000-54,999	18,496	59.9	9,044	48.9	69.6	755	4.1	69.7	890	4.8	64.0	1,425	7.7	60.7
55,000-59,999	12,626	67.6	6,075	48.1	76.7	460	3.6	76.9	630	5.0	70.9	1,009	8.0	69.0
60,000-64,999	12,435	75.3	5,367	43.2	82.9	450	3.6	83.9	611	4.9	77.6	967	7.8	77.1
65,000-69,999	10,368	81.6	4,296	41.4	87.9	326	3.1	89.0	527	5.1	83.3	705	6.8	82.9
70,000-74,999	9,107	87.2	3,472	38.1	91.9	258	2.8	93.0	480	5.3	88.6	699	7.7	88.7
75,000-79,999	5,656	90.6	2,181	38.6	94.5	133	2.4	95.1	295	5.2	91.8	455	8.0	92.5
80,000-84,999	5,276	93.9	1,673	31.7	96.4	124	2.4	97.0	255	4.8	94.6	330	6.3	95.2
85,000-89,999	2,965	95.7	944	31.8	97.5	58	2.0	97.9	140	4.7	96.1	200	6.7	96.9
90,000-94,999	1,108	96.4	333	30.1	97.9	26	2.3	98.3	51	4.6	96.7	73	6.6	97.5
95,000-99,999	2,371	97.8	727	30.7	98.7	56	2.4	99.2	121	5.1	98.0	137	5.8	98.6
≧100,000	3,569	100.0	1,102	30.9	100.0	54	1.5	100.0	183	5.1	100.0	168	4.7	100.0
Total	163,314	100.0	86,162	52.8	100.0	6,426	3.9	100.0	9,155	5.6	100.0	12,058	7.4	100.0

Notes: Each figure in the "C%" column represents the cumulative total percentage of each designated group in the public service workforce (all employees, women, Aboriginal peoples, persons with disabilities, and persons in a visible minority group) in the identified salary band or lower. Other percentages are a designated group's share of each salary band (rows). For example, in the "C%" column one finds that 69.6 per cent of all women earned less than $55,000 in fiscal year 2002-03. The figure in the column to the left (48.9 per cent) represents the percentage of women in this salary band, that is, the $50,000-$55,999 range.

Source: Canada, Treasury Board of Canada, 2003: 41.

cent earned more than $80,000 per year, and only 2.2 per cent earned over $100,000 per year. While public service salaries have tended to be viewed by the general public and the media as "good" salaries and while senior officials do make handsome incomes, most public servants earn only ordinary incomes, and public service management salaries pale in comparison to those found in the private sector.

The gender difference in these salaries is significant. It is common knowledge that women generally earn less than men. Roughly speaking, the lowest third of all employees, male and female, earned just over $40,000 per year, but 45 per cent of women earned $45,000 or less. Roughly three-quarters of all female employees earned less than $60,000 per year, while three-quarters of all employees made $65,000 or less. Similarly, the top 10 per cent of all employees earned over $75,000 per year, while the top 10 per cent of female earners began around the $70,000 range. Both occupational and age dynamics come into play here. Women tend to be congregated in administrative support roles—secretaries, clerks, cleaners—and thus in lower paid occupations, while older men dominate the higher paying executive, professional, and technical occupations and so generally outrank women in terms of remuneration. But once again, these dynamics are changing; as more women move into more senior positions within the public service, these wage discrepancies will become more muted.

Box 8.5 categorizes the federal public service by region of work and employee designation. As with the general Statistics Canada figures for the regional distribution of all those involved in the public service, these Treasury Board figures demonstrate how the population distribution of the federal public service tends to mirror that of the general Canadian population with one obvious exception—roughly 41 per cent of all federal public servants work within the national capital region of Ottawa-Hull, and nearly 70 per cent of all those in executive positions work within this region. Two basic findings can be drawn from this information.

1. First, roughly 60 per cent of all federal public servants live and work outside of the country's capital. For all the common talk of the federal government being "out of touch" with the regions, it is important to realize that the bulk of all federal policies and programs are administered by federal employees working throughout all the regions of Canada. Regional offices, in turn, are in direct and steady contact with their head offices in Ottawa-Hull, meaning that the senior leadership of departments and agencies located in the National Capital Region can and do maintain a close liaison with all their field offices spread across the country.

BOX 8.5

Distribution of Federal Public Service Employees by Designated Group and Region of Work (as at March 31, 2003)

PSSRA I-I, Indeterminate, Terms of Three Months or More, and Seasonal Employees

Region of Work	All Employees #	Women #	Women %	Aboriginal Peoples #	Aboriginal Peoples %	Persons with Disabilities #	Persons with Disabilities %	Persons in a Visible Minority Group #	Persons in a Visible Minority Group %
Newfoundland and Labrador	3,119	1,301	41.7	124	4.0	151	4.8	29	0.9
Prince Edward Island	1,730	1,069	61.8	43	2.5	160	9.2	32	1.8
Nova Scotia	8,619	3,507	40.7	219	2.5	610	7.1	414	4.8
New Brunswick	5,521	2,902	52.6	154	2.8	267	4.8	69	1.2
Quebec (without the NCR*)	19,362	9,759	50.4	298	1.5	620	3.2	850	4.4
NCR* (Quebec)	19,292	11,085	57.5	845	4.4	1,025	5.3	1,322	6.9
NCR*	68,396	37,932	55.5	2,024	3.0	3,721	5.4	5,378	7.9
Ontario (without the NCR*)	20,535	11,300	55.0	776	3.8	1,470	7.2	2,281	11.1
NCR* (Ontario)	49,104	26,847	54.7	1,179	2.4	2,696	5.5	4,056	8.3
Manitoba	6,068	3,329	54.9	691	11.4	386	6.4	357	5.9
Saskatchewan	4,239	2,253	53.1	509	12.0	229	5.4	133	3.1
Alberta	8,723	4,709	54.0	634	7.3	540	6.2	597	6.8
British Columbia	14,572	7,020	48.2	709	4.9	910	6.2	1,787	12.3
Yukon	287	183	63.8	53	18.5	20	7.0	5	1.7
Northwest Territories	558	306	54.8	124	22.2	28	5.0	22	3.9
Nunavut	157	81	51.6	45	28.7	2	1.3	5	3.2
Outside Canada	1,428	511	35.8	23	1.6	41	2.9	99	6.9
Total	163,314	86,162	52.8	6,426	3.9	9,155	5.6	12,058	7.4

* "NCR" stands for "National Capital Region."
Source: Canada, Treasury Board of Canada, 2003: 40.

2. Second, however, Ottawa-Hull is the political and administrative heart of the country. The National Capital Region is where the executive leadership of the federal government is found; thus, it is not surprising to find that the single largest agglomeration of federal executives and senior officials is located in the capital. Here one finds deputy ministers, associate and

assistant deputy ministers, senior managers, and advisors responsible for the policy and administrative operations of the government's departments and agencies. Though the federal public service has roots in every part of the country, executive power is firmly attached to this particular centre.

In Box 8.6, the distribution of the federal public service across departments, agencies, boards, and commissions shows the great range in size of various federal institutions. Some offices and boards—such as the Civil Aviation Tribunal and the registry of the Competition Tribunal—are tiny, having only a handful of employees; others have comparatively huge numbers of employees—National Defence, Human Resources Development, Public Works, and Fisheries and Oceans. When CCRA was established as a special agency of the federal government to replace Revenue Canada, thus abstracting its 37,000 employees from the statistics, the single largest department of the federal government, in terms of employees, became Human Resources Development Canada (HRDC). Even between departments, there can be great differences in population size. The ones just mentioned are among the largest, and they stand in high relief above Finance (1,034 employees), Solicitor General (276 employees), Veterans Affairs (3,511 employees), and Justice (4,734 employees).

But staff size does not correlate with importance and political influence. As we have seen, the single most powerful department in the government is Finance because of its central role in budgetary policy and financial management. Likewise, although the departments of Justice and Foreign Affairs and International Trade (3,799 employees), for example, are comparatively small, their policy subject matters are of great importance to any government because they are critical both to the government's domestic and international policy agenda; this significance is recognized by most Canadians. These departments have influence greater than other small departments such as Veterans Affairs and Heritage simply on the basis of what they do.

A basic truth, however, should not be ignored here. This listing of departments and agencies reveals the policy fields and policy issues that the current government has inherited from past governments and which it wishes to continue. What one observes here, in total, is a reflection of the matters that the current federal government believes to be worthy of consideration, management, and development. This range of activities is broad and expansive, extending from management development to international development, from the regulation of fisheries and oceans to the regulation of transportation and public works, from the administration of national archives to the administration of multiculturalism and citizenship, health

BOX 8.6

Distribution of Federal Public Service Employees by Designated Group According to Department or Agency (as at March 31, 2003)

PSSRA I-I, Indeterminate, Terms of Three Months or More, and Seasonal Employees

Department or Agency	All Employees #	Women #	Women %	Aboriginal Peoples #	Aboriginal Peoples %	Persons with Disabilities #	Persons with Disabilities %	Persons in a Visible Minority Group #	Persons in a Visible Minority Group %
Human Resources Development Canada	23,434	16,363	69.8	831	3.5	1,861	7.9	1,749	7.5
National Defence*	18,909	7,102	37.6	430	2.3	1,066	5.6	883	4.7
Correctional Service Canada	14,303	5,946	41.6	938	6.6	755	5.3	662	4.6
Public Works and Government Services Canada	12,750	6,467	50.7	298	2.3	686	5.4	981	7.7
Fisheries and Oceans Canada	10,062	3,067	30.5	318	3.2	465	4.6	385	3.8
Health Canada	8,506	5,599	65.8	576	6.8	380	4.5	1,017	12.0
Statistics Canada	5,833	2,989	51.2	122	2.1	323	5.5	641	11.0
Agriculture and Agri-Food Canada†	5,772	2,597	45.0	131	2.3	238	4.1	385	6.7
Industry Canada	5,629	2,765	49.1	125	2.2	284	5.0	506	9.0
Environment Canada	5,499	2,258	41.1	123	2.2	240	4.4	491	8.9
Citizenship and Immigration Canada	5,117	3,261	63.7	119	2.3	298	5.8	715	14.0
Department of Justice Canada	4,734	3,067	64.8	163	3.4	251	5.3	421	8.9
Royal Canadian Mounted Police (Civilian Staff)	4,631	3,579	77.3	183	4.0	232	5.0	242	5.2
Transport Canada	4,495	1,846	41.1	107	2.4	206	4.6	358	8.0
Natural Resources Canada	4,408	1,679	38.1	103	2.3	187	4.2	375	8.5
Department of Foreign Affairs and International Trade	3,799	1,836	48.3	92	2.4	181	4.8	289	7.6
Indian and Northern Affairs Canada	3,656	2,289	62.6	1,144	31.3	239	6.5	197	5.4
Veterans Affairs Canada	3,511	2,444	69.6	110	3.1	309	8.8	264	7.5
Canadian Heritage	1,924	1,304	67.8	74	3.8	88	4.6	154	8.0
Canadian International Development Agency	1,548	923	59.6	35	2.3	56	3.6	130	8.4
Public Service Commission of Canada	1,534	1,035	67.5	52	3.4	122	8.0	174	11.3
Passport Office	1,219	869	71.3	25	2.1	43	3.5	125	10.3
Treasury Board of Canada Secretariat	1,068	633	59.3	20	1.9	82	7.7	88	8.2
Department of Finance Canada	1,034	519	50.2	12	1.2	34	3.3	72	7.0
Immigration and Refugee Board	946	639	67.5	22	2.3	44	4.7	207	21.9
Privy Council Office	724	422	58.3	22	3.0	26	3.6	36	5.0
National Archives of Canada	658	332	50.5	19	2.9	37	5.6	26	4.0
Canadian Grain Commission	609	212	34.8	30	4.9	47	7.7	49	8.0
Atlantic Canada Opportunities Agency	602	337	56.0	12	2.0	21	3.5	9	1.5
Canadian Space Agency	518	197	38.0	5	1.0	8	1.5	56	10.8
National Library of Canada	493	322	65.3	15	3.0	32	6.5	28	5.7

BOX 8.6 CONTINUED

Distribution of Federal Public Service Employees by Designated Group According to Department or Agency (as at March 31, 2003)

Department or Agency	All Employees	Women		Aboriginal Peoples		Persons with Disabilities		Persons in a Visible Minority Group	
	#	#	%	#	%	#	%	#	%
Registry of the Federal Court of Canada	458	308	67.2	10	2.2	29	6.3	41	9.0
Communication Canada	438	259	59.1	11	2.5	11	2.5	17	3.9
Economic Development Agency of Canada for the Regions of Quebec	413	230	55.7	7	1.7	13	3.1	23	5.6
Canadian Radio-television and Telecommunications Commission	403	230	57.1	9	2.2	34	8.4	19	4.7
Western Economic Diversification Canada	354	201	56.8	20	5.6	25	7.1	39	11.0
National Parole Board	309	238	77.0	15	4.9	17	5.5	17	5.5
Office of the Chief Electoral Officer	296	142	48.0	13	4.4	19	6.4	16	5.4
Solicitor General Canada	276	162	58.7	13	4.7	13	4.7	14	5.1
Canadian Transportation Agency	262	153	58.4	5	1.9	17	6.5	12	4.6
Canadian Human Rights Commission	212	139	65.6	9	4.2	28	13.2	18	8.5
Transportation Safety Board of Canada	209	65	31.1	1	0.5	11	5.3	23	11.0
Canadian Centre for Management Development	188	127	67.6	8	4.3	7	3.7	9	4.8
Office of the Registrar of the Supreme Court of Canada	157	105	66.9	8	5.1	11	7.0	14	8.9
Office of the Secretary of the Governor General	152	94	61.8	1	0.7	13	8.6	7	4.6
Offices of the Information and Privacy Commissioners	147	91	61.9	4	2.7	13	8.8	7	4.8
Office of the Commissioner of Official Languages	129	82	63.6	6	4.7	5	3.9	1	0.8
Tax Court of Canada	119	76	63.9	5	4.2	8	6.7	8	6.7
Status of Women Canada	116	109	94.0	3	2.6	10	8.6	14	12.1
Canadian Environmental Assessment Agency	108	61	56.5	6	5.6	1	0.9	7	6.5
Canada Industrial Relations Board	94	64	68.1	1	1.1	4	4.3	9	9.6
Canadian International Trade Tribunal	80	42	52.5	0	0.0	3	3.8	4	5.0
Office of the Commissioner for Federal Judicial Affairs	57	40	70.2	4	7.0	3	5.3	2	3.5
Canadian Dairy Commission	56	32	57.1	1	1.8	0	0.0	7	12.5
Office of Indian Residential Schools Resolution of Canada	56	35	62.5	6	10.7	5	8.9	2	3.6
Royal Canadian Mounted Police Public Complaints Commission	39	27	69.2	1	2.6	3	7.7	1	2.6

BOX 8.6 CONTINUED

Distribution of Federal Public Service Employees by Designated Group According to Department or Agency (as at March 31, 2003)

Department or Agency	All Employees #	Women #	Women %	Aboriginal Peoples #	Aboriginal Peoples %	Persons with Disabilities #	Persons with Disabilities %	Persons in a Visible Minority Group #	Persons in a Visible Minority Group %
Patented Medicine Prices Review Board Canada	35	20	57.1	0	0.0	3	8.6	2	5.7
Canadian Forces Grievance Board	33	23	69.7	1	3.0	0	0.0	2	6.1
International Joint Commission	32	12	37.5	0	0.0	2	6.3	1	3.1
Hazardous Materials Information Review Commission Canada	27	14	51.9	0	0.0	1	3.7	2	7.4
Canadian Intergovernmental Conference Secretariat	23	12	52.2	0	0.0	0	0.0	0	0.0
Military Police Complaints Commission	22	15	68.2	0	0.0	0	0.0	0	0.0
Canadian Human Rights Tribunal	18	12	66.7	1	5.6	1	5.6	0	0.0
Law Commission of Canada	12	8	66.7	1	8.3	2	16.7	0	0.0
National Farm Products Council	12	7	58.3	0	0.0	0	0.0	0	0.0
Registry of the Competition Tribunal	12	7	58.3	0	0.0	2	16.7	0	0.0
Canadian Artists and Producers Professional Relations Tribunal	10	5	50.0	0	0.0	0	0.0	1	10.0
NAFTA Secretariat, Canadian Section	10	6	60.0	0	0.0	0	0.0	4	40.0
Copyright Board Canada	8	4	50.0	0	0.0	0	0.0	1	12.5
Civil Aviation Tribunal of Canada	4	4	100.0	0	0.0	0	0.0	0	0.0
Royal Canadian Mounted Police External Review Committee	3	2	66.7	0	0.0	0	0.0	0	0.0
Total	163,314	86,162	52.8	6,425	3.9	9,155	5.6	12,058	7.4

* Civilian staff only. Data for members of the Canadian Forces are not included because the Treasury Board is not their employer.

Fisheries and Oceans Canada data include data for the Canadian Coast Guard.

† Data for the Agriculture Canada Prairie Farm Rehabilitation Administration are included.

Source: Canada, Treasury Board of Canada, 2003: 38.

and welfare, and human resources. Box 8.6, in short, is as much a listing of basic government priorities as it is a notation of the employment distribution of federal public servants.

8.1.1 Departmental Evolution

Another point to be gleaned from Box 8.6 is that the organizational structure of the government changes over time. This current list of departments, agencies, and offices is significantly different from the structure of the Trudeau and Mulroney ministries. The short-lived Progressive Conservative government of Kim Campbell undertook a major reorganization of the federal public service in 1993, changes largely retained by the Chrétien government. As part of this downsizing initiative, the number of departments was reduced from 32 to 23, with six "new" departments being created, eight "old" departments being abolished, and 15 being substantially redesigned. This type of restructuring is common in the history of Canadian public administration, as governments seek not only to "spruce-up" an administration and respond to demands for greater economy and efficiency but also to address new and emerging policy concerns. Hence, HRDC was created in 1993 to improve the delivery of federal policies and programs respecting employment, unemployment, job retraining, and skills development through the merger of portions of the former departments of Employment and Immigration, Labour, Health and Welfare, and the Secretary of State. In 2003, when Paul Martin became prime minister, HRDC was altered once again, being divided into two new departments: Human Resources and Skills Development Canada, primarily responsible for employment policy, unemployment assistance programs, and job retraining; and Social Development Canada, responsible for broad matters of social policy such as child care. Likewise, the alteration of the status of Revenue Canada into the CCRA reflects, at best, an initiative to refashion this institution into a more dynamic and responsive agency of the federal government. At worst, such a change might be viewed as a cynical attempt to camouflage the true nature and size of the federal public service.

As such changes occur in Canadian administrative history, they reveal changing and developing government policy priorities as well as a growing role for the state in society, with a corresponding increase in public service employment. At the time of Confederation, the federal public service was just a shadow of what it has become in the late twentieth century. In 1867 the federal government consisted of 13 departments employing around 5,000 persons (Inwood, 2004: 127). As Box 3.2 illustrated, these original departments reflected a period of limited government, the *laissez-faire* state as highlighted in Chapter 2, in which the role of the federal government was perceived as encompassing the provision of law, order, and security (Justice and Defence), the coordination of government services (Privy Council, Secretary of State, Finance, Customs, and Inland Revenue), and the provision of certain communication and economic infrastructure (Public Works, Post Office, Agriculture, and Marine and Fisheries). While most of these departments have continued to exist in one form or another into the present day, this limited government of the Victorian era gave way over the twentieth century to the form and scope of government associated with the reform liberal welfare state.

The precursors of this change in the role and size of the federal government were the department of Labour in 1900 and that of Health in 1918. The major growth of the federal public sector, though, came in the 1960s and 1970s as governments responded both to rising public expectations of government services as well as to robust finances and grand visions of the public service leading a "just society." This period saw the separate establishment of the Treasury Board (1966) and the creation of Manpower and Immigration (1966). Consumer and Corporate Affairs, Regional Economic Expansion, and the Department of the Environment were established in 1967; Communications in 1968; and Energy, Mines, and Resources in 1970. The 1970s and 1980s also witnessed the development of various ministries of state such as those for Urban Affairs, Science and Technology, Economic Development, Social Development, and Economic and Regional Development. These bodies were designed to be policy planning, research, and coordinating institutions assisting departments with their work (Dyck, 1996: 486-88; Kernaghan and Siegel, 1999: 394-96).

In even so quick a recitation of departmental evolution over the last century as this, one notices that the structures, scope, and sheer population size of the federal government has dramatically altered over time. This pattern at the federal level was replicated during the same time period at the provincial level. Over this century, governments evolved into major actors in the social and economic life of this country. The growth of this workforce has been important not only for its role in providing new and desirable socio-economic services, but also for the personnel management questions that governments have been compelled to address as they became significant employers in their own right.

8.2 Traditional Issues in Public Sector Human Resources Management

Many of the great historical and contemporary debates surrounding the ways and means to improve the quality of government services and to enhance the accountability of government to the people have revolved around the management of the public sector personnel system. Issues that have been addressed and that still elicit much heated discussion include patronage and meritocracy, staffing and hiring policy, personnel training, and public service renewal. These matters will be explored in the remainder of this chapter. In the next chapter, attention will be focused on yet other important though contentious policy matters, such as public sector representativeness, bilingualism and multiculturalism, the impact of human rights policy, gender equity, employment equity, collective bargaining, and the right to strike.

8.2.1 The Patronage System

In 1867 not only were the federal and provincial public services small in numerical terms compared to what they are today, but their dominant organizational principle was **political patronage** (Simpson, 1988: Introduction). All appointments to the federal or provincial public services, as well as the letting of government contracts and licences, were ultimately grounded in the political affiliations of prospective employees or grantees and in the partisan interests of the government of the day. In the half-century following Confederation, it was commonplace for newly elected governments to fire the vast majority of those public servants they had inherited from the previous administration in order to give these jobs to their own relatives, friends, and supporters. This approach to public service management, also known as the "spoils system" (from the American President Andrew Jackson's famous rationalization for his patronage practices: "to the victors go the spoils of the battle") sent a number of clear signals to those directly involved as well as to the general public.

- Public sector employment and the gaining of government contracts was contingent on partisan support for the governing party.
- Education, work experience, and personal attributes—merit—were usually insufficient factors in enabling a person to gain and maintain public service employment or contracts or licences. Usually the key

determinant in employment was not "what you knew" but "who you knew."

- Public service work was not, in any way, "professional," that is, related to professional standards and qualifications. Rather, public service was viewed as the "property" of the government of the day to be used and manipulated by that government for its own partisan ends.

- The public service was in no way considered to be independent of the government. It had no identity of its own, because it could not promote professionalism based on merit; it had no control over the appointment process, meaning that it was inherently transitory, the refuge of "political hacks" and those with "connections."

- Finally, individuals interested in government employment learned that the route to such employment was through support for the governing party or the party that would gain this title. Thus, individual political activity during this time period was influenced by direct material considerations.

Thus, many people supported and worked for a political party not out of ideological or policy considerations but because of what they hoped to gain from such support. A patronage connection existed between parties and their supporters. The latter would offer their loyalty, money, or labour in return for material benefits—jobs, contracts, or licences—once the former gained power. And party leaders knew these expectations existed, since they had created and nurtured them, and they knew these expectations had to be satisfied if they were to retain the support of their "loyalists" (Simpson, 1988: chs. 3,4).

The patronage system, though, was not without its detractors, and it began to come under increasing criticism in the late Victorian period. Patronage was attacked as being both immoral and inefficient. Critics from universities, churches, and social reform movements, including early feminist leaders such as Nellie McClung, challenged the morality of patronage on the grounds that the bureaucracy was used and abused for the political advantage of the governing party, rather than used in the public interest for the benefit of the entire society. At the turn of the century, critics also attacked the system as being grossly inefficient since favouritism, nepotism, and partisan manipulation meant that the bureaucracies in the country were far from being professional and rational organizations staffed with competent officials undertaking their responsibilities in light of the needs for economy, efficiency, and effectiveness. In this sense, the push for a merit-based system of personnel administration was one of the first examples of a demand for a rationalist approach to public sector management.

8.2.2 The Development of the Merit Principle

It was at the federal level that this patronage system first came under sustained attack, and it was here where the organizing principle of meritocracy first became established in Canadian public sector management. The very first half-hearted attempts at public service reform occurred in the 1880s when the Macdonald government, responding to public criticism of patronage, established a Board of Civil Service Examiners, designed to help ministers and their deputies in the selection of public servants. The impact of this institution was minimal, however, in that ministers retained full control over the criteria for employment and final hiring decisions. By the first decade of the twentieth century, though, public criticism of patronage had reached such a level that the Laurier government passed the Civil Service Act of 1908, which, for the first time, recognized the importance of the merit principle in the management of the federal public service (Simpson, 1988: 117–22; Kernaghan and Siegel, 1999: 557).

The **merit principle** contains two related considerations:

- all Canadian citizens "should have a reasonable opportunity to be considered for employment in the public service"; and
- all employment decisions must be based "exclusively on merit or fitness to do the job" (Jackson and Jackson, 1998: 388).

Decisions about hiring, promotion, demotion, and dismissal were to be based on a rational assessment of education, experience, competence, and professionalism, rather than on past political or personal affiliations. In order to implement this new approach to personnel management, the Civil Service Act also created a new institution, the Civil Service Commission, responsible for enforcing the merit principle within Ottawa through the necessary processes of job postings, classifications, setting criteria, examinations, interviews, assessments, evaluations, and decision-making.

While this reform is significant in the history of the merit principle, the act was flawed in that it applied only to Ottawa. At this time the federal public service was divided into two categories: the Inside Service, comprising those employees situated in Ottawa, and the Outside Service, comprising all those employed elsewhere in the country. The provisions of this Civil Service Act were only applicable to the Inside Service. Given that five-sixths of all federal employees were in the Outside Service, the vast majority of the federal public service still was subject to the rules of the old game. But times were changing.

The First World War finally brought the application of the merit principle across the full federal public sector. During the war there were numerous government scandals regarding the management of the war effort and the manner by which the Canadian forces were financed and equipped. Bureaucratic foul-ups caused by a combination of administrative incompetence, graft, self-interest, and corruption resulted in troops being provided with substandard clothing and food, flawed and hazardous munitions, and unreliable rifles. In peacetime such "SNAFUs" would have been embarrassing, the stuff of political finger-pointing and debate; during the war they too often led to unnecessary hardships, wounds, and deaths, the news of which enraged many political actors on the home front, including patriotic group leaders, social reformers, church leaders, the media, opposition party spokesmen, and large numbers of the general public. As public sector incompetence was uncovered, the demands for the ends of patronage and the introduction of rationalist meritocracy throughout the entire federal public service became a common refrain. Thus, in 1918, the Union government of Robert Borden brought forth a new Civil Service Act, extending the application of the merit principle throughout the entire federal government and strengthening the enforcement powers of the Civil Service Commission (Simpson, 1988: 123-32; Kernaghan and Siegel, 1999: 557).

8.3   Professionalization and the Public Service Commission

Since 1918, the task of the Civil Service Commission—renamed the Public Service Commission (PSC) in 1967—has been the nurturing, maintenance, and promotion of a professional public service free from partisan interference, insulated from the evils of patronage, and capable of providing meritorious service to the Canadian public. To accomplish these objectives, the PSC established a highly complex and rationalistic merit system to replace patronage. As the latter was superseded, an important but little understood dynamic in public personnel management took place. The establishment of a professional, merit-based system of personnel relations required highly codified rules and procedures regarding staffing. Rationalism in public sector personnel management thus came at the expense of simplicity and expedience in decision-making.

If all persons are to be treated equally in employment opportunities, with individual capabilities being the primary criteria for selection, employment decision-making must be open and subject to relatively "objective" standards of evaluation regarding merit. The benefit of this is that the personnel system is fair and is perceived as being fair by all interested observers. The drawback is that the system becomes highly bureaucratized and cumbersome and, correspondingly, more expensive and time-consuming to operate. As is commonly known, to hire or fire anyone in the federal public service is an extremely complex and rather slow process—much less "efficient" than similar decision-making in the private sector. Just as we observed the development of very complex systems of rationalist financial management in the previous two chapters, here we observe the intricacies and difficulties of rationalist personnel management in this and the next chapter. It is always important to bear in mind, however, that regardless of the growing complexities in the personnel system, such bureaucratic rules and regulations have all developed from the common goal of eliminating the worst features of patronage. And always remember that "efficient" decision-making may not be "just" decision-making.

Through its responsibility for the implementation of the merit principle, the PSC and its predecessor established a complex system of personnel management comprised of certain managerial processes:

- job classification;
- **human resource planning**, staffing, training and development;
- and performance evaluation.

All these matters are central to the role of the PSC, yet are fraught with difficulties, highlighting how challenging the task of the commission and personnel policy rationalism truly is.

8.3.1   Job Classification

Job classification involves the ordering of all public service positions into particular occupational categories, groups, and subgroups for the purposes of establishing job criteria for employment decision-making and wage and salary considerations. As noted in Box 8.7, the six main occupational categories within the federal public service are divided into a further 72 occupational groups and 106 subgroups, highlighting the wide and varied range of work that public servants undertake. The difficulties with such classification, however, lie in the establishment and evaluation of relevant job criteria. At the heart of the merit principle is the assessment of the ability of a particular person to meet the criteria of a given job. The criteria

BOX 8.7

Distribution of Federal Public Service Employees by Designated Group According to Occupational Category and Group (as at March 31, 2003)

PSSRA I-I Indeterminate, Terms of Three Months or More, and Seasonal Employees

Occupational Category and Group		All Employees	Women		Aboriginal Peoples		Persons with Disabilities		Persons in a Visible Minority Group	
		#	#	%	#	%	#	%	#	%
Executive		4,209	1,424	33.8	114	2.7	193	4.6	177	4.2
Scientific and Professional										
AC	Actuarial Science	4	1	25.0	0	0.0	0	0.0	0	0.0
AG	Agriculture	7	1	14.3	1	14.3	1	14.3	0	0.0
AR	Architecture and Town Planning	237	60	25.3	5	2.1	6	2.5	28	11.8
AU	Auditing	188	60	31.9	2	1.1	4	2.1	35	18.6
BI	Biological Sciences	1,747	712	40.8	31	1.8	54	3.1	191	10.9
CH	Chemistry	422	164	38.9	2	0.5	8	1.9	93	22.0
DE	Dentistry	11	0	0.0	0	0.0	1	9.1	0	0.0
DS	Defence Scientific Service	564	88	15.6	1	0.2	9	1.6	71	12.6
ED	Education	737	444	60.2	74	10.0	27	3.7	51	6.9
EN	Engineering and Land Survey	2,577	351	13.6	34	1.3	82	3.2	414	16.1
ES	Economics, Sociology and Statistics	5,396	2,411	44.7	119	2.2	238	4.4	674	12.5
FO	Forestry	96	19	19.8	1	1.0	5	5.2	3	3.1
HR	Historical Research	131	53	40.5	2	1.5	4	3.1	3	2.3
LA	Law	2,574	1,310	50.9	68	2.6	134	5.2	207	8.0
LS	Library Science	426	312	73.2	9	2.1	21	4.9	28	6.6
MA	Mathematics	341	127	37.2	0	0.0	16	4.7	53	15.5
MD	Medicine	248	84	33.9	3	1.2	13	5.2	28	11.3
MT	Meteorology	522	87	16.7	3	0.6	14	2.7	36	6.9
ND	Nutrition and Dietetics	37	37	100.0	2	5.4	0	0.0	0	0.0
NU	Nursing	1,541	1,300	84.4	129	8.4	42	2.7	114	7.4
OP	Occupational and Physical Therapy	49	39	79.6	0	0.0	0	0.0	3	6.1
PC	Physical Sciences	1,924	709	36.9	37	1.9	55	2.9	168	8.7
PH	Pharmacy	14	9	64.3	0	0.0	0	0.0	1	7.1
PS	Psychology	325	160	49.2	2	0.6	12	3.7	18	5.5
SE	Scientific Research	1,867	303	16.2	8	0.4	51	2.7	295	15.8
SG	Scientific Regulation	595	284	47.7	3	0.5	25	4.2	88	14.8
SW	Social Work	50	37	74.0	4	8.0	2	4.0	1	2.0
UT	University Teaching	211	30	14.2	1	0.5	5	2.4	26	12.3
VM	Veterinary Medicine	39	20	51.3	0	0.0	2	5.1	4	10.3
Total		22,880	9,212	40.3	541	2.4	831	3.6	2,633	11.5

BOX 8.7 CONTINUED
Distribution of Federal Public Service Employees by Designated Group According to Occupational Category and Group (as at March 31, 2003)

Occupational Category and Group	All Employees #	Women #	Women %	Aboriginal Peoples #	Aboriginal Peoples %	Persons with Disabilities #	Persons with Disabilities %	Persons in a Visible Minority Group #	Persons in a Visible Minority Group %
Administration and Foreign Service									
AS	Administrative Services	19,965	14,794	74.1	790	4.0	1,118	5.6	1,027	5.1
CA	Career Assignment Program	150	84	56.0	16	10.7	11	7.3	38	25.3
CO	Commerce	2,974	1,203	40.5	89	3.0	129	4.3	220	7.4
CS	Computer Systems Administration	11,004	3,303	30.0	216	2.0	529	4.8	1,191	10.8
FI	Financial Administration	3,039	1,531	50.4	83	2.7	135	4.4	400	13.2
FS	Foreign Service	1,130	404	35.8	17	1.5	39	3.5	113	10.0
IS	Information Services	2,634	1,789	67.9	75	2.8	115	4.4	133	5.0
MM	Management Trainee	185	114	61.6	1	0.5	9	4.9	23	12.4
OM	Organization and Methods	218	135	61.9	3	1.4	12	5.5	8	3.7
PE	Personnel Administration	3,227	2,359	73.1	158	4.9	299	9.3	283	8.8
PG	Purchasing and Supply	2,339	1,184	50.6	74	3.2	147	6.3	167	7.1
PM	Program Administration	17,010	10,855	63.8	1,004	5.9	1,207	7.1	1,182	6.9
TR	Translation	1,139	764	67.1	2	0.2	39	3.4	32	2.8
WP	Welfare Program	2,375	1,279	53.9	162	6.8	174	7.3	134	5.6
Total		67,389	39,798	59.1	2,690	4.0	3,963	5.9	4,951	7.3
Technical									
AI	Air Traffic Control	13	1	7.7	0	0.0	0	0.0	1	7.7
AO	Aircraft Operations	518	42	8.1	10	1.9	9	1.7	13	2.5
DD	Drafting and Illustration	240	90	37.5	4	1.7	19	7.9	19	7.9
EG	Engineering and Scientific Support	6,287	1,738	27.6	144	2.3	264	4.2	343	5.5
EL	Electronics	1,147	40	3.5	22	1.9	51	4.4	40	3.5
EU	Educational Support	25	22	88.0	4	16.0	0	0.0	0	0.0
GT	General Technical	2,081	588	28.3	97	4.7	102	4.9	59	2.8
PI	Primary Products Inspection	240	50	20.8	9	3.8	22	9.2	14	5.8
PY	Photography	19	4	21.1	0	0.0	1	5.3	0	0.0
RO	Radio Operations	348	62	17.8	12	3.4	14	4.0	4	1.1
SI	Social Science Support	3,474	2,186	62.9	141	4.1	198	5.7	252	7.3
SO	Ships' Officers	999	61	6.1	23	2.3	18	1.8	12	1.2
TE	RCMP Special Group	722	416	57.6	3	0.4	4	0.6	6	0.8
TI	Technical Inspection	1,444	145	10.0	33	2.3	57	3.9	117	8.1
Total		17,557	5,445	31.0	502	2.9	759	4.3	880	5.0

BOX 8.7 CONTINUED

Distribution of Federal Public Service Employees by Designated Group According to Occupational Category and Group (as at March 31, 2003)

Occupational Category and Group	All Employees #	Women #	Women %	Aboriginal Peoples #	Aboriginal Peoples %	Persons with Disabilities #	Persons with Disabilities %	Persons in a Visible Minority Group #	Persons in a Visible Minority Group %
Administrative Support									
CM Communications	71	23	32.4	1	1.4	5	7.0	0	0.0
CR Clerical and Regulatory	30,179	24,912	82.5	1,525	5.1	2,353	7.8	2,582	8.6
DA Data Processing	383	234	61.1	14	3.7	25	6.5	29	7.6
OE Office Equipment Operation	22	12	54.5	1	4.5	5	22.7	1	4.5
ST Secretarial, Stenographic, Typing	1,931	1,893	98.0	71	3.7	111	5.7	129	6.7
Total	32,586	27,074	83.1	1,612	4.9	2,499	7.7	2,741	8.4
Operational									
CX Correctional Services	6,169	1,427	23.1	582	9.4	258	4.2	300	4.9
FR Firefighters	405	7	1.7	12	3.0	10	2.5	4	1.0
GL General Labour and Trades	5,162	218	4.2	158	3.1	268	5.2	102	2.0
GS General Services	3,068	1,069	34.8	113	3.7	201	6.6	128	4.2
HP Heat, Power and Stationary Plant Operation	478	3	0.6	9	1.9	35	7.3	25	5.2
HS Hospital Services	637	362	56.8	47	7.4	23	3.6	60	9.4
LI Lightkeepers	110	4	3.6	4	3.6	1	0.9	0	0.0
PR Printing Operations	47	12	25.5	1	2.1	2	4.3	3	6.4
SC Ships' Crews	1,288	70	5.4	23	1.8	47	3.6	28	2.2
SR Ship Repair	1,329	37	2.8	18	1.4	65	4.9	26	2.0
Total	18,693	3,209	17.2	967	5.2	910	4.9	676	3.6
Total Federal Public Service	163,314	86,162	52.8	6,426	3.9	9,155	5.6	12,058	7.4

Source: Canada, Treasury Board of Canada, 2003: 32.

to be met must be as clear, specific, and measurable as possible. This, however, is often not the case, as the development of criteria relating to the duties, responsibilities, demands, skills, and requirements of jobs has tended to be excessively general, given that it is usually very difficult to specifically codify all the requirements of particular jobs. But, as job criteria are left codified in general terms, the evaluation of the match between a particular person and a given job becomes more subjective, as differing persons interpret general terms in differing manners. This issue is one that poses great practical problems for the PSC, public servants, would-be employees, and political analysts.

8.3.2 Human Resource Planning

The PSC is also actively involved in human resource planning (Kernaghan and Siegel, 1999: 563-64). The PSC and all personnel managers in departments and agencies engage in a process of analyzing their current and future personnel needs and developing managerial strategies to meet these needs. Such decision-making involves the PSC in assessing

- the anticipated quantity and quality of public sector work;
- the number and types of persons needed to undertake this work;
- the nature of recruitment, selection, and training required to meet these needs;
- the financial implications of such initiatives; and
- the appropriate management structures and systems needed to ensure that these goals are met.

While departments and other agencies, boards, and commissions are primarily interested in satisfying immediate personnel needs, the PSC must adopt a more expansive approach to thinking about personnel management.

The leadership of the PSC is responsible for the well-being of the public service personnel system as an institution. Thus, it must be concerned not only with immediate staffing concerns but with broader issues such as

- the development and promotion of staff training;
- the constant upgrading of the technological skills of employees;
- the "graying" of the public service as a greater proportion of employees congregate in the "older" age bands, leading to a need to promote greater hiring of the young;
- the rejuvenation and renewal of the public service following the decade-long process of job cuts in the 1990s;
- the promotion of certain groups of people that have been historically underrepresented within the public service (francophones, women, visible minorities, the disabled, and Aboriginal peoples); and,
- the constant maintenance and protection of the merit principle in all personnel decision-making.

In seeking to meet all these objectives, however, tensions arise regarding how these goals are to be met, and, in particular, whether policies of employment equity are consistent with the merit principle.

8.3.2.1 STAFFING

While the PSC has many roles, the bulk of its work has always centred around the staffing process (Kernaghan and Siegel, 1999: 564-66). All decisions regarding the hiring, promotion, demotion, and firing of public servants fall within its jurisdiction. To ensure that decisions are based on a fair assessment of merit, in light of all other representational considerations, requires a complex system of evaluation mechanisms. The staffing process calls for the rigorous use of such matters as publicized job postings and invitations for applications, written examinations, personal interviews, formal reviews of qualifications and past experience, and assessments of current job performance. Through the systematization of these staffing undertakings, their application in light of established job criteria, and a rigorous evaluation of a candidate's merit to do the job, the PSC and its predecessor has been able to substantially reduce the practice of patronage found within the federal public service.

This is an accomplishment of much importance, yet even here the staffing process is not without criticism. Again, the drawback is a formalized, bureaucratized system that can be slow, inflexible, inefficient, and difficult to put into operation. Indeed, these are among the criticisms of the federal staffing system as expressed by senior managers themselves. As the system has become more rule-oriented to reduce the discretionary judgement at the heart of patronage, merit has been susceptible to administrative "sclerosis"—decisions get made but only very slowly and with much red tape. A further criticism with the staffing process is that, despite the efforts to reduce discretionary and arbitrary decision-making, the system is still open to significant discretionary judgement. Job criteria tend to be defined in general terms, and the assessment of the match between the criteria and a given person is the responsibility of those managers delegated by the PSC to this task. In performing it, they have been subjected to much criticism. As Kernaghan and Siegel note, questions have arisen regarding the proper extent to which managers gauge "knowledge, abilities, sensitivity, potential for advancement, and seniority" (Kernaghan and Siegel, 1999: 557). Questions have also arisen about the adequacy of the training of personnel managers and the fairness and efficacy of written examinations and interview techniques. As is widely suspected within the public service and among job applicants, personnel managers have predispositions regarding the type of person they wish to hire and support. As a former public service commissioner has argued, some managers favour their own staff or the people they know. Others tend to select and promote in their own image, creating hurdles and barriers for those unlike them (Kernaghan and Siegel, 1999: 557).

This problem is one identified by feminist analysts in explaining the historic underrepresentation of women in the public service, and this assessment has been embraced by those concerned with the underrepresentation of other social groups.

These criticisms lead to reflections on the concept of bureaucratic patronage. While the staffing system may now work admirably well in controlling and suppressing partisan patronage, it is still possible for senior managers to manipulate the personnel system to suit their interests and to favour their preferred candidates, provided they possess the basic credentials required for the position. Formal examinations and interviews may lead to a position or promotion going not to the most meritorious person but to the person with the best bureaucratic connections to senior managers, while these managers are in a position to justify their subjective selection through their control of the objective examination and interview process. Thus, despite the many advances in staffing processes over the last century, the process is still one fraught with controversy and problems.

8.3.2.2 TRAINING AND DEVELOPMENT

Within any organization intent on progressing into the future in a stable and effective manner, it is not good enough to continue with current employees with current skills. Rather, those organizations that are successful at managing the adaptations required by changing times are those that place priority not only on current staffing decisions but also on staff training and development to meet future needs. The federal government is no different in this respect, and the PSC has always been responsible for training and development initiatives designed to provide employees with "knowledge, skills, and experience" enabling them to do their present jobs efficiently and effectively while preparing them for future responsibilities (Kernaghan and Siegel, 1999: 558). The PSC supports both formal classroom training in universities and colleges and on-the-job training. Courses range from computer skills upgrading to financial management and accounting, from effective communications and public speaking to courses in public administration and public policy.

The problem with such training and development initiatives, however, is that they tend to be undervalued by governments because, while they are immediately costly in terms of fees and time away from current duties, their benefits in terms of increased employee efficiency, effectiveness, capability, job satisfaction, and future flexibility may not be observed for months or years. Training and development initiatives are equivalent to investments that can be evaluated only over the long term. Unfortunately, most govern-

BOX 8.8
The Canada School of Public Service

The Canada School of Public Service (formerly known as the Canadian Cen-tre for Management Development) dates back to 1991. Since then this institu-tion has been active in a wide range of skills development, training initiatives, and research undertakings designed to promote best management practices within the federal public service. The following is the legislative mandate of the CSPS:

S.4 The Objects of the School are:
  (a) to encourage pride and excellence in the Public Service and to foster in managers and other Public Service employees a sense of the pur-poses, values and traditions of the Public Service;
  (b) to help ensure that those managers have the analytical, creative, advisory, administrative and other managerial skills and knowledge necessary to develop and implement policy, respond to change, including changes in the social, cultural, racial and linguistic charac-ter of Canadian society, and manage government programs, services, and personnel efficiently, effectively and equitably;
  (c) to help managers and other Public Service employees to develop successful cooperative relationships at all levels through leadership, motivation, effective internal communications and the encourage-ment of innovation.
  (d) to develop within the Public Service and to attract to the Public Service, through the School's programs and studies, persons who are of high calibre and who reflect the diversity of Canadian society, and to support their growth and development as public sector managers and employees committed to the service of Canada;
  (e) to formulate and provide training, orientation and development programs for public sector managers and employees, particularly for those in the Public Service;
  (f) to assist deputy heads in meeting the learning needs of their organi-zation, including by way of delivering training and development programs;
  (g) to study and conduct research into the theory and practice of public sector management and public administration; and
  (h) to encourage a greater awareness in Canada of issues related to public sector management, public administration and the role and functions of government and to involve a broad range of individu-als and institutions in the School's pursuit of excellence in public administration.

Source: The Public Service Modernization Act, 2002-2003, *Statutes of Canada*, 2002-2003, c. 22.

ments place too little stress on future training and development, especially in times of financial restraint when all programs are under scrutiny and all organizations are supposed to trim expenditures. All too often, training and development budgets are among the first to be cut, because such reductions do not result in immediate institutional problems and pain. But persistent failure to prepare for the future will produce problems and pain in the future, as government institutions realize that their employees are inadequately skilled to meet the demands of future policies, programs, government needs, and public expectations.

In 1988, in an effort to address the training and development needs of the federal public service, the government established the Canadian Centre for Management Development (CCMD) (Inwood, 2004: 295). This organization, renamed in 2004 the **Canada School of Public Service** (CSPS), engages in multifaceted approaches to enhancing management training, skills development, policy and program analysis, and strategic planning and leadership. All these matters are important to any organization, and the CCMD/CSPS has sought to carve out a niche for itself as a small but vital component in the development of the collective managerial wisdom of the Public Service of Canada. Through its numerous training sessions, seminars, courses, and publications, it promotes, as its broad mandate, the development of the intellectual capital of the public service, while also providing public sector managers with a forum where they can come together, learn from one another, review and challenge existing forms of managerial thinking, and interact with academic analysts also interested in the world of government and public sector management. Such noble aspirations, however, are not always welcomed within the inner circles of the Ottawa establishment. As Donald Savoie has argued, officials in the department of Finance made a point of not attending CCMD activities, believing that its management courses were generally to be avoided (Savoie, 1999: 161). This pointed lack of interest in the work of the CCMD/CSPS by the most significant department in the government is telling, as is the willingness of senior officials "at the centre" to control the work of the CCMD/CSPS with respect to controversial matters of current policy. Savoie has documented a case that occurred in the early 1990s when the secretary of the Treasury Board contacted the head of the CCMD to insist that a special project on management-labour relations be dropped due to ongoing management-labour disputes. The CCMD complied with this "request" (Savoie, 1999: 235). Despite such resistance to the work of the school, and the delicate path that its officials must follow as they negotiate the process of studying and analyzing federal management from the inside, the CCMD/CSPS has proven itself nevertheless to be a valuable element in the management training process of the federal public service. It is sufficiently important to the current government that it escaped closure as part of Program Review and has even witnessed an expanded training and development role, as the federal government seeks to rejuvenate the public service and its management component.

8.3.3   Performance Evaluation

The final managerial process in the personnel system is performance evaluation (Kernaghan and Siegel, 1999: 569-70). In a system in which demonstrated merit is central to all personnel decisions, the regular periodic review and assessment of employee performance is essential to all other decision-making. Performance evaluation should enable management to rationally assess the strengths and weaknesses of employee performance, capabilities for future assignments, necessary upgrading and training, and recommendations for pay increases and promotion. The evaluation process is also a means to facilitate formal communication between managers and employees, stipulating that management must address these matters while guaranteeing to employees that they will receive feedback on the quality of their work. Within the federal public service permanent employees tend to be evaluated annually while temporary and probationary employees are evaluated more frequently.

Despite the need for and potential benefits of performance evaluation it remains, like so many other matters in the personnel system, a controversial subject. Just as decision-making regarding job classification and staffing is susceptible to subjective factors, so too is employee evaluation. The PSC calls for evaluations to be standardized and to rank employees on a five-point scale: outstanding, superior, fully satisfactory, satisfactory, and unsatisfactory. Experience has shown, however, that differing managers will exhibit differing approaches to these terms, with some being more generous and others less so in their rankings. There is no clear objective standard as to what constitutes satisfactory behaviour and how the adjective "fully" affects this evaluation. The subjectivity that enters into this process when one must evaluate others on such general and variable criteria—hence, the process itself—is open to much criticism. Many employees complain that the system is unfair, since managers have wide discretion to reward favourites while harming the career prospects of those not so ingratiating. Many managers, however, complain that the process is of questionable worth because, all too often, managers provide inflated appraisals of employees as a means of enhancing worker morale and pre-empting the possibility of drawn-out and uncomfortable challenges to critical employee evaluations. Homogenized good grades, though, eventually defeat the purpose of evaluation when they come to be accepted as normal, with most employees expecting and receiving similar rankings. How then does management differentiate better employees from weaker ones?

Rationalistic performance evaluation is an important part of personnel management and is required if a bureaucracy is to effectively understand its workforce and organize it for future development, while expecting and rewarding demonstrated merit. Yet, as is so often the case, the realization of this theoretical ideal is surrounded with difficulties. Subjectivity can hardly be avoided when one set of persons is evaluating another set's personal and interpersonal skills and capabilities. Because any merit-based system of personnel management requires a process of performance evaluation, the existence of good, well-trained managers is integral. If the process hinges on human judgement, humans themselves will determine how well it works. This situation re-emphasizes the importance of developing and maintaining a strong corps of senior managers who understand the importance of performance evaluation, the complexities and difficulties inherent in the process, the problems that can be encountered by flawed evaluations and the benefits that accrue to competent evaluations, and the need to balance objective and subjective criteria of evaluation. In short, the system calls for the wise exercise of discretionary judgement.

8.4 Merit in Perspective

The merit principle stands as the first great organizing principle of the modern, professional public service. After it became entrenched in federal law in 1918, the Civil Service Commission was able to eliminate the worst excesses of political patronage. Through the application of the principles and practices of job classification, personnel planning, open merit-based selection, and ongoing monitoring, evaluation, and training, the federal government has developed a public service noted for its professionalism and freedom from partisan bias. Indeed, from the reform of 1918 one can trace the evolution of a career public service in which talented individuals are attracted to many diverse, interesting, and important fields of work in which demonstrated merit is the key organizing principle determining one's admission and subsequent career development. Prior to the First World War the patronage system prevented the emergence of such a professional ethos, but in the decades following it, the Civil Service Commission and leading prime ministers—Mackenzie King, St. Laurent, and Pearson—and public servants—O.D. Skelton, Robert Bryce, Mitchell Sharp, and Gordon Robertson—worked to transform the public service into a meritocracy. The leadership and vision they displayed helped make the federal government the dominant governmental actor within this country through most of the twentieth century, with these attributes subsequently emulated by the provincial governments.

However, on a cautionary note, the development of the merit principle has neither guaranteed that merit will always be the determining factor in personnel management, nor has it fully eliminated the practice of political patronage. As we have just seen, meritocracy is easier said than done. Difficulties arise in classifying jobs, evaluating the merit of applicants, and of assessing the performance of those already employed. In all of these managerial functions, the goal of "objective" analysis confronts the "subjective" nature of decision-making when human beings are involved. The problem is not simply one of establishing coherent job requirements and conducting fair evaluations of education, talent, and experience. Such activities can be rigorously overseen through well-publicized guidelines and multiple factors of evaluation assessed by a variety of analysts, with all decisions subject to a right of appeal to independent and knowledgeable superiors. The most difficult issue respecting the implementation of the merit principle is not discounting political favouritism and distinguishing strong from weak applicants or employees but distinguishing between applicants and employees whose education, skill, and achievement profiles are virtually identical. What do personnel managers do when, say, 400 persons apply for one "policy analyst" position, and the top 30 applicants all possess superior qualifications?

The question becomes one of how the merit principle is to be interpreted and applied. Does the principle necessitate that the "best" candidate be identified, or does it simply require that a "qualified" candidate be found? If the first view prevails, one enters into the difficult world of seeking distinguishing characteristics of merit from among those who are all roughly comparable. This process of distinction-making can be highly subjective, as differing personnel managers assign differing weights and emphasis to differing personal, educational, and experiential characteristics. It is this very search for "best" candidates that has been responsible for the demonstrated inflation in job requirements and credentials in the public service, as managers search for distinguishing characteristics and applicants seek to make their resumes stronger than those of the "competition." Hence, administrative positions that three decades ago may have required, as an educational minimum, just a high school diploma will now normally require a university degree or college diploma; policy positions that a generation ago only required a BA may now require an MA or a PhD. And even then, personnel managers often find the selection process difficult, as numerous candidates for the same position will possess such credentials.

The thrust to find distinguishing characteristics of merit thus heightens the quest for credentials and experience on all sides, leaving personnel managers confronting the same problem as at the outset: how to distinguish between comparably well-qualified candidates? And, again, the resolution to this dilemma has tended to be found in recourse to criteria that do not necessarily fit well with the traditional understanding of the merit principle, namely, individual connections, bureaucratic patronage, and conformity to an established administrative culture. One can wonder whether this reality undermines the organizational purpose underlying the merit principle; one can also wonder whether this reality can be altered.

If, however, the second approach to merit is adopted, and personnel managers seek "qualified" candidates, the problem of selection becomes fierce because countless numbers of applicants will be qualified for any one position, and many current employees will be qualified for promotion. When there is an overabundance of qualified candidates, some other criteria of selection must come into play. As we have seen, some criteria may simply be "connections" or "bureaucratic favouritism" or various forms of bias in discounting women, ethnic minorities, Aboriginal peoples, or the disabled. Clearly, such viewpoints have constituted criteria in the selection process in the past and are still found within certain public sector organizations. While stringent efforts have been underway for over a decade to eliminate systemic bias in personnel management, it has been and will be extremely difficult to eliminate the factors of connections and bureaucratic favouritism. With respect to these latter two concepts, personnel managers clearly favour those they know over those they do not, and they clearly favour those who emulate the values, attitudes, and undefined values of their given organization as it now exists. And this is not necessarily wrong.

Discrimination based on innate characteristics is wrong and is actively prohibited by human rights law (Howe and Johnson, 2000), but selection based on conformity to general institutional needs and practices is perfectly legitimate. It is important and desirable for an organization to hire, retain, and promote those who fit the legitimate "corporate culture," since this is necessary for maintaining the long-term stability and effectiveness of the organization. Thus, those with the "fit" will be advantaged, the "fit" meaning those currently doing well within the public service or those who are viewed as possessing values and attitudes similar to those currently within the organization. Such persons benefit from their connections, because they are among the first who will be made aware of insider information respecting upcoming job opportunities, and they can be schooled in their personal presentation and the interests and predispositions of those decision-makers on selection committees. If all this sounds rather informal and subjective—personnel decision-making tied to personal contacts, inclinations, and desires—it is. And it is this way because simply being educationally or technically qualified for a position is insufficient means for obtaining employment. Other selection criteria do come into play: some sinister, others merely bureaucratic.

8.4.1   Merit, Senior Political Appointments, and Patronage

These difficulties in the application of the merit principle constitute only one of the limitations of the principle found in the federal government. A second problem is that the principle—and the corresponding role of the PSC—does not apply to all positions in the broader federal public service. The PSC's jurisdiction extends only to the public service comprising those persons employed by government departments and certain major agencies. It does not possess jurisdiction over personnel management respecting Crown corporations or regulatory agencies. While these institutions will normally follow the merit principle in their routine staffing decisions, the appointment of senior executives remains a prerogative of the government of the day. This is also the case of all appointments to the Senate, the federally appointed judiciary, ambassadorships and missions abroad, and all those appointed under "Orders in Council." Thus, literally thousands of positions from the significant to the obscure remain subject to patronage appointment. Also, much government contractual work—from legal and accounting services to advertising and management consulting services—are subject to the preference of the government of the day. It is common, for example, for Liberal governments to favour professional firms with Liberal connections and Progressive Conservative governments to favour those with Conservative credentials.

One must be careful in assessing the nature of patronage with respect to these forms of appointment-making and contractual obligations. The traditional form of partisan patronage can still be found on occasions when governments bestow positions or benefits on party loyalists of dubious merit, which was often the charge brought against both the Trudeau and Mulroney governments with respect to appointments to certain regulatory agencies, such as the Canadian Immigration and Refugee Board and the Canadian Parole Board. This old style of patronage, though, is waning, the victim of media scrutiny, public anger, professional need, and political sensitivity. It is important to bear in mind that governments now seldom hire or retain persons simply because they are party loyalists if they are also unqualified to adequately perform the tasks of a given position. Such hirings, when they do occur, are clearly the worst form of patronage and arouse professional, media, and public criticism, as Mulroney learned from the scathing political and media criticism of many of his Order-in-Council appointments (Simpson, 1988: ch. 13; Cameron, 1995).

But criticisms of patronage cannot and should not extend so far as to deny governments the right to hire persons qualified to perform senior managerial tasks who are also supporters of the government of the day. As Jeffrey Simpson (1988) has long argued, some may consider this patronage, but it is not illegitimate patronage. Rather, governments of all political orientations will routinely look to qualified persons they know and trust to fill senior positions in regulatory agencies and Crown corporations, for example. This ensures that important governing institutions are subject to the direction of good managers who also share the same broad ideological orientation and policy perspective of the government and who will not have motivations to sabotage the work of the governing party. Such hiring practices are sensible and should not be labelled with the epithet of illegitimate patronage. In appointing senior directors and managers to regulatory agencies and Crown corporations, for example, one should not expect a Liberal government to pass over qualified professionals who happen to be Liberal supporters in favour of other qualified professionals who are Progressive Conservatives or New Democrats or Blocistes, or strictly neutrals. Likewise, the various provincial governments of Lucien Bouchard and Bernard Landry (Parti Québécois), Ralph Klein and John Hamm (Progressive Conservative) and Lorne Calvert and Gary Doer (NDP) all favoured their own qualified loyalists over all others as they sought to create senior agency leaderships loyal and trustworthy to their governments.

That this approach to senior appointment-making is routinely followed by governments should not be surprising since it makes eminent political sense for governments to appoint to senior positions qualified persons whom they trust. Illegitimate patronage arises when demonstrably underqualified persons are appointed to positions solely on account of their political connections, but such incidents are now exceedingly rare. Governments tend to refrain from hiring the less competent for two reasons. First, to do so exposes them to a variety of public criticisms, while also placing important institutions in the hands of substandard management, a condition that may return to haunt the government. Secondly, governments now do not need to hire loyalists who are of substandard professional calibre because, in this time of an increasingly well-educated and experienced workforce, they can find loyalists who are also well-qualified to do the work. The old form of patronage has become increasingly rare not only because it is morally offensive, but also because it is practically unnecessary and counterproductive.

For an overview of the merit system in the provinces, please see the Thinking Government web site.

8.5   Human Resources Management Reform and Management Renewal

While the development and application of the merit principle has been the signature dynamic in the history of the federal public service over the past century, a variety of other important issues have also attracted the attention of those concerned with the management of public servants. The next chapter will address such matters as the representativeness of the Public Service of Canada, the extent to which employment equity is utilized within it, and the nature and working of the federal system of labour relations and collective bargaining. For the remainder of this chapter, however, attention will be directed to the broad issue of management reform and renewal and its implications for personnel policy.

Just as there have been many rationalistic attempts to redesign the federal system of financial management, so too has the federal public service been the focus of repeated reform and renewal initiatives, all aimed at fundamentally improving the quality of government services, the work of government personnel, and the managerial relationships between departments, Crown agencies, and central agencies. The overall success of most of these initiatives has been limited, at best, though the most recent undertaking, the La Relève exercise and its aftermath, may prove to have the most impact, though in an incremental fashion. This short narrative on management renewal begins some 40 years ago.

8.5.1   The Glassco Commission

In 1960 the Diefenbaker government established the Royal Commission on Government Organization (named the Glassco Commission after its chairman) to study and report on ways and means to improve the personnel management system in the public service. Its hallmark catch-phrase was its admonition to "let the managers manage" (Inwood, 2004: 326). The Glassco Report (Canada, 1962) criticized an excessive and mechanistic approach to centralized control over department management, resulting in cumbersome bureaucratic procedures that frustrated rather than promoted sound management principles and administration. The report called for the decentralization of managerial authority down to line departments and their executive ranks so that those managers closest to the daily routine of policy and program development and implementation would be able to exert decisive control over such matters of management.

Though the Pearson government eventually came to endorse much of the thrust of the Glassco Commission, especially its recommendations on the establishment of collective bargaining in the public sector, and while this and all subsequent federal governments have enunciated their support for the principle of "letting the managers manage," tensions have always existed between two competing positions. First is the belief in the efficiency and effectiveness of decentralized program management in the hands of department executives expert in their given policy field; second is the demand by central agencies and the political leaders of a government—the forces of the centre—to maintain effective command and control over all major financial and personnel decision-making of all departments to ensure that the core policy and administrative interests of the government do not suffer from inappropriate decisions made by line departments and their staff. As Savoie (1999) has argued in his study of the federal public service, these basic tensions continue to this day, as we shall observe, but always with the forces of the centre maintaining a firm hand on the evolution of government policy and management direction. This general trend can be observed through a recitation of some of the major reports and initiatives on government reform over the past quarter-century.

8.5.2 The Lambert Report

In 1979, the Royal Commission on Financial Management and Account-ability (known as the Lambert Commission) released its Final Report (Canada, 1979a). This document attacked what the commission saw as a serious malaise in management deriving from "an almost total breakdown in the chain of accountability"(Canada, 1979a: 21). It found

- that general management practices in the federal government were deficient;

- that excessive centralized controls vitiated departmental initiative while confusing lines of responsibility;
- that senior executives tended to be more interested in policy than program management;
- that both financial and personnel management systems were far from the rational systems they were meant to be;
- that deputy ministers should be viewed and evaluated more like senior executives in the private sector;
- that central agencies were failing to provide an open and responsive environment within which departments and their managers could flourish; and
- that all the accountability relationships between department managers, deputy ministers, central agencies, and ministers had to be much more rigorously defined, implemented, and evaluated.

The Lambert Report, in essence, called for a massive overhaul of the government's management system and system of accountability.

Needless to say, this report was met with a frosty reception in Ottawa, with the Trudeau government rejecting almost all of its findings. Savoie writes that senior officials gave the Lambert Report very low marks. They considered it to have an overwhelming private sector influence, with very little application to the public sector. Very quickly after its release the Report was viewed to be of little significance (Savoie, 1999: 207). While these conclusions unfairly represent the Lambert Report in that its analysis of the meaning and importance of accountability in government was very thought-provoking and still merits reading today, this reaction was typical. The impact of the report in Ottawa was minimal, as Savoie suggests, because it sought to do too much, was unfocused, and tried to substantially challenge and reorganize the authority of the centre.

8.5.3   The D'Avignon Report

In sharp contrast to the Lambert Report was the Report of the D'Avignon Committee—the Special Committee on the Review of Personnel Management and the Merit Principle—also released in 1979 (Canada, 1979b). It met with a much more favourable reception in Ottawa, being much more focused and limited in scope while advocating a policy approach that fit well with the current thinking of central agencies and the PSC. The D'Avignon Report narrowly concentrated on reforms to the public service appointment and promotion systems, stressing the need for greater consideration to be given to such factors as "sensitivity to the public" and the ability of employees to interact well with the public. The simple tone of these recommendations differ dramatically from those of the Lambert Commission, but there was one major recommendation that was eventually seized upon by the Trudeau government and its successors. The D'Avignon Report strongly criticized the lack of representativeness in the federal public service with respect to women, ethnic and visible minorities, the handicapped, and Aboriginal Canadians. In seeking a means to redress such underrepresentation and the related problem of systemic discrimination, the report endorsed the concepts of affirmative action and employment equity. These matters, and their policy and practical implications, will be addressed more fully in the next chapter.

8.5.4 The Productivity Improvement Program

In its last years the Trudeau government launched an initiative to address some of the accountability and management problems highlighted in the Lambert Report. More recent reports of the auditor general also had directed attention to "undue red tape" and bureaucratic procedures that tended to hamper, rather than enhance, the efficient and effective delivery of government programs. Through the Productivity Improvement Program (Inwood, 2004: 310-11), the Treasury Board was assigned the task of investigating how central agencies imposed accountability controls on departments; how such controls could be streamlined; and the degree to which bureaucratic rules and regulations could be rewritten, revamped, reduced, or removed altogether to improve government productivity. Inwood notes, however, that this initiative was short-lived, dying with the Liberal governments of Pierre Trudeau and John Turner. The newly elected Progressive Conservative government of Brian Mulroney launched a number of its own projects to deal with management reform.

8.5.5 The Ministerial Task Force on Program Review

The first in a variety of management reform undertakings by the Mulroney government was the Ministerial Task Force on Program Review (Inwood, 2004: 310-11). This Program Review initiative was an abject failure in comparison to its namesake a decade later. In 1984, Prime Minister Mulroney established this task force under the leadership of Deputy Prime Minister Eric Nielson. The goal of this group, comprising four of the most senior members of the Mulroney government, was to review, assess, and reduce government expenditure by cutting "red tape," streamlining organizations, eliminating unnecessary bureaucratic procedures, and introducing private sector business practices into the running of government departments and agencies. The results, as Inwood highlighted, were disappointing to those who expected the government to make deep cuts to programs and personnel. Following the work of 19 study teams, whose members came from both the public and private sectors, by 1986 the Nielson Task Force had identified only $500 million in budgetary savings to be gained through the elimination of minor programs while making the simple recommendation that the government should initiate a policy of "contracting-out" for government services (Inwood, 2004). In reality, all departments consulted by the task force groups vigorously defended their current program activities and levels of expenditures, and the task force itself had neither the power, nor inclination, nor support from the prime minister himself to push for major cutbacks to program spending. The Mulroney government was slowly coming to realize that reforming the public service would not be as easy a task as it had first anticipated.

8.5.6 Increased Ministerial Authority and Accountability

In 1986, the Mulroney government launched its second public service reform initiative, entitled Increased Ministerial Authority and Accountability (IMAA) (Inwood, 2004). This initiative, which had some limited success, was a two-pronged policy undertaking sponsored by the Treasury Board and designed to promote flexibility in departmental operations, reduce bureaucratic reporting requirements to the Treasury Board, and generally to simplify the policy-making process. The first component of the IMAA undertaking was a modest reform to the operational control procedures of the Treasury Board. It gave line departments greater autonomy in sponsoring conferences, letting out competitive contracts, classifying departmental positions other than those in the executive category, and reducing the number of departmental reports required to be filed with the Treasury Board. As part of this increased departmental autonomy, the government also agreed to enable departments to carry forward into the next fiscal year up to 5 per cent of their capital budgets.

The second part of IMAA involved the negotiation of Memoranda of Understanding (MOUs) between particular departments and agencies and the Treasury Board. These MOUs outlined the department's increased authority and range of operation free from direct Treasury Board oversight while also noting specific accountability requirements to be met by departments and Crown agencies. The MOU specified objective program service targets and set performance measurements for the evaluation of the degree to which departments or agencies had fulfilled established goals. As an incentive for departments and agencies entering into such MOUs, Treasury Board gave the commitment that should any participating organization realize financial savings as a result of IMAA activity, it would be free to keep such monies for future program use (Savoie, 1999).

Despite the supposed benefit of IMAA, this initiative was also short-lived. Savoie writes that few departments ever signed a MOU and that those that did quickly came to regret the decision due to the disconnect between the amount of paperwork required to produce a MOU and the limited tangible benefits from engaging in the process (Savoie, 1999: 208-09).

The limited success of IMAA in reducing some centralized controls over line departments could not mask the reality that these departments were still subject to substantial oversight and direction by central agencies. These agencies—the guardians—still insisted on defending their core accountability powers over line departments—the spenders—and the concept of "letting the managers manage," though a noble principle to department managers, was one that had to be married to the other equally noble principles of government accountability and centralized direction and control of broad departmental policies and programs undertaken in the name of the government.

8.5.7   PS2000

The third and last of the Mulroney government's attempts at major organizational reform was **PS2000**, designed to establish a reinvigorated public service by the turn of the century. PS2000 was launched in 1989 by the prime minister and Paul Tellier, his Clerk of the Privy Council and Secretary to Cabinet. Ten task forces were established, each headed by a deputy minister and each mandated to study a particular component of the public service and to develop ways and means to "simplify personnel policies, to loosen central agency controls and increase managerial freedom of department managers, and to increase efficiency and program delivery" (Inwood, 2004: 312). The task of PS2000 was sweeping in its scope and vision. In Inwood's words:

> It was in PS2000 that the suggestion was found that each department should produce that '90s business-school contrivance, the

mission statement. Managers would delineate specific service-oriented goals, as well as reflect notions of participatory management. PS2000 called for department managers to consult broadly not only with their own employees but also with citizens, to establish service standards and a more service-oriented culture. And organizational reform was achieved by flattening structures so that no more than three executive levels existed under each deputy minister.... The goal here was to improve communication and to empower managers. Furthermore, it was suggested that the number of categories and levels within groups be reduced to simplify both personnel matters and decision-making procedures. Finally, the government decided to reinforce the importance of new organizational models of service delivery, called Special Operating Agencies (SOA), which had been introduced earlier by the Treasury Board. (Inwood, 2004: 312)

As with its predecessors, however, PS2000 never fulfilled the visions of its creators. Its call for greater decentralization of decision-making, to "let the managers manage," caused in-fighting between central agencies and departments as well as between central agencies themselves. The Treasury Board was especially resistant to the grand nature of the PS2000 reform proposals. Line managers also came to distrust the sincerity of the call for greater participatory management and the move to "empower" all public servants as a means to greater program effectiveness. Though these concepts had entered into the literature of management reform in the 1980s and early 1990s, one might have thought any serious attempt to introduce into the Public Service of Canada such systems as participatory management, democratized administration, and the decentralization of decision-making through the empowerment of junior managers and line staff would meet with many theoretical and practical problems. As, indeed, it did. On the theoretical side, the long-standing debate between operational departmental autonomy and relative managerial independence to engage in the best forms of action as understood by such management and their staff still ran counter to the principle of centralized control of departments and the imposition and maintenance of strict accountability processes over departments and Crown agencies. Within this worldview, the concepts of participatory management and the democratization of decision-making represented an abdication of responsibility on behalf of guardians, while jeopardizing the ability of any government and its senior bureaucratic and political leadership to control and direct the actions of its many parts.

As these theoretical debates were flourishing, the operational implementation of PS2000 ran into a series of practical nightmares for its proponents. Following months of task force consultations with line managers and staff, the release of its recommendations came at the same time as the Mulroney government declared a public service wage freeze and a unilateral reduction in its management ranks by 10 per cent (Savoie, 1999: 212). Notwithstanding the participatory rhetoric of PS2000, as the government confronted its growing financial management crisis and the problem of the deficit and debt, it turned to what it considered to be the most effective means of quickly and seriously addressing the problem through a top-down command approach to crisis management. The procedure followed by the government here, with its lack of consultation with affected management and staff, was an object of criticism by those affected second only to the actual freeze and layoffs themselves.

The final nail in the PS2000 coffin was the 1991 Al-Mashat affair. As the project was ongoing, stressing the need for managers to be innovative, creative, and not averse to taking risks, the media announced that senior officials in the departments of External Affairs and Immigration had allowed Al-Mashat, Iraq's ambassador to the United States and principal spokesman during the Gulf War, to enter Canada on a landed immigrant visa. Although the decision was perfectly legal, it elicited much hostile media and opposition party criticism. Rather than accept ministerial responsibility for the decision, however, the three central political actors in the story—Joe Clark, Barbara McDougall, and Brian Mulroney himself—all disavowed the action of their senior staff, attacked the decision, and blamed senior bureaucratic incompetence for the action. This ministerial refusal to accept responsibility and to publicly attack public officials for their actions sent a chill throughout the senior ranks of the Public Service of Canada. In an assessment of the Al-Mashat affair and its implications for PS2000, Gene Swimmer observed:

> Senior executives now heard a mixed message from the government: We want you to take risks, we expect you to make mistakes sometimes; but if you screw up, we may hang you out to dry publicly. The refusal of ministers Joe Clark and Barbara McDougall to take responsibility in the traditional manner for departmental errors reinforced public service caution and scepticism about taking risks. (Swimmer, 1994: 172)

By 1992, PS2000 was effectively dead. What began as an ambitious attempt to transform the Public Service of Canada fundamentally quickly descended to a project of, at best, some noble aspirations that had run up against the grinding realities of profound theoretical differences between the proper relationships of departments with central agencies, the appropriate manner by which accountability can and should be exercised in government, the manner by which senior bureaucratic and political leaderships should and will relate to subordinates, and the practical realities of how governments will actually make decisions in the "real world" of power politics. With the demise of PS2000, the Mulroney government's efforts at management renewal also came to an end.

8.5.8   Program Review and La Relève

For those working within the federal public service in the 1990s, Program Review was the most significant and most painful of any federal reform initiative of the past quarter-century. Apart from major cutbacks to most departmental budgets, as recounted in Chapter 7, Program Review also resulted in an overall employment decrease for the Public Service of Canada of 39,305 positions, or 17.4 per cent. This reduction in personnel over the four years from 1995 to 1999 was dramatic, yet it was not the only major change affecting those employed in the public service. For most of the past decade public servants experienced unilaterally imposed pay freezes, wage rollbacks, and the suspension of collective bargaining (see Chapter 9), as well as severe limitations on all new hirings for the public service. The cumulative result of all such impacts, which some would call the "bashing" and "battering" of the public service (Inwood, 2004: 307), was the development of a "quiet crisis" within public service ranks.

The term "quiet crisis" came from none other than Jocelyne Bourgon, Clerk of the Privy Council and Secretary to Cabinet, in her 1997 report to the prime minister on the Public Service of Canada (Canada, 1997a: 39, 44). In explaining the genesis of this problem at the heart of the government's system of personnel management, she affirmed a number of causes: "the loss of talent through many years of downsizing; a demographic skew after years of limited recruitment; constant criticism of the public sector which seriously affected morale; many years of pay freezes; and increasing interest by the private sector in acquiring the skills of public servants. It was also evident that the corrective action necessary to offset these pressures had not been taken" (Canada, 1997a: 42-44). In her assessment of the "malaise" facing the public service, she confronted some disturbing truths:

The problem is showing up in various forms.

- After years of downsizing, some public servants, for the first time, are questioning their career choice.
- Others are not convinced that their skills and abilities are being used effectively.
- Still others, after an exemplary career, would not advise their children to follow in their footsteps.
- Some students would not consider a career in the Public Service if presented with other options (Canada, 1997a).

A number of these points bear reiteration. As Bourgon argued, the public service, at all ranks, is aging at a remarkable and dangerous rate, the dual results of the demographic reality of the babyboomer generation nearing retirement age and the intake of younger staff over the past two decades being minimal at best. She explicitly warned the prime minister that "over 30 per cent of the current executive group will be in a position to retire by the year 2000, and this will rise to 70 per cent by 2005. A similar pattern exists in some of the professional and scientific categories" (Canada 1997a: ch. 6). She continued her analysis of the problems facing the public service by stressing that those who remain in government service, both executives and staff, have faced the depressing prospects of stunted career paths and limited opportunities for professional growth. "Mobility, particularly interdepartmental mobility," she argued, "is at an all-time low despite the fact that the changing nature of service delivery and policy issues requires managers and policy analysts to acquire a broad diversity of knowledge and experience. As a result, excellent employees have not been given the chance to prepare adequately for future needs." And the problem here, she maintained, is that as existing personnel leave the public service through retirement, especially through early retirement or severance packages, the government is then faced with the unpleasant reality that there are actually insufficient numbers of younger, well-trained, and experienced managers and staff persons to assume their places. The result is an organization that does not fully possess the "human capital," in terms of experience, training, and intelligence, to adequately meet the increasing policy and program challenges that it is called upon to address. "To perform well," Bourgon wrote, "the public service must constantly retain, motivate, and attract a corps of talented and dedicated public servants. There are indications that this could be the most difficult challenge that the Public Service of Canada will face over the coming years" (Canada, 1997a).

The most senior leadership within the federal government clearly accepted this message. Recruitment and staff renewal became top priorities, the PCO being given a lead role in this policy dynamic. In seeking to address the "quiet crisis," a major reform initiative known as **La Relève** was launched. This name, which is French for "relief and reawakening" is also an acronym for Leadership, Action, Renewal, Energy, Learning, Expertise, Values, and Experience. The La Relève exercise, much like other reform undertakings before it, involved a broad series of consultations and group analyses, this time led by the PCO. It aimed to find means by which the public service could be improved, morale enhanced, program efficiency and effectiveness furthered, the relationship between staff and management bettered (especially through the use of more participatory and democratic forms of organizational decision-making), and greater leadership skills among public service managers developed (Canada, 1997b).

Through the work of La Relève, one can observe two broad streams of action:

1. *A stress on renewal, recruitment, retraining, and improved remuneration across the federal public service.* Faced with the prospect of an aging workforce increasingly depleted by retirement and severance policies, the federal government has now endorsed a number of special programs to bring new, younger people into the public service and to train and improve the managerial skills of junior executives already in the service. The PSC and the Treasury Board have established policies to recruit university graduates and professionals with specialized skills to enter the public service and begin accelerated programs of management development. In turn, the PCO and the CSPS have initiated a number of specialized programs for those within the public service, such as the Management Trainee Program, the Accelerated Executive Development Program, and the Career Assignment Program. All these initiatives are designed to bring new people into the public service, especially into its junior management ranks; to train them in the broad array of policy and program skills required by the public service; and to give them valuable work experience as they begin to pursue careers in the public service. As a part of these broad renewal initiatives, moreover, the government has made a commitment to improve the salary levels of all public servants. Following years of pay freezes and wage roll-backs, the Treasury Board has been authorized to engage in renewed collective bargaining with unionized staff to address demands for pay increases; it has also been mandated the task of improving executive salary scales both as a

means to adequately remunerate senior staff and to help the public service retain officials who are being actively recruited by the private sector.

2. A focus on senior executive training and promotion. In 1998, as part of the La Relève exercise, the PCO established the "Leadership Network," in part to support the "collective management of assistant deputy ministers." This initiative marked a significant change in the manner by which deputy ministers were appointed, trained, and promoted to the levels of assistant, associate, or full deputy minister. Whereas in the past assistant deputy ministers had been appointed to a given "position" within a given department, now, as part of the Leadership Network approach, such persons were first appointed to the "level" of assistant deputy minister and then assigned to a department. The formal appointment, however, is to the level, not to the department position. In defending this action, the PCO stressed the need for a broad array of senior managers at the assistant deputy minister level who are generalists in the field of management, who have a diversified work experience, who are capable of engaging in horizontal career paths as they move across departments, and who are capable and interested in developing and furthering a government-wide "corporate" approach to the work of the public service. This is all in contrast to the more traditional view of deputy ministers as senior department executives more narrowly tied into the work and mindset of a particular department, its needs, and its organizational and policy ethos. In other words, an organizational change in the nature of the senior appointment process, which seems innocuous at first appearance, has deep implications for all power relations between departments and central agencies. This reform marked a significant change in the role of assistant deputy ministers, how they perceive themselves, and how they are perceived by other senior actors in the system. As Savoie (1999: 231) explained this reform, these officials are now considered to be, first and foremost, policy and program generalists whose primary strategic vision is to be centred on the government overall, not any given department.

It is interesting to note, however, that by 2004, this approach of appointment to rank rather than to position had been effectively discontinued by Clerk of the Privy Council Alex Himmelfarb. In what many Ottawa insiders stress as a victory for the traditional assistant deputy minister appointment process and the reassertion of the relative autonomy of individual departments and their senior executives, the appointment process into the ranks of senior management has reverted to appointment to position, a method placing greater power and influence into the hands of senior departmental management when the time comes for them to decide who they want as a new assistant deputy minister for their department.

8.5.9   The Public Service Modernization Act

In November 2003 the latest federal human resources reform initiative was launched with the passing of the **Public Service Modernization Act** (PSMA). The policies and programs deriving from this act, according to senior officials in the TBS represent "The most significant reform in public service human resources management in more than 35 years. The changes brought about by this legislation will transform the way the government hires, manages and supports the men and women who make up the public service" (Canada, 2005).

The PSMA has four main goals:

- To modernize staffing through a new Public Service Employment Act
- To foster collaborative labour management relations through a new Public Service Labour Relations Act
- To clarify roles and strengthen accountability for deputy heads and their managers
- To Provide a more integrated approach to learning development for employees through the formation of the new Canada School of Public Service (Canada, 2005).

The PSMA also vests leading responsibility for the development and management of federal human resources policy and programming into the hands of the newly created **Public Service Human Resources Management Agency of Canada** (PSHRMAC). The PSHRMAC (more commonly referred to by Ottawa insiders as "pushermac") is a subagency of the TBS, with its staff being mandated the task of providing advice and assistance to all departments, agencies, boards, and commissions as they develop their new approaches to human resources management. In fulfilling this role, the PSHRMAC is also called upon to collaborate closely with the TBS, the PCO, the PSC, and the CSPS in the development and implementation of human resources policy.

The PSMA seeks to make staffing decisions easier and more timely for departments by devolving upon deputy heads of departments greater flexibility in hiring by giving them the ability to have greater control over setting job requirements, running job ads, and assessing merit based upon the principle of hiring "qualified" candidates for a job rather than having to struggle to find "the best" candidate for a job. This shift in focus with respect to the application of the merit principle to the actual practice of hiring in the real world of the public service hearkens back to the discussion found earlier in section 8.4 above. In all such hiring activities, however, the human resources management actions taken by senior departmental officials must be based upon departmental human resources plans which have been approved by the PSC and have been reviewed by the PSHRMAC. All departments are thus called upon to develop fairly extensive long-term human resource development plans highlighting the types of personnel they need; how they will seek to attain, train, and develop such personnel; and how they will apply and promote the merit principle in their human resource decision-making.

Staff training is also an important consideration in this new human resources regime, with the CSPS as the key institution providing centralized and corporate-wide training to all public servants. The CSPS offers a wide variety of courses to a wide variety of different types of public servants from newly hired personnel through to senior managers and deputy heads. Its curriculum shifts from general background information on government structures, the basics of financial management, human resources management, information technology management, and privacy issues to advanced courses, geared to senior management, devoted to such matters as leadership, policy development, and ethics and accountability.

As the federal government works to implement the policies and programs associated with the PSMA, a number of issues bear watching. How well are the public service unions involved in the decision-making processes? A number of the unions have been highly critical of the concept of giving management greater "flexibility" in hiring, hinting that this might be a means for management to seek to tilt the hiring process more to their favour at the expense of procedural fairness for all employees. We will look at this issue more closely in the next chapter. There may also be concern at senior levels as to whether too much authority for the management of human resources has now been delegated back down to departmental level. The concern is that a desire for greater departmental "flexibility" may harm the concept of overall system-wide consistency in the application of the merit principle as well as of overall centralized leadership of human resources policy and human resources renewal throughout the federal government. Once again we see here the ongoing tension between centralization and decentralization of decision-making authority within any large and complex bureaucracy.

8.6 Human Resources Reform in Retrospect

Of all the human resources reform initiatives reviewed in the previous pages, it is instructive to note that the La Relève exercise has had and likely will continue to have the greatest impact on the Public Service of Canada. There is a renewed commitment within the government to bring new people into the public service, to bolster public service employment, to enhance employment opportunities within government, and to promote the management corps of the public service, albeit with a much more centralized focus. In this sense, the downsizing and cutbacks of the 1990s are over, and the government is seeking to repair some of the damage that it inflicted upon itself in these and earlier years. It is important, however, to bear in mind Inwood's assessment of this general situation. The turnaround in the attitude and policy of the federal government is contingent on its financial management reforms, the elimination of the deficit, and the new era of budgetary surpluses. For the first time in nearly two decades, senior managers within the public service can begin to plan the future of personnel policy without having to think about funding restrictions, service reductions, and the need for employee downsizing. Public service reform is very much connected to the fiscal capacity of the government and its willingness to devote public monies to these ends (Inwood, 2004: 297-98).

In looking at the broader history of public service reform attempts over the past quarter-century, however, a cautionary note must be sounded. Indeed, anyone viewing the plethora of initiatives, reports, and "new" undertakings to renew, revitalize, rejuvenate, and reform the public service over these years, with special emphasis being placed on the elimination of "red tape" and unnecessary bureaucratic procedures and with the desire to make the public service more efficient, effective, responsive, participatory, or managerially sound must be taken aback by the record of these attempts. "There has not been one reform effort introduced in recent years that has lived up to expectations" (Savoie, 1999: 232). Savoie's conclusion is sobering and illustrative of a number of important, general conclusions. One is the difficulty of engaging in rationalistic reform of the personnel system. Just as one can document the trials and tribulations of rationalism with respect to financial management policy, as in Chapter 7, so too can the problems inherent in attempting to engage in wholesale rationalistic reforms to the personnel system be documented. Problems of comprehension, definition, agreement on policy ends, direction, the tension between departmental managerial autonomy and centralized governmental control, sincerity, trust, and the realities of managerial and political power relations can all impede the best-laid plans of rationalist policy analysts. Calls to "let the managers manage" will always have an appeal to those seeking to reform the process of government and department administration, yet the claim for greater managerial autonomy as a stepping stone to greater government efficiency and effectiveness will always be met by the equally important claim for government accountability and centralized control. Those in central agencies and in the centre of government will always stress the need for the government, overall, to retain a firm grip on the work of departments and Crown agencies so as to ensure that their actions are consistent with general government policies and priorities and that departmental undertakings are always subject to the political will of the elected cabinet. The tension between these competing visions of management and government are inherent in the very nature of a government that blends a wide array of line departments and Crown agencies with centralized forms of policy and program development and control. Likewise, calls for greater participatory management and democratization of decision-making by strengthening liaison between senior management and staff will remain more rhetoric than reality, given the nature of power relations in any government bureaucracy. While the policy aim resonates well with liberal democratic principles of public involvement in decision-making, it also runs counter to the bureaucratic principles of effective and responsible decision-making vested in the hands of central authorities and the political executive, which is, in turn, responsible to Parliament for the exercise of government power.

This is not to say, however, that no progress can be made in altering and reforming the methods and substance of personnel management or the operational relationships between departments and central agencies. We have seen some significant changes and improvements in personnel administration over these years as the La Relève initiative has demonstrated and as the next chapter will highlight. Notice, however, that all these changes and reforms are much more easily understood as emerging from an incrementalist rather than a rationalist system of management development. This finding is not meant to belittle the impact of rationalist initiatives in seeking profound changes and reforms to the system of personnel management. As the record indicates, every government over the past quarter-century has sought to rationalize and improve the nature and working of the public service and its huge complement of employees. Every government has sought to enhance the efficiency and effectiveness of its operations, and many have made efforts to consciously improve the ability of the public service to represent Canadians, to be responsive to the needs and interests of particular social groups, to be fair and equitable in its dealings with minority groups, and to be fair and just in its relationship with its own employees. In the next chapter we will review the history of these initiatives towards public service representativeness and equity.

Key Terms

Canada School of Public Service (CSPS): The CSPS is the formal centralized educational agency of the federal public service designed to provide employee training and management development courses for public servants. Formerly known as the Canadian Centre for Management Development, the CSPS plays an important role in management renewal policy.

human resources planning: That aspect of management devoted to the recruitment, training, retention, mobilization, and promotion of personnel. Good human resources planning is essential to the development of an effective, competent, and successful public service.

La Relève: A human resources reform policy developed in 1997 to address the perceived "quiet crisis" confronting the federal public service following the Program Review of the mid-1990s. La Relève sought to rejuvenate the federal public service by attracting younger Canadians to enter the public service while also enhancing management training and the centralization of senior executive training within the federal public service.

merit principle: The concept and practice that all decision-making respecting the hiring, training, promotion, demotion, and firing of public servants should be undertaken strictly according to objective assessments of competence usually related to education and demonstrated successful job experience rather than to subjective assessments of a person's political affiliations or personal connections. The merit principle became the dominant organizing principle of public service human resource policy from the time of the First World War to the present.

PS2000: A human resources reform policy launched by the Mulroney government designed to reinvigorate the federal public service by the turn of the last century. PS2000 was a highly rationalistic approach designed to bring the human resource planning of the federal public service more into line with similar practices found in the private sector.

political patronage: The concept and practice that decision-making respecting the hiring, training, promotion, demotion, and firing of public servants should be undertaken according to subjective assessments of a person's political affiliations or personal connections rather than the person's demonstrated competence to do the job. The political patronage system dominated federal human resource policy from Confederation to the First World War.

Public Service Commission (PSC): The key agency responsible for all hiring, promotion, lateral transfer, demotion, and dismissal from the federal public service.

The PSC, created in 1967, was originally called the Civil Service Commission, which was established in 1918 with the mandate to promote and protect the merit principle in all human resource decision-making within the federal public service.

Public Service Modernization Act (PSMA): Passed in 2003, the Public Service Modernization Act marks the federal government's latest human resources policy initiative. The PSMA is designed to promote more efficient staffing decision-making, to streamline public service labour relations, to improve accountability, and to promote greater management training and development through the work of the CSPS.

Public Service Human Resources Management Agency of Canada (PSHRMAC): Known as "Pushermac," the PSHRMAC was established by the PSMA as the key federal agency with responsibility for human resources development policy in the federal public service. The PSHRMAC falls within the overall jurisdiction of the TBS.

References and Suggested Reading

Adamson, Agar, and Ian Stewart. 1996. "Party Politics in the Not So Mysterious East." In Hugh G. Thorburn, ed., *Party Politics in Canada*. 7th ed. Scarborough, ON: Prentice-Hall Canada. 514-33.

Adie, Robert F., and Paul G. Thomas. 1987. *Canadian Public Administration: Problematical Perspectives*. 2nd ed. Scarborough, ON: Prentice-Hall Canada.

Cameron, Stevie, 1995. *On The Take: Crime, Corruption and Greed in the Mulroney Years*. Toronto: Seal Books.

Canada. 1962. Royal Commission on Government Organization. *Report*. 5 vols. Ottawa: Queen's Printer.

Canada. 1979a. Royal Commission on Financial Management and Accountability. *Final Report*. Ottawa: Supply and Services.

Canada. 1979b. *Report of the Special Committee on the Review of Personnel Management and the Merit Principle*. Ottawa: Supply and Services.

Canada. 1997a. *Fourth Annual Report to the Prime Minister on the Public Service of Canada*. Ottawa: Privy Council Office.

Canada. 1997b. *La Relève: A Commitment to Action*. Ottawa: Privy Council Office.

Canada. 1998. *First Progress Report on La Relève: A Commitment to Action*. Ottawa: La Relève Task Force.

Canada. 2005. *Public Service Management Act General Overview*. Ottawa: Public Service Human Resources Management Agency of Canada.

Canada, Treasury Board of Canada. 2003. *Annual Report on Official Languages, 2002-03*. Ottawa: Supply and Services.

Drabek, Stan. 1995. "The Federal Public Service: Organizational Structure and Personnel Administration." In Robert M. Krause and R.H. Wagenberg, eds., *Introductory Readings in Canadian Government and Politics*. 2nd ed. Toronto: Copp Clark.

Dyck, Rand. 1996a. *Canadian Politics: Critical Approaches*. 2nd ed. Toronto: Nelson.

—. 1996b. *Provincial Politics in Canada: Towards the Turn of the Century*. 3rd ed. Scarborough, ON: Prentice-Hall Allyn and Bacon Canada.

Howe, R. Brian, and David Johnson. 2000. *Restraining Equality: Human Rights Commissions in Canada*. Toronto: University of Toronto Press.

Inwood, Gregory J. 2004. *Understanding Canadian Public Administration: An Introduction to Theory and Practice*. 2nd ed. Scarborough, ON: Prentice-Hall Allyn and Bacon Canada.

Jackson, Robert J., and Doreen Jackson. 1998. *Politics in Canada: Culture, Institutions, Behaviour and Public Policy*. 4th ed. Scarborough, ON: Prentice-Hall Allyn and Bacon Canada.

Kernaghan, Kenneth, and David Siegel. 1999. *Public Administration in Canada: A Text*. 4th ed. Toronto: Nelson.

McRoberts, Kenneth. 1993. *Quebec: Social Change and Political Crisis*. 3rd ed. Toronto: McClelland and Stewart.

Savoie, Donald J. 1999. *Governing from the Centre: The Concentration of Power in Canadian Politics*. Toronto: University of Toronto Press.

Simpson, Jeffrey. 1988. *Spoils of Power: The Politics of Patronage*. Toronto: Collins Publishers.

Swimmer, Gene, *et al.* 1994. "Public Service 2000: Dead or Alive?" In Susan Philips, ed., *How Ottawa Spends 1994-95*. Ottawa: Carleton University Press.

Related Web Sites

PUBLIC SERVICE COMMISSION OF CANADA
   <http://www.psc-cfp.gc.ca>

PUBLIC SERVICE HUMAN RESOURCES MANAGEMENT AGENCY OF CANADA
   <http://www.hrma-agrh.gc.ca>

CANADA SCHOOL OF PUBLIC SERVICE
   <http://www.myschool-monecole.gc.ca>

THE LEADERSHIP NETWORK
   <http://www.hrma-agrh.gc.ca/leadership/>

TREASURY BOARD SECRETARIAT
   <http://www.tbs-sct.gc.ca>

CHAPTER 9
The Representative and Equitable Public Service

The previous chapter has provided a general overview of the federal human resources management system, its origin, the problematic aspects of patronage, the development and nature of the merit system, and some of the major initiatives in human resources management reform over the past quarter-century. This chapter directs attention to a number of more specific yet controversial aspects of the human resources system within the Public Service of Canada. If the first great administrative reform to modernize human resources management within the federal government was the push for the merit principle, the second has been the drive for a public service that is generally representative of the society it serves and equitable in its relationships to citizens and employees. While the objective of entrenching the merit principle within the federal public service has ceased to be a point of debate, the aim of creating a representative and equitable bureaucracy has always tended to elicit sharp divisions of opinion. Though most Canadians will not quarrel with the principle that the modern federal government, and indeed all provincial governments, should be representative of the general society it serves and should be equitable in its dealings with those around it and within it, many will debate the merits and demerits of particular policy means chosen by governments to reach these ends. Such substantive policy initiatives as official bilingualism, multiculturalism, the recognition and promotion of human rights, **employment equity** policy, public service unionization, **collective bargaining**, and the right of public servants to strike have been matters of great debate, with some of these issues remaining controversial to the present time.

As the federal government has moved to develop policies for these matters, increasing complexity in human resources management and the expectations placed on administrators have been a result. The federal human resources management system is complicated in the extreme; it comprises many major policies and programs, principles, and values, only one of which, though a dominant one, is the merit principle. Since the 1960s, the merit system has been augmented by other human resources-related policy initiatives—bilingualism, anti-discrimination provisions and human rights promotion, employment equity, and collective bargaining—all of which were designed, in one fashion or another, to enhance either the **representativeness or equitable nature of the federal public service**. Each of these initiatives emerged from a distinct context, each was a response to real and deep problems in government, each represented a government commitment to human resources policy reform, and each has remained a major element of the human resources system of the federal government. The cumulative effect of these initiatives is a multifaceted—and operationally cumbersome—system of human resources management. The most basic of personnel functions—the hiring, promotion, demotion, and dismissal of staff—and such management routines as remuneration, discipline, and normal work procedures are far more complicated than any such system found in the private sector. All decisions affecting the organization and management of staff must comply with a multitude of policies and principles, which, in theory, ensure that the federal public service is staffed not only upon merit but on representativeness and equity. The breadth of essential human resource policies not only makes the federal human resources system one that is often difficult to comprehend, but one that is open to conflict during the application of its principles and prescriptions. Does the policy of employment equity vitiate the merit principle? Does public service collective bargaining and the right to strike promote equity and fairness in personnel relations or threaten merit and the provision of service to the public? Does the principle of a representative public service run counter to the principle of an efficient public service? Indeed, is the very concept of a representative public service logical to the bureaucratic setting, let alone practicable? To understand the full nature of the federal human resources system, one must delve into the major personnel policies that persist alongside the merit principle and study their application and interrelationships. We begin this review with an archetypal Canadian issue, the question of French-English representation and tensions around French-Canadian attitudes to and concerns about the federal public service.

9.1   Bilingualism and Biculturalism

From Confederation through the 1960s the composition of the federal public service was overwhelmingly English Canadian and the common language of work in Ottawa was English. As Jean Chrétien mentioned in his autobiography (Chrétien, 1986: 16-18), the Ottawa of the early 1960s was far from a national capital in which French Canadians could feel at home. Though francophones comprised roughly 25 per cent of the total population, they represented only some 12 per cent of the members of the federal public service. They were even more poorly represented in senior management ranks; immediately following the Second World War, for example, the number of francophone deputy ministers was precisely zero (Kernaghan and Siegel, 1999: 584-85). Such underrepresentation was not perceived as a national problem until the Quiet Revolution of the 1960s and the resurgence of French-Canadian nationalism. During these years the French-Canadian media and intelligentsia came increasingly to criticize the discriminatory environment faced by French Canadians within the federal public service, arguing that it could not hope to serve the interests of French Canadians if it did not represent them. At this time, the Public Service of Canada was viewed by most French Canadians as a foreign entity, staffed primarily by, and essentially serving and promoting the interests of, English Canadians; in short, it was an organization in which few French Canadians could or would want to build a career.

The criticism of the unrepresentativeness of the federal public service cut deeply against the liberal vision of the modern state, especially at this time of growing French-Canadian nationalism and cultural reawakening. According to critics of the status quo, the state should represent all major groups and social interests within society, and the federal public service should broadly represent the society it serves. Thus, if roughly one-quarter of the Canadian population is francophone, then roughly one-quarter of the workforce of the federal public service, across all occupational levels, should also be francophone. Anything less than this would not only be discriminatory but would suggest that the federal government could not adequately understand the needs and interests of French Canadians and could not effectively develop and administer policies and programs for them. The Glassco Royal Commission on Government Organization, undertaken in the early 1960s, went far in endorsing this way of thinking, recognizing that francophones were greatly underrepresented in the federal public service and that, in order to promote cultural representativeness, "a career at the centre of government should be as attractive and congenial to French-speaking as to English-speaking Canadians" (Canada, 1962: 29).

By the mid-1960s the Liberal government of Lester Pearson had committed itself to the policy of promoting **bilingualism and biculturalism** across the country generally and within the public service in particular. As the Royal Commission on Bilingualism and Biculturalism was studying these concepts and planning ways by which the federal government could be more inclusive of French Canadians, Pearson stated, in 1966, that "the linguistic and cultural values of the English-speaking and French-speaking Canadians will be reflected through civil service recruitment and training" (Canada, 1966: 3915). In inheriting and defending this policy, Prime Minister Pierre Trudeau was to pronounce that "the atmosphere of the public service should represent the linguistic and cultural duality of Canadian society, and ... Canadians whose mother tongue is French should be adequately represented in the public service—both in terms of numbers and in levels of responsibility" (Canada, 1970: 84-87). Bilingualism and biculturalism were fully entrenched into the federal public service by the **Official Languages Act, 1969** and the Official Languages Program of the Treasury Board, which was developed the same year. These initiatives stipulated

- that the federal government was committed to operating in both official languages;
- that, when dealing with federal government offices, citizens had the right to be served in either official language;
- that public servants should be able to work in the official language of their choice; and
- that the federal public service should become broadly representative of Canada's cultural and linguistic identity.

Since 1969, these goals have largely been met. Indeed, as of 1982, official federal bilingualism has been constitutionally entrenched in the Charter of Rights and Freedoms. Federal departments and agencies pride themselves on their ability to provide services in both official languages, and the government, generally, through active policies of francophone recruitment, has been able to bring the level of francophone representation in the public service up to its proportion of the overall national population. Box 9.1 highlights the linguistic distribution of federal public service employment between 1978 and 2003. Over this period, the proportion of anglophones in the Public Service of Canada declined from 75 per cent in 1978 to 69 per cent as of 2003, while the corresponding proportion of francophones in the government increased from 25 to 31 per cent. These numbers reveal that francophones are actually *overrepresented* in the federal government by

BOX 9.1

Participation of Anglophones and Francophones in the Public Service by Region

The terms "Anglophones" and "Francophones" refer to employees in terms of their first official language. The first official language is the language declared by employees as the one with which they have a primary personal identification (that is, the official language in which they are generally most proficient).

Region	1978		1984		2002		2003	
	Anglo.	Franco.	Anglo.	Franco.	Anglo.	Franco.	Anglo.	Franco.
Canada and Outside Canada	75%	25%	72%	28%	69%	31%	69%	31%
Total		211,885		227,942		159,948		163,287
Western provinces and Northern Canada	99%	1%	98%	2%	98%	2%	98%	2%
Total		49,395		52,651		35,087		35,612
Ontario (excluding NCR)	97%	3%	95%	5%	95%	5%	95%	5%
Total		34,524		36,673		20,295		20,366
National Capital Region	68%	32%	64%	36%	59%	41%	59%	41%
Total		70,340		75,427		64,564		67,008
Quebec (excluding NCR)	8%	92%	6%	94%	8%*	92%	8%*	92%
Total		29,922		32,114		20,136		20,323
New Brunswick	84%	16%	73%	27%	62%	38%	61%	39%
Total		6,763		7,698		5,386		5,417
Other Atlantic provinces	98%	2%	96%	4%	95%	5%	96%	4%
Total		19,212		21,802		13,186		13,334
Outside Canada	76%	24%	74%	26%	71%	29%	69%	31%
Total		1,729		1,577		1,294		1,227

* On March 31, 2003, the participation of Anglophones in Quebec (excluding the NCR) stood at 1,550 employees compared to 1,512 the previous year. This figure is different from that on page 22 because it has been rounded off.

Source: Canada, Treasury Board of Canada, 2003a: 42.

roughly eight percentage points. (As of the 2001 census, French Canadians accounted for 22.9 per cent of the Canadian population; CCMD, 2003.) This overrepresentation is usually explained by the greater degree of bilingualism held by French Canadians compared to their English-Canadian compatriots, meaning that French Canadians can more effectively compete for public service positions that require bilingual language competency. It is interesting to note the impact of official bilingualism on the federal public service in both the **National Capital Region** and in New Brunswick, reflecting the strength of the Acadian population in that province and the substantial proportion of francophones that now work in the nation's capital. Ottawa is far different from what it was in the early 1960s, illustrating the type of social changes that can be wrought by the consistent application of policy commitment over time. Also evident from Box 9.1 is the linguistic homogeneity found in Quebec *vis-à-vis* the predominantly English-Canadian provinces. These figures reveal the linguistic divisions in this country, hinting at the "two solitudes."

In looking more closely at the language requirements for positions in the federal public service, Box 9.2 shows the changing linguistic requirements nationwide from 1978 through 2003. What is most noticeable is the steady increase in the proportion of federal positions that are classified as "bilingual." As of 2003, fully 38 per cent of all such positions now require a working facility in both official languages. This figure, however, can be interpreted in two ways. One is to welcome the growing degree of bilingualism within the federal government. The other is to protest that the vast majority of federal positions do not require bilingual skills, but rather are classified either as "English-essential," which accounts for 51 per cent, or "French-essential," which accounts for only 5 per cent. These figures reflect the more unilingual status of federal government services to the public outside of the National Capital Region and New Brunswick.

In light of this finding, though, the information in Box 9.3 bears scrutiny. It highlights language requirements by region, revealing that, as of 2003, fully 63 per cent of all federal positions in the National Capital Region were classified as bilingual. This figure unmistakeably illustrates the importance of bilingual capability within the headquarters of government departments, Crown agencies, and central agencies, strongly suggesting that anyone who wishes to pursue a career in the federal public service and who wishes to rise through the ranks of bureaucratic power would be well advised to become proficient in both official languages. The table also highlights the importance of bilingual positions in both Quebec and New Brunswick and, most notably, the overwhelming importance of bilingual capabilities for

BOX 9.2
Language Requirements of Positions in the Public Service

All positions in the Public Service of Canada are designated as bilingual or unilingual, depending on their specific requirements and according to the following categories:

- bilingual — a position in which all, or part, of the duties must be performed in both English and French;
- English essential — a position in which all the duties must be performed in English;
- French essential — a position in which all the duties must be performed in French; and
- either English or French essential ("either/or") — a position in which all the duties can be performed in English or French.

Year	Bilingual	English essential	French essential	English or French essential	Incomplete records	Total
1978	25%	60%	8%	7%	0%	
	52,300	128,196	17,260	14,129	0	211,885
1984	28%	59%	7%	6%	0%	
	63,163	134,916	16,688	13,175	0	227,942
2002	37%	51%	6%	5%	1%	
	59,790	81,823	8,977	8,380	978	159,948
2003	38%	51%	5%	6%	0%	
	61,896	83,380	8,584	8,766	661	163,287

Source: Canada, Treasury Board of Canada, 2003a: 31.

those employed in the Foreign Service outside Canada. Fully 77 per cent of all federal positions held abroad are classified bilingual. Again, the message is clear. The Foreign Service is essentially a bilingual service, and anyone seriously considering a career in this branch of the federal government should be fluent in both French and English.

The foregoing boxes and the reality they depict reveal that the federal public service has become increasingly bilingual, especially with regard to its operations within the National Capital Region and abroad, as well as in the provinces of Quebec and New Brunswick. In this sense, the policy aims of bilingualism and biculturalism, at least with respect to the federal public service, have largely been fulfilled. The Public Service of Canada has become one in which French Canadians are far from discriminated

BOX 9.3
Language Requirements of Positions in the Public Service by Region

The heading **Unilingual Positions** represents the sum of the three following categories: English essential, French essential, and either English or French essential.

Since all rotational positions abroad, which belong primarily to the Department of Foreign Affairs and International Trade, are identified as unilingual, the language requirements have been determined by the incumbents' linguistic proficiencies rather than by the requirements of the positions.

Region	Bilingual positions	Unilingual positions	Incomplete records	Total
Western provinces and Northern Canada	4% 1,573	96% 34,014	0% 25	35,612
Ontario (excluding NCR)	10% 1,998	90% 18,346	0% 22	20,366
National Capital Region (NCR)	63% 42,281	36% 24,272	1% 455	67,008
Quebec (excluding NCR)	58% 11,805	42% 8,499	0% 19	20,323
New Brunswick	48% 2,612	51% 2,752	1% 53	5,417
Other Atlantic provinces	10% 1,368	89% 11,879	1% 87	13,334
Outside Canada (linguistic capacity)	77% 945	23% 282	0% 0	1,227
Region not specified	0% 0	0% 0	0% 0	0

Source: Canada, Treasury Board of Canada, 2003a: 33.

against and treated as second-class citizens. Rather, over the past three decades, French Canadians have come to be well-represented, even over-represented at times and in certain occupational categories, including the influential management level. The achievement of such representativeness with respect to francophones, however, does elicit some troubling questions about the practice and theory of public service representativeness. Has such representation of French Canadians within the federal public service made the federal government more responsive to the needs and interests of French Canadians since 1969? Has the federal government been better able to develop policies and programs for French Canadians than was hitherto the case? Do French Canadians view the federal government as being more responsive and open to them now than was the case prior to the enactment of official bilingualism policy? And does the relative over-representation of French Canadians within elements of the public service and the stress on official bilingualism cause problems for English Canadians? Are the needs of English Canadians being effectively served by such federal policy? These, of course, are very difficult questions. Any answer is likely to depend on whether the respondent is French Canadian or English Canadian and on his or her views on the broader questions of Québécois nationalism, federalism, the role of the federal government within Quebec, and whether requirements of official bilingualism for federal employment are perceived as an unfair imposition upon those English Canadians who happen to be unilingual.

In thinking about the real practice of official bilingualism in the federal public service, however, it is important for English Canadians to appreciate how many French Canadians working in the government perceive the effectiveness of this policy. In *French to Follow: Revitalizing Official Languages in the Workforce*, a report prepared by the Canadian Centre for Management Development, the authors stress that while the federal public service professes to offer substantial bilingualism in its working environment, the reality is that all too often English dominates the routine life of federal offices due to the limited effective bilingual capabilities of English-Canadian employees; this is even regrettably true of those English Canadians who have undertaken French language training. Common complaints raised by French Canadian employees regarding the effectiveness of official bilingualism in reality are:

- the absence of work tools in the employee's chosen official language, e.g., directives, manuals, internal memos, working papers, training guides, telephone messages;
- the absence of computer tools such as software in both official languages;
- the linguistic profile of bilingual positions does not always reflect genuine needs related to the tasks to be performed in the second language;

- information sessions and meetings that take place in one language only;
- the unilingualism (English) of supervisors and senior managers;
- draft documents circulate all too often in only one language, usually English;
- to ensure that they are understood, French-speaking employees must work in English;
- once English-speakers complete their language training, they find it hard to maintain and consolidate their knowledge of French (CCMD, 2003: 7-8).

Grievances such as these highlight the practical difficulties in making official bilingualism work in a society where, for a wide variety of reasons, second-language capabilities are far more entrenched and prevalent within the French-Canadian community than the English-Canadian one. And just as many English Canadians complain about the burdens and limitations imposed upon them by official bilingual requirements for entry into and promotion within the federal public service, so too many French Canadians will complain of a hollow bilingual reality in the federal public service where, in reality, English remains the dominant language of work.

Regardless of these difficulties respecting the implementation of official bilingualism, what remains clear is that the federal public service is a much more welcoming environment for French Canadians, and they have increasingly entered it since 1969. Whether their increased presence has made the federal policy more responsive to Québécois interests is, however, a point of great debate. On one hand, broad support for Québécois nationalism has increased over these decades, resulting in its near victory in the 1995 Quebec referendum. On the other hand, support for the federal government and the federal presence in Quebec remains relatively strong, as evinced by two referendum defeats for the sovereignty position and the inability of the Parti Québécois to develop the "winning conditions" for sovereignty. Whether any of this is related to official bilingualism policy and the status of French Canadians within the federal government, however, is an open question. Such policy, though, has long been a concern for unilingual English Canadians who do see their chances for employment in the federal government restricted by federal language policy, especially for those seeking advanced positions in the Ottawa bureaucracy or the Foreign Service. As the federal public service becomes even more bilingual, and as the general English-Canadian public becomes more aware of the disproportionate share of federal employment now held by francophones, will this public become disenchanted by official bilingualism, complaining that the current federal government is becoming less responsive and open to them? Such a line of thinking is not far-fetched when attention is directed to the representativeness of the federal public service and its responsiveness to broader social groups.

9.2   Representative and Responsive Government: A First Analysis

Thinking along these lines ushers in further theoretical, yet disquieting, concerns about the representativeness of public service (Kernaghan and Siegel, 1999: 575-80; Inwood, 2004: 276-78). Is government responsiveness to various social and economic issues contingent on particular forms of social group representation within the public sector? Is this an accurate statement, and is it a desirable concept in public sector management? Can only members of a particular social group effectively represent that group, meaning that governments can only respond to, and be responsive to, various social groups when the public service is a mirror image of the society it serves? And is this possible or even desirable?

If it is held that socio-economic and cultural policy responsiveness is contingent on the socio-economic and cultural representativeness of the public service and that public servants should be representatives of their particular socio-economic and cultural groups, can it also be true that the attitudes of public servants representing a particular group are consistent with the attitudes of that group in general? In other words, do all French-Canadian public servants think and act on behalf of all French Canadians in Canada? This line of reasoning, in turn, raises the question as to whether any social group thinks and acts in a homogenous manner. Do all French Canadians think alike with respect to federal public policy and public services? Of course, the answer to this is no. Opinions range widely among this large group about the merits and demerits of the various public policy approaches that might be taken to be the role of the federal government in French Canada, especially on the issue of Quebec and Québécois nationalism. If, however, one believes in the representative theory of public service, does this not necessarily mean that the federal government should be promoting the hiring of French Canadians *and* that the French Canadians hired should be representative of the diversity of socio-economic and cultural opinion among all French Canadians? The latter notion would mean that at least one-quarter of all francophone Québécois in the federal public service should be hard-line separatists, with a further 10 to 15 per cent soft sovereigntists. No federal government has ever taken the representative principle this far, and none ever will for both practical and purely political reasons. But the theoretical issue here is not lost on the Parti Québécois and its supporters, who have long argued that the supposed increasing representation of French Canadians in the federal public service really masks a growing representation of federalist francophone opinion within the federal public service, meaning that this public service is increasingly unrepresentative of those Québécois who are *not* federalist.

The representative theory of government responsiveness is also problematical with respect to the role of individual public servants and their backgrounds and duties. Can and should individual public servants deriving from a particular socio-economic and cultural group be expected to reflect even the general attitudes of the ancestral group? Or is this idea dubious to the point of impossibility on sociological grounds, namely, that those entering the public service will tend to be much better educated than the members of the ancestral group overall, thus making them unrepresentative of the general group from the very start? Moreover, once various members of a particular group have entered the public service, they are exposed to work experiences, professional expectations, educational processes, and value judgements that shape, and have the purpose of shaping and conditioning, their thought and practices as public servants. So, by the very nature of their career choice, these persons will become increasingly unrepresentative of the general group from which they derived. This intensifies the question as to whether these persons can be seen as accurate representatives of broader groups or even as those who are most likely to make government policy more responsive to those groups of origin. Is it the role of any one public servant, or any one group of public servants, to represent a given socio-economic and cultural group, to tailor public policy development and/or program implementation to the benefit of one distinct group in society? Should the public duty of the public servant be to serve the interests and respond to the needs of one distinct socio-economic and cultural group? Or is the duty of the public servant to serve the interests of the society overall and to respond to the collective needs of all citizens? The representative theory of public sector management ultimately runs up against the concept of the public interest as a whole and the duty of the public servant; that is, the public servant is to serve the state by serving the *general* public interest through general policy-making and program implementations. The *public* servant is to serve all citizens equally regardless of socio-economic and cultural background, meaning that, in theory, an English Canadian should be, and indeed is expected to be, just as responsive and open to the policy and program needs of French Canadians as those directed at English Canadians, Aboriginal Canadians, or any other subgroup of the Canadian body politic.

The troubling practical and theoretical problems touched on here with respect to official language policy mark only the beginning of a debate on the theory and practice of representative and responsive government. Over the past 30 years support for several initiatives designed to defend, support, and promote the socio-economic and cultural interests of particular groups have led the federal government to develop a number of policies and programs aimed at making the federal public service a more representative, responsive, and equitable bureaucracy in its relations with particular groups.

9.2.1   Representation and Employment Equity

Over the past three decades concern for a representative public service has extended from a focus on language and the equitable representation of French and English Canadians in the public service to one embracing the interests of such groups as women, Aboriginal peoples, people with disabilities, and visible minorities. The genesis of this broadening focus can be traced to a number of factors, including the growing multicultural reality in this country; the increasing political awareness of this reality, as expressed in federal multicultural policy dating from 1971 and the official recognition of equality rights in the 1982 Charter of Rights and Freedoms; and the growing political awareness and influence of institutionalized groups representing these people who have suffered discrimination.

As these groups grew and developed over the 1970s and 1980s, they directed much critical commentary against the systemic discrimination they perceived in the ranks of the federal public service, which was attacked for being unrepresentative of their particular branch of Canadian society. The criticism of all these groups, furthermore, was that the public service was essentially dominated by white, able-bodied males. Such men were perceived as maintaining a grip on major positions and occupations within the public service; women, for example, were found in government service usually in clerical and administrative support roles—the "pink-collar ghettoes"—and so were among the lowest paid of government employees. These criticisms carried much validity. Academic studies ranging from the works of John Porter (1968), Wallace Clement (1983), Dennis Olsen (1980), and Kernaghan and Siegel (1999) repeatedly demonstrated that a "number of important groups are under-represented in the service, and both the senior and middle echelons are unrepresentative of the general population" (Kernaghan and Siegel, 1999: 570). In all these studies it was agreed that the most underrepresented were those from the four groups listed above—all among the historically disadvantaged in this society.

In the 1970s and 1980s, however, leaders from these groups, as well as certain journalists, academics, and political leaders, began to demand the righting of past wrongs and the creation of a public service truly not discriminative but representative of the entire society. With the example of the policy initiatives respecting official bilingualism, other advocates learned that policies of multiculturalism and employment equity might likewise be successful in reconfiguring the public service. These analysts rejected the criticisms of the representational principle and advanced claims for much greater initiatives to alter the composition of the public service fundamentally. The proponents and defenders of employment equity policy in particular have persistently maintained

- that major socio-economic and cultural groups should be equitably represented within the ranks of all governments;
- that such representation is integral to governments' being responsive to the needs and interests of these groups; and
- that individual public servants deriving from these groups will be seen, and should be seen, and should see themselves as ambassadors of their group.

Moreover, where past social and government discrimination has hindered the ability of members of these groups to gain entry into and promotion within governments, then positive policies of affirmative action should be employed by the state to rectify such past abuses. Such policies are further defended as representing a clear government and public statement to the effect

- that past social discrimination was wrong and hurtful to those individuals and groups affected;
- that society in general and governments in particular thus were handicapped in failing to make full use of the wealth of "human capital" available to them; and
- that all those social groups that have suffered from discrimination had and have valuable contributions to make to society.

Therefore, all governments must now reach out to these historically discriminated groups through a policy of reconciliation. Discrimination on unjust grounds must be prohibited, past discrimination must be admitted and condemned, and the current and future work of governments must be founded upon the principles of equitable representation and responsiveness.

Federal government initiatives to address these representational issues began in 1977 with the passage of the Canadian Human Rights Act, which prohibits discrimination within federal institutions and federally regulated industries on the basis of gender, colour, religion, ethnic and national origin, age, or disability. In 1979 the D'Avignon Special Committee on the Review of Personnel Management and the Merit Principle endorsed the concept of employment equity, stressing that the federal public service in the past had not been fair in its dealings with women and visible minority groups and that it had not supported true equality of opportunity for all citizens. The committee argued in favour of the creation of special programs to open the public service for such groups by specifically targeting and recruiting their members for employment in the federal public service and accelerating their career paths within the service. Recognizing that such special programs would run into the criticism that they constituted policies of reverse discrimination against men and non-minorities and that they also ran counter to the merit principle, the D'Avignon Committee further stressed that, at times, merit "can and should be temporarily suspended by parallel provision for special treatment of members of designated groups in support of eventual real equality of opportunity":

> The committee went further in its efforts to enshrine the new principle of special treatment for the members of certain groups. They recommended amending the Public Service Employment Act to allow preference in appointment for members of designated groups with minimum qualifications, and for the "suspension of certain qualifications" which could later be obtained through training on the job. The merit principle, according to the committee, was to remain, but it was to operate along with other principles such as equality of opportunity, efficiency, effectiveness, sensitivity, responsiveness and equity. (Adie and Thomas, 1987: 82)

Support for such equity policy was further advanced by the 1984 Royal Commission on Equality in Employment (known as the Abella Commission). Its report introduced the complexities surrounding the concept of equality and of the differing means to counter inequality:

Sometimes equality means treating people the same, despite their differences and sometimes it means treating them as equals by accommodating their differences....

We now know that to treat everyone the same may be to offend the notion of equality.... Equality means nothing if it does not mean that we are of equal worth regardless of differences in gender, race, ethnicity or disability.... Ignoring differences and refusing to accommodate them is a denial of equal access and opportunity.

It is discrimination. (Canada, 1984: 3)

As did the D'Avignon Report, the Abella Commission argued that in addressing the issue of past systemic discrimination suffered by distinct groups, justice required more than simply prohibiting future discrimination against individuals. Rather, in order to create the foundations for justice and equality, the government was urged to recognize the collective nature of discrimination: particular groups that have suffered from systemic discrimination should be accorded collective support for their future claims to equal treatment, and specific programs of affirmative action should be endorsed by the government to rectify past discrimination and to ensure that members of historically discriminated-against groups are now welcomed and encouraged to enter the public service. Such programs of affirmative action were viewed as not only eliminating the harmful effects of past discrimination but of sending important messages both to the general society and to minority groups. To the former, the message was that past discrimination was wrong and that all minority groups deserve equal treatment and respect, including the support of special affirmative action programs to help them to overcome the effects of historic abuse. To the latter, the message was that society now recognizes the wrongs that were perpetrated against them; that these groups are valued elements of the broader society, deserving of respect, dignity, and affirmation; and that the state will actively support their integration into society fully, including the structures of the public service.

Such affirmative action programs were given constitutional recognition and protection under the Charter of Rights and Freedom. Section 15(1) reads, in part: "Every individual is equal before and under the law and has the right to the equal protection and benefit of the law without discrimination...." But Section 15(2) reads, in whole: "Subsection (1) does not preclude any law, program or activity that has as its object the amelioration of conditions of disadvantaged individuals or groups including those that are disadvantaged because of race, national or ethnic origin, colour, religion, sex, age, or mental or physical disability." Programs of employment equity were thereby exempt from Charter challenge, even if it was argued that they, in themselves, constituted policies of reverse discrimination.

The federal government adopted policies of employment equity with regard to hiring and promotion in the mid-1980s, with all these initiatives being formalized in the Employment Equity Act of 1995. Both the Public Service Commission (PSC) and the Treasury Board have responsibilities for the development and implementation of employment equity programs. The PSC defines employment equity as "employment practices designed to ensure that the regular staffing process is free of attitudinal and systemic barriers in order that the Public Service reflects all groups present in the Canadian labour force, and designed to ensure that corrective measures are applied to redress any historical disadvantage experienced by certain designated groups." The Treasury Board has as its operational role the tasks of

> eliminating barriers to the employment and advancement of designated groups; establishing positive policies and practices to enable the equitable representation and distribution of the designated groups in the Public Service; providing advice and assistance to departments in developing and implementing their employment equity plans; and, establishing strategies to help departments deal with under-representation. (Canada, 1994: 6)

Given these mandates, the PSC and the Treasury Board have undertaken vigorous initiatives to promote employment equity. Persons from designated groups are actively sought during the hiring process, and candidates from such groups are accorded special supportive treatment and standing. Equity initiatives are designed to facilitate training and development, leading to accelerated promotion. The Treasury Board offers a number of programs geared to support the training of women and Aboriginal persons, for example, while the PSC operates specific offices such as the Women's Careering Counselling and Referral Bureau and the Office of Native Employment. The Treasury Board has also established two task forces—a Task Force on an Inclusive Public Service and a Task Force on the Participation of Visible Minorities in the Federal Public Service—while the PSC also encourages all departments to establish "mentoring programs" for members of designated groups, whereby younger employees from such a group are "taken under the wing" of older employees and given support,

BOX 9.4

Representation of Women, Aboriginal Peoples, Persons with Disabilities, and Visible Minority Groups in the Federal Public Service, 1988-2003

Representation of Women, 1988–2003 (%)

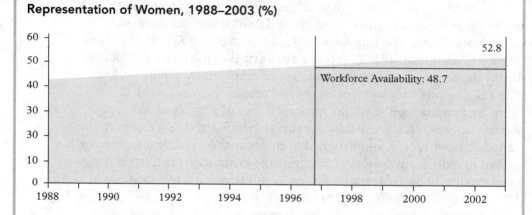

Representation of Aboriginal Peoples, 1988–2003 (%)

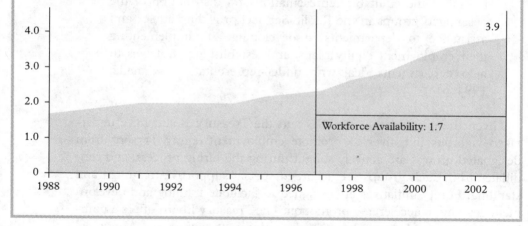

BOX 9.4 CONTINUED

Representation of Persons with Disabilities, 1988–2003 (%)

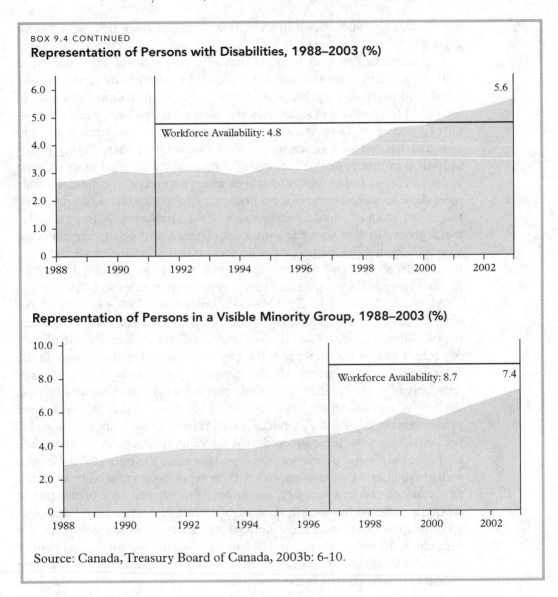

Workforce Availability: 4.8

5.6

Representation of Persons in a Visible Minority Group, 1988–2003 (%)

Workforce Availability: 8.7   7.4

Source: Canada, Treasury Board of Canada, 2003b: 6-10.

encouragement, and advice in the development of their skills and knowledge.

It is important to bear in mind that all equity policies are designed to work in tandem with the merit principle. In decision-making affecting hiring and promotion, principles of equity are not to trump principles of merit, but the two sets of principles are to co-exist and be applied compatibly. Concerns of merit are always front and centre in all personnel decision-making, but so too are the concerns of equity policy. Equity policy in itself does not justify the hiring of a demonstrably non-competent job applicant, for example, but in instances where a number of candidates fully meet the established criteria for a position, equity considerations are to be taken into account should one or more of the applicants be from a designated group. In this way, the principles of merit and equity are expected to work together, leading to a public service that is both representative of the broader society and reflective of the best talent that society has to offer. Box 9.4 records the results of all such equity undertakings as of 2003.

As can be seen, as of 2003, women constituted 52.8 per cent of the federal public service, which is proportionate to their share of the general population while higher than their overall workforce availability rate of 48.7 per cent. The box also highlights the increase in female participation in the federal public service since 1988. Aboriginal persons also had an overall representation rate higher than their general workforce availability rate. Persons of Aboriginal heritage accounted for 3.9 per cent of the federal public service as of 2003, while their workforce availability rate was 1.7 per cent. Again, we see a marked increase in the proportion of Aboriginal people in the federal public service, especially since the mid-1990s. Persons with disabilities have also exceeded their workforce availability over the first years of the new century, accounting for 5.6 per cent of the public service in 2003 with a workforce availability rate of 4.8 per cent. Persons in a visible minority remain most underrepresented, accounting for only 7.4 per cent of the public service in 2003 though accounting for 8.7 per cent of the available workforce; however, the trend line is favourable for reaching equitable representation in the near future.

The figures from Box 8.3 (page 431) reveal the occupational segregation of women within the public service as of 2003. As already noted above, women generally comprise almost half of the public service, but they account for only 33.8 per cent of the executive category. They account for 59.1 per cent of those employed in the administrative and foreign services, but only 40.3 per cent of the scientific and professional category. Most notable, however, is the vast overrepresentation of women in the administrative support category, at 83.1 per cent. To feminist advocates of employment equity, these figures reveal an historic pattern of discrimination in which women have generally been consigned to the more menial and less well-paying positions of clerks, secretaries, typists, data processors, and office equipment operators.

It is interesting to note, also from Box 8.3, that a roughly parallel dynamic is found among the other designated groups. Though all such groups tend to be underrepresented in most occupational categories and especially the executive group, Aboriginal persons tend to be overrepresented in the categories of operations and administrative support—again, the categories with more jobs requiring lower skills and educational levels, thereby those with lower remuneration rates. Likewise, persons with disabilities achieve their highest representational score in the administrative support category. Persons in a visible minority, however, achieve their highest score in the scientific and professional category; roughly one-quarter of such persons are employed within this category, engaged in such fields as auditing, chemistry, engineering and land surveying, mathematics, medicine, scientific research, and scientific regulation. This is evidence of the interest among first- and second-generation immigrants in acquiring professional skills as the key to success and entry into Canadian middle-class life. Since maths and sciences constitute a universal language and minimize the English language expertise and social knowledge requisite to other disciplines, they are a popular choice among new Canadians. As such education is obtained, career paths in the public service become obtainable.

Age is an issue, especially as it relates to the factor of the underrepresentation of women within the executive category (see Box 8.3). While women represent only 33.8 per cent of senior managers, one can observe that such underrepresentation is most pronounced within the older age bands, that is, among those who experienced the occupational, systemic discrimination of the postwar era up to the 1980s. Of all executives aged 60-64, which includes those who are among the most senior in the government, women account for only 12.6 per cent. But younger women—those who entered the public service in the last two decades and who are now benefitting from employment equity programs—account for much larger proportions of the executive ranks within their age bands. For all executives in their forties, women account for roughly 40 per cent of the total, and, for those in their late thirties, they have almost achieved occupational parity. Current federal policy leads us to expect these women, over time, to filter into the most senior executive ranks. These figures suggest two conclusions.

1. The current very low representation of older women in senior executive positions will become a thing of the past. As they retire, they will be replaced by those rising through the organization, the younger age bands increasingly equitably representative of women. Indeed, one can predict that within 25 years the gender disparity within the executive ranks of the federal public service will have ceased to exist.

2. Governments will continue to promote employment equity policies for women, notwithstanding the current achievement of gender parity within the public service overall, until women account for half of all executive positions across all age bands.

9.2.2 Pay Equity

Distinct from employment equity policy, which deals with the equitable hiring and promotion of persons from historically discriminated-against groups, is the policy of **pay equity** (Kernaghan and Siegel, 1999: 590-92; Inwood, 2004: 284-85). "Pay equity" refers to "equal pay for work of equal value" and, over the past two decades, has become a policy issue of great concern to female employees of governments, as elsewhere. As mentioned above, most women employed in the federal public service—and in provincial public services—have been congregated in administrative and clerical jobs, which tend also to be among the lowest paid in the public service. Over the 1970s and 1980s feminist critics devoted increasing attention to the discrepancies between income levels between men and women and the tendency for female-dominated job categories to be less well paid in comparison to male-dominated job categories. They argued that such disparities, generally resulting in women earning only two-thirds of what men earned, were the result of discriminatory attitudes to the value accorded the work of women in comparison to men and that the value of all work should be judged free from sexist stereotyping. As advanced by its supporters, pay equity policy aims to achieve four interrelated goals:

- the identification of jobs that are predominantly female and male, that is, job categories that are 70 per cent or more dominated by one sex;
- the evaluation of the work requirements of these jobs, with this evaluation devised and undertaken in a way that is gender neutral;
- the comparison of these jobs in light of such factors as education and skills required, effort, responsibilities, and working conditions, with female-dominated and male-dominated job categories requiring

roughly equal professional expectations of employees being flagged for closer analysis as to pay; and

- the analysis of pay levels between job categories that call for roughly equal capabilities and work from their employees.

If discrepancies in pay are found between jobs that possess roughly equal employee requirements, worth, and value, these discrepancies are to be addressed by bringing the lower paid group of employees up to the pay level of the higher paid, with provision for appropriate back-pay. As feminist analysts predict, most discrepancies indicate discriminatory treatment of female employees, meaning that women will tend to be the greatest beneficiaries of the application of pay equity policies.

The federal government endorsed the principle of pay equity in the 1977 Canadian Human Rights Act (s.11), and most provincial governments followed suit in provincial human rights legislation over the subsequent two decades. Endorsing the principle and actually living up to legal obligations, however, can be very different concepts. While the federal government had undertaken a number of investigations and had agreed to pay out some $1 billion in pay equity back-pay by 1977, it had also waged a protracted, decade-long pay equity battle with some 65,000 clerks, secretaries, data processors, and other office workers, all mainly female employees represented by the Public Service Alliance of Canada. This union, the major one in the public service, eventually brought legal action against the federal government before the Canadian Human Rights Commission, claiming systemic, decades-long pay discrimination totalling upwards of $42 billion dollars. In 1997, the commission ruled in favour of the union on the general merits of the claim, though it drastically reduced the compensation amount to some $4 billion. On appeal to the Federal Court of Canada in 1998, the government once again lost, and, in 1999, it reached a negotiated settlement with the union to disburse between $3.3 and $3.6 billion in retroactive pay to those current and past employees affected by the decision. This marks the single greatest pay equity initiative in Canadian history and a great victory, not only for the designated women and their union, but for the policy itself and the Canadian Human Rights Commission (Inwood, 2004: 284).

9.3 Representative and Responsive Government: A Second Analysis

Equity policies such as those of the federal government have also been undertaken by all provincial governments over the past decade. In all jurisdictions, however, while such policies have had their supporters they have also experienced criticisms, criticisms so strong that in the fall of 1995 the Progressive Conservative government of Mike Harris announced the abolition of employment equity programs within the Ontario public service. The theory and practice of employment equity in particular has become one of the most controversial and debatable public policy issues in recent years, such that no understanding of contemporary personnel management is complete without some knowledge of the arguments for and against it.

Those who attack employment equity programs raise four interrelated points (Howe and Covell, 1994; Roberts, 1994).

1. *Employment equity hiring and promotion practices run counter to the merit principle,* because all candidates are not evaluated equally on their individual merits and capabilities; some are given preferential treatment while others are downgraded—discriminated against—solely on the basis of innate personal characteristics such as gender, race, colour, or non-disability. The argument here is that giving some candidates preferred status on the basis of innate personal characteristics has nothing whatsoever to do with the capability for doing a particular job and that in any hiring or promotion process, attention should be focused only on matters of merit: education, experience, and aptitude.

The counter-claim advanced by defenders of employment equity is that the policy supports rather than detracts from the merit principle, in that it serves to bring down prejudicial barriers that for too long dominated the personnel system. In this sense, supporters of equity policy stress that the merit system never worked properly in the past, because it failed both to prevent the development of systemic discrimination and to enable women and members of minority groups to enter the public service in a fair and representative manner. The old approach to merit masked discriminatory attitudes that led to all public services being unrepresentative of the society they were to serve. Employment equity policy is designed to overcome these barriers, to ensure that the public service is representative of the broader society, and to assure that the public sector is staffed by a full complement of people reflective of the broader society and thus capable of responding to the needs and interests of that broader society. To defenders of equity policy, this more collectivist approach to personnel policy will lead to a meritocratic public service. Defenders of the policy also stress that the principle of equity policy in no way runs counter to the principle of merit, that the two principles can be married through the application of both equity and merit systems of personnel management, and that those hired as a result of equity initiatives are fully competent and meritorious members of the public service.

2. *Such collectivist distinction-making, designed to give affirmative promotion to members of certain designated groups over the interests of other non-designated groups, constitutes "reverse discrimination."* In an effort to combat past discriminatory practice, most governments now have reversed the focus of discrimination, being prejudiced in favour of those they previously harmed, while now discriminating against all others, mainly white, able-bodied young males. Though such policy is designed to combat discrimination and promote equality and understanding, it is argued that it does neither, but continues to endorse discriminatory treatment that further divides and embitters the persons negatively affected by the policy. The proof of the discriminatory nature of the policy is the special constitutional protection that it requires: Section 15(2) of the Charter, the provision that specifically shields employment equity policies from constitutional challenges. Critics assert that these policies violate the equality rights of individuals not protected by the equity provisions and that the requirement for special constitutional protection sends an unmistakable signal that the operational working of equity policy is so discriminatory against large numbers of affected individuals (white, able-bodied males), that it could only survive by virtue of a special constitutional exemption to equality rights.

Defenders of the policy, of course, reject all these claims, calling equity policy not "reverse discrimination" but "affirmative action" (Agócs, 1994; Agócs, Burr, and Somerset, 1992). The aim of equity policy is to right historic wrongs; to ensure that the personnel systems of public services are finally open and fair to all people, regardless of innate personal characteristics; and to ensure that public services are representative of the society they serve. These collective goals, however, call for collective measures of enforcement, at least at the very initiation of equity policies, and it is this collectivist orientation of the policy that is protected by 15(2) of the Charter. The Charter is a document that protects and advances individual rights, so 15(2) is seen by defenders of equity policy as the necessary counterweight to ensure that a policy reform initiative with such a collectivist orientation can survive legal challenge.

3. *The policy is demeaning to all individuals, especially those in the designated groups, in that it suggests that individuals are to be assessed and evaluated for hiring and promotion not solely on the basis of individual merit but also on account of their group affiliation.* And it is argued that this has resulted, in many cases, in less qualified individuals from designated groups receiving appointments and promotions over other more qualified candidates. These actions result not only in bitterness from those suffering from the reverse discrimination but sends signals to all persons that members of the designated groups need special status and treatment because it is believed they cannot succeed on their own merits. Thus, a policy designed to promote equality and better relations between social groups acts counter to these goals by stigmatizing members of non-designated groups by hiring practices and by stigmatizing underqualified members of designated groups by not so subtly informing them that they require special assistance in order to succeed in life.

Advocates of employment equity argue that equity policies do not send out such signals, that persons hired as a result of such policies are as well-qualified and meritorious as others hired, and that those who continue to hold discriminatory attitudes to the members of designated groups simply show their continuing prejudicial ways of thinking. Defenders of equity policy have long argued that the policy does result in better and more harmonious working relationships between employees and that historic social barriers and social attitudes that unfortunately have existed between people are brought down by the policy, leading differing peoples to get to know each other better and members of majority groups to understand and relate to members of minority groups. Through such interaction, all people come to realize that they are more or less the same with respect to the fundamentals of thoughts and beliefs, aspirations and desires, and that any concern respecting those innate personal characteristics that formerly served to divide them tends to fade away.

4. *The best means to combat discriminatory treatment in personnel management is through the rigorous use of human rights legislation prohibiting discrimination on the basis of gender, race, colour, ethnic or national origin, religion, age, disability, or sexual orientation.* The collective measures found in this policy are far more effective in addressing the problems of historic systemic discrimination and in creating a representative public service than is the move to endorse a policy of individualistic application. Legal penalties can be imposed on those found transgressing the law, and its enforcement would send clear signals to everyone that all persons are to be considered and

treated equally, regardless of innate personal characteristics. Through this approach to personnel management, these critics stress, the merit principle can be advanced by focusing attention on individuals and their skills, attributes, and capabilities, not on their group identities.

While advocates of employment equity generally support the application of human rights law, they will stress that the problem with such an approach to fairness in hiring and representation is that it is reactive, requiring an affected person to complain about discrimination after the fact, rather than being proactive, as is equity policy. The proactive approach is held to be more progressive by equity advocates in that it seeks to promote a fair and just workforce as a matter of initial policy, not as a reaction to costly and time-consuming complaints.

This debate on the merits and demerits of employment equity policy is long-standing and will likely continue for as long as the policy remains in place. What are the dynamics of these differing viewpoints? One is the central importance of individualist versus collectivist ways of thinking with respect to the policy. Equity policy reflects a collectivist world view and is thereby promoted and supported by those who are ideologically comfortable with a more collectivist orientation to the nature and working of society and the role of the state. Most defenders of equity policy tend to the left of the ideological spectrum. Its critics tend to the right, to be those who are much more attuned to and supportive of individualistic forms of thinking and action. These more conservative analysts always emphasize the importance of individual merit and the establishment of systems for measuring individual merit and prohibiting individual discrimination. Social democrats and leftist liberals, however, assert the importance of more collectivist means for addressing the problem of systemic discrimination through active state intervention and the importance of the development of a public service that is broadly representative of the general society.

The arguments at this point return to the theoretical issues of representativeness and social responsiveness we discussed above. All the concerns and problems with respect to official bilingualism policy—group representation, the representativeness of the public service, the ability of a representative public service to be more responsive to society, and the appropriate role of individual public servants—also apply to equity policy, perhaps even more so. Beyond the debate about the actual fairness of the implementation of equity policy, the greatest theoretical problems it confronts are those of the representation/responsiveness debate. It is a matter of record that the federal government has endorsed equity policy for the better part of two decades now and that over this time the face of the federal public service has been noticeably changing, as the boxes in this chapter have demonstrated. It is also a matter of record that the federal government has consciously sought to soften the sharp edges of the ideological debate that equity policy engenders through reference to what it terms "managing diversity." Through the language of "managing diversity," the federal government emphasizes the "removal of barriers" to employment prospects and promotion for all people in order to accommodate greater access and career mobility for traditionally disadvantaged groups while avoiding the techniques of "hard" employment equity, especially numerical targets or quotas that emphasize the collectivist goal of group representation.

Through this softer approach to equity policy the federal personnel system has become much more representative of Canadian society, and this policy dynamic is continuing. But, more troubling questions remain. Is this personnel system more responsive to Canadian society? Is it more responsive to the interests of the designated groups? Have the long-term socio-economic and cultural interests of these broader groups been better served by the federal government as a result of the federal public service being more representative of these groups? Do individual public servants, and especially those deriving from these designated groups, actually perform as ambassadors of their group and act to promote and advance the interests of their group? Or is the role of every public servant always and only to be the furtherance of the broad public interest? These questions remain at the core of the representative/responsiveness debate, and they will linger long into the future. At this point it is also important to note, however, that concern for the equitable treatment of employees did not begin either with employment equity policy or official bilingualism policy. The concept of equity is multifaceted, and it can be approached, understood, and advanced in a variety of manners. So far we have assessed two of these approaches. But there is a third, more traditional, approach to the advancement of workplace equity and fairness and that is through the processes of unionization and collective bargaining.

9.4 Equity and Labour Relations: The Public Service and Unionization

Many features distinguish the public and private sectors; one of the most notable is that the vast majority of public sector employees are unionized, possessing the right to engage in collective bargaining. This is true across all levels of government—federal, provincial, and municipal—and across all formats of public service organization—traditional departments, regulatory agencies, and Crown corporations. As Kernaghan and Siegel (1999: 597) have observed, while public service employees constitute less than one-quarter of the total Canadian labour force, they comprise almost half of all union members in the country. By extension, the three largest unions in Canada represent public servants: the Canadian Union of Public Employees, the National Union of Public and General Employees, and the Public Service Alliance of Canada.

At the federal level, full unionization and collective bargaining rights were extended to public servants employed in traditional departments and related offices in 1967. But many other employees had been long unionized and able to engage in collective bargaining by virtue of their being employed in Crown corporations. As previously noted in Chapter 3, these institutions—such as the CBC, Canada Post, and the NFB—are free to develop their own independent approaches to labour relations, and many did recognize staff unions and collective bargaining rights under general labour relations legislation. Within the regular federal public service prior to the 1960s, employee initiatives for involvement in labour relations decision-making took the form of various public service staff associations formed in the late nineteenth and early twentieth centuries. In 1944, as part of its move to garner the support of organized labour and left-leaning voters, the Liberal government of Mackenzie King agreed to formalize its consultations with staff associations through the creation of the National Joint Council of the Public Service of Canada. This institution promoted communication and consultation between the government and leaders of staff associations, but it was only an advisory body (Kernaghan and Siegel, 1999: 598).

By the early 1950s the staff associations, dissatisfied with this advisory system, desired a greater role in the formal management of labour relations, so they began to call for full collective bargaining rights. In the 1963 federal election campaign, public service collective bargaining became an election issue, with the Pearson Liberals promising that they would unionize the federal public service and extend full collective bargaining rights to its members. Pearson won a minority government that year and was dependent on the NDP to sustain his government in the House of Commons. One of the prices of NDP support was fulfilling this election pledge, so in the following years the Pearson government established a Prefatory Committee on Collective Bargaining, which was charged with the task of researching ways and means of introducing unionization and collective bargaining into the federal public service. This committee's work led to the enactment in 1967 of the **Public Service Staff Relations Act** (PSSRA), the

Public Service Employment Act (PSEA), and amendments to the Financial Administration Act (FAA). These legislative initiatives provided the framework for the system of collective bargaining found today in the federal government (Kernaghan and Siegel, 1999: 598-99).

9.4.1 The Federal Collective Bargaining System

This system of labour relations is unique in that, while it gives employees the right to engage in collective bargaining and, under certain circumstances, to take strike action, it also imposes many restrictions on the scope and substance of collective bargaining. Although the vast majority of federal employees are unionized, in contrast to the proportion of unionization in the private sector, these unionized employees do not possess the same range of rights and powers as held by unionized workers in the private sector. This is a fact often overlooked by certain political actors, media analysts, and citizens concerned with the nature of labour relations within the federal government. And, as will be seen, overshadowing this entire collective bargaining system is the federal government and Parliament itself. In circumstances where the government is both employer and governor, commanding the will of Parliament, it is common for major labour relations disputes to become major political disputes, with the balance of power residing securely in the hands of the government.

Although the working of this system of collective bargaining is quite complex, the basic structure of the process can be quickly outlined. The PSSRA established the **Public Service Staff Relations Board** (PSSRB), a quasi-judicial regulatory agency that bears responsibility for:

- establishing bargaining units of employees,
- certifying recognized bargaining agents (unions),
- overseeing the settlement of contract negotiations (known as interest disputes) and of grievances launched during the life of a contract (known as rights disputes), and
- resolving all disputes respecting unfair or improper bargaining behaviour or conflicting interpretations of labour relations law.

The legislation stipulates that the bargaining units are to be based on the occupational groups and categories recognized by the Treasury Board and the PSC, meaning that there are some 70 bargaining units covering the federal public service. The Treasury Board is the official employer for the purposes of negotiations, with Treasury Board officials being assisted in this work by senior management from departments and offices specifically concerned with particular bargaining units.

The PSSRA also stipulates that certain classes of public servants are to be excluded from collective bargaining. The excluded comprise all managers in the executive category, all legal officers in the Department of Justice, the officials in Treasury Board, and all those acting as management advisors with respect to labour relations, staffing, and classification. Such exclusions, in the name of distinguishing management from labour, elicit little criticism, but other provisions respecting the scope of bargaining rights have proven very controversial. The act distinctly limits collective bargaining to a set of matters much more narrow than that found in private sector labour relations.

The PSSRA confirms that collective bargaining can be undertaken with respect to such matters as "rates of pay, hours of work, leave entitlements, standards of discipline, other directly related terms and conditions of employment, grievance procedures, check-off of union dues, occupational health and safety, and career development." Excluded, however, are all matters respecting the organization of the public service, the assignment of duties, the classification of positions, and job evaluation. These are considered management prerogatives. Also excluded are all matters falling within the jurisdiction of the PSC as denoted by the Public Service Employment Act. This means that all matters of recruitment, promotion, transfers, demotion, and firing are excluded from collective bargaining. This approach to structuring the system is designed to preserve the special role of the PSC in overseeing the administration of the merit principle. This is a laudable objective, but it imposes substantial limitations on bargaining units wishing to bring a union perspective to such matters as recruitment, promotion, and transfer. What one sees here are the difficulties encountered when governments establish systems designed to meet numerous goals— here, a labour relations system designed to adhere both to the merit principle and the rationale of collective bargaining. The system can be made to work tolerably well, as has been the general case in recent decades, but the very nature of the compromises required to establish it remain a source of tension and limitation.

9.4.2   Collective Bargaining Tracks

In addressing matters that can be bargained, bargaining units have a choice of procedure for dealing with the employer: an arbitration track or a conciliation/strike track. The choice of which track to follow is at the discretion

---

BOX 9.5

Federal Public Service: Collective Bargaining Tracks

Arbitration Track	Conciliation/Strike Track
Negotiation agreement, or conciliator appointed	Negotiation agreement, or conciliator appointed
Fact-finding	Fact-finding
Arbitration board established	Conciliation undertaken
Arbitral award	Agreement or strike action

---

of the union, and, once chosen, it cannot be changed during the course of negotiations.

As Box 9.5 shows, the first three steps in both tracks are identical. Should negotiations encounter difficulties, either party may request the PSSRB to appoint a conciliator to assess their positions and to advise on how an agreement might be reached. The report of the conciliator is normally provided to the board and the parties within 14 days. A further advisory option open to the parties is that of fact-finding. This step is optional, but, if it is invoked, it must precede either arbitration or conciliation requests. A third-party fact-finder, similar to a conciliator and appointed by the PSSRB, has the duty of communicating with the parties involved, assessing their positions, and offering advice on how to obtain a settlement. Unlike the conciliator, though, the fact-finder must report to the board within 30 days; if the parties fail to reach an agreement within 15 days after submission of the fact-finder's report, it is made public. This procedure, involving the knowledge of both sides that the fact-finder's report will be publicized if the parties fail to come to an agreement, is designed to promote conciliation, as no party wishes to be publicly labelled as unreasonable.

If no agreement has been reached following these steps, relevant procedure then diverges depending on which track has been endorsed. If the arbitration track is followed, the parties are asked to obtain agreement on as many issues as possible, and all matters remaining in dispute are handed to an arbitration board acting under the auspices of the PSSRB. These boards are tripartite, consisting of one representative chosen by each of the parties and a third nominee from the PSSRB selected by these labour and management representatives. The arbitration board then reviews the matters in dispute, hears arguments from each side, and has the duty of deciding the merits of these outstanding issues and of fashioning a collective agreement. This agreement, known as an arbitral award, is final and legally binding on all parties for the duration of the contract.

If the conciliation/strike track is followed, if agreement has not been reached after the conciliation and fact-finding stage, either party may request the formation of a conciliation panel. This body, also tripartite in the manner of the arbitration board, is designed to give the parties one last chance to reach an agreement. This conciliation board is mandated to report back to the PSSRB on its work, usually within 14 days. If either party finds the advice of the conciliation board unacceptable, the bargaining unit has the right to strike following a seven-day "cooling off" period after the PSSRB receives the conciliation report. Should a strike occur, the union and management essentially act out the drama common to any strike action: pickets, management continuing to work, protests, press conferences, accusations and counter-accusations, negotiations, mediation, and, eventually, settlement.

9.4.3   Public Sector Collective Bargaining in Practice

The system described above is one that has evolved over decades and that worked quite well until the 1990s. It is geared to facilitate the right to strike of unionized employees while providing non-strike options for negotiations and numerous advisory and conciliation mechanisms to help the parties reach agreement short of the disruption of public services. Just as in the private sector, most labour-management negotiations towards a new contract result in an amicable negotiated settlement, absent any strike action. Public sector strikes are rare, arising in less than 5 per cent of contractual bargaining situations. But, for all the sense of balance between labour and management drafted into the system, a number of its features, both legislative and political, have served to tip the balance of power distinctly in favour of the employer, that is, the government.

The first major limitation is that of "official designation." Under the PSSRA, when a bargaining unit opts for the conciliation/strike track, the employer has the right to designate a certain proportion of the unionized positions of that bargaining unit as essential for the provision of necessary public services. The legislation stipulates that designated positions are those "having duties consisting in whole or in part of duties the performance of which at any particular time, or after any specified period, is or will be necessary in the interests of the safety or security of the public." Those employees holding a "designated" position are forbidden to engage in strike action. The power of designation is established to ensure that essential services—such as health and safety inspections, border controls, and prison operations—will not be jeopardized through strike action. The power, however, has been advantageous to the employer in weakening the power of the bargaining units, and over the past 15 years differing federal governments have aggressively expanded the scope of designated positions. While in the 1970s only some 15 per cent of bargaining units were designated as essential, by the late 1980s this figure had risen to 40 per cent, and, in some instances—air traffic controllers, for example—the designation is as high as 100 per cent. Such designations weaken and, in extreme instances, effectively eliminate the employees' right to strike (Kernaghan and Siegel, 1999: 608).

Beyond the power of designation, however, the federal government has one overriding power clearly giving it the whip hand in dealing with strikes: this is its power as a government commanding the confidence of a majority in Parliament. Should a strike become too controversial, should it be perceived by influential segments of the business community and large segments of the public and the media as being unduly harmful to society, the government has the right to introduce "back to work" legislation. If the government possesses a parliamentary majority, the passage of such legislation is a foregone conclusion, as is the termination of the strike. While the Canadian government has not used this power as a matter of routine, as this, too, would vitiate the practical impact of the right to strike, it has used the power on numerous occasions. For example, in October 1991, some 70,000 members of the Public Service Alliance of Canada undertook a legal strike across the country, causing significant disruption to federal public services. Following four weeks of strike action, the Progressive Conservative government of Brian Mulroney legislated its employees back to work and to binding arbitration of the matters in dispute, and this move was largely supported by the general public.

This broad legislative power gives the federal government the legal power to suspend or abolish any and all provisions of the collective bargaining system as it has been outlined here. The first legislated suspension of collective bargaining occurred in 1975 with the Trudeau government's wage and price control policy. The next action was in 1982 when the Trudeau government again suspended bargaining rights during another program of wage restraint. The third suspension was initiated by the Mulroney government in 1991, when it imposed major limitations on public policy salary increases. The government stipulated that all collective agreements would be extended for 24 months following their expiration, with only a 3 per cent pay increase being awarded in the second year. It was this legislated action that precipitated the strike of that year, a strike the unions lost. In 1993, the Progressive Conservative government extended this collective bargaining suspension for a further two years, and when the Liberals came to power in late 1993 they accepted and prolonged the suspension to 1997 while also freezing all incremental salary increases (Kernaghan and Siegel, 1999: 610-11). This suspension was lifted by the Chrétien government in early 1997, with the government citing its much improved fiscal condition and the advent of balanced budgets as justification. Skeptics also noted, however, that this action came just prior to the calling of a general election for the spring of that year. With the reintroduction of full collective bargaining throughout the federal public service and with the government now concerned with such personnel matters as employee morale and retention and public service renewal, the Treasury Board is now officially committed to the negotiation of collective agreements that are winning the first pay increases for federal public servants in a decade. The unions have much ground to make up, but while the employer now has much healthier finances than at any time in the past quarter-century, the Treasury Board strongly holds the view that negotiated pay increases should be tied to increases in the cost of living. Future negotiations will reveal whether public sector unions can win greater than national average pay increases from the government.

As noted in Chapter 8, the Public Service Modernization Act, 2003 (PSMA) has, as one of its goals, the streamlining of the collective bargaining system. This legislation is designed to enhance flexibility in hiring by enabling human resource managers to base staffing decisions on the selection of persons "qualified" to do a given job rather than on the more laborious process of seeking the "best" person for a given job. This redefinition of merit, taken with the support of the PSC, may have the effect of greatly expediting the hiring process, but it may also result in a greater number of grievances being filed by disgruntled employees who have been passed over for a promotion they believe they deserve. The act is also designed to promote greater mediation as a means to resolving disputes, by providing for public interest commissions in lieu of conciliation boards when grievances arise between bargaining agents and the employer. While the TBS, as the official employer for the federal government, is enthusiastically trumpeting the virtues of the PSMA, questions remain as to how well it will be implemented, how it will be received by the public sector unions, and whether it will actually expedite the process of staffing and streamline the labour-management system within the federal public service. As of the time of writing, the jury is still out on these matters.

9.4.4 Collective Bargaining in Perspective

Although the foregoing has focused on the nature and working of the collective bargaining system within the federal government, one should note that public service collective bargaining has been an important and at times controversial issue in the provinces as well. The provinces display a variety of approaches to regulating public service collective bargaining, ranging from treating public sector unions no differently from their private sector counterparts (as is the case in Manitoba and Saskatchewan) to formal public sector models of collective bargaining in which public sector unions are created and treated distinctly from private sector unions, public service strikes are prohibited, and contract negotiations are undertaken through a process of tripartite arbitration. This has been the system followed in Nova Scotia, Prince Edward Island, Alberta, and, until 1991, in Ontario. Between these two extremes are two modified versions. In British Columbia and Quebec, public service employees are subject to the same labour legislation as their private sector counterparts, but they must also adhere to "essential services" legislation restricting the scope of their right to strike. The systems in Newfoundland, New Brunswick, and for the moment in Ontario are similar to that found in Ottawa. Public sector unions possess a right to strike, but the legislation under which they operate is separate from that of private sector unions. In these provinces, public sector unions also confront a two-track system, with the government possessing a wide power to designate positions for essential services.

As can be observed from this review of public sector collective bargaining systems, there is no one correct way to organize the process. Also, there is certainly no consensus either within the public or within differing governments as to whether public servants should be accorded the right to strike. Critics of a conservative orientation usually maintain that the work performed by public servants is special, akin to a public trust, within which the right to strike is contrary to the principle of public service. Many conservatives claim that public servants should be denied the right to strike and that, where such rights do exist, the relevant legislation should be amended so as to strip the right from public servants and their unions. Those of a more liberal or social democratic orientation defend the right to strike, at least in theory, as being an entitlement that should be shared by all workers within a democracy as a means of protecting their interests in the management of workplaces. Liberals and social democrats thus uphold the principle of the right to strike, stressing that it is a fundamental aspect of labour rights and workplace equity, and that, in practice, public sector strikes are rare occurrences that seldom jeopardize the delivery of core services to the public.

Here, though, theory has often conflicted with practice. The federal Liberal government of Jean Chrétien saw fit to continue the suspension of collective bargaining rights that it inherited from its Progressive Conservative predecessor, and even NDP provincial governments such as those of Bob Rae in Ontario and Glen Clark in British Columbia undertook collective bargaining suspensions as means to address public sector deficit problems. This delineates the precarious position of public service collective bargaining within this country. The "right to strike" is not universally recognized, and governments of all political persuasions have proven they will not hesitate to suspend and curtail established entitlements of public service employees if such actions are deemed to be financially and socially necessary. It is also apparent from such actions across the federal and provincial landscapes that the general public will be at least ambivalent if not outright supportive of such restrictive measures. Public sector union leaders across this country learned over the 1990s that they can count on limited public sympathy when they confront employer-governments and that these adversaries are prepared to engage in harsh negotiations and are always willing and able to legislate as a last resort.

This is not to be read, however, as meaning that the public sector collective bargaining system is dead or that it has not produced significant benefits for ordinary unionized public servants. Quite the contrary. Over the past 30 years, public sector unions have been responsible for considerable benefits enjoyed by their members. Grievance procedures for work assignments and discipline are well-established and ongoing, regardless of restrictions on contractual negotiations. Furthermore, through earlier rounds of collective bargaining, public service unions have been able to acquire for their members quite generous benefits of maternity and parental leave, sick-time, vacations, and severance packages. In these areas, public service unions have led the way in the development of employee benefits. Over this time period, it is also fair to say that public service compensation levels have been quite decent in comparison to the private sector, although it must be remembered from our earlier review of public sector salary levels that the majority of public servants possess ordinary incomes, which place them squarely within the ranks of Canada's low- to middle-income earners.

In the 1990s, however, public sector compensation levels stagnated, if not declined, because of collective bargaining suspensions and wage roll-backs experienced in certain provinces. And, where collective bargaining remained in play, the whole tone of negotiations was markedly different. This was dramatically revealed in Ontario in the winter of 1996 when negotiations between the Ontario Public Service Employees Union (OPSEU) and the provincial Progressive Conservative government resulted in a six-week strike noted for its bitterness and open confrontation between strikers and police. The new tone was also demonstrated in the focus of substantive negotiations. The primary focus was not on wage and benefit increases but on employee downsizing and the ways and means to facilitate a 12,000 to 15,000-person reduction in the size of the Ontario public service. The new reality of fiscal restraint, tough economic times, and government restructuring was aptly displayed by OPSEU leaders, who proclaimed victory on the grounds of the severance package and employee "bumping" privileges they had negotiated with the Harris government. Another OPSEU strike in the spring of 2002 only served to demonstrate the continued animosity between Ontario's unionized public servants and their government employer and their difficulty in gaining significant wage increases.

As we enter the fifth decade of public service collective bargaining, we see a system under strain. It has been responsible for certain major gains by unionized employees, but it is also a system that governments from all parties have found, at times, awkward and undesirable. Thus, governments have been quite willing to short-circuit the system when they believed such actions to be financially desirable and politically saleable. Yet, despite collective bargaining suspensions, wage rollbacks, and general public hostility to public service unions, the basic contours of the collective bargaining system have remained in place across this country. Public servants are generally unionized, collective bargaining processes remain entrenched in law (even if they were circumvented through most of the 1990s), and grievance procedures and undertakings remain an important regulatory feature of the routine relationship between public service employees and employers. All this suggests that, while the process of collective bargaining has been severely limited in past years, especially at the federal level, the system of collective bargaining and public service unionization remains a fundamental part of employer-employee relations; with the advent of a new era of balanced budgets and fiscal health across most governments, and the federal government in particular, these relations will continue to evolve as the actors in the systems return to a more normal set of circumstances surrounding collective bargaining and the negotiation of pay rates and working conditions.

9.5   Public Human Resource Management: A Retrospective

The federal human resource system assessed in these last two chapters is multifaceted and complex. In fact the system has become so complex that it has become the butt of jokes, as people mock the bureaucratic red tape involved in taking almost any action from hiring to firing. But what is viewed as insufferable bureaucratise by one person can be viewed as fundamental due process to another. It is this issue of perspective that has led to the personnel system becoming so involved.

The system as it now stands requires federal human resource managers to concern themselves with the matters of merit, official bilingualism, human rights policy, employment equity policy, contractual obligations, collective bargaining, and grievance procedures. The range of institutions, actors, and policies involved in the management of this system is truly staggering. Any major decision respecting human resources reform in any one department or agency would and could involve the department or agency itself, the Treasury Board, the Public Service Commission, the Office of the Official Language Commissioner, the PSSRB, the Canadian Human Rights Commission, public service unions, and such policy matters as the merit principle, official bilingualism, multiculturalism, human rights policy, employment equity policy, and collective bargaining policy. The system clearly would be far more efficient if managers did not have to address these matters; it would be far more efficient if managers could simply hire and fire at will, while making all other personnel decisions according to their discretionary judgement. Such a laissez-faire, more conservative, management-oriented system would obviously be more timely and less prone to formal disputes, but would it be desirable? Indeed, such a system once existed, prior to the First World War, and that system came to be universally scorned as patronage-ridden and ineffective.

It is important to bear in mind that each of the human resource policies and programs adopted since the early decades of the twentieth century were designed to protect and promote specific values, ethical goals, and practical ends deemed important by governments and large numbers of the public. In this sense, the system can be seen as the by-product of rationalist thought, discussion, and action as to how best to organize the federal public service. Each of the personnel policies and programs that have been reviewed above have emerged from a particular political, administrative, and social context, with each initiative being broadly supported by governments and interests groups both at the point of inception and thereafter, hence the continuation of these policies and programs over time. Each initiative has been designed to respond to a given practical problem, with each new policy and program approach being, in theory, rationally conceived to address the problem and to advance a much better, more efficient, effective, equitable, and rational approach towards the management of human resources. Administrative complexity, however, has been the by-product of these initiatives, each successively designed to improve and regularize personnel management in keeping with the principles of meritocracy, bilingualism, respect for human rights, representativeness and responsiveness, equity, and the rights and interests of organized labour.

Governments have sought to promote these principles through the development and application of formal rules and procedures. Thus, we have rules respecting the enforcement of merit, which call for hiring and promotion to be undertaken according to open competitions, examinations, interviews, and an impartial assessment of candidates' backgrounds and capabilities. These rules directly circumscribe the discretionary judgement of managers. Similarly, decisions respecting staffing, deployment, training, and promotion must now also take into account official language requirements, anti-discrimination provisions, and policies of employment equity. And, as managers balance all of these matters, they must also be aware and respectful of the requirements of collective bargaining and contractual obligations. The work of human resource managers is thus intricate and involved, leading the human resource management system to be complicated and often slow in operation. But what to the untrained eye appears to be gross inefficiency is often, in reality, a necessarily complex system operating to meet and serve a host of standards and requirements far exceeding those that have to be addressed by the private sector.

In this sense, the public sector human resource management system has been established to do different things and to accomplish more—to be more open, meritocratic, representative, and equitable—than private sector personnel systems attempt. As such, it seeks to be far more institutionally rational. Of course, one can debate the rationalistic merits of particular elements of this system, with most critical public attention in recent years being directed to the issues of public sector representativeness, responsiveness, employment equity, and the right to strike; one can also question whether the evolution of the personnel system has been more in keeping with principles of rationalist or incrementalist development, for, despite the claims of systematic rationalist developments, the actual evolution of the system, as outlined in the past two chapters, suggests a strong incremental orientation. One can appreciate the complexity of the federal human resource management system by understanding its origins, rationale, and policy direction. And one should always be wary of those who too hastily criticize the public sector personnel system for being inefficient. While there can always be room for improvement with respect to the application and operationalization of all policies and programs, the principles underlining the public human resource system have evolved over decades of debate, discussion, and practical implementation, and these important principles are now well-embedded in the nature and working of the Canadian state. If the basic concepts and rules of meritocracy, representativeness and responsiveness, official bilingualism, multiculturalism, human rights policy, employment equity policy, and collective bargaining did not exist, the vast majority of Canadians would likely, once again, invent them.

Key Terms

bilingualism and biculturalism: The policy idea that French Canada and English Canada are two of the founding nations of the country and that the languages and broad cultures of these founding nations should be represented in the framework of the federal parliament, government and public service.

collective bargaining: The legal concept of recognizing the right of employees to form unions and to formally negotiate with the representatives of their employer with respect to pay and benefits, terms and conditions of work, and grievance procedures. Collective bargaining in the federal public service is both extensive compared to the Canadian private sector but also limited by the nature and working of the merit principle and the role of the Public Service Commission of Canada.

employment equity: The policy that certain socio-demographic groups that have suffered historical discrimination in this country—notably women, Aboriginal peoples, persons of a visible minority, and persons with disabilities—should be afforded special recognition as the government strives to alleviate such historical discrimination by seeking to ensure that these groups are represented in the federal public service in the same proportion as these groups exist in the general population.

National Capital Region: The combined cities of Ottawa and Hull. The National Capital Region (NCR) forms the administrative and executive heart of the federal government. Whereas the vast majority of federal public servants work outside of the NCR, the vast majority of senior managers and executives work within home departments and agencies domiciled therein.

Official Languages Act, 1969: Federal legislation stipulating that both French and English are the official languages of Canada, that the federal public service is to be able to function in both official languages, and that Canadians have the right to receive public services from the federal Public Service in the official language of their choice.

pay equity: The policy concept that women are to receive the same pay for work of equal value as that received by men. Where there is a demonstrable imbalance in pay rates between men and women, corrective action by the government is to be taken.

Public Service Staff Relations Act (PSSRA): Federal legislation dating from 1967 that recognizes the right of most federal public servants to engage in collective bargaining with their employer, represented by the Treasury Board Secretariat.

Public Service Staff Relations Board (PSSRB): The board, established by the PSSRA, mandated with the role of overseeing collective bargaining within the federal public service and addressing complaints and grievances from the actors within the collective bargaining system.

representativeness of public service: The concept that the membership of the public service should be representative of the society it serves; in other words, that the membership of the public service should reflect the socio-demographic diversity of the general population so as to reflect and represent the various major social groups (gender, linguistic, race, religion, colour, region, handicapped status, etc.) that comprise the broader society.

References and Suggested Reading

Adie, Robert F., and Paul G. Thomas. 1987. *Canadian Public Administration: Problematical Perspectives.* 2nd ed. Scarborough, ON: Prentice-Hall Canada.

Agócs, Carol. 1986. "Affirmative Action, Canadian Style: A Reconnaissance." *Canadian Public Policy* 12: 148-62.

—. 1994. "Employment Equity: Is it Needed? Is It Fair?" In Mark Charlton and Paul Barker, eds., *Crosscurrents: Contemporary Political Issues.* 2nd ed. Toronto: Nelson.

Agócs, Carol, Catherine Burr, and Felicity Somerset. 1992. *Employment Equity: Cooperative Strategies for Organizational Change.* Scarborough, ON: Prentice-Hall Canada.

Canada. 1962. Royal Commission on Government Organization. *Report.* 5 vols. Ottawa: Queen's Printer.

—. 1966. *House of Commons Debates.* 6 April.

—. 1970. *House of Commons Debates.* 23 June.

—. 1984. Royal Commission on Equality in Employment. *Report.* Ottawa: Supply and Services.

—. 1994. Treasury Board. *Employment Equity in the Public Service: Annual Report 1992-93.* Ottawa: Supply and Services.

Canada, Treasury Board of Canada. 2003a. *Annual Report on Official Languages, 2002-03.* Ottawa: Supply and Services.

Canada, Treasury Board of Canada. 2003b. *Employment Equity in the Federal Public Service, 2002-03.* Ottawa: Supply and Services.

CCMD. 2003. *French to Follow: Revitalizing Official Languages in the Workforce.* Ottawa: Canadian Centre for Management Development.

Chrétien, Jean. 1986. *Straight from the Heart.* Toronto: Seal Books.

Clement, Wallace. 1983. *Class, Power and Property: Essays on Canadian Society.* Toronto: Methuen.

Dyck, Rand. 1996. *Provincial Politics in Canada: Towards the Turn of the Century.* 3rd ed. Scarborough, ON: Prentice-Hall Canada.

Howe, Brian, and Katherine Covell. 1994. "Making Employment Equity Legitimate." *Inroads* 3: 70-79.

Inwood, Gregory J. 2004. *Understanding Canadian Public Administration: An Introduction to Theory and Practice.* 2nd ed. Scarborough, ON: Prentice-Hall Allyn and Bacon Canada.

Kernaghan, Kenneth, and David Siegel. 1999. *Public Administration in Canada: A Text.* 4th ed. Toronto: Nelson Canada.

Love, J.D. 1979. "Personnel Organization in the Canadian Public Service: Some Observations on the Past." *Canadian Public Administration* 22.3: 402-14.

Olsen, Dennis. 1980. *The State Elite.* Toronto: McClelland and Stewart.

Porter, John. 1958. "Higher Public Servants and the Bureaucratic Elite in Canada." *Canadian Journal of Economics and Political Science* 24, 4: 483-501.

—. 1968. "The Economic Elite and the Social Structure of Canada." In B.R. Blishen *et al.*, eds., *Canadian Society: Sociological Perspectives.* 3rd ed. Toronto: Macmillan. 754-72.

Roberts, Jack. 1994. "Employment Equity—Unfair." In Mark Charlton and Paul Barker, eds., *Crosscurrents: Contemporary Political Issues.* 2nd ed. Toronto: Nelson.

Siegel, David. 1988. "The Changing Shape and Nature of Public Service Employment." *Canadian Public Administration* 31.2: 159-93.

Related Web Sites

THE TREASURY BOARD OF CANADA
  <http://www.tbs-sct.gc.ca>

THE PUBLIC SERVICE HUMAN RESOURCES MANAGEMENT AGENCY OF CANADA
  <http://www.hrma-agrh.gc.ca>

THE LEADERSHIP NETWORK
  <http://www.hrma-agrh.gc.ca/leadership>

THE OFFICE OF THE COMMISSIONER OF OFFICIAL LANGUAGES
  <http://www.ocol-clo.gc.ca>

PSAC
  <http://www.psac-afpc.org>

CHAPTER 10
Contemporary Issues in Management Reform

The past quarter-century has experienced significant change in public sector management in Canada. As we have observed in previous chapters, over the 1980s and 1990s there was widespread concern about the growth of the state, its increasing presence in social and economic life, and burgeoning public sector deficits and debts. The rising prominence and influence of conservative thought over these years resulted in the promotion of ideas supportive of smaller government and of government that would be less intrusive and interventionist in the private sector and more supportive of the interests and values of private enterprise. These ideas, in turn, spurred demand that government be more "businesslike" in all its operations—that it be more economical and efficient in all its actions; that it do "more with less"; and that, in dealing with the public, it be more service-oriented. Rather than government being perceived as sets of large, impassive, and staid bureaucracies engaged in traditional forms of policy-making and routine, systematized program implementation, there were calls for it to be more innovative in serving public needs and individual demands for service while maintaining a smaller, leaner public service that would be more intelligent, productive, and accountable. Through all these changes, moreover, government was expected to refocus attention on the politics/administration dichotomy, with clearer lines being drawn between the roles of politicians as policy-makers and public servants as managers and administrators. Managers, in this view, were to be concerned with management, not policy development, and at the same time they were expected to redesign and transform the ability of government to better serve the needs of its clients. This was a tall order indeed.

The theory and practice of government and public sector management have undergone a major rethinking and reworking over the past quarter-century, as previous chapters have noted. Here, we will consider these new approaches to government and management, examining the ideas underlying them, the theoretical debates surrounding them, and the practical impact they have had on Canadian governments, particularly the federal government. Governments have had time now to implement these new approaches and methods, so with the benefit of hindsight we can look at the merits and shortcomings of this paradigmatic shift to a "leaner and friendlier" public service. These new concepts of governance have brought about some changes in the structure and role of government, but such changes have been more evolutionary than revolutionary, demonstrating more the reform of government rather than its substantive "reinvention." The idea that government can be, or even should be, "reinvented" to become more like the private sector is highly contested, and we will probe this debate. The changes within the federal government itself are more modest and reformist in nature, but this does not diminish their significance or their impact on both the government and the broader society. These new approaches and reforms, however, have had little effect on the actual exercise of executive power within government; to its critics, the centralized command-and-control mode of decision-making remains firmly entrenched in the working of the federal government. To begin our analysis, we first must review these new approaches to government and management. The logical starting point is what is known as the New Public Management.

10.1 New Public Management

New Public Management refers to an approach to the theory and practice of government and public sector management that first emerged in the Conservative government of Margaret Thatcher in Britain. As Peter Aucoin (1995: 1-2) has outlined, Thatcher came to power in 1979, stressing that three dimensions of British government had to be reformed:

- the power of the public service had to be diminished to make government more subject and responsive to the will of elected ministers, not career bureaucrats;

- private sector management practices were to be introduced into the public sector to enhance the economy and efficiency of government programs; and
- all public services were to be rethought and redesigned to make them more responsive to the needs and concerns of individual citizens, ensuring that matters of service delivery and service quality were primary concerns for all public officials.

As the Thatcher government began implementing these broad policy priorities through such specific actions as privatization, deregulation, public sector downsizing, the contracting-out of public services, expenditure restraint initiatives, and the introduction of user fees and the commercialization of public services, this new approach to government gained enormous attention in the media, both in Britain and abroad, as well as internationally among academics. While the policy and program undertakings of her government elicited much debate and controversy in Britain over the 1980s, Prime Minister Thatcher held firm in her commitment to reshape and reform the British government, and this she largely achieved (Aucoin, 1995: 3-5; Savoie, 1994: 200-13). What was to many conservatives a much desired and long-awaited neo-conservative revolution in Britain following upon decades of social democratic/reform liberal approaches to government and the role of the state was something to be emulated elsewhere. Such was the case with President Ronald Reagan in the United States and, to a lesser degree, Prime Minister Brian Mulroney in Canada, as these leaders sought to capture the vision and direction of the "Iron Lady." As these Thatcherite initiatives came to dominate government action in Britain and influenced government behaviour in other countries as well, they came under increasing academic attention and scrutiny. Christopher Hood (1991) coined the term the "New Public Management" (NPM) to refer to this approach to government.

The NPM, according to Hood, is centred on a number of key assumptions and understandings:

1. *The roles of politicians and public sector managers must be clearly distinguished,* with the former having the decisive lead in policy-making, while the latter focus almost exclusively on matters of management and program implementation. In the past, so this perspective maintains, senior managers exerted too great an influence on matters of policy, thereby not only distorting and limiting the role of ministers but also distracting senior management from what should be their primary responsibility—the active

and effective management of government activities. Managers, thus, are expected to devote most of their attention to management, not policy, and within this refocused role they are to stress and promote improved administrative performance. Governments are to set explicit goals, standards, and measures of performance for management, and managers are to work to ensure that these objectives are met in the most economical, efficient, and effective manner possible.

2. *Governments and their managers are to stress the importance of adopting and using private sector modes of operation and management.* As much as possible, the NPM calls for government to be run like business, with governments creating competitive environments within which their bureaucracies are to operate and with public sector managers expected to think and act similarly to their private sector counterparts.

3. *In achieving these goals, management is admonished to concentrate on, and to achieve, objective results.* Government "outputs" are now to matter much more than "inputs," though the efficient and economical use of resources is always to be a primary consideration. This often calls for the fundamental redesign of government organizations, the downsizing of bureaucracies, the disaggregation of bureaucratic units, and the decentralization of bureaucratic power through the promotion of participatory management.

4. *The development and promotion of systems of participatory management are viewed as essential to liberating the productive potential of government organizations,* thereby making them progressive and innovative bodies much better able to achieve higher levels of results, and customer service. This is in keeping with much of the literature on contemporary organizational theory, as noted in Chapter 5.

Through all of these actions, as one can imagine, there is a concern for accountability. These managerial reconfigurations are designed to enhance the calibre of accountability and responsiveness of government bureaucracies both to their political masters and to the broader public. Through the application of the principles and practices of the NPM, it is claimed that public sector management will become more faithful and subject to the direction and leadership of elected politicians—ministers and parliamentarians—while also devoting much greater attention and concern to the quality of public services made available to citizens.

10.1.1   Reinventing Government

As the NPM came to be the dominant new approach to thinking about and restructuring the process of government in the Western world, it gained a number of academic proponents. While Hood was the first to give the concept a coherent theoretical form, by far the most influential and well-known advocates of NPM have been two Americans, David Osborne and Ted Gaebler. Their *Reinventing Government: How the Entrepreneurial Spirit is Transforming the Public Sector* (1993) became a bestseller in the United States (no small feat for a book on public sector management!), thereby not only disseminating the ideas of the NPM across a wide popular audience but also enhancing the perceived legitimacy and popularity of these ideas among government leaders—both politicians and managers—in the United States and beyond.

In this landmark work Osborne and Gaebler contend that governments can be and are becoming "reinvented" through the application of entrepreneurialism to their managerial forms and operations. By stressing the development of more streamlined, flexible, and responsive forms of policy-making and management, founded on such concepts as empowerment, competition, enterprise, anticipation, and market-orientation, they stress that the structures of governments can be radically changed and their program results fundamentally improved. In advancing these claims, Osborne and Gaebler present 10 principles of **reinventing government** that, if embraced by governments and managers, can turn public sector managers into public sector entrepreneurs.

BOX 10.1
Osborne and Gaebler's 10 Elements of Reinventing Government

- Catalytic government: steering rather than rowing
- Community-owned government: empowering rather than serving
- Competitive government: injecting competition into service delivery
- Mission-driven government: transforming rule-driven government
- Results-oriented government: funding outcomes, not inputs
- Customer-driven government: meeting the needs of the customer, not the bureaucracy
- Enterprising government: earning rather than spending
- Anticipatory government: prevention rather than cure
- Decentralized government: from hierarchy to participation and teamwork
- Market-oriented government: leveraging change through the market

1. *Catalytic government: steering rather than rowing.* The role of government and management, according to Osborne and Gaebler, is to be proactive and innovative, not reactive and traditional. Rather than dealing with issues and problems as they arise and engaging in standardized, bureaucratic forms of decision-making and program delivery—the routine tasks of administrative "rowing"—governments are encouraged to be catalytic:

- They should approach the tasks of governing and managing by seeking new and creative ways to achieve desired public goals.
- They should deal with issues and problems by going beneath the surface and beyond standard administrative actions to probe their deeper causes and natures, thus seeking newer and better ways to address these matters. In all their actions, governments and management should aim to "steer" rather than "row."
- Rather than engaging in routine work designed to cope with a given issue, they should bring other concerned actors—individuals, interest groups, and businesses—together, so that all these concerned parties can "brainstorm" and work together in developing new approaches, programs, and means of program delivery.
- Rather than government viewing itself as the necessary means of service delivery, these other actors themselves may be able to develop other program means for dealing with the issue at hand, with state actors simply acting as the catalyst for such innovation.

Governments and their management then are to be perceived as leaders and innovators, encouraging new and alternative policy and program design and facilitating new policy and program implementation—with such service delivery being vested in the public service, the private sector, the voluntary sector, or a mixture of public/private partnerships. The core foundation of catalytic government is thus quite simple: government and management must be prepared

- to innovate,
- to break from past and traditional forms of thought and action,
- to encourage all other interested parties to work with government and its management in the redesign of governmental policies and programs, and
- to be ready and willing to promote and embrace new means of policy and program development and implementation towards the goal of better, more responsive, and accountable public services.

2. *Community-owned government: empowering rather than serving.* In keeping with the goal of catalytic and innovative government is the aim of establishing new and deeper linkages between government and the communities it serves. Traditional forms of bureaucratic action imply that governments have answers for particular issues and problems, that governments and their management control the means of public policy and program implementation, and that citizens are passive recipients of state initiatives. Such thought and behaviour, however, result in the creation and perpetuation of dependency between citizens and communities and their governments.

Rather than maintain this approach of simply "serving" the public, governments and management, according to Osborne and Gaebler, should "empower" citizens and communities to claim ownership of public policies and program initiatives. People should come to see themselves as "clients," "customers," or "consumers" of government services, with distinct interests and stakeholder claims to particular policy fields and the desire and need to be involved in decision-making with respect to these fields. The citizen as client should view government and public sector management as a means to facilitate all individuals, social groups, businesses, and the community as a whole in taking responsibility for these policy fields and, ultimately, for their own lives. Again, the role of government and management is catalytic in promoting such changes and new attitudes to citizen-state relations.

3. *Competitive government: injecting competition into service delivery.* As a means of achieving better government, Osborne and Gaebler stress that public sector managers

- are to be encouraged to recognize the limitations of government;
- are counselled to think of new ways to deliver programs and to draw on the vast array of service providers within the broader society;
- need to realize, as public sector entrepreneurs, that governments attempting to provide every traditional public sector service not only drain public resources but cause public organizations to overextend their operational capabilities, thus reducing service quality and effectiveness.
- must promote service delivery by a wide variety of organizational actors—public, private, voluntary or non-profit, and combinations thereof.

By breaking the monopoly of all public services being provided by large, traditional government bureaucracies, public sector entrepreneurs can create an environment whereby a large number of varied service providers can compete among themselves for the right to deliver certain services to specified program quality standards for a contractually limited period of time and for a set amount of money, with the lowest service bidder receiving the contract. The result, it is supposed, is an operational system of program implementation marked by greater economy and efficiency, service responsiveness, and innovation.

4. *Mission-driven government: transforming rule-driven government.* In providing better and more intelligent government, public sector managers are also encouraged to promote mission-driven government. Rather than governments and public sector organizations being dominated by concerns for existing rules and standard operating procedures, they are expected to refocus their attention on new ways of achieving their fundamental mission. The purpose of the organization, its fundamental *raison d'être*, should become the driving force behind all of its actions, with public sector entrepreneurs then structuring all necessary rules and regulations regarding operational procedures, financial and personnel management, and legal administration around the mission of the organization. The overall aim here is to create innovative government institutions, and a system of government itself, in which public goals, directions, and vision, not the application of standardized bureaucratic rules, are the chief characteristics of government and its work.

5. *Results-oriented government: funding outcomes, not inputs.* The quest for mission-driven government naturally flows into results-oriented government. Through this concept, public sector entrepreneurs are challenged to dedicate themselves and their organizations to attaining substantive policy goals—the mission of the organization—as opposed to concentrating almost exclusively on the control of public resources expended in routine bureaucratic operations. The priority of the public sector is to be the successful realization of desired ends—policy and program results—rather than the routine oversight of organizational means. While the careful management of such means will always remain an important consideration for managers, Osborne and Gaebler urge them to place greater stress on operational performance and the ability of organizations to achieve results, as opposed to simply administering resources. In this sense, all organizations should view the management of institutional inputs as means to the greater end of the organizational mission, with the organization and its management ultimately evaluated on the degree to which they can economically, efficiently, yet effectively realize their goals.

6. *Customer-driven government: meeting the needs of the customer, not the bureaucracy.* As government changes and is reinvented through the application of all these principles, the relationship between government organizations and citizens also changes. In this new, improved system of government, citizens as "customers" or "clients" engage with government bodies in transactional modes, where the key role of the government actor is to serve the needs of the customer first. In traditional forms of government organization and operation, so Osborne and Gaebler argue, the exact opposite was usually the case, with large bureaucracies believing and acting on the principle that "their" interests and needs in self-preservation and self-advancement were first and foremost and that it was their duty to decide how best to define and deal with the needs of citizens, with such citizen needs being dealt with in routine and systematized manners. In reinvented government, this traditional approach is turned on its head, with all government organizations and their employees viewing citizens as customers and believing that serving the needs and interests of these customers should be their central focus and objective.

7. *Enterprising government: earning rather than spending.* With fundamental changes in the form and operations of government there also emerges a major rethinking of how government programs can be and should be funded. With existing limitations on financial resources and the reluctance of governments and the general public to accept new tax increases, Osborne and Gaebler emphasize that governments and public sector entrepreneurs must "do more with less." This demands innovation in financial management and, in particular, borrowing financial concepts from the private sector. Public sector entrepreneurs are advised to think more about "earning" than "spending" money and are encouraged to bring the profit motive into the operations of their institutions. User fees are promoted as a way of raising revenues. Likewise, government organizations are urged to experiment with systems of bureaucratic savings as means of creating alternative forms of revenue generation. Rather than being expected to spend all their annual appropriations by the end of each fiscal year or see the unused portion returned to general government coffers (in Canada, the Consolidated Revenue Fund), public sector managers are to be assisted in saving allocated monies for future use by the organization. If they can realize savings through the development of more economical and efficient means of performing required work, such savings are to remain with the organization, to be used and deployed as its managers deem best in the service of the organizational mission. These savings can be used in any manner of

ways, but one creative and long-standing one would be to create a capital pool for investment purposes, with the organization then deriving a return on investment that can be used to fund organizational activities. In these ways, and countless other financial innovations, bureaucracies are expected to be less traditional and more enterprising in the task of attaining, using, and developing financial resources.

8. *Anticipatory government: prevention rather than cure.* In keeping with the principles of a reinvented government, and especially a government that is "catalytic," public sector entrepreneurs, according to Osborne and Gaebler,

- are expected to be forward-looking and progressive in their policy and program thinking, not backward-looking and traditional;
- are to be dynamic and anticipatory, rather than dealing with issues and problems, once they have arisen, through standard operating procedures;
- are to engage in close communication and mutual education with all interested parties, actors, and customers in a given policy field; learn about the field; and gain such expertise and awareness about the field, its players, and their needs as to enable the government organization to anticipate developments.

In this manner, rather than reacting to changes in their environment, public sector entrepreneurs are to direct and lead change, managing the needs of their given field and preventing problems from arising in the first instance. Rather than coping with pre-existing problems in a "rowing" manner, they should be "steering" change and promoting policy and program initiatives that ensure positive and progressive developments.

9. *Decentralized government: from hierarchy to participation and teamwork.* As government is reinvented, public sector managers are also encouraged to promote and realize the benefits of organizational decentralization. Rather than viewing bureaucratic organizations as being naturally founded on the principles of hierarchy and highly centralized command-and-control systems of power relations and decision-making, Osborne and Gaebler assert that those in the public sector should recognize how organizations are changing and how they can operate more economically, efficiently, and effectively if they are decentralized and made more participative. Advances in information technology, improved communications systems,

and increases in workforce quality and managerial capabilities can lead to more flexible, intelligent, and productive team-based organizational work and development. Public sector entrepreneurs are challenged to build "smart organizations" that can make full use of all the material and human resources available to the institution through the promotion of participatory management. In this way, operational decision-making can be extended throughout the organization, being placed in the hands of those who are most aware of practical realities and how basic organizational goals can be fine-tuned to meet and serve customer needs and wants more successfully. Thus, tactical decision-making regarding the operation of the organization can be decentralized down to those most knowledgeable about these matters, while overall strategic direction can remain firmly in the control of senior management—but this senior managerial/entrepreneurial leadership will have close communication links with middle management and field-level "customer service agents."

10. *Market-oriented government: leveraging change through the market.* The final principle of reinvented government advanced by Osborne and Gaebler is its orientation to the market. Instead of the traditional view that the public sector is fundamentally different from the private sector, with the former having its own distinct traditions, values, principles, and modes of operation, public sector managers are advised to think of all facets of socio-economic life in holistic terms. In this sense, life is not divided into public and private spheres *per se*, but into markets, with all markets—international, national, regional, and local—representing a collection of people, interests, and socio-economic forces. The task of public sector workers is to realize that these markets, because of the ever-increasing complexity of socio-economic life and the interplay of people and forces within them, are now beyond the control of any single government body. According to Osborne and Gaebler, those in the public sector

- should use the logic of market economics as a means of promoting change within society and ensuring social and economic growth and prosperity, rather than seeking to control and regulate these markets through conventional policy and programs;
- should structure public policies and programs to be consistent with the nature of dominant market forces in society, with governments seeking to work with, rather than against, these forces and their underlying assumptions and trends.

Hence, government policies and programs must be more like those in the private sector, the better to dovetail with private sector actors and their dominant strategic and tactical considerations in regard to desired public policies. In this way, according to Osborne and Gaebler, governments need to interact and work with market behaviour to advance their own missions while also serving the long-term needs of their customers and the broader social and economic system within which all these actors exist.

These 10 principles of reinventing government stand not only as a widely popularized manifesto for the redesign of public sector bureaucracies and their operations, but also as a fundamental challenge to the traditional understanding of government and the nature and role of the public sector. As Osborne and Gaebler have argued, they provide a new conceptual framework for government and public sector management—an analytical checklist of ways and means and forms of thought for developing a new paradigm of government and management. They explain that, "What we are describing is nothing less than a shift in the basic model of governance used in America. This shift is underway all around us, but because we are not looking for it—because we assume that all governments have to be big, centralized and bureaucratic we seldom see it. We are blind to the new realities because they do not fit our preconceptions" (Osborne and Gaebler, 1993: 321).

These "new realities" of reinvented government call for government

- to be smaller, yet more focused;
- to be "mission-driven" and "results-oriented"; and
- to be geared to "customer service" through the use of "market-oriented" approaches to public service founded on "competition," "enterprise," "entrepreneurialism," "anticipatory" action, "community empowerment," and "participatory management."

In short, government and public sector management are expected to be more businesslike, which, besides being more economical, efficient, and effective, also involves being responsive and accountable to those they serve.

10.1.2 Reinventing Government: The Canadian Perspective

The idea that contemporary government can be and should be "reinvented" along market lines is not foreign to this country. In Canada, the reinvention thesis has been supported by various analysts, including most notably

Sandford Borins (1995a, 1995b) and Bryne Purchase and Ronald Hirshorn (1994). In defending the NPM, Borins is quick to stress that the concept of reinventing government is not a "simplistic Big Answer" to government problems nor a panacea for dealing with fiscal management difficulties. Rather, he sees it as a theoretically and practically valid manner for reconfiguring public sector management. In keeping with the basic position of Osborne and Gaebler, Borins (1995a: 122-32) contends that a growing body of Canadian evidence suggests that, through major innovations in service delivery, managerial autonomy, administrative empowerment, and the use of performance indicators geared to competitive, entrepreneurial models of program management, the nature and quality of government services can be dramatically altered and improved. These new dynamics of innovation, spurred both by the public's demand for greater service and by government needs to restrain costs, are now, according to Borins, a fundamental part of the organizational environment of all governments in Canada. In keeping with this line of thinking "reinvention" is the shape of things to come.

Purchase and Hirshorn (1994: 43) agree: "reinvention" is part of the "post-bureaucratic paradigm" in public sector management, in which the core concepts of the old bureaucratic framework—the "public interest," "administration," "functions, authority and structure," and "cost-justification"—are transcended by other, stronger principles. In this new mode of thinking, public sector management is centred on such principles and considerations as "results citizens value," "quality and value," "production," the identification of "missions, services, customers and outcomes," and the provision of "value." And the means to these ends are many and varied. They include

- restructuring bureaucratic organizations and reconfiguring public sector managerial orientations;
- redesigning government programs and responsibilities,
- using private sector approaches to policy and program implementation more extensively; and
- encouraging a governmental and broader socio-economic environment conducive to smaller government with a more market-oriented, entrepreneurial, and businesslike attitude to public service and public sector management.

More recently, Kernaghan, Marson, and Borins (2000: 23-24) have highlighted the breadth of ideas and concepts captured under the rubric of the NPM within the Canadian perspective. Remaining quite sympathetic to the broad strategic goals of the NPM, they stress that the concept embraces three approaches to public sector governance:

- an emphasis on the importance of reducing the role of the state in society through such practices as privatization, deregulation, and contracting-out of services;
- the importance of restructuring and reforming the nature and working of government organizations; and
- the importance of improving management capabilities and practices within the public sector through participatory decision-making and employee empowerment.

All three of these approaches derive from and inform NPM thinking, yet, as these authors indicate, specific NPM initiatives found within any one government can be broader or narrower and more or less expansive or radical in their implications for government and for citizens dealing with that government.

The choice of policy application in these cases, then, depends on the degree of support within government for substantial change to its way of organizing and delivering public services. In typical Canadian fashion, most Canadian governments, especially the federal government, have been more moderate and centrist in their application of NPM approaches, stressing managerial reforms over the wholesale reinvention of government systems. While initiatives deriving from NPM thought on the nature of government have been influential in this country, especially in relation to specific managerial practices and dynamics, they have not amounted to a substantial reconfiguration of the working of government. Such restraint in the application of the NPM derives, in part, from the many criticisms of the approach that emerged in the 1990s, as well as from a recognition, among certain policy-makers, of the inherent limitations of the broadest NPM reforms and in the ability to make fundamental changes in governmental organizations.

10.1.3   Reinvention, the New Public Management, and the Critics

The proponents of government reinvention and the NPM have been effective in publicizing their views over the past two decades to the point that, in this country, a number of governments have seized on these approaches and the ideas flowing from them as guidelines for restructuring their own institutional structures and managerial operations. Changes brought about by the Klein government in Alberta (see Bruce *et al.*, 1997) and the former Harris government in Ontario have been the most significant provincially in pursuing the principles of the reinvention/NPM paradigm. Prior to a review and analysis of these initiatives at the federal level, however, it is important to recognize the sharp rejoinders that the reinvention/NPM thesis have elicited from critics.

A number of authors in this country have been highly critical of the NPM, but none has been more eloquent than Donald Savoie (1995). Influenced by the work of the American critic James Q. Wilson, Savoie contends that NPM is "basically flawed" in that it purports to offer a highly rationalistic, less bureaucratic, more market-oriented, and commercialized approach to government and public sector management, but in reality it fails to recognize and understand the basic yet important differences between the public and private sectors. As noted in Chapter 5, there are fundamental differences between public and private sector organizations. Savoie contends that these differences cannot be, and should not be, glossed over, ignored, or rejected in the quest to make the public sector more like the private sector. Many critics of government have long argued that public sector organizations should be operated and managed along private sector lines, with much greater attention devoted to such business considerations as the promotion of economy and efficiency in all government operations. Indeed, as seen in Chapter 2, such considerations have been a long-standing part of conservative thought, with much of the basic thrust of NPM thus standing as an ideologically conservative approach to government reform.

Savoie (1995: 112-16) warns all those interested in the NPM to beware of this ideological orientation and the claims of the reinvention thesis that it can lead to a fundamental "paradigm shift" in the nature and working of government. While he does assert that many operational improvements can be made in how governments work and that much progress can be effected in making governments and their public sector management more economical, efficient, effective, socially responsive, and accountable, such reforms will not and should not come at the expense of the core traditions, roles, and duties of the public service. As Savoie argues, governments and the public service have important roles to play in the socio-economic, cultural, and political life of this country, and the public sector cannot be viewed simply as something that should be essentially indistinct from the private sector. Rather, the public sector has a distinct purpose in the development and implementation of public policy designed to serve the collective interests of society. The role of government, therefore, is not to promote private interests as defined by the logic of profit-seeking entrepreneurs but to pursue public interests as determined through the process of democratic politics culminating in the decision-making of democratically elected governments and legislatures. In this sense, the traditional paradigmatic concepts and understandings of the public sector are to be recognized and accepted as important features of social life distinct from their private sector counterparts. In other words, the purpose of government is fundamentally different from the purposes of private sector firms, and, given this profound simplicity, the core operational concepts of the latter will be ill-suited to the former.

Contrary to the logic of the private sector, as Savoie stresses, governments are expected to view people first and foremost as citizens with equal rights and interests, not primarily as consumers or clients with individualized wants. The work of government should be seen primarily as a public service and the fulfillment of the public interest rather than as the management of private markets and the servicing of client needs. Government itself should be seen as an important institution and process within society, promoting the broad goals of democracy, accountability, social responsiveness, equity, due process, the rule of law, and the serving of collective needs, rather than as an institution that should be as small and unintrusive as possible, with operational processes as businesslike as possible. Thus, social purpose and the public good matter more than private interest, just as the provision of public services to citizens as a right is more important than concerns of profitability and cost-effectiveness. The fear that Savoie, among others, expresses is that the ideological values of the NPM will weaken governments, making them smaller and less significant actors in the life of society and thus diminishing the public realm, the public interest, and the public good.

Savoie (1995: 117-21) is also quick to stress the managerial and political limitations of the NPM. In many ways the values and principles of the NPM, and the reinvention thesis in particular, are simplistic and fail to account for the political and administrative complexity of the public sector, policy-making, and program administration. In such a complex environment, as reviewed in Chapters 3 to 5, radical and revolutionary change as envisioned through the reinvention thesis is unlikely to occur or to survive for long. This is because government policies and programs exist, as Savoie argues, within a world of political and legal constraints, including public expectations of service standards, the established practices and professional understandings of political and bureaucratic actors, and judicially recognized rights to particular administrative procedures. In such a world in which practical wisdom, respect for the political-legal trade-offs that have spawned existing policies and programs, and command-and-control power relations are as important as concern for managerial economy and efficiency, administrative decision-making is inherently incremental and restrained. It is unlikely, as Savoie suggests, that public servants will seek to transform radically how they engage in routine policy and program management, just as it is unlikely that particular client groups of specified departments, agencies, and programs will seek fundamental changes to those programs to which they have become accustomed. It is also highly unlikely that senior managers and their political superiors will embrace the proclamations of participatory management and the decentralization and democratization of decision-making power in contrast to the command-and-control mode of power relations with which they are accustomed. Such a substantial transfer of power and authority from centralized authorities at the apex of government institutions to those further down the institutional hierarchies, Savoie claims, is highly unlikely, despite supportive rhetoric to the contrary. A clear example of this can be seen in the revamping of Ontario's education system by the former Progressive Conservative government in that province; despite claims of giving more control to those closest to the operational end of the system (parents, students, and teachers), in fact the changes were a centralizing power grab by the government that stripped autonomy from school boards and gave greater control to the provincial education ministry. Of course, so much of the power relations that we have reviewed and assessed throughout this text suggest that this is, in fact, the dynamic at work.

Savoie's general conclusion is that while change does and will occur within government, such change will be incremental in nature. This approach to the development of public sector management not only meshes with empirical reality but is theoretically desirable: cautious, gradual reform, rather than rationalist reinvention, allows for the development of accumulated wisdom sensitive to specific political, legal, and administrative contexts. This, in turn, provides ongoing intelligence to managers in regard to whether any given procedural or substantive alteration to existing policy is valuable, viable, and capable of being successfully implemented in any given policy and program field.

This incrementalist and gradualist defence of political and managerial reform over reinvention is also reflected in the works of Michael Trebilcock (1994) and Paul Thomas (1993). While Trebilcock, like Savoie, is quite supportive of the need for governments to perform their duties more economically and efficiently, he contends that "institutional evolution, rather than revolution in the way governments do their work is all that we can reasonably aspire to" (Trebilcock, 1994: 6). In addition to the constraints of accepted policy and program understandings and given legal procedures towards the implementation of policy, Trebilcock stresses the importance of established administrative culture within bureaucracies and the interrelationship between this and the broader political environment within which any given institution exists. It is important to recall the key concepts of this established administrative culture within the public service: public duty, citizen equality, due process, rights to public services, public accountability, and the understanding that the state stands apart and distinct from any particular private interest, operating along lines geared solely to the service and promotion of the public interest. Since these concepts, according to Trebilcock, are embedded in Canada's political environment, a radical alteration of one is unlikely, unless it is supported and influenced by a like change in the others. But, as Trebilcock suggests, a fundamental reinvention of the nature of democratic politics and public expectations of public service and the role of the state is not to be found in this society. There is public concern for greater efficiency and economy in the way public bureaucracies perform their duties, but, as we observed in Chapter 2, there is no broad public consensus for a radically altered, commercialized, and downsized public sector (Trebilcock, 1994: 68-73).

Thomas (1993: 55) echoes these concerns, stressing that change within any organization, public or private, is contingent upon a host of factors, including "size, structure, process, leadership and culture." Adaptation to changing environmental concerns and demands is important for any organization, he stresses, but one should beware the allure of fundamentalist, holistic prescriptions for such change. In Thomas's analysis, substantial organizational change "tends to be disorderly, disjointed and problematic. There is no magic recipe for success" (Thomas, 1993: 57). Bureaucratic reconfiguration within the public sector is again viewed as emerging incrementally from an environment in which managers respond to pressures for reform as well as to the political and institutional expectations, rules, and conventional understandings regarding the appropriate role of the state in society. And, as with Trebilcock, Thomas affirms the importance of administrative culture to the process of change. "Culture has replaced structure as the most popular variable in the organizational change process" (Thomas, 1993: 57). Significant alterations to government organizations thus depend on their meshing with and supporting established and respected institutional values, attitudes, and beliefs. As Savoie emphasized, the culture of the public sector is fundamentally different from that of the private sector, with these differences existing, as Thomas suggests, for important and valid reasons. Thomas recognizes that these cultural values and understandings can change and evolve, but such changes tend to be incremental in nature. The pace of change, then, is slow and measured rather than quick and radical. And as with Trebilcock and Savoie, Thomas sees no real basis in Canadian society for a fundamental rethinking of the values and understandings that most people have of governments and their roles. He argues that no revolution is underway with respect to how most people think about the desired nature of public sector management, nor have public expectations changed significantly regarding policy and program development and implementation. Rather than witnessing the reinvention of government, at best, Thomas suggests, we will observe its reform.

10.2 The New Public Management in Practice: Certain Initiatives, Uncertain Success

Despite the debate over the merits and demerits of the NPM and the concept of reinventing government, governments in this country, most notably both the Mulroney Progressive Conservative and Chrétien Liberal governments, have undertaken initiatives influenced by these new ways of thinking about government and public sector management. Financial and personnel management reforms during the 1980s and 1990s have been considered in previous chapters; here we will consider these initiatives as examples of how government has redesigned and reconfigured policy in keeping with the basic logic of NPM. Certain changes promoted by both the Mulroney and Chrétien governments have resulted in significant changes to the structure and operation of federal government institutions. Substantial privatization, some deregulation, and the downsizing of the federal public service through the process of Program Review in the mid-1990s are the main examples of these structural changes. The actual methods of government decision-making, however—the exercise of centralized leadership and the nature of managerial control within public sector organizations—appear to have changed little. Initiatives designed to empower employees and to promote participative forms of management and operations have been, by and large, abject failures.

10.2.1 The New Public Management and the Mulroney Government

As we saw in Chapter 8, the Progressive Conservative government of Brian Mulroney launched a number of initiatives to reconfigure and redirect the nature of the federal government along more businesslike and business-friendly lines of action. By far the most significant and influential actions of this government restructuring related to privatization and deregulation. As outlined in Chapters 2 and 3, the Mulroney government oversaw the full or partial privatization of a substantial number of Crown corporations, including de Havilland, Canadair, Teleglobe, Eldorado Nuclear, Canadian Arsenals, Air Canada, and Petro-Canada. It also promoted deregulation in several major economic fields, as highlighted in Chapter 3, including the oil and gas industry, foreign investment screening, transportation, and financial services. All these initiatives fit into a broader conservative understanding of the desired role of the state and reflected a belief in the efficacy of reducing the size and scope of government and of enhancing and promoting the interests of business, the private sector, and free enterprise. These values and objectives, of course, conform to the general logic of the NPM, its stress on creating more economical and efficient government systems, and its support of the entrepreneurial and market-oriented ethos of the private sector.

The structural reforms effected by the federal government through privatization and deregulation represented major alterations—a reconstitution of the federal government—still observed and felt to this day. In this respect, certain NPM undertakings of the Mulroney government were significant and, as far as their proponents were concerned, successful. Indeed, the record of privatizations by this government and their effect on its broad structure can be seen as revolutionary when compared to the pattern of Crown corporation activity that had gone before. In this sense, and with regard to the commercial functions of the federal government via Crown corporations, these privatizations can be seen as a reinvention of the federal state. The same conclusion cannot be drawn, however, with respect to certain initiatives undertaken by this government to restructure its internal workings and the nature of its management functions. Chapter 8 illustrated a number of these initiatives, such as the Ministerial Task Force on Program Review, Increased Ministerial Authority and Accountability (IMAA), and PS2000. All three can be understood as emerging from the basic values, ideas, and policy proposals of the NPM, yet not one was an unqualified success. In fact, quite the opposite is true. The Ministerial Task Force on Program Review failed to instil fiscal discipline and market-oriented program management techniques. While IMAA was innovative in granting some departments and their management greater control over program activities, internal personnel decision-making, and unused capital budget appropriations, it failed to attract widespread support within government.

In particular, it failed to restructure the power relations between departments and central agencies, resulting in the former still being subject to strict reporting and control regimes imposed by the latter, contrary to the concepts of decentralization, power-sharing, and participatory management as advocated by the NPM.

The PS2000 initiative was by far the grandest of the Mulroney government's attempts to transform the federal public service and its management. It was also specifically rooted in the logic of the NPM. Its overall objective was to improve how government functions

- by making it, according to the rubric of NPM thought, more economical, efficient, and effective;
- by making public service bureaucracies more innovative and service-oriented;
- and by making the government more responsive and accountable to the needs of its "customers" and "clients."

Through this, the public service was to be restructured, so that departments and their managers would be empowered to make decisions on their own. Central agency controls were to be loosened, administrative procedures simplified, and participatory management encouraged. As observed in Chapter 8, however, the PS2000 venture collapsed on itself within two years, a victim both of the theoretical problems inherent in the concept of participatory management, empowerment, and decentralized control within bureaucracies and of the practical problems of governments and ministers insisting on maintaining effective command and control over their bureaucratic institutions. Contrary to the noble aspirations of PS2000, all of its calls for empowerment, decentralization, and participatory management ran counter to the dominant trends in the Canadian federal government towards the maintenance of centralized and hierarchical command-and-control approaches to departmental/agency decision-making and an ever-increasing concentration of power in the hands of a select number of officials and ministers co-existing around the figure of the prime minister. Against this reality of centralized and concentrated power, the values of participatory management and decentralized decision-making appear, at best, as naive evocations of a managerial ideal; at worst, they may be seen, as Inwood suggests, as cynical attempts by senior officials to manipulate management and staff to "buy into" faddish reform initiatives while seeking to demonstrate to the general public that a major improvement in the functioning of the federal government was at hand (Inwood, 2004). All the while, the true nature of power relations within the federal government remained unchanged.

10.2.2 The New Public Management and the Chrétien Government

While the Mulroney government achieved some significant restructuring through privatization and deregulation, the most substantial alterations to the nature and working of the federal government in the past quarter-century have occurred in the past 15 years. As with their Progressive Conservative predecessors, the Chrétien government had been motivated by the general logic of the NPM and sought to renew the federal government and to make it, according to the now common rhetoric of managerial change, more economical and efficient; more capable of doing "more with less"; and more responsive, participatory, and accountable. The major projects undertaken towards these ends, as discussed in Chapters 7 and 8, were Program Review and La Relève.

Program Review was the more substantial and influential of these initiatives. Through it, the federal government

- eliminated some 45,000 positions from the Public Service of Canada and the military;
- made expenditure reductions of $29 billion between 1995 and 1998;
- effected the downsizing of such departments as National Defence, Human Resources Development Canada, Environment, Canadian Heritage, Transportation, Industry, Agriculture and Agri-Food Canada, and Natural Resources;
- unilaterally disbanded both the Established Programs Financing system and the Canada Assistance Plan, replacing them with the Canada Health and Social Transfer (CHST);
- reduced its fiscal commitment to the CHST by $4.5 billion;
- revamped the Unemployment Insurance system, renaming it Employment Insurance, and introduced stricter requirements for making claims and reduced coverage amounts for those receiving benefits;
- privatized the national system of air traffic control;
- off-loaded to local authorities the responsibility for airports and harbour authorities; and
- downsized federal agencies responsible for such matters as environmental protection, housing development, and food products and consumer protection.

Program Review, in short, marked the single greatest move to reform, restructure, and reduce the size and scope of the federal government in Canadian history. And through such action, as noted in Chapter 7, it was heralded as the means by which the Chrétien government established control over the nation's finances, reduced and eventually eliminated the deficit, and built the framework for recent budgetary surpluses.

The La Relève initiative can be seen as a consequence of Program Review. Given the substantial restructuring of the federal government and the downsizing of the public service during these years, morale, confidence, and even the operational capabilities of the federal public service began to suffer, as noted in Chapter 8. With the decline in staff, coupled with years of pay freezes and moratoria on new staff and managerial hirings, there was a growing concern that the federal public service had not been renewing itself in that it had not been recruiting, training, promoting, and rewarding the new staff and management required to meet the policy and program needs of the government in the future. There was also a fear that the quality of public services and their delivery mechanisms were being eroded and that service quality was suffering. The changes wrought during the early and mid-1990s had resulted in an overall sense of malaise, a sense that the public service had lost its way, that it was no longer a relevant and driving force in the socio-economic life of the country, and that it had not been maintaining itself as an organizationally healthy body with a human resource talent pool that could lead it forward into the future. These concerns led the Clerk of the Privy Council in 1997 to speak of a "quiet crisis" in the Public Service of Canada that needed immediate and constructive attention. La Relève was launched to address these problems and to renew and revitalize the public service through new hiring programs, the promotion of management training, the improvement of pay and working conditions, and the promotion of greater management-staff participation in organizational decision-making. While La Relève was in no way as ambitious a project as Program Review, it was important in its own right and offered some hope for better working conditions, organizational stability, and future growth. The La Relève exercise can also be seen as borrowing certain ideas from the NPM in relation to the promotion of organizational efficiency and effectiveness, participatory management, and improved service delivery.

In regard to both Program Review and La Relève, however, certain serious questions can be raised as to the degree to which these ventures conformed to and supported the concepts of the NPM and the reinvention of government. No one can deny the profound impact of Program Review on the federal government and on the country. In its early incarnation, it was demonstrably influenced by NPM. The six tests of Program Review, outlined in Chapter 7, are representative of core NPM concerns, with all government departments and agencies being expected to engage in rational program evaluation and redesign to meet them and, consequently, to develop a more economical, efficient, and smaller government that would be more commercialized and attuned to the needs and interests of citizens, businesses, and the private sector. As mentioned in Chapter 7, however, Program Review never lived up to these expectations as a means of reconfiguring the machinery of the federal government because central governmental authorities, primarily located in the Department of Finance, saw and used the process as a "rough and ready" means to achieve major, albeit incremental, budget-cutting. Rather than departments and agencies engaging in a thoughtful and reflective assessment of the merits and demerits of the six tests with respect to their particular policies and programs, they were confronted with ad hoc budget cuts dictated by Finance; these "notional" cutback levels, in turn, were persistently and consistently supported by the minister of finance and the prime minister as vital means to the end of deficit reduction. This objective, and not a major rethinking and reconfiguration of the system of governance, became the operational logic of Program Review.

Most analysts, therefore, see Program Review as a failed NPM exercise. It failed to support a comprehensive and rationalistic reappraisal of government along NPM lines and also fell short of generating empowerment and participation of department and agency middle management and staff in the change process. Rather than being involved as key players in this process, these officials were passive recipients of policy and program decisions made for them by a few centralized authorities. Nothing in the operational results of Program Review, moreover, fundamentally sought to alter the process of decision-making and the exercise of power within government. While the NPM and reinvention thesis devote much attention to the concepts of decentralizing power and authority within bureaucracies and empowering management and staff to be more active in leading policy and program development, these values and attitudes were never met by the actual exercise of power through the Program Review process. As Savoie has argued, rather than witnessing the decentralization and sharing of power, the process only demonstrated the increasing centralization of power in the hands of a small number of lead bureaucratic and political authorities and the continued presence of the command-and-control mode of decision-making.

Given the reality of centralized power that effectively dominates the federal bureaucracy, one can wonder about the ability of the La Relève project to make any significant change to the established order. Indeed, given the practical reality by which executive power is exercised in Ottawa, it is not surprising that an analyst such as Inwood (2004: 73) suggests that official efforts to promote administrative decentralization and participatory management are symbolic reform initiatives, more indicative of governments seeking to appeal to the latest "fad" in organizational theory than an honest attempt at fundamental transformation of the decision-making processes. Those in the public service who lived through PS2000 and Program Review and their purported involvement of line management and staff in the redevelopment and redesign of operational activities may be excused for being somewhat cynical in their attitudes to senior executive proclamations about the empowerment of employees and the promotion of participatory management. With respect to both of these initiatives, "empowerment" and "participatory management" became empty buzzwords lost amid the exercise of real power emanating from lead authorities.

Despite much rhetoric in favour of empowerment, decentralization of decision-making, and participatory management, real managerial and governmental power remains with those few individuals who are directly responsible and accountable for the exercise of such power, and it is highly doubtful that the La Relève initiative changed this. While it may be beneficial for senior officials to consult widely with subordinate management and staff, and while the general attitudes and approaches of the organic-humanistic model of organizational theory are embraced by these officials, it is rare for any of these leaders to disavow the command-and-control approach to leadership and responsibility—quite the contrary, since senior management and its political leadership stress, by their actions if not their words, the primary and vital importance of centralized, hierarchical, and authoritative leadership. And yet, through this, certain of the basic principles of the NPM and reinvention thesis have been, in practical terms, abandoned.

10.2.3 The New Public Management and the Martin Government

When Paul Martin became prime minister in December 2003, he and his government inherited the public service management reform initiatives of his predecessor. While the leadership rivalry between Chrétien and Martin had become legendary by this time, the differences between them in no way extended to the substance of management reform. Rather, the Martin government continued to champion the management reform agenda of the Chrétien government, stressing the importance of the modernization of the public service while also promoting greater systems of accountability and financial controls respecting the spending of public monies.

In speaking in regard to the Martin government's 2005 budget and its reiteration of the need for more open, responsive, and accountable government, Reg Alcock, President of the Treasury Board, asserted:

> Our goal is to offer Canadians the best public service possible. We must "work smart," pay attention to the needs of Canadians, and react more quickly to change. We will support public servants as they deliver services to Canadians. Coordinated efforts in all of these areas will serve to strengthen trust, accountability, and the value-for-money that Canadians receive from their government. They will ensure that the Government continues to strengthen Canada's competitive advantage in the world and position the country for the future. (Canada, 2005)

In its public service modernization initiative, the Martin government stressed that its reforms were rooted to the values of transparency, quality, and efficiency. There were three main themes to this initiative:

- modernizing and improving service delivery,
- strengthening transparency and accountability, and
- improving financial management.

With respect to service delivery the government is committed to the ever-increasing use of the Internet as a means of communication and interchange between citizens, businesses, and the public service. The Canada Site at <http://www.canada.gc.ca> provides links to a vast array of services listed by client, topic, and department, and the telephone information portal of 1-800 O-Canada provides up-to-date information on all federal programs and services. The ultimate goal of the government is to be able to offer to Canadians a "one-stop" information service available by phone, Internet, or in person with respect to all major government programs and services. Of course, as the federal government becomes more reliant and capable with respect to the use of electronic forms of communication, this places an added burden on it to offer such forms of communication and transaction in a secure fashion. Through its government on-line undertakings the federal government has had to develop systems of information infrastructure security that can assure both members of the public and those public servants dealing with them that the citizen-government Internet interconnection is one that is safe, private, and secure. As more Canadians take advantage of the Canada Customs and Revenue Agency's ability to file tax returns on-line, the importance of this concern is only magnified.

As the Martin government struggled with concerns about ethics (see the next chapter), it sought to promote greater transparency and accountability in its operations. Its new Management Accountability Framework sought

- to clarify the relationships between ministers and Crown corporations,
- to strengthen the accountability regimes of Crown corporations,
- to make the government appointment process more transparent,
- to improve the government's reporting relationship to Parliament, and
- to promote a more stringent approach to respecting values and ethics within the work of the public service.

Closely tied to these reform initiatives are those designed to improve the government's financial management. The TBS was mandated the role of strictly scrutinizing all government expenditures for ways and means of finding savings and efficiencies, and the Office of the Comptroller General was re-established within the TBS to provide leadership across the government respecting improved financial management, accounting policies, and internal audits. Cabinet's Expenditure Review Committee was also charged with responsibility for maintaining balanced budgets overall, more effectively aligning financial resources with governmental priorities, and searching for better operational mechanisms for promoting program efficiency (Canada, 2005).

10.3 Program Review, La Relève, and Public Service Modernization: Reinventing Government?

The substance and processes of the policy and program changes inherent to Program Review, La Relève, and current initiatives in public sector modernization are open to question. Have they and their related policy and program changes represented the advent of a coherent NPM approach to government? And more pointedly, do they represent a reinvention of government along the lines advanced by Osborne and Gaebler? These questions are central to much contemporary analysis and debate about the nature of government in this country, how it is changing, and whether such changes are for the better or not.

The impact of Program Review on the federal government, and on the country in general, certainly has meant change in how and what government operates over the past decade. La Relève and the public sector modernization initiatives of the Martin government promised more modifications in the future. The question, however, is whether these alterations would represent a fundamental transformation in government and its role or a more gradual reform, as suggested in the writings of Savoie, Trebilcock, and Thomas. While Program Review has had a great impact, and though Borins and Purchase and Hirshorn stress that the NPM "is here to stay" (Kernaghan and Siegel, 1999: 78), the question is the degree to which changes reflect and support a coherent NPM approach. As Kernaghan, Marson, and Borins have argued, a variety of ideas and approaches inform NPM in Canada, ranging from fundamental government reinvention to more modest management reforms (Kernaghan *et al.*, 2000: 24), and the latter are more reflective of the changes that have occurred and are occurring in Ottawa. The values of the NPM are found more in micro- and meso-level management enhancement practices than in major macro-level alterations to the structure and configuration of government and its relationship to citizens. As all these NPM developments and initiatives are relatively new, this remains a field of inquiry still in need of thorough research, but one can raise certain questions and observe certain dynamics that cast doubt on some of the more grandiose claims of the advocates of the NPM and especially of the reinvention thesis.

It is important to recall what a reinvented government would look like:

- Its departments and agencies would be "catalytic."
- They would "steer" policy development and program implementation by fashioning new ways of providing public services, consulting and working with "clients" and "empowering" them to assume greater responsibility for the creation and management of services.
- These changes would be effected through public/private partnerships; rewards and incentives for those customers dealing with the organization; and the innovative use of new information technologies, communication services, and service delivery mechanisms.
- Many new forms of service delivery would be countenanced and practised, including privatization, deregulation, contracting out of

government services, and even volunteer labour to provide public services.

- Departments and agencies would also be "community-owned," closely tied to community and business groups, with these group members and their leaders sharing fully in the management and administration of government organizations.
- These organizations would strongly promote "client" access to their operations and would encourage close and effective "customer service."
- Departments and agencies would also stress "competitive" government, promoting the commercialization and marketing of government activities through such initiatives as privatization and deregulation, as well as contracting out and downsizing government services.
- Departments and agencies would also be "mission-driven" and "results-oriented." Management would focus more on "results" than "rules and regulations" and would be constantly seeking new and innovative ways to develop policies and deliver services more economically, efficiently, and effectively.
- Organizations would stress "competitive" means for delivering services and would aggressively promote methods by which they could generate revenue through such devices as user fees, capital pools, and investment funds.
- In all their actions, departments and agencies would concentrate on people as "consumers" and "clients" more so than as citizens, with the responsibility of any given government institution being to service the needs of such customers and clients, much like any other private sector firm.

Taken together, these approaches would establish "enterprising" and "anticipatory" government organizations that blend public service with an entrepreneurial mentality. Such organizations would be expected to combine service delivery effectiveness with financial stability and profitability, thus promoting their own financial well-being while anticipating and responding to changes in the policy and program environment. Ultimately, all government organizations would see their organizational environments as sets of markets, with their role being to interact with these markets to service the needs of market actors in a businesslike manner.

A "reinvented" government, in short, would be a radically transformed government. It would be recast as a result of a clear, rationalistic, and economistic effort to restructure its organization and action to achieve a vision of a new and coherent operational reality. Given the manner and depth of change required for such a fundamental transformation, one can and should question the extent to which the federal government, or any government, has been able to reinvent itself.

We have noted many changes to, and reconfigurations of, the federal government and its departments and agencies over the past decade, including

- increased privatization and deregulation,
- the downsizing of government organizations,
- the off-loading of certain responsibilities and functions,
- the contracting out of certain services,
- the increased usage of user fees for services,
- the development of public/private partnerships in certain fields,
- the interest in and promotion of new forms of service delivery to government "customers,"
- the increasing government concern for economy and efficiency in all its actions, and
- the advancement of precise and effective forms of program evaluation so as to better measure results achieved.

All of these matters, as Borins (1995) and Purchase and Hirshorn (1994) assert, can be seen as evidence of the NPM. And with the privatization of federal Crown corporations, it is fair to assert that we have witnessed a reinvention of the nature and working of the federal government. If other policy and program fields were to emulate the transformative changes found in this policy field, we would see the full reinvention of government and the unquestioned triumph of the NPM as a new and revolutionary approach to government organization and functioning. Most of the initiatives undertaken to date, however, are consistent with the more modest proposition that the government is simply engaged in a process of evolutionary administrative reform rather than revolutionary change. This reform can be explained more in terms of incrementalism, or bounded rationalism, or mixed scanning, than of comprehensive rationalism. This "reform thesis" of government change, as advocated most strongly by Thomas (1993), also helps to explain certain weaknesses and limitations in government attempts to transform fundamentally how it engages in policy and program development and implementation.

Most of the recent changes to government structures and operations, as Savoie, Trebilcock, and Thomas argue, can be explained as being evidence of government reform, not reinvention. The downsizing of the federal government, the reduction in personnel, the cutting of budgets, and the off-loading of certain programs and responsibilities can all be understood as efforts to deal with the deficit and debt, not to transform how government works. Thus, Program Review was more an exercise in deficit control and elimination than an attempt at profound restructuring. User fees, various public/private partnerships, and increased concern and attention for improved service delivery have also been explained along these reformist lines as having been designed to make more modest, albeit important, changes to the workings of government. Concern for economy, efficiency, and program effectiveness; the promotion of anticipatory change; and the quest for more open, participative forms of management and communication, both inside and outside any given organization—all predate the advent of the NPM and reinvention thesis. Governments and their bureaucracies have long had an interest in developing innovative and better means for realizing these ends. Interest in results-based management founded on mission statements and rigorous systems of performance evaluation is also a long-standing feature of government reform initiatives, just as is interest in better and more up-to-date forms of service delivery. In all these respects, the reform thesis can explain much of what has transpired within the federal government over the past decade. And it can also explain much of what did not happen.

Over the past decade, for example, have we truly witnessed a transformation in the nature of managerial decision-making geared to the promotion of greater participation of management, staff, interest groups, and clients, resulting in the sharing of decision-making power and the serious involvement of these latter three groups in setting priorities for government institutions? The short answer is no. Decision-making authority in government has been increasingly centralized in recent decades, leading to what Savoie refers to as the dominance of the centre and the strategic prime ministership. Within each department or agency, ministers and their senior staff maintain a tight grip on all matters of strategic importance to the organization, the minister, and the government overall. In such a realm of centralized authority, participatory management is perceived as being co-management, or the sharing of decision-making power among elected officials, senior management, middle management, and line staff. While participatory management may be a signal component element of the NPM and the theory of reinventing government, such an approach simply does not conform either to the theory of accountability based on the concept of ministerial responsibility or to the practical realities of power politics.

In theoretical terms, as outlined in Chapter 5, participatory management challenges the accountability of senior managers and elected ministers by involving more and more officials and players in decision-making, making the process more convoluted and the lines of responsibility more complex. If senior officials truly share decision-making power with subordinates, this raises questions as to where power lies within an organization and who is officially responsible and accountable for actions taken if problems arise from such actions. And with respect to elected officials, if they are sharing decision-making responsibility with subordinates, questions can and will arise as to whether they are properly exercising democratic control over the assigned bureaucratic entity for which they are responsible to Parliament.

All such theoretical considerations become most germane, of course, when there are explicit questions about responsibility for decision-making when those decisions are seen to be problematic. When questions arise as to the failures of particular government actions, of who must bear responsibility for them and who must right perceived wrongs, claims of participatory management quickly tend to evaporate. As we have seen in Chapter 4, responsibility for policy and program decision-making rests with senior management within each department or agency, with ultimate responsibility being borne by elected ministers accountable to Parliament. Since these officials are responsible for decision-making and ultimately responsible and accountable for bureaucratic problems, it is of little surprise that elected politicians seek to retain and exercise effective command and control over such decision-making, notwithstanding the noble ideals of participatory management. This, then, becomes the practical reality of power relations within government, and one with which all administrative change initiatives such as PS2000, Program Review, and La Relève have had to contend.

Through the changes of the 1990s can it also be said that federal departments and agencies have become "catalytic" actors engaged more in strategic leadership than tactical program administration? Have we witnessed the creation of "competitive" government in which private sector models of service delivery are advanced and departments and agencies respond to people more as customers and clients than as citizens? Have the changes of the past decade resulted in the creation of a more enterprising and entrepreneurial government geared to market-oriented solutions to societal problems? In short, has the essence of government changed over the past decade so that it is today fundamentally different from that which existed just a decade or more ago? The general response to all such questions again must be no.

While certain departments and agencies have been and may be experiencing some greater and deeper changes than others, it is difficult to argue that the nature, work, and role of government has been fundamentally reinvented. Reforms and changes over the past two decades have not risen to the height of reinvention. While the federal government has been downsized, and while some of its roles and responsibilities have been reduced and its operational capabilities made more limited by policies of fiscal restraint, it is important to note the continuities in the nature and practice of government across the decades of the latter half of the twentieth century. Indeed, little has changed with respect to fundamental public service values, and core social, economic, and cultural policies and programs of previous governments have continued to define the core responsibilities of current governments. In addition, basic attitudes regarding the appropriate role of the state in society remain entrenched among the general public.

Far from federal departments and agencies viewing people essentially as customers and clients to be dealt with in individual, transactional manners, these organizations are encouraged, by the government itself, to view people as citizens, bearing rights to and interests in public services designed to respond to the socio-economic needs of themselves individually and the broader society in which they live (Canada, 2000a). And far from federal departments and agencies seeing the role of government in strongly competitive, entrepreneurial, and market-oriented perspectives, much evidence suggests that, despite the reductions and restrictions on government institutions and activities over the past decade, the organizations of the federal government have not lost sight of the essential characteristics of public service or of the important distinctions between the public and the private sectors. For example, despite the impact of Program Review and financial restraint, the federal government still maintains a major and vital presence in health, education, and social welfare, with the nature of its public policy role being essentially unchanged. In health policy, the federal government remains committed to the principles of the Canada Health Act and to the preservation of a public system of medical care. Federal government opposition to the establishment of a two-tiered health-care system founded on substantial private sector for-profit service delivery is supported, in turn, by most opposition parties, most provincial governments, and widespread public opinion. The results of the 2000 and 2004 federal elections confirmed general public opposition to, and rejection of, the idea of two-tiered health care. While health policy has clearly been undergoing some major reforms, basically attributable to funding reductions, it is hard to sustain the argument that we have been witnessing its reinvention, a point that supporters of the reinvention thesis would likely lament.

Similar findings can be advanced with respect to education and social welfare policy. Despite funding cutbacks, the federal government remains committed to substantial support for the nation's post-secondary college and university system through the block funding of the Canada Health and Social Transfer, and specialized support for colleges and universities comes from various programs, including the support of student loans, the promotion of research in the arts and sciences, and support for technological innovation. And despite funding cutbacks to social welfare policies, the federal government remains committed to such policies and programs as the Canada Pension Plan, support for seniors, Employment Insurance and support for those who are unemployed, continued federal transfers to the provinces in support of provincially administered social assistance and welfare programs, and federal-provincial equalization policy. In all these respects the core nature of federal responsibilities and obligations has not changed, nor has widespread public support for these government roles diminished. Quite the contrary in fact, public concern for maintaining and enhancing such a federal role has grown as federal spending cuts in all these fields have been felt over the past decade. Such cutbacks represented incremental changes dictated more by financial pressures than by attempts to restructure in any fundamental way how government works. This broad dynamic can be observed in the working of Human Resources Development Canada and employment skills training policy. Rather than being "reinvented" out of existence in favour of more "market-oriented" approaches to labour market management and skills development, Human Resources Development remains a major portfolio in the federal government despite Program Review cutbacks. Indeed, this department has been given increased responsibilities for preparing Canadian workers for the demands of the "new economy."

The point about policy and program change here is subtle yet important. Major cutbacks to federal policies and programs as a result of deficit reduction policy have substantially affected these policies and programs to the point that many critics contend that the quality of public services across most fields of government activity has seriously declined over the past decade. Any such decline, however, is far from being evidence of comprehensive government reinvention. Program Review, after all, certainly was not an undertaking of reinvention—government has not sought to transform fundamentally its policy and program role within society. At most, it has sought to maintain its core responsibilities while downsizing its financial support for these responsibilities; at worst, it can be argued that it is neglecting its responsibilities in the quest for fiscal balance while not having the courage to embrace fully the market logic of reinvention. In either case, however, the government is not consciously engaged in reinvention, and, as the ten principles enunciated by Osborne and Gaebler indicate, such rational and conscious engagement is a necessary hallmark of reinvention.

Programs and policies in the Environment and Heritage Canada portfolios also indicate that the more things change, the more they stay the same. While federal funding for both these policy fields was sharply reduced over the past decade, leading to much public concern in regard to the quality of environmental protection and heritage preservation, such funding cutbacks and the more restricted role of the federal government in these areas simply brought increased criticism of the government and growing demands for a greater state commitment to promote environmental policy and heritage conservation. The Walkerton, Ontario, water quality scandal increased such popular demands for all governments—municipal, provincial, and federal—to take environmental policy more seriously and to decrease popular support for policies of environmental regulatory off-loading, deregulation, and privatization. Similarly, growing public concern about the quality and preservation of national parks and heritage sites, ranging from Banff National Park in Alberta to Fortress Louisbourg in Cape Breton, has served to increase calls and demands from concerned groups and individuals for the federal government to do more again to protect and nurture these sites of natural beauty and national heritage.

The evidence that the federal government has been engaged in a fundamental transformation—a reinvention—of its basic roles and responsibilities is thus hard to find. Government changes, for all their significance, have been more incremental than rational, more modest and reform-oriented than comprehensive and reventionist, and more motivated by short-term considerations of budget-cutting than by long-term interests in systematically transforming the nature of government. It is important, here, to remember a point made in Chapter 3: no government inherits policies and programs with a clean slate. Rather, all governments assume most of their policy and program responsibilities from their predecessors, with many of these policies and programs dating back years, if not decades. Governments will thus inherit series of more or less coherent policy initiatives designed to address major socio-economic problems, needs, wants, and interests. The Chrétien government, for example, inherited such pre-existing policies and programs as

- the Canada Health Act and the medicare system;
- the Canada Pension Plan;

- the system of federal-provincial Established Programs Financing;
- environmental protection policy;
- official bilingualism and multiculturalism policy;
- regional equalization and regional development policy;
- agricultural, fisheries, and industrial development policy;
- free trade policy;
- national defence policy;
- heritage and cultural policy; and
- human rights policy.

With respect to each of these policy fields, and all the others that, combined, account for the full range of federal policy and program responsibilities, the government also inherited fully fledged sets of government institutions and bureaucratic actors specifically designed and charged with responsibility for developing and administering all existing, and any new, policy and program initiatives of the government. These institutions and the people that work within them have well-founded understandings of their roles and responsibilities, their legal obligations to policy and program development and implementation, and the forms of actions that are expected of them. They also possess a clear awareness and preference for well-established standard operating procedures needed to fulfil their duties and obligations, as well as for the appropriate relationships they should have with the various interested parties within their policy community. Within these issue areas such policies and programs will also have long-established track records and pre-existing clientele interested in maintaining the services they have come to expect. Indeed, these clientele often are organized into distinct interest groups—such as business and industry associations or special interest non-governmental organizations—dedicated to maintaining and enhancing their group relationship to relevant state organizations.

So, policies and programs exist within complex and pre-established institutional environments with various and competing organizational actors seeking to advance their interests within the policy field in question. Interest groups outside of government advance their claims for improved policy and program services while demanding the preservation of services beneficial to their members. Likewise, bureaucratic actors within government organizations advance their interests in policy and program design and action beneficial to their long-term personal and institutional self-interest. In most cases this involves public servants seeking to preserve existing systems of bureaucratic organization and action on the grounds of familiarity, ease of operation, successful past experience, and the fear of change.

The public choice model of decision-making posits that neither politicians nor public servants will advance organizational reforms that could fundamentally alter and limit their responsibilities and powers; such actions are counterproductive to the material self-interest of these actors.

Both the bureaucratic politics and policy networks models of decision-making also offer insights into how decisions get made and the complex environments within which public servants must operate as they engage in policy and program decision-making. A further aspect of any government's policy and program "inheritance," moreover, is its pre-existing system of labour relations and collective bargaining. These matters constrain and limit the administrative changes that can be made within any government institution in that substantial alterations to personnel work patterns will involve contractual negotiations with public sector unions, with these unions being committed to defending and promoting the best interests of employees. Initiatives to advance reinventionist changes to work patterns, such as through the contracting out of public services and the use of volunteer community-based labour, will thus likely invite hostile public service union reaction and employee resistance to any such changes. Within this complex world of pre-existing organizations and interests, policies, programs, public servants, unions, and citizens, effecting any type of policy change is a complicated and difficult task; effecting radical and transformative reinventionist change is even more difficult, if not impossible.

The difficulties of dealing with change within an environment of long-established policies and programs, procedures, and interests have been explored by Brian Howe and David Johnson (2000) with respect to human rights policy and the functioning of human rights commissions at the federal and provincial levels. This work offers support for the reform thesis of government change in recent years. The federal Human Rights Commission and its provincial counterparts have undergone major restructuring of their methods of program delivery and service to citizens, but these initiatives are better understood as emerging from an environment of incrementalist change than as being the result of comprehensive rationalism aimed at the reinvention of human rights policy.

An important dynamic illustrated in this work is the pivotal influence of a legislative policy and program framework providing "rights" to individual citizens, with a government body—a human rights commission—being legally obligated to serve and promote these rights while also dealing with transgressions of such rights according to set legal procedures. Within such a legal framework, which is not unique to human rights commissions, the ability of any bureaucratic organization to transform its structure and operations is strictly limited by its legal duty to adhere to its legislative mandate, to operate through pre-established forms of organization, and to implement and enforce pre-established legal rights and duties. Fidelity to law becomes a restraint on organizational change to the extent that any and all change must be consistent with established legal norms and procedures. And any change or organizational action that appears to be inconsistent can and likely will be subject to legal challenge. In this sense, the federal Human Rights Commission, for example, cannot unilaterally impose user fees on complainants and respondents, cannot restructure its complaint adjudication process to involve private mediation services engaged in more "market-oriented" and "entrepreneurial" decision-making, and cannot levy fines on guilty parties so as to create an investment capital pool. All such changes would be illegal under the Canadian Human Rights Act. These sorts of changes could only be legislated into existence by Parliament, acting on proposals of the responsible minister.

Any attempt at radically altering the long-standing and historic balance of interests between human rights advocacy groups and the business community to refashion the substantive and procedural nature of human rights policy, however, would result in great debate and acrimony. If a government were to support the fundamental reinvention of human rights policy, meaning that it was willing to "go back to square one" in determining human rights policies and procedures, how would interest groups concerned with these matters respond? Rights advocacy groups would very likely press for greater rights coverage and protections; the easier ability to "prove" cases of discrimination; and a stronger, larger, and better funded human rights commission specifically dedicated to promoting the interests of rights advocates and complainants and capable of more rigorously and effectively implementing the law and punishing wrongdoers. Business groups, in turn, would likely argue in favour of the outright abolition of the Human Rights Commission as a first preference or, failing this, for more restricted approaches to the substantive and procedural applications of rights policy; stricter rules and regulations governing the "proving out" of alleged discriminatory practices, and a smaller, less well-funded commission specifically mandated to devote special concern to the interests of business respondents. Any minister and government contemplating a major reconfiguration of rights policy and procedures would be moving into a hornet's nest of controversy and debate with little prospect of finding a middle ground of compromise and balance.

For these reasons neither the federal nor any provincial human rights commission has made a concerted attempt to transform and reinvent its structure and operations. Governments have clearly avoided any such effort for fear of the uncontrolled and undesired results that would likely ensue. Rather, more modest yet still significant changes and reforms have addressed operational problems and opportunities such as improved public education programs and case-flow management, but these changes and reforms emerge much more incrementally than rationalistically. While any organization and any government may, in theory, be free to engage in any transformative change agenda it wishes to pursue, in reality all of their actions are governed by institutional traditions, past practices, and established understandings of what constitutes sound policy and program action. These actions will also be structured by assessments of what is viable and doable, serving the long-term interests of both the organization and the government while also advancing public policy aims and meeting with relative support from stakeholder groups, the media, and the general public.

10.4   Reforming Government: The Broad Contours of Change

Though it is hard to argue that we have been witnessing the reinvention of government in this country at the federal, provincial, or municipal levels, this is not to suggest that significant changes in governance have not been occurring. In fact, important changes and reforms are still evolving and developing, with some of these changes falling within the broad, reformist parameters of the NPM while others simply reflect long-standing aims and desires for government to be more economical, efficient, and effective—three classical objectives of any management system. In looking at the changes that have transpired and are still developing within the federal government, one can distinguish between matters that are more micro- or meso-operational and tactical in orientation and those that are oriented more towards macro-changes, policy-oriented and strategic in direction.

10.4.1   Service Delivery

All departments and agencies of the federal government have been expected to find ways to improve their economy and efficiency in all their policy and program actions. As a consequence of the Program Review constraints, most agencies and departments have been required to refashion their program delivery to fit within smaller budget allocations. They have been expected—some would say forced—to prioritize their various program activities, stressing the development of better management practices, new and better methods of program delivery, and more streamlined and targeted approaches to addressing their main policy objectives. Though the concept of "doing more with less" hardly constitutes reinvented government, it is a key component of the NPM that was embraced by the Chrétien government and remains a touchstone of the Martin government.. As the Treasury Board (1997: 2, 8) document, *Getting Government Right*, stated:

> Nowhere has change been more dramatic than in the public sector. We have built complex systems of social support, economic development promotion, health and education, scientific research, cultural development and environmental management. Many of these services are central to our conception of who we are as Canadians. And, after a long period of expenditures too great for the economy to bear, we are learning how to provide them within our means. We are learning that fiscal prudence is compatible with the society our elders struggled to build.... Delivering high-quality federal government services essential to Canadian society remains a bedrock of government policy and the raison d'être of the government's program spending plans. The focus on change, efficiency and re-engineering should not obscure the fact that the government remains committed to service excellence.

In introducing this report in 1997 President of the Treasury Board Marcel Massé reiterated this concern for balancing public needs for high-quality policies and programs with the requirements of fiscal prudence. "In today's global marketplace," he wrote, "the federal government must manage change and emphasize efficiency in administration. Our collective challenge is to master new ways of doing things while safeguarding the rights of Canadians" (Canada, 1997: President's Message).

In working to meet these goals from a management perspective, the federal government has initiated a number of programs designed to address two major concerns: the promotion of service quality and the enhancement of policy capacity. With respect to the first concern, as part of the La Relève program, the government established the Service Improvement Initiative. This five-year program (2000-05) is designed to promote "citizen-centred service delivery" by providing "easier, more convenient, more seamless 'access' to government services; and higher levels of 'quality and performance' in service delivery by government organizations" (Canada, 2000b). It calls for all departments and agencies to set service standards for all principal public services, to measure operational performance against

BOX 10.2
Service Delivery

The Canadian Centre for Management Development has engaged in some interesting research on Canadian attitudes to service delivery and service quality in studies specifically comparing public and private sector services. Contrary to much conventional wisdom these studies have found that public sector service quality does not rank far below that of the private sector. Rather, most Canadians surveyed found that, on average, the general quality of public sector service delivery was roughly comparable to that of private sector service delivery, and that, in certain instances, specific types of public sector services far outranked private sector services. In fact, the most highly rated services were three delivered by the public sector.

Citizens' Satisfaction with Public and Private Sector Service Quality
(Service satisfaction, on a scale of 0–100; N = 2,900)

	Service Quality		Service Quality
Fire Departments	86	Public-Sector Average[1]	62
Libraries	77	Private-Sector Average[2]	62
Garbage Disposal	74	Colleges/Universities	58
Supermarkets	74	Customs	58
Provincial Parks	71	Canada Post	57
Canada Pension/OAP	69	Taxis	57
RCMP	68	Revenue Canada, Tax	57
Passport Office	66	Insurance Agencies	55
Motor Vehicle Licence	66	Hospitals	51
Telephone Companies	63	Banks	51
Health Card	62	Road Maintenance	45

[1] Combined average of specific municipal, provincial, and federal services.
[2] An average of seven services.

Note: For both public sector and private sector services, the ratings are for those services used by respondents in the past year.

Adapted from CCMD 1999: 6.

these standards, and, over five years, to show a 10 per cent improvement in citizen/client satisfaction with such service delivery.

Senior officials in the PCO, the TBS, the Canada School of Public Service (CSPS), and line departments and agencies have recognized through the Service Improvement Initiative the importance of service quality to citizens and the need for government institutions always to stress the primary importance and place of citizens/clients in everything these institutions do. While this focus on service improvement clearly resonates with the broad NPM literature and, in its current manifestation borrows heavily from the language of the NPM, the concept is far from new. As the Treasury Board (1997: 11) argued:

> Many initiatives to modernize the delivery of services are under-way in the Public Service. These efforts do not focus on cost-cutting alone, but rather on ensuring that Canadians receive an ever-improving mix of government services that meet their needs, and that the government provides these services within a stable expenditure base. Just as the private sector has had to innovate continually to provide goods and services tailor-made for the individual consumer, so must the government tailor its goods and services to the interests of citizens. The design and delivery of government programs must be oriented toward the citizen, and not toward the needs of the Public Service, the con-straints of current management styles or outmoded production processes.

How well the current government lives up to these expectations remains to be seen, but it is committed to improving service quality through a wide range of means. These extend from the most traditional ones of depart-ments and agencies working on program implementation efficiency to enhanced use of information technology and the Internet to link citizens/clients to government initiatives and programs. As we have seen, the Gov-ernment On-Line Project means to provide "one-stop access to Govern-ment of Canada information services," so that by 2004 "Canadians will be able to request and receive all key federal services through secure, interac-tive and timely on-line transactions" (Canada, 2001: Minister's Message). This is to be achieved through high-speed, broadband Internet connec-tions linking citizens/clients to government web sites, with the former able to access these services through their own private or business computers' Community Access Program (CAP) sites, established government offices, or Service Canada centres. The latter are to be located in a host of federal government offices, post offices, public libraries, and community centres across the country. At the heart of all such Internet access to government services, of course, is the Government of Canada web site, which serves as an information and communication link between the government and citizens/clients. The planners of the project envision that it will increasingly become a service link, the beginning of a system of "e-government" allowing citizens and clients to interact with specific government institutions and programs and engage in service transactions that would otherwise have to be undertaken through more traditional means of communication. They anticipate that, in time, such matters as diverse as applying for passports, registering to vote, seeking information on jobs and skills training, filing income tax returns, and making claims for program entitlements such as student loans, Employment Insurance, or seniors' pensions will be increasingly undertaken via the Internet.

As Kernaghan, Marson, and Borins (2000: 236-45) have argued, the development of **e-government**—that is, the growing use of information technology in the initiation and delivery of services to the public—is an increasingly important feature of government in Canada. Yet, while information technology offers many means to facilitate enhanced communication flows between citizens and the public service, certain problems and tensions, both managerial and ethical, may come from it. The use of information technology to provide public services is still new and developing, and it brings many "growing pains." As these authors note, various information technology projects in the past have been marked by implementation failures, the inability of the technology to do the prescribed job, or the relative inability of management and staff to embrace and support fully the new technological innovations. It is also worth noting that information technology projects are skills-intensive, requiring technological and staff training support networks, not all of which have been present in various governmental initiatives. One problem common to all governments is the difficulty in gaining and retaining skilled information technology specialists. Employees with these skills are very "hot" commodities in the job market, and in most instances they can gain far more remunerative work in the private sector. One of the great challenges to the public sector, then, is finding ways to keep their skilled personnel, and this highlights once again the importance of enhancing employee working conditions, including salaries, as mentioned in Chapter 8.

With respect to ethical considerations, a number of issues deserve mention. One is that the increased use of information technology in public service delivery requires that most people are familiar with and have access to the means of information technology. Yet not all Canadians are "technologically literate," and knowledge of and access to information technologies is highly contingent on both income level and age. Poorer Canadians and the elderly are much less likely to be willing or able to make use of the new service delivery systems. This poses a serious question of fair access to services. While initiatives such as the CAP site programs seek to make computer technology available to the widest number of citizens, they are still in their infancy, with most Canadians likely being unaware of their existence. A further ethical issue is that of privacy and security. As more government services come to be offered on-line, there is a corresponding need for governments to ensure that such services can guarantee a citizen's legitimate expectation of privacy. If a citizen is filing a tax return over the Internet, there is an expectation that the government server is secure and that the information so provided will only be viewed and used by those officials responsible for tax-filing measures. As governments generate more and more advanced databases, however, there are concerns that such information may be pooled and used by other officials for a variety of reasons, ranging from simple information-gathering through data mining to security investigations into possibly fraudulent activities. One then confronts a tension between the privacy considerations of citizens versus certain considerations of managerial efficiency and effectiveness in policy development and program delivery.

These are thorny issues that will have to be addressed as governments move further into the field of information technology. And a final point here, of course, is the very security of such information technology systems themselves. Citizens who use them will expect them to be fully secure and free from tampering. If citizens are to make increasing use of processes of "e-government," they must be assured that the systems themselves are as secure as possible from the improper access and manipulation known as "hacking." One only needs to ponder the prospect of on-line voting for federal or provincial elections, and the possible problems that such an initiative might face, to gain perspective on the limitations and fears associated with the use of information technology in certain fields of public service.

Apart from these high-technology/information technology approaches to new methods of service delivery, the federal government has also promoted a variety of more traditional approaches to **alternative service delivery** (ASD), many of which we have already reviewed in previous chapters. Alternative service delivery at the intermediate level of policy and managerial action can range from "selecting a different federal government organizational option," such as a service agency, Crown corporation, or other "mission-driven entity" designed to provide a "more tailored policy, management and organizational framework that allows the government to focus more clearly on services, streamline operations and improve accountability," to policies of devolution (off-loading), commercialization, deregulation, and privatization (Kernaghan and Siegel, 1999: 297-98). These policies of privatization and commercialization have dramatically affected the presence of Crown corporations in this country; indeed, they have been the closest thing to the "reinvention" of government in Canada. Though there has been less dramatic change with respect to deregulation, some important and widely felt deregulation initiatives have been pursued, especially in the trade, energy, and transportation sectors. Program devolution, through the downloading of federal responsibilities to other levels of government and the commercialization of remaining federal activities through greater stress on revenue generation, user fees, and contracting out have also led to significant changes in certain policy and program operations. This is especially true in relation to environmental and transportation policy, though such changes have also elicited much public criticism regarding the declining role of the state in providing public services and public oversight of major policy fields. While there was widespread public acceptance of the privatizations of the 1980s and 1990s, it is much less pronounced with respect to policies of deregulation, downloading, and commercialization. This dynamic is most vividly displayed by public anger over the Walkerton, Ontario, and North Battleford, Saskatchewan, water scandals.

A further means of ASD is through partnerships with other levels of government or with the private sector. The partnership approach is encouraged by the federal government as a way of achieving certain desired goals in a more economical and efficient manner by involving other stakeholders. Such partnership initiatives over the past decade have included

- the Canada Infrastucture Works Program, which brings all three levels of government together in the planning and execution of public works projects;
- the reform of the Canadian Food Inspection Agency and the increased use of private sector testing, monitoring, and regulation of food safety;
- the creation of federal-provincial public service access centres modelled on the Service Canada prototype; and
- the involvement of private sector actors in such new public works undertakings as the redevelopment of Toronto's Pearson Airport and

the construction of the Confederation Bridge linking Prince Edward Island and New Brunswick (Canada, 1997: 14).

These reforms have proven significant to the federal government and have represented a new and different manner by which it can engage in policy and program action in a number of undertakings. Of course, not everyone agrees with the direction of such initiatives nor with the quality of program performance or service delivery achieved. Nonetheless, these service delivery reforms indicate a government seeking to effect major changes in how it interacts with its policy environment and how it can balance demands for quality services and fiscal prudence. They also become the subject of ideological debate over the appropriate role of the state in society and the degree to which the government's actions are consistent with or harmful to strong leadership within the social and economic life of this society and the effective management of its public policies and programs.

10.4.2 The Leadership Network

The concept of leadership highlights one more micro-management initiative in regard to public service reform over the past decade. As part of La Relève the federal government created the Leadership Network, as noted in Chapter 8. This body, officially a new government agency closely affiliated with both the CSPS and the Committee of Senior Officers representing the deputy minister community, has been charged with promoting leadership throughout the public service. The Leadership Network

- brings together management and staff of like rank and responsibilities,
- encourages open communication within and between such networks on organizational leadership opportunities and problems,
- hosts training seminars on the theory and practice of leadership, and
- disseminates best leadership practices throughout the public service.

Thus, the network is a catalyst for development, awareness, and change within the public service, not only promoting important managerial skills but enhancing a collective sense of identity, a common vision, and an understanding of leadership within government. In defining and encouraging leadership, the network explicitly views it as comprising and relating to six particular managerial skills, all of which can be studied, analyzed, and taught: communication, team-building and facilitation, flexibility and innovation, "win-win negotiations," the "ability to see the big picture," and risk-taking (Canada, 1998a).

In promoting leadership the network is officially dedicated to the advancement of a "knowledge-based organization" within which management and staff share and participate in the ongoing work and development of their organizations. As Jocelyne Bourgon, the Clerk of the Privy Council, wrote in 1998, the newly emerging Public Service of Canada is confronting a much more complex operational environment than ever seen in the past, one demanding that government organizations be ever more creative, intelligent, and capable in administering their assigned tasks, in dealing with problems, and in developing new and better operational means for achieving desired policy and program ends. "Employees are expected to look for solutions, contribute ideas, share information with others, innovate and make a contribution. They are also expected to share with their home organization a responsibility for keeping their skills, knowledge, and expertise current and for contributing to the development of others" (Canada, 1998b: Pt 3, p.4).

Through this developmental and humanistic approach to organizational action, management is likewise called upon to show participative, creative, and even democratic leadership. Bourgon states:

> With all the power and authority in the world, one cannot "command and control" creativity and innovation. One cannot "order" new results to emerge. A new approach to management is called for. This approach requires a climate of trust, encourages collaboration, and favours inclusiveness. It recognizes the importance of sharing power in exchange for having everyone gain a greater sense of collective responsibility. This management model is much more complex than the one we have inherited from the industrial era. (Canada, 1998b: 4-5)

This new management approach, of course, is not new at all, since it emerges from the participatory management theories advanced by such authors as Douglas McGregor, Chris Argyris, and Peter Drucker, as noted in Chapter 5. Whether this initiative in participatory management will prove any more successful than previous efforts remains to be seen, but with the past record of such initiatives and the theoretical and practical managerial and political problems associated with them, one should not be overly surprised if this reform initiative also fails to meet expectations. Indeed, Bourgon's use of the phrase "command and control" is intriguing since it is this approach to decision-making and the exercise of power, according to

Savoie, that characterizes the dominant form of decision-making within the federal government.

This recognition of *realpolitik*, however, should not distract from the broader reform implications of the Leadership Network and its impact on public sector management. In focusing on the six basic elements of management enumerated above as variables that can be acted on and improved, the network is endeavouring to enhance, in practical ways, the operational calibre of managerial leadership throughout the public service. Such a reform initiative is ambitious, as it commits the network, and by extension the government, to a process of leadership education, training, and renewal that is bold in design yet uncertain in terms of final results. The goals, however, of developing better managerial leaders and of promoting and encouraging better, more creative, innovative, and effective leadership are clearly important and desirable, especially after years of leadership malaise within the federal public service. The work of the Leadership Network, then, also marks a conscious effort by the senior officials driving the La Relève and public sector modernization initiatives to improve the operational morale of the public service. This is to be achieved by reinvigorating its sense of purpose, its professional ethos, and its belief that the Public Service of Canada needs and deserves skilled leadership at all levels if it is to meet its many goals and duties. Concern for the promotion of leadership marks an important development in the recent history of the federal public service, marking the end of a period of sharp restraint and retrenchment and the advent, possibly, of a period where creative leadership is once again expected and desired of public sector managers.

10.5   Creative Leadership: Building Policy Capacity

While initiatives to promote improved service delivery quality stand as significant micro- and meso-level managerial reforms of recent years, there have also been some important macro-level reforms within the federal public service designed to enhance the overall policy capacity of the government. In 1995, the Clerk of the Privy Council admitted that "the core role of policy development" within the public service had been neglected in recent years, due to the fiscal problems confronting the government, and was in need of substantial improvement (Canada, 1995: 3). These reforms were to take the shape of improved medium- and long-term policy development initiatives within departments and agencies as well as the promotion of horizontal and collaborative policy networks spanning and linking together such institutions, allowing for policy research, investigation, and development to be thematic and holistic in a "real world" sense rather than being divided along institutional/jurisdictional lines.

By 2002 this focus on improving policy capacity had resulted in two government-wide initiatives, one rather modest, the other more expansive. The modest one is the Policy Research Development Program, an undertaking sponsored by the PCO and designed to "recruit, develop and retain highly qualified individuals" to serve as policy analysts and researchers within the federal public service. This program was created

- to support the recruitment of new talent into the public service,
- to promote the development of their policy research skills, and
- to augment the policy analysis strength of the PCO.

Although the program was designed to be additional to and supportive of existing policy development initiatives within each department and agency, it was also crafted to give participants exposure to "corporate-wide policy research skills," "experience working on research initiatives that cross sectors, disciplines, and departments and methodologies," and "an appreciation of the role of central coordinating agencies and other key players in the federal system" (Policy Research Development Program, 2001). The modesty of this program, however, lies in the fact that no more than ten recruits will be hired in any one year, with each serving a three-year training period. In thinking of this program and its central agency orientation, it is useful to recall Savoie's analysis of the growing power and influence of "the centre" and the move by central agencies and those they directly serve to enhance their command-and-control authority across the entire breadth of the public service.

The more expansive policy undertaking of the federal government is its Policy Research Initiative (PRI). Its basic objective is to strengthen the policy research capacity of the federal government by building policy networks. Its ultimate goals are to "develop a stronger base of longer term policy research on cross-cutting issues" and to "strengthen a culture of partnership in the policy research community across Canada." The PRI is, in its own words, "a catalyst" that brings together policy analysts and researchers from "over 30 federal departments and agencies, provincial governments, numerous think tanks, and many universities" (Policy Research Initiative, 2001). In keeping with its origins as a PCO initiative, the PRI management team ultimately reports directly to the Clerk of the Privy Council, while it also maintains close operational linkages with the CSPS.

The PRI has sponsored a number of policy-related publications, including *Horizons*, a magazine aimed at keeping its readers abreast of the latest developments in policy research, and *Isuma: Canadian Journal of Policy Research*, a publication that addresses policy research in the social sciences and encourages "multidisciplinary" and "horizontal" ways of looking at and thinking about the policy issues and problems confronting Canadian society and, by extension, Canadian governments (Isuma, 2001). The major work of the PRI to date, however, has been to sponsor three major research projects into medium- and long-term policy and program concerns that will define the shape of public policy well into the future. These three projects have been devoted to policy matters relating to North American linkages and free trade, social cohesion, and sustainable development.

These projects, and those that will follow, identify the important policy issues confronting the federal government and the continuing public demand that the government show leadership in addressing the tensions, problems, and opportunities found in these fields. They also illustrate the need for the federal government to have skilled policy staff and managers capable of providing departments, agencies, central agencies, and the political executive with effective policy advice on courses of action and for promoting the long-term public interest as well as the best interests of the government and public service. In so doing, they underscore and accentuate the all-important linkages between management and policy. As discussed in Chapter 1, all governments confront major policy fields where they are required to exercise choice in advancing the public interest. In making these policy and program choices, and in implementing and administering desired initiatives, all governments must rely on their staff, especially senior management, for administrative and policy leadership. Management must then be conversant in a host of policy matters respecting their fields of responsibility in particular, as well as in broad matters affecting the government overall. Such concern, it should be noted, runs directly counter to one of the basic propositions of the NPM: that there should be a sharp distinction between management and policy, with the role of managers being simply to manage. This NPM goal of re-establishing a clear politics/administration dichotomy has been shown, by the practice of the federal government, to be naive. Rather than seeking to differentiate and divide policy-making from program implementation and administration, the initiative to build policy capacity is a recognition by government that matters of policy and administration are inextricably linked and that public sector management needs to be as well-versed and competent in the one as the other.

As we enter a new century with a self-proclaimed "reformed" and "revitalized" federal government, it is instructive to reflect on some of the major and self-defined policy concerns of that government and the consequent demands placed on management regarding the development of policy and program advice.

10.5.1   North American Linkages and Free Trade

North American linkages and free trade is one of the greatest issues confronting not only Canada but also the government and its role in the socio-economic life of the country. With the advent of trade liberalization, free trade, and globalization, the role that any government can play in regulating the economy and providing financial subsidies to particular firms is called into direct question. The North American Free Trade Agreement (NAFTA) specifically prohibits any state action that constitutes a barrier to trade and/or that creates discriminatory treatment against the firms of the other NAFTA partners (Johnson, 1994: ch. 4). NAFTA requires all partner states to accord "national treatment"—that is, equal treatment and consideration—to the firms of the other partner countries just as if those firms were domestic in the host country. As such, direct state subsidies of specific Canadian industries is no longer a valid tool of either federal or provincial industrial policy, because such subsidies discriminate against other competitor firms of the other partner countries. Questions also arise as to whether federal restrictions on for-profit health care facilities under the Canada Health Act constitute illegal restraints on American firms wishing to offer private health care services in Canada, or whether Canada Post's operation of a courier service in direct competition with American courier providers, such as UPS, constitutes illegal cross-subsidization of a national firm. Such questions also come up in regard to a number of other matters. Does the Canadian practice of allowing lumber producers to cut trees on Crown land for a set fee constitute unfair state subsidy on the grounds that these "stumpage fees" are lower than similar fees found in the United States, where most timberlands are privately owned? Do Canadian health care and workers' compensation systems constitute unfair subsidization of Canadian firms on the grounds that the state is bearing responsibility for the costs of employee medical and compensation insurance and care, costs that are otherwise a fiscal responsibility of private firms in the United States? And are Canadian laws that protect Canadian cultural industries and restrict the sale of bulk water exports to the United States valid under free trade?

These are issues that all Canadian governments, especially the federal government, must deal with on a regular basis as they endeavour to manage NAFTA relations, deal with the United States, and move towards further trade liberalization through the American hemisphere. With respect to all of these subjects, relevant public sector managers are called on to become expert in particular fields of trade relations and legitimate versus illegitimate state actions. These managers are then expected to advise their superiors and responsible ministers on appropriate courses of action and the development and maintenance of policies and programs consistent with NAFTA and other trade regulations while also serving and advancing Canadian public interests and the goals of the government.

In recognizing the importance of these issues and the significance of trade liberalization to the current and future roles of government, we must keep in mind two considerations.

1. *Trade liberalization clearly does restrict the range of policy and program actions available to any government.* Simply put, direct subsidization of domestic firms and discriminatory treatment of foreign firms are now explicitly forbidden by a growing number of trade treaties. These restrictions do not mean, however, that governments have lost all ability to engage in industrial policy to regulate the economy or to promote specific Canadian-based socio-economic policy (Russell, 1993; Johnson, 1994: 512-21).

2. *The critical task of governments and their policy advisors is to develop and defend those policies and programs that can satisfy NAFTA and other trade laws while also advancing Canadian interests.* The key here, arguably, is the concept of general availability and general application of law to all economic actors—foreign and domestic. Industrial incentives and support programs—for example, for business, entrepreneurs, skills training, research and development, and exports—that are made broadly available to all firms, domestic and foreign, acting within a particular economic sector within the country or to all firms existing within the country or a particular province or region will have a high likelihood of surviving NAFTA challenges. The logic is that such support programs are equivalent to the general benefits of public education and public health care systems, which are generally available to all firms doing business within Canada.

If these policies and programs can survive within the world of liberalized trade, as they have done, then the logic of these initiatives should be transferable to other socio-economic policies and programs, provided that program implementation remains true to the concept of general availability.

In similar fashion, the provision of state support to particular firms in the guise of business services made available through commercial transactions between a given firm and a designated state agency, for example, would also likely survive NAFTA challenge on the grounds that such a transaction was conforming to accepted market principles. As such, a federal or provincial Crown corporation providing business support services, management information, regulatory advice, and export development support for a competitive fee could survive within the realm of trade liberalization. In this respect, note the continuing role and work of the Export Development Corporation. State ability to engage in socio-economic regulation is also likely secure on the grounds that it applies equally to all affected firms while bestowing benefits to all firms in an equal manner. Thus, regulatory regimes ranging from labour relations, workers' compensation, human rights law, and environmental protection policies have all continued to exist under a system of free trade simply because they are policies of general applicability. These examples of pre-existing or possible policies and programs are indicative of the types of state actions that remain possible and viable under a regime of free trade. Should a government wish to engage in creative, innovative, and progressive policies to advance federal or provincial social or economic interests, it is far from being hamstrung, as some critics of trade liberalization would suggest, but can undertake and maintain various and important roles in the socio-economic life of the country. Public sector management must not only be aware of this environment and of the continuing scope of action and power held by governments but be capable of developing and defending innovative policy and program options serving public and governmental interests.

10.5.2   Social Cohesion

Just as changing trade relations have posed challenges to Canadian governments, so too have changing and evolving socio-economic relations confronted these governments with demands for creative leadership (Dyck, 2000: chs. 3, 6-8). Throughout this text we have documented many of the problems that Canadian governments, especially the federal government, face as they deal with the realities of modern life in this country. Demands for fiscal restraint and balanced budgets have led to significant government cutbacks, the downsizing of both federal and provincial public services, and consequent restrictions in the extent of the social welfare "safety net." At the federal level in particular, these cutbacks have affected such major policy fields as health, education, social assistance, skills training, regional development, and culture and heritage. As these cutbacks were imposed, they not only helped to balance the federal budget but also elicited major criticisms regarding the changing face of social policy in this country.

There have been growing concerns that the quality of government services in all these policy fields, as well as others, has seriously deteriorated; that rather than "doing more with less" the federal government is, in fact, "doing less with less"; and that in such areas as health care, post-secondary education, and social assistance and housing, for example, Canadians are worse off now than they were a quarter-century ago. Such attitudes give rise to concerns about "social cohesion": as the social safety net frays, society increasingly becomes polarized between the "haves" and "have-nots," with the federal government playing a more limited and restricted role in seeking to bridge this divide. Growing poverty, homelessness, youth unemployment, spiralling post-secondary education costs and student indebtedness, hospital waiting lists, the number of persons without family doctors—these are just some of the most common issues surrounding the debate on the changing nature of Canadian society. And all such concerns question the role and actions of government and the competency of government reactions to such problems, as well as whether the state has a valid role in addressing these policy concerns or whether greater reliance should be placed on private sector solutions.

Such concerns have posed major challenges to all governments, especially the federal government, as budgetary deficits have given way to budgetary surpluses. To what degree is "social cohesion" a problem in Canada, and what can be and should be the role of the federal government in addressing this problem? What are the policy and program options that present themselves to the federal government to enable it to play a more active and progressive role in such matters as health care policy, post-secondary educational support, social welfare assistance policy, and regional development initiatives? And what of the other long-standing aspects of social cohesion policy: national unity, federalism and balanced federal-provincial relations, the role of Quebec within the federation, bilingualism and biculturalism, multiculturalism, race relations, gender equity, and general concern for the promotion of human rights? All of these policy matters are part of the "social cohesion" policy field, and all deserve attention.

10.5.3 Sustainable Development

The same types of concerns and policy dynamics are also found in regard to concerns for sustainable development (Paehlke, 1990; Brooks, 1998). While governments are fully expected to serve and promote the economic development of this country, they are also expected to achieve this goal in such a manner as not to jeopardize the long-term security and viability of the natural environment. In this sense, just as social policy must be juxtaposed and balanced with concerns for financial stability, so too must economic development be balanced with concerns for environmental protection and preservation. Thus, governments and their management are expected to develop policies and administer programs capable of meeting these different yet interrelated objectives. Striking such a balance is difficult, however, with interests on both sides often being highly critical of compromises that restrict the gains that each can make.

The practice of sustainable development remains a work of government still in its infancy. The federal government and its environmental policy-makers, for example, must work to integrate environmental concerns and considerations into all government policy-making and program administration. This, of course, is no easy task given what we now know of interdepartmental rivalry and competition. The Department of the Environment, moreover, must also contend with the power and influence of Finance and its approaches both to macro-economic development policy and to the funding and promotion of other departments within government. And, given the holistic and transborder nature of environmental concerns and problems, any serious effort to address environmental policy must, of necessity, be multigovernmental, bringing together as many jurisdictions as possible towards the realization of common environmental objectives.

The nature of such a complex policy environment, however, highlights the problems, difficulties, and challenges that environmental policy-makers must confront as they develop policies and programs. Such policy-makers must first gain some consensus within government and among its many and various institutional actors on desirable and achievable environmental policy. They must then gain some reasonable level of consensus from various economic, environmental, and other interest groups concerned with environmental policy and its relationship to economic matters. And they must gain and maintain broad popular support for whatever initiatives they bring forward.

With most environmental policy and program matters, the federal government must interact and negotiate with other Canadian governments—provincial, territorial, and municipal—as well as with other national and international bodies. Given the shared border, intergovernmental relations with the United States will always be a priority, and, with the international dynamics of such matters as global warming, species habitat protection, and marine preservation, international agreements such as the Kyoto Protocol will be a necessity. The obvious problem, of course, is the great difficulty in managing within such a complex policy environment of sovereign actors with their own distinct interests, needs, wants, and ideological perspectives. Gaining any form of strategic and operational consensus in such a multi-organizational and intergovernmental environment is difficult in the extreme. This difficulty, however, only accentuates the importance of sound management in this field and the requirement that all governments have highly qualified and talented people dealing with these matters. The significance of a sustainable environment to global well-being demands nothing less.

10.5.4   Aboriginal Self-Government

One last, broad policy concern deserving mention is the development of Aboriginal self-government (Asch, 1997; Canada, 1996; Long and Dickason, 1996). The concept of First Nations, as recognized by the Royal Proclamation of 1763 and as affirmed by the Constitution Act, 1982, has resulted in the federal government entering into negotiations with various groups representing Aboriginal peoples. These protracted discussions have involved the negotiation or renegotiation of treaty rights and land claim settlements and the negotiation of self-government agreements. In all these instances, the federal government and its agents must recognize the special status of Aboriginal peoples, respect the inherent Aboriginal right to self-government, and affirm and defend Aboriginal treaty rights where they are found to exist. The relationship between Canada's First Nations and the federal government is thus unique, unlike any other relationship between the government and any other social group for the simple reason that Aboriginal peoples are not like any other "group" in society but are, in fact, members of First Nations that pre-exist any other government in this land. The federal government has to deal with the interests of these First Nations in a way that both satisfies the rights and needs of these nations and also serves the long-term best interests of the broader, non-Aboriginal community.

In seeking to strike this balance and make policy in this context, policy-makers have to be knowledgeable and aware of First Nations' history, rights, and interests; sensitive to the needs and socio-economic and cultural problems experienced by many First Nations' communities; and both courageous and creative in recognizing the right to First Nations' self-government and in developing means to achieve this end. The fulfilment of such requirements has never been an easy task for this government and its officials. The history of federal relations *vis-à-vis* the First Nations is marked by varying degrees of disinterest, distrust, paternalism, racism, non-recognition, and neglect. In recent years this relationship has been changing and evolving as the federal government and certain provincial governments have sought to improve mutual contact and cooperation between non-Aboriginal and First Nations governments. There have been a number of successes, including land claim settlements in the northern territories and British Columbia, the establishment of Nunavut as a separate territory, the establishment of Aboriginal self-government power in Manitoba, and the recognition of Aboriginal rights in the Constitution Act, 1982. But there have also been problems, from the continuing poverty and social exclusion experienced by most Aboriginal peoples to disagreements over the application of treaty rights, most notably witnessed in the aftermath of the *Marshall* decision on the Mi'kmaq fishery. While much has been accomplished among federal, provincial, and First Nations' governments, much more remains to be done, and the role of knowledgeable and sensitive public sector managers is vital to policy and program success.

10.6   Government Reform: Final Reflections

As we have just seen, whether at the micro-managerial or macro-policy level, the federal government is undergoing, or seeking to undergo, certain major alterations in how it engages with Canadians and undertakes its public duties. As a result, the nature of government has changed and is changing. Many people can and will have sharply differing opinions as to the merits and demerits of these changes, these opinions deeply rooted both in individual ideological understandings as to the appropriate role of the state in society and in practical assessments of these changes and whether they enhance, diminish, or leave relatively unchanged the quality of public services in this society.

Regardless of these varied assessments, a number of points stand out. Contrary to the more grandiose claims of the advocates of the NPM, we are witnessing more the reform of government than its reinvention. While certain aspects of the NPM approach can be discerned within the micro, meso, and macro changes underway within government, these aspects, combined, have not resulted in a comprehensive and revolutionary change in the way government is exercised and public services delivered. Despite the more modest and evolutionary changes associated with the reform thesis of government change, the reforms that we have witnessed, and those still occurring, have been substantial and important. While generally maintaining broad continuity with past practices and policies, they have nevertheless reshaped the working of government by significantly diminishing its size, by "reordering" and "reforming" the processes of public service delivery, and by compelling the government to refocus and rebuild its policy capacity.

In addition, as the federal government has been undergoing change and reformation, major concerns have arisen regarding the concept of government accountability, whether the government is properly, adequately, and effectively fulfilling its responsibilities to the Canadian people and whether it possesses managerial leadership of the highest calibre. Accountability and leadership are two of the overarching points of consideration with respect to any analysis of the nature and working of government, and these issues are the subject of our final chapters.

Key Terms

alternative service delivery (ASD): An approach to the operational side of public sector management in which policy analysts seek to determine other, more efficient, and more effective means of providing public services. ASD often involves privatization, deregulation, commercialization, and devolution of services.

e-government: The operational process whereby access to government services are provided via Internet connections. The federal government operates a massive web site (<http://www.canada.gc.ca>) that provides a vast array of information and access to federal government services.

New Public Management (NPM): A wide ranging approach to rethinking public sector management that emerged in Britain and the United States in the late 1980s and early 1990s. The thinking respecting the NPM can run from a conservative approach to seeking to make the public sector operate more like the private sector through to more liberal approaches in which the public sector is accepted as a unique environment for the delivery of goods and services but where such operational delivery can still be made more economical, efficient and effective.

reinventing government: A reformist concept to thinking about government reform widely promoted by American authors David Osborne and Ted Gaebler. The reinventing government thesis advocated by these authors involves governments seeking to adopt ten major reform initiatives as listed in Box 10.1.

References and Suggested Reading

Some short passages from this chapter respecting the New Public Management have been borrowed, adapted, and reworked from R. Brian Howe and David Johnson, 2000. *Restraining Equality: Human Rights Commissions in Canada*. Toronto: University of Toronto Press.

Asch, Michael, ed. 1997. *Aboriginal and Treaty Rights in Canada: Essays on Law, Equality and Respect for Difference*. Vancouver: University of British Columbia Press.

Aucoin, Peter. 1995. *The New Public Management: Canada in Comparative Perspective*. Ottawa: Institute for Research on Public Policy.

Borins, Sandford. 1995a. "The New Public Management is Here to Stay." *Canadian Public Administration* 38: 122-32.

—. 1995b. "Public Sector Innovation: The Implications of New Forms of Organization and Work." In B. Guy Peters and Donald J. Savoie, eds., *Governance in a Changing Environment*. Montreal and Kingston: Canadian Centre for Management Development/McGill-Queen's University Press.

Brooks, Stephen. 1998. *Public Policy in Canada: An Introduction*. 3rd ed. Toronto: Oxford University Press.

Bruce, Christopher J., Ronald D. Kneebone, and Kenneth J. McKenzie, eds. 1997. *A Government Reinvented: A Study of Alberta's Deficit Elimination Program*. Toronto: Oxford University Press.

Canada, Privy Council Office. 1995. *3rd Annual Report to the Prime Minister on the Public Service of Canada*. Ottawa: Supply and Services.

—. 1997. *Getting Government Right*. Ottawa: Supply and Services.

—. 1998a. *Renewal of the Public Service of Canada: Sustaining the Momentum with the Leadership Network*. <http://www.leadership.gc.ca>.

—. 1998b. *5th Annual Report to the Prime Minister on the Public Service of Canada*. Ottawa: Supply and Services.

—. 2000a. *7th Annual Report to the Prime Minister on the Public Service of Canada*. Ottawa: Supply and Services.

—. 2000b. Treasury Board Secretariat. *A Policy Framework for Service Improvement in the Government of Canada*. Ottawa: Supply and Services.

—2005. Treasury Board Secretariat. *Budget 2005: Strengthening and Modernizing Public Sector Management*. Ottawa: Supply and Services.

Canada, Royal Commission on Aboriginal Peoples. 1996. *Report of the Royal Commission on Aboriginal Peoples*. Ottawa: Supply and Services.

Canada, Treasury Board. 2001. *Government On-Line*. Ottawa: Government of Canada Web Site, <http://www.canada.gc.ca>.

Canadian Centre for Management Development (CCMD). 1999. *Citizen-Centred Service: Responding to the Needs of Canadians*. Ottawa: CCMD.

Dyck, Rand. 2000. *Canadian Politics: Critical Approaches*. 3rd ed. Toronto: Nelson.

Hood, Christopher. 1991. "A Public Management for all Seasons?" *Public Administration* 69: 3-19.

Howe, R. Brian, and David Johnson. 2000. *Restraining Equality: Human Rights Commissions in Canada*. Toronto: University of Toronto Press.

Inwood, Gregory J. 2004. *Understanding Canadian Public Administration: An Introduction to Theory and Practice*, 2nd ed. Scarborough, ON: Prentice-Hall Allyn and Bacon Canada.

Isuma. 2001. *About Isuma*. Ottawa: Government of Canada Web Site, <http://www.canada.gc.ca>.

Johnson, Jon R. 1994. *The North American Free Trade Agreement: A Comprehensive Guide*. Aurora, ON: Canada Law Book.

Kernaghan, Kenneth, Brian Marson, and Sandford Borins. 2000. *The New Public Organization*. Toronto: Institute of Public Administration of Canada.

Kernaghan, Kenneth, and David Siegel. 1999. *Public Administration in Canada: A Text.* 4th ed. Toronto: Nelson.

Long, David, and Olive Dickason. 1996. *Visions of the Heart: Canadian Aboriginal Issues.* Toronto: Harcourt Brace.

Osborne, David, and Ted Gaebler. 1993. *Reinventing Government: How the Entrepreneurial Spirit is Transforming the Public Sector.* New York: Plume Books.

Paehlke, Robert. 1990. "Environmental Policy in the 1990s." In G. Bruce Doern and Bryne B. Purchase, eds., *Canada at Risk?: Canadian Public Policy in the 1990s.* Toronto: C.D. Howe Institute.

Policy Research Development Program. 2001. *FAQs.* Ottawa: Government of Canada Web Site, <http://www.canada.gc.ca>.

Policy Research Initiative. 2001. *Overview.* Ottawa: Government of Canada Web Site, <http://www.canada.gc.ca>.

Purchase, Bryne, and Ronald Hirshorn. 1994. *Searching for Good Governance.* Kingston: School of Policy Studies, Queen's University.

Russell, Brian R. 1993. "Industrial Policy, Subsidies, and Trade Law: Troubling the Waters of Trade." In A.R. Riggs and Tom Velk, eds., *Beyond NAFTA: An Economic, Political and Sociological Perspective.* Vancouver: Fraser Institute.

Savoie, Donald J. 1994. *Thatcher, Reagan, Mulroney: In Search of a New Bureaucracy.* Toronto: University of Toronto Press.

—. 1995. "What is Wrong with the New Public Management?" *Canadian Public Administration* 38: 112-21.

Thomas, Paul G. 1993. "Coping with Change: How Public and Private Organizations Read and Respond to Turbulent Environments." In F. Leslie Seidle, ed., *Rethinking Government: Reform or Reinvention?* Montreal: Institute for Research on Public Policy.

Trebilcock, Michael J. 1994. *The Prospects for Reinventing Government.* Toronto: C.D. Howe Institute.

Related Web Sites

GOVERNMENT OF CANADA
<http://www.canada.gc.ca>

PRIVY COUNCIL OFFICE
<http://www.pco-bcp.gc.ca>

PUBLIC SERVICE HUMAN RESOURCES MANAGEMENT AGENCY OF CANADA
<http://www.hrma-agrh.gc.ca>

GENERAL HUMAN RESOURCES
<http://govinfo.library.unt.edu/npr>

CHAPTER 11

Public Sector Accountability: Responsibility, Responsiveness, and Ethics

As this book has shown, governments in Canada play an enormously important role in the political, social, and economic life of all Canadians. Unless one lives as a hermit, it is impossible to escape contact with the state—public policy and public sector management are all around us. Debate over the appropriate role of government is fundamental to Canadian politics, with the evolution of the state being greatly influenced by the ebb and flow of ideological beliefs held by Canadians and reflected through their political and electoral choices. The presence of the state is felt in all aspects of life. From health, education, and welfare policy to national and regional economic development, and including such policy fields as immigration, culture and heritage, human rights, national defence, and the environment, the impact of the state is immense, and this is still the case despite a decade of significant government downsizing.

Given the significance of this state presence in society, its management remains of profound importance. All governments, all political parties, most major interest groups, and most citizens interested in the work of governments care, to varying degrees, about the management of the public sector, stressing the importance of public services that will operate in the most economical, efficient, and effective manner possible to serve and advance public needs and wants. Concern for policy, then, is inextricably connected to matters of administration and management; the one cannot exist without the other, with the quality of the former very much shaped and conditioned by the quality of the latter. In this sense, the operational world in which governments exist and within which they will be evaluated is one blending matters of policy with those of management. All Canadian governments hold great yet varied responsibilities. They are judged by the quality of their policy and program development and by the quality of their policy and program implementation and administration. They are evaluated not only by how well their actions serve the needs and wants of Canadians, but also by how well these actions are undertaken. And through all of these actions the responsibility of the state remains, at heart, quite simple: to advance the socio-economic well-being of Canadians and to promote "the public interest."

This is clearly the ultimate goal of government as understood by common citizens, and it is the primary reason for the existence of governments in the first instance. In terms of democratic theory, governments are human creations established to meet important needs and provide key goods and services as defined and desired by citizens themselves. The process of identifying and agreeing on such needs, goals, and services—of establishing the appropriate role of the state—thus forms the heart of the democratic political process as recounted in Chapters 1 and 2. The achievement of such goals, in turn, forms the core of the policy and management processes as dealt with in this book.

Despite the importance of these goals, however, and the recognition within both government and the broader public that a key function—if not *the* key function—of government is the fulfilment of public needs to serve the public interest, there is great debate about the degree to which governments have fulfilled these goals. Those both inside and outside of government stress the important role of government within society, but many question whether those in government are properly fulfilling the responsibilities and objectives entrusted to them.

We are all aware of the common criticisms levelled against governments, political leaders, and public servants: they are wasteful; they are out of touch; they are arrogant and self-serving; they are stupid; they all too often engage in folly; and, at times, their actions are unethical or even criminal. What is disconcerting is that each of these criticisms can be supported by some form of documented evidence:

- the administration of the Montreal 1976 Olympic Games was wasteful;
- the Ontario NDP's employment equity policy was out of touch with general public opinion;

- the corruption scandals associated with the Mulroney government indicate that certain persons in that government were arrogant and self-serving;
- the ham-fisted efforts of the Department of National Defence to conceal and destroy evidence of wrongdoing with regard to the Somalia scandal are viewed by many, including some in the military, as being the height of stupidity and folly;
- cases of expense account padding, ritual hazings, and the use of public office for private gain are documented examples of unethical practices in the military, just as the convictions of various soldiers for the killing of a Somali youth are evidence of criminal misbehaviour by public officials; and
- although Jean Chrétien came to power in 1993 promising a government that would be above reproach, bringing a new sense of ethics to public sector management, by the end of his tenure as prime minister in 2003 his government had become the subject of enormous criticism over the degree to which it fulfilled this promise: questions about the security arrangements for the Asia-Pacific Economic Cooperation (APEC) summit in Vancouver in 1997, the management of public monies associated with the Canada Jobs Fund administered by Human Resources Development Canada (HRDC), and, worst of all, allegations of fraud and corruption associated with the sponsorship scandal of the late 1990s had all tarnished, to the minds of many, the reputation of the Chrétien Liberal government, with this criticism flowing over to taint the successor Martin administration.

Public concern over such real or alleged examples of government misbehaviour tend to be two-pronged. On one hand there is direct concern or disgust over the actual event or decision in question. There is anger that a wasteful or stupid or unethical act was committed. On the other hand, and somewhat deeper, there is concern that such actions reveal a malaise in government in that good, proper, desirable, economical, efficient, and effective decisions in the public interest are not being made by those in authority. There is a disconcerting recognition by many in the public and in government that, at times, governments, political leaders, and public servants do not live up to the ideals of democratic government and public service. Public power, designed ideally to benefit society, can be maligned, twisted, or perverted to benefit the few who wield power.

For these reasons such scandals become newsworthy and lead many, both inside and outside of government, to seek ways to control and punish government and administrative misbehaviour and to establish account-ability systems to prevent such misbehaviour from occurring in the first instance.

11.1   Accountability: Basic Concepts and Issues

In the *Final Report* of the 1979 Royal Commission on Financial Manage-ment and Accountability, the commissioners defined **accountability** as:

> the essence of our democratic form of government. It is the lia-bility assumed by all those who exercise authority to account for the manner in which they have fulfilled responsibilities entrusted to them, a liability ultimately to the Canadian people owed by Parliament, by the Government and, thus, every gov-ernment department and agency.
>
> Accountability is the fundamental prerequisite for prevent-ing the abuse of delegated power and for ensuring, instead, that power is directed toward the achievement of broadly accepted national goals with the greatest degree of efficiency, effective-ness, probity and prudence. (Canada, 1979: 21)

This definition stresses the importance of government officials being liable—being held responsible—for both the procedural and substantive merit of their decisions. This is crucial in any democratic system in which the bureaucracy is designed to serve and advance specified socio-economic needs and interests as determined through the working of political and parliamentary processes. The definition acknowledges that accountability is a process of control in which all government officials, from top to bottom, must be subject to scrutiny, review, analysis, and discipline in regard to their exercise of power; this control does not relate simply to the procedural matters of making economical and efficient decisions in accordance with due process, but to the broader criteria of whether the decisions of governments and government actors were substantively sound: Were they effective? Were they desirable? Were they just? And did they appropriately address the problems and issues the government was seeking to resolve? As can be seen, concern for accountability does go to the very "essence of our democratic form of government." Indeed, an assessment of the quality of accountability found in any government will consider the practical and moral worth of that government itself.

11.1.1 Traditional Perspectives

The crucial importance of accountability has resulted in a vast literature on the best approaches for understanding and assessing accountability in practice. The traditional starting point is the famous exchange of articles in American public administration journals between Carl Friedrich and Herman Finer between 1935 and 1941. Both authors were occupied with developing appropriate means to enhance accountability in liberal democratic governments to forestall the abuse of bureaucratic power, but they came to sharply different conclusions as to how this goal could best be met.

Finer (1941) argued that accountability was best achieved by subjecting bureaucratic officials to strict and detailed rules, regulations, controls, and sanctions.

- In exercising their duties, public servants must follow stringently the standard operating procedures as explicitly detailed in written rules and regulations.
- As much as possible discretionary judgement was to be avoided through the provision of formal rules designed to cover all possible courses of action, but if and when an exercise of discretion was required, it would be made by a superior official, in turn responsible to his or her superior.
- Thus, government is perceived as a hierarchy of authority in which all officials owe a duty of responsibility to their immediate superior, who must account to other officials further up the chain of command, with this chain eventually culminating in the hands of elected leaders answerable and accountable to democratically elected legislatures.
- In this system all public officials know who their superior is, what their duties entail, and that they can be subjected to direct control and sanction by that superior should they fail to fulfil their duties adequately.

This all sounds rather militaristic; in fact, Finer's thinking was very much influenced by the Weberian approach to bureaucratic organization outlined in Chapter 5.

Friedrich (1940) attacked this approach for being both too simplistic and inattentive to the overriding importance of self-direction and self-regulation of public servants. Friedrich, influenced by the organic-humanistic approach to management, argued that the type of detailed rules, regulations, and strict controls advocated by Finer were simply unworkable.

- Detailed regulations could not be drafted to cover all situations, nor could such controls be applied consistently in all circumstances.
- Standard operating procedures could not be expected to cover all possible exercises of discretionary judgement.
- A rigid application of formal rules to the myriad circumstances of real-life situations could result in ill-designed government responses to difficult problems.

Beyond these operational criticisms, Friedrich also challenged Finer's basic theoretical approach. To Friedrich, the key to accountability was not external control over public servants, but internal wisdom within public servants. This wisdom directed them to make good decisions as a matter of routine.

In short, Friedrich adopted the philosophic position that, rather than directing and forcing people to do good, governments need to establish administrative systems that encourage wisdom and good operational behaviour from people in the first instance. Thus, we see these authors expressing two rather different perspectives on human nature that, in turn, influence the approach to accountability that each advances. Friedrich is a philosophical liberal, stressing that people tend to be inherently good and wise and that an accountability system need only be developed to encourage public servants always to be thinking about how and whether their actions are contributing to the public good and the public interest. In his world view, accountability is promoted when the public service possesses an administrative culture in which the objectives of serving the public interest and being responsive to broad social and economic needs stand at the fore. Public servants identify with these goals as a matter of inner, moral choice, and, as this occurs, their external actions, their exercise of state power, likely will be in accordance with broad public desires for good governance.

Of course, Finer never accepted this moral approach to accountability as being a workable system of accountability in the "real world." In practice, he believed that one has to be concerned not with the "moral" actor but with the problematic one, the one who does not necessarily share a common vision of good public sector management and public service but is, rather, motivated by a very narrow self-interest: simply doing the job with as little fuss and in as little time as possible; trying to make the job as easy as possible; doing the bare minimum of work and offering the bare minimum of effort to accomplish given tasks; and also, possibly, seeking to maximize individual access to perquisites, benefits, and material gain from one's work. Finer was much more philosophically conservative in stressing that most persons were flawed, often motivated by the baser instincts of human nature. For these people, whom he believed to be far more prevalent in society than Friedrich would concede, the only effective means of control were strict external rules and regulations directly enforced by superior officers.

In the 1960s, Frederick Mosher (1968) sought to clarify thinking about accountability by focusing attention on the two broad concepts that flow through the work of Finer and Friedrich, namely, objective responsibility and subjective responsibility. Mosher stressed that both forms of responsibility were integral to good government, but that only the former was directly related to accountability. As he argued,

- objective responsibility "connotes the responsibility of a person or an organization to someone else, outside of self, for some thing or some kind of performance. It is closely akin to 'accountability' or 'answerability.' If one fails to carry out legitimate directives, he is judged irresponsible and may be subjected to penalties" (Mosher, 1968: 7-10).
- subjective responsibility directs attention "not upon to whom and for what one is responsible (according to law and the organization chart) but to whom and for what one 'feels' responsible and 'behaves' responsibly. This meaning, which is sometimes described as 'personal' responsibility, is more nearly synonymous with identification, loyalty, and conscience than it is with accountability and answerability" (Mosher, 1968: 7).

Objective responsibility thus entails rules and regulations that directly establish lines of communication, obligation, and control within government. Officials are assigned duties to perform and objectives to achieve, and their performance will be measured; success will be rewarded, and failure criticized or punished. The external, objective nature of this form of control led Mosher to stress that this management process was best suited to establishing a clear accountability framework. But Mosher did not underestimate the importance of the psychological dynamic of subjective responsibility. All organizations possess a set of common values, ideas, and beliefs that provide its philosophical foundation, establishing why it exists, what its broader social purpose is, why membership in it is important, and what is expected of its members. As such values, ideas, and beliefs are inculcated in public servants, for example, they provide a moral framework to guide and direct them in the process of public decision-making, so that socially desirable decisions are rendered in the first instance, thereby negating any need to undertake the formal processes of reviews and controls at the centre of objective responsibility. Objective controls stand as a fallback mechanism to be brought into play if and when the dictates of subjective responsibility fail and persons need to be held to account and disciplined for their actions.

This focus on objective and subjective responsibility leads to thinking about accountability in terms of formal and informal lines of control and lines of influence. As Finer and Mosher suggest, formal controls and formal lines of authority and responsibility are important to any accountability system. Officials need to know that they exist within an organization where all actors possess obligations and responsibilities to set superiors for given undertakings and that if these obligations and responsibilities are not properly fulfilled, formal controls and disciplinary action can be imposed on the irresponsible actor. But, as Friedrich and Mosher also emphasize, the world of informal controls and responsibility is also significant. The establishment of a shared value system providing a set of ideals and standards accepted by public servants as the foundation for their decision-making is a basic requirement of any public service. Such a world of subjective responsibility results in other informal lines of control and responsibility being nurtured and respected, as officials develop moral obligations and expectations in relation to other actors and forces in the political system. In this respect it is not surprising to know that public servants develop an informal loyalty or identity to such actors or forces as the media and social interest groups, the concepts of human rights and the rule of law, and the principles of public participation and decision-making in the public interest.

11.1.2   A Synthetic Approach

The above-mentioned theories on and approaches to accountability and responsibility are important and offer useful insights. It is not reasonable, however, to insist that any of these approaches offer the one correct way to understand and attain accountability. Rather, a full appreciation of accountability must encompass all of these concepts, blending objective and subjective, formal and informal approaches into one comprehensive and inclusive view.

Clearly, an important requirement in accountability is that government officials, from public servants to political leaders, must be subject to a set

BOX 12.1

Accountability: The Synthetic Approach

Elements	Political responsiveness	Legal responsiveness	Social responsiveness
Main concept	Ministerial responsibility	Rule of law	Public interest
Main systems of implementation	Formal controls	Formal controls	Informal controls
	Rules and regulations	Judicial review	Subjective ideals/ political action
Main actors	Governments	Governments	Governments
	Ministers	Public servants	Public servants
	Senior officials	Courts	Political parties
	Political parties	Tribunals	Interest groups
	Parliament	Litigants	Citizens
	Media	Media	Media
Main problems	Evaluation	Cost/complexity	Evaluation
	Imposing discipline	Assessing merit of courts over tribunals	Subjectivity leading to ongoing debate
Main strengths	Direct political control over bureaucracy	Maintenance of impartial legal control over bureaucracy	Allowing for ongoing public assessment of government
	Ministers and officials can be held responsible	Bureaucratic power subject to law	Public admin. at heart of democratic process

of formal, objective expectations by which their performance can be monitored and, if need be, controlled. Within parliamentary systems of government this approach to accountability is given life through the concept of **ministerial responsibility**, in which a chain of obligations and controls links all public servants to their superiors, who are in turn responsible to their superiors, up to and including the political leadership of the government. The cabinet itself is subject to the authority and control of Parliament, which is ultimately subject to the sanction of the people as expressed through regular democratic elections. Ministerial responsibility, examined in Chapters 3 and 4, thus stands as one of the core elements of accountability.

But this is not the only system of formal obligations and controls that governs the actions of public servants and political leaders. As we see in the chapter on Administrative Law found on the Thinking Government web site, various procedural and substantive requirements must be met by decision-makers prior to their decisions being accorded legal legitimacy. Any disputes, furthermore, over whether or not such decision-makers have met their legal obligations are subject to judicial review, meaning that the courts have the ultimate authority to determine that any and all government decisions conform to law. A further significant element of accountability, then, is the legal responsiveness of government actors as expressed through the rule of law and judicial review.

These two elements of accountability essentially reflect the formal objective obligations and controls advocated by Finer and Mosher. But one cannot neglect the importance of informal subjective obligations and controls. Contrary to Mosher's perspective, the ideals and values of democratic government are an important part of the theory and practice of accountability. In this respect, accountability does not simply mean that public servants and political leaders are subject to formal political and legal obligations and controls, but that their actions must also be in accordance with broadly accepted norms of democratic government and socio-economic goals consistent with "the public interest." Thus, the final significant element of accountability is that public servants and political leaders must demonstrate social responsiveness to fundamental democratic ideals and the socio-economic needs and interests of the public.

Government accountability can then be viewed as encompassing three distinct yet interrelated concepts: political responsiveness, legal responsiveness, and social responsiveness. Each of these concepts will be assessed more fully below.

11.1.3   Political Responsiveness

The concern that government actors should be **politically responsive** to superior authorities has resulted in the creation of and adherence to the doctrine of ministerial responsibility. In theory, the cabinet is collectively responsible to Parliament for government policy-making and administration. If a cabinet loses the confidence of Parliament, either in a formal vote of non-confidence or by failing in its attempt to pass a major monetary bill or the annual budget, constitutional convention dictates that it must resign, usually resulting in an election for a new government. The doctrine furthermore holds that each cabinet minister is generally responsible for the policy and administrative actions of his or her department and is answerable to Parliament for all undertakings occurring within the department or any related agency. In this respect, the political head of the department is vested with superior political and administrative authority within the department, thereby possessing the formal power to set the direction and to oversee the working of the department, or any agency, in accordance with the political interests of the cabinet. In this manner, each department is ultimately subject to the executive leadership of an elected cabinet minister who is, in turn, subject to the authority of the prime minister and cabinet. And, of course, the government must answer to Parliament.

This is just one important aspect of the accountability relationship. The second is that all public servants working within a department or agency are required to assist, support, and implement the policy and administrative actions desired by the minister. All officials, from the most senior to the most junior, are expected to help the department as a whole in fulfilling its collective obligation to the minister and the cabinet. Thus, senior officials pass commands and requirements down the departmental or agency chain of command, with the expectation that such commands and requirements will be properly executed by the appropriate officials and with each manager holding his or her subordinates responsible for the successful implementation of department policies and programs. Failure to meet these obligations can result in criticism and disciplinary action within the department, up to and including demotion or dismissal from the public service, though this must be done in accordance with the rules of the Public Service Commission and the Public Service Staff Relations Board, as outlined in Chapter 8. Through the working of this administrative aspect of ministerial responsibility, the government is promised that all administrative actors within a department or agency will exercise their authority and duties in accordance with the wishes of the department's political head and subject to the immediate managerial oversight of superior officials.

In theory this is a basically sound method for ensuring political responsiveness within government. There are, however, certain practical difficulties with the operation of this approach to accountability.

The major problem, as recognized by analysts such as Kernaghan and Siegel (1999), Jackson and Jackson (1998), and Dyck (1996), is that of the role and capabilities of the minister. The theory compels the minister to adopt a superhuman position as head of the department, ultimately responsible for all political and administrative actions of all members of the department and any related agency. But, as seen in Chapter 8, many departments have hundreds, if not thousands, of employees, sometimes spread far across the country, and they make thousands of executive decisions and tens of thousands of routine administrative decisions every year. The work of regulatory agencies only adds to these totals. Ministers, though, will be directly involved in only a small proportion of such annual decision-making, usually concerned with around 200 of the most important policy and administrative decisions of their department (Jackson and Jackson, 1998: 273). All other decisions are made without the prior knowledge of the minister, being undertaken, in theory, in the belief that they are in accordance with broad departmental policy.

But what happens when a "stupid" decision is made or a decision that seemed right at the time turns out to be a mess? If the minister was directly involved in the decision-making process, the doctrine of ministerial responsibility holds that he or she must take responsibility for the action and answer to Parliament and to his/her immediate boss, the prime minister; in the case of a serious error or abuse of power, the minister will be asked to resign. Such was the fate of John Fraser, the Minister of Fisheries and Oceans in the early Mulroney years, who became embroiled in the "Tunagate scandal" of 1985, in which tainted canned tuna was distributed to consumers. But what if the minister was not directly involved in the decision—indeed, knew nothing of the decision—with the error of judgement resting with subordinate officials? Is the minister expected to resign in these cases?

The balance of opinion now is that in such cases ministers must remain answerable to Parliament, but they should not be held directly responsible for actions in which they did not play a direct role. Rather, if a mistake was perpetrated deep within the departmental organization by certain subordinate officials, the disciplinary system within the department or agency will deal with those directly responsible and their immediate superiors who allowed a problem to develop. This was the course of action followed in the alleged Canada Jobs Fund/HRDC scandal of the late 1990s that came to a head in 2000. In this case, allegations of departmental wrongdoing and sloppy administrative and financial management procedures resulted in widespread departmental administrative reforms, with senior managers being well informed that stricter controls over funding initiatives were to be imposed. The minister responsible for the department, Jane Stewart, did not, however, have to resign her position over this issue on the grounds that she was not the minister responsible for the department in the mid-1990s when these financial management problems began to arise and that she was instrumental in beginning the reform process in the department once she assumed the portfolio in 1998.

It is interesting to note the flow of ministerial events surrounding the sponsorship scandal of the late 1990s and the tenure of Minister of Public Works Alphonso Gagliano, the key political official responsible for the Sponsorship Program in Quebec. When this scandal began to break in the early years of the new century Prime Minister Chrétien defended his minister as an exemplary member of cabinet. When opposition, media, and public pressure became too hot for the government, Chrétien removed Gagliano from cabinet but gave him a diplomatic posting as Canadian ambassador to Denmark in 2002. Chrétien stood firm despite much public criticism of the propriety of this appointment, but his successor as party leader and prime minister, Paul Martin reversed the decision a year later. One of his first executive decisions was to call a public inquiry into the so-called sponsorship scandal as well as removing Gagliano from his ambassadorial posting.

The exceptional nature of these actions surrounding the application of ministerial responsibility to the sponsorship scandal suggest that the more lenient approach to the doctrine of ministerial responsibility has become the norm. If this is the case, however, questions do arise as to whether ministers now face appropriate political discipline for poor decision-making. The problem is that with the complexity of major decision-making, in which dozens of senior officials may be involved and in which a "decision" involves dozens of factors and considerations delegated to various officials for analysis and preparation, reasonable arguments can be made that in any given "problem" case, other officials and not the minister should be held responsible. The argument is often made that a minister cannot be expected to double- and triple-check the quality of all the work of all of his or her senior advisors; ministers, rather, must trust their senior officials to produce sound work, and if this trust is violated, the fault must lie with the subordinate official and not the beleaguered minister. In fact, ministers are seldom called upon to resign for policy or administrative malpractice, even when strong evidence suggests that he or she was either aware of, or should have been aware of, such malpractice. This, of course, was the opposition parties' claim against Jane Stewart with respect to the HRDC scandal. They argued that she misled the House of Commons with respect to the severity of the problems in her department and that she should have known of these problems much sooner than she did.

The Somalia affair of the mid-1990s, involving military abuse of authority, the events leading to the deaths of Somali teenagers at the hands of Canadian airborne troops in 1992, and the subsequent alleged cover-up of military wrongdoing is a classic case in point (Desbarats, 1997). While a number of enlisted men and officers were subsequently punished for their roles in these events, concerns about a cover-up and the manipulation and destruction of possible evidence implicating senior officials within the Department of National Defence were never fully aired in public. Though the Chief of Defence Staff was forced to resign over this affair in 1996, opposition calls for the resignation of the minister went unheeded; that same year the government announced the termination of the commission of inquiry investigating the Somalia affair just as it was preparing to examine the roles and responsibilities of senior officials in Ottawa. It is interesting to note that although shutting down a commission inquiry prior to the conclusion of its work was unprecedented in Canadian history, this decision of the Chrétien government elicited little public criticism. Most critical commentary came from the media and the academic community, but the general public appeared uninterested, and in the 1997 federal election the Somalia affair barely registered as an issue.

Ministers still will be expected to resign, however, if they are directly implicated in allegations of personal wrongdoing. The most recent example of this was the resignation from cabinet of Judy Sgro, Minister of Immigration in the Martin government, in 2005. In 2004 Sgro had been attacked by the opposition and media for showing personal and partisan favouritism in the awarding of ministerial permits designed to allow landed immigrants to remain in Canada. Facing mounting pressure, she stepped down from her position while an investigation was conducted into her actions by the federal Ethics Commissioner; this investigation eventually exonerated her of all serious charges.

As ministers overall, however, face lessened expectations or responsibility one would expect that the requirements of responsibility then fall to administrative officials within departments and agencies. This is generally true, yet even here there are controversies regarding the application of responsibility. While there have been calls for deputy ministers to be made officially responsible for the administrative work of departments, such initiatives have not been implemented in legislation for fear of diminishing the tradition of ministerial responsibility and politicizing the role of deputy ministers. Thus, the formal accountability expectations imposed on administrative officials remain subject to the traditional understanding of ministerial responsibility and the discretionary judgement of senior officials in deciding how, when, and in what manner discipline should be imposed on department officials suspected of poor decision-making and administrative malpractice. As mentioned above, though, as any one action or decision may have dozens of officials involved in its creation or implementation, it can often be extremely difficult to determine exact responsibility for inappropriate and undesirable decision-making. In short, there is protection and concealment for incompetents in numbers and complexity.

Consequently, the effectiveness of the doctrine of ministerial responsibility as a means of imposing political responsiveness over government institutions can be questioned. Certain analysts—for instance, Denton, 1979; Sutherland, 1991—have spoken of a growing problem of accountability in this regard. They argue that ministers should be more responsible for the administrative cultures they either create or tolerate within their departments and agencies. While the current Canadian practice is now rather lenient, the British, operating with the same principles of ministerial responsibility within a similar parliamentary system, are much more rigorous and demanding in their expectations of ministerial behaviour and responsibility for both general and specific department decisions. We could follow this example, setting much higher standards for ministerial behaviour than we do at present. With respect to internal departmental discipline, though, one should not underestimate the effectiveness of internal review, analysis, and discipline. It can be difficult and often slow and unseen to the public, but if senior officials have the will to act, the process can work and can be significant in either exonerating or penalizing those public servants suspected of poor performance. Any public servant who has experienced such investigations can testify to this.

11.1.4 Legal Responsiveness

As with the doctrine of ministerial responsibility, the concept of **legal responsiveness**—the rule of law and the procedural and substantive requirements of administrative law—stand as a second major set of formal objective standards that must be adhered to by public servants and their political superiors. As can be seen in the chapter on Administrative Law found on the Thinking Government web site, there are numerous and important legal obligations borne by government officials engaged in administrative decision-making. Such decision-making must be undertaken in accordance with the established rules of administrative law, and any dispute as to whether or not government authorities have properly fulfilled their legal obligations can be decided through judicial review by superior courts. In this sense, all legal decisions of government bodies can be made subject to the scrutiny and evaluation of the law. In other words, all administrative decision-makers know that they can be held to account for the quality of their legal decision-making by the courts, with the courts possessing the authority to overrule any decisions determined to be unjust.

Thus, the law is a crucial element of the accountability system within which every department and agency finds itself (Boyd, 1995; Gall, 1996). Ministers and public servants are either patently aware of their need to be responsive to the procedural or substantive requirements of administrative law as a matter of general government knowledge, or they will be made aware of this requirement through adverse criticism by the courts. The study of administrative law has not been at the centre of studies in public administration in this country. This is an oversight in need of correction, since the formal objective requirements of accountability are not fully satisfied by the doctrine of ministerial responsibility; indeed, the routine application of administrative law is clearly as important to ensuring government accountability as is the application of the rules of ministerial responsibility.

Debates on the appropriate balance of power to be struck between the courts and specialized quasi-judicial administrative tribunals are of special significance. The pivotal issue in these debates is that of accountability: Does legal accountability necessitate the rigid adherence to judicial review as exercised by the courts, or can such tribunals be trusted to be effective, economical, just, and accountable legal decision-makers in their own right? Courts, tribunals, and governments have struggled over this issue for the better part of three decades, reaching a rough equilibrium at the present time in which the courts maintain the unhindered right to review all administrative actions that pass the threshold of administrative law, but they may defer to tribunal decisions if they believe such decisions to be procedurally sound and generally reasonable in law.

This approach to tribunal accountability highlights three important features:

- systems of accountability can be flexible and are subject to interpretation and change;
- accountability is related to concerns about the quality of formal procedures and control systems; and
- thought regarding accountability often focuses on the socio-economic and political quality of government decisions.

In this respect, accountability is not just about due process and formal control, but about the substantive content of governmental action. At the heart of the judicial deference doctrine is the understanding that, at times, regulatory agencies and tribunals, and not the courts, are the most effective, economical, expert, and pragmatic bodies to provide legally sound and just decision-making.

11.1.5   Social Responsiveness

Social responsiveness is at once the broadest and the most controversial element in the accountability equation. In contrast to political and legal responsiveness, which essentially address formal objective standards of controls, the concept of social responsiveness touches on the subjective world of understanding and evaluation that so concerned Friedrich and Mosher.

From this perspective, a department or agency is considered to be accountable when the substance of its policy and program actions is in accordance with broadly understood social and economic needs, interests, and concerns. Accountability exists when the government decision-maker exercises its power so as to meet and serve societal goals understood to be in "the public interest." In contrast to ministerial responsibility and the rule of law, concern for accountability here is focused not generally on whether appropriate procedures, processes, and controls were followed, but whether the substantive quality of government decision-making actually served to benefit society and promote the long-term interests of socio-economic development.

As one can see, this approach is vast and clearly subjective, far exceeding the much narrower confines of accountability as generally understood by politics and the law. However, it is no less valid, and it is central to the thinking of many inside and outside of government. Accountability as social responsiveness is primarily advocated by political parties, interest groups, and the media, as they constantly evaluate the substantive merits of government action in addressing the current and future social and economic needs and interests of society. When a government is deemed to be appropriately responsive, it will be judged to be accountable, and when it is not so judged, its actions and inactions will be attacked as being undesirable and unaccountable. From this perspective one can observe that daily media coverage of national and provincial politics and government is part of an ongoing accountability process through which governments are judged in light of expectations and possibilities and with respect to their ability to offer good public service.

Of course, a deep current of subjective analysis runs through this approach. Any understanding of what "the public interest" means will depend on the ideological perspective of the given evaluator. Moreover, the assessment of the degree to which a given government's actions either serve or hinder "the public interest" is contingent on the political viewpoint of the evaluator and the values, attitudes, and beliefs that he or she brings to such an assessment. Simply put, a conservative's assessment of "the public interest" and the merit of a given government will be sharply different from that of a social democrat. Thus, the ideological concepts discussed in Chapter 2 exist not only as the core principles for understanding politics and government but also for understanding and assessing government accountability. Indeed, this ideological approach to viewing accountability as being inextricably tied to social responsiveness is the most common approach used by parties, groups, the media, and common citizens in assessing the quality of government actions. Governments live in this constant world of diverse opinions and subjective evaluations of their actions and whether they are being appropriately responsive to the broad socio-economic needs and interests of society. This approach to accountability thus connects the evaluation of government action and inaction directly to the broader political processes of party politics, interest group debates and activities, media scrutiny and evaluation, academic studies, and the shaping of general public opinion that ultimately become the focus of electoral campaigns and outcomes.

This approach is not restricted to political leaders and those outside of the government itself. There is ample evidence that many public servants share this approach to accountability in that they perceive their role as being not simply to carry out orders in accordance with due process but to develop and/or implement policies and programs that will promote and advance the broad interests of society. Studies indicate that many public servants perceive themselves as "servants" of the public interest and that many senior managers stress that they possess a loyalty not only to their departments and agencies and the law but to the ideals of the public service and to the promotion of the public good (Canada, 1979: 458, 471). These ideals—honesty, fairness, impartiality, justice, economy, efficiency, effectiveness, sensitivity, and compassion—can act as important motivational factors to public servants and guide them in how they will actually undertake and fulfil their responsibilities.

Concern for the public interest also influences how external societal parties and groups assess the working of government just as the same concern determines how officials understand and approach their duties. The social responsiveness approach to accountability thus highlights the importance of both external and internal actors in the process of decision-making as well as the significance of subjective considerations in the evaluation of the merit of governmental actions.

11.1.6   Accountability: Further Reflections

All three aspects of accountability—political, legal, and social—point out important obligations borne by government leaders and public sector managers as well as significant public concerns about the quality of government services they receive. A synthetic approach to accountability highlights the various forces to which (or for which) accountability is owed. With respect to political and legal responsiveness, accountability is essentially owed to specific superior bodies—either ministerial or political superiors in the case of ministerial responsibility or superior courts in the case of legal responsibility. But with social responsiveness there is a much broader understanding of the object of accountability: it is owed by public servants and governments to society itself and is evaluated by the leading political actors in society—political parties, interest groups, the media, and common citizens.

This synthetic approach to accountability stresses the multifaceted nature of accountability relationships and the importance of looking at accountability in light of both objective and subjective, formal and informal patterns of interaction. Certain initiatives designed to enhance accountability will not and should not be easily pigeonholed into this three-part categorization, which is simply an aid in thinking about accountability relationships in government and society. In certain instances, accountability initiatives will bridge these categories as well as blend the concepts of objective and subjective, formal and informal.

11.2   Other Forms of Accountability

11.2.1   Public Participation

A long-standing criticism of public sector management in particular and democratic government more generally is that it is too closed and elitist so that decision-making is far removed from the ordinary citizens ultimately affected by government policies and programs; the result of this is often held to be that governments are out of touch with popular sentiments and concerns and that, consequently, governments are inadequately accountable to the people. Many analysts, such as Osborne and Gaebler, and political leaders from across the ideological spectrum, such as Tommy Douglas, René Lévesque, Stockwell Day, and Stephen Harper, have called for greater public participation in the process of government decision-making. Greater participation, in this sense, can range from holding referendums on major issues of public policy, to a greater use of broad-based public hearings in advance of major decision-making, and to state support for social interest groups to allow them to become institutionalized actors roughly comparable to business groups and thus more effective participants in the policy-making process. Greater participation can also be achieved by involving interest groups in making policy and implementing programs. As we observed in the previous chapter, this is one of the reinvention principles of Osborne and Gaebler—community-owned government—and it stresses the point that those who are directly affected by such state actions should be directly involved in making the decisions dealing with these actions. Public participation from this viewpoint can include

- public consultations by government,
- more formal liaisons between governmental decision-making bodies and major interest groups concerned with the work of government, and
- the formal integration of social interest groups into the institutions of government (Johnson, 1993).

Though more informal manners of consultation have tended to dominate Canadian practice regarding public participation, there has been some experimentation with "corporatist" systems of formal group integration into government decision-making bodies. Most of this experimentation has been at the provincial level in such bodies as labour relations and workers' compensation boards and appeal tribunals, where board membership is divided equally among representatives of government, business, and labour. Through the institutionalization of such interests into the decision-making structure of these agencies there is the expectation that better policy and program implementation will result, with these interests working together to establish policies that better reflect the balance of interests.

Advocates of enhanced public participation in government seek to advance their goal in various ways, with all such initiatives having their strengths and weaknesses. The essential point is that all participatory initiatives can be seen as attempts to enhance the accountability of governments in ways that bridge the existing categories of accountability, usually through the subjective social responsiveness of governments, although some have broader implications. Public hearings before decisions are made and the funding of interest groups will directly affect the objective practice of administrative law, as more groups enter the field and have an impact on the legal responsiveness of governments. Likewise, greater use of public hearings and referendums and the development of corporatist forms of policy-making may influence the formal practice of ministerial responsibility if decision-making power flows out from traditional departments and agencies to non-traditional decision-making bodies and processes. Are ministers to be held responsible for policies they have had only a minority influence in shaping? If not, though, who or what is to be held responsible? In this respect, initiatives of public participation may affect the nature of political responsiveness of governments, forcing analysts to ponder the accountability implications of such initiatives from a variety of perspectives.

Having raised this issue of public participation in government decision-making, we need to make an important caveat. Rather than government power and decision-making authority becoming decentralized and being made more open and participatory, the reverse has been true in recent years. While there has been, and likely always will be, much political and administrative rhetoric in favour of enhanced public participation in government decision-making, the reality is that this participation will remain subject to the tight rules of ministerial responsibility and the authority of responsible officials and those senior managers who directly report to them. As we saw in Chapters 5 and 10, significant theoretical and practical problems associated with the participatory model of public sector management militate against its use in most government settings.

It is interesting, then, to reflect on the existence of corporatist forms of organization in certain regulatory agencies. Such participatory forms of interest group representation tend to be found in regulatory agencies dealing with highly specialized forms of policy and law, with the relevant policy field dominated by a few major and competing sets of interests. This is clearly visible with respect to both labour relations and workers' compensation boards, which are characterized by the presence of long-established interests representing both business and organized labour. In these policy settings, all provincial governments have found it advantageous to bring such groups together, to give them official representation in the regulatory agencies, and to encourage them to work together with government representatives to develop and implement sound and responsive labour and workers' compensation policy and administration. While there have been initiatives to expand such corporatist approaches, they have been few and far between. Rather than being a harbinger of a new and generally applicable participatory approach to government, such corporatist initiatives will likely remain intriguing counter-examples of the dominant trend to traditional and centralized government decision-making.

11.2.2 Freedom of Information

A further means of enhancing government accountability is through the development of legislation designed to allow citizens to gain access to government documents. Many provinces have freedom of information legislation and the federal Parliament approved its Access to Information Act in 1983 (Kernaghan and Siegel, 1999: 512-17). Through this law, citizens, groups, businesses, and, most importantly, the media have a right to obtain and examine most government documents and records. This act specifically provides:

> a right to access to information in records under the control of a government in accordance with the principles that government information should be available to the public, that necessary exceptions to the right of access should be limited and specific and that decisions on the disclosure of government information should be reviewed independently of government. (Canada, Access to Information Act, Schedule I)

While the Access to Information Act provides Canadians with a general right of access to federal government information, it exempts

- all matters dealing with national security and cabinet confidentiality;
- all matters of either personal or business confidentiality; and
- all matters dealing with intergovernmental relations, both in international terms and between the federal government and its provincial counterparts.

These various exemptions are designed to maintain the security of communications between governments and the confidentiality of communications between governments and citizens and businesses as well as between ministers and their senior aides and advisors. Apart from these exemptions, however, the general public and the media now have a right to gain access, for a price, to the vast majority of documents produced in the policy-making and implementation processes.

This legislation was explicitly developed to enhance the accountability of government, and most clearly it falls within the parameters of the social responsiveness aspect of accountability. Subject to the restrictions found in the act, its essential purpose is to open up the process of government to the public by making available the government's documentary record. Its operative principles are that

- government decision-making should be public;
- the actions of the bureaucracy should be subject to public scrutiny, or, in most cases, to media scrutiny made available to the public; and
- better, more socially responsive government will result from such openness and scrutiny.

In this sense, openness and the knowledge that most government actions and decisions can be subject to public scrutiny act as an impetus to fair and decent decision-making that conforms to established law and ethical principles.

But, again, the impact of this legislation extends beyond the ambit of enhancing social responsiveness. Decision-making concerning its application and the invocation of its exceptions brings one directly into the field of legal responsiveness and administrative law. In those cases where a request for information is denied by a relevant department or agency, the act provides for a two-tiered review mechanism. The first stage is for the federal Information Commissioner to investigate the complaint, interview the parties to the complaint, and assess the validity of the arguments for and against releasing the given material to the public. Following this investigation the commissioner will issue a recommendation as to whether or not the information should be made public. The commissioner's judgement, however, is advisory only; he or she cannot compel the release of government information. Following a decision that information should be released, if the government body still refuses to do so, the complainant, or the commissioner with the complainant's consent, can apply to the Federal Court of Canada for judicial review of the government's action. The court has the full legal power to either compel the release of documents or to accept the opinion of the relevant government body.

The increased political and legal scrutiny of ministerial and bureaucratic decision-making involved here enhances the pressure faced by both ministers and public servants in being called on to explain and justify their actions. In this respect, such freedom of information legislation has a ready bearing not only on the legal responsiveness of government actors but also on their political responsiveness. Once again, a policy initiative can have crosscutting impacts on the various accountability issues.

11.2.3 Ombudsmen

Another multifaceted initiative to promote greater accountability in government is the creation of ombudsmen's offices (Kernaghan and Siegel, 1999: 433-34). Such an office is a general public service complaints' bureau to which citizens can bring grievances concerning the way they have been treated by those in the public service. The ombudsmen's staff are given legislative authority to investigate all complaints they deem to have merit, requiring those officials responsible for decisions, or non-decisions, to explain their actions and to consider the consequences of these actions. Ombudsmen have no legislative power to quash a questionable decision or to order that a new one be made, so they are not akin to judges, nor can they choose to make what they believe to be a better decision on their own, as they are not given legal responsibility for such first-order decision-making. Rather, the authority of the ombudsman is investigative and reflective, giving responsible officials an opportunity for considered second thought, re-evaluation, and change—or, if they choose not to, then perhaps bringing them unwanted media attention.

All provinces with the exception of Prince Edward Island have instituted ombudsmen's offices within their public services, but despite significant lobbying the federal government has not followed suit, arguing that other specialized offices such as the Office of the Official Languages Commissioner, the Canadian Human Rights Commission, and the Office of the Information Commissioner already address the needs that would be served by an ombudsman. It is interesting to note, however, that the federal government has established an ombudsman's office for the Canadian military with a mandate of hearing complaints from service personnel respecting their treatment both from peers and more senior officers. This may represent the beginning of a larger role for an ombudsman within the federal public service.

Notably, ombudsmen address all forms of responsiveness expected by governments. Through their reviews they clearly assess the substantive merit of administrative decisions in light of their social responsiveness, but they also assess whether the objective matters of due process and/or ministerial responsibility have been duly exercised. Ombudsmen's reviews can be a shortcut towards ensuring legal responsiveness without having to go through the complex processes of judicial review and a reminder to those in authority that ministerial responsibility, control, and leadership must be appropriately followed in all decision-making. Again, accountability involves all of these matters.

11.3 Accountability and Government Ethics

One cannot discuss accountability without considering the theory and practice of **government ethics**. Though many people smirk at this term, claiming it to be an oxymoron, such laughter itself belies the latent public interest in, and recognition of, the importance of ethical behaviour in government. It is true that, as Jackson and Jackson (1998: 367) suggest, while many Canadians are suspicious and distrustful of the quality of ethical behaviour in government, they rightfully expect that those in government should exercise their authority and power in manners that are legal, just, proper, and, quite simply, moral. Very few Canadians expect, as a basic rule, that all political leaders and public servants will be immoral and corrupt, hence the public concern over ethical behaviour when evidence of wrongdoing is brought to light through one or more of the elements of accountability mentioned above. The sponsorship scandal of the late 1990s and the Gomery Commission investigation of 2005 into allegations of wrongdoing associated with the federal sponsorship program in Quebec are evidence of this fact.

The concept of government ethics encompasses a number of diverse concerns. First, those who are political leaders and public servants, having access to greater or lesser domains of state power and authority, should exercise this power and authority in a just and fair manner. There is a broad social recognition that those in government should not lie, cheat, steal, embezzle, or otherwise place their private interest ahead of the public interest; they should also be law-abiding and respectful and supportive of the dominant Canadian political ideals of democracy, equality, liberty, and belief in individual human rights while being responsive to the broad needs and interests of the Canadian people as expressed through the democratic political process. This is a tall order, but these expectations do exist, although most Canadians are not conscious of them until they hear of government officials from this or other countries who do not share such values.

Public demand for ethical behaviour of Canadian government officials is also coupled with a recognition that such high standards of ethical behaviour are not always met by political leaders and public servants. Media stories of ministers lying to or deceiving the public and of public sector managers receiving bribes from private interests in return for favours or covering up evidence of government blunders and illegality naturally enrage the general public, resulting in public demands for the stricter enforcement of ethical standards within government. Canadian political history has been replete with scandals and rumours of scandals, including such historic examples as John A. Macdonald and the CPR, the Canadian government choice of the Ross rifle during the First World War, and the abuse of regulatory power in the Quebec of Maurice Duplessis. Numerous other instances of corruption have involved such matters as liquor licensing, government contracting, influence peddling, favouritism, and nepotism. More contemporary examples of scandals and alleged scandals are those that plagued the Mulroney government, resulting in certain ministerial resignations, notably those of John Fraser and Sinclair Stevens, the laying of criminal charges in a variety of influence-peddling matters, and much public debate over the Airbus affair. The Chrétien government experienced the Somalia/Canadian Airborne affair, the HDRC/Canada Jobs Fund affair, and allegations of prime ministerial wrongdoing in the Auberge Grand-Mère (also known as the Shawinigate affair), and, of course, the sponsorship scandal of the late 1990s and the Gomery Commission investigation of these matters in 2005.

All real or alleged scandals have tended to spur public demands for ethical reforms, with these reforms having a dual focus. The most common government action has been to draft codes of ethics to control conflict-of-interest situations. These arise when a political leader or public servant directly places personal interest ahead of the public interest by using his or her public position to gain private wealth or other benefits.

Codes of ethics

- routinely prohibit ministers and public servants and their families from receiving money, gifts, property, trips, and any other benefit from any other private or public party; the aim is to ensure that the professional integrity of the public official is not impugned by either the reality or the appearance of bias in favour of a specific force or interest external to the government and to the public interest;
- routinely require ministers and other elected officials to disclose their financial assets and interests to allow either the public or selected ethics officers to scrutinize their private financial interests and to be watchful for any alleged conflict of interest between these private interests and the official's public responsibilities (Greene and Shugarman, 1997: ch. 6).

BOX 11.2
Ten Principles of Public Sector Ethics

(As highlighted in the federal *Conflict of Interest Code, Statutes of Canada*, 1994.)

Ethical standards
Public office holders shall act with honesty and uphold the highest ethical standards so that public confidence and trust in the integrity, objectivity, and impartiality of government are conserved and enhanced.

Public scrutiny
Public office holders have an obligation to perform their official duties and arrange their private affairs in a manner that will bear the closest public scrutiny, an obligation that is not fully discharged by simply acting within the law.

Decision-making
Public office holders, in fulfilling their official duties and responsibilities, shall make decisions in the public interest and with regard to the merits of each case.

Private interests
Public office holders shall not have private interests, other than those permitted pursuant to this Code, that would be affected particularly or significantly by government actions in which they participate.

Public interest
On appointment to office, and thereafter, public office holders shall arrange their private affairs in a manner that will prevent real, potential, or apparent conflicts of interest from arising but if such a conflict does arise between the private interests of a public office holder and the official duties and responsibilities of that public office holder, the conflict shall be resolved in favour of the public interest.

Gifts and benefits
Public office holders shall not solicit or accept transfers of economic benefit, other than incidental gifts, customary hospitality, or other benefits of nominal value, unless the transfer is pursuant to an enforceable contract or property right of the public office holder.

Preferential treatment
Public office holders shall not step out of their official roles to assist private entities or persons in their dealings with the government where this would result in preferential treatment to any person.

Insider information
Public office holders shall not knowingly take advantage of, or benefit from, information that is obtained in the course of their official duties and responsibilities and that is not generally available to the public.

Government property
Public office holders shall not directly or indirectly use, or allow the use of, government property of any kind, including property leased to the government, for anything other than officially approved duties.

Post-employment
Public office holders shall not act, after they leave public office, in such a manner as to take improper advantage of their previous office.

- regulate outside employment, prohibiting public officials from engaging in other work that may directly affect their ability to undertake their public duties properly;
- impose restrictions on post-employment, requiring certain senior public servants to refrain, for a certain amount of time (usually six to 12 months), from joining a private firm subject to the regulation or direct commercial dealing with the official's former department or agency; such a "cooling-off" period is designed to allow for a space of time to arise between former officials and their old institutions and institutional actors.
- can also regulate the types of contact that government officials have with certain other officials, most commonly prohibiting contact with adjudicative officers: politicians and public servants are forbidden to contact judges and other quasi-judicial officers serving on regulatory agencies about the merits of particular cases currently before these adjudicative decision-makers; as can be seen in the Administrative Law chapter on the Thinking Government web site, such interventions constitute bias and are grounds for judicial review of any affected decision.

The system of enforcement of such ethics codes varies from one jurisdiction to another (Inwood, 2004: 351-55). In certain instances, with respect to elected officials, enforcement falls within the jurisdiction of a specially appointed conflict-of-interest or ethics commissioner. At the federal level, conflict-of-interest rules and regulations affecting ministers are, as of 2004, overseen by a Federal Ethics Commissioner who reports directly to Parliament. Prior to this date, however, the key official responsible for the application of ethics guidelines was an ethics counsellor appointed by the prime minister and who reported solely to the prime minister (Greene and Shugarman, 1997:155-56). As the controversy over Chrétien's financial relationship respecting the Grand-Mère Inn and golf course rose in intensity in the spring of 2001, this reporting relationship came to be a focus of critical attention, since it was felt that the counsellor could not be an independent officer serving the public interest if this person serves under the prime minister, must report to the prime minister, and has his or her tenure in office subject to the control of the prime minister. Over the spring of 2001 there were many calls for the reform of ethics laws as they apply to cabinet ministers and the prime minister, with most critics speaking in favour of the establishment of an independent ethics commissioner appointed by Parliament with a reporting relationship to Parliament,

BOX 11.3

The Sponsorship Scandal

Following the "near-death experience" of the 1995 Quebec referendum, the federal government under the leadership of Prime Minister Jean Chrétien established a special fund, the Sponsorship Program, designed to channel federal monies into Quebec so as to promote the federal government and Canada in Quebec-based advertising.

This program was placed under the leadership of the federal Department of Public Works. By October of 2000, internal Public Works audits were indicating that the department was not closely supervising a number of the Quebec-based advertising firms that were receiving substantial amounts of sponsorship funding.

In May 2002 Auditor General Sheila Fraser released a preliminary report into the Sponsorship Program that was highly critical of waste, mismanagement, and lack of proper bureaucratic and political oversight of public monies. In a subsequent report in February 2004, she asserted that out of total program spending of $200 million, up to $80 million may have been misappropriated or otherwise wasted by advertising agencies.

Also in February 2004, Prime Minister Paul Martin, just three months into his new position as leader of the government, called a special inquiry into the scandal to be led by Justice John Gomery of the Quebec Superior Court. In testimony before this inquiry there were widespread allegations that millions of dollars of public monies were funneled into Quebec-based advertising agencies with most, if not all, of these firms having close ties to the Quebec wing of the federal Liberal Party. There were also allegations that substantial amounts of these monies were re-routed back to the federal Liberal Party, contrary to the Canada Election Act.

In his report on this scandal, Justice Gomery was called upon

- to explore the nature of this scandal,
- to assess how this problem came to exist in the first place,
- to advise on greater controls over public spending,
- to advise on tighter means of ministerial responsibility,
- to advise on tighter forms of governmental accountability, and
- to promote greater transparency in government.

Having read the Gomery Commission Report, how well do you believe these goals were served? Do its recommendations help to promote greater accountability and ethics in government? Does the promotion of ethics in government require greater formal and objective controls or better, more subjective training and mentoring in ethical political and bureaucratic behaviour?

not to the prime minister. It should come as no surprise that Prime Minister Chrétien consistently refused these demands for the diminution of his power and authority, stressing that all cabinet ministers serve at his pleasure and that the prime minister alone should be the final arbiter of their tenure in office. And with respect to his own position, he stressed that questions regarding the ethical propriety of a prime minister were strictly political matters to be dealt with through the established means of political accountability, namely, parliamentary Question Period, political debate, media scrutiny, and, ultimately, the judgement of the people via democratic elections. Chrétien was able to survive the criticisms launched against him with respect to this matter, and he clearly was reluctant to forgo any of the prerogatives of power centred in his office. In all of this, he once again demonstrated the command mode of authority long noted as a hallmark of prime ministerial government.

With the change in power from the Chrétien to the Martin ministry came a change in attitude and focus with respect to the application of federal ethics rules as they applied to ministers, MPs, and senior public servants. With the establishment of the Office of the Ethics Commissioner in 2004, there is now, in Ottawa, a senior public servant who is functionally independent of the government of the day, with a reporting relationship directly to Parliament, who possesses the duty of assessing and making rulings with respect to whether any politician or public servant has violated the standards of federal ethics legislation. It is anticipated that with the new status of the Ethics Commissioner as an independent Officer of Parliament, there will now be a more serious approach taken to the promotion and enforcement of ethics among cabinet ministers and MPs than was observed during the Chrétien years. The sponsorship scandal has only served to highlight the need and importance for more vigilant oversight, enforcement, and education across the government with respect to the theory of governmental ethics and their application on a routine basis by those in positions of authority.

When attention shifts from elected ministers to public servants, however, the enforcement of ethics codes generally falls under the jurisdiction of senior management within the given department or agency. At the federal level, the Conflict of Interest and Post-Employment Code for Public Office Holders is administered by such officials within each department and agency, although any disciplinary action against a public servant for violation of ethics standards must be consistent with the rules and regulations of the Public Service Commission, responsible for the merit principle, and the Public Service Staff Relations Board, responsible for the implementation and enforcement of collective agreements and their grievance procedures. As a central agency, the Treasury Board Secretariat has taken a lead role in coordinating departmental and agency initiatives regarding ethics enforcement; in promoting information, jurisprudence, and "best practices" regarding ethics matters; and in establishing common benchmarks and standards for the application of rules. In promoting this work, the Treasury Board, in its own words, is committed to reinforcing ethical leadership by "clarifying the principle of ministerial responsibility and the responsibilities of officials, and identifying the responsibilities of senior and line managers for promoting sound values and ethics." It is also dedicated to the reinvigoration of "an extensive dialogue on values and ethics that emphasizes the primacy of the principles of respect for the law, the public interest, and public service as a public trust" (Canada, 2000: 2) As an overriding goal:

> Our objective is to stimulate sustained and transparent discussion and action on values and ethics by Canadians and members of the federal public sector.... we focus on values and ethics initiatives that promote ethical decision-making as part of a comprehensive approach to good governance in federal entities.... Values and ethics initiatives are not sustainable without leadership at the highest levels and a commitment to act. Thus, one of our primary concerns [is] the leadership responsibilities of parliamentarians, ministers, and heads and managers of federal entities. (Canada, 2000: 12, 20, 21)

Conflict of interest has become the dominant issue covered in codes of ethics. This issue is obviously important, and federal, provincial, and municipal governments have expended much effort in establishing formal objective rules rather than leaving such situations to be governed by the subjective understandings of the persons directly involved. This latter approach to ethics regulation, as explained through the ideas of Friedrich, had been the preferred traditional approach of all governments prior to the 1970s, but increasing government and public concern regarding the quality of ethics in governments over the past 20 years has led to the greater reliance on an objective formalistic approach to enforcement as championed by Finer. Most analysts, including Kernaghan and Siegel (1999: 374-75), stress the value and effectiveness of written codes in addressing matters of conflict of interest. Today, the move away from subjective to objective approaches to responsibility and ethical control is a fact of government life. It would be inconceivable now for any government to disestablish ethical codes of conduct. In fact, as recent alleged scandals in Ottawa have shown, news of such events tends to result in opposition party, media, and much public demand for stronger ethics codes with stricter enforcement.

This being acknowledged, a further point begs mention. While recent scandals have attracted much critical public attention to the ethical behaviour of public servants, they have also reinforced the fact that such scandals are actually rare in Canadian government and that the vast majority of Canadian public servants never run afoul of ethical guidelines. In fact, public servants will often be the most critical of misbehaviour by their fellow colleagues in that the unethical behaviour of the few will adversely affect the general public opinion in which all public servants are viewed. Perception is very important, and all public servants know that the media will seldom, if ever, report on a public servant doing a routine job in a very good, professional, and ethical manner although this is the routine working reality for the vast majority of them. But when one public servant gets caught behaving in an unethical manner, this is likely to make national news with all public servants then being tainted through guilt by association. The public anger at such lapses of ethical behaviour, however, nevertheless affirms that most members of the public expect high standards of professionalism from public servants and will be very annoyed when such standards have been violated. What one needs to remember is that such violations are the exceptions to the rule.

The issue of ethics enforcement, in general, raises many difficult questions pertaining both to the application of ethical rules and regulations and to the scope and nature of these rules in the first instance. Most codes of ethics mention the importance of public servants undertaking their responsibilities in light of obligations to the rule of law, honesty, integrity, respect for fundamental human rights, and respect for superior political and administrative authority. All of these values are desirable and necessary within the public service, but the basic problem confronting those concerned with such government ethics is that in the real world it is often difficult to know how to turn theory into practice. Ethics implementation can be problematic; in certain instances, reasonable people will reasonably disagree as to whether a particular administrative action results in a breach of ethical standards requiring some form of discipline. Consider some hypothetical examples derived from real cases.

1. *Is it ever permissible for public servants to accept money or gifts from interest groups or businesses with which they must interact?* The basic answer is no. All federal and provincial ethics codes prohibit the acceptance of gifts, hospitality, or other benefits that could either influence employees in their judgement and performance of their official duties or raise an appearance of a conflict of interest among the general public were they to become aware of the action. Indeed, bribery of public officials has long been a prohibited ground of action under the Criminal Code, with the illegality being both the issuance and the acceptance of a bribe. But what if the receiver is

a Canadian ambassador abroad, and the "gift"—an artwork—is from the host country as a symbol of goodwill between the two countries. Should the ambassador refuse to accept the gift, possibly insulting the giver? Here, the considered opinion is that such a gift can and should be accepted but in a very public way, with the gift understood as being a gift to the Canadian people and not to the particular diplomatic official himself or herself.

2. *Is it ever permissible for a public servant to use government facilities and working hours to engage in personal activities unrelated to the work of the given office?* Should a public servant, for example, use such facilities and time to promote and assist the private business interests of his or her spouse? Or should a public servant use such facilities, and the knowledge gained from such work, to promote his or her own personal interests? Is it permissible for a public servant to engage in public consultation with firms dealing with his or her department, with the public servant trading on confidential information gained through the work process? Or is it permissible for a public servant to use his or her access to public records or his or her influence in official decision-making to undertake "favours" for family members of friends? Is it acceptable, for example, for an official in the Department of Immigration and Citizenship to fast-track a claim for landed immigrant status made by a family friend?

In all such instances the answer is no, the rule being that a public servant is not to use public office for any type of private gain or to bestow favouritism upon family and friends. The principle here—impartial and equal application of rules and regulations established by law—is derived from the Weberian logic of bureaucracy. Yet, even here the hard and fast application of such rules can become blurred by human behaviour. While public servants are rightfully admonished not to use their access to public office for private gain, in many small ways such actions are a routine part of office life. Not all public servants use government phone lines for "official" business only, just as office supplies and photocopiers not infrequently are used for non-official matters. The salient point here becomes the degree of such non-official usage. Most managers tend to turn a blind eye to minor infractions of these rules but will rightfully attack the flagrant misuse of public office and its perquisites. With respect to the use of influence by public servants, while the use of influence, as suggested in the example above, is clearly prohibited and rarely found, other forms of influence being exploited can be more problematic. Is it wrong, for example, for senior officials to "coach" certain junior officials in interview techniques and tactics as a means of assisting them in the quest for promotion? At what point does the "mentoring" of one official end and the unfair discrimination against other officials begin?

3. *Is it ever permissible for public servants to lie, or misrepresent the truth, to members of the public and elected officials?* The immediate response of most Canadians would be to say no. But what about times of war or peacekeeping operations, when matters of national security are at stake? For obvious security reasons, the Canadian government routinely lied to or misled the Canadian public with respect to the operations of North Atlantic convoys during the Second World War. Most Canadians condone such an exception to the normal standard of ethical conduct of public servants as a necessary response to abnormal and dangerous circumstances.

Similarly, must police officers or immigration officers always speak the truth to criminal suspects or detainees? On many occasions, as a part of criminal investigations or other interrogations, law enforcement officers may tell a lie to a suspect or detainee to see the type of response the lie will elicit. A standard technique used when two or more suspected accomplices are being questioned separately by police is for the officers to tell each suspect that one of the others has confessed and implicated him or her. Even though nothing of the sort has happened, such a tactic may result in the suspect confessing or providing other useful information for the progress of the investigation. Is this type of behaviour unethical? Most Canadians seem willing to accept it, holding that the standard ethical rule can be justifiably departed from in these cases on the grounds of a greater public interest. But it must be recognized here that the ethical rule against lying is being relaxed, at least in these circumstances, and this can raise problems over the long term if law enforcement officers come to believe that "normal" ethical standards do not apply to them.

4. *Is the government ever justified in proceeding surreptitiously with a policy which it deems in the public interest even when some of the public may be inconvenienced by this action?* Consider the following: a provincial community and social services agency has identified a need for a halfway house or a group home for young offenders or the mentally challenged. The logic of such institutions is that they should be located in residential neighbourhoods to allow their residents gradually to reintegrate into the larger society. The authorities realize, though, from much past experience, that such transition houses are vehemently opposed by neighbourhood community groups, who may approve of the policy of reintegration in principle but not the practice of placing a group home in their neighbourhood. The common

community reaction in such cases is termed the NIMBY syndrome—Not In My Back Yard!

Since the government authorities are aware that this reaction is likely, are they justified in proceeding with their initiative? Is it ethical in such a case for the authorities to purchase a property quietly and to turn it into a group home without notifying the local community? If certain persons in the local community become suspicious and begin asking questions about the intentions of the government agency, is it acceptable for these officials to lie or to mislead these questioners? Does it make a difference if the questioner is a common citizen or an elected municipal leader? What if the questioner is a member of the provincial or federal legislature or Parliament? Reasonable people can reasonably disagree as to the proper course of action in a matter such as this.

These cases have frequently occurred in Canada, and they will continue to do so as the needs of social welfare authorities clash with the interests of local communities. The problem is that there is no clearly right answer to such a dispute—one's perspective will be coloured by one's pre-existing attitudes to social welfare policy and community interests. This highlights the difficult terrain that one must sometimes traverse in determining whether certain actions by public servants are ethical or not.

5. *Finally, is it ever permissible for a public servant to violate his or her oath of confidentiality and leak information to opposition parties, specific interest groups, and/or the media on the grounds that such information should be in the public realm but is being subjected to a government "cover-up"?* While such whistle-blowing has always been a feature of life for government, public interest in it has come to the fore in recent years at the same time as widespread cynicism about the trustworthiness of governments has increased. The issues are complex: by blowing the whistle on an alleged government cover-up, a public servant deliberately breaks the law and violates his or her oath of office by releasing confidential information to non-governmental sources without any form of due process. On its face, any such action is improper and will be and has been met, in practice, with guilty parties being subjected to internal discipline ranging from financial penalties and demotions to outright dismissal. But there are times when the public might support the actions of such whistle-blowers, when the information being made public indicates illegal activities within a government body, gross waste and mismanagement, or direct threats to public health and safety coupled with evidence of attempts, by senior officials, to prevent such information from being made public. In such instances, many people will turn a blind eye to

the breach of official procedure by the self-proclaimed "public defender" and will accept the legitimacy of the whistle-blowing because of the public good being promoted. In this sense, whistle-blowing will be judged on very utilitarian grounds, with any would-be whistle-blower needing to be careful in judging the public assessment of such an action prior to its being undertaken.

In short, the assessment of the merits of any particular case of such illegal disclosure of information is inherently political, with all interested parties to the case, as well as the general public, judging its merits in light of a balance between the severity of the procedural irregularity in relation to the importance of the substantive information obtained from the action. The nature of this political assessment of any case of whistle-blowing, however, points out the difficulty of trying to establish any form of rules or procedures to govern such instances. Given its political nature, whistle-blowing will likely remain a feature of bureaucratic life that is afforded few, if any, special rules and regulations or protections. Also, it is likely to remain a fact of life faced by all governments, with public opinion ultimately determining the moral merits and demerits of particular cases.

11.4 Accountability: Final Reflections

The seemingly simple concept of accountability, which is found in journalistic accounts and political debate on an almost daily basis, is far from straightforward when one begins to investigate it and probe for its meaning. Rather than trying to impose a one-dimensional definition, this chapter has proposed a multifaceted synthetic approach. Accountability has political, legal, and social dimensions, and it includes concerns of ministerial responsibility and the development and functioning of a ministerial chain of command and discipline, along with broader questions about the responsiveness of public policies to the needs and interests of society. But accountability relates to more than this. It is also about the rule of law and whether government actions have been undertaken and implemented with due respect for the procedural and substantive rules of administrative law.

Accountability, then, is an enormous concept with a broad reach of concerns and issues. We address issues of accountability

- when we question whether ministers have properly fulfilled their responsibilities and whether public servants are subject to an appropriate system of command and discipline;

- when we question whether government decision-making has been undertaken within the concept of the rule of law and the dictates of natural justice and fairness, jurisdiction, and error of law;
- when we, as citizens, ask if government decisions are wise, just, and sound, effectively dealing with the social and economic concerns of the country, or the province, or the municipality;
- when we assess whether the actions of governments are ethical, whether the actions of public servants are wise and just, and whether, in cases such as whistle-blowing, the greater good being achieved, as determined by a maverick public servant, can outweigh the procedural harm caused by the action.

The concept of accountability is broad simply because the responsibilities of any government are great, calling for effective yet sensitive and just decision-making on political, legal, and social grounds. And how any one individual answers the basic question as to whether a government overall—or particular institutions, policies, programs, or actions of a government and its officials—is indeed accountable will very much depend on that person's political and ideological views. Different people can and will have differing understandings of the requirements of ministerial responsibilities, just as they can have opposing approaches to the application of the rules of administrative law. Simply put, though accountability is a central concept pertaining to the theory and practice of government and management, it is inherently political and thus subject to continuous interpretation and debate. Interpretations and debates, in turn, become the substance of further political discussion about the merits and demerits of government action, with this discourse becoming a part of the accountability process itself.

Key Terms

accountability: The broad concept that all officials of government, both elected cabinet ministers and unelected public servants, are responsible for the procedural and substantive merit of their decision-making. All such officials are called upon to undertake their responsibilities in accordance with law, the concept of ministerial responsibility, and social responsiveness.

government ethics: The broad concept of appropriate forms of political and bureaucratic decision-making within government. The basic principles of government ethics stress that politicians and public servants are to undertake their duties in light of serving the public interest, maintaining fidelity to law, and avoiding having their private interests interfere with their public duties.

legal responsiveness: A principle of accountability stressing that all cabinet ministers and public servants must be responsive to all the rules of administrative law when exercising administrative and executive authority.

ministerial responsibility: The principle that cabinet ministers are individually responsible for all matters dealing with the running of their departmental portfolios as well as being collectively responsible for all policy and program decisions made by cabinet on behalf of the government.

political responsiveness: A principle of accountability stressing that all cabinet ministers and public servants must be responsive to the rules of individual and collective ministerial responsibility when exercising administrative and executive authority.

social responsiveness: A principle of accountability that all cabinet ministers and public servants must be responsive to the broad social needs and interests of the communities they are serving when exercising administrative and executive authority. Of course, the application of this principle is highly subjective.

References and Suggested Reading

Bennis, Warren. 1994. *On Becoming a Leader*. Reading, MA: Addison-Wesley.

Boyd, Neil. 1995. *Canadian Law: An Introduction*. Toronto: Harcourt Brace Canada.

Canada. 1979. Royal Commission on Financial Management and Accountability. *Final Report*. Ottawa: Supply and Services.

—. 2000. Report of the Auditor General. *Values and Ethics in the Federal Public Sector*. Ottawa: Supply and Services, Oct.

Denton, T.M. 1979. "Ministerial Responsibility: A Contemporary Perspective." In R. Schultz *et al.*, eds. *The Canadian Political Process*. 3rd ed. Toronto: Holt, Rinehart and Winston. 344-62.

Desbarats, Peter. 1997. *Somalia Cover-Up: A Commissioner's Journal*. Toronto: McClelland and Stewart.

Dixon, Norman. 1979. *On The Psychology of Military Incompetence*. London: Futura.

Dyck, Rand. 1996. *Canadian Politics: Critical Approaches*. 2nd ed. Toronto: Nelson Canada.

Finer, Herman. 1941. "Administrative Responsibility in Democratic Government." *Public Administration Review* 1: 335-50.

Friedrich, Carl J. 1940. "Public Policy and the Nature of Administrative Responsibility." In Carl J. Friedrich and Edward S. Mason, eds. *Public Policy*. Cambridge, MA: Harvard University Press. 3-24.

Gall, Gerald. 1996. *The Canadian Legal System*. 4th ed. Toronto: Carswell.

Greene, Ian, and David P. Shugarman. 1997. *Honest Politics: Seeking Integrity in Canadian Public Life*. Toronto: James Lorimer.

Ingstrup, Ole, and Paul Crookall. 1998. *The Three Pillars of Public Management: Secrets of Sustained Success*. Montreal and Kingston: McGill-Queen's University Press.

Inwood, Gregory J. 2004. *Understanding Canadian Public Administration: An Introduction to Theory and Practice*. 2nd ed. Scarborough, ON: Prentice-Hall Allyn and Bacon Canada.

Jackson, Robert, and Doreen Jackson. 1998. *Politics in Canada: Culture, Institutions, Behaviour and Public Policy*. 4th ed. Scarborough, ON: Prentice-Hall Canada.

Johnson, David. 1993. "The Canadian Regulatory System and Corporatism: Empirical Findings and Analytical Implications." *Canadian Journal of Law and Society* 8: 95-120.

Kernaghan, Kenneth, and David Siegel. 1999. *Public Administration in Canada: A Text*. 4th ed. Toronto: Nelson Canada.

Mancuso, Maureen, and Michael M. Atkinson, André Blais, Ian Greene, and Neil Nevitte. 1998. *A Question of Ethics: Canadians Speak Out*. Toronto: Oxford University Press.

Mosher, Frederick. 1968. *Democracy and the Public Service*. New York: Oxford University Press.

Mowen, John C. 1993. *Judgement Calls: High Stakes Decisions in a Risky World*. New York: Simon and Schuster.

Rynard, Paul, and David Shugarman, eds. 2000. *Cruelty and Deception: The Controversy over Dirty Hands in Politics*. Peterborough, ON: Broadview Press.

Spears, Larry C., ed. 1995. *Reflections on Leadership*. New York: John Wiley and Sons.

Sutherland, Sharon. 1991. "Responsible Government and Ministerial Responsibility." *Canadian Journal of Political Science* 24: 91-120.

Wills, Garry. 1994. *Certain Trumpets: The Nature of Leadership*. New York: Simon and Schuster.

Yukl, Gary. 1998. *Leadership in Organizations*. 4th ed. Saddle River, NJ: Prentice-Hall.

Related Web Sites

OFFICE OF THE ETHICS COMMISSIONER
<http://www.parl.gc.ca/oec-bce>

PRIVY COUNCIL OFFICE
<http://www.pco-bcp.gc.ca>

TREASURY BOARD SECRETARIAT
<http://www.tbs-sct.gc.ca>

CHAPTER 12
Public Sector Management: The Challenges of Leadership

This book began with the presentation of a paradox. On the one hand, most Canadians tend to have a very critical, skeptical, even hostile attitude towards government and the work of public servants. They may express the view that governments are uneconomic, inefficient, incompetent, or wasteful. They think, or say, that government institutions—departments, agencies, offices—are confusing, awkward, and bloated bureaucracies staffed by people who are overpaid, underworked, and generally self-serving. This widespread and cynical attitude treats public administration as a joke and public sector management as, in essence, boring, tedious, uninteresting, and ultimately unimportant.

Yet, paradoxically, most Canadians also hold deeply felt attitudes and beliefs ultimately very favourable to the role of governments and their work—the social and economic service outcomes of government policies and programs. We are proud of the general quality of life found in this country, even in comparison to that found in our wealthy southern neighbour. Most of us take pride in our health care and public education systems, just as we also value our system of social welfare. And we comment favourably on other building blocks of Canadian social life: gun control, human rights legislation, multiculturalism policy, environmental regulation, health and safety regulation, regional equalization and development policy, and support for indigenous arts and culture.

The irony, of course, is that all these distinguishing and important elements of the Canadian quality of life are matters of public policy and public administration. They are all features of the Canadian state, created and maintained for all of us through the work of public-sector management. Why do Canadians exhibit such contradictory attitudes with respect to the state, the work of government, and the nature of public-sector management in this country? We take up this question again as an epilogue to the review and analysis that has gone before.

12.1   Making Sense of the Paradox

It may be that the paradox has a solution, that the seemingly contradictory aspects of the puzzle can be resolved, and that an understanding can be derived from it. How? Two considerations deserve attention, one that is rather simple, the other much deeper and more profound.

From our study of government, we recognize that some aspects of the public criticism of governments, public services, and public servants are unfounded, based more on prejudice towards stereotypes than considered or substantial judgements. As we saw in Chapter 8, for example, it is hard to sustain a rational argument that most public servants are overpaid and underworked when one actually looks at public sector wage rates. Most employees in the public sector earn relatively modest salaries, and most public sector managers are qualified to garner much higher salaries in the private sector. Indeed, relative wage rates have become a major issue with respect to employee retention in the public sector, with the federal government recognizing that one of its key priorities in the first decade of this new century will be the enhancement of public service salaries and working conditions.

It is also difficult to sustain the position that the actions of the public service are inherently inefficient and uneconomic or that the quality of service standards in the public service are consistently inferior to those found in the private sector. While certain bureaucratic organizations and programs may have problems in these ways at times, it is not just to engage in generalization. As we saw in Chapter 10, the quality of service standards in some public organizations are very high, and when one compares certain public and private organizations with respect to service quality, the results can be surprising. In a number of instances, public sector bureaucracies clearly outrank private sector enterprises in service delivery.

It is also hard to sustain arguments that governments and their bureaucracies are largely ineffective, incompetent, unresponsive, or unaccountable. Of course, these matters are all very much enveloped with political understandings and conditioned by ideological predispositions with respect as to how any one individual views the appropriate role of the state and the actions of government in any particular case, but, again, one would be unjust to generalize. While particular governments and particular public sector organizations may be guilty of ineffective, incompetent, unresponsive, and unaccountable actions in particular instances, such a finding cannot sustain a blanket condemnation of most government undertakings and the broader role of the state in this society. The substantial and widespread public support for the central policies and programs of governments in this country—the second element of the public sector management paradox—remains indicative of a deep public recognition of the importance and value of state action and how most governments in our society have been able, most of the time, to meet and fulfill their essential responsibilities to the public in a generally desirable and acceptable manner.

So, in certain respects, the criticism of the state, of governments, and of public servants found in the first part of the paradox simply does not withstand critical review. Indeed, as developed in Chapters 1 and 2, one must always be aware of the political and ideological underpinnings of arguments critical of the nature and working of the state, just as one should be aware of the same biases raised in defence of the state and its actions. None of the foregoing is meant to suggest, however, that the paradox with respect to government and public sector management is simply a myth, created and maintained by those with an ideological predisposition hostile to a creative and active state in this society. Though certain aspects of the general public's criticism of government can be overdrawn for political and ideological reasons, and one should be cognizant of this fact, the paradox standing at the heart of public sector management in this country is real and is deserving of serious consideration and reflection.

On a deeper level this paradox confronts us with a profound critique of government that must be and should be of great concern to all those working within governments in this country, as well as to all citizens interested in and affected by the work of these governments. Most people in this society do have serious criticisms of the quality of governance and are concerned about issues of economy, efficiency, and effectiveness in the administration of government activities. Most people do harbour doubts about the quality of public services and whether governments are appropriately fulfilling their obligations to the public. And most people do express legitimate concerns as to whether governments and their bureaucratic organizations are properly responsible and responsive to the public and the public interest. In short, most Canadians do wonder whether our governments are appropriately accountable to the people of Canada and want to know what these governments and their political and administrative leaderships can do to ensure that the highest standards of accountability are found.

It is at this level of analysis one might discover the resolution of the paradox. Criticism of the state and government as well as support for the essential work of the state and government can be seen as opposite sides of the same coin. Most people in this society exhibit a general respect for the fundamental policies and programs of governments, once they think about them, and rightly view these policies and programs as cornerstones of Canadian society. But they are also critical of much of the routine operations of governments and their bureaucracies. They want governments to be more economical, efficient, and effective in their work and to pay more attention to matters of service quality and service delivery—in other words, to be more responsible and responsive to the needs of the public. Simply put, most people, through their criticisms of governments, are expressing a demand that governments be more accountable to them and to this society, to do their work better, and to be better servants of the public trust. And if people believe that trust is not being well served, they will complain about it, whether they possess the knowledge of details to do so fairly, or not.

At this level of analysis the paradox ceases to exist, because these broad goals are also those of governments themselves. All governments in this society are committed to providing Canadians with high quality public services and to doing so with the highest standards of accountability. All governments recognize

- the vital importance of accountability in everything they do;
- that public respect and support for the work of governments will be contingent upon governments displaying to the public that their actions are accountable in all possible senses of the term;
- that their actions must be as economical, efficient, and effective as possible;
- that their actions must be responsible and prudent;
- that their policy and program decisions must be well-designed, well-implemented, and consistent with all legal obligations borne by the state; and
- that they must be ultimately responsive to the social and economic needs of the broader society and the various interest groups within it.

Thus, governments and their public servants are called upon to display the highest calibre of policy and program administration in the name of the public. Politicians and public servants are expected to provide nothing less than excellent management of public services. All governments are pledged to these ends, in the name of service to the public, and the most important means to these ends is the effective exercise of leadership.

12.2   Public Sector Management and Leadership

Leadership has always been at the heart of effective organizational management, and in recent years interest in leadership has been one of the most important issues in management reform in both the private and public sectors. There is a vast and growing literature on leadership within organizations, and one need only go to the management section of any bookstore or library to see dozens of volumes on the subject. Authors such as Mowen (1993), Bennis (1994), Wills (1994), Spears (1995), Wren (1995) Champy (1995) Yukl (1998), and Ingstrup and Crookall (1998) are but a few of the more notable writers in this field. All these works, in one manner or another, probe the nature of leadership in organizations, and, depending on whether one is looking at the private or public sectors, certain common traits emerge as vital elements of good leadership. We will now begin to probe these traits as they relate to the public sector within this country, but we will do so by first looking at the broad characteristics associated with leadership failures and bureaucratic incompetence.

12.3   Accountability and Leadership: Bureaucratic Competence and Incompetence; Why Things Go Wrong

As outlined in Chapter 5, analysts of management theory have directed their attention to broad organizational and procedural dynamics that can result in better or weaker approaches to management, especially in relation to government. These approaches to thinking about the merits and demerits of various methods of management are important and worthy of study and reflection, but here the focus of analysis is on the very special factor of the leadership capabilities of senior officials. As we saw in Chapter 11, the federal government is committed to improving the leadership calibre of the federal public service, and all other provincial governments echo this concern for the development of leadership skills and capabilities throughout their public services. As the Clerk of the Privy Council has asserted, effective leadership is vital to the sound administration of current policies and programs as well as to the promotion and development of new initiatives necessary for seeing this country and its government advance into the future. Leadership thus stands at the heart of good governance, meaning that leadership is vital to the fulfilment of accountability within government. To appreciate the nature of good leadership much can be learned from reviewing the theory and practice of poor leadership. We wish to probe the psychology of bureaucratic incompetence not only as a means to gain knowledge about bureaucratic failures but also to understand its opposite, namely, the nature of bureaucratic competence and sound effective leadership.

Quite interesting work on this subject matter has been advanced by the English psychologist Norman Dixon (1979). Although his work was restricted to the issues surrounding military incompetence, much of his commentary and analysis offer fruitful insights into the origins of government incompetence generally and, conversely, the nature of effective government leadership. Here, we will rework some of his terminology to broaden the scope of analysis. The following is a derivative listing of Dixon's conclusions about organizational incompetence and failed leadership, with certain Canadian examples provided for practical emphasis.

12.3.1   Bureaucratic Pathologies

1. *A lack of concern for wasting resources.* The problem here, as Dixon suggests, is that a government or bureaucratic leader may show little interest in the efficient use of public resources—people, money, and material—because of the official's awareness that such resources do not come out of "his or her" pocket and that they "can always be replenished." The official may feel that spending demonstrates significance and power in that "the more you have, the more you can use, and thus the more important you look." Think, for example, of the financial fiasco of the Montreal Olympics of 1976. Critics of the Chrétien government's administration of the Sponsorship Program in the late 1990s also argue that senior officials in the Department of Public Works showed wanton disregard for rules of sound financial management in that the political imperatives for supporting certain advertising programs as well as supporting certain partisan "friends" were far more important than administering control and audit functions over such spending.

2. *A fundamental conservatism and a clinging to outworn traditions.* It is always dangerous, Dixon asserts, for leaders to be fixated on the past and on past ways of dealing with problems—the attitude that the best way is "the way we have always done it." As times change and new problems arise, they may very well require that new ways of thinking and problem-solving techniques be developed to cope with the changed situation. Many ana-

lysts view the history of federal and provincial support for the Cape Breton coal and steel industries to promote Cape Breton regional development as a classic example of governments being fixated on outworn and non-viable solutions to current problems. Rather than supporting the industries of the past through massive subsidy programs, it would have been far better for Cape Breton had governments allowed these industries to pass away earlier rather than later, while supporting the development of new industries for the new Cape Breton economy, namely, information technology, specialized manufacturing, tourism, and oil and gas development.

3. *Preconceptions based on narrow ways of thinking.* We all go through life, Dixon suggests, with preconceptions gained through upbringing, education, and life experience with regard to what is good, just, and proper in a given circumstance. If leaders have policy-making and administrative preconceptions founded on stereotypical ways of thinking marked by arrogance, ignorance, intolerance, or prejudice, problems will likely ensue, as these preconceptions result in leaders either failing to gain "intelligence" or clashing with those with differing viewpoints. Think of the feminist and ethnic minority critique of past hiring practices in the public sector as recounted in Chapter 9. Their criticism was that senior managers had deeply entrenched sexist and racist preconceptions leading them to discriminate against women and visible minorities, with the result that the public service did not represent these important segments of society, eventually leading to great tensions between these groups and governments over hiring practices. One need look no further than the Canadian military to see an institution that is struggling to overcome deeply entrenched prejudices held by many within its ranks respecting the proper roles and places for women and members of visible minority groups.

4. *Underestimating problems and adversaries and overestimating one's own capabilities and solutions.* This is often a common human failing, so Dixon argues. Political and bureaucratic leaders may become so immersed in their own undertakings and so convinced of their own intelligence and wisdom that they begin to operate in a bubble of their own making, increasingly divorced from the real world around them. This can result in leaders failing to see the true complexities of issues or the true strengths of those opposed to them, hence ignoring or dismissing information unpalatable or wrong simply because it conflicts with their preconceptions of themselves and their ideas of good policy and management. Consider the failure of the Charlottetown Accord. This was a classic example of first ministers being

so wrapped up in the esoteric world of constitutional policy-making that they cut themselves off from the reality of mainstream Canadian public opinion at the grassroots, failing to recognize the deep antagonisms held by most people across the country toward the terms and conditions of the accord. Of more recent vintage and of broader scale, consider the public furore that erupted over the United States-led invasion of Iraq in 2003, an invasion for which President George W. Bush sought Canadian support. Many critics argued that the American administration was rushing into a conflict without a sufficient justification for war as well as a lack of a long-term plan on how to deal with Iraq once the invasion was complete. Most Canadians, as recorded in opinion polls, have demonstrated their satisfaction that the Canadian government refused to participate in this conflict that seems to have no end.

5. *An obstinate persistence in a given task despite contrary evidence to its worthiness.* In certain instances and for certain reasons, leaders may become committed to a particular course of action and may adhere to such commitment despite strong evidence that the direction being followed is undesirable. In certain respects, as Dixon contends, such obstinacy may be attributed to a passionate belief in the rightness of a policy, but in others it may result from a combination of ignorance and arrogance, a lack of awareness of broader dynamics, and a refusal to admit that one may have been mistaken. I am personally aware of one nice little example of such incompetence at the micro-bureaucratic level. As late as the mid-1980s, a particular provincial office manager in one of the smaller provinces steadfastly refused to support the computerization of her office on the grounds that computers were "confusing" and a "passing fad." Rather than promoting the use of office computers, this official argued in favour of retaining electronic typewriters. This position probably reflects her unfamiliarity and fear of this technology rather than any considered assessment of it; moreover, once she had staked out her position, she likely felt she would lose face if she had to retract. Of course, this is what eventually happened, as computer technology came to reshape the practice of office work, but in the meantime this office had made questionable purchases of machinery already obsolete.

6. *Believing in simple solutions to complex problems.* Certain political and bureaucratic leaders may well come to be overwhelmed by their responsibilities and by the problems facing them. Their personal, intellectual, and professional background may be insufficient to enable them to cope with the realities of their situation. Complex problems are complex for the very

reason that they are multifaceted and highly involved, possessing various antecedents, characteristics, and possible outcomes; another feature of complex problems is that their solutions, likewise, will tend to be complex. By definition a complex problem will be one that does not have a simple solution, meaning that those who must address themselves to the resolution of such problems must be willing and able to deal with complexity, comprehend the nature of a multifaceted and involved problem, and devise sophisticated approaches for resolving the problem. The signs of leaders being "in over their heads," then, is that they thrash about, latching on to simple answers and solutions because they are the ones they can understand and advocate; of course, such simple solutions rarely, if ever, stand up to scrutiny or are effective for change. For example, the various "Just Say No" campaigns against drug use and teen sex testify to the inability of certain leaders to understand and effectively address the problems of the illicit drug industry and teen pregnancy rates.

7. *Not encouraging critical thinking.* Those political and bureaucratic leaders that may be guilty of certain of these other tendencies of incompetence will likely be the type, Dixon writes, who also feel threatened by critical thinking, because thought and criticism may directly confront them with evidence of their own weakness, failure, and incompetence. We all know stories of leaders who surround themselves with "yes men" who will tell the boss what he or she wants to hear. Such behaviour perpetuates established and accepted organizational patterns, practices, traditions, and ways of thought even when such factors may be in need of criticism and reform. While the encouragement and promotion of critical thinking is one of the most important features of leadership, it is a challenging position to take, because the leader may become the very target of such thought. In certain instances, leaders will not encourage such thought or even punish those around them who engage in it. Recall the tensions surrounding the Diefenbaker cabinet in the early 1960s or some of the complaints surrounding the actions of Ontario Premier Mike Harris with respect to cutbacks to environmental regulations and the monitoring of water quality in Ontario prior to the Walkerton scandal.

8. *Suppress or distort "bad news."* This is an all-too-common phenomenon within organizations marked by poor leadership, Dixon argues. Rather than admit to mistakes and confront the reality of policy and program weakness and the need for reform, most incompetent leaders react to such problems by denying their existence or, if this proves impossible, by seeking to cover

them up. In this manner it is hoped that the problem will go away or be concealed and forgotten. Such actions may only exacerbate the problem, resulting in a greater mess to be dealt with by appropriate authorities in the future. This, in a nutshell, characterizes the response of senior officials in the Department of National Defence to the Somalia affair. Rather than admit to serious breaches of discipline and a failure of training and command ascribed to the Canadian Airborne Regiment, senior officials sought to suppress the whole issue through a not-too-elaborate deception manoeuvre that ultimately made for an even worse scandal for the military.

9. *Indecisiveness followed by frenzy in times of crisis*. Many officials who are otherwise competent political and bureaucratic leaders in times of normal conditions may, however, fail the acid test of leadership in times of crisis. When circumstances arise that are wholly unexpected or unpredictable, in which past experience and knowledge offer no clear sense of direction to be followed, but in which decisions must be made "now," officials are thrust into a very difficult environment. Those who are accustomed to "go by the book" suddenly find that "the book" is useless. They are called upon to innovate in an intelligent and thoughtful manner, but many find such action intimidating and beyond their capabilities. They postpone making decisions or vacillate from one stance to another as events evolve around them. Such indecisiveness coupled with an awareness that indecision in a time of crisis is wrong will push poor leaders into weak and frenzied decisions that lack objectivity or a sense of the whole picture. Often, such decisions simply make matters worse. The decisions and non-decisions of senior officials in the Canadian Red Cross with respect to the contamination of the blood supply in the mid-1980s may come to be regarded as a classic case in point.

10. *Looking for scapegoats and conspiracies.* When poor leaders are confronted with the objective evidence of failure—lost elections, discredited policies, programs that either collapse or simply persist but with no desirable impact on the given problem—they will often respond by denying personal responsibility for the failure. Rather than admit to mistakes and difficulties and commit to studying to learn from past mistakes, such leaders, Dixon maintains, will search for persons or things (scapegoats) on which they can lay blame, thereby absolving themselves of responsibility for failure. This dynamic of shifting responsibility can also result in leaders claiming that either internal or external "enemies" conspired against them, thereby bringing them down through some devious plot. With this argument the

conclusion is supposed to be clear: the impugned leader did no wrong; rather, he or she was "stabbed in the back" by malicious forces who could not tolerate his or her superiority or understand his or her wisdom. In reflecting on this tendency it is interesting to compare the short prime ministership of Kim Campbell and her autobiographical evaluation of what went wrong in the federal election of 1993 with the assessments of most journalists and political commentators in analyzing her findings concerning these events.

12.3.2 Accountability and Leadership

A review of these bureaucratic pathologies is useful on two counts. First, they highlight failings and weaknesses commonly associated with policy and administrative breakdowns. By thinking about these tendencies and applying them to real government problems, one can gain a more incisive understanding of the difficulties confronted by governments and the behavioural traits of poor political and bureaucratic leaders. A study of bureaucratic pathologies enables one to better understand why certain policies, programs, and undertakings fail or suffer grave difficulties and how one can think through and analyze such failures and difficulties. Inquiries into problems associated with the Canadian blood supply, the Canadian Airborne Regiment, and the sponsorship scandal at the federal level and the Walkerton water supply system at the provincial level in Ontario are noteworthy examples of the importance of reviewing and analyzing government problems. Such undertakings are important not only because they seek to understand what went wrong and to attach responsibility for failures, but also because they discover the qualities of good accountable leadership that we expect from public officials.

We come to the second reason for studying bureaucratic pathologies: by isolating behaviour that is commonly considered problematical, we gain understanding of the commonly understood attributes of sound leadership. By reversing Dixon's tendencies associated with incompetence, we can highlight those tendencies associated with political and managerial competence. What are the requirements of sound leadership? What are the leadership traits that the federal government is seeking to promote and inculcate in all federal managers through the work of the Canada School of Public Service and its Leadership Network? What is the basic nature of a good leader in any setting? The following tendencies derived from Dixon's work are generally confirmed by other studies of leadership, such as those by Bennis (1994); Wills (1994); Mancuso, Price, and Wagenberg (1994); Spears (1995); Yukl, (1998); and Ingstrup and Crookall (1998).

Good leadership entails:

- forethought, having a clear vision of short-range and long-range objectives and goals that will benefit society;
- a definite ability to understand the contours of such vision and to be able to articulate and explain this vision to others;
- an ability to motivate;
- a willingness to embrace new ideas;
- a tendency to be broad-minded, free from and critical of prejudicial and stereotypical thinking;
- an openness to new information even when such information is critical of you and your own established thought and practices;
- a deep interest in understanding the problems you are confronting as well as the positions and strengths of your adversaries;
- a willingness to change your plans, to be flexible when evidence suggests flexibility and change is required, but the courage to persist with sound plans even if others waver through indifference or fear or lack of vision;
- the ability to engage in complex thought, to recognize that there are no simple solutions to complex problems but rather more or less complex solutions that need to be clearly understood and articulated;
- maintaining a close concern for human, financial, and material resources;
- the willingness to be self-critical and to encourage others around you to be self-critical and always willing to engage in critical analysis of all ideas, policies, plans, programs, and undertakings;
- the willingness to learn from others and the courage to admit your own mistakes;
- an ability to exploit opportunities, to engage in new ways of doing things, and to innovate when innovation is reasonably called for;
- the strength to not be fearful of breaking from old traditional ways of thinking and acting;
- the willingness to listen to, and learn from, bad news; and,
- the ability to be decisive and wise in times of crisis through having a strong theoretical and practical foundation informing you of what is right and proper action.

In reflecting upon all such leadership traits, Ingstrup and Crookall (1998) have provided an interesting schema of leadership in public sector management. They contend that there are "three pillars" to effective management in the public sector: aim, character, and execution.

1. By "aim" they stress that the best public sector organizations have a clear sense of mission, a coherent strategic vision informing and guiding all their actions. The mission, in turn, provides the foundation for all mechanisms of accountability, with the strategic direction of any organization establishing the framework for judging whether or not the organization is accountable for achieving its set ends in acceptable and desirable manners.

2. By "character" they assert that all successful public sector actors need to make effective use of people, communications, and trust. Effective public service managers need to manage their employees in order to train them, direct them, inspire them, and learn from them how best to run the organization so as to meet its mission goals. Key to this is effective communications, with good managers using multiple channels of communication—both formal and informal—in maintaining and enhancing liaison with employees, partner organizations, and those citizens the organization is serving. Such open and responsive communication patterns, in turn, are seen as integral to building trust in an organization. Effective public sector management requires employees to trust their management leaders just as these leaders are expected to trust their staff. Such trust helps to bind an organization together, with all its actors believing that they are part of a greater whole, working together to further important ends.

3. Finally, Ingstrup and Crookall speak of "execution." This refers to the tactical means used to achieve desired organizational ends. Good execution

- is centred on management tools, teamwork, and change management; good managers do not subscribe to one and only one management approach, but are willing to learn from, use, and adapt a variety of management approaches and management tools, capable of promoting the ends of the organization;
- witnesses an organization moving to achieve its ends through the development, elaboration, and implementation of administrative means that are economical, efficient, and effective;
- features organizational leaders observing past methods of action, learning from them, and fine-tuning current management procedures to provide for better policy and program delivery in the future.

BOX 13.1
The Leadership Network

The Leadership Network of the federal government was established in 1998, under the auspices of the prime minister, to carry forward the renewal initiatives begun by La Relève.

Its mandate is "To promote, develop and support networks of leaders throughout the Public Service of Canada, and to assist them in the ongoing challenge of La Relève."

Operating principles
- Report functionally to the Committee of Senior Officials (COSO), which represents the deputy minister community
- Work in close partnership with other stakeholders, including departments and agencies, regions, functional communities, learning advisory panels, Public Service Commission, Treasury Board Secretariat, and the Canadian Centre for Management Development
- Draw on knowledge, expertise, and talent throughout the Public Service
- Build on the momentum of earlier La Relève initiatives

Organizational structure consists of three horizontally integrated components
- Leadership Network Development
- La Relève Action Support
- Assistant Deputy Minister Corporate Secretariat

Key areas of focus
- Nurture existing leadership networks and create others
- Reach out to leaders at all levels of the public service
- Strengthen traditional communication techniques
- Enhance dialogue among leaders
- Assist departments and agencies in La Relève implementation
- Promote and support action throughout the Public Service in key areas such as
    - pride and recognition
    - values and ethics
    - demographics
    - challenges of middle managers and executives
    - workforce of the future
    - regional and national engagement in public service reform

For more information see http://leadership.gc.ca

Source: Canada, TBS, 1998.

With all of this, teamwork is a vital feature of organizational life in that the organization is called upon to work cooperatively, strategically, and tactically together to meet desired ends through the most intelligent application of viable means. Thus, good organizational leadership is held to be ever cognizant of change. Institutions are always subject to change as organizational environments alter and evolve and as policy and program orientations change and transform. Change is ever present in governments. Public sector managers manage change by being responsive to altering strategic and tactical organizational conditions and by being willing and able to alter and adapt changing institutional means to evolving organizational ends.

Through all of this, particular features of effective leadership come to the fore:

- vision, mission, accountability, sound human resource management, respect for people, effective use of communications, inspiration, trust, sound financial management, the promotion of economy, efficiency, and effectiveness in all actions;
- the assertion of flexibility in management;
- the promotion of teamwork; and
- the ability to anticipate, respond to, and take advantage of change.

These characterize effective managers and leaders in public sector organizations.

Admittedly all these leadership traits establish very high standards for any individual to be considered a good leader and for any organization to be viewed as displaying effective leadership. Good effective leadership is integral to accountability; state power should be exercised in ways responsive to political, legal, and social issues, because that is in the best interests of society. Citizens in this country expect that their governments will be accountable to them, and their expectations of leadership are high.

It is interesting, then, to reflect upon current and past Canadian political and administrative leaders in light of these criteria. While everyone's list will be slightly different, reflecting personal, ideological, pragmatic, and sentimental impressions of particular leaders, we may find that many of us view most of our political and administrative leaders as failing to measure up to the ideal criteria listed here. The paradox comes into play once again. However, we do acknowledge that, at the heart of all government activity lies the concept of leadership, and good leadership is vital to accountability. Public concern is justified inasmuch as through good leadership a society gains accountable government; by demanding accountability in government, one encourages the conditions promoting the rise of good leadership.

12.3.3 Accountability and Leadership: Final Reflections

All those in governments, be they elected political leaders or members of the public service, have a vested interest in enhancing the quality of their leadership for this will directly affect the degree to which their work is efficacious and responsible as well as being worthy of public respect and support. If a government ever loses such public support and respect, its days will be numbered. If and when public servants and the public sector loses such broad public support, they run the risk of new governments coming to power with political agendas highly critical and dismissive of their work.

Thus, good leadership is of interest to everyone concerned with the public sector in this society and its ability to serve the public interest. As Garry Wills (1994) has long argued, one cannot speak of "leadership" without also speaking of "followership." The group that follows the leader ranges from a few people to an entire nation. Followers need leaders but, equally so, one cannot be a leader without followers. Leaders need to inspire their followers, convince them of the soundness and merit of their strategic vision, allay their fears and give them reasonable hope, and motivate them to work for a greater good. By displaying these and all the other traits of effective leadership, leaders can forge deep and abiding bonds with their followers, helping to build and maintain a relationship of power and purpose through which important goals can be realized of benefit to both the leader and the led.

But this relationship, as Wills stresses, is symbiotic. Good leadership requires good followership. Good leadership within government, to be precise, requires followers—public servants as well as citizens—who are intelligent and knowledgeable about the state, the role of government, the demands and expectations of policy and program development and implementation, the limitations and trade-offs in government decision-making, and the nature of accountability in government. At the deepest level, citizens as followers who show little to no informed interest in these matters will be ignorant citizens and poor followers, with these qualities affecting the type of leaders and leadership they receive. Citizens who show little interest in the nature and working of their own governments, who demonstrate little concern for the quality of the public sector management they receive, and who have little interest in the accountability of government will receive governments and leaders who will sooner or later take them for granted and provide them with second-rate levels of public service, management, and leadership.

However, citizens—followers—who take all these matters seriously and who are concerned with the nature and working of government in this society and in the quality of public sector management designed to serve the public interest will maintain high expectations of the quality of government leaders. Citizens who are well-informed are citizens who are a vital part of the broader system of accountability. They will be more likely to elect good men and women to office and more likely to demand that good men and women staff and manage the public service. Good leadership in government is vital to the realization of accountability in government, and such leadership, in turn, is contingent upon the actions of good citizens as followers.

We are looking at a symbiotic relationship in which we all have a part to play. And this highlights the importance of the subject matter of this text. This book has offered a review and analysis of public sector management in Canada. There is an old adage that people get the government they deserve. We deserve the very best quality of government, and, to this end, we as citizens have a civic duty to be interested in the nature of government. We have a duty to be well-informed, sensitive, and critical of the functioning of government and the quality of public sector management we receive from the government. We possess a duty, in short, to promote good government in this society, and the first and last element of this duty is to be aware.

12.4 Accountability, Government, and Management: Confronting the Future

As we enter a new century, this country and its governments confront many challenges and many opportunities. The host of major public policy concerns that have defined elements of political debate and government action in this country are still with us. Canadian-American relations and free trade, globalization, and the regulatory capacity of the state remain subjects of great concern, as are the policy matters of social cohesion, sustainable development, and First Nations' policy with the promotion and establishment of viable systems of Aboriginal self-government. To these matters must now be added heightened concern for national defence and security and intelligence policy in the wake of the 9/11 terrorist attacks in the United States. Following a decade of major cutbacks to government services at both the federal and provincial levels of organization, we also witness great concern expressed over the state of health, education, and social assistance policy; regional development and industrial support policy; and such other diverse policy fields as human rights promotion, culture and heritage protection, agricultural policy support, infrastructure redevelopment, and national defence. In all these fields and others, there are calls for governments to reinvest in public services in order to promote the public good. The calls for governments to do more and to reclaim their place as progressive leaders in the development of Canadian society and in the promotion and protection of a liberal social welfare state remain strong.

As governments confront these demands for the development of better public policies and programs, they also face demands for the promotion of stronger economic growth; the promotion of the interests of the private sector as the main engine of the economy; and the promotion of tax cuts, debt reduction, and a smaller government that seeks to do "more with less." There remain strong forces on the right of the ideological spectrum insisting that the significant shift in focus over the past quarter-century away from a centre-left perspective on the role of the state to one that is centre-right is desirable and important and should be maintained and even strengthened. All governments confront a complex policy and program environment in which they are faced with many options. While the role of the state in the social and economic life of this society has been redefined and reduced over the past quarter-century due to a variety of reasons ranging from concern over rising deficits and debts to the rising prominence of conservative thought, the future role of the state still remains an open question.

In spite of these forces of the right, there are also strong liberal and social democratic forces in favour of a revitalization of the state and its pro-active role in socio-economic policy development and regulation. As most governments now have tamed the deficits and debt that bedevilled them for most of the past 25 years, they now face choices about what to do with the new budgetary flexibility that balanced and even surplus budgets provide. Should strong revenue streams be geared primarily to tax cuts and debt reduction or to reinvestment in social, economic, and national defence programs? Or should there be some balanced, 50/50 compromise position between these two contrasting options? If there is to be a reinvestment in social services, where should that money go? Health care? The environment? Education? Transportation? But if the allure of tax cuts wins out over program reinvestment, at what point might it be necessary to argue that, if Canadians want the quality of public services to which they have become accustomed, we might have to consider the possibility of marginal tax increases? Questions such as these will dominate political debate in this country over the next decade, and, indeed, we have already seen the advent of this debate at the federal level during the elections of 2000 and 2004.

Regardless of the course that Canadian governments adopt with respect to these broad matters of policy directions, there will be increasing demands that the public sector respond to these changing policy and program priorities with the highest degree of economy, efficiency, and effectiveness. While public services may not be reinvented but rather reformed as a result of the political and socio-economic pressures confronting modern governments, they will still be expected to perform all the traditional functions of public sector management to the best, most professional degree possible. Though the development of policy capacity is currently a major concern of the federal government, so too will be the maintenance and enhancement of administrative capacity respecting financial management policy and operations, personnel management policy and operations, and the sound management of government legal obligations under the terms and conditions of administrative law. In all these managerial fields, managers and staff will be expected to deliver services and meet government and public expectations for sound and accountable public service, with these officials operating in accordance with the best traditions and practices of ministerial responsibility, legal responsibility, and social responsiveness. All these features of the broad accountability system will continue to exert their synthetic influence over the nature and working of public sector management, with all government institutions, managers, and staff called to account for the manner by which they exercise power.

Concerns about democracy and bureaucracy will remain a constant, as will the issue of the proper relationship between elected ministers and non-elected officials. The concept of ministerial responsibility will remain a foundational principle of Canadian government, with all public servants being aware that they live within an organizational system in which ultimate policy and administrative decision-making rests with elected ministers. In the routine life of bureaucratic organizations, however, the operational influence of senior public servants respecting routine decision-making will likely remain pronounced, highlighting a sharp division of labour between elected and non-elected officials in the decision-making process. In looking at this process overall, we will see in all likelihood the command mode of executive decision-making continue in Ottawa, with the concentration of executive power among a few senior officials at the very head of the government. The senior officials with such power, both elected and non-elected, will be unlikely to willingly relinquish it, and, as past decades have illustrated, they will probably continue to acquire even more power. We will also continue to see criticism of this trend, with critics asserting that, while this dynamic may benefit and promote the decision-making authority of those "at the centre," such a concentration distorts the concepts and practices of cabinet government and parliamentary democracy while placing excessive power in too few hands. Whether such a concentration of power at the centre is desirable or not for the long-term health of the government of Canada will thus likely remain a topic of intense political debate in this country until it is resolved. There will be those who will call for a diminution of such power "at the centre" and for much greater emphasis on participation by various interests and groups in the making of public policy. Such calls for participation, however, will likely continue to abut against the *realpolitik* of concentrated power and those who desire and benefit from such concentration.

Concerns about bureaucracy and law will also remain at the forefront of accountability, with all government institutions and their public servants being morally and legally obligated to exercise state power according to the pre-established rules of administrative law as overseen by superior courts. With respect to the law, we will likely see not only the continuation of the importance of judicial review of administrative actions as a significant control over state action but also the increased use, by government institutions, of the practice of structuring discretion as a means of establishing rules of decision-making process prior to engaging in actual decision-making, with such structuring activities being open to various social and economic interests concerned with the work of particular institutions. In this way we will likely observe some greater participation in the work of government, blending state interests and societal groups in a dialogue respecting the future development of state policy and procedures.

There will also be continuing concern regarding accountability and the social responsiveness of governments in the eyes of opposition parties, socio-economic interest groups, the mass media, and the general public. All such groups tend to judge governments and their managements by the degree to which public policy and program implementation responds to social and economic needs and either promotes or hinders the socio-economic development of this country. Of course, the assessment of all such matters is inherently subjective, geared to each analyst's ideological presuppositions and understandings as to the desired role of the state in society and the best forms by which policies and programs can and should be developed to serve the public interest. As such, while all such interests will continue to judge governments by their social responsiveness, and while all such interests will continue to demand that governments act in socially responsive manners, debate will ensue, as a natural part of political discourse, as to what social responsiveness actually means and how it is to be measured and assessed. And within this environment of subjective political debate and discourse, public sector managers will be called upon to act in the public interest and will continue to see this as a fundamental part of their *raison d'être*. They will then be called upon and will serve not only the government of the day, by virtue of the rules and logic of ministerial responsibility, but, through their leadership, they will also serve and attend to the wider needs and concerns of the larger society.

As government changes and evolves, in accordance with changing public attitudes to the appropriate role of the state in society and changing understandings as to what types of policies and programs are considered necessary and/or acceptable and/or desirable by the general public, any government, federal or provincial, will respond to such changes and develop policies and programs in at least partial conformity with such expressions of political will. And, in doing so, each government will be expected to meet its socio-economic and political responsibilities in an accountable fashion. Public sector managers and staff will be called upon to serve the government of the day in the most professional manner possible. They will be expected to conform to and support the policy direction of the government, serving its ministers faithfully and fully, while assisting them in the development and implementation of new policy and program initiatives. They will also be expected to undertake their duties and administrative responsibilities in full accordance with established legal responsibilities, showing conformity to the law in all their actions and ensuring that all state decision-making is in compliance with all the rules of administrative law. And they will be required to serve the broad public interest by promoting the development of socially responsive policies and programs and responding to the concerns and feedback of social interests regarding the application and impact of such policies and programs.

This is the fundamental nature of accountability in government. It is an amalgamation or synthesis of ministerial responsibility, legal responsibility, and social responsibility. Given the nature of these concepts and their component dynamics, accountability is a feature of government that is never concluded. It is a process of actions, undertakings, and responses to a variety of political, legal, and social stimuli, with these actions and undertakings either making for better or worse government. Accountability involves government figures—elected ministers and public servants—making choices and taking decisions in their exercise of state power. The process of making choices and supporting such policy initiatives with sound program implementation and administration is then a matter of leadership, with such leadership being judged on the basis of whether such policy and program actions achieve desired ends, whether they respond to and serve social needs, and whether they attract the support and consent of a broad majority, or at least a consistent plurality, of the general public. Leadership is thus at the centre of accountability, with the relative success or failure of governments and public sector management being inextricably tied to the calibre of leadership emerging from their ranks.

In judging the merits and demerits of governments and their management, we judge the nature and working of their leadership, and this, as we have seen throughout this text, is a ceaseless task. As governments respond to changing socio-economic, political, and ideological dynamics, they develop new policies and programs, or reaffirm existing policies and programs, that reflect government choice respecting desired options, directions, and undertakings. Such choices become the foundation of government decision-making, providing the substance of policies and programs to be implemented, administered, and managed by the public service. All such actions—both the exercise of policy decision-making and the application of managerial authority designed to turn policy goals into program results—call for and demand critical understanding of the methods and processes of decision-making and policy and program implementation and management as well as a critical awareness of how and why such methods and processes have arisen, how well they work in practice, their strengths and weaknesses, their possible alternatives and their constraints, and the nature and working of government leadership.

I hope that, through this text, your ability to understand government action and government leadership has been enhanced. In the broadest sense, critical public awareness of government and its management is a fundamental part of accountability. Any government serving an informed and constructively critical citizenry will be a better government; it will be one more conscious of its public duties while also being more socially responsive. A critical awareness of the nature and working of government is a vital component of good citizenship, with such knowledge benefitting all those affected by state action: politicians, public servants, governments, interest groups, and citizens.

References and Selected Reading

Bennis, Warren. 1994. *On Becoming a Leader*. Reading, MA: Addison-Wesley.

Bennis, Warren, and Robert Townsend. 1995. *Reinventing Leadership: Strategies to Empower the Organization*. New York: William Morrow and Co.

Canada, Treasury Board of Canada Secretariat. 1998. *The Leadership Network*. Ottawa: Treasury Board Secretariat.

Champy, James. 1995. *Reengineering Management: The Mandate for New Leadership*. New York: Harper Business.

Dixon, Norman. 1979. *On the Psychology of Military Incompetence*. London: Futura.

Ingstrup, Ole, and Paul Crookall. 1998. *The Three Pillars of Public Management: Secrets of Sustained Success*. Montreal and Kingston: McGill-Queen's University Press.

Kouzes, James M., and Barry Z. Posner. 1995. *The Leadership Challenge: How to Keep Getting Extraordinary Things Done in Organizations*. San Francisco, CA: Jossey-Bass.

Laschinger, John, and Geoffrey Stevens. 1992. *Leaders and Lesser Mortals: Backroom Politics in Canada*. Toronto: Key Porter Books.

Mancuso, Maureen, Richard G. Price, and Ronald Wagenberg, eds. 1994. *Leaders and Leadership in Canada*. Toronto: Oxford University Press.

Mowen, John C. 1993. *Judgement Calls: High Stakes Decisions in a Risky World*. New York: Simon and Schuster.

Paquet, Gilles. 1999. *Governance Through Social Learning*. Ottawa: University of Ottawa Press.

Spears, Larry C., ed. 1995. *Reflections on Leadership*. New York: John Wiley and Sons.

Wills, Garry. 1994. *Certain Trumpets: The Nature of Leadership*. New York: Simon and Schuster.

Wren, J. Thomas. 1995. *The Leader's Companion: Insights on Leadership Through the Ages*. New York: Free Press.

Yukl, Gary. 1998. *Leadership in Organizations*. 4th ed. Saddle River, NJ: Prentice-Hall.

Index